THE CAMBRIDGE EDITION OF THE WORKS OF
JONATHAN SWIFT

THE CAMBRIDGE EDITION OF THE WORKS OF
JONATHAN SWIFT

THE CAMBRIDGE EDITION OF THE WORKS OF
JONATHAN SWIFT

JONATHAN SWIFT

English Political Writings
1711–1714

THE CONDUCT OF THE ALLIES
AND OTHER WORKS

Edited by

BERTRAND A. GOLDGAR and IAN GADD

CAMBRIDGE
UNIVERSITY PRESS

CAMBRIDGE UNIVERSITY PRESS
Cambridge, New York, Melbourne, Madrid, Cape Town, Singapore, São Paulo, Delhi

Cambridge University Press
The Edinburgh Building, Cambridge CB2 8RU, UK

Published in the United States of America by Cambridge University Press, New York

www.cambridge.org
Information on this title: www.cambridge.org/9780521829298

First published 2008

Printed in the United Kingdom at the University Press, Cambridge

A catalogue record for this publication is available from the British Library

Library of Congress Cataloguing in Publication data
Swift, Jonathan, 1667–1745.
English political writings, 1711–1714 : the conduct of the allies and other
works / Jonathan Swift ; edited by Bertrand A. Goldgar and Ian Gadd.
p. cm. – (The Cambridge edition of the works of Jonathan Swift)
Includes bibliographical references and index.
ISBN 978-0-521-82929-8
I. Goldgar, Bertrand A., 1927– II. Gadd, Ian Anders. III. Title. IV. Series.
PR3722G64 2008
828′.509–dc22 2008015473

ISBN 978-0-521-82929-8 hardback

This edition is supported by the
Arts and Humanities Research Council

Arts & Humanities
Research Council

CONTENTS

ILLUSTRATIONS

THE CAMBRIDGE EDITION OF THE WORKS OF
JONATHAN SWIFT

GENERAL EDITORS' PREFACE

The Cambridge Edition of the Works of Jonathan Swift is the first fully annotated scholarly edition ever undertaken of Swift's complete works in both verse and prose. The great editions of Swift by Herbert Davis and Harold Williams have remained standard for over half a century. We are all greatly indebted to them, but the time has come to replace or revise their texts and commentary in the light of subsequent historical, biographical and textual knowledge. Davis's fourteen-volume edition of the Prose Writings offered valuable introductions but no annotation. The commentary to his separate edition of *The Drapier's Letters*, and Williams's commentaries to the *Poems* and *Journal to Stella*, though excellent in their time, must now be supplemented by a considerable body of more recent scholarship. The Cambridge Edition's detailed introductions, notes and appendices aim to provide an informed understanding of Swift's place in the political and cultural history of England and Ireland, and to establish the historical, literary and bibliographical contexts of his immense achievement as a prose satirist, poet and political writer. The editors of individual volumes include distinguished historians, as well as leading scholars of eighteenth-century literature.

For the Cambridge Edition, Swift's texts will be collated and analysed afresh, with attention to new evidence of drafts, autographs, transcripts and printed editions, including revisions of Swift's own *Works*. All lifetime editions will be investigated for their authority. The choice of the version to be printed will be based on an assessment of the work's nature and of the particularities of its history. As a general rule the last authoritative version of the work will be chosen, but in the case of works that are bound in tightly to an immediate context of controversy (polemical tracts, for example), the first edition will usually be chosen instead. In all cases editors will have regard to Swift's overall conception of his text, including issues of typography and illustration. All substantial authorial variants will be recorded in the apparatus, along with those accidental variants editors deem significant, and full introductions will provide the history of the text and the rationale for editorial decisions.

ACKNOWLEDGEMENTS

In working on this edition I am in a sense returning to my beginnings, since I started my scholarly career four decades ago by writing about Swift's relationships with Addison and Steele. That work took shape as a dissertation directed by the great Swift scholar Louis Landa, to whose memory my portion of this volume is dedicated.

In the course of this journey backwards I have incurred many obligations to other scholars of the eighteenth century. I would like to thank first of all my daughter Anne Goldgar, who not only helped with particular points of Dutch history but also gave me constant support and encouragement throughout my research in London. I am grateful, as always, to Thomas Lockwood for taking time from his research on Fielding to suggest ways of dealing with my own difficulties. Ian Higgins, one of the general editors of these volumes of Swift, suggested helpful revisions to my Introduction, and James McLaverty, the textual editor, carefully read and helped me revise the introduction and the notes. I am grateful to Claude Rawson, also a general editor, for arranging for me to change my editorial assignment early in the game. James Woolley, a fellow volume editor, kindly furnished essential information about some of the political verse attributed to Swift. Linda Bree, the press editor, offered prompt and friendly advice whenever needed. And my co-editor, Ian Gadd, not only did more than his share of the labour but also patiently and successfully worked to make our long-distance partnership a happy one.

For helpful information and advice in preparing the notes I am also indebted to A. R. Braunmuller, J. A. Downie, Michael Harris, Christoph von Ehrenstein, Clyve Jones, David Onnekink, Angus Ross, Adam Rounce and Melinda Zook. I am grateful to the staffs of the British Library, particularly Giles Mandelbrote and Karen Limper, and of the Institute of Historical Research. Gretchen Revie of Lawrence University Library offered consistently valuable assistance, and Lawrence University made possible several trips to England by generous research funds. Corinne, who stayed behind on these trips, nevertheless made them more bearable by her patience and her wit.

BERTRAND A. GOLDGAR

My primary debt of gratitude is to Jim McLaverty, who persuaded me to undertake this project and also encouraged and supported me throughout. My patient and generous co-editor, Bert Goldgar, proved an exemplary collaborator; I have learned much from him about Swift in particular and about scholarship in general. The rest of the editorial team – the general editors and the two postdoctoral fellows, Paddy Bullard and Adam Rounce – also deserve thanks for their energy and tolerance. At Cambridge University Press, Linda Bree and Maartje Scheltens proved forbearing, indefatigable and thorough editors.

I am very grateful to my colleagues at Bath Spa University, especially Tracey Hill and Tim Middleton, for their support, and to the Arts and Humanities Research Board (now the Arts and Humanities Research Council) who generously granted me a Research Leave award in 2005, without which this project would not have been completed on time. Randall McLeod taught me how to use an optical collator. Chloë Trueman and Claire Drake provided invaluable service in checking collations in the final stages of the project. Rulers were generously wielded on my behalf by Jason McElligott in Dublin and Joseph Marshall in Edinburgh, and Alex Barber made me think again about the events surrounding the prosecution of John Barber in 1714. Shef Rogers offered insightful comments about my hypotheses concerning the printing of *The Conduct of the Allies*, while my perplexity over the format of *Conduct*'s first edition was eased by the helpful advice of David L. Vander Meulen and David Gants. I am grateful too, to Michael Turner, for providing information about Michael Treadwell's unpublished notes on members of the London book trade.

I am also grateful to the following for their assistance and for precise responses to my questions: Giles Mandelbrote and his colleagues at the British Library; the staff of Lambeth Palace Library; Mari Takayanagi of the House of Lords Record Office; the staff of the National Art Library, Victoria & Albert Museum; the staff of Bodleian Library, Oxford (especially those in Duke Humfrey); Christine Ferdinand of Magdalen College, Oxford; Norma Aubertin-Potter of All Souls College, Oxford; Naomi van Loo of New College, Oxford; Jill Whitelock and her special collections colleagues at Cambridge University Library; David McKitterick and his colleagues at Trinity College, Cambridge; Caroline Pilcher and Carol Dery of the Founders' Library at the University of Lampeter; Joseph Marshall, Helen Vincent and colleagues at the National Library of Scotland; the library staff of Trinity College, Dublin (especially Charles Benson), the National Library of Ireland, the Royal Irish Academy and the Honourable Society of King's Inn, Dublin; Alvan Bregman of the Rare Book and Manuscript Library,

University of Illinois at Urbana-Champaign; and Daniel Traister of Van Pelt Library, University of Pennsylvania.

Finally, I owe a great deal to my parents and to Fiona, who sustained, cajoled, fretted, advised, and occasionally even photocopied.

IAN GADD

CHRONOLOGY

1664 Marriage in Dublin of Swift's parents, Jonathan Swift the elder and Abigail Erick.

Birth of John Vanbrugh. Katherine Philips, *Poems* (pirated).

1665 Second Anglo-Dutch War (until 1667). Commencement of *Philosophical Transactions* by Royal Society. Plague in London.

1666 Fire of London. John Bunyan, *Grace Abounding*; Nicolas Boileau-Despréaux, *Satires*; Molière, *Le Misanthrope*.

1667 March or April: Swift's father dies; 30 November: birth of Swift in Dublin.

Dismissal of Edward Hyde, first Earl of Clarendon; the 'Cabal' administration of the government (until 1673). Death of Abraham Cowley. Birth of John Arbuthnot. John Dryden, *Annus Mirabilis, Indian Emperor, Of Dramatick Poesy*; John Milton, *Paradise Lost* (1st edn); Thomas Sprat, *History of the Royal Society*.

1668 Dryden appointed Poet Laureate. Beginning of *Mercurius Librarius* (*Term Catalogues*); Cowley, *Works*, with life by Sprat.

1670 Birth of William Congreve. Milton, *The History of Britain*; Blaise Pascal, *Pensées*; Izaac Walton, *Lives*.

1671 Milton, *Paradise Regained, Samson Agonistes*.

1672 Third Anglo-Dutch War (until 1674); second Declaration of Indulgence. Births of Joseph Addison and Richard Steele. John Sheffield, first Duke of Buckingham, *Rehearsal*; Andrew Marvell, *Rehearsal Transpros'd* (Pt II, 1673).

1673–82 Swift at school at Kilkenny

1673 Second Declaration of Indulgence withdrawn, and Test Act signed. End of Cabal.

1674 Death of Milton. Opening of Theatre Royal. Boileau, *L'Art Poetique*; Milton, *Paradise Lost* (2nd edn, in 12 books); Thomas Shadwell, *Enchanted Island*.

1675 William Wycherley, *Country Wife*.
1676 George Etherege, *Man of Mode*;
Shadwell, *Virtuoso*.
1677 Aphra Behn, *The Rover*, Pt I (Pt II,
1681); Wycherley, *Plain Dealer*.
1678 Popish Plot. Death of Marvell;
birth of George Farquhar. Bunyan,
Pilgrim's Progress, I (Pt II, 1684); Samuel
Butler, *Hudibras*, III.
1679 Exclusion Crisis (until 1681). Birth
of Thomas Parnell. Gilbert Burnet, *History
of the Reformation* (vols. II and III, 1681
and 1715).
1680 Deaths of Butler, John Wilmot,
second Earl of Rochester, François La
Rochefoucauld. Sir Robert Filmer,
Patriarcha; Rochester, *Poems*; Wentworth
Dillon, fourth Earl of Roscommon,
Horace's Art of Poetry Made English; Sir
William Temple, *Miscellanea*, I.
1681 Thomas Burnet, *Telluris Theoria
Sacra*, Books I and II; John Oldham,
Satires Upon the Jesuits; Dryden, *Absalom
and Achitophel*.

1682 April: Swift admitted to Trinity
College Dublin. He remains there until
the outbreak of war between James II and
William III.

Death of Sir Thomas Browne. Dryden,
*The Medall, Religio Laici, Mac Flecknoe,
Absalom and Achitophel*, II; Lucretius, *De
rerum natura* (tr. Thomas Creech);
Thomas Otway, *Venice Preserv'd*; Sir
William Petty, *Essay Concerning the
Multiplication of Mankind*.
1683 Rye House Plot. Death of Oldham.
1684 Behn, *Love-Letters Between a
Noble-Man and his Sister* (1684–7).
1685 February: Death of Charles II and
Accession of James II. June to July:
Monmouth Rebellion. October: Edict of
Nantes revoked. Birth of John Gay; birth
of George Berkeley. *Sylvae* (including
contributions by Dryden); Dryden, 'To the
Pious Memory of Mrs Anne Killigrew',
Threnodia Augustalis.

1686 Swift takes his bachelor's degree by
speciali gratia from TCD

Behn, *The Lucky Chance*; Dryden, *The
Hind and the Panther*, 'Song for St.
Cecilia's Day'.
1687 April: James II's Declaration of
Indulgence. Isaac Newton, *Principia*.

1688   Civil war breaks out in Ireland.

Glorious Revolution. November: William of Orange invades England; December: James II flees to France (transfer of the crown to William and Mary in 1689). Birth of Alexander Pope; death of Bunyan; Shadwell named Poet Laureate in succession to Dryden. Charles Perrault, *Parallèle des Anciens and des Modernes* (completed 1697).

1689   January: Swift leaves for England; employed in Sir William Temple's household at Moor Park, near Farnham, Surrey; meets Esther Johnson (Stella), then eight years old.

Accession of William and Mary. Birth of Samuel Richardson; death of Behn. John Locke, *First Letter on Toleration*.

1690   May: Swift returns to Ireland, on doctors' advice, after first appearance of Ménière's disease.

James II defeated by William III in Ireland (Battle of the Boyne) and flees to France. Dryden, *Don Sebastian*; Locke, *Two Treatises of Government*, *Essay Concerning Human Understanding* (enlarged 1694–1700), *Second Letter on Toleration*; Petty, *Political Arithmetick* (see 1682); Temple, *Miscellanea*, II, includes 'An Essay upon the Ancient and Modern Learning', which triggers Phalaris controversy (rev. edn 1692).

1691   Swift, *Ode. To the King*. Returns to Moor Park by end of year.

Treaty of Limerick ends war in Ireland.

1692   Swift, *Ode to the Athenian Society* (in supplement to *Athenian Gazette*, vol. V). Swift takes degree of MA at Oxford, for future purpose of ordination.

Death of Shadwell. Locke, *Third Letter on Toleration*; Thomas Rymer, *Short View of Tragedy*.

1693   Beginning of National Debt. Congreve, *Old Batchelor*; Dryden, 'Discourse Concerning Satire', prefixed to trs. of Juvenal and Persius; Locke, *Thoughts Concerning Education*.

1694   Swift returns to Ireland, takes deacon's orders.

Death of Mary II; Founding of Bank of England. Congreve, *Double Dealer*; *Dictionary* of French Academy; William Wotton, *Reflections on Ancient and Modern Learning*.

1695   January: Swift ordained priest, and becomes prebendary of Kilroot, near Belfast.

Death of Henry Purcell. Richard Blackmore, *Prince Arthur*; Charles Boyle, ed., *Epistles of Phalaris*; Congreve, *Love for Love*; Locke, *Reasonableness of Christianity* and *Vindication of the Reasonableness of Christianity* (second *Vindication*, 1697); Thomas Southerne, *Oroonoko*.

1696–9 Swift at Moor Park, at work on *A Tale of a Tub* and related writings.

1697 Birth of William Hogarth. Richard Bentley, 'Dissertation upon the *Epistles of Phalaris*' (in 2nd edn of Wotton's *Reflections*, see 1694); Blackmore, *King Arthur*; Dryden, *Works of Virgil*; Vanbrugh, *Provok'd Wife*.
1698 Boyle, *Dr Bentley's Dissertations on the Epistles of Phalaris and the Fables of Aesop Examin'd*; Jeremy Collier, *Short View of the English Stage*; Daniel Defoe, *Enquiry into Occasional Conformity*; William Molyneux, *The Case of Ireland Stated*.

1699 January: death of Temple. August: Swift returns to Ireland as chaplain to Earl of Berkeley, Lord Justice of Ireland. Writes 'When I come to be Old'. November: Swift's edition of Temple's *Letters* (dated 1700) is published.

Bentley, *Dissertation upon the Epistles of Phalaris, with an Answer to the Honourable Charles Boyle*; Samuel Garth, *The Dispensary*.

1700 February: Swift appointed Vicar of Laracor, Co. Meath. October: appointed prebendary of St Patrick's Cathedral, Dublin.

Death of Charles II of Spain; final statute against Catholics; dispute over Irish forfeitures; Act of Resumption; death of Duke of Gloucester; Partition Treaty. Death of Dryden; birth of James Thomson. Blackmore, *Satire against Wit*; Miguel de Cervantes, *Don Quixote*, tr. Peter Motteux; Congreve, *Way of the World*; Dryden, *Fables* and *Secular Masque*; François Fénelon, *Dialogue des Morts*; James Harrington, *Works*, with life by John Toland; Matthew Prior, *Carmen Seculare*.

1701 April: Swift goes to England with Lord Berkeley; August: Esther Johnson's move to Dublin; September: Swift moves back to Dublin with Rochester, new Lord Lieutenant. October: Swift, *Contests and Dissensions in Athens and Rome*; Swift's edition of Temple, *Miscellanea*, III.

Death of James II; his son, James Francis Edward (b. 1688), 'Pretender' to the throne, recognized by Louis XIV; Act of Settlement; general election (Tory landslide); Impeachment of John, Baron Somers; general election (Whig recovery). Addison, 'Letter to Halifax' (written); Charles Davenant, *Essay on the Balance of Power*; John Dennis, *Advancement of Modern Poetry*; Steele, *Christian Hero*.

1702 February: Swift takes the degree DD, Trinity College, Dublin. April: travels to England. August: writes 'Meditation on a Broomstick' (published in *Miscellanies*, 1711). October: returns to Ireland.

Death of William III, accession of Anne; Tory ministry; Godolphin–Marlborough influence; Edward Harley Speaker of the House of Commons; War of Spanish Succession. Clarendon, *History of the Great Rebellion* (1702–4); Defoe, *Shortest-Way with the Dissenters*; William King, *De Origine Mali*; *Observator* (1702–12); *Poems on Affairs of State* (1702–7); Anthony Ashley Cooper, first Earl of Shaftesbury, *Paradoxes of State*.

1703 November: travels to England, and stays until May 1704. Swift's edition of Temple, *Letters to the King*.

First Occasional Conformity Bill defeated in Lords; campaign in Flanders; Great Storm (27 November); Defoe imprisoned, pilloried and released. Abel Boyer, *History of the Reign of Queen Anne* (1703–13); Steele, *The Lying Lover*; Ned Ward, *London Spy* (collected edn, eighteen monthly parts, November 1698–1703).

1704 May: publication of *Tale of a Tub*, containing also 'Battle of the Books', and 'Mechanical Operation of the Spirit'. Second and third edns follow this year. 1 June: arrives back in Dublin; there or in Laracor until November 1707.

Battle of Blenheim; Queen Anne's bounty; Ministry of Daniel Finch, second Earl of Nottingham, resigns; Harley Secretary of State; Henry St John Secretary at War; death of Locke. Defoe, *Review* (1704–12); Dennis, *Grounds of Criticism in Poetry* and *Liberty Asserted*; Wycherley, *Miscellany Poems*.

1705 *Tale of a Tub*, fourth edn.

General Election, Whig victory, 'Junto' administration; John Churchill, first Duke of Marlborough breaks through lines of Brabant; 'Church in Danger'; Haymarket Opera House opened by Vanbrugh; Addison Commissioner of Appeals. Addison, *The Campaign* and *Remarks on Italy*; Samuel Clarke, *Being and Attributes of God*; Bernard Mandeville, *The Grumbling Hive*; Steele, *The Tender Husband*; Toland, *Socinianism Truly Stated*; Vanbrugh, *The Confederacy*; Wotton, *Reflections upon Ancient and Modern Learning*, 3rd edn, with a *Defense of the Reflections*, including 'Observations upon *The Tale of a Tub*'.

1706 Act of Succession; Battle of Ramillies; Charles Spencer, third Earl of Sunderland, Secretary of State; Steele made Gazetteer; death of John Evelyn; birth of Benjamin Franklin. Addison, *Rosamond*; Farquhar, *The Recruiting Officer*; Locke, *Conduct of Understanding*, *On Miracles* and *Fourth Letter on Toleration*; White Kennett, *Complete History of England* (1706–19).

1707 April: Swift writes 'Story of the Injured Lady'. August: writes 'Tritical Essay'. November: Swift in London on Church of Ireland business; meets Addison, Steele and other authors; writes tracts on political and ecclesiastical issues; begins friendship with Esther Vanhomrigh (Vanessa).

Union of England and Scotland; births of Henry Fielding and Charles Wesley. Colley Cibber, *Comical Lovers*, *The Double Gallant* and *The Lady's Last Stake*; Defoe, *Modest Vindication of Present Ministry*; Farquhar, *The Beaux' Stratagem*; Delarivier Manley, *Almyna*; John Philips, *Ode to Bolingbroke*; Prior, *Poems on Several Occasions* (pirated); Thomas Tickell, *Oxford*.

1708 January: Swift, *Predictions for 1708*; March: *Elegy on Partridge, Account of Partridge's Death*; December: *Letter concerning the Sacramental Test*; writes *Sentiments of a Church of England Man* (published 1711); writes *Argument against Abolishing Christianity*.

Battle of Oudemarde; Harley and St John resign; Catalonia Campaign; Somers returns to office; Naturalization Act; Addison Keeper of Records, Dublin Castle. Joseph Bingham, *Origines Ecclesiasticae*; Collier, *Ecclesiastical History of Great Britain* (1708–14); Bernard Le Bovier, sieur de Fontenelle, *Dialogues of the Dead*, tr. John Hughes; Locke, *Letters*; John Philips, *Cyder*; Shaftesbury, *Letter Concerning Enthusiasm*; Lewis Theobald, *Persian Princess*.

1709 April: Swift, *Famous Prediction of Merlin, A Vindication of Isaac Bickerstaff, Project for the Advancement of Religion*. 'Baucis and Philemon' published in various locations. Steele starts *The Tatler* (12 April); Swift's 'A Description of the Morning' appears in No. 9 (30 April). Swift's edition of Temple, *Memoirs* III. June: returns to Dublin.

Charles XII defeated at Pultawa; Henry Sacheverell's sermon, *The Perils of False Brethren*; births of Samuel Johnson and George Lyttelton; Copyright Act (first, fourteen-year term, renewable for another fourteen if author is alive); Steele dismissed from the *Gazette*. Berkeley, *New Theory of Vision*; Manley, *The New Atalantis*; Ambrose Philips, 'Pastorals' and Pope, 'Pastorals', published in the Tonson *Poetical Miscellanies* VI; Prior, *Poems on Several Occasions*; Nicholas Rowe's edn of Shakespeare (1709–10); Shaftesbury, *The Moralists*.

1710 *Tale of a Tub*, fifth edn. Swift arrives in London on 1 September, travelling on behalf of the Church of Ireland soliciting for a remission of some financial imposts on the clergy of the Church of Ireland; begins epistolary diary known as *Journal to Stella*, 1710–13; Swift's letter on corruptions of style published as *The Tatler*, No. 230. October: meets Harley, leader of the new Tory government; still dining regularly with Addison and Steele; 'A Description of a City Shower' appears in *The Tatler*, No. 238; November: takes over pro-government paper, *The Examiner*.
1711 February: Swift attends Harley's 'Saturday Club' dinners; publishes *Miscellanies in Prose and Verse* (includes 'Sentiments of a Church-of-England Man' and 'Argument Against Abolishing Christianity'). September: Death of Swift's

January: Marlborough threatens to resign commission over Tory influence of Abigail Masham at court. March: trial of Sacheverell ends disappointingly for Whig managers. August: Sidney, first Earl of Godolphin dismissed as Lord Treasurer, replaced by Tory treasury under Robert Harley. October: landslide victory brings Tories to power. Samuel Clements, *Faults on Both Sides*; Berkeley, *Principles of Human Knowledge*; September: Addison begins *The Whig Examiner*. Pierre Bayle, *Dictionary*, first English edn; Congreve, *Collected Works*; Manley, *Memoirs of Europe*. January: Peace conference at Utrecht begins. February: Tory 'October Club' attacks Harley for perceived moderation. March: assassination attempt by Marquis de Guiscard on Harley. May: Robert Harley created Lord Treasurer and Earl of friend Anne Long. November: Swift, *Conduct of the Allies*.

1712   May: Swift, *Proposal for Correcting the English Tongue*. August: Swift, *Some Remarks on the Barrier Treaty*. Formation of the 'Scriblerus Club' with Pope, Gay, Parnell and Arbuthnot.
1713   January: Swift, *Mr. C[olli]ns's Discourse of Free-Thinking, put into Plain English*. May: public acrimony between Swift and Steele. June: Swift installed as Dean of St Patrick's Cathedral, Dublin. October: Swift, *Importance of the Guardian Considered*; composes 'Cadenus and Vanessa'.

1714   February: Swift, *Public Spirit of the Whigs*; declared 'seditious and scandalous libel' by Lords; Swift Governor of Bethlehem Hospital ('Bedlam'). March: Swift helps draft Queen's speech. June: Swift leaves London for Letcombe Basset, Berkshire; writes *Some Free Thoughts* (not published until 1741). August: sails for Dublin, beginning of six-year break from publication.
1719   March 13: Swift writes birthday verses for Stella.
1720   Swift, *Proposal for the Universal Use of Irish Manufacture*; at subsequent trial of its printer, Edward Waters, Chief Justice Whitshed refuses to accept 'not guilty' verdict from jury.

1721   April: earliest references to writing of *Gulliver's Travels*, in a letter to Charles Ford. Swift travels over four hundred miles on his 'Summer Rambles' in Ireland.

1722   July: patent to strike copper coins for Ireland granted to William Wood. August: Francis Atterbury implicated in Jacobite 'Layer's Plot'.

Oxford. November: Nottingham (Swift's 'Dismal') breaks with Harley. December: Marlborough dismissed. Pope, *Essay on Criticism*; Steele, *The Tatler* final number, January; Addison and Steele, *The Spectator* (1 March 1711 – 6 December 1712); Shaftesbury, *Characteristicks*.
July: St John created Viscount Bolingbroke. October: Oxford and Bolingbroke clash in cabinet. Pope, *Rape of the Lock* (two-canto version); Arbuthnot, *Proposal for an Art of Political Lying*.
March: Peace and commerce treaties signed by Britain and France at Utrecht. August: Bolingbroke's bid to control ministry defeated by Harley; general election, another Tory victory. December: Queen Anne seriously ill. Pope, *Windsor-Forest*; Gay, *Rural Sports*; Parnell, *Essay on the Different Styles of Poetry*; Addison, *Cato*; Steele, *The Guardian, The Englishman*.
January: Steele, *Crisis*. July: Oxford dismissed by Queen Anne. August: death of Queen Anne; accession of George I. Beginning of Whig supremacy.
1715   June: Pope, *Iliad*, first books published.
1717   January: Pope, Gay and Arbuthnot, *Three Hours After Marriage*. Pope, *Works*.
1718   Death of Parnell.

June: death of Addison.

March: Declaratory Act (that the British parliament may make laws binding on Ireland). August: collapse of the 'South Sea Bubble'. November: John Trenchard and Thomas Gordon begin publishing *Cato's Letters*.
Emergence of Robert Walpole as *de facto* Prime Minister. September: death of Prior. December: Parnell, *Poems on Several Occasions*, with Pope's 'Epistle to Oxford' as preface.

1723   June: Death of Vanessa; Swift begins four-month tour of southern Ireland.

1724   January: Swift finishes book four of *Gulliver's Travels*, and begins book three. March: *Letter to the Shopkeepers of Ireland* (first *Drapier's Letter*). August: *Letter to Harding* (second *Drapier's Letter*). September: *Some Observations* (third *Drapier's Letter*). October: *Letter to Whole People of Ireland* (fourth *Drapier's Letter*). December: *Letter to Molesworth* (fifth *Drapier's Letter*)

May: death of Oxford. October: £300 reward offered for naming of the author of fourth *Drapier's Letter*. Burnet, *History of his Own Time*.

1725   April: Swift created freeman of City of Dublin. April–October: Swift and Stella at Quilca with Sheridan family; completion of *Gulliver's Travels*.

April: Bolingbroke returns from exile in France. September: cancellation of William Wood's patent. Pope's edition of Shakespeare and translation of Homer's *Odyssey* (to 1726).

1726   March: Swift travels to London. April: Audience with Princess of Wales. Meetings with patriot members of opposition, and with Walpole. May: at Pope's Twickenham villa with Gay and Martha Blount; visits Richard Temple, first Viscount Cobham at Stowe; Stella seriously ill. August: returns to Dublin amid public acclamation. 28 October: first edn of *Gulliver's Travels*.

March: Lewis Theobald, *Shakespeare Restored*. December: William Pulteney and Bolingbroke launch opposition periodical *The Craftsman*.

1727   January: Swift attempts to correct early editions of *Gulliver*. April: travels to London for his last English visit. June: Pope/Swift *Miscellanies*, vols. 1 and 2. August: returns to Ireland, writing 'Holyhead Journal' during a week of delays before crossing.

June: death of George I, accession of George II. Autumn: floods and crop failures in Ireland. Death of Newton. Gay, *Fables*.

1728   January: Death of Stella. Swift, 'On the Death of Mrs Johnson'. March: 'last' volume of Pope/Swift *Miscellanies*; Swift, *A Short View of the State of Ireland*. May: Swift and Sheridan begin *The Intelligencer*, runs until May 1729.

January: Gay's *Beggar's Opera* begins triumphant run at Lincoln's Inn Fields. May: Pope, *Dunciad*; numerous printed attacks on Pope.

1729   October: Swift, *A Modest Proposal*. December: Swift meets Laetitia Pilkington, author of *Memoirs* (1748–54) concerning Swift, and her husband Matthew.

April: Pope, *Dunciad Variorum*.

1730   February: Swift tells Pope of his friendship with a 'triumfeminate' of Dublin literary Bluestockings (Mary Barber, Constantia Grierson, Mrs Sican).

Charles, second Viscount Townshend resigns as Secretary of State. Trial of Francis Charteris. Cibber made Poet Laureate.

1731 Swift works on *Verses on the Death of Dr Swift* (published 1739) and the scatological poems published in 1734.
1732 April: Swift, *Life and Character of Dr Swift*. June: Swift, *The Lady's Dressing Room*. October: Pope/Swift *Miscellanies*, 'third' vol.; Swift has met his future biographer, the Earl of Orrery.
1734 A letter of commendation from Swift appears as preface to Mary Barber's *Poems on Several Occasions*. November: George Faulkner begins to publish Swift's *Works* in Dublin. December: Swift, *A Beautiful Young Nymph Going to Bed* published with 'Strephon and Chloe' and 'Cassinus and Peter'.
1735 Death of Swift's faithful housekeeper, Mrs Brent. Faulkner publishes first four volumes of *The Works of J.S., D.D, D.S.P.D.*, with revised/restored *Gulliver's Travels* as vol. III.
1736 December: Swift tells Pope that 'I now neither read, nor write; nor remember, nor converse. All I have left is to walk, and ride.' June: *A Character of the Legion Club*.
1737 August: Swift created freeman of the City of Cork.

1738 Spring: Swift, *Genteel and Ingenious Conversation*; fifth and sixth volumes of the Faulkner *Works*.
1739 January: Swift, *Verses on the Death of Dr Swift*, edited by Pope and William King, followed by Dublin edition in February.
1740 May: Swift makes his last will, on the brink of his final decline; bequests to Rebecca Dingley (Stella's companion), Martha Whiteway (guardian during his final years), and others; land purchased for St Patrick's Hospital. First printing of the Swift–Pope letters.
1742 November: Swift's understanding 'quite gone'.

1745 19 October: death of Swift.

December: Pope, *Epistle to Burlington*. First issue of *Gentleman's Magazine*. Death of Defoe.
December: death of Gay. Hogarth, *Harlot's Progress*.
1733 January: Pope, *Epistle to Bathurst*. February: Pope, first *Imitation of Horace*; *An Essay on Man*. Excise Crisis.
January: Pope, *Epistle to Cobham*. Hogarth, *Rake's Progress* (engravings published 1735).

January: Pope, *Epistle to Arbuthnot*. February: death of Arbuthnot. Bolingbroke returns to France. April: Pope, *Works* II.

Porteous Riots; repeal of Test and Corporation Acts defeated. Joseph Butler, *Analogy of Religion*.

May: Pope's edn of his letters. Prince of Wales expelled from court; death of Queen Caroline.
October: death of Thomas Sheridan. Pope visited by Bolingbroke. Last report of Society for Reformation of Manners. October: War of Jenkins' Ear.

War of Austrian Succession.

March: Pope, *The New Dunciad* (i.e. book IV).
1744 May: death of Pope. Death of Walpole. Jacobite rebellion.

ABBREVIATIONS

*   copy physically examined
§   copy collated using optical collator
†   copy manually collated
¶   copy checked against list of variants

Account Books	Paul V. Thompson and Dorothy J. Thompson (eds.), *The Account Books of Jonathan Swift*, Newark: University of Delaware Press, 1984
Arbuthnot, *John Bull*	John Arbuthnot, *The History of John Bull*, ed. Alan W. Bower and Robert A. Erickson, Oxford: Clarendon Press, 1976
Ball, *Correspondence*	*The Correspondence of Jonathan Swift, D. D.*, ed. F. Elrington Ball, 6 vols., London: G. Bell & Sons, 1910–14
BJECS	*British Journal for Eighteenth-Century Studies*
BL	British Library
BLJ	*British Library Journal*
Bodl	Bodleian Library, Oxford
Bolingbroke, *Letters*	*Letters and Correspondence of Henry St John, Lord Viscount Bolingbroke*, ed. Gilbert Parke, 4 vols., London, 1798
Bond	Maurice F. Bond (ed.), *The Manuscripts of the House of Lords, Volume X: 1712–1714*, London: HMSO, 1953
Boyer, *State*	Abel Boyer, *The Political State of Great Britain*, 38 vols., London, 1711–29
Chalmers	John P. Chalmers, 'Bodleian Copyright Deposit Survivors of the First Sixteen Years of the Copyright Act of Queene Anne 10 April 1710 to 25 March 1726', unpublished M.Litt. thesis, University of Oxford (1974)
CJ	*Journals of the House of Commons, from November the 8th 1547*, 101 vols., 1803–52
CUL	Cambridge University Library
CWJS	*Cambridge Edition of the Works of Jonathan Swift* (2008–)
Davis	*The Prose Writings of Jonathan Swift*, ed. Herbert Davis *et al.*, 16 vols., Oxford: Basil Blackwell, 1939–74
ECCO	*Eighteenth Century Collections Online*, Thomson Gale, online subscription database
Ehrenpreis	Irvin Ehrenpreis, *Swift: The Man, His Works, and the Age*, 3 vols., London: Methuen, 1962–83

ELH	*English Literary History*
Ellis, *Discourse*	*A Discourse of the Contests and Dissentions between the Nobles and the Commons in Athens and Rome*, ed. Frank H. Ellis, Oxford: Clarendon Press, 1967
Ellis, *Examiner*	*Swift vs. Mainwaring: 'The Examiner' and 'The Medley'*, ed. Frank H. Ellis, Oxford: Clarendon Press, 1985
Englishman	Richard Steele, *The Englishman: A Political Journal*, ed. Rae Blanchard, Oxford: Clarendon Press, 1955
ESTC	*English Short Title Catalogue*
Fischer, 'Legal Response'	John Irwin Fischer, 'The Legal Response to Swift's *The Public Spirit of the Whigs*', in John Irwin Fischer, Hermann J. Real and James Woolley (eds.), *Swift and his Contexts*, New York: AMS Press, 1989, pp. 21–38
Ford	*The Letters of Jonathan Swift to Charles Ford*, ed. David Nichol Smith, Oxford: Clarendon Press, 1935
Gaskell	Philip Gaskell, *A New Introduction to Bibliography*, Oxford: Clarendon Press, 1972
GM	*The Gentleman's Magazine*, 1731–1907
Gregg	Edward Gregg, *Queen Anne*, London: Routledge & Kegan Paul, 1980
Guardian	*The Guardian*, ed. John Calhoun Stephens, Lexington: University Press of Kentucky, 1982
Heawood	Edward Heawood, *Watermarks: Mainly of the 17th and 18th Centuries*, Hilversum: Paper Publications Society, 1950
Higgins	Ian Higgins, *Swift's Politics: A Study in Disaffection*, Cambridge: Cambridge University Press, 1994
HLQ	*Huntington Library Quarterly*
HMC	Historical Manuscripts Commission
Holmes	Geoffrey Holmes, *British Politics in the Age of Anne*, London: Macmillan, 1967
HP 1690–1715	Eveline Cruickshanks, Stuart Handley and D. W. Hayton (eds.), *The History of Parliament. The House of Commons 1690–1715*, 5 vols., Cambridge: Cambridge University Press, 2002
LJ	*Journals of the House of Lords, Beginning Anno Primo Henrici Octavi*, 79 vols., London, 1771
Loeb	The Loeb Classical Library
McKenzie, *1641–1700*	D. F. McKenzie (ed.), *Stationers' Company Apprentices 1641–1700*, Oxford: Oxford Bibliographical Society, 1974
McKenzie, *1701–1800*	D. F. McKenzie (ed.), *Stationers' Company Apprentices 1701–1800*, Oxford: Oxford Bibliographical Society, 1978
Macpherson, *Papers*	James Macpherson, *Original Papers; Containing the Secret History of Great Britain, from the Restoration, to the Accession of the House of Hanover*, 2nd edn, 2 vols., London, 1776

Maner	Martin W. Maner, 'An Eighteenth-Century Editor at Work: John Nichols and Jonathan Swift', *PBSA* 70 (1976), 481–99
Marlborough–Godolphin	Henry L. Snyder (ed.), *The Marlborough–Godolphin Correspondence*, 3 vols., Oxford: Clarendon Press, 1975
Maynwaring	*The Life and Posthumous Works of Arthur Maynwaring, Esq; Containing Several Original Pieces and Translations in Prose and Verse*, London, 1715
MP	*Modern Philology*
Münster	Hermann J.Real *et al.* (eds.), *Reading Swift: Papers from the Münster Symposium*, Munich: Fink, 1985, 1993, 1998, 2003
N&Q	*Notes and Queries*
Nichols (1801)	*The Works of the Rev. Jonathan Swift, D. D.*, ed. John Nichols, 19 vols., London, 1801
NLI	National Library of Ireland
NLS	National Library of Scotland
n.s./o.s.	new-style/old-style dating – see note on dates
ODNB	*The Oxford Dictionary of National Biography*
OED	*Oxford English Dictionary*
Parliamentary History	William Cobbett and John Wright, *Cobbett's Parliamentary History of England from the Norman Conquest in 1066 to the year 1803*, 36 vols., London, 1806–20
PBSA	*Papers of the Bibliographical Society of America*
POAS	*Poems on Affairs of State: Augustan Satirical Verse, 1660–1714*, ed. G. deF. Lord *et al.*, 7 vols., New Haven: Yale University Press, 1963–75
Pollard	M. Pollard, *A Dictionary of the Dublin Book Trade, 1550–1800, Based on the Records of the Guild of St Luke the Evangelist, Dublin*, London: Bibliographical Society, 2000
Quinlan	Maurice J. Quinlan, 'The Prosecution of Swift's *Public Spirit of the Whigs*', *Texas Studies in Literature and Language* 9 (1967), 167–84
RES	*Review of English Studies*
Review	*Defoe's Review*, ed. Arthur W. Secord, 22 vols., New York: Columbia University Press for The Facsimile Society, 1937, 1965
RIA	Royal Irish Academy, Dublin
Rivington	Charles A. Rivington, *'Tyrant': The Story of John Barber*, York: William Sessions Limited, 1989
Ross and Woolley	*Jonathan Swift: Major Works*, ed. Angus Ross and David Woolley, Oxford: Oxford University Press, 1984

Rothschild Library	*The Rothschild Library: A Catalogue of the Collection of Eighteenth-century Printed Books and Manuscripts Formed by Lord Rothschild*, privately printed at Cambridge University Press, 1954
SB	*Studies in Bibliography*
Scott (1814)	*The Works of Jonathan Swift*, ed. Walter Scott, 19 vols., Edinburgh, 1814
Scott (1824)	*The Works of Jonathan Swift*, ed. Walter Scott, 2nd edn, 19 vols., Edinburgh, 1824
Spectator	*The Spectator*, ed. Donald F. Bond, 5 vols., Oxford: Clarendon Press, 1965
SR	Stationers' Register
SStud	*Swift Studies*
Steele, *Correspondence*	*Correspondence of Richard Steele*, ed. Rae Blanchard, Oxford: Oxford University Press, 1941
Steele, *Tracts*	*The Tracts and Pamphlets of Richard Steele*, ed. Rae Blanchard, Baltimore: Johns Hopkins University Press, 1944
SwJ	Alexander Lindsay, 'Jonathan Swift 1667–1745', in *Index of English Literary Manuscripts, Vol. III, Part 4*, London, Mansell, 1997
Szechi	D. Szechi, *Jacobitism and Tory Politics 1710–14*, Edinburgh, John Donald, 1984
TCC	Trinity College, Cambridge
TCD	Trinity College Dublin
Temple Scott	*The Prose Works of Jonathan Swift*, ed. Temple Scott, 12 vols., London, 1897–1908
Tilley, *Proverbs*	Morris P. Tilley, *A Dictionary of the Proverbs in England in the Sixteenth and Seventeenth Centuries*, Ann Arbor: University of Michigan Press, 1950
TLS	*Times Literary Supplement*
Treadwell, 'Swift's Relations'	Michael Treadwell, 'Swift's Relations with the London Book Trade to 1714', in Robin Myers and Michael Harris (eds.), *Author/Publisher Relations During the Eighteenth and Nineteenth Centuries*, Oxford: Oxford Polytechnic Press, 1983, pp. 1–36
Treadwell, 'Trade Publishers'	Michael Treadwell, 'London Trade Publishers 1675–1750', *The Library* 6th ser., 4 (1982), 99–134
Trevelyan	George M. Trevelyan, *England under Queen Anne*, 3 vols., London: Longman, 1930–4
TS	H. Teerink, *A Bibliography of the Writings of Jonathan Swift*, 2nd edn, ed. Arthur H. Scouten, Philadelphia: University of Pennsylvania Press, 1963
TSLL	*Texas Studies in Literature and Language*

Wentworth Papers	James J. Cartwright (ed.), *The Wentworth Papers 1705–1739*, London: Wyman and Sons, 1882
Wheeler	*The Conduct of the Allies*, ed. C. B. Wheeler, Oxford: Clarendon Press, 1916
Williams, *Corr.*	*The Correspondence of Jonathan Swift*, ed. Harold Williams, 5 vols., Oxford: Clarendon Press, 1963–5
Williams, *JSt*	*Journal to Stella*, ed. Harold Williams, 2 vols., Oxford: Clarendon Press, 1948
Williams, *Poems*	*The Poems of Jonathan Swift*, ed. Harold Williams, 2nd edn, 3 vols., Oxford: Clarendon Press, 1958
Woolley, 'Canon'	David Woolley, 'The Canon of Swift's Prose Pamphleteering, 1710–1714, and *The New Way of Selling Places at Court*', *Swift Studies* 3 (1988), 96–123 (and foldout endpaper)
Woolley, *Corr.*	*The Correspondence of Jonathan Swift, D. D.*, ed. David Woolley, 4 vols., Frankfurt am Main: Peter Lang, 1999–
Woolley, 'Dialogue'	David Woolley, '*A Dialogue upon Dunkirk* (1712) and Swift's "7 penny Papers"', in Hermann J. Real and Richard H. Rodino (eds.), *Reading Swift: Papers from the Second Münster Symposium on Jonathan Swift*, Munich: W. Fink, 1993, pp. 215–23
Woolley, 'Forster's *Swift*'	David Woolley, 'Forster's *Swift*', *The Dickensian* 70 (1974), 191–204
Woolley, *Intelligencer*	Jonathan Swift and Thomas Sheridan, *The Intelligencer*, ed. James Woolley, Oxford: Clarendon Press, 1992

Shortened forms of Swift's works included in this volume

Conduct	*The Conduct of the Allies*
Defence	*A Defence of Erasmus Lewis* or *The Examiner* (2 February 1713)
Dialogue	*A Dialogue upon Dunkirk, between a Whig and a Tory*
Discourse	*A Discourse concerning the Fears from the Pretender*
Hue and Cry	*A Hue and Cry after Dismal*
Humble Address	*The Humble Address of. . . Lords* (11 April 1713)
Importance	*The Importance of the Guardian Considered*
It's Out at Last	*It's Out at Last: Or, French Correspondence Clear as the Sun*
Letter	*A Letter from the Pretender, to a Whig-Lord*
New Way	*The New Way of Selling Places at Court*
Publick Spirit	*The Publick Spirit of the Whigs*
Some Advice	*Some Advice Humbly Offer'd to the Members of the October Club*

Some Considerations	*Some Considerations upon the Consequences hoped and feared from the Death of the Queen*
Some Free Thoughts	*Some Free Thoughts upon the Present State of Affairs*
Some Reasons	*Some Reasons to Prove . . . In a Letter to a Whig-Lord*
Some Remarks	*Some Remarks on the Barrier Treaty*
Vote of Thanks	*Vote of Thanks* by the House of Lords (9 April 1713)

NOTE

The year's beginning has been taken as January throughout. Britain followed the Julian (or Old Style) calendar until 1752; however, by 1700, most of mainland Europe followed the Gregorian (or New Style) calendar which was eleven days ahead. Dates of events taking place on mainland Europe have been marked with '(n.s.)'. All other dates are Old Style but are not marked as such unless the context is not clear.

All biblical quotations are taken from *The Bible: Authorized King James Version* (Oxford: Oxford University Press, 1997); all classical quotations are taken from the Loeb Classical Library except where noted.

Place of publication for pre-1800 items cited in the Introduction and the notes is London unless noted otherwise.

INTRODUCTION

1. *The Conduct of the Allies, Tory politics, and the Barrier Treaty*

On 8 September 1711 Swift, in a letter to his friend Charles Ford, remarked casually of Queen Anne, 'I find no body expects she can live long; and that is one great Reason why they would hasten a Peace.' Then he adds, ''Tis thought by State Astronomers that we shall have a scribbling Winter; but perhaps I shall then be far enough off', and finally, before his adieu, 'I am at least twice oftner with th[e] M—rs than when you was here, yet You see nothing comes of it' (Woolley, *Corr.*, vol. I, p. 381). These lines can all serve in some ways as keynotes for his life that autumn. Whatever the Queen's health, the movement towards Peace which would culminate in the treaty of Utrecht in 1713 was on its way; it was indeed a scribbling winter with Swift as a major scribbler; and though his familiarity with the chief ministers Harley and St John had not yet produced the preferment he was hoping for, what did come of it was his place as the most successful political writer of the Queen Anne period, a period dominated in its final years by the two overriding issues of the peace and the Succession.

Swift was ready for an important new task. On 7 June he had published the last *Examiner* paper totally his own, a review of the accomplishments of the Tory Parliament which was to end five days later; and though there was no announcement that he would be succeeded by another hand, Swift did say that the main design he had had in writing those papers had been now 'fully executed' (Ellis, *Examiner*, p. 470). Though perhaps he did not know it in June, by September he had an important new assignment. On the next day after writing to Ford, in fact, Swift in his *Journal* mentions to Stella that he had hoped to stay at Windsor a week 'to be at leisure for something I am doing' (Williams, *JSt*, p. 356). The nature of that 'something' was made very clear in his comments to her over the next month. On the 28th he wrote to her, 'We have already settled all things with France, and very much to the honour and advantage of England; and the queen is in mighty good humour. All this news is a mighty secret; the people in general know that a Peace is forwarding' (p. 356). The job he had been set was to make the people in general, and especially the members of Parliament, who would be returning

1

to town in November, not only realize that a peace was forwarding but accept the idea that England was proceeding with negotiations for peace with France without the knowledge and agreement of the Dutch, the Austrians and the other Allies – all contrary to the Eighth Article of the Grand Alliance (1701), which stipulated that peace must be agreed to by all the allied powers. In the next sentence he made the problem plain to Stella: 'The earl of Strafford is to go soon to Holland and let them know what we have been doing: and then there will be the devil and all to pay; but we'll make them swallow it with a pox' (p. 372). His project for the next two months was to make them swallow it, to force it down their throats with facts, figures and cool disdain without directly addressing the question of underhand dealing by the ministers, a question which made even St John uneasy (Holmes, p. 79). Instead of discussing the prospects for peace or Britain's relations with France, Swift would need to focus on the Conduct (or misconduct) of the Allies themselves.

It was a project on which he spent several months, as is made plain by his frequent reference to this 'business' in his letters to Stella from September until November. He was not acting alone; there are plenty of comments about the role of both St John and Oxford in urging him on and furnishing help: 'the ministers reckon it will do abundance of good, and open the eyes of the nation, who are half bewitched against a Peace' (Williams, *JSt*, p. 397). 'Three or four great people', he reports on 10 November, 'are to see there are no mistakes in point of fact' (p. 408). Oxford and St John did more than correct facts or read proof, of course; both furnished ideas. There are even a few verbal similarities between Swift's *Conduct of the Allies* and an earlier tract by Harley (Oxford) called 'Plaine English', and the Lord Treasurer continued to make alterations after the book had gone through three editions (pp. 428–9).[1] As he was writing, Swift made constant visits to consult his printer in the City (John Barber), all duly reported to Stella, with one of the six sheets corrected by St John (Woolley, *Corr.*, vol. I, p. 396). Finally on 27 November, ten days before the opening of parliament, the first edition of *Conduct*, Swift's most influential and successful political pamphlet, was published, the 'great men' having received their copies the night before (Williams, *JSt*, p. 421).

The subject of the pamphlet would not be taking the town by surprise, since all through the autumn of 1711 printers were kept busy churning out writings about the possibility of Peace. In a pamphlet published in early November, just a few weeks before *Conduct* itself finally appeared, Defoe, himself now

1 J. A. Downie, '*The Conduct of the Allies*: the Question of Influence', in Clive Probyn (ed.), *The Art of Jonathan Swift* (London: Vision, 1978), pp. 120–4.

a ministerial writer, gave his impression of the feverish atmosphere of the Town as it spoke of little except the possibility of peace: 'Unhappy Nation! What End can these Things lead us to? Not a Publick Society, not a Coffee-house, not a Meeting of Friends, not a Visit, but like *Jehu* to *Jezabel, who is on my Side?* Who? Who is for Peace? Who is for carrying on the war?'[2] Even back in June 1711 Defoe had noted in his *Review*, 'Peace is now all the Discourse of the Town, what Ground we have for it I confess I don't see' (vol. VIII, p. 141).

But the real furore had started with the signing of the Preliminary Articles from France on 27 September, which were then, to the dismay of the ministry, revealed to the public on 13 October by the Whiggish *Daily Courant*, having been placed there by the imperial envoy Count Gallas. By coincidence on the same day, Addison sent a letter to Edward Wortley enclosing a copy of the Tory *Post Boy* and commenting, 'I send you Enclosed a paper of Abel Roper's, which every body looks upon as Authentick: we talk of nothing but a peace.'[3] October was then marked by a succession of pamphlets, their titles fairly well revealing their political bent: *The Taxes not Grievous, and therefore not a Reason for an Unsafe Peace* (2 October); Defoe's *Reasons why this Nation Ought to Put a Speedy End to this Expensive War* (6 October); *Anguis in Herba; Or, The Fatal Consequences of a Treaty with France* (advertised on 29 October, but actually a reprint of a much earlier pamphlet by Henry Maxwell); *Reflections upon the Examiner's Scandalous Peace* (probably by Abel Boyer in September 1711). On 16 October Swift found himself abused in another pamphlet by Boyer, *An account of the State and Progress of the Present Negotiation of Peace*, which nastily attacks Swift's political tergiversation, his ambition and even his bad French. Swift mentioned this work to Stella, carefully noting that he had had the 'French dog' taken up by a messenger and that St John had promised he would 'swinge' him (Williams, *JS*, p. 384). Not all the Whig tracts in these months resorted to abuse, however, since they had their own ironist. Arthur Maynwaring's *Vindication of the Present M—y, from The Clamours rais'd against them* (1711) deftly pretends to defend the Preliminaries against an enraged town. His opening sentence might even have made Swift smile:

> Among the many restless Endeavours of the Ruin'd Party [the Whigs] to sink the Reputation of the present M——y, there is none in which they discover their Good-will to them more than in the Violence they shew in attacking the new Preliminaries, which tho they are such weak wretched

2 *An Essay at A Plain Exposition Of That Difficult Phrase A Good Peace* (1711), p. 7.
3 Walter Graham (ed.), *Letters of Joseph Addison* (Oxford: Oxford University Press, 1941), pp. 265–6.

things that they must fall of themselves, without any opposition made to them, yet these angry Men run upon them with all their might.   (p. 3)

Less than a week after Swift's book was published, Peter Wentworth wrote with concern to his brother the Earl of Strafford, a plenipotentiary at the Utrecht conference, 'there's so many of the Allies to satisfie, that it will be almost impossible to make a fast, honourable, and lasting Peace in any short time' (*Wentworth Papers*, p. 217). Swift's major task, then, was to depict the Allies' demands in an unfavourable light. Yet his full title makes plain that not only the Allies but the 'late Ministry' as well are to blame for beginning and carrying on the war. After Swift lays bare in the first half of his pamphlet all the follies and mistakes in the conduct of the war, all the 'weak and foolish Bargains with our Allies', he asks, how did it happen that we have thus become the '*Dupes* and *Bubbles*' of Europe? Was it our stupidity? And the answer is that they are in a war of this duration because of the 'Family', the leaders of the Whig 'Junto' and the Marlboroughs (Godolphin's only son was married to Marlborough's oldest daughter, and the Earl of Sunderland was married to his second daughter), and because of the 'Monied Men', who had raised vast sums by trading stocks and lending at exorbitant rates. These people are the 'real Causes of our present Misery', Swift says (below, pp. 81–7).

But even after exposing the causes, he still needs to address those MPs who may favour peace but only a 'good' one, which for many of them was defined by the cry, 'No Peace without Spain', that is, without restoring Spain to the House of Austria. Although this had been the principle accepted by both parties for most of the war, the defeat and capture of Earl Stanhope in the battle of Brihuega in 1710 had ended the support of most Tories for that slogan, and the Emperor's death in April of 1711 made it militarily unrealistic and politically undesirable to think that the new Emperor Charles VI could also become King of Spain (see Holmes, pp. 77–9). Even if that could be accomplished, it would mean the end of the Balance of Power, one of the principles behind the Grand Alliance, and Austria would replace France as the superpower of Europe. In *Conduct* Swift quotes the Eighth Article of the Grand Alliance to emphasize that it contains no suggestion that a peace must include guaranteeing Spain for the Austrians. Unfortunately, as it turned out, Swift's arguments on this point were put to the test and failed with some readers little more than a week after *Conduct* first appeared; on the first day of the new session in the House of Lords, the Earl of Nottingham successfully moved that a motion thanking the Queen for her Address include a clause rejecting any peace in which Spain and the West Indies were allotted to the

House of Bourbon. This political blow to the administration created near-panic in Swift and other supporters of the ministry, until 29 December, when Queen Anne resolved the crisis by creating 'no less than twelve lords to have a majority', as Swift exulted to Stella (Williams, *JSt*, p. 450).

In all other ways, however, this pamphlet which had cost him 'so much time and trouble' (Williams, *JSt*, p. 420) was having all the success he could have hoped for. It was intended to be ready for the sitting of Parliament, but Parliament, he reported on 25 November, is 'to be prorogued for eight or nine days; for the Whigs are too strong in the house of lords' (p. 421). Even so, almost as soon as it was published it began 'to make a noise' (p. 423), and the printers began working night and day to get a second edition ready. 'They sold a thousand in two days,' and by its third day of life he could claim, 'the pamphlet makes a world of noise, and will do a great deal of good: it tells abundance of most important facts which were not at all known' (pp. 423–4). As the third edition began printing, Oxford made some alterations; in a day half the third edition was already sold. Naturally, the Whigs and representatives of the Allies were less happy. St John told Swift that the Dutch envoy intended to complain about it, and on 3 December Swift heard 'the Whigs are resolved to bring that pamphlet into the house of lords to have it condemned' (p. 429).

Swift was perhaps taken aback by the threat of condemnation, especially when he learned that it had nothing to do with the Allies or Spain but with the Succession. In the first three editions, he had said that if a foreign power were called in to guarantee the Succession of the crown as stipulated in the Barrier Treaty, 'we put it out of the Power of our own Legislature to change our Succession, without the Consent of that Prince or State who is Guarantee, how much soever the Necessities of the Kingdom may require it'. Swift appears to have been truly surprised when Lord Chief Justice Parker considered that passage possibly treasonable and sent for John Morphew, named in the imprint, to try to find the author. Swift wrote a long-winded and perhaps disingenuous substitute passage, which he used in the fourth and subsequent editions, and then in a postscript he protested Parker's reading, pointing out that it goes against the Revolution principles of the Whigs themselves. Finally, in the midst of his next pamphlet, *Some Remarks on the Barrier Treaty*, he protested again, making a distinction between his argument and the Whigs' view of the grounds for altering the Succession: 'The *Whigs* are for changing the Succession when they think fit, though the entire Legislature do not consent; I think it ought never to be done but upon great Necessity, and that with the Sanction of the whole Legislature' (see pp. 129–31). But his protests did little good; even a month and a half later, he reported to Stella, 'A Whig Membr took out the Conduct of the Allyes, and read that Passage about the Succession, with great Resentmt, but none seconded him' (Williams, *JSt*, p. 488). And of course almost every 'Answer' to *Conduct*, which an eminent modern Dutch historian has called Swift's 'venomous pamphlet', delightedly complained of that passage, and even attacks on Swift that did not focus on *Conduct* managed to drag it in.[4]

It may be difficult for modern readers to understand either why his enemies seemed so outraged or why Swift seemed so persistent on this point, which in subsequent editions he repeated with more elaborate language but without softening his position. Yet though today it may seem harmless enough, in the last years of Queen Anne even to talk about the Succession was to touch on sensitive issues, for the fear of Jacobitism was always present, and the statutes on treason enacted since the Revolution made such talk potentially dangerous. It was of course treasonable to try to hinder anyone named in the Act of Settlement (1700) from succeeding to the Crown, but it was also high treason for a person 'maliciously, advisedly, and directly, by writing or printing', to maintain and affirm that any other person has any right or title to the Crown otherwise than according to the Act of Settlement, or that the Kings or Queens of the realm, with the authority of Parliament, 'are not able to make laws and statutes of sufficient force and validity to limit and bind the Crown and the descent thereof' (1707, An Act for the Security of her Majesty's Person, 6 Anne c. 7). Swift may not seem to be in violation of such laws, but in assuming the possibility of 'legislative defeasibility', as it was called, i.e., in assuming that the legislative body could alter the hereditary succession of the Crown, he was going further than even a Whig Chief Justice could comfortably tolerate. Again, this may seem paradoxical, since to a modern reader it may at first appear, as Swift suggests, very much to the taste of a Whig, but in 1711 any meddling with the Succession immediately smacked of efforts to put the Jacobite pretender on the throne.

Yet Swift persisted in claiming that the passage was completely innocent. When Stella's companion Rebecca Dingley took alarm at it, Swift protested to Stella, 'I here take leave to tell politick Dingley, that the passage in the *Conduct of the Allies* is so far from being blameable, that the secretary designs to insist upon it in the house of commons, when the Treaty of Barrier is debated there' (Williams, *JSt*, pp. 477–8). I have not found that St John especially insisted on it during the debate on the Barrier Treaty, not even

---

4 Pieter Geyl, *The Netherlands in the Seventeenth Century: Part Two* (London: Ernest Benn, 1964), p. 321. See, for example, Thomas Burnet (attrib.), *The Thoughts of a Tory Author, Concerning the Press* (1712), p. 4.

after, as noted already, a Whig member protested about it. But the alarm or pseudo-alarm over the passage continued, and Swift continued unrepentant.

Modern scholars in commenting on this episode have been of several minds, and since their comments are mostly determined by their views of Swift's entire political orientation, their arguments must be sketched here only briefly. Thus Ian Higgins sees Swift's ministerial writing as ambivalent on the Act of Settlement, 'reflecting his (and the Tory party's) reservations about the House of Hanover and perhaps a calculated attempt to keep legislative alterations of the succession a theoretically open possibility' (Higgins, p. 89 and see pp. 90–5).[5] And Higgins believes that the ministers who 'vetted' Swift's tract allowed the passage to go forward to keep the Jacobites among the Tory members of Parliament content and cooperative in their parliamentary votes. On the other hand, Daniel Eilon argues that the passage is an expression of Swift's consistently 'old Whig' attitudes to the Revolution, in which the 'legislature had the power and prerogative to institute a hereditary succession and also to repeal it in cases of extreme necessity'. Eilon points out that Swift's insistence here on the 'parliamentary defeasibility of the succession', though a source of embarrassment in *Conduct*, was later to become a useful ironic tool against Steele in Swift's *Publick Spirit of the Whigs*, even enabling Swift sarcastically to charge Steele with high treason.[6]

In short, since we obviously cannot know what exactly was in Swift's mind when he insisted on retaining in *Conduct* the substance of a passage which aroused so much concern, today's reader, though recognizing the reason for some suspicion, will also understand that the issue is secondary to Swift's major task in the pamphlet, which was of course to detach the English from the cause of the Allies in an effort to move them further along the road to peace. And it was mainly for that reason, rather than because of concern about the Succession, that it had to be answered effectively.

Although there were numerous others, the major answerer to Swift was Francis Hare, Marlborough's chaplain, his 'stupid priest', as St John called him (Bolingbroke, *Letters*, vol. I, p. 367), who had already published a defence of Marlborough called *The Management of the War* (1711). Now he 'continues to spoil paper' (St John again), attacking Swift in a four-part series under the general title of *The Allies and the late Ministry Defended against France and the Present Friends of France*, appearing from 5 December 1711 to 5 March 1712. The pamphlets are not lively reading, despite some help from Arthur

---

5 On Swift's 'Jacobitism', see below.
6 Daniel Eilon, 'Did Swift Write *A Discourse on Hereditary Right?*', *MP* 82 (1985) 381–4, and his *Factions' Fictions: Ideological Closure in Swift's Satire* (Newark: University of Delaware Press, 1991), p. 103.

Maynwaring, since Hare attempts to move through *Conduct*, answering Swift point by point, after first over-simplifying and reducing Swift's arguments to three: 'To go into the Grand alliance was wrong in it self. 2. The Terms of it don't oblige us to insist upon the *Restitution of the Spanish Monarchy*. 3. The Allies are a Pack of Rogues' (p. 31). Along the way, however, he does point out Swift's mishandling of documents: his omission, for example, of a phrase in the Eighth Article of the Grand Alliance and his misquotation of the first Separate Article of that treaty. But St John had spoken with cold and accurate assurance when he said of Hare and others who protested the dismissal of Marlborough, 'They had best for their patron's sake as well as their own, be quiet. I know . . . how to revive fellows that will write them to death' (Bolingbroke, *Letters*, vol. I, p. 365).

In the first few weeks following its publication, in addition to attacks in the Whig press like the *Observator*, there were also pamphlet attacks by writers less verbose than Hare but no less ineffective: *Remarks on a False, Scandalous, and Seditious Libel, Intituled, The Conduct of the Allies, and of the Late Ministry* (perhaps by John Oldmixon), such an incoherent, rambling, hit-and-miss response that it is hard to believe Maynwaring had any share in it, as some have suggested; and *A Defence of the Allies and the Late Ministry: or, Remarks on the Tories New Idol* (1712), once said to be by Defoe, Swift's fellow labourer in the Tory vineyard, an interesting attribution because the author is scathing on the subject of Swift's 'voluminous' style as he comes 'blustering upon the Stage, shouted in by the whole Tory Mob' (p. 3) – but Defoe's authorship has recently been firmly disputed.[7] (The following June Defoe did apparently write *A Further Search Into the Conduct of the Allies*, but it is a sequel, not an answer, a Tory piece attacking the Dutch memorial of April 1712.) Several of the hostile pamphlets hint that Swift, or sometimes just 'the Examiner', is their opponent, and they do what they can to capitalize on his 'suspect' comment about the Protestant Succession. But they can do little in the face of Swift's assured rhetoric.

Swift had promised in the postscript to the fourth edition of *Conduct* that 'whatever Objections of Moment' he could find in any of the answers, including Hare's, would be fully answered in a paragraph at the end of the Preface in the next edition. But of course since he never responded, he means us to assume he found no such objections of moment in any of them. And indeed they are not a brilliant bunch. As Douglas Coombs pointed out long ago, their problem was their audience; Swift preaches to the half-converted,

7 P. N. Furbank and W. R. Owens, *Defoe De-Attributions* (London: Hambledon, 1994), pp. 52–3.

to those who were already willing to believe the worst of the Allies because they were tired of the war. Essays which tried to counter his appeal to their feelings of impatience by reminding them that they should always be grateful to the Dutch for their role in the Revolution or by slurring him as a Jacobite were doomed to be ineffective.[8] By February 1712, Swift's triumph was complete; he saw his work bear fruit in the House of Commons. Though ten days later one member attempted to diminish its effect by reading the passage about the Succession, Swift could report to Stella on 4 February, 'The house of commons have this day made many severe votes about our being abused by our allies. Those who spoke, drew all their arguments from my book, and their votes confirm all I writ; the Court had a majority of a hundred and fifty: all agree, that it was my book that spirited them to these resolutions' (Williams, *JSt*, p. 480). And that view was seconded several years later in a short, hostile pamphlet by Robert Walpole, a man who was to dominate the political scene during the major decades of Swift's later productive career. In his *Short History of the Parliament* (1713) Walpole reflected on the effect of Swift's political 'masterpiece':

> This Master-piece, fill'd with Falsities and Misrepresentations, was no sooner dispers'd and canvass'd in the World, but it produc'd the desir'd Effect, affording Arguments for artful and ill-designing Instruments to . . . prejudice the Minds of weak and deluded People, and firing others, who had no Leisure or Opportunity to be better inform'd, with Resentment and Indignation against the Allies.   (p. 8)

Walpole's harping on the 'Falsities' of Swift's masterpiece was echoed much later in a passage in volume II of Bishop Burnet's *History of His Own Time* (1724–34); Swift, the 'mercenary Pen', defamed the Dutch in his *Conduct* with 'much Art, but with no regard to Truth', claiming that England was so exhausted that the war was impossible to carry on and that the Allies, especially the Dutch, had failed the English repeatedly (p. 581). To this charge Swift responded in his margin only by a single, emphasized comment: *'It was all true'* (Davis, vol. V, p. 293).

   Near the end of *Conduct* Swift refers again to the Barrier Treaty with the States, 'which deserveth such Epithets as I care not to bestow: But may per-haps consider it, at a proper Occasion, in a *Discourse* by it self' (p. 91). In the event it was February 1712 before the Commons called for the treaty to be considered, although St John's letters make it plain that it had been a topic high on the ministerial agenda for almost a year. In the meantime Swift served

---

8 Douglas Coombs, *The Conduct of the Dutch* (The Hague: Nijhoff, 1958), pp. 287–8.

the Court and diverted himself by addressing in print an issue of internal Tory politics, the impact of the high-Church high-Tory parliamentary group called 'The October Club'. In February 1711, almost a year before the piece was written, Swift had described the group in this way to Stella:

> We are plagued here with an October Club, that is, a set of above a hundred parliament-men of the country, who drink October beer at home, and meet every evening at a tavern near the parliament, to consult affairs, and drive things on to extreams against the Whigs, to call the old ministry to account, and get off five or six heads. The ministry seem not to regard them, yet one of them in confidence told me, that there must be something thought on to settle things better.   (Williams, *JSt*, pp. 194–5)[9]

Their activities were not limited to talk; they planned debating tactics, packed committees, and organized slates for elections to parliamentary commissions, and by early in the new year they were causing delays in Harley's plans for money and supply. By the end of 1711 they numbered over 140, and had won significant concessions from Harley, now since May the Earl of Oxford and Lord Treasurer.[10] Apparently on his own, with no ministerial prompting, Swift used his arts of impersonation to help quiet these barking dogs.

He knew his target, for he was on good terms with some of the members; in April 1711, while still writing *The Examiner*, he had been invited to dine with them and been forced to decline the invitation as improper, considering his friendship with the ministers. On 12 and 13 April he wrote to Stella of the Tory complaints that the ministry did too little to get rid of Whigs in place and find appointments for Tories, adding significantly 'and indeed I think they have some reason to complain' (Williams, *JSt*, pp. 241–2). In short, putting himself in the mind of an 'October man' in order to preach moderation in his little pamphlet required, I think, only a short imaginative step. Indeed, in *Memoirs* Swift admits his belief that 'if this body of men could have remained some time united, they would have put the crown under a necessity of acting in a more steady and strenuous manner' (Davis, vol. VIII, p. 125). But Oxford, who best understood the Queen's dispositions, had to break their measures, he goes on to say, and though never named it is the Lord Treasurer who is the hero of Swift's *Some Advice Humbly Offer'd to the Members of the October Club*; the Duke and Duchess of Somerset (now the Queen's favourite) are the antagonists; and the Queen herself is the weak pawn in this little drama in which the narrator says, sympathetically, yes, we

9 See H. T. Dickinson, 'The October Club', *HLQ 33* (1970), 155–73.
10 *HP 1690–1715*, pp. 460, 470; Dickinson, 'The October Club', 163–4.

are right, but prudence and practicality demand that we back off a bit, lest we ruin everything by ruining 'the *Person on whom we so much depend*' (p. 111).

Swift pretends on the title page that *Some Advice* is offered in a letter 'from a Person of Honour' because members of the October Club apparently took special pride in being gentlemen of the best families and having fixed, unchanging principles, all of them patriots who act from honour, 'Men of Birth, Fortune and Principles'.[11] From the outset also, his tone, as Irvin Ehrenpreis has described it, is that of an insider admitting the rank and file to the secrets of the inner circle, while also asking for his readers to be calm and patient. Swift took special care to keep his authorship secret, even from Barber, perhaps because of his acquaintance with some of the October men or perhaps, as Ehrenpreis suggests (vol. II, pp. 522–5), because he did not want to endanger his relations with St John, who is not depicted here as favourably as Oxford. As it turned out, however, both ministers received the piece well without (apparently) knowing its author; 'the secretary read a great deal of it to lord treasurer', Swift reported, and 'they all commended it to the skies' (Williams, *JSt*, p. 470).

Although the Preface included by Faulkner in 1737 claimed the letter was 'very seasonably published with great Success' (Davis, vol. VI, p. 188), its success seems to have been fairly limited. Swift complained to Stella on 28 January 1712 that it did not sell well despite being 'finely written' (Williams, *JSt*, p. 474). By 1 February, sales began to pick up (p. 478), which the preface to the work in Swift's 1801 *Collected Works* (Nichols, vol. III, p. 251) attributes to an apparent belief that Harcourt had written it. Ehrenpreis says the piece was reprinted by Boyer in his *Political State*, but that is misleading, since Boyer did not include it until the 1718 edition of his compilation. Nonetheless, *Some Advice* did not make much of an impact in the political press. Advertisements for the second edition ran in *The Examiner* for many weeks in January and February 1712, perhaps a sign that it did not attract many readers. Some may have confused it briefly with *A Letter to a Member of the October-Club, Shewing, That to Yield Spain to the Duke of Anjou by a Peace, would be the Ruin of Great Britain* (1711), but as the title makes plain that letter was not about the October Club but an ultra-Whiggish tract (by Francis Hare), and about as far from Swift's work as anything could be.

Finally, in January and February 1712, as the Commons began looking at the Barrier Treaty of 1709, Swift could follow up on his stated intention in *Conduct* and turn his attention again in that direction. Although the precise

11 See *The Character and Declaration of the October Club* (1711), p. 4, and *Considerations upon the Secret History of the White Staff* (1714), p. 22.

meaning of 'Barrier' was a point of dispute, in basic terms the Dutch Barrier was a collection of cities and fortresses in the French border area and in the Spanish Netherlands which the Dutch were allowed by this treaty to garrison as a protection against French invasion, in return for which the Dutch pledged military support for the Hanoverian Succession, should it be necessary. The treaty in question was negotiated in 1709, with Viscount Townshend and the Duke of Marlborough acting for the British; the latter, however, refused to sign the treaty, writing to his Duchess on 8 August 1709 (o.s.) that he wished the Queen to know his position so that he 'might not be obliged to signe what I think so very prejudiciall to England', adding that Townshend misjudges the Dutch, for as soon as they have their Barrier they will make peace as soon as possible (Marlborough–Godolphin, pp. 1334–5). To Godolphin (the Lord Treasurer) Marlborough predicted even more 'exorbitant' demands from the Dutch, asserting that Townshend's position would prove fatal to the interest of the Queen and England (p. 1336). And on 23 September he wrote to the Duchess that the friendship between Holland and England must continue, 'for I think without it we are all undone; but to that end we must not pretend to wash a blackemore white, which I take the business of the Barier to bee' (p. 1375). The treaty was completed without his signature on 29 October 1709.

If the British general and hero of the Whigs could reach the conclusion that the Barrier Treaty of 1709 was a wretched bargain for his country, little wonder that the Tory ministry made it a prime target. In April 1711, almost a year before the matter was heard in Parliament, St John wrote to Lord Raby that the treaty 'was the measure of a faction, who made their Court to Holland, at the expence of Britain. I will undertake to show, in almost every article of it, something more or less scandalous' (Bolingbroke, *Letters*, vol. I, p. 153). This view was predominant in the Commons in the winter of 1711–12 and summed up in the Representation (written by Sir Thomas Hanmer with Swift's help) which the Commons presented to the Queen on 4 March 1712 and which Swift quotes in his *History* (Davis, vol. VII, pp. 90–4; see Swift's comments, pp. 78–9). About the same time a Whig writer unsympathetically summed up the general feeling to which the Commons was responding and to which Swift sympathetically appeals in his tract: 'It is a general Cry, What have we been Fighting for? What are we to have after all? We have conquered 30 or 40 Towns for the *Dutch*; what for our selves? We are only to have *Dunkirk* demolished and *Newfoundland*.'[12]

---

12 John Oldmixon (attrib.), *The Dutch Barrier Our's* (1712), p. 11.

Swift's *Some Remarks on the Barrier Treaty* was, like *Conduct*, a piece which he was specifically asked to write for the Tory ministry, or so one infers from his report to Stella on 12 February: 'I dined in the City with my Printer; to consult with him about some Paprs Ld Tr— gave me last night, as he always does, too late; However, I will do something with them' (Williams, *JSt*, pp. 486–7). He called it 'too late' because the treaty had already been laid before the House; but there was still plenty he could do to explain the ministry's case to the public. A set of resolutions censuring the treaty and calling Lord Townshend and others involved in it 'Enemies to the Queen and the Kingdom' was passed on 16 February, and, on 19 February, the States General wrote to the Queen promising to rectify some of the problems complained about, a letter which (Boyer reports unconvincingly) 'did wonderfully reconcile' the Dutch to the 'Generality of the People' (*State*, vol. III, p. 74). It was Swift's task to make sure the generality of the people took a sharply different view.

He had a wonderful weapon at hand, the 'Counter-Project', which, as he explains in the Preface, was the outline of an alternative treaty which the British Court had drawn up and given to Townshend and Marlborough to use in the negotiations with the Dutch. To show how they had ignored, exceeded or otherwise altered their instructions, Swift had only to print the relevant articles of the Counter-Project and call the reader's attention to the contrast between them and the text of the 1709 Barrier Treaty, which itself he was making available to readers for the very first time, since the Commons did not order it to be printed until several days after Swift's pamphlet appeared (*CJ*, vol. IV, p. 261). For additional documentary support, Swift includes the remarks of Prince Eugene and Count Sinzendorf (Zinzendorf), the Austrian general and the Austrian diplomat, both of whom had objected to the Barrier discussions early in 1709, while the negotiations were still in progress. To end this parade of pieces of documentary evidence, Swift closes his case with a 'Representation' of English merchants in Flanders, who complain about the effect of the treaty on their trade. As John Oldmixon scornfully remarks, 'The Author of the *Conduct* has one admirable way of proving what he says, he imitates those Historians, who to knock down all Opponents, Print Appendixes at the End of their Works, with Copies of the Records to which they refer.'[13] But these records, of course, were furnished to this historian by those who were making the history.

---

13 John Oldmixon (attrib.), *Remarks upon Remarks* (1711), p 8; for the objections of the Austrians, see Marlborough–Godolphin, p. 1254.

To prepare the way for all those documents Swift presents an incisive commentary, short but scathing. Its very opening image, I think, sets this writer off from the horde of other political pamphleteers in the period, very few of whom could have written it: he imagines 'a reasonable Person in *China*' who reads the Barrier Treaty and concludes that the States General must be some vast commonwealth like Rome and the Queen of England a petty prince under the protection of the Dutch – the image is carried out through a long brilliant paragraph that sets up unforgettably the power relations that seem implied by a treaty in which so much seems given by Britain in return for so little, a 'wild Bargain' which, he insinuates, could only have resulted from bribery or other crass methods of persuasion (p. 124). As I have already indicated, along with his indictment of the treaty Swift takes occasion here to defend himself from attacks on the passage in *Conduct* which Chief Justice Parker and others seemed to think could be taken to impugn the Protestant Succession. Indeed, a good bit of the essay portion of *Some Remarks* is given over to comments about that passage on the Succession and to saying 'a few Words' to the gentleman (Francis Hare), who was still in the process of answering *Conduct*. These topics are certainly not digressions, but they do add to the somewhat leisurely manner Swift adopts in this pamphlet, a manner which heightens rather than lessens the tone of lofty contempt with which he takes stock of the Whigs and their Barrier Treaty.

Whether or not he really intended to bait his critics by returning to his earlier remarks about the Succession, it is the case that some of the hostile responders to this pamphlet chafe and fume about what they are quick to call the Jacobite implications of *Some Remarks* as well as about his comments on the Dutch Barrier itself. Thus *Remarks upon Remarks*, attributed to John Oldmixon, has as one of its major points that Swift and his friends are opposed to the Barrier Treaty only because it guarantees the Succession to the British throne, indeed saying that his attacks on the Dutch are not his real point. Oldmixon even begins his response by re-hashing Parker's claim that one line in *Conduct* may be treasonable, and he goes into gleeful detail later in describing the scene in the Commons when *Conduct* was attacked because of it. Arthur Maynwaring's *Short Account and Defence of the Barrier-Treaty* was posthumously published and not part of the public debate, but interestingly it argues forthrightly that the Succession is the only point that matters in the treaty, that if there were no Pretender to the Crown it would be unnecessary to engage the Allies at all.[14]

---

14 Printed in Maynwaring (1715).

However, the longest response, *The Barrier Treaty Vindicated* (1712), thought now to be by Stephen Poyntz though once mistakenly attributed to Hare, does not play that card, although it does assume that only a foreign alliance (and he means the Dutch) can protect Britain from the Pretender. Poyntz, who had been tutor to the sons of Townshend and thus had special interest in the Barrier Treaty, does not refer by name to Swift but does quote from the preface of his 'Libel'. Poyntz in turn was answered by two essays in *The Examiner* (1 and 18 December 1712), questioning whether we need a foreign alliance to secure the Succession and whether the Dutch barrier is really a good one – the point of the treaty, says *The Examiner*, was to keep the Dutch steady in the war and to strengthen the Whigs. Those papers in turn (we are now months after Swift's pamphlet, and he no longer figures in the public discussions) were answered by *An Answer to the Examiner's Cavils Against the Barrier Treaty* (1713), and so the debate continued to swirl, until at least the end of January 1713, when Swift's young friend William Harrison, now Queen's Secretary at the Hague, brought back a new barrier treaty (Williams, *JSt*, p. 611).

But in a way the most interesting and amusing reaction to Swift's pamphlet is one which Davis (vol. VI, pp. xv–xvi) took to be a criticism but which I think is simply another prong in the Tory attack, *Some Remarks on the Letters Between the L—d T—nd, and Mr Se—tary B—le* (1712), in a letter to the author of *Some Remarks*. This is a nice piece of irony, published by Morphew,[15] and the criticism is all tongue-in-cheek; the writer says to Swift, in effect, 'you didn't go far enough; why did you leave out these incriminating letters and yet quote the likes of Count Zinzendorf?' Much of this sounds like someone close to Swift, if not a spoof in which he had a hand, such as the side-assault on Chief Justice Parker, who is made to argue that even those who first created the Succession would be guilty of treason if they tried to alter it, and the 'criticisms' of Swift's pamphlet which are not really criticisms at all, just ways of 'piling it on': 'Nor have you touch'd upon the Weakness of the Treaty itself, which was certainly worth your Observation' (p. 12). The speaker, in short, professes to be very disappointed by this tract from the 'incomparable' author of *Conduct*, who actually might have enjoyed it if it had come to his attention, just as he enjoyed Arbuthnot's very funny parody of the treaty in the second of his *John Bull* pamphlets (17 March), in which Nicholas Frog (the Dutch) agrees to ensure that John Bull's last Will remain unalterable even by John Bull himself, and for that purpose will be allowed

---

15 Published, that is, in the eighteenth-century sense of the term; see the Textual Introduction, pp. 330–2, for more information.

to '*enter his House at any Hour of the Day or Night, to break open Bars, Bolts and Doors, Chests of Drawers and strong Boxes*' (*John Bull*, p. 31).[16]

2. Court scandal, ministerial conflicts and 'penny papers' on Dunkirk

With the Barrier Treaty firmly dealt with, Swift could 'sitt and be idle now', which he says he had not been for over a year. However, he added in his *Journal*, 'I will stay out the Session, to see if they have any further Commands for me' (Williams, *JSt*, p. 499). Although he thought Parliament would rise by April, the session continued until July. During that period he did not have 'further Commands' from the ministers, unless one counts some work with St John followed by consultations with Barber in late February and early March, presumably involving his collaboration with Sir Thomas Hanmer on the Representation to the Queen. Otherwise, as he reported with pleasure several times to Stella, he had 'no large work' on his hands.

But on 28 March he was with Erasmus Lewis 'getting Materials for a little Mischief' (Williams, *JSt*, p. 526), an indication that some satiric publication would be forthcoming. Yet it has not previously been clear what piece of mischief that might be, especially if it was something for which an Under-Secretary of State might furnish materials. The most likely candidate, I think, is *The New Way of Selling Places at Court. In a Letter from a Small Courtier to a great Stock-Jobber*, a work recently attributed to Swift by David Woolley and accepted by the present editors. It was not published until 13 May – Swift was extremely ill all through April – but it is based on an incident at Court which he reported to Stella in his *Journal* for 23 March, just five days before he went to Lewis for help with his mischief. Here is the relevant passage:

> Did I tell you of a Scoundrel about the Court, that sells Employnts to ignorant People, and cheats them of their Money. he lately made a Bargain for the Vicechamberlns Place for 7000ll, and had receivd some Guinneas Earnest, but the whole Thing was discoverd tothr day, and Examination taken of it by Ld. Dartmouth, & I hope he will be swingd. The Vicechambrln told me sevrll Particulars of it last night at Ld Mashams.
>
> (Williams, *JSt*, p. 522)

The fact that the examination was taken by Lord Dartmouth, Secretary of State, explains why Swift would have consulted Lewis, since Lewis was Under-Secretary to Dartmouth and would have had access to papers on the

---

16 For Swift's approval, see Williams, *JSt*, p. 516.

case. Moreover, thanks to the gossipy Peter Wentworth we now know the identity of the Scoundrel; on 28 March, in a passage unnoticed by Woolley, Wentworth wrote to his brother the Earl of Strafford,

> Isreel Feilding has had a complaint made of him by the Vice-chamberlain, for his giving out that his place was to be sold. He had got a bouble as he thought, who he told he had the disposal of that place for 7,000, two thousand was to be given to Mr Cook, and the rest to a great[er?] lady then my Lady Masham, that was to say more in favour with the Queen . . .
>
> (*Wentworth Papers*, p. 282)[17]

Moreover, Israel Fielding was, apparently, a 'creature' of Harley's, or at least one who solicited Harley for preferment or family favours; he appears in Harley's correspondence as early as 1707, and even after Queen Anne's death Fielding wrote to him asking his help in getting his son into Charterhouse as a 'Queen's Boy' (HMC *Portland*, vol. II, p. 456; vol. III, p. 497). His connection with Harley might have been one more reason for Swift to consult Erasmus Lewis, who was close to the Lord Treasurer. Israel Fielding, as Swift hints in his essay, had a near-permanent place in the Court because his wife, Margery, was the Queen's 'foster-sister', that is, she was the daughter of a woman who had been Anne's wet nurse, and she also served the Queen in the royal household (for example, as a 'bedchamber woman' in 1702) until her death in 1713 (Gregg, p. 5; compare Marlborough–Godolphin, p. 139). Swift's 'little Mischief' covered a wider range than one might first think.

His other piece of prose published in May (aside from his *Proposal for Correcting . . . the English Tongue*) was the 'threepenny Pamphlet' *Some Reasons to Prove, That no Person is obliged by his Principles, as a Whig, to Oppose Her Majesty or her Present Ministry. In a Letter to a Whig-Lord*, published by Morphew on 31 May. This pamphlet has attracted some uncommon disagreement among major Swift scholars, with Herbert Davis describing it as Swift's political writing at its best (vol. VI, p. xviii) and Irvin Ehrenpreis finding it not only dull but too worldly and cynical in its assumptions to be persuasive (vol. II, p. 564). But whom was it really intended to persuade? Various figures known to Swift have been suggested as the 'Whig Lord' to whom the piece is addressed. The two principal ones are Lord Ashburnham, son-in-law of the Duke of Ormond, married to one of Swift's favourite young women and (though earlier a strong Whig) under her Tory thumb until her death in 1713; and Lord Radnor, a Whig who had financial obligations to

---

17 Compare Arbuthnot, *John Bull*, p. 70 and p. 216 n., for another attack on Fielding, which appeared on 16 April.

Oxford and the Court and with whom Swift spent three hours trying to 'bring him over' in December 1711, even though personally he did not care if the 'scoundrel' was hanged (Holmes, pp. 49, 227 and n.; Williams, *JSt*, pp. 451–2, 454). Davis suggests Ashburnham but then seems to reject him, and Ehrenpreis favours Radnor, but, as Davis implies, it is quite possible Swift did not intend any specific figure despite the apparently personal comments from time to time in the pamphlet. Would Swift indeed have wanted a piece that might quickly be attributed to him (for example, because published by Morphew) to contain identifiable allusions to Tory or Whig peers? If his desire, as Davis describes it, is to lay out a moderate point of view that is beyond 'party', he would not want particular figures to be easily identified as his intended audience.

Yet is his pamphlet actually intended to be so 'moderate'? To be sure, he argues firmly against 'party' distinctions, the only issues being whether one is for peace or war, for the old Whig ministry or against it. And he manages to suggest that some objections to the Oxford ministry that might be considered based on principle are only strategic or expedient, such as the vote on Nottingham's 'No peace without Spain' motion in December 1711 or complaints about 'Oxford's dozen', the Queen's creation of twelve new peers. Moreover, both by implication and direct comment Swift manages to indict the Whigs for a whole series of recent positions and actions: stirring up the City against the ministry, encouraging foreign ministers to give directions to the British Queen, urging on Grub-Street writers to attack figures in great employments, capitalizing politically, or trying to, on the dismissal of Marlborough, supporting the bill for a General Naturalization which would make us be overrun 'by Schismaticks and Beggars', and persistently trying to repeal the Test Act, a repeal which would level the Church 'with every sniveling Sect in the Nation' (p. 172). Those last phrases sound more like a member of the October Club than someone trying to persuade a member of the House of Lords that the only real difference between the parties is their attitude towards the Royal Prerogative. If this was the language Swift used in arguing for three hours with Lord Radnor, little wonder that we never learn whether he succeeded in 'curing' him.

A month later we find Swift 'very desponding', though the men of affairs laugh at him for it. His anxiety, as expressed in his letter to Archbishop King on 26 June 1712 (Woolley, *Corr.*, vol. I, p. 426), had to do with possible delays in British troops under the Duke of Ormond taking possession of Dunkirk. That occupation was to be a step in the peace process arising from a series of deaths in the French royal family in 1711 and the spring of 1712, deaths that left Philip V, King of Spain and grandson of Louis XIV, as the next heir in succession to the Duke of Anjou. Since one of the major aims of the war had been to prevent the union of France and Spain in the House of Bourbon, Anne insisted that before the peace negotiations could continue, Philip must formally renounce the kingdom of France, and that was to be done with the agreement of the States of Spain. When that was accomplished, she promised, there could be a suspension of arms, provided that the French handed over Dunkirk to the British as a pledge. The French did agree to these proposals, whereupon the Queen (i.e., St John in her name) sent the notorious 'restraining orders' which secretly forbade the Duke of Ormond from engaging in further battle with the French; however, until Philip agreed to the renunciation, the British forces could not take possession of Dunkirk or declare an armistice. Swift explains in his *History* that Anne expected an immediate decision from Philip, and though she knew Prince Eugene might attack the allied forces, she 'could not endure to think that perhaps some Thousands of Lives of her own Subjects and Allies might be sacrificed without Necessity' (Davis, vol. VII, pp. 125, 129). Most modern historians have been less understanding about these orders, which for some are the work of 'perfidious Albion'. In any case, on 6 June the Queen made a long speech to both Houses setting out the terms of a general Peace between France and Britain, terms which Swift quotes in *History*. Ormond then undertook a march to the sea before sending a detachment to occupy Dunkirk, along the way taking possession of Ghent and Bruges as security in case of Dutch reluctance to come to terms. Finally, on 8 July, Swift's friend General John Hill, brother of Lady Masham, entered Dunkirk and took possession.

Swift was relieved. His state of anxiety during the final stages of this event is recorded in his letters to Stella: 'I wish it were over . . . If we have Dunkirk once, all is safe' (Williams, *JSt*, p. 544). 'I am just now told that the Governr of Dunkirk has not orders yet to deliver up the Town to Jack Hill and his Forces, but expects them daily . . . I do not like these Stoppings in such an Affair' (pp. 546–7). Moreover, he had some anxiety in the spring of 1712 over another sort of 'restraining order', one that seemed to threaten the press. The Queen's speech on 17 January had included complaint about the 'great licence taken in publishing false and scandalous Libels' (*Parliamentary History*, vol. VI, p. 1092), but as far back as 31 January 1711 Swift had been somewhat alarmed at the prospect: 'They are here intending to tax all little printed penny papers a half-penny every half-sheet, which will utterly ruin Grub-street, and I am endeavouring to prevent it' (Williams, *JSt*, pp. 177–8). When, after the Queen's message, Parliament took up the matter seriously, he was saying more anxiously, 'so farewel to Grub-street' (p. 466). And a few weeks later, 'I have now nothing to do; and the Palnt by the Qu—'s

Recommendation is to take some Method for preventing Libells &c, which will include Pamphlets I suppose' (p. 499); on 10 March he writes that the Commons are being slow to act, 'and the Pamphleteers make good use of their Time for there come out 3 or 4 every day' (p. 510). On 29 March he reports that he has remonstrated with Oxford and Benson (Chancellor of the Exchequer) about this measure, arguing that 'instead of preventing small Papers and Libels, it will leave nothing else for the Press' (Woolley, *Corr.*, vol. I, p. 420).

But the Act passed on 10 June, to be effective on 1 August, and on 19 July Swift speaks of the imminent death of Grub-street since 'an Act of Parlmt takes place, that ruins it, by taxing every half sheet at a halfpenny' (Williams, *JSt*, p. 551). Finally, on 7 August, we hear, 'Grubstreet is dead and gone last Week' (p. 553). To one accustomed to Scriblerian satire it may seem a bit odd to find Swift even half-jokingly mourning the death of Grub-street, but he had, first of all, some scepticism about the efficacy of the new law, and secondly a clear concern that it might stop his own pen from flowing (thus his obvious worry that it would affect pamphlets). And could it be that there was a part of Swift which took pleasure in the give and take of political lampooning? 'Since Dunkirk has been in our Hands, Grubstreet has been very fruitfull: pdfr [Swift] has writt 5 or 6 Grubstreet papers this last week' (p. 548); this comment (from 17 July) and others like it sound like a writer thoroughly enjoying himself and not too concerned about a Grubean label, as does his letter saying to General Hill himself that he can neither punish nor reward him for the gift of a snuff box, since 'Grub-street is no more: for the Parliament has killed all the Muses of Grub-street, who yet, in their last moments, cried out nothing but Dunkirk' (Woolley, *Corr.*, vol. I, p. 434).

Whatever the case, Swift did express his exultation over the occupation of Dunkirk in a series of 'penny papers', so that on 7 August he could write to Dingley and Stella, 'I plyed it pretty close the last Fortnight, and publisht at least 7 penny Papers of my own, besides some of other Peoples' (Williams, *JSt*, p. 553). Indirectly, to Stella, he indicates his authorship of a handful of them: 'Have you seen Toland's Invitation to Dismal, or a Hue & cry after Dismal, or a Ballad on Dunkirk, or an Argument that Dunkirk is not in our Hands Poh, you have seen nothing' (p. 548). David Woolley, who was the major modern scholar to work on identification of these papers, lists them as follows: two poems, *Peace and Dunkirk* and *Toland's Invitation to Dismal*, and the five prose broadsides, all published between 10 and 19 July: *A Dialogue upon Dunkirk*, *It's Out at Last*, *A Hue and Cry after Dismal*, *Dunkirk Still in the Hands of the French* (no copy extant), and *A Letter from the Pretender*

('Canon'). The four extant prose pieces are included in this volume, and each deserves a brief comment.

The *Dialogue* between a Whig and a Tory is set on 6 July, when in fact Swift is believed to have written the piece. The arguments on both sides are predictable, but Swift must have enjoyed parodying the Whig press in his character's sneering incredulity first about the news of the imminent surrender of the town and citadel, then his pooh-poohing the news as an item of no importance, and at the end his move to the usual Whig effort at a *coup de grâce*, an accusation of Jacobitism. Along the way Swift works in the anti-Dutch themes that were almost obligatory in England in 1712, when some even talked of a war with the Dutch. In addition to these themes David Woolley has pointed to the pleasure Swift seems to take here in using with great particularity information that only someone in the confidence of the government was likely to have ('Dialogue', p. 218).

In the somewhat more amusing *It's Out at Last*, published on or before 10 July, Swift again uses a Whig persona, but that is only the beginning of the joke. For this speaker appears to live in a time zone many months behind that of Swift's audience. Harold Williams comments (*JSt*, p. 554 n.) that ordinary readers might have taken the piece literally and read it as an attack on the ministry; Herbert Davis disagrees, pointing to the fact that it was advertised in *The Examiner* (vol. VI, p. xx). But surely both scholars are saying less than necessary, since the speaker's great discovery that the 'M—stry *Corresponded* with *France*' is one that any reader at the time would have immediately found ridiculous anyway; for by July 1712 everyone knew that the Ministry 'corresponded' with France, no matter in what sense one takes 'corresponded'. The peace negotiations were well underway. Matthew Prior's trip carrying overtures to France over a year earlier had become public knowledge despite efforts to keep it secret, Preliminaries had been signed in October 1711 and the Congress at Utrecht had been meeting for six months. Indeed, according to Defoe, some 'have all along been . . . positive that the Peace was already made, and has been made a great while' (*Review*, 31 May 1712). By June 10 Defoe was denying that a *separate* peace had been made by Great Britain, without the Allies, and this was indeed still a fear that the government had to allay.

It is possible, faintly, that by the MP's outrage Swift is mimicking the outrage over the 'restraining orders' to Ormond, which had been debated in the House of Lords in May. In that case 'correspondence' might be literally intended as 'secret letters' as well as simply 'Relation between persons or communities; usually qualified as good, friendly, fair, ill, etc.' (*OED*). Or perhaps Swift intends readers to recall the furore in Parliament a month earlier, over an Address by the Lords thanking the Queen for her speech on 6 June laying out conditions of peace. When several Lords entered a protest against the exclusion of phrases that would have England join with the Allies in a 'mutual Guaranty', their protest began with the claim that the 'terms of peace that are offered, have proceeded from a separate negociation, carried on by the ministers with France, without any communication thereof to the . . . States-General' (*Parliamentary History*, vol. VI, p. 1148). This protest was expunged on 13 June, but printed anyway, with an Order then to discover the printer and publisher. All this was just a month before Swift's pamphlet about 'correspondence'. Nevertheless, these readings are probably over-ingenious. Swift was writing a broadside in which the satire is funny but, well, broad, and in which his main object was most likely only to score points about the Dunkirk success and to laugh at Whig paranoia about the ministry's dealings with the French.

The next 'penny paper', appearing on or before 17 July, was *A Hue and Cry after Dismal*, a piece of mock-journalism, being a 'full and true Account' of strange doings in Dunkirk, written not by a Whig this time but by one who has been 'certainly informed' of the bizarre behaviour of a Whig Lord disguised as a chimney-sweeper who is caught and taken before the Governor, General Hill (p. 195). To see Swift's purpose we have to recall that on the opening day of this session of Parliament, 7 December 1711, Daniel Finch, 2nd Earl of Nottingham and heretofore a high-Church Tory, signalled his defection by arguing that the vote of thanks to the Queen carry with it condemnation of any peace that left the house of Bourbon in possession of Spain and the West Indies. Even before the event Swift had reported to Stella, 'Lord Nottingham, a famous Tory and speech-maker, is gone over to the Whig side: they toast him daily, and lord Wharton says, It is *Dismal* (so they call him from his looks) will save England at last'; and the day before Nottingham spoke Swift parodied the intended speech in *An Excellent New Song*, a ballad 'two degrees above Grubstreet' (Williams, *JSt*, pp. 430–1). Nottingham did not take such jokes in good humour: Peter Wentworth wrote to his brother the Earl of Strafford, 'My Lord N— made a complaint of a grub street speech they had cry'd about, as spoke by him in the house, of which he said he had not spoke one word, and now they cry up and down a sham speech of his vindication from the former' (*Wentworth Papers*, p. 225). A few weeks before this 'penny paper' in prose, Swift used the name 'Dismal' in a verse satire on Nottingham, *Toland's Invitation to Dismal to Dine with the Calves Head Club*, in which a notorious free thinker invites the high-Church Nottingham to a meeting of a republican club (the members are all important Whigs) to celebrate the anniversary of the execution of Charles I – a gathering of figures Nottingham would find abhorrent. In *Hue and Cry* also his 'Apostasy' is explicitly attacked, and the Dutch are again hit at, but the mood is more comic than satiric (see Ehrenpreis, vol. II, pp. 560–1). The press paid no attention to Swift's piece, but there was one pitiful Tory attempt to capital-ize on it, *The Description of Dunkirk with Squash's and Dismal's Opinion how easily Prince Eugene may Retake it, and many Other Matters of the Last Impor-tance* (1712), a ballad which concludes with this reference to Swift's prose piece:

> *Eugene* will take't Cries *Squash* by Mars,
> As Easily as Kiss his A—se.
> Which I can the more safely swear,
> Since I and my dear Lord were there,
> Like Chimney Sweepers Drest that we
> Might with our Dismal Hopes agree.

The final 'penny paper' appeared on 19 July, when Swift spoke of it to Stella in this way: 'To day there will be anothr Grub; a Letter from the Pretendr to a Whig Ld' (Williams, *JSt*, pp. 550–1). Unlike most of his preceding 'Grubs', it was not about Dunkirk but Jacobites, an effort to turn the tables on the Whigs by accusing them of correspondence with the Pretender. The familiar Whig cry was that the Tories and their ministers were plotting with the Pretender and engaging in just the kind of correspondence Swift parodies here. This broadside, then, is a fake letter from the Pretender at the Jacobite Court of St Germains to Lord W—, easily recognizable as Swift's old *bête noire*, Thomas Earl of Wharton, stalwart Whig leader and one of the least likely of all members of the House of Lords to be serving as an agent of the Pretender. The letter uses ciphers for proper names, as was common in diplomatic correspondence in the period; Swift, of course, did not necessarily intend his readers to make specific identifications of all the 'Whigs' alluded to in the letter; a few would be enough to make his point. It is not meant to be a hoax, and it is most unlikely that he expected anyone to take it seriously. Two decades later he 'fancied' he had not written it, but it was recognized at the time of its first publication as an effort to turn the tables on a common Whig manoeuvre; after first presenting a genuine Jacobite document, Abel Boyer reprinted this piece in his *Political State*, with this introductory remark: 'On the other hand, the High Church Party endeavour'd to throw off the Odium of the Design of bringing in the *Person who pretends to disturb the Succession in the House of* Hanover, on their Antagonists the *Whigs*; for which purpose they publish'd . . . the following *supposed LETTER from the PRETENDER to a* Whig-Lord' (vol. IV (1712), pp. 37–8).

From the late summer of 1712 to the late spring of 1713, Swift's political writing was almost completely taken up with working on the long document that was to be his *History of the Four Last Years of the Queen*, a work unlike almost all of his previous writing during the Oxford ministry because written not only to persuade the present public but also to lay down the record for posterity, which he clearly foresaw would condemn the Treaty of Utrecht and the ministry that brought the peace (Davis, vol. VII, p. x). Throughout this period he had to suffer delays and difficulties from both Oxford and Boling-broke, both of whom he consulted from time to time about his manuscript in progress. A comment in the *Journal* for 7 January 1713 is typical: 'the Ministers have got my Papers & will neithr read them nor give them to me, & I can hardly do any thing' (Williams, *JSt*, p. 597). At the same time, of course, he continued to despair at the quarrels of the two chief ministers and at his inability to bring them together, quarrels which he was perhaps aware of early but which he later dated from Guiscard's attack on Harley in 1711.[18] And so, on 15 September 1712, he complained, 'I am again endeavouring as I was last year to keep People from breaking to pieces, upon a hundred misunderstandings. One cannot withold them from drawing different ways while the Enemy is watching to destroy both' (p. 556); on 28 October: 'I have helped to patch up these people together once more. God knows how long it may last' (p. 568). He longed to be rid of the problem, out of sheer weariness. 'I dislike a million of things in the course of publick Affairs; & if I were to stay here much longr I am sure I shoud ruin my self with endeavoring to mend them . . . Tis impossible to save People against their own will; and I have been too much engaged in Patch-work already' (p. 580). On New Year's Day, he was again despairing: 'But burn Politicks. & send me from Courts & Ministers' (p. 593). To the pressure of trying to keep peace between the ministers was added his increasing feeling that they were going to do absolutely nothing about his own search for preferment. And, most vexing of all, like everyone else he had to endure the long wait for the parties at Utrecht to come to agreement and sign a general Peace. Finally the Peace came in April, and by the end of that month preferment for Swift. In June he left for Ireland to be installed as Dean of St Patrick's; as he remarked wryly to William Diaper, a young poet he had taken under his wing, 'The Prints will tell you that I am condemned to live again in Ireland, and all that the Court or Ministry did for me, was to let me chuse my Station in the Country where I am banished' (Woolley, *Corr.*, vol. I, p. 481).

---

18 See *An Enquiry into the Behaviour of the Queen's Last Ministry* (Davis, vol. VIII, pp. 145–6), and H. T. Dickinson, *Bolingbroke* (London: Constable, 1970), pp. 77, 81.

During this long period (September 1712–May 1713) Swift's only formal 'political' writing for a public audience was confined to one essay in *The Examiner* and a handful of notices and items in *The Post Boy* and *The Evening Post*. However, his work behind the scenes and his close connections with the ministers, especially with Oxford, continued throughout this period while he was writing his *History*. Though it was once thought he was 'employed, not trusted'[19] by the Oxford ministry, we now know that he gave assistance to the Lord Treasurer in preparing two of the most important speeches of the Queen, that he also wrote an Address by the House of Lords to the Queen and the Vote of Thanks to her at the time when the peace was ready to be announced (both are included in this volume), and that he was involved somehow in Oxford's thinking about management of the House of Lords. Evidence presented by J. A. Downie and David Woolley shows that he made slight changes and corrections in the texts both of her speech of 9 April 1713, announcing the signing of the peace treaties, and that of 2 March 1714, her last speech during Oxford's treasurership. Further evidence provided by Clyve Jones shows that two important lists of the allegiances of members of the House of Lords were drawn up by Oxford in the spring of 1713 but are in Swift's hand, perhaps taken down as Oxford dictated them.[20]

Since Swift's role, though thus demonstrably significant, was limited to advice, corrections and possible consultations, the Queen's speeches themselves are not included in this volume, nor are two other pieces printed by Davis.[21] One is *The Examiner* of 16 January 1713, blaming the Dutch and the Emperor for the delays in the peace negotiations and developed from a 'hint' Swift says he furnished the editor; but there is no evidence Swift had a hand in writing it, and the present editors agree with David Woolley that the writing is 'poor stuff'. The second piece is the Address of the Lords on 11 March 1714, an Address condemning the writer of *Publick Spirit*, i.e. Swift himself. However, his items for the newspapers and the one *Examiner* essay we are reprinting touch on some important incidents or issues during this long wait for peace and preferment (Woolley, 'Canon', 110).

One item he furnished is completely personal, a short notice of the death of Anne Long, a young woman friend of Swift's whom he knew through

---

19 John Boyle, Lord Orrery, *Remarks on the Life and Writings of Dr Jonathan Swift* (1752), ed. João Fróes (Newark: University of Delaware Press, 2000), p. 47.

20 J. A. Downie and David Woolley, 'Swift, Oxford and the Composition of the Queen's Speeches', *BLJ* 8 (1982), 121–46; Downie, 'Swift and the Oxford Ministry: New Evidence', *SStud* 1 (1986), 2–8; Clyve Jones, 'Swift, the Earl of Oxford, and the Management of the House of Lords in 1713: Two New Lists', *BLJ* 16 (1990), 117–30.

21 For further discussion about attribution, see the Textual Introduction, pp. 335–6.

Esther Vanhomrigh; she was a famous beauty, toast of the Kit-Kat Club. Swift was more moved by her death than the newspaper notice suggests, writing to Stella, 'I never was more afflicted at any death', and adding the following:

> I have ordered a paragraph to be put in the *Post-boy*, giving an account of her death, and making honourable mention of her; which is all I can do to serve her memory: but one reason was spite; for, her brother would fain have her death a secret, to save the charge of bringing her up here to bury her, or going into mourning.   (Williams, *JSt*, pp. 445–6)

He also wrote to the Norfolk clergyman in the town where Miss Long had died, asking him to arrange a suitable memorial, and his account book gives the draft of an inscription, with such lines as 'She was the most beautifull | Person of the Age, she lived in' (Woolley, *Corr.*, vol. I, pp. 405–6).

As this and other such entries make clear, Swift had some sort of authority over Abel Roper, editor of the Tory *Post Boy*, though we do not know any details of their relationship. 'Roper is my humble Slave,' he wrote on 21 March 1712 (Williams, *JSt*, p. 519), and since most of the items he wanted printed were politically sensitive such a slave proved very useful, especially if we speculatively view Swift as a sort of manager of Tory propaganda. Two incidents requiring political management and special handling of the press occurred in November 1712, the so-called 'Band-Box plot', involving a deadly device sent to Oxford and opened by Swift, and the tragic duel between the Duke of Hamilton and Lord Mohun, in which both men were killed. Swift's account to Stella of his 'Escape' on 4 November when he opened the Band-Box says the 'Prints have told a thousand Lyes' about the episode and that a 'true account' has been furnished to *The Evening Post*, 'onely I would not suffer them to name me.' He did not need to be named, since the story and his part in it quickly spread through the town. The Whig reaction, of course, was uniformly sceptical and joking, though some Tory readers were apparently sympathetic. Williams cites both a ballad and *The Flying-Post* as Whig pieces which suggested Swift made the whole thing up (*JSt*, pp. 572–3, and notes). Abel Boyer wrote a pamphlet bringing together both of these affairs and the duel. *A True and Impartial Account of the Duel . . . And, some Previous Reflections on Sham-plots* (1712) connects the publicity about both events with Tory paranoia: '*An Iron-Pin*, can't be missing in the Roof of a Cathedral; Preparations for the Anniversary of a Popular Rejoycing can't be made . . . a *Band-Box* with a few Squibs can't be sent' (p. 3) and a duel can't be fought without *The Examiner* and *The Post Boy* making it a Whig conspiracy. And, Boyer claims, no efforts have been made to trace the persons who sent the band-box, no proclamation with a reward has been promulgated, and the great man himself has turned off all questions with a smile. In reaction to such infuriating disbelief, Swift complained to Stella that he had been abused by the Whig papers: 'God help me; what could I do; I fairly ventured my Life' (Williams, *JSt*, p. 579). As for the duel, Boyer argues it arose from private animosities and was not a party-quarrel, despite the fact that Hamilton was scheduled to go to France as an ambassador and despite the efforts of Swift (he thinks) in *The Examiner* to make it seem one. Of course, Swift in his account for *The Post Boy* made sure Mohun's second, General Maccartney, who he thought was responsible for Hamilton's death, was given an account 'as malicious as possible, and very proper for Abel Roper', a self-judgment well borne out by the second excerpt we are reprinting about the duel (Williams, *JSt*, p. 574). Swift himself was greatly distressed by the event and included it, with some apologies, as material fit for his *History*.

The selection from *The Examiner* written during this winter period deals with a problem that Swift would be confronting in almost all of his remaining political writing in the Queen Anne period: the charge that the Tory leaders were actively seeking to bring in the Pretender. In the case of his essay of 2 February 1713, he felt also a strong personal motivation, since one of his closest friends, Erasmus Lewis, was the object of a smear campaign, though it may have begun from a simple error. Swift summed it up for Stella in this way:

> My Friend Mr Lewis has had a Lye spread on him by the mistake of a Man who went to anothr of his name to give him thanks for passing his privy seal to come from France; that tother Lewis, spread about that the Man brought him thanks from Ld Perth, & Ld Melfort, (two Lds with the Pretender) for his great Services &c. the Lds will examine that tother Lewis to morrow in Council, and I believe you will hear of it in the Prints, for I will make Abel Roper give a Relation of it.   (Williams, *JSt*, p. 609)

Swift does not mention that the visitor from France, Charles Skelton, was also an officer in the French army and a Roman Catholic – those details obviously fed the flames of the conspiracy-mongers.

According to Daniel Szechi, the publicity given this 'entirely fabricated' affair was part of a larger Whig 'scare campaign' developed for this election year. This same month, Szechi adds, Oxford was informed by Toland that the Whig leaders were starting a whispering campaign to prove that the Lord Treasurer was a covert Jacobite (Szechi, p. 145). It was quickly obvious that Swift or someone else badly needed to counter the rumours by some journalistic effort of the sort he provided in *The Examiner*. On 14 February, for example, Defoe wrote to Oxford to report the distress of a dissenting minister in Lincolnshire about Jacobite accusations in *The Flying Post* and *The Daily Courant*: 'The first', says Defoe's informant, 'is the Affair of Mr Lewis which has made So much Noise in Town and Country . . . I Wish you would Explain That affair to us, for he [*The Daily Courant*] Insinuates a Direct Correspondence by it between Our Court and That of St Germans.'[22] Lord Berkeley of Stratton, a moderate Tory, described to the Earl of Strafford how Henry Lewis had repeated his story to twenty people in a chocolate house, but also added significantly that if there had been any substance to it the parties involved would have been taken up. In a later letter, however, he reported that despite substantial efforts to disprove the story, many would not be 'persuaded out of it' (*Wentworth Papers*, pp. 316, 318). Even Abel Boyer was moved to give a fairly even-handed account of the affair, explaining that the episode occurred when the public was already agog over a fire destroying the house of the French ambassador and other such 'Insolencies'; Boyer prints the counter-advertisement Henry Lewis inserted in *The Daily Courant* in answer to the depositions printed in other papers by Skelton and by Swift's close friends Erasmus Lewis and Charles Ford. After reporting on the Privy Council's examination of H. Lewis, Boyer surprisingly concludes 'so that the whole matter appear'd to be only a foolish and malitious Invention of Mr Henry Lewis' (*State*, vol. V, p. 49).

One tactic of both Swift's essay and of the depositions of his two friends is to assume that Henry Lewis, a 'Hamburg merchant' (one who trades with Hamburg), is actually named 'Levi', i.e., that he is a Jew. Whether accurate or not, this was intended, one supposes, to cast general doubt on his truthfulness, and it also enabled Swift in *The Examiner* to imply specifically that any oath Lewis takes on the gospels will be meaningless. But the Whig *Flying Post* responded in kind. One of a series of nasty questions posed by a letter in that paper on 3 February reads, 'Whether Mr. Henry Lewis has not as great a Right to be credited upon his Oath as ever Sir S—n M—na could pretend to?' 'If he has, what can the *Examiner* mean by his unmannerly and impious Jest upon Mr. *Henry Lewis*, by calling him *Levi*?' The reference is to Sir Solomon de Medina, a Jewish merchant who furnished bread to the allied armies and paid a commission to the Duke of Marlborough, which the Duke later claimed was used for secret service. Medina's testimony in the Commons in 1711 helped to discredit Marlborough, and the Whig tactic in response to Swift's 'Levi' usage is obvious enough.

Boyer, finally, had claimed, that none of these testimonies or affidavits was enough to overcome the 'stubborn Incredulity of some People' (*State*,

---

22 *Letters of Daniel Defoe*, ed. G. H. Healey (Oxford: Clarendon Press, 1955), p. 398.

vol. V, p. 49). He was right. The story continued to circulate, and long after the death of the Queen, a collection called *Political Merriment* printed two ballads ridiculing Erasmus Lewis and the Tories, one entitled 'The Rare Show' and the other 'Lewis upon Lewis, or the Snake in the Grass'. The first stanza of that second ditty concludes,

> On *L—s* the Scribe I now must treat,
> And *L—s* the Whig in *Marlborough-street*,
> And *Sk—ton* the Vassal of L—s the Great,
> *Oh! Tories, what are ye contriving?*[23]

They were contriving a Peace. And as Swift worked with Oxford on the Lord's Address to the Queen in April he could have looked back with satisfaction on his role in bringing about the conclusion which he, at least, had been anticipating with pleasure. Even Trevelyan, no great admirer of the Dean, admits, '*The Conduct of the Allies* materially helped to obtain peace for Europe on the only possible terms' (Trevelyan, vol. III, p. 192). I think it is also the case that after two and a half years of labouring for the ministry, Swift was a thorough-going adherent to the Tory party. To be sure, he made a show sometimes of despising party labels when trying to win over moderates, he speaks of a 'Curse of Party' (Williams, *JSt*, p. 589) and he continued throughout life to think of himself as having 'old whiggish principles' (Woolley, *Corr.*, vol. II, p. 361). But there is abundant evidence in his letters to Stella that in practical, day-to-day terms in 1713 his real attitude had hardened and that he spoke from the heart when he said, 'I avoid all Conversation with the othr Party. it is not to be born' (Williams, *JSt*, p. 634). Nevertheless, Swift's party loyalty, his close relationship with the ministers, his devoted work for both Oxford and Bolingbroke and unceasing efforts to keep them together, did not produce the preferment in the Church for which he had hoped. He admitted to Stella, 'I confess I thought the Ministry would not let me go; but perhaps thy cant help it' (p. 662). Perhaps they couldn't. But in any case, with more and more public anxiety about the safety of the Protestant Succession, with the power struggle between the Tory leaders worsening, and with Richard Steele devoting himself single-mindedly to party warfare, it was not long before they asked him to come back.

3. Swift vs. Steele: the Peace and the Succession

Swift returned to England on 1 September, but it was two months before he published another political pamphlet in prose. Although a new Parliament

---

23 *Political Merriment: or, Truths told to Some Tune* (1714–15), p. 41.

had been summoned for November, it was prorogued three times, and the session did not begin until 16 February 1714. However, the Court did meet in Windsor most of the autumn, and Swift travelled back and forth continually between London and Windsor in those months. Thus he had continued contact with both Bolingbroke and Oxford. There was, however, no more 'journal' to Stella and her companion, and so we have no close record of his political and social life during this, his last prolonged stay in England during the reign of Queen Anne and his last period of political writing in support of her government. And such a record is all the more a loss because this time which began in such an apparently relaxed fashion was in fact a period of fierce and tense political struggle between Whigs and Tories and also, for Swift and others close to the centres of power, between the leaders of that government.

There were now two principal issues at the heart of the party struggle, one the problem of Dunkirk, growing out of a single provision of the Treaty of Utrecht, and the other the charge of Jacobitism against the ministry. The latter, in fact, was the most serious issue with which Swift and his party had to contend in the final eleven months before the Queen's death. Indeed, fending off the charges of Jacobitism now got dragged into every other political dispute, not surprisingly given the Queen's poor health. Swift himself, as author of *The Examiner* and *Conduct*, had 'Jacobite' levelled at him by his contemporaries, partly, as already noted, because of his comments about the Dutch as 'guarantees' of the Hanoverian Succession.

'Jacobite' is a label that has in recent years surfaced again in Swift scholarship, although to my knowledge no modern scholar has claimed he participated in any plot to bring in the Pretender at the death of the Queen, even though some of his close friends (Ormond, Ford, Barber) were active Jacobites at various times. The scholarly dispute has been more about his ideological leanings than his practical politics, and as such need not concern readers of his political writings from this period.[24] More problematical, however, is the role of those he liked, trusted and worked for, especially the two chief ministers. One common claim is that Bolingbroke and Oxford were both Jacobites busily seeking a return of the Pretender and that Swift simply was ignorant of their plans; as though anticipating this view, Swift wrote to Archbishop King in 1716, 'Had there been ever the least Overture or Intent of bringing in the Pretend' during my Acquaintance with the Ministry, I think I must have been very stupid not to have pickt out some

---

24 See Higgins, especially chapters I and II, and J. A. Downie, 'Swift and Jacobitism', *ELH* 64 (1997), 887–901.

discoveryes or Suspicions.' And he adds, "I look upon the coming of the Pretender as a greater Evil than any we are like to suffer under the worst Whig Ministry that can be found' (Woolley, *Corr.*, vol. II, p. 205). Modern historians have confirmed that both ministers had dealings with the Jacobite Court, but they have differed as to the degree. The most 'Whiggish' reaction is that of Edward Gregg (chapters 13–14), but his bias is atypical. In fact the most authoritative and specialized account paints a very different picture: Szechi's *Jacobitism and Tory Politics 1710–14* argues cogently that Oxford and Bolingbroke, the latter a late arrival to the Jacobite camp, tried to manipulate both the Jacobite Court and the Jacobites in Parliament for their own ends in domestic politics. Far from plotting to bring in the Stuart Pretender, Szechi says, right up to the moment of the Succession both were trying to 'lull the Jacobite Court into inaction' (p. 183). And Tim Harris, a decade later, writes that although Oxford and Bolingbroke 'seemed to flirt with Jacobitism', 'they were never sincere, and their actions must be set in the context of their attempts to rally disparate groups of Tories behind them in their own personal struggle for dominance'.[25] Apparently, then, it was not that Swift was 'stupid', only that there really was not very much for him to have known about.

Controversy over the demolition of Dunkirk brought Swift into direct conflict with his old friend Richard Steele, one of the 'Whig Wits' who, as Swift predicted soon after his arrival in London in 1710, was about to lose his post as Gazetteer for 'engaging in parties' in his *Tatler* (Williams, *JSt*, p. 13). Steele continued to participate more and more in partisan writing, though he kept his other post as a Stamp Office Commissioner until July 1713, when he resigned to stand for Parliament. As he did for a number of other Whig writers, Swift tried to speak on his behalf to the Harley administration, not knowing that Steele had met Harley privately; and when Steele missed an appointment Swift vowed, 'I shall trouble myself no more about him' (p. 129).[26] There were some efforts at a rapprochement, but relations remained cool until May 1713, when they became heated. Steele refused to believe that Swift no longer wrote *The Examiner*, and in his own new organ *The Guardian* he signed his name to a paper (no. 53, 12 May) which had this to say about the authorship of *The Examiner*:

> I will give my self no manner of Liberty to make Guesses at him, if I may say him; for tho' sometimes I have been told, by familiar Friends, that they

25 Tim Harris, *Politics under the Later Stuarts* (London: Longman, 1993), p. 226.
26 On the relations of Swift and Steele, see B. Goldgar, *The Curse of Party* (Lincoln: University of Nebraska Press, 1961).

saw me such a Time talking to the *Examiner*, others, who have rally'd me upon the Sins of my Youth, tell me it is credibly reported that I have formerly lain with the *Examiner*. I have carried my Point . . . and it is nothing to me, whether the *Examiner* writes against me in the Character of an estranged Friend, or *an exasperated Mistress.*   (*The Guardian*, p. 210)

The references in the last line are, first, to Swift himself and secondly to Delarivier Manley, Swift's colleague in Tory propaganda and mistress of his printer friend John Barber.

After this the letters began to fly (Woolley, *Corr.*, vol. I, pp. 483–97, throughout). Swift wrote to Addison (13 May) complaining. 'Now, Sir, if I am not author of the *Examiner*, how will Mr. Steele be able to defend himself from the imputation of the highest degree of baseness, ingratitude, and injustice?' Steele then wrote back to Swift (19 May), with an opening line not only insulting him but certain to make him feel foolish for trying to help Steele: 'They laugh at you, if they make you believe your interposition has kept me thus long in office', but closing 'I am heartily glad of your being made Dean of St. Patrick's.' Swift replied angrily on 23 May, alluding five times to Steele's phrase 'they laugh at you', detailing his efforts to solicit favours with the ministry on Steele's behalf, and denying once more any connection with the present *Examiner*. On the same day that Swift wrote, 23 May, Steele published another *Guardian* essay (no. 63) under his own name, one no doubt as offensive to Swift as the first one. If any gentleman has been named as the author of *The Examiner*, Steele says, then let him do himself justice in public, and as for Mrs Manley, if he is wrong, he can offer her no reparation but in 'begging her Pardon, that I never lay with her'. There was one more exchange of letters between the two (26 and 27 May), in somewhat more restrained tones, with Swift claiming that their quarrel was not about political principles but political leaders. And that was the end; there was never again any correspondence between them. The personal quarrel had by now become public, with *The Examiner* in its issue of 22 May pointedly absolving Swift ('a *certain Gentleman*') of having any share in its authorship. The friendship was over, but it had really ceased to be possible in any case in 1710, when Swift began writing for the government and no longer moved in Whig circles.

All this had been in May and was past history by the time Swift returned from Ireland. Before his return, Steele suddenly used *The Guardian* of 7 August to enter into a dispute over the demolition of Dunkirk, which seemed essential to the Whigs because it would remove not only a threat to Britain's security but a possible point of origin for a Jacobite invasion. Their suspicions increased when a M. Tugghe, representing the magistrates of Dunkirk, circulated a memorial asking that the harbour be spared. Steele's *Guardian* of that day (no. 128), in the form of a letter from 'English Tory' to the persona Nestor Ironside, gives the usual Whig arguments, but its tone is singular: three times Steele says, 'The *British* Nation expect the immediate Demolition' of Dunkirk. The word 'expect' was seized upon by the Tories (e.g. in *The Examiner* for 24 August) as a direct attack on the royal prerogative.

Steele's protest was annoying to the Ministry not only because of its tone but also because they themselves were unhappy about developments in Dunkirk in this early phase of what was to continue to be a point of dispute between them and the French authorities. Steele was actually right, the demolition was indeed being delayed by design, or so Bolingbroke's correspondence with Prior in September indicates (Bolingbroke, *Letters*, vol. IV, pp. 283–4, 314–15).[27] Abel Boyer saw at once how unsettling Steele's piece would be to the ministry: 'These severe Reflections were, no doubt, a great Mortification to Monsieur *Tugghe*; but how they were relish'd by the *British* Court, is neither easy to guess, nor, perhaps, safe to relate. But this I will adventure to say, that the Apprehension that *Dunkirk* might not be demolish'd began about this time to raise strange Jealousies in People's Minds' (*State*, vol. VI, pp. 66–7). So of course the British Court began to respond. One answer was *The Honour and Prerogative of the Queen's Majesty Vindicated and Defended Against the Unexampled Insolence of the author of the Guardian*, once thought to be Defoe's but now de-attributed; in Steele's defence was *Dunkirk or Dover*, supposedly by the deist John Toland, a 'worthy Advocate for such a Man and such a Cause', quipped *The Examiner* (2 October 1713). On 23 September Steele himself rambled onto the stage with *The Importance of Dunkirk Consider'd: In Defence of the Guardian of August the 7th*. It was addressed to the Bailiff of Stockbridge, the borough from which Steele had been returned to Parliament on 25 August. In the course of this tract, as much a compilation as anything else, he attacked a recent Tory pamphlet, *Reasons concerning the Immediate Demolishing of Dunkirk* (1713; probably Defoe's), in terms that suggest he thought Swift had written it.[28] Defoe here takes the line that the French are obliged to demolish the fortifications, but the

27 On the Dunkirk dispute, see J. R. Moore, 'Defoe, Steele, and the Demolition of Dunkirk', *HLQ* 13 (1950), 279–302, and P. Hyland, 'A Breach of the Peace: the Controversy over the Ninth Article of the Treaty of Utrecht', *BJECS* 22 (1999), 51–66.
28 On Defoe's authorship and non-authorship of these titles, see Furbank and Owens, *Defoe De-Attributions*, p. 61, and *A Critical Bibliography of Daniel Defoe* (London: Pickering and Chatto, 1998), p. 140.

British are not, and he give strong reasons why it may be useful to the British to keep them intact; he also ridicules Steele at some length, so that it is not surprising that 'the *worthy* Mr *Steele*' (p. 14) saw Swift's hand in it.

But Swift had taken no part in any of the early stages of the Dunkirk controversy, having just returned to London and found the Court in some disarray over the Bolingbroke–Oxford quarrel. He had also come back to find Richard Steele now the leading Whig propagandist and a recently elected MP. On 1 October Steele had dropped *The Guardian* and started publication of the totally political *Englishman*, a move of some concern to his friend Addison, who wrote to John Hughes on 12 October, 'I am in a thousand troubles for poor Dick, and wish that his zeal for the public may not be ruinous to himself; but he has sent me word that he is determined to go on.' Their quarrel continued to be public, with a sort of pamphlet warfare being waged between Steele in *The Englishman* and 'Swift' (as Steele thought erroneously) in *The Examiner*.[29]

The growing suspense was finally broken on 2 November when Swift published *The Importance of the Guardian Considered*, dedicated to the demolition of Richard Steele. It is a masterpiece of Swift's wit and also frankly *ad hominem*; at the same time, Swift does make some salient points about the Dunkirk controversy, suggesting that the Whigs themselves have circulated M. Tugghe's petition and, of course, questioning Steele's right as a subject to impugn the Queen's prerogative. That last point was something Swift seems to have meant seriously; a few months earlier (28 March) he had written to Archbishop King, 'you will please to consider, that this Way of every Subject interposing their Sentiments upon the Management of foreign Negotiations, is a very new Thing among us, and the Suffering it, has been thought in the Opinion of wise Men, too great a Strain upon the Prerogative' (Woolley, *Corr.*, vol. I, p. 472). Nevertheless, this work's reputation arises from its literary merit, not from its function as a political pamphlet. There is no evidence that Swift's ministerial friends encouraged it (though the sources that might give such evidence are lacking), and it did not create much of a stir. Steele himself, except for including it in a list of enemy works, did not respond to it directly, only to *The Examiner*, which for the rest of November was in a paper war with him. Of course, Swift was more and more being identified as the writer of that paper, just at the time that its authorship had become a major personal issue between him and Steele. Indeed their actual personal relationship by this time was irrelevant; in the world of political journalism

29 Addison, *Letters*, p. 280; for examples of the pamphlet war, see *The Englishman* No. 1 (6 Oct.), and *Examiners* for 2, 12, 16 Oct. and 2 Nov.

in late 1713 they had become at least figuratively the chief representatives and spokesmen for the warring sides.

November was a busy month for both parties. After Swift's *Importance*, appeared *Two Letters concerning the Author of the Examiner*, in which one letter suggests that perhaps Mr Examiner is a French Jesuit, and the second explains that all anonymous authors fall into two camps, one (bad) with the *Tale of a Tub*, *The Review*, *The Mercator*, and *The Examiner*, and the other (good) with the *The Tatler*, *The Spectator*, *The Guardian*, *The British Merchant*, and so on. In the middle of the month the *Character of Richard Steele* appeared, by 'Toby Abel's Kinsman' (William Wagstaffe), a very abusive document with no mention of Swift; naturally enough, he was accused of writing it by his enemies, and Steele quotes from it extensively in his extraordinarily self-righteous final number to *The Englishman* (no. 57, 15 February 1714) which hints broadly that Swift is the offending author:

> I think I know the Author of this, and to shew him I know no Revenge but in the method of heaping Coals on his head by Benefits, I forbear giving him what he deserves; for no other reason, but that I know his Sensibility of Reproach is such, as that he would be unable to bear Life it self under half the ill Language he has given me.   (p. 235)

And so the battle continued, reaching its climax in January and February 1714, with an elaborate build-up and advertising campaign in advance of Steele's major work, *The Crisis*. In early December Swift parodied the alarmism and crisis-mongering of Steele and other Whigs in his *Preface to the B----p of S--r--m's Introduction*; and the carefully engineered brouhaha, which had begun as far back as October, was further satirized in a poem, in some respects Swift-like but probably not Swift's, imitating the First Ode of the Second Book of Horace. It was published by Morphew on 7 January 1714, and Steele probably thought it was Swift's, since the tone is as condescending and patronizing as Swift's had been in *Importance*.[30] Finally, after all the build-up, *The Crisis* itself was published on 19 January, its subtitle worth quoting as a précis of Steele's intention: 'Representing, From the most Authentick Records, the Just Causes of the late Happy Revolution: and the several Settlements of the Crowns of England and Scotland on Her Majesty . . . with some Seasonable Remarks on the Danger of a Popish Successor'. As in his *Importance of Dunkirk*, Steele favours quotation and compilation over the effort of organized comment, and his first section, after

---

30 On the authorship of the poem, see Woolley, 'Canon', p. 97, n. 5. James Woolley has kindly advised me that *CWJS* will treat the poem as unlikely to be Swift's.

a dedication to the clergy of the Church of England (which of course infuri-
ated Swift), is a series of extracts and quotations from all the laws and edicts
from the past quarter of a century that can possibly bear on the question
of the Succession. After this 'tedious but impressive recital', as his modern
editor calls it (*Tracts*, p. 125), Steele sounds the alarm and recites the threats
to England and Protestantism; he is at pains also to deplore the apparent
national indifference in the face of imminent dangers, dangers which must
have seemed especially real because the Queen had been seriously ill over
Christmas. Pages are spent in ecstatic praise of Marlborough, Steele being
unaware that his hero, like the Tory ministers, was constantly in correspondence with the Jacobite Court (Szechi, pp. 8, 38−9). In his response Swift
moves through Steele's points seriatim, but it is worth noting that, in the
course of warning of British unpreparedness for the Pretender's imminent
invasions, Steele complains of 'treasonable Books' circulating almost without notice from most people, books raising questions about the birth of the
Pretender and *Hereditary Right*; moreover, he complains, 'The Author of the
Conduct of the Allies has dared to drop Insinuations about altering the Succession' (*Tracts*, p. 176). Swift responds only briefly to his inclusion among
so many dangers, but by this time he cannot have been surprised to find the
usual distortion of his meaning repeated by Steele, and he throws into his
response a counter-charge about the early Jacobitism of Chief Justice Parker,
who had complained about the passage in 1711. Steele's tract then ends with
a brief but gory recital of 'the Barbarous Cruelties of Papists' (pp. 178−9)
to show his audience what they can expect if they fail to heed his warning.

The *Crisis* is almost unreadable today, but it was published by subscription
and widely circulated by Whig leaders in the Hanover Club and by Hanoverian agents, in fact possibly financed by the Elector himself. Steele wrote
to his wife that it was being circulated 'all over the Kingdom' (Steele, *Correspondence*, pp. 292−3). There were some interesting answers to *The Crisis*
even before Swift's; 'One of the Clergy', for example, wrote *Remarks . . . In a
Letter to the Author* (1714) which makes the obvious but telling point that the
very acts of Settlement inserted in Steele's pamphlet make it a self-refuting
document, so that it is really aimed only at denigrating the ministry. The
same argument explains what seems at first to be a very odd remark made by
the Earl of Strafford to the Princess Sophia, the Electress, in claiming that
the landed men and churchmen are heartily in her interest: 'I need no better
proofs, than that famous book of Steel's called, The Crisis, which the Whigs
cry up so much, and which I think is demonstration to your Royal Highness,
that you have nothing to fear from the Tories'; all the Tories, Strafford goes
on, are sworn to her succession and have abjured the Pretender. Again, we

have a neat turning upside down of Steele's alarmism (Macpherson, *Papers*, vol. II, pp. 568–9).

The Princess may have been convinced, but the stature of Steele's pamphlet was such that whether actually read or merely circulated it had to be answered in a powerful way, and Swift, as the leading man on the ministerial side, was clearly the writer to do it. He had finished his *History*, but there was still no publication in sight, and at the same time that *The Crisis* was being readied for circulation, he was soliciting Bolingbroke and Oxford to intercede in his effort to be appointed Historiographer Royal, an effort which ultimately proved as useless as his efforts to get the *History* published quickly. Did he also discuss with them beforehand his response to Steele, soon to be published as *The Publick Spirit of the Whigs*? We simply do not know, but on balance it seems likely. Since the public was expecting and awaiting a major Tory response to *The Crisis*, and since, given the recent writings over Dunkirk they were expecting Swift to furnish it, surely one of the two ministers would have been involved in offering help. J. A. Downie, echoing a point made earlier by Maurice Quinlan, argues that if the ministers had seen it they would have censored any offensive passages about the Union with Scotland, but this seems to ignore the fact that Swift's powerful friends had gone over *Conduct* with great care, and yet Parker had still found that objectionable passage about the Succession, a passage which continued to bedevil Swift until the death of the Queen.[31] In this case it was not the entire passage about the Union that gave offence, since dissolving the Union had been the subject of debate in Parliament only a year earlier and commonly discussed; the problem was only one paragraph about the Scottish people, a passage which as Swift pointed out later to Peterborough might have been missed in a quick reading of a long tract. One must remember too that Swift had been summoned to return to England because the ministry had 'further service' for him; that Defoe wrote to Oxford about *Publick Spirit* in terms that assumed Swift ('That Gentleman') was Oxford's agent; and that Swift spoke sarcastically of the price on his head as what happens to those who 'scribble for the Government' (Woolley, *Corr.*, vol. I, pp. 513, 516, 519, 602).[32] But without a 'Journal' or letters, we cannot be sure.

Whatever the level of government assistance or control, Swift's pamphlet, which appeared on 23 February 1714, his last political pamphlet published before the death of Queen Anne, is generally given high marks, though the sarcasm seems laboured in some parts. Ehrenpreis, who calls it one of Swift's finest works, gives it a careful and masterful analysis. But of course it

31 Downie, 'Swift and the Oxford Ministry', 8.   32 Defoe, *Letters*, p. 432.

also proved to be Swift's most troublesome pamphlet, since his long passage on the Union got him into deep difficulties almost before any journalistic answers could even appear. On 2 March, after complaint was made to the House of Lords by the Earl of Wharton and 'several Paragraphs' were read, the House resolved that it was a 'false, malicious, and factious Libel, highly dishonourable and scandalous to the *Scotch* Nation' and injurious to the Queen; Morphew was ordered to be brought into custody (*LJ*, vol. 19, pp. 627–8). There was a comical aspect to Wharton's role that Swift may have enjoyed if he knew; here is Peter Wentworth's description:

> Lord W— was out in his intended introduction of the matter, for he begun by telling the house, as he past thro' the court of request this Book was put into his hand and lighting accidentally upon the 20th and 21st page were [*sic*] the reflection upon the whole Scotch Nation is; but when he came to read the words he had bought a second edition, were [*sic*] those pages were left out, so he was forc't to call to some lords that had the first edition in their pockets.

And he adds, 'the Whigs guesses it to be Dr Swift's'; but he claims, as an afterthought, if the worst comes 'they' have a man who will own up to it and 'save the Doctor's Bacon' (*Wentworth Papers*, p. 359). It was a dangerous business, and Swift was no doubt rather worried about his bacon. In the next few days Barber's and Morphew's servants were examined (even Barber's compositors); on 11 March an Address to the Queen asked that she issue a reward to discover the author since Barber would answer no questions about him. At that point, on 11 March, a motion was made (by Lord Guernsey) to insert the words 'because the Author . . . pretends to know the Secrets of Your Majesty's Administration' (*LJ*, vol. 19, pp. 631–4). Happily for Swift it was defeated.

It is not clear how closely Swift himself followed all this, but Oxford had sent him on 3 March funds to 'answer such exigencys as their case may immediatly require', intended for Barber and his men presumably (Woolley, *Corr.*, vol. I, p. 589). As late as 16 March one peer had no new developments to report; the Tory Lord Berkeley of Stratton, who knew Swift, wrote as follows to Strafford: 'The house of Lords hath been taken up with a book call'd the publick Spirit of the Whigs, where the Scotch are most unsufferably abus'd, but doe not shew half the resentment that other people shew. Much bustle hath been made to find the Author to noe purpose. It is imagin'd to be Swift, who hath more wit then judgment' (*Wentworth Papers*, p. 361). And a proclamation was issued to discover the author, with a reward of three hundred pounds. The story that has grown up about all this (originating perhaps in Boyer's account) is that the Earl of Mar, Secretary of State and temporary employer of Erasmus Lewis, had prosecuted Barber so that no further inquiries could be made. But recent research by John I. Fischer ('Legal Response'), though inconclusive on many points, has shown Mar to be Swift's main enemy in this affair, although apparently Swift himself never realized it. The author's own sardonic conclusion in writing to Peterborough on 18 May was, 'The fault was, calling the Scots a fierce poor northern people. So well protected are those who scribble for the Government' (Woolley, *Corr.*, vol. I, p. 602).[33]

Outside of Parliament Swift's pamphlet got reactions along party lines, with Boyer naming him as '*Jonathan*', suggesting that the offensive passages were written to 'gratify the Spleen of a Lord' who loves his mischief better than his meat (Bolingbroke?), and explaining how the writer temporarily escaped punishment 'being under the Wings of some great Men' (Boyer, *State*, vol. VII, p. 223). From within the Tory camp an unusual reaction came from Defoe (probably), who as a champion of the Union wrote a strongly worded attack on Swift (no longer 'That Gentleman'), *The Scots Nation and Union Vindicated from the Reflections cast on them in an Infamous Libel* (1714); stepping aside from the Steele–Swift war Defoe objects to the 'Man-Monster' that has 'fired side ways at the Lookers on' (p. 7). Perhaps with a grain of truth, he says Swift's passions have left his reason in the lurch, and 'however he may escape with his Knavery, his best Friends will never excuse his Folly' (p. 12). Ironically, Defoe was at the same time helping Oxford get rid of Steele by sending him (on 10 March) a 'Collection of Scandal' drawn from Steele's writing that formed the basis for an indictment. On 18 March, by a heavy vote, Steele was expelled from the House of Commons. Even in the midst of the debate on his expulsion, he put forward a motion about Dunkirk. Little wonder that in his *Apology* (1714) he wrote, 'I have mentioned *Dunkirk* till I am sick.'[34]

4. Jacobitism and looking back: Swift's final writing in Queen Anne's England

But Swift himself was to scribble for the government no more, at least not scribble anything for public consumption that could have an impact on public opinion. His other writings during the rest of Queen Anne's life were

---

33 The printing, publication, 'censoring', and prosecution of *Publick Spirit* are recounted in detail in the relevant textual account in this volume (pp. 446–57).

34 Defoe, *Letters*, pp. 433–8; Steele, *Tracts*, p. 280.

retrospective and reflective, although some were intended for an immediate audience which circumstances did not allow them to have. His letters reveal his changes in mood as the summer approached. By May 1714 he had decided to leave London for the country; on 18 May he wrote to Peterborough, 'I never led a life so thoroughly uneasy as I do at present', adding that their enemies could not have contrived a situation worse for them (Woolley, *Corr.*, vol. I, p. 600). He had given up in despair his efforts to reconcile Bolingbroke and Oxford, 'from the quarrel between which two great men all our misfortunes proceeded' (memorandum attached to *Some Free Thoughts*), and in the first week of June, taking his *History* with him, he retired to Letcombe Bassett, Berkshire, away from the 'Courts and Ministers, and Business and Politicks' of which he was 'weary to death' (p. 611). In reflecting on life at Court, he now could write, to Arbuthnot, 'I have a Mind to be very angry, and to lett my anger break out in some manner that will not please them, at the End of a Pen . . . You must try another Game; this is at an End. Your Ministry is fourscore and ten years old, and all you can endeavor at is an Euthanasia, or rather it is in a deep Consumption at five and twenty' (p. 618). In this mood of uneasy detachment and controlled anger he began to let his mood break out at the end of a pen.

Even before he left London he produced a brief fragment, dated 20 February and headed *A Discourse concerning the Fears from the Pretender*. One may assume, as Davis does, that it was a false start to his main pamphlet at this time, *Some Free Thoughts upon the Present State of Affairs*, or one may accept it, as does D. Nichol Smith (*Ford*, p. 216), as the beginning of a pamphlet about the Pretender which Swift then abandoned. In any case its date was just after the election of a Speaker in the Commons and just before the Queen was to address the opening of Parliament (2 March). On 20 February *Publick Spirit* had not yet appeared, and Swift of course did not know that one order of business would be a protest in the Lords at his own most recent work. So, fresh from responding to Steele's *The Crisis*, he began writing a discourse on what was obviously the major point of contention between Whigs and Tories, the Protestant Succession, an issue on which the Tories were at a disadvantage if only from the difficulty of demonstrating a negative proposition. But as Swift well knew, and as he pointedly says in the final sentence of the fragment, the level of threat posed by the Pretender was for most people the crucial issue. A year earlier Bolingbroke had written to Shrewsbury, 'The clamour of Jacobitism seems to be the only resource of our enemies' (Bolingbroke, *Letters*, vol. III, p. 489). But it was a potent resource.

How much Swift could do to add to or supplant that fragment is unclear, but it is plain that he finished it at Letcombe close to 1 July. On that day he dispatched *Some Free Thoughts* in a MS printer's copy to Ford with extraordinary instructions to send it secretly to John Barber without any sign to him or to Erasmus Lewis that Ford or Swift had any connection with it. For the fairly remarkable and convoluted history of the MS after that point, including Bolingbroke's editorial interventions, please see the relevant textual account (pp. 480–2).

After Ford had read the pamphlet, he commented, 'I really think it is at least equal to any thing you have writ, & I dare say it will do great service as matters stand at present' (Woolley, *Corr.*, vol. I, p. 634). The 'great service' would have been bringing peace between Oxford and Bolingbroke and thus peace to the Tory party. But Swift's 'anger' was such that even this calm and deliberate analysis of the problems could not fail to alienate both sides, and it is thus unsurprising that on 11 July he wrote to Ford, 'as for Service it will do, a Fiddlestick. It will vex them, and that's enough' (Woolley, *Corr.*, vol. II, p. 1). Indeed, it could not have done much service with regard to the two ministers and is clearly designed as a political pamphlet for a wider audience. As well as finding fault with Oxford, and maybe less so with Bolingbroke, it also lays out a hard Tory line, combining (or trying to combine) full-fledged Tory doctrines (passive obedience, non-resistance, hereditary right, for example) with unhesitating acceptance of the Hanoverian Succession. Also a passage like that at the end, detailing what the British nation has a right to 'expect' from the Elector, surely cannot have been meant seriously by Swift; for those demands are not remotely connected to the reality of the political situation and thus (unlike his actual proposal of the Elector's grandson coming over) must have been intended to score points by contrast with the actual behaviour of the Whigs and their demands. The political particulars are also combined with passages of general political wisdom, such as the one (intended of course to reflect on Oxford's uncommunicativeness) beginning 'Every Man must have a Light sufficient for the Length of the Way he is appointed to go' (p. 299). Such passages not only show Swift's writing at its best, they also cast an ironic light on the failure of his powerful friends' efforts to secure him the post of Historiographer Royal, a failure he learned of only on 20 July, in an almost casual mention in a letter from Ford; when Arbuthnot had written Swift on 17 July about his efforts on the Dean's behalf, the appointment had already been made (vol. II, p. 15).

In the rest of the summer events affecting Swift moved quickly. Oxford was finally dismissed on 27 July and replaced by Shrewsbury. But Bolingbroke's triumph was a very short one, for on 1 August the Queen died, and Bolingbroke to no one's surprise was not among the nineteen lords named by the Elector to serve as Regents until his arrival; as Swift wrote to Bolingbroke on 7 August, 'the events of five days last week might furnish morals for another volume of Seneca' (Woolley, *Corr.*, vol. II, p. 56). In a letter of 3 August, Bolingbroke had entreated him to come to London, but the death of the Queen meant Swift had to go to Ireland to take the oaths; in reply he did make an offer of sorts, 'if your Lordship thinks my service may be of any use in this new world, I will be ready to attend you by the beginning of winter'. On the same day he wrote to Ford in terms that suggest he was indeed expecting to return from Ireland in a short time; and he added, 'I am breeding anoth^r Pamphlet, but have not writt a Word of it. The Title will be something like this—Some Considerations upon th[e] Consequences apprehended by th[e] Qu—s Death.' He tells Ford that he will write it in Letcombe and during his journey and then send it from Ireland (pp. 58, 60–1). Swift's final political writing before his return to Ireland was undertaken, then, with great deliberation and sense of purpose (he put aside polishing an imitation of Horace in order to 'breed' this pamphlet); he gave birth, however, to only a fragment, though he called it 'a good piece' of the whole when writing to Ford again on 12 August. There was no further mention of the pamphlet in his letters before he returned to Ireland at the end of August. The fragment, entitled *Some Considerations upon the Consequences hoped and feared from the Death of the Queen*, is dated 'Aug. 9. 1714' and was not printed until 1765. Swift's original intentions in this piece are now obscured; both Davis (vol. VIII, p. xxix) and Ehrenpreis (vol. III, p. 108) think he meant to defend the (by then) very unpopular Oxford, but although his account begins with the early history of Harley's coming to power in 1710, there is no way to know in what direction Swift would have moved had he stayed with it. It is hard to believe that what remains could be a 'good piece' of anything of moment, much less something that would have been able to 'rally the party behind Oxford', as Ehrenpreis suggests. We can only agree with Swift's curses on 14 September when he wrote to Bolingbroke, whose dismissal from office on 31 August he had just learned about, 'The — take this country; it has, in three weeks, spoiled two as good sixpenny pamphlets, as ever a proclamation was issued out against . . . I shall be cured of loving England, as the fellow was of his ague, by getting himself whipt through the town' (Woolley, *Corr.*, vol. II, p. 79). The pamphlets, obviously, were *Some Free Thoughts* and *Some Considerations*.

'Confound all Politicks', Swift wrote to Ford on 12 August, as he readied himself to return to Ireland. 'Have I had enough of them or no?' (Woolley, *Corr.*, vol. II, p. 66). He had certainly had enough of English politics in this 'new world', and though he continued to speak of returning to England if his friends had need of him, it was never a strong possibility, as he probably realized. But another political world awaited him, one in which his 'evil instrument', as he called his pen, would again work wonders. On 3 July he had written a heartfelt letter to Oxford which ends on this note: 'I have said enough, and like one at Your Levee having made my Bow, I shrink back into the Crowd' (vol. I, p. 629). It may be too much to say with Samuel Johnson that in the reign of Queen Anne Swift 'dictated for a time the political opinions of the English nation';[35] but shrinking back into the crowd was never to be his way.

35 Samuel Johnson, *The Lives of the Most Eminent English Poets; with Critical Observations on their Works*, ed. Roger Lonsdale, 4 vols. (Oxford: Clarendon Press, 2006), vol. III, p. 208.

THE CONDUCT OF THE
ALLIES

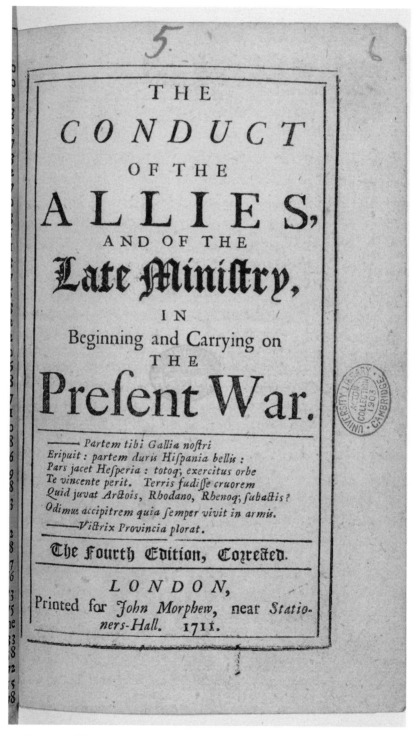

THE
CONDUCT
OF THE
ALLIES,
AND OF THE
Late Ministry,
IN
Beginning and Carrying on
THE
Present War.

——— Partem tibi Gallia nostri
Eripuit : partem duris Hispania bellis :
Pars jacet Hesperia : totoq; exercitus orbe
Te vincente perit. Terris fudisse cruorem
Quid juvat Arctois, Rhodano, Rhenoq; subactis?
Odimus accipitrem quia semper vivit in armis.
———Victrix Provincia plorat.

The Fourth Edition, Corrected.

LONDON,
Printed for *John Morphew*, near *Statio-*
ners-Hall. 1711.

Figure 1. Title page of the fourth edition: CUL, Acton.d.25.1001 (6).

THE PREFACE

I cannot sufficiently admire the Industry of a sort of Men, wholly out of Favour with the Prince and People,[1] *and openly professing a separate Interest from the Bulk of the Landed Men, who yet are able to raise, at this Juncture, so great a Clamour against a Peace, without offering one single Reason, but what we find in their* Ballads.[2] *I lay it down for a Maxim, That no reasonable Person, whether* Whig *or* Tory *(since it is necessary to use those foolish Terms)*[3] *can be of Opinion for continuing the War, upon the Foot it now is, unless he be a Gainer by it, or hopes it may occasion some new Turn of Affairs at home, to the Advantage of his Party; or lastly, unless he be very ignorant of the Kingdom's Condition, and by what Means we have been reduced to it. Upon the two first Cases, where Interest is concerned, I have nothing to say: But as to the last, I think it highly necessary, that the Publick should be freely and impartially told what Circumstances they are in, after what Manner they have been treated by those whom they trusted so many Years with the Disposal of their Blood and Treasure, and what the Consequences of this Management are like to be upon themselves and their Posterity.*

Title page mottos] *Partem tibi Gallia nostri / Eripuit: partem duris Hispania bellis: / Pars jacet Hesperia: totoq; exercitus orbe / Te vincente perit. Terris fudisse cruorem / Quid juvat Arctois, Rhodano, Rhenoq; subactis?*: Lucan, *The Civil War*, V.264–8: 'Some of us were snatched from you by Gaul, others by the hard campaigns in Spain; others lie in Italy; over all the world you are victorious and your soldiers die. What boots it to have shed our blood in Northern lands, where we conquered the Rhone and the Rhine?' (trans. J. D. Duff).

    Odimus accipitrem quia semper vivit in armis: Ovid, *The Art of Love*, II.147: 'We hate the hawk, because he ever lives in arms' (trans. J. H. Mozley).

    Victrix Provincia plorat: Juvenal, *Satires*, I.50: '[While you] poor Province, win your cause and weep!' (trans. G. G. Ramsay).

1 *admire*: 'wonder at'.

2 *Ballads*: cf. Williams, *JSt*, p. 394 (24 October 1711): 'The Whig party are furious against a Peace, and every day some ballad comes out reflecting on the ministry on that account.' Swift's complaint on this point moved one answerer to the *Conduct* to respond, 'as if *Nonsense, Contradiction, Falshood, Ignorance* and *Impudence* deserv'd any other Treatment' (*Remarks on a . . . Libel, Intituled, The Conduct of the Allies* (1711), p. 6).

3 *those foolish Terms*: cf. Swift's ridicule of those 'two fantastick Names of *Whig* and *Tory*' in one of his last *Examiner* papers (31 May 1711) and his comment early in his *History* that by 1711 disputes about principles between Whigs and Tories had been dropped 'and those Fantastick Words ought in justice to have been so too' (Davis, vol. VII, p. 3). See also *Examiners* for 16 November 1710, and 8 and 22 March 1711.

Those who, either by Writing or Discourse, have undertaken to defend the Proceedings of the Late Ministry, in the Management of the War, and of the Treaty at Gertruydenburg,[4] *have spent time in celebrating the Conduct and Valour of our Leaders and their Troops, in summing up the Victories they have gained, and the Towns they have taken. Then they tell us what high Articles were insisted on by our Ministers and those of the Confederates, and what Pains both were at in persuading* France *to accept them. But nothing of this can give the least Satisfaction to the just Complaints of the Kingdom. As to the War, our Grievances are, That a greater Load has been laid on Us than was either just or necessary, or than we have been able to bear; that the grossest Impositions have been submitted to for the Advancement of private Wealth and Power, or in order to forward the more dangerous Designs of a* Faction, *to both which a Peace would have put an End; And that the Part of the War which was chiefly our Province, which would have been most beneficial to us, and destructive to the Enemy, was wholly neglected. As to a Peace, We complain of being deluded by a* Mock Treaty;[5] *in which those who Negotiated, took care to make such Demands as they knew were impossible to be complied with, and therefore might securely press every Article as if they were in earnest.*

These are some of the Points I design to Treat of in the following Discourse; with several others which I thought it necessary, at this time, for the Kingdom to be informed of. I think I am not mistaken in those Facts I mention; at least not in any Circumstance so material, as to weaken the Consequences I draw from them.

After Ten Years War, with perpetual Success, to tell us it is yet impossible to have a good Peace, is very surprising, and seems so different from what hath ever hapned in the World before, that a Man of any Party may be allowed suspecting, we have either been ill used, or have not made the most of our Victories, and might therefore desire to know where the Difficulty lay: Then it is natural to enquire into our present Condition; how long we shall be able to go on at this Rate; what the Consequences may be upon the present and future Ages; and whether a Peace, without that impracticable Point[6] *which some People do so much insist on, be really ruinous in it self, or equally so with the Continuance of the War.*

---

4 *Treaty at Gertruydenberg*: the peace conference held at Gertruydenberg (Geertruidenberg) September 1709–March 1710, which resulted in Preliminaries agreed to by the Allies on 28 May 1709. Louis XIV then accepted all the sections except Article Thirty-Seven, which demanded that all of Spain (currently ruled by his grandson Philip of Anjou) be given up to the Austrian Archduke Charles, who would then be acknowledged by the French as Charles III, King of Spain. In the face of his unsurprising refusal, the war continued.

5 *deluded by a Mock Treaty*: that negotiated at Gertruydenberg. Swift amplifies this point below (pp. 91–2). For Swift's ridicule of the unreasonable demands made of the French, see also *A New Journey to Paris* (1711).

6 *that impracticable Point*: i.e., 'No Peace without Spain', which Swift discusses near the end of this pamphlet (pp. 87–106).

THE
CONDUCT
OF THE
ALLIES, &c.

The Motives that may engage a wise Prince or State in a War, I take to be one or more of these: Either to check the overgrown Power of some ambitious Neighbour; to recover what hath been unjustly taken from Them; to revenge some Injury They have received; (which all Political Casuists allow); to assist some Ally in a just Quarrel; or lastly, to defend Themselves when They are invaded. In all these Cases, the Writers upon Politicks admit a War to be justly undertaken.[7] The last is what hath been usually called *pro aris & focis*;[8] where no Expence or Endeavour can be too great, because all we have is at stake, and consequently, our utmost Force to be exerted; and the Dispute is soon determined, either in Safety or utter Destruction. But in the other four, I believe, it will be found, that no Monarch or Commonwealth did ever engage beyond a certain Degree; never proceeding so far as to exhaust the Strength and Substance of their Country by Anticipations[9] and Loans, which, in a few Years, must put them in a worse Condition than any they could reasonably apprehend from those Evils, for the preventing of which they first entred into the War: Because this would be to run into real infallible Ruin, only in hopes to remove what might perhaps but appear so by a probable Speculation.

And, as a War should be undertaken upon a just and prudent Motive, so it is still more obvious, that a Prince ought maturely to consider the Condition he is in, when he enters on it: Whether his Coffers be full, his Revenues clear of Debts, his People numerous and rich by a long Peace and free

---

7 *Writers . . . undertaken*: the writers whom Swift and his contemporaries would most likely have in mind were Hugo Grotius (1583–1645) and Samuel von Pufendorf (1632–94). See Pufendorf, *De officio hominis ex civis juxta legem naturalem* (1682), bk. II, ch. xvi, and see esp. Grotius, *De jure belli ac pacis* (1625), bk. II, ch. i, from which Swift's comments seem directly derived.

8 *pro aris et focis*: 'for our altars and our homes', a phrase frequently used as a motto and deriving from Cicero, *Nature of the Gods*, III.40.94.

9 *Anticipations*: money used before it is actually 'at one's disposal' (*OED*).

Trade, not overpressed with many burthensom Taxes; No violent Faction
ready to dispute his just Prerogative, and thereby weaken his Authority at
Home, and lessen his Reputation Abroad. For, if the contrary of all this
happen to be his Case, he will hardly be persuaded to disturb the World's
Quiet and his own, while there is any other way left of preserving the latter
with Honour and Safety.

Supposing the War to have commenced upon a just Motive; the next
Thing to be considered, is, When a Prince ought in Prudence to receive the
Overtures of a Peace: Which I take to be, either when the Enemy is ready
to yield the Point originally contended for, or when that Point is found
impossible to be ever obtained; or when contending any longer, though
with Probability of gaining that Point at last, would put such a Prince and
his People in a worse Condition than the present Loss of it. All which
Considerations are of much greater Force, where a War is managed by an
Alliance of many Confederates, which in the variety of Interests, among
the several Parties, is liable to so many unforeseen Accidents.

In a Confederate War it ought to be considered, which Party has the
deepest share in the Quarrel: For though each may have their particular
Reasons, yet one or two among them will probably be more concerned than
the rest, and therefore ought to bear the greatest part of the Burthen, in
proportion to their Strength. For Example: Two Princes may be Competitors for a Kingdom, and it will be your Interest to take the Part of Him, who
will probably allow you good Conditions of Trade, rather than of the other,
who possibly may not. However, that Prince whose Cause you espouse,
though never so vigorously, is the Principal in that War, and You, properly
speaking, are but a Second. Or a Commonwealth may lie in danger to be
over-run by a powerful Neighbour, which, in time, may produce very bad
Consequences upon your Trade and Liberty: 'Tis therefore necessary, as
well as prudent, to lend them Assistance, and help them to win a strong
secure Frontier; but, as They must in course[10] be the first and greatest Sufferers, so, in Justice, they ought to bear the greatest Weight. If a House be
on fire, it behoves all in the Neighbourhood to run with Buckets to quench
it; but the Owner is sure to be undone first; and it is not impossible that
those at next Door may escape, by a Shower from Heaven, or the stillness
of the Weather, or some other favourable Accident.

10 *in course*: i.e., 'in due course'.

But, if an Ally, who is not so immediately concerned in the good or ill Fortune of the War, be so generous, as to contribute more than the Principal Party, and even more in proportion to his Abilities, he ought at least to have his Share in what is conquered from the Enemy: Or, if his Romantick Disposition transports him so far, as to expect little or nothing of this, he might however hope, that the Principals would make it up in Dignity and Respect; and he would surely think it monstrous to find them intermedling in his Domestick Affairs, prescribing what Servants he should keep or dismiss, pressing him perpetually with the most unreasonable Demands, and at every turn threatning to break the Alliance, if he will not comply.[11]

From these Reflections upon War in general, I descend to consider those Wars, wherein *England* hath been engaged since the Conquest. In the Civil-Wars of the *Barons*, as well as those between the Houses of *York* and *Lancaster*, great Destruction was made of the Nobility and Gentry, new Families raised, and old ones extinguished, but the Money spent on both was employed and circulated at Home; no Publick Debts contracted; and a very few Years of Peace quickly set all right again.

The like may be affirmed even of that unnatural Rebellion against King *Charles* I. the Usurpers maintained great Armies in constant Pay, had almost continual War with *Spain* or *Holland*, but managing it by their Fleets, they encreased very much the Riches of the Kingdom, instead of exhausting them.

Our Foreign Wars were generally against *Scotland* or *France*; the first being upon our own Continent, carried no Money out of the Kingdom, and were seldom of long continuance. During our first Wars with *France*, we possessed great Dominions in that Country, where we preserved some Footing till the Reign of Queen *Mary*; and though some of our latter Princes made very chargeable Expeditions thither, a Subsidy, and two or three Fifteenths, cleared all the Debt. Beside, our Victories were then of some Use as well as Glory; for we were so prudent to Fight, and so happy to Conquer, only for our selves.

The *Dutch* Wars, in the Reign of King *Charles* II. though begun and carried on under a very corrupt Administration, and much to the Dishonour of the Crown, did indeed keep the King needy and poor, by discontinuing

11 *intermedling . . . comply*: a pointed remark; see below (p. 86), where Swift describes the efforts of the Dutch and the Imperial representatives to influence the Queen because of their concern over the fall of public credit after Sunderland was dismissed in 1710.

or discontenting his Parliament, when he most needed their Assistance; but neither left any Debt upon the Nation, nor carried any Mony out of it.

At the *Revolution*, a general War broke out in *Europe*, wherein many Princes joined in an Alliance against *France*, to check the ambitious Designs of that Monarch; and here the *Emperor*, the *Dutch*, and *England* were Principals. About this time the Custom first began among us of borrowing Millions upon Funds of Interest: It was pretended, That the War could not possibly last above one or two Campaigns; and that the Debts contracted might be easily paid in a few Years, by a gentle Tax, without burthening the Subject. But the true Reason for embracing this Expedient, was the Security of a new Prince, not firmly settled on the Throne: People were tempted to lend, by great Premiums[12] and large Interest, and it concerned them nearly to preserve that Government, which they trusted with their Money. The Person said to have been Author of so detestable a Project,[13] is still living, and lives to see some of its fatal Consequences, whereof his Grand-Children will not see an end. And this pernicious Counsel closed very well with the Posture of Affairs at that time: For, a Set of Upstarts, who had little or no part in the *Revolution*, but valued themselves by their Noise and pretended Zeal when the Work was over, were got into Credit at Court, by the Merit of becoming Undertakers and Projectors of Loans and Funds: These, finding that the Gentlemen of Estates were not willing to come into their Measures, fell upon those new Schemes of raising Mony, in order to create a Mony'd-Interest, that might in time vie with the Landed, and of which they hoped to be at the Head.

The Ground of the first War, for ten Years after the *Revolution*, as to the Part we had in it, was, to make *France* acknowledge the late King,[14] and to recover *Hudson's-Bay*. But during that whole War, the Sea was almost entirely neglected, and the greatest Part of *Six* Millions Annually employed to enlarge the Frontier of the *Dutch*. For the King was a General, but not an Admiral; and although King of *England*, was a Native of *Holland*.

After ten Years Fighting to little purpose; after the Loss of above an hundred thousand Men, and a Debt remaining of twenty Millions, we

12 *Premiums*: sums paid in addition to the interest as an inducement for the lender to make a loan.
13 *Author of . . . Project*: Gilbert Burnet (1643–1715), Bishop of Salisbury. See Swift's comments in *History* (Davis, vol. VII, pp. 68–69) on this 'Expedient', which he says Burnet learned in Holland.
14 *the late King*: William III.

at length hearkned to the Terms of a Peace,[15] which was concluded with great Advantages to the *Empire* and *Holland*, but none at all to us; and clogged soon after by the famous Treaty of *Partition*;[16] by which, *Naples, Sicily*, and *Lorain*, were to be added to the *French* Dominions; or if that Crown should think fit to set aside the Treaty, upon the *Spaniards* refusing to accept it, as they declared they would, to the several Parties at the very time of transacting it; then the *French* would have Pretensions to the whole Monarchy. And so it proved in the Event; for, the late King of *Spain* reckoning it an Indignity to have his Territories cantoned out into Parcels, by other Princes, during his own Life, and without his Consent, rather chose to bequeath the Monarchy entire to a younger Son of *France*: And this Prince was acknowledged for King of *Spain* both by Us and *Holland*.

It must be granted, that the Counsels of entring into the present War were violently opposed by the *Church-Party*, who first advised the late King to acknowledge the Duke of *Anjou*; and particularly, 'tis affirmed that the Earl of *G——n*,[17] who was then in the Church-Interest, told the King in *November*, 1701, That since his Majesty was determined to engage in a War so contrary to his private Opinion, he could serve him no longer, and accordingly gave up his Employment; though he happened afterwards to change his Mind, when he was to be Lord High Treasurer, and have the sole Management of Affairs at home; while those abroad were to be in the hands of *One*, whose Advantage, by all sorts of Ties, he was engaged to promote.[18]

The Declarations of War against *France* and *Spain*, made by Us and *Holland*, are dated within a few Days of each other.[19] In that published by

15 *Terms of a Peace*: the Treaty of Ryswick, September 1697, between Britain, France, the United Provinces and Spain, cost Louis XIV most of his conquests since 1679 and recognized William as King of England.
16 *Treaty of Partition*: in 1698 and again (because of the death of the Electoral Prince of Bavaria) in 1700 treaties involving the partitions of the Spanish Empire were made necessary by the failure of the Treaty of Ryswick to settle the question of a successor to the dying Spanish King Charles II, who was without an heir. Naples, Sicily and Lorraine were to be French dominions, but the throne of Spain was to go to the Archduke Charles, a son of the Austrian Emperor. However, as Swift goes on to say, Charles II thwarted this settlement by bequeathing Spain to the Duke of Anjou, grandson of Louis XIV.
17 *Earl of G——n*: Sidney Godolphin, first Earl of Godolphin (1645–1712), Lord Treasurer in the Whig administration until 1710, when he fell after the Sacheverell trial.
18 *hands of One . . . promote*: Marlborough; Swift calls attention to ties of blood as well as politics; Godolphin was part of the 'Family', since his only son married Marlborough's oldest daughter.
19 *the Declarations . . . other*: made in 1702, the Queen's on 4 May, the Dutch on 8 May. In his attack on the *Conduct*, Francis Hare (1671–1740), Chaplain to the Duke of Marlborough

the *States*, they say very truly, That *they are nearest, and most exposed to the Fire*; that *they are blocked up on all sides, and actually attacked by the Kings of* France *and* Spain; that *their Declaration is the Effect of an urgent and pressing Necessity*; with other Expressions to the same purpose. They *desire the Assistance of all Kings and Princes*, &c. The grounds of their Quarrel with *France*, are such as only affect themselves, or at least more immediately than any other Prince or State; such as, *the* French *refusing to grant the Tariff promised by the Treaty of* Ryswick; *the loading the* Dutch *Inhabitants settled in* France, *with excessive Duties, contrary to the said Treaty; the Violation of the* Partition-Treaty, *by the* French *accepting the King of* Spain's *Will, and threatning the* States, *if they would not comply; the seizing the* Spanish Netherlands *by the* French *Troops, and turning out the* Dutch, *who by Permission of the late King of* Spain *were in Garrison there; by which means that Republick was deprived of her Barrier, contrary to the Treaty of* Partition, *where it was particularly stipulated, that the* Spanish Netherlands *should be left to the Archduke.* They alledged, that *the* French *King governed* Flanders *as his own, though under the Name of his Grandson, and sent great Numbers of Troops thither to fright them: That he had seized the City and Citadel of* Liege, *had possessed himself of several Places in the Archbishoprick of* Cologne, *and maintained Troops in the Country of* Wolfenbuttel, *in order to block up the* Dutch *on all sides; and caused his Resident to give in a Memorial, wherein he threatned the* States *to act against them, if they refused complying with the Contents of that Memorial.*

The Queen's Declaration of War is grounded upon the *Grand Alliance*, as This was upon the unjust Usurpations and Encroachments of the *French* King; whereof the Instances produced are, *His keeping in Possession a great Part of the* Spanish *Dominions, seizing* Milan *and the* Spanish *Low-Countries, making himself Master of* Cadiz, *&c. And instead of giving Satisfaction in these Points, his putting an Indignity and Affront on Her Majesty and Kingdoms, by Declaring the Pretended Prince of* Wales[20] K. *of* England, *&c.* which last was the only personal Quarrel we had in the War; and even

and later Bishop of St Asaph and Bishop of Chichester, points out, correctly, that Swift omits the phrase in the Queen's Declaration which says that the French King 'exercises an absolute Authority over all that Monarchy', claiming that Swift's intent is to minimize the Duke of Anjou's succession to that monarchy as an occasion of the quarrel (Hare, *The Allies and the Late Ministry Defended*, Part I, 3rd edn (1712), p. 42).

20 *Pretended Prince of Wales*: i.e., the 'Old Pretender', the Chevalier de St George (1688–1766), son of James II.

This was positively denied by *France*, That King being then willing to Acknowledge Her Majesty.

I think it plainly appears, by both Declarations, that *England* ought no more to have been a Principal in this War, than *Prussia*, or any other Power, who came afterwards into that Alliance. *Holland* was first in the Danger, the *French* Troops being at that time just at the Gates of *Nimeguen*. But the Complaints made in our Declaration, do all, except the last, as much or more concern almost every Prince in *Europe*.

For, among the several Parties who came first or last into this Confederacy, there were few but who, in proportion, had more to get or to lose, to hope or to fear, from the good or ill Success of this War, than We. The *Dutch* took up Arms to defend themselves from immediate Ruin; and by a successful War, they proposed to have a larger Extent of Country, and a better Frontier against *France*. The *Emperor* hoped to recover the Monarchy of *Spain*, or some part of it, for his younger Son, chiefly at the Expence of Us and *Holland*. The King of *Portugal* had received Intelligence, that *Philip* designed to renew the old Pretensions of *Spain* upon that Kingdom, which is surrounded by the other on all sides, except towards the Sea, and could therefore only be defended by *Maritime Powers*. This, with the advantageous Terms offered by King *Charles*,[21] as well as by Us, prevailed with that Prince to enter into the Alliance. The Duke of *Savoy's* Temptations and Fears were yet greater: The main Charge of the War on that side, was to be supplied by *England*, and the Profit to redound to him. In case *Milan* should be Conquered, it was stipulated that his Royal Highness should have the Dutchy of *Montferrat*, belonging to the Duke of *Mantua*, the Provinces of *Alexandria*, and *Valentia*, and *Lomellino*, with other Lands between the *Po* and the *Tanaro*, together with the *Vigevenasco*, or in lieu of it, an Equivalent out of the Province of *Novara*, adjoining to his own State; beside whatever else could be taken from *France* on that side by the Confederate Forces. Then, he was in terrible Apprehensions of being surrounded by *France*, who had so many Troops in the *Milanese*, and might have easily swallowed up his whole Dutchy.

The rest of the Allies came in purely for Subsidies, whereof they sunk considerable Sums into their own Coffers, and refused to send their

---

21 *offered by King Charles*: i.e., by the Archduke Charles of Austria, son of the Emperor and claimant to the Spanish throne.

Contingent to the *Emperor*, alledging their Troops were already hired by *England* and *Holland*.

Some time after the D. of *Anjou*'s succeeding to the Monarchy of *Spain*, in breach of the *Partition* Treaty, the Question here in *England* was, Whether the Peace should be continued, or a new War begun. Those who were for the former, alledged the Debts and Difficulties we laboured under; that both We and the *Dutch* had already Acknowledged *Philip* for King of *Spain*; that the Inclinations of the *Spaniards* to the House of *Austria*, and their Aversion for that of *Bourbon*, were not so surely to be reckoned upon, as some would pretend; that We rightly thought it a piece of Insolence, as well as Injustice, in the *French*, to offer putting a King upon Us; and the *Spaniards* would conceive, we had as little Reason to force one upon Them; That it was true, the Nature and Genius of those two People differed very much, and so would probably continue to do, as well under a King of *French* Blood, as one of *Austrian*; but, if we should engage in a War for Dethroning the D. of *Anjou*, we should certainly effect what, by the Progress and Operations of it, we endeavoured to prevent, I mean an Union of Interest and Affections between the two Nations; For the *Spaniards* must of necessity call in *French* Troops to their Assistance: This would introduce *French* Counsellors into King *Philip*'s Court; and this, by degrees, would habituate and reconcile the two Nations: That, to assist King *Charles* by *English* or *Dutch* Forces, would render him odious to his new Subjects, who have nothing in so great an Abomination, as those whom they hold for *Hereticks*: That, the *French* would by this means become Masters of the Treasures in the *Spanish West-Indies*: That, in the last War, when *Spain*, *Cologne*, and *Bavaria* were in our Alliance, and by a modest Computation brought Sixty thousand Men into the Field against the Common Enemy; when *Flanders*, the Seat of War, was on our side, and his Majesty, a Prince of great Valour and Conduct, at the Head of the whole Confederate Army; yet we had no Reason to boast of our Success: How then should we be able to oppose *France* with those Powers against us, which would carry Sixty thousand Men from us to the Enemy, and so make us, upon the Balance, weaker by One hundred and twenty thousand Men, at the beginning of this War, than of that in the Year 1688?

On the other side, those whose Opinion, or some private Motives, inclined them to give their Advice for entring into a new War, alledged how dangerous it would be for *England*, that *Philip* should be King of

Spain; that we could have no Security for our Trade, while that Kingdom was subject to a Prince of the *Bourbon* Family; nor any hopes of preserving the Balance of *Europe*, because the Grandfather would, in effect, be King, while his Grandson had but the Title, and thereby have a better Opportunity than ever of pursuing his Design for Universal Monarchy. These and the like Arguments prevailed; and so, without offering at any other Remedy, without taking time to consider the Consequences, or to reflect on our own Condition, we hastily engaged in a War which hath cost us sixty Millions; and after repeated, as well as unexpected Success in Arms, hath put us and our Posterity in a worse Condition, not only than any of our Allies, but even our conquered Enemies themselves.

The part we have acted in the Conduct of this whole War, with reference to our Allies abroad, and to a prevailing Faction at home, is what I shall now particularly examin; where I presume it will appear, by plain Matters of Fact, that no Nation was ever so long or so scandalously abused by the Folly, the Temerity, the Corruption, the Ambition of its domestick Enemies; or treated with so much Insolence, Injustice and Ingratitude by its foreign Friends.

This will be manifest by proving the Three following Points.

First, That against all manner of Prudence or common Reason, we engaged in this War as Principals, when we ought to have acted only as Auxiliaries.

Secondly, That we spent all our Vigour in pursuing that Part of the War which could least answer the End we proposed by beginning of it; and made no Efforts at all where we could have most weakned the Common Enemy, and at the same time enriched our Selves.

Lastly, That we suffered each of our Allies to break every Article in those Treaties and Agreements by which they were bound, and to lay the Burthen upon us.

Upon the first of these Points, That we ought to have entered into this War only as Auxiliaries. Let any Man reflect upon our Condition at that time: Just come out of the most tedious, expensive and unsuccessful War that ever *England* had been engaged in; sinking under heavy Debts, of a Nature and Degree never heard of by Us or Our Ancestors; the Bulk of the Gentry and People heartily tired of the War, and glad of a Peace, though it brought no other Advantage but it self: No sudden Prospect of lessening our

Taxes, which were grown as necessary to pay our Debts, as to raise Armies: A sort of artificial Wealth of Funds and Stocks in the Hands of those who for Ten Years before had been plundering the Publick; Many Corruptions in every Branch of our Government, that needed Reformation. Under these Difficulties, from which Twenty Years Peace, and the wisest Management, could hardly recover us, we declare War against *France*, fortified by the Accession and Alliance of those Powers I mentioned before, and which, in the former War, had been Parties in our Confederacy. It is very obvious what a Change must be made in the Balance, by such Weights taken out of Our Scale and put into Theirs; since it was manifest by Ten Years Experience, that *France* without those Additions of Strength, was able to maintain it self against us. So that Human Probability ran with mighty odds on the other side; and in that case, nothing under the most extreme Necessity should force any State to engage in a War. We had already acknowledged *Philip* for King of *Spain*; neither does the Queen's Declaration of War take notice of the Duke of *Anjou's* Succession to that Monarchy, as a Subject of Quarrel; but the *French* King's governing it as if it were his own; his seizing *Cadiz, Milan,* and the *Spanish Low Countries*, with the Indignity of Proclaiming the *Pretender*. In all which we charge that Prince with nothing directly relating to us, excepting the last: And this, although indeed a great Affront, might have easily been redressed without a War; for the *French* Court declared they did not acknowledge the *Pretender*, but only gave him the Title of *King*, which was allowed to *Augustus* by his Enemy of *Sueden*, who had driven him out of *Poland*, and forced him to acknowledge *Stanislaus*.[22]

'Tis true indeed, the Danger of the *Dutch*, by so ill a Neighbourhood in *Flanders*, might affect us very much in the Consequences of it; and the Loss of *Spain* to the House of *Austria*, if it should be governed by *French* Influence, and *French* Politicks, might, in time, be very pernicious to our Trade. It would therefore have been prudent, as well as generous and charitable, to help our Neighbour; and so we might have done without injuring our selves: For by an old Treaty with *Holland*,[23] we were bound to assist

---

22 *Augustus . . . Stanislaus*: Charles XI of Sweden, who had conquered Poland early in the Northern War, secured the election of Stanislaus Leszczynski, a nobleman, as King of Poland, and expelled Augustus II (Elector of Saxony), who was forced to give up the crown in 1706.
23 *by an old Treaty with Holland*: Swift is referring to 'A Treaty of a Defensive Alliance between Charles II, King of England, and the States General of the United Provinces of

that Republick with Ten thousand Men, whenever they were attacked by the *French*; whose Troops, upon the King of *Spain*'s Death, taking Possession of *Flanders*, in right of *Philip*, and securing the *Dutch* Garrisons 'till they would acknowledge Him, the *States-General*, by Memorials from their Envoy here, demanded only the Ten thousand Men, we were obliged to give them by virtue of that Treaty. And I make no doubt but *Holland* would have exerted themselves so vigorously, as to be able, with that Assistance alone, to defend their Frontiers: Or, if they had been forced to a Peace, the *Spaniards*, who abhor dismembring their Monarchy, would never have suffered the *French* to possess themselves of *Flanders*. At that time they had none of those Endearments to each other which this War hath created; and whatever Hatred and Jealousie were natural between the two Nations, would then have appeared. So that there was no sort of necessity for Us to proceed further, although We had been in a better Condition. But our Politicians at that time had other Views, and a new War must be undertaken, upon the Advice of those, who with their Partisans and Adherents, were to be the sole Gainers by it. A Grand Alliance was therefore made between the Emperor, *England*, and the *States-General*; by which, if the Injuries complained of from *France* were not remedied in two Months, the Parties concerned were obliged mutually to assist each other *with their whole Strength.*[24]

Thus We became Principal in a War, in Conjunction with two Allies, whose share in the Quarrel was, beyond all Proportion, greater than Ours. However, I can see no Reason from the Words of the Grand Alliance, by which we were obliged to make those prodigious Expences we have since been at. By what I have always heard and read, I take the *whole Strength of*

---

the Netherlands, concluded at Westminster, March the 3rd, 1677/8', and specifically to Separate Article 1 of that treaty, which specifies that England will assist the States (and vice versa) if they are attacked by providing 6,000 foot soldiers, well armed, and twenty men of war (*A General Collection of Treatys, Declarations of War, Manifestos, and other Publick Papers* (1710), vol. II, p. 187). Swift's point is that if the English government had met the terms of this treaty instead of joining in the second Grand Alliance in 1701, the Dutch would have been satisfied and the ruinous war avoided. See the next note.

24 *with their whole Strength*: quoting the treaty of the Grand Alliance. The phrase is not present in exactly that form in every translation, but it is in the Queen's declaration of war on 4 May 1702, summarizing this portion of the Grand Alliance treaty: 'And it being provided by the third and fourth Articles of the fore-mention'd Alliance, that if in the space of two Months ... the Injurys complain'd of were not remedy'd, the Partys concern'd shou'd mutually assist each other with their whole strength' (*A General Collection of Treatys*, vol. I, p. 421).

the Nation, as understood in that Treaty, to be the utmost that a Prince can raise Annually from his Subjects; if he be forced to Mortgage and Borrow, whether at Home or Abroad, it is not, properly speaking, *his own Strength*, or that of the Nation, but the entire Substance of particular Persons, which not being able to raise out of the annual Income of his Kingdom, he takes upon Security, and can only pay the Interest; and by this Method one Part of the Nation is pawned to the other, with hardly a Possibility left of being ever redeemed.

Surely it would have been enough for us to have suspended the Payment of our Debts contracted in the former War, to have continued our Land and Malt Tax, with those others which have since been mortgaged: These, with some Additions, would have made up such a Sum, as, with prudent Management, might, I suppose, have maintained an Hundred thousand Men by Sea and Land; a reasonable Quota in all conscience for that Ally, who apprehended least Danger, and expected least Advantage. Nor can we imagine that either of the Confederates, when the War begun, would have been so unreasonable, as to refuse joyning with us upon such a Foot, and expect that we should every Year go between three and four Millions in Debt (which hath been our Case) because the *French* could hardly have contrived any Offers of a Peace so ruinous to us as such a War. Posterity will be at a loss to conceive what kind of Spirit could possess their Ancestors, who after ten Years Suffering, by the unexampled Politicks of a Nation, maintaining a War by annually Pawning it self; and during a short Peace, while they were looking back with Horrour on the heavy Load of Debts they had contracted; universally condemning those pernicious Counsels which had occasioned them; racking their Invention for some Remedies or Expedients to mend their shattered Condition: That these very People, without giving themselves time to breath, should again enter into a more dangerous, chargeable, and extensive War, for the same, or perhaps a greater Period of Time, and without any apparent Necessity. It is obvious in a private Fortune, that whoever annually runs out, and continues the same Expences, must every Year mortgage a greater Quantity of Land than he did before; and as the Debt doubles and trebles upon him, so doth his Inability to pay it. By the same Proportion we have suffered twice as much by this last ten Years War, as we did by the former; and if it were possible to continue it five Years longer at the same rate, it would be as great a Burthen as the whole Twenty. This Computation, so easy and trivial as it is almost a shame to mention, Posterity will think that those who first advised the War, had either not the Sense or the Honesty to consider.

And as we have wasted our Strength and vital Substance in this profuse manner, so we have shamefully misapplied it to Ends at least very different from those for which we undertook the War, and often to effect others which after a Peace we may severely repent. This is the second Article I proposed to examine.

We have now for Ten Years together turned the whole Force and Expence of the War, where the Enemy was best able to hold us at a Bay;[25] where we could propose no manner of Advantage to our selves; where it was highly impolitick to enlarge our Conquests; utterly neglecting that Part which would have saved and gained us many Millions, which the perpetual Maxims of our Government teach us to pursue; which would have soonest weakened the Enemy, and must either have promoted a speedy Peace, or enabled us to go on with the War.

Those who are fond of continuing the War cry up our constant Success at a most prodigious rate, and reckon it infinitely greater than in all human Probability we had reason to hope. Ten glorious Compaigns are passed, and now at last, like the sick Man,[26] we are just expiring with all sorts of good Symptoms. Did the Advisers of this War suppose it would continue Ten Years, without expecting the Successes we have had; and yet at the same time determine, that *France* must be reduced, and *Spain* subdued, by employing our whole Strength upon *Flanders*? Did they believe the last War left us in a Condition to furnish such vast Supplies for so long a Period, without involving Us and our Posterity in unextricable Debts? If after such Miraculous *Doings*, we are not yet in a Condition of bringing *France* to our Terms, nor can tell when we shall be so, though we should proceed without any Reverse of Fortune; What could we look for in the ordinary course of Things, but a *Flanders* War of at least Twenty Years longer? Do they indeed think a Town taken for the *Dutch*, is a sufficient Recompence

25 *at a Bay*: i.e., in great distress, as a hunted animal (*OED*).
26 *the sick Man*: alluding to an Aesop fable, called 'A Doctor and His Patient' in the version of Sir Roger L'Estrange (1692, no. 95). After a doctor congratulates his patient on his increasingly serious symptoms, the sick man says to a concerned friend that he is doing so well that he is 'e'en ready to die, of I know not how many good Signs and Tokens'. Mainwaring and Oldmixon had used the same fable in the *Medley* for 20 November 1710; see Ellis, *Examiner*, pp. 46–7.

to us for six Millions of Money? which is of so little Consequence to the determining the War, that the *French* may yet hold out a dozen Years more, and afford a Town every Campaign at the same Price.

I say not this, by any means, to detract from the Army or its Leaders. Getting into the Enemy's Lines, passing Rivers, and taking Towns, may be Actions attended with many glorious Circumstances: But when all this brings no real solid Advantage to us, when it hath no other End than to enlarge the Territories of the *Dutch*, and encrease the Fame and Wealth of our *General*,[27] I conclude, however it comes about, that Things are not as they should be; and that surely our Forces and Money might be better employed, both towards reducing our Enemy, and working out some Benefit to our selves. But the Case is still much harder, We are destroying many thousand Lives, exhausting all our Substance, not for our own Interest, which would be but common Prudence; not for a Thing indifferent, which would be sufficient Folly, but perhaps to our own Destruction, which is perfect Madness. We may live to feel the Effects of our Valour more sensibly than all the Consequences we imagine from the Dominions of *Spain* in the Duke of *Anjou*. We have Conquered a noble Territory for the *States*, that will maintain sufficient Troops to Defend it self, feed many hundred thousand Inhabitants, where all Encouragement will be given to introduce and improve Manufactures, which was the only Advantage they wanted; and which, added to their Skill, Industry and Parsimony, will enable them to undersell us in every Market of the World.

Our Supply of Forty thousand Men, according to the first Stipulation, added to the Quota's of the Emperor and *Holland*, which they were obliged to furnish, would have made an Army of near Two hundred thousand, exclusive of Garrisons; enough to withstand all the Power that *France* could bring against it; and we might have employed the rest much better, both for the common Cause and our own Advantage.

The War in *Spain* must be imputed to the Credulity of our Ministers, who suffered themselves to be persuaded by the Imperial Court, that the *Spaniards* were so violently affected to the House of *Austria*, as upon the first Appearance there, with a few Troops under the Archduke, the whole Kindom would immediately revolt. This we tried, and found the Emperor to have deceived either Us or Himself: Yet there we drove on the War at

27 *our General*: Marlborough.

a prodigious Disadvantage, with great Expence; And by a most corrupt Management, the only General, who by a Course of Conduct and Fortune almost miraculous, had nearly put us into Possession of the Kingdom, was left wholly unsupported, exposed to the Envy of his Rivals, disappointed by the Caprices of a young unexperienced Prince, under the Guidance of a rapacious *German* Ministry, and at last called home in Discontent:[28] By which our Armies, both in *Spain* and *Portugal*, were made a Sacrifice to Avarice, Ill-conduct, or Treachery.

In common Prudence, we should either have pushed that War with the utmost Vigor, in so fortunate a Juncture, especially since the gaining that Kingdom was the great Point for which we pretended[29] to continue the War, or at least when we had *found* or *made* that Design impracticable, we should not have gone on in so expensive a Management of it; but have kept our Troops on the Defensive in *Catalonia*, and pursued some other way more effectual for distressing the Common Enemy, and advantaging Ourselves.

And what a noble Field of Honour and Profit had we before us, wherein to employ the best of our Strength, which, against all the Maxims of *British* Policy, we suffered to lie wholly neglected? I have sometimes wondered how it came to pass, that the Style of *Maritime Powers*, by which our Allies, in a sort of contemptuous manner, usually couple us with the *Dutch*, did never put us in mind of the Sea; and while some Politicians were shewing us the way to *Spain* by *Flanders*, others by *Savoy* or *Naples*, that the *West-Indies* should never come into their Heads. With half the Charge we have been at, we might have maintained our original Quota of Forty thousand Men in *Flanders*, and at the same time, by our Fleets and Naval Forces, have so distressed the *Spaniards* in the North and South Seas of *America*, as to prevent any Returns of Mony from thence, except in our own Bottoms.[30] This is what best became us to do as a Maritime Power: This, with any common-degree of Success, would soon have compelled *France* to the Necessities of a Peace, and *Spain* to acknowledge the Archduke.

---

28 *General . . . in Discontent*: Charles Mordaunt, 3rd Earl of Peterborough, friend of Swift and Pope, who had been successful in capturing Barcelona in 1705 despite difficulties with the Archduke Charles and the 'unexperienced' Prince George of Hesse-Darmstadt, former governor of Catalonia. He was recalled to England in 1707 to explain his military conduct, by which time he had become connected to the Tories.

29 *pretended*: i.e., 'intended, purposed' (*OED*).   30 *our own Bottoms*: i.e., ships (*OED*).

But while We, for Ten Years, have been squandring away our Mony upon the Continent, *France* hath been wisely engrossing all the Trade of *Peru*, going directly with their Ships to *Lima*, and other Ports, and there receiving Ingots of Gold and Silver for *French* Goods of little Value; which, beside the mighty Advantage to their Nation at present, may divert the Channel of that Trade for the future, so beneficial to us, who used to receive annually such vast Sums at *Cadiz*, for our Goods sent thence to the *Spanish West-Indies.* All this we tamely saw and suffered, without the least Attempt to hinder it; except what was performed by some private Men at *Bristol*,[31] who inflamed by a true Spirit of Courage and Industry, did, about three Years ago, with a few Vessels, fitted out at their own Charge, make a most successful Voyage into those Parts, tooke one of the *Aquapulco* Ships, very narrowly mist of the other, and are lately returned laden with unenvied Wealth; to shew us what might have been done with the like Management, by a publick Undertaking. At least we might easily have prevented those great Returns of Mony to *France* and *Spain*, though we could not have taken it our selves. And if it be true, as the Advocates for War would have it, that the *French* are now so impoverished; in what Condition must they have been, if that Issue of Wealth had been stopped?

But great Events often turn upon very small Circumstances. It was the Kingdom's Misfortune, that the Sea was not the Duke of *Marlborough*'s Element, otherwise the whole Force of the War would infallibly have been bestowed there, infinitely to the Advantage of his Country, which would then have gone hand in hand with his own. But it is very truly objected, That if we alone had made such an Attempt as this, *Holland* would have been Jealous; or if we had done it in Conjunction with *Holland*, the House of *Austria* would have been discontented. This hath been the Style of late Years; which whoever introduced among us, they have taught our Allies to speak after them. Otherwise it could hardly enter into any Imagination,

31 *private Men at Bristol*: in 1708 one Christopher Shuter and fifteen other merchants in Bristol sent Captain Woodes Rogers on a privateering expedition to attack Spanish ships engaged in the South Sea trade; sailing in two ships and piloted by the experienced William Dampier, on 22 December 1709 off California they captured a rich Spanish 'Manila Ship' bound for Acapulco, though a larger one escaped them. In 1711 they returned to England with their profits and with Alexander Selkirk, the original of 'Robinson Crusoe', whom they had rescued from the island of Juan Fernandez and who became one of their officers. See Woodes Rogers, *A Cruising Voyage round the World; first to the South Seas; thence to the East-Indies, and homeward by the Cape of Good Hope; begun in 1708, and finished in 1711* (1712) (Reprint, Amsterdam: Da Capo Press, 1969).

that while we are Confederates in a War, with those who are to have the whole Profit, and who leave a double share of the Burthen upon Us, we dare not think of any Design, though against the Common Enemy, where there is the least Prospect of doing Good to our own Country, for fear of giving Umbrage and Offence to our Allies; while we are ruining our selves to Conquer Provinces and Kingdoms for Them. I therefore confess with Shame, that this Objection is true: For it is very well known, that while the Design of Mr. *Hill*'s Expedition[32] remained a Secret, it was suspected in *Holland* and *Germany* to be intended against *Peru*; whereupon the *Dutch* made every where their Publick Complaints, and the Ministers at *Vienna* talked of it as *an Insolence in the Qu——— to attempt such an Undertaking*; which, however it has failed, partly by the Accidents of a Storm, and partly by the Stubbornness or Treachery of some in that Colony, for whose Relief, and at whose Entreaty it was in some measure designed, is no Objection at all to an Enterprize so well concerted, and with such fair Probability of Success.

It was something singular that the *States* should express their Uneasiness, when they thought we intended to make some Attempt in the *Spanish West-Indies*; because it is agreed between us, that whatever is Conquered there, by Us or Them, shall belong to the Conqueror: Which is the only Article that I can call to mind, in all our Treaties or Stipulations, with any view of Interest to this Kingdom; and for that very Reason, I suppose, among others, hath been altogether neglected. Let those who think this too severe a Reflection, examin the whole Management of the present War by Sea and Land with all our Alliances, Treaties, Stipulations and Conventions, and consider, whether the whole does not look as if some particular Care and Industry had been used, to prevent any Benefit or Advantage that might possibly accrue to *Britain*.

This kind of Treatment from our two Principal Allies, hath taught the same Dialect to all the rest; so that there is hardly a petty Prince, whom we half maintain by Subsidies and Pensions, who is not ready, upon every Occasion, to threaten Us, that He will recal His Troops (though they must

---

32 *Mr. Hill's Expedition*: a disastrous attempt in May 1711 to take Quebec undertaken by John Hill, brother of the Queen's favourite, Lady Abigail Masham, and set in motion by St John partly as a way of gaining her favour. On the hold which a maritime strategy exercised over Tory thinking, see Holmes, p. 75. Despite what he writes here, when the expedition (which was opposed by Harley) first set off, Swift wrote to Stella, 'I believe it will come to nothing' (Williams, *JSt*, p. 257).

rob or starve at home) if we refuse to comply with Him in any Demand, however so unreasonable.

Upon the Third Head I shall produce some Instances, to shew how tamely we have suffered each of our Allies to infringe every Article in those Treaties and Stipulations by which they were bound, and to lay the Load upon Us.

But before I enter upon this, which is a large Subject, I shall take leave to offer a few Remarks on certain Articles in three of our Treaties; which may let us perceive, how much those Ministers valued or understood the true Interest, Safety, or Honour of their Country.

We have made two Alliances with *Portugal*,[33] an Offensive and Defensive: The first is to remain in force only during the present War; the second to be Perpetual. In the Offensive Alliance, the Emperor, *England*, and *Holland* are Parties with *Portugal*; in the Defensive only We and the *States*.

Upon the first Article of the Offensive Alliance it is to be observed, that although the Grand Alliance, as I have already said, allows *England* and *Holland* to possess for their own, whatever each of them shall Conquer in the *Spanish West-Indies*; yet here we are quite cut out, by consenting, that the Arch-Duke shall possess the Dominions of *Spain* in as full a manner as their late King *Charles*. And what is more remarkable, we broke this very Article in favour of *Portugal*, by subsequent Stipulations; where we agree, that King *Charles* shall deliver up *Estremadura*, *Vigo*, and some other Places to the *Portuguese*, as soon as we can Conquer them from the Enemy. They who were guilty of so much Folly and Contradiction, know best whether it proceeded from Corruption or Stupidity.

By two other Articles (beside the Honour of being Convoys and Guards in ordinary to the *Portuguese* Ships and Coasts) we are to guess the Enemies

33 *two Alliances with Portugal*: by the offensive alliance of the 'Methuen treaties' of 1703, it was agreed that Portugal would maintain at its own expense 15,000 men and raise 13,000 more, to be paid by the Allies, who were to add some of their own troops. The maritime powers also obliged themselves to keep men of war on the coast of Portugal to defend ports and protect trade as well as to defend Portuguese dominions abroad. The defensive alliance had similar articles affecting British ships; but Francis Hare, from whom these details are drawn, accuses Swift of ignoring the eighth article, which specifies that if the ships of the three nations act in conjunction in any common expedition, then the commander that has the most ships under him will act as admiral to the whole. See Hare, *The Allies and the Late Ministry Defended*, Part II, 2nd edn (1711), pp. 21–39.

Thoughts, and to take the King of *Portugal*'s Word, whenever he has a Fancy that he shall be invaded: We also are to furnish him with a Strength superior to what the Enemy intends to invade any of his Dominions with, let that be what it will: And, 'till we know what the Enemy's Forces are, His *Portuguese* Majesty is sole Judge what Strength is superior, and what will be able to prevent an Invasion; and may send our Fleets, whenever he pleases, upon his Errands, to some of the furthest Parts of the World, or keep them attending upon his own Coasts till he thinks fit to dismiss them. These Fleets must likewise be subject, in all things, not only to the King, but to his Viceroys, Admirals and Governours, in any of his foreign Dominions, when he is in a Humour to apprehend an Invasion; which, I believe, is an Indignity that was never offered before, except to a Conquered Nation.

In the Defensive Alliance with that Crown, which is to remain perpetual, and where only *England* and *Holland* are Parties with them, the same Care, in almost the same Words, is taken for our Fleet to attend their Coasts and foreign Dominions, and to be under the same Obedience. We and the *States* are likewise to furnish them with twelve Thousand Men at our own Charge, which we are constantly to recruit, and these are to be subject to the *Portuguese* Generals.

In the Offensive Alliance we took no care of having the Assistance of *Portugal*, whenever we should be invaded: But in this, it seems, we were wiser; for that King is obliged to make War on *France* or *Spain*, whenever we or *Holland* are invaded by either; but before this, we are to supply them with the same Forces, both by Sea and Land, as if he were invaded himself: And this must needs be a very prudent and safe Course for a Maritime Power to take upon a sudden Invasion; by which, instead of making use of our Fleets and Armies for our own Defence, we must send them abroad for the Defence of *Portugal*.

By the Thirteenth Article we are told, what this Assistance is which the *Portugueze* are to give us, and upon what Conditions. They are to furnish Ten Men of War; and when *England* or *Holland* shall be invaded by *France* and *Spain* together, or by *Spain* alone; in either of these Cases, those Ten *Portugueze* Men of War are to serve only upon their own Coasts; where, no doubt, they will be of mighty Use to their Allies, and Terror to the Enemy.

How the *Dutch* were drawn to have a Part in either of these two Alliances, is not very material to enquire, since they have been so wise as never to observe them, nor, I suppose, ever intended it, but resolved, as they have since done, to shift the Load upon us.

Let any Man read these two Treaties from the beginning to the end, he will imagine, that the King of *Portugal* and his Ministers sat down and made them by themselves, and then sent them to their Allies to Sign; the whole Spirit and Tenor of them, quite thro', running only upon this single Point, What We and *Holland* are to do for *Portugal*, without any mention of an Equivalent, except those Ten Ships, which at the time when we have greatest need of their Assistance, are obliged to attend upon their own Coasts.

The Barrier-Treaty[34] between *Great Britain* and *Holland*, was concluded at the *Hague* on the 29th of *October*, in the Year 1709. In this Treaty, neither Her Majesty, nor Her Kingdoms, have any Interest or Concern, farther than what is mentioned in the Second and the Twentieth Articles: By the former, the States are to assist the Queen in Defending the Act of Succession; and by the other, not to Treat of a Peace 'till *France* acknowledges the Queen and the Succession of *Hanover*, and promises to remove the *Pretender* out of his Dominions.

As to the first of these, It is certainly for the Safety and Interest of the *States-General*, that the Protestant Succession should be preserved in *England*; because such a Popish Prince as we apprehend, would infallibly join with *France* in the Ruin of that Republick. And the *Dutch* are as much bound to support our Succession, as they are tied to any Part of a Treaty of League Offensive and Defensive, against a Common Enemy, without any separate Benefit upon that Consideration. Her Majesty is in the full peaceable Possession of Her Kingdoms, and of the Hearts of Her People; among whom, hardly one in five hundred are in the *Pretender*'s Interest. And whether the Assistance of the *Dutch*, to preserve a Right so well established, be an Equivalent to those many unreasonable exorbitant Articles in the rest of the Treaty, let the World judge. What an Impression of our Settlement must it give Abroad, to see our Ministers offering such Conditions to the *Dutch*, to prevail on them to be Guarantees of our Acts of Parliament! Neither perhaps is it right, in point of Policy or good Sense, that a Foreign Power should be called in to confirm our Succession by way

---

34 *Barrier-Treaty*: the terms are detailed by Swift in the following passages, and the treaty itself is printed below, at the end of Swift's *Some Remarks* (pp. 136–53).

of Guarantee;[35] but only to acknowledge it. Otherwise we put it out of the Power of our own Legislature to change our Succession, without the Consent of that Prince or State who is Guarantee;[36] however our Posterity may hereafter, by the Tyranny and Oppression of any succeeding Princes, be reduced to the fatal Necessity of breaking in upon the excellent and happy Settlement now in force.

As to the other Article, it is a natural Consequence that must attend any Treaty of Peace we can make with *France*; being only the Acknowledgment of Her Majesty as Queen of Her own Dominions, and the Right of Succession by our own Laws, which no Foreign Power hath any Pretence to dispute.

However, in order to deserve these mighty Advantages from the *States*, the rest of the Treaty is wholly taken up in directing what we are to do for them.

By the Grand Alliance, which was the Foundation of the present War, the *Spanish Low-Countries* were to be recovered and delivered to the King of *Spain*: But by this Treaty, that Prince is to possess nothing in *Flanders* during the War: And after a Peace, the *States* are to have the Military Command of about twenty Towns with their Dependances, and four hundred thousand Crowns a Year from the King of *Spain* to maintain their Garrisons. By which means they will have the Command of all *Flanders*, from *Newport* on the Sea to *Namur* on the *Maese*, and be entirely Masters of the *Pais de Waas*, the richest part of those Provinces. Further, they have liberty to Garrison any Place they shall think fit in the *Spanish Low-Countries*, whenever there is an Appearance of War; and consequently to put Garrisons into *Ostend*, or where else they please, upon a Rupture with *England*.

35 *Guarantee*: 'a person or party that makes a guaranty or gives a security; a guaranteeing party' (*OED*).
36 *Otherwise we ... Guarantee*: this passage was widely attacked. Lord Chief Justice Sir Thomas Parker, later 1st Earl of Macclesfield (*c.* 1666–1732), found it open to a treasonable interpretation, in which he has been followed by at least one modern scholar (Higgins, p. 91). In response to criticism, Swift softened the text in the fourth edition and added a postscript giving his rationale. But as late as 14 February he reported to Stella that a Whig MP read 'that Passage about the Succession' in the House of Commons 'with great Resentmt, but none seconded him' (Williams, *JSt*, p. 488). See his restatement of the position in his *Remarks* on the Barrier treaty, along with a further rationale and an unrepentant account of the reaction (pp. 129–30). Note also his quip in Williams, *JSt*, p. 568 (October 1712) about sitting just under Parker while attending a trial and handing him his pen when it dropped: 'I was going to whisper him that *I had done good for evil; for he would have taken mine from me.*'

By this Treaty likewise, the *Dutch* will, in effect, be entire Masters of all the *Low-Countries*, may impose Duties, Restrictions in Commerce, and Prohibitions at their Pleasure; and in that fertile Country may set up all sorts of Manufactures, particularly the Woollen, by inviting the disobliged Manufacturers in *Ireland*, and the *French* Refugees,[37] who are scattered all over *Germany*. And as this Manufacture encreases abroad, the Cloathing People of *England* will be necessitated, for want of Employment, to follow; and in few Years, by help of the low Interest of Mony in *Holland, Flanders* may recover that beneficial Trade which we got from them: The Landed Men of *England* will then be forced to re-establish the Staples of Wool abroad; and the *Dutch*, instead of being only the Carriers, will become the original Possessors of those Commodities, with which the greatest Part of the Trade of the World is now carried on. And as they increase their Trade, it is obvious they will enlarge their Strength at Sea, and that ours must lessen in Proportion.

All the Ports in *Flanders* are to be subject to the like Duties the *Dutch* shall lay upon the *Scheld*, which is to be closed on the side of the *States*: Thus all other Nations are, in effect, shut out from Trading with *Flanders*. Yet in the very same Article it is said, That the *States* shall be *favoured in all the Spanish Dominions as much as Great Britain, or as the People most favoured*. We have Conquered *Flanders* for them, and are in a worse Condition, as to our Trade there, than before the War began. We have been the great Support of the King of *Spain*, to whom the *Dutch* have hardly contributed any thing at all; and yet *they are to be equally favoured with us in all his Dominions*. Of all this the Queen is under the unreasonable Obligation of being Guarantee, and that they shall possess their Barrier, and their four hundred thousand Crowns a Year, even before a Peace.

It is to be obscrvcd, That this Treaty was only Signed by one of our Plenipotentiaries:[38] And I have been told, That the other was heard to say, He would rather lose his Right-hand, than set it to such a Treaty. Had he

---

37 *French Refugees*: i.e., Huguenots.
38 *one of our Plenipotentiaries*: only Townshend signed the Barrier Treaty for Britain, for Marlborough refused; his comment about preferring to lose his right hand was supposedly made to the Queen (Gregg, p. 288). Writing to his wife on 19 August 1709 (n.s.), the Duke explained, 'our best friends will think that I am partial to the house of Austria; but I call God to witness, that my concern proceeds from the love I have for the intrest of my country, and my concern for such of my friends as are now in the ministry'. And again on 7 September (n.s.), making a point Swift makes here, 'as a good Englishman I can never think it reasonable or wise to lett

spoke those Words in due season, and loud enough to be heard on this side the Water, considering the Credit he then had at Court, he might have saved much of his Country's Honour, and got as much to himself: Therefore, if the Report be true, I am inclined to think He only SAID it. I have been likewise told, That some very necessary Circumstances were wanting in the Entrance upon this Treaty; but the Ministers here rather chose to sacrifice the Honour of the Crown, and the Safety of their Country, than not ratify what one of their Favourites had transacted.

Let me now consider in what manner our Allies have observed those Treaties they made with Us, and the several Stipulations and Agreements pursuant to them.

By the Grand Alliance between the Empire, *England* and *Holland*, we were to assist the other two, *totis viribus*,[39] by Sea and Land. By a Convention subsequent to this Treaty, the Proportions which the several Parties should contribute towards the War, were adjusted in the following manner. The Emperor was obliged to furnish ninety Thousand Men against *France*, either in *Italy*, or upon the *Rhine*: *Holland* to bring sixty Thousand into the Field in *Flanders*, exclusive of Garrisons; and we forty Thousand. In Winter, 1702. which was the next Year, the Duke of *Marlborough* proposed the raising of Ten Thousand Men more, by way of Augmentation, and to carry on the War with greater Vigour; to which the Parliament agreed, and the *Dutch* were to raise the same Number. This was upon a *Par*, directly contrary to the former Stipulation, whereby our Part was to be a Third less than theirs; and therefore it was granted, with a Condition, that *Holland* should break off all Trade and Commerce with *France*. But this Condition was never executed, the *Dutch* only amusing us with a specious Declaration till our Session of Parliament was ended; and the following Year it was taken off, by concert between our General and the *States*, without any Reason assigned for the Satisfaction of the Kingdom. The next and some ensuing Campaigns, further additional Forces were allowed by Parliament for the War in *Flanders*; and in every new Supply, the *Dutch* gradually lessened their Proportions; though the Parliament addressed the Queen that the *States* might be desired to observe them according to Agreement; which had no other Effect, than to teach them to elude it, by making their Troops

---

them have Dendermond or Ostend, if we have any consideration for our trade in Flanders, or what goes from thence to Germany' (Marlborough–Godolphin, pp. 1336, 1356).
39 *totis viribus*: 'with our whole strength'; see pp. 59–60.

Nominal Corps, as they did by keeping up the Numbers of Regiments, but sinking a fifth Part of the Men and Mony. So that now things are just inverted, and in all new Levies we contribute a third more than the *Dutch*, who at first were obliged to the same Proportion more than us.

Besides, the more Towns we Conquer for the *States*, the worse Condition we are in towards reducing the Common Enemy, and consequently of putting an end to the War. For they make no Scruple of employing the Troops of their Quota, towards Garrisoning every Town as fast as it is taken, directly contrary to the Agreement between us, by which all Garrisons are particularly excluded. This is at length arrived, by several Steps, to such a Height, that there are at present in the Field, not so many Forces under the Duke of *M*——'s Command in *Flanders*, as *Britain* alone maintains for that Service, nor have been for some Years past. The Troops we maintain in *Flanders*, (as appears by the Votes of the House of Commons for the Year, 1709.) are Forty thousand the original Quota; Ten thousand the first Augmentation; three thousand *Palatines*; four thousand six hundred thirty nine *Saxons*; *Bothmer*'s Regiment of eight hundred Men; and a further Augmentation taken that Year into the Service of about two thousand; making in the whole upwards of sixty thousand: And it is well known, that the Battles of *Hochstet* and *Ramellies* were fought with not above Fifty thousand Men on a side.

The Duke of *Marlborough* having entered the Enemies Lines, and taking *Bouchain*,[40] formed the Design of keeping so great a Number of Troops, and particularly of Cavalry, in *Lisle, Tournay, Doway*, and the Country between, as should be able to harass all the Neighbouring Provinces of *France*, during the Winter, prevent the Enemy from erecting their Magazines, and by consequence, from Subsisting their Forces next Spring, and render it impossible for them to assemble their Army another Year, without going back behind the *Soame*[41] to do it. In order to effect this Project, it was necessary to be at an Expence extraordinary of Forage for the Troops, of building Stables, finding Fire and Candle for the Soldiers, with other incident Charges. The Queen readily agreed to furnish Her Share of the first Article, that of the Forage, which only belonged to Her. But the *States* insisting, that Her Majesty should likewise come into a Proportion of the

40 *Bouchain*: The French garrison surrendered 14 September 1711; for other problems with the Dutch in this engagement see *Publick Spirit*, below (p. 271).
41 *Soame*: the Somme.

other Articles, which in Justice belonged totally to them: She agreed even to that, rather than a Design of this Importance should fail.[42] And yet we know it hath failed, and that the *Dutch* refused their Consent, 'till the time was past for putting it in Execution, even in the Opinion of those who proposed it. Perhaps a certain Article in the Treaties of Contributions,[43] submitted to by such of the *French* Dominions as pay them to the *States*, was the principal Cause of defeating this Project; since one great Advantage to have been gained by it, was, as before is mentioned, to have hindred the Enemy from erecting their Magazines: and one Article in those Treaties of Contributions is, that the Product of those Countries shall pass free and unmolested. So that the Question was reduced to this short Issue, Whether the *Dutch* should lose this paultry Benefit, or the Common Cause an Advantage of such mighty Importance?

The Sea being the Element where we might most probably carry on the War with any Advantage to our selves, it was agreed that we should bear five Eighths of the Charge in that Service, and the *Dutch* the other three: And by the Grand Alliance, whatever we or *Holland* should Conquer in the *Spanish West-Indies*, was to accrue to the Conquerors. It might therefore have been hoped, that this *Maritime Ally* of ours, would have made up in their Fleet, what they fell short in their Army; but quite otherwise, they never once furnished their Quota either of Ships or Men; or if some few of their Fleet now and then appeared, it was no more than appearing, for they immediately separated to look to their Merchants and protect their Trade. And we may remember very well when these *Guarantees of our Succession*, after having not one Ship for many Months together in the *Mediterranean*, sent that part of their Quota thither, and furnished nothing to us, at the

---

42 *Design of this Importance should fail*: Marlborough himself attacked the Dutch attitude towards this 'Project': preparing to besiege the fortress Le Quesnoy, as a first step, he wrote to Oxford, 'As the loss of time on their part has made it impracticable to provide what they proposed, I think they cannot reasonably expect her majesty should bear any part of the extraordinary charge [except that of the forage for the troops in her own pay].' A few days later he wrote that the next proposal of the Dutch on the issue was 'unreasonable' and 'impracticable', complaining 'it would keep us a month longer in the Field to make all the enquiries' (BL, Add. MSS. 61125, fos. 123, 125 (letters of 22, 26 October 1711), bracketed words inserted in same hand after 'charge').

43 *Treaties of Contributions*: 'contribution' in the military sense, 'An imposition levied upon a district for the support of an army in the field, to secure immunity from plunder, or for similar purposes' (*OED*), in this case agreements or 'treaties' for such levies by the Dutch upon the 'Neighbouring Provinces of *France*' in which they had forces.

same time that they allarmed us with the Rumour of an Invasion.[44] And last Year, when Sir *James Wishart*[45] was dispatched into *Holland* to expostulate with the *States*, and to desire they would make good their Agreements, in so important a part of the Service; he met with such a Reception as ill became a Republick to give, that lies under so many great Obligations to us; in short, such a one, as those only deserve, who are content to take.

It hath likewise been no small Inconvenience to us, that the *Dutch* are always slow in paying their Subsidies, by which means the weight and pressure of the Payment lies upon the Queen, as well as the Blame, if Her Majesty be not very exact; nor will even this always content our Allies. For in *July* 1711, the King of *Spain* was paid all his Subsidies to the first of *January* next; nevertheless he hath since complained for want of Mony; and his Secretary threatned, that if we would not further supply his Majesty, he could not answer for what might happen; although K---g C——s had not at that time, one third of the Troops for which he was paid; and even those he had, were neither Paid nor Cloathed.

I shall add one Example more, to show how this Prince has treated the Q——n, to whom he owes such infinite Obligations. Her Maj---y borrowed Two hundred thousand Pounds from the *Genoese*, and sent it to *Barcelona*, for the Payment of the *Spanish* Army: This Mony was to be re-coined into the current Species of *Catalonia*, which by the Allay[46] is lower in Value 25*l. per Cent*. The Q——n expected, as she had Reason, to have the Benefit of this Recoinage, offering to apply it All to the Use of

---

44 *remember . . . an Invasion*: as C. B. Wheeler points out in his edition of *Conduct* (1916), p. 94, even Francis Hare was unsure of the exact event to which Swift is alluding here, but Hare suggests it refers to the winter of 1709–10, when the Dutch fleet in the Mediterranean returned home for the winter after the orders for them to stay went awry, upon which the Dutch promptly sent another squadron to replace them (see Hare, *The Allies and the Late Ministry Defended*, Part II, pp. 56–8). For rumours of an invasion in late March 1709, see Marlborough–Godolphin, p. 235 n.

45 *Sir James Wishart*: Wishart, an Admiral knighted in 1704, was made a Lord Commissioner of the Admiralty in 1710, Commander in Chief of the Mediterranean Fleet in 1713–14, and was later a Tory MP for Portsmouth 1711–15. In February 1710–11 he had been sent to Holland to negotiate the quota of Dutch men of war (BL, Add. MSS. 31146, fo. 300). He was ill received because, on orders from his government, he also sought to persuade the Dutch to disrupt French trade in the South Seas. St John complained in letters of Wishart's cold reception, so that he was most likely Swift's source for the remark; on 20 March 1711 he wrote to an English friend in Holland, 'We are not pleased with the usage of Sir James Wishart' (Bolingbroke, *Letters*, vol. I, p. 112). See also the account by Paula Watson, in *HP 1690–1715*, vol. V, pp. 904–5.

46 *Allay*: 'Inferior metal mixed with one of greater value' (*OED*).

the War; but K---g C——s, instead of consenting to this, made a Grant of the Coinage to one of his Courtiers; which put a stop to the Work: And when it was represented, that the Army would Starve by this Delay, his Majesty only replied, *Let them Starve!* and would not recal his Grant.

I cannot forbear mentioning here another Passage concerning Subsidies, to shew what Opinion Foreigners have of our Easiness, and how much they reckon themselves Masters of our Mony, whenever they think fit to call for it. The Queen was by Agreement to pay Two hundred thousand Crowns a Year to the *Prussian* Troops, the *States* One hundred thousand, and the Emperor only Thirty thousand, for Recruiting, which his Imperial Majesty never paid. Prince *Eugene* happening to pass by *Berlin*, the Ministers of that Court applied themselves to him for Redress in this Particular; and his Highness very frankly promised them, that in Consideration of this Deficiency, *Britain* and the *States* should encrease their Subsidies to Seventy thousand Crowns more between them, and that the Emperor should be punctual for the time to come: This was done by that Prince, without any Orders or Power whatsoever. The *Dutch* very reasonably refused consenting to it; but the *Prussian* Minister here, making his Applications at our Court, prevailed on us to agree to our Proportion, before we could hear what Resolution would be taken in *Holland.* It is therefore to be hoped, that his *Prussian* Majesty,[47] at the end of this War, will not have the same grievous Cause of Complaint, which he had at the Close of the last; that his Military-Chest was emptier by Twenty thousand Crowns, than at the time that War began.

The Emperor, as we have already said, was by Stipulation to furnish Ninety thousand Men against the Common Enemy, as having no Fleets to maintain, and in Right of his Family being most concerned in the Success of the War. However, this Agreement hath been so ill observed, that from the Beginning of the War to this Day, neither of the two last Emperors had ever Twenty thousand Men, on their own Account, in the Common Cause, excepting once in *Italy*; when the Imperial Court exerted it self in a Point they have much more at heart than that of gaining *Spain* or the *Indies* to their Family.[48] When they had succeeded in their Attempts on the side of *Italy*, and observed our blind Zeal for pushing on the War at all

47 *his Prussian Majesty*: the Elector Frederick of Brandenburg.
48 *a Point . . . Family*: i.e., reconquering Italian and other Mediterranean territories for the Empire.

Adventures, they soon found out the most effectual Expedient to excuse themselves. They computed easily, that it would cost them less to make large Presents to one *single Person*,[49] than to pay an Army, and turn to as good Account. They thought they could not put their Affairs into better Hands; and therefore wisely left us to fight their Battles.

Besides, it appeared by several Instances, how little the Emperor regarded his Allies, or the Cause they were engaged in, when once he thought the Empire it self was secure. 'Tis known enough, that he might several Times have made a Peace with his discontented Subjects in *Hungary*, upon Terms not at all unbefitting either his Dignity or Interest: But he rather chose to sacrifice the whole Alliance to his private Passion, by entirely subduing and enslaving a miserable People, who had but too much Provocation to take up Arms to free themselves from the Oppressions under which they were groaning:[50] Yet this must serve as an Excuse for breaking his Agreement, and diverting so great a Body of Troops, which might have been employed against *France*.

Another Instance of the Emperor's Indifference, or rather Dislike to the Common Cause of the Allies, is the Business of *Toulon*.[51] This Design was indeed discovered here at home, by a Person whom every body knows to be the Creature of a certain *Great Man*,[52] at least as much noted for his

49 *one single Person*: Marlborough; after Blenheim he was given by Emperor Leopold the principality of Mindelheim, and in 1706 Emperor Joseph offered him the Governorship of the Spanish Netherlands, worth £60,000 a year, a gift which he was forced to decline because of protests from the Dutch.

50 *under which . . . groaning*: despite Marlborough's urging, the Emperor, acting on the views of Jesuit advisors, consistently refused to make peace with rebelling Hungarian Protestants and Constitutionalists.

51 *Business of Toulon*: the failure of the siege of Toulon occurred in August 1707 and was a major disappointment for the Allies. Prince Eugene and the Austrian Court, believing that the attack on Toulon was mostly for the benefit of England and Holland, had postponed the effort from the spring until midsummer. Victor Amadeus II, the Duke of Savoy (1666–1732), though at first in favour of attacking the French forces of Marshal Tessé, despaired after Eugene showed himself reluctant. See Trevelyan, vol. II, pp. 307–9.

52 *Creature of a certain Great Man*: the 'Great Man' is Godolphin, Lord Treasurer in 1707. As his 'Creature' one scholar suggests James Brydges, Paymaster of the Forces Abroad, who apparently gambled on the outcome of the siege (G. Davies, 'The Seamy Side of Marlborough's War,' *HLQ* 15 (1951), 21–44). But a much better candidate, suggested by Ross and Woolley (p. 654), is Arthur Mainwaring, MP, Auditor of the Imprest, and a figure strongly loyal to Godolphin (see the recent sketch in *HP 1690–1715*, vol. IV, pp. 781–8). Mainwaring, who was also one of the many wagering on the siege, asked his friend the Duchess of Marlborough to give him confidential information on its progress to help him win bets (see Marlborough–Godolphin, p. 1081 n.). Despite the Ross–Woolley identification, there is no evidence that

Skill in Gaming as in Politicks, upon the base mercenary End of getting Mony by Wagers; which was then so common a Practice, that I remember a Gentleman in Employment, who having the Curiosity to enquire how Wagers went upon the *Exchange*, found some People, deep in the Secret, to have been concerned in that kind of Traffick, as appeared by Præmiums named for Towns, which no body but those behind the Curtain could suspect. However, although this Project had gotten wind by so scandalous a Proceeding, yet *Toulon* might probably have been taken, if the Emperor had not thought fit, in that very Juncture, to detach twelve or fifteen thousand Men to seize *Naples*, as an Enterprize that was more his private and immediate Interest. But it was manifest that his Imperial Majesty had no mind to see *Toulon* in Possession of the Allies; for even with these Discouragements the Attempt might have yet succeeded, if Prince *Eugene* had not thought fit to oppose it; which cannot be imputed to his own Judgment, but to some Politick Reasons of his Court. The Duke of *Savoy* was for attacking the Enemy, as soon as our Army arrived; but when the Mareschal *de Thesse's* Troops were all come up, to pretend to besiege the Place, in the Condition we were at that time, was a Farce and a Jest. Had *Toulon* fallen then into our Hands, the Maritime Power of *France* would, in a great measure, have been destroyed.

But a much greater Instance than either of the foregoing, how little the Emperor regarded Us or Our Quarrel, after all we had done to save his Imperial Crown, and to assert the Title of his Brother to the Monarchy of *Spain*, may be brought from the Proceedings of that Court not many Months ago. It was judged, that a War carried on upon the side of *Italy*, would cause a great Diversion of the *French* Forces, wound them in a very tender Part, and facilitate the Progress of our Arms in *Spain*, as well as *Flanders*. It was proposed to the Duke of *Savoy* to make this Diversion; and not only a Diversion during the Summer, but the Winter too, by taking Quarters on this side of the Hills. Only in order to make him willing and able to perform this Work, two Points were to be settled. First, It was necessary to end the Dispute between the Imperial Court, and his Royal Highness; which had no other Foundation, than the Emperor's refusing to

Mainwaring 'discovered' the design to anyone, but if Swift really had a specific creature in mind, he seems the most likely candidate. On wagers about Toulon, see also Defoe's *Review*, 13 September 1707; and on the personal allusion, see Swift's exchange with Francis Hare, *Some Remarks*, below (p. 134).

make good some Articles of that Treaty, on the Faith of which the Duke engaged in the present War, and for the Execution whereof *Britain* and *Holland* became Guarantees, at the Request of the late Emperor *Leopold*.[53] To remove this Difficulty, the Earl of *Peterborow* was dispatched to *Vienna*, got over some part of those Disputes, to the Satisfaction of the Duke of *Savoy*, and had put the rest in a fair way of being accomodated, at the time the Emperor *Joseph* died. Upon which great Event, the Duke of *Savoy* took the Resolution of putting himself immediately at the Head of the Army, though the whole Matter was not finished, since the Common Cause required his Assistance; and that until a new Emperor were Elected, it was impossible to make good the Treaty to Him. In order to enable him, the only thing he asked was, that he should be reinforced by the Imperial Court with eight Thousand Men, before the end of the Campaign. Mr. *Whitworth*[54] was sent to *Vienna* to make this Proposal, and it is credibly reported, that he was impowered, rather than fail, to offer forty Thousand Pounds for the March of those eight Thousand Men, if he found it was want of Ability, and not Inclination, that hindered the sending them. But he was so far from succeeding, that it was said, the Ministers of that Court did not so much as give him an Opportunity to tempt them with any particular Sums; but cut off all his Hopes at once, by alleging the Impossibility of complying with the Queen's Demands, upon any Consideration whatsoever. They could not plead their old Excuse of the War in *Hungary*, which was then brought to an end: They had nothing to offer but some general Speculative Reasons, which it would expose them to repeat; and so, after much Delay, and many trifling Pretences, they utterly refused so small and seasonable an Assistance; to the Ruin of a Project that would have more terrified *France*, and caused a greater Diversion of their Forces, than a much more numerous Army in any other Part. Thus, for want of eight Thousand Men, for whose Winter Campaign the Queen was willing to give forty Thousand Pounds; and for want of executing the Design I lately mentioned, of hindring the Enemy from erecting Magazines, towards which Her Majesty was ready, not only to bear Her own Proportion, but a Share of that which the *States* were obliged to, our Hopes of taking Winter-Quarters in the North and

53 *that Treaty . . . Leopold*: a treaty made between the Emperor and Victor Amadeus II, Duke of Savoy, in October 1703, which brought Savoy over to the Allies from the French.
54 *Whitworth*: Charles Whitworth (1675–1725), a leading diplomat, had been an envoy to Russia 1704–10 and ambassador to Poland and Austria in 1711.

South Parts of *France* are eluded, and the War left in that Method, which is like to continue it longest. Can there an Example be given in the whole Course of this War, where we have treated the pettiest Prince, with whom we had to deal, in so contemptuous a manner? Did we ever once consider what we could afford, or what we were obliged to, when our Assistance was desired, even while we lay under immediate Apprehensions of being invaded?

When *Portugal* came, as a Confederate, into the Grand Alliance, it was stipulated, That the Empire, *England* and *Holland*, should each maintain Four thousand Men of their own Troops in that Kingdom, and pay between them a Million of Pattacoons[55] to the King of *Portugal*, for the Support of Twenty eight thousand *Portugueze*; which number of Forty thousand, was to be the Confederate Army against *Spain* on the *Portugal* side. This Treaty was ratified by all the Three Powers. But in a short time after, the Emperor declared himself unable to comply with his part of the Agreement, and so left the Two thirds upon Us; who very generously undertook that Burthen, and at the same time Two Thirds of the Subsidies for Maintenance of the *Portugueze* Troops. But neither is this the worst Part of the Story: For, although the *Dutch* did indeed send their own particular Quota of Four thousand Men to *Portugal* (which however they would not agree to, but upon Condition, that the other Two thirds should be supplied by us;) yet they never took care to recruit them: For in the Year 1706. the *Portugueze, British* and *Dutch* Forces, having marched with the E. of *G———y* into *Castile*, and by the noble Conduct of that General, being forced to retire into *Valencia*,[56] it was found necessary to raise a new Army on the *Portugal* side; where the Queen hath, at several times, encreased Her Establishment to Ten thousand five hundred Men, and the *Dutch* never re-placed one single Man, nor paid one Penny of their Subsidies to *Portugal* in six Years.

The *Spanish* Army on the side of *Catalonia* is, or ought to be, about Fifty thousand Men (exclusive of *Portugal*): And here the War hath been carried on almost entirely at our Cost. For this whole Army is paid by the Queen, excepting only seven Battalions and fourteen Squadrons of *Dutch* and *Palatines*; and even Fifteen hundred of these are likewise in our Pay;

55 *Pattacoons*: a 'Portuguese and Spanish silver coin, worth, in the 17th c., about 4s. 8d. English' (*OED*).

56 *retire into Valencia*: after defeat in Spain and the failure of 'King' Charles to become established in Madrid, Galway and the allied army retired to Valencia (September 1706).

besides the Sums given to King *Charles* for Subsidies and the Maintenance of his Court. Neither are our Troops at *Gibraltar* included within this number. And further, we alone have been at all the Charge of Transporting the Forces first sent from *Genoa* to *Barcelona*; and of all the Imperial Recruits from time to time: And have likewise paid vast Sums as Levy-Mony,[57] for every individual Man and Horse so furnished to Recruit, tho' the Horses were scarce worth the Price of Transportation. But this hath been almost the constant Misfortune of our Fleet, during the present War; instead of being employed on some Enterprize for the Good of the Nation, or even for the Protection of our Trade, to be wholly taken up in Transporting Soldiers.

We have actually Conquered all *Bavaria, Ulm, Ausburg, Landau*, and a great part of *Alsace*, for the Emperor: And by the Troops we have furnished, the Armies we have paid, and the Diversions we have given to the Enemies Forces, have chiefly contributed to the Conquests of *Milan, Mantua* and *Mirandola*, and to the Recovery of the Dutchy of *Modena*. The last Emperor drained the Wealth of those Countries into his own Coffers, without encreasing his Troops against *France* by such mighty Acquisitions, or yielding to the most reasonable Requests we have made.

Of the many Towns we have taken for the *Dutch*, we have consented, by the Barrier-Treaty, that all those which were not in Possession of *Spain*, upon the Death of the late Catholick King, shall be part of the *States* Dominions, and that they shall have the Military Power in the most considerable of the rest; which is, in effect, to be the absolute Sovereigns of the whole. And the *Hollanders* have already made such good use of their Time, that, in Conjunction with our G——l, the Oppressions of *Flanders* are much greater than ever.

And this Treatment, which we have received from our two principal Allies, hath been pretty well copied by most other Princes in the Confederacy, with whom we have any Dealings. For Instance, Seven *Portugueze* Regiments after the Battle of *Almanza*,[58] went off, with the rest of that broken Army, to *Catalonia*; the King of *Portugal* said, he was not able to pay them, while they were out of his Country; the Queen consented therefore

---

57 *Levy-Mony*: 'bounty-money paid to recruits' (*OED*).
58 *Battle of Almanza*: on 25 April 1707 (n.s.) Galway attacked a superior French and Spanish force under the command of the Duke of Berwick; his defeat ended all chance that the Archduke Charles (now Emperor Charles VI) would become 'Charles III' of Spain.

to do it Herself, provided the King would raise as many more to supply their Place. This he engaged to do, but never performed. Notwithstanding which, his Subsidies were constantly paid him by my Lord *G*————*n,* for almost four Years, without any Deduction upon Account of those Seven Regiments; directly contrary to the Seventh Article of our Offensive Alliance with that Crown, where it is agreed, that a Deduction shall be made out of those Subsidies, in Proportion to the number of Men wanting in that Complement, which the King is to maintain. But whatever might have been the Reasons for this Proceeding, it seems they are above the Understanding of the present Lord Treasurer; who not entring into those Refinements, of paying the *publick* Money upon *private* Considerations, hath been so uncourtly as to stop it. This Disappointment, I suppose, hath put the Court of *Lisbon* upon other Expedients of raising the Price of Forage, so as to force us either to lessen our number of Troops, or be at double Expence in maintaining them; and this at a time when their own Product, as well as the Import of Corn, was never greater; And of demanding a Duty upon the Soldiers Cloaths we carry over for those Troops, which have been their sole Defence against an inveterate Enemy; and whose Example might have infused Courage, as well as taught them Discipline, if their Spirits had been capable of receiving either.

In order to augment our Forces every Year, in the same Proportion as those, for whom we Fight, diminish theirs, we have been obliged to hire Troops from several Princes of the Empire, whose Ministers and Residents here, have perpetually importuned the Court with unreasonable Demands, under which our late Ministers thought fit to be Passive. For those Demands were always backed with a Threat to recall their Soldiers, which was a Thing not to be heard of, because it might *Discontent the Dutch.* In the mean time those Princes never sent their Contingent to the Emperor, as by the Laws of the Empire they are obliged to do, but gave for their Excuse, that we had already hired all they could spare.

But if all this be true: If, according to what I have affirmed, we began this War contrary to Reason: If, as the other Party themselves, upon all Occasions, acknowledge, the Success we have had was more than we could reasonably expect: If, after all our Success, we have not made that use of it, which in Reason we ought to have done: If we have made weak and foolish Bargains with our Allies, suffered them tamely to break every Article, even in those Bargains to our Disadvantage, and allowed them to treat us with

Insolence and Contempt, at the very Instant when We were gaining Towns, Provinces and Kingdoms for them, at the Price of our Ruin, and without any Prospect of Interest to our selves: If we have consumed all our Strength in attacking the Enemy on the strongest side, where (as the old Duke of *Schomberg*[59] expressed it) *to engage with* France, *was to take a Bull by the Horns*; and left wholly unattempted, that part of the War, which could only enable us to continue or to end it. If all this, I say, be our Case, it is a very obvious Question to ask, by what Motives, or what Management, we are thus become the *Dupes* and *Bubbles*[60] of *Europe*? Sure it cannot be owing to the Stupidity arising from the coldness of our Climate,[61] since those among our Allies, who have given us most Reason to complain, are as far removed from the Sun as our selves.

If in laying open the real Causes of our present Misery, I am forced to speak with some Freedom, I think it will require no Apology; Reputation is the smallest Sacrifice Those can make us, who have been the Instruments of our Ruin; because it is That, for which in all Probability they have the least Value. So that in exposing the Actions of such Persons, I cannot be said, properly speaking, to do them an Injury. But as it will be some Satisfaction to the People, to know by whom they have been so long abused; so it may be of great use to Us and our Posterity, not to trust the Safety of their Country in the Hands of those, who act by such Principles, and from such Motives.

I have already observed, that when the Counsels of this War were debated in the late King's Time, my Lord *G———n* was then so averse from entring into it, that he rather chose to give up his Employment, and tell the King he could serve him no longer. Upon that Prince's Death, although the Grounds of our Quarrel with *France* had received no manner of Addition, yet this Lord thought fit to alter his Sentiments; for the Scene was quite

---

59 *Duke of Schomberg*: Frederick Herman, 1st Duke of Schomberg (1615–90), a German soldier of fortune, assisted William III in 1688, was killed in the Battle of the Boyne and buried at St Patrick's Cathedral, Dublin, with an inscription written by Swift describing his family's refusal to pay for the monument. He was in French military service himself from the early 1650s until after 1685, when as a Protestant he left because of the revocation of the edict of Nantes.

60 *Bubbles*: i.e., dupes, gulls.

61 *coldness of our Climate*: not a joke; the notion that a cold climate dulls one's intelligence or genius had a long tradition, going back to Aristotle's *Politics* (VII.6.1). Cf. Milton's worry over the possibility, *Paradise Lost* IX.44–5, or Addison's *Spectator*, no. 160, published 3 September 1711, just a few months earlier than this tract.

changed; his Lordship, and the Family with whom he was engaged by so complicated an Alliance, were in the highest Credit possible with the Q——n:[62] The Treasurer's Staff was ready for his Lordship, the Duke was to Command the Army, and the Dutchess, by her Employments, and the Favour she was possessed of, to be always nearest Her Majesty's Person; by which the whole Power, at Home and Abroad, would be devolved upon that Family. This was a Prospect so very inviting, that, to confess the Truth, it could not be easily withstood by any who have so keen an Appetite for Wealth or Ambition. By an Agreement subsequent to the Grand Alliance, we were to assist the *Dutch* with Forty thousand Men, all to be Commanded by the D. of *M*. So that whether this War were prudently begun or not, it is plain, that the true Spring or Motive of it, was the aggrandizing a particular Family, and in short, a War of the *General* and the *Ministry*, and not of the *Prince* or *People*; since those very Persons were against it when they knew the Power, and consequently the Profit, would be in other Hands.

With these Measures fell in all that Sett of People, who are called the *Monied Men*; such as had raised vast Sums by Trading with Stocks and Funds, and Lending upon great Interest and Præmiums; whose perpetual Harvest is War, and whose beneficial way of Traffick must very much decline by a Peace.

In that whole Chain of Encroachments made upon us by the *Dutch*, which I have above deduced, and under those several gross Impositions from other *Powers*, if any one should ask, why our G——l continued so easy to the last? I know no other way so probable, or indeed so charitable to account for it, as by that unmeasurable Love of Wealth, which his best Friends allow to be his predominant Passion.[63] However, I shall wave any

62 *Family . . . with the Q——n*: the Marlboroughs, to whom the 'late Ministry was closely joined . . . by Friendship, Interest, Alliance, Inclination and Opinion' (*The Examiner* for 23 November 1710). Godolphin's only son was married to Marlborough's oldest daughter, and Sunderland was married to his second daughter. Cf. also Swift's comments on the relationships when attacking the Duchess of Marlborough in *The Examiner* for 19 April 1711, and see his comments on the 'Alliances' of the two figures to the Marlboroughs in *History*, Davis, vol. VII, pp. 8–9.

63 *Love of Wealth . . . Passion*: cf. Swift's notorious *Examiner* for 23 November 1710 which gives an 'account' of the perquisites, rewards and gifts acquired by the Duke in contrast to those of a Roman general. When *Conduct* was published in late 1711, Marlborough was on the brink of being dismissed. 'Two and an half *per Cent*.', mentioned by Swift a few sentences later, was the amount a report to Parliament claimed he had appropriated from the pay of foreign mercenaries serving the Queen in Flanders; see *History*, Davis, vol. VII, p. 66.

thing that is Personal upon this Subject. I shall say nothing of those great Presents made by several Princes, which the Soldiers used to call *Winter Foraging*, and said it was better than that of the Summer; of Two and an half *per Cent.* substracted out of all the Subsidies we pay in those Parts, which amounts to no inconsiderable Sum; and lastly, of the grand Perquisites in a long successful War, which are so amicably adjusted between Him and the *States.*

But when the War was thus begun, there soon fell in other Incidents here at home, which made the Continuance of it necessary for those who were the chief Advisers. The *Whigs* were at that time out of all Credit or Consideration: The reigning Favourites had always carried what was called the *Tory Principle*, at least, as high as our Constitution could bear; and most others in great Employments, were wholly in the Church-Interest. These last, among whom several were Persons of the greatest Merit, Quality, and Consequence, were not able to endure the many Instances of Pride, Insolence, Avarice and Ambition, which those Favourites began so early to discover, nor to see them presuming to be the sole Dispensers of the Royal Favour. However, their Opposition was to no Purpose; they wrestled with too great a Power, and were soon crushed under it. For, those in Possession finding they could never be quiet in their Usurpations, while others had any Credit, who were at least upon an equal Foot of Merit, began to make Overtures to the discarded *Whigs,* who would be content with any Terms of Accomodation. Thus commenced this *Solemn League and Covenant,*[64] which hath ever since been cultivated with so much Application. The great Traders in Mony were wholly devoted to the *Whigs,* who had first raised them. The Army, the Court, and the Treasury, continued under the old *Despotick* Administration: The *Whigs* were received into Employment, left to manage the Parliament, cry down the Landed Interest, and worry the Church. Mean time, our Allies, who were not ignorant, that all this artificial Structure had no true Foundation in the Hearts of the People, resolved to make their best use of it, as long as it should last. And the General's Credit being raised to a great height at home, by our Success in *Flanders*, the *Dutch* began their gradual Impositions; lessening their Quota's, breaking their

---

64 *Solemn League and Covenant*: in using this term to describe accommodation with the Whig Junto, Swift is being bitingly contemptuous, for the 'Solemn League and Covenant' was the agreement in 1643 between the Parliamentarians and the Scots which established Presbyterianism as the legal religion of England, Scotland and Ireland.

Stipulations, Garrisoning the Towns we took for them, without supplying their Troops; with many other Infringements: All which we were forced to submit to, because the General was *made easie*; because the Monied Men at home were fond of the War; because the *Whigs* were not yet firmly settled; and because that exorbitant degree of Power, which was built upon a supposed Necessity of employing particular Persons, would go off in a Peace. It is needless to add, that the Emperor, and other Princes, followed the Example of the *Dutch*, and succeeded as well, for the same Reasons.

I have here imputed the Continuance of the War to the mutual Indulgence between our General and Allies, wherein they both so well found their Accounts; to the Fears of the *Mony-changers*, lest their *Tables should be overthrown*;[65] to the Designs of the *Whigs*, who apprehended the Loss of their Credit and Employments in a Peace; and to those at home, who held their immoderate Engrossments of Power and Favour, by no other Tenure, than their own Presumption upon the Necessity of Affairs. The Truth of this will appear indisputable, by considering with what Unanimity and Concert these several Parties acted towards that great End.

When the Vote passed in the House of Lords, against any Peace without *Spain* being restored to the *Austrian* Family, the Earl of *W———n* told the House, That it was indeed impossible and impracticable to recover *Spain*; but however, there were *certain Reasons*, why such a Vote should be made at that time; which Reasons wanted no Explanation: For the General and the Ministry having refused to accept very Advantagious Offers of a Peace, after the Battle of *Ramellies*, were forced to take in a Set of Men, with a previous Bargain, to skreen them from the Consequences of that Miscarriage.[66] And accordingly upon the first succeeding Opportunity, which was that of the Prince of *Denmark*'s Death,[67] the Chief Leaders of the Party were brought into several great Employments.

---

65 *Tables . . . overthrown*: from Matthew 21:12, in which Jesus goes into the Temple and overthrows the tables of the moneychangers, calling it in the next verse a 'den of thieves'.

66 *Consequences . . . Miscarriage*: this vote was in December 1707. Addison wrote on 23 December, 'There was a great Debate in the House of Lords on Friday last', a debate to which Lord Somers put an end 'by proposing that they shoud Resolve no peace was to be made with France . . . till the Spanish monarchy was separated from the Bourbon Family, wch was carried nemine contradicente' (Walter Graham (ed.), *The Letters of Joseph Addison* (Oxford: Oxford University Press, 1941), p. 85). There was in fact one negative vote in the Lords (Holmes, pp. 77–8). See below, pp. 88–90, and 95–103 throughout.

67 *Prince of Denmark's Death*: George of Denmark, the Prince Consort, died 28 October 1708, after which the Whig Junto (the 'Set of Men' Swift refers to) took over the major cabinet

So when the Queen was no longer able to bear the Tyranny and Insolence of those ungrateful Servants, who as they *wexed the Fatter*, did but
kick the more;[68] our two great Allies abroad, and our Stock-jobbers at home,
took immediate Alarm; applied the nearest way to the Throne, by Memorials and Messages,[69] jointly directing Her Majesty not to change Her
Secretary or Treasurer; who for the true Reasons that these officious Inter-
medlers demanded their Continuance, ought never to have been admitted
into the least Degree of Trust; since what they did was nothing less than
betraying the Interest of their Native Country, to those Princes, who in
their Turns, were to do what they could to support Them in Power at
home.

Thus it plainly appears, that there was a Conspiracy on all sides to go on
with those Measures, which must perpetuate the War; and a Conspiracy
founded upon the Interest and Ambition of each Party; which begat so firm
a Union, that instead of wondring why it lasted so long, I am astonished to
think, how it came to be broken. The Prudence, Courage, and Firmness of
Her Majesty in all the Steps of that great Change, would, if the Particulars
were truly related, make a very shining Part in Her Story: Nor is Her
Judgment less to be admired, which directed Her in the Choice of perhaps
the only Persons who had Skill, Credit, and Resolution enough to be Her
Instruments in overthrowing so many Difficulties.

Some would pretend to lessen the Merit of this, by telling us, that
the Rudeness, the Tyranny, the Oppression, the Ingratitude of the late

---

positions; Somers became Lord President of the Council, Wharton Lord Lieutenant of
Ireland, and Pembroke Lord High Admiral, the post which had been Prince George's.
68 *wexed . . . kick the more*: Deut. 32:15 'But Jeshurun waxed fat, and kicked: thou art waxen fat,
thou art grown thick, thou art covered with fatness; then he forsook God which made him,
and lightly esteemed the Rock of his salvation.'
69 *Memorials and Messages*: after Sunderland's dismissal in June 1710, the States presented a
resolution appealing to the Queen to make no further changes in her ministry; this was badly
received, the Queen finding such a proceeding extraordinary (Marlborough–Godolphin,
p. 1548 n.). Similar expressions of concern came from the Bank of England over the fall of
public credit as well as from the Dutch and Imperial envoys. The Queen replied that she
had no present intentions to make further changes but if other ministers were changed it
would be 'no prejudice to the Bank or to the common cause' (William Coxe, *Memoirs of . . .
Marlborough* (London: Bohn, 1848) vol. III, p. 98; cf. Gregg, p. 317). The vagueness of this
reply produced more reassurance than was justified, with misunderstanding on the part of
the Allies; so that Marlborough had to admit, 'I am of opinion as in most things, the less
on[e] medles the better' (Marlborough–Godolphin, p. 1551). Swift attacked this meddling
in *The Examiner* for 18 January 1711.

Favourites towards their Mistress, were no longer to be born. They produce Instances to shew, how Her M——y was pursued through all Her Retreats, particularly at *Windsor*; where, after the Enemy had possessed themselves of every Inch of Ground, they at last attacked and stormed the Castle, forcing the Q——n to fly to an adjoining Cottage, pursuant to the Advice of *Solomon*, who tells us, *It is better to dwell in a corner of the Housetop, than with a brawling Woman in a wide House.*[70] They would have it, that such continued ill Usage was enough to enflame the meekest Spirit: They blame the Favourites in point of Policy, and think it nothing extraordinary, that the Queen should be at an end of Her Patience, and resolve to discard them. But I am of another Opinion, and think their Proceedings were right. For nothing is so apt to break even the bravest Spirits, as a continual Chain of Oppressions: One Injury is best defended by a second, and this by a third. By these Steps, the old *Masters of the Palace* in *France* became *Masters of the Kingdom*;[71] and by these Steps, a *G——l during Pleasure*, might have grown into a *General for Life*, and a *G——l for Life* into a *King*.[72] So that I still insist upon it as a Wonder, how Her M——y, thus besieged on all sides, was able to extricate Her self.

Having thus mentioned the real Causes, though disguised under specious Pretences, which have so long continued the War; I must beg leave to reason a little, with those Persons who are against any Peace, but what they call a *Good One*; and explain themselves, that no Peace can be *good*,

---

70 *Solomon . . . House*: Proverbs 21:9.

71 *Masters . . . of the Kingdom*: alluding to those called 'Majores Domus' or Mayors of the Palace in the Merovingian dynasty (448–751) of the Franks, who held the power of presenting petitions to the King; the office became powerful and hereditary, gradually supplanting that of the kings, who were mere figureheads.

72 *G——l . . . King*: in 1709 Marlborough sought to be made 'Captain General for Life', a request which the Queen refused; Tories depicted the Duke as seeking to be a perpetual dictator and compared him to Cromwell. Swift lists the incident for Stella as an example of the Duke's covetousness and ambition (Williams, *JSt*, p. 145, 31 December 1710). In *The Examiner* for 21 December 1710 Swift laid it down as a maxim obeyed by all wise governments, 'That no *private* Man should have a Commission to be *General for Life*, let his Merit and Services be ever so great'. Swift later claimed that the Queen reacted with alarm and talked 'as if she apprehended an attempt upon the crown' (*Memoirs*, Davis, vol. VIII, pp. 114–15), but in *History* he says the Duke's chief motive was 'the Pay and Perquisites by continuing the War', since 'he had *then* no Intentions of settling the Crown in his Family', his only son having died some years before (Davis, vol. VII, p. 7).

without an entire Restoration of *Spain* to the House of *Austria*. It is to be supposed, that what I am to say upon this Part of the Subject, will have little Influence on those, whose particular Ends or Designs of any sort, lead them to wish the Continuance of the War. I mean the General and our Allies abroad; the Knot of late Favourites at home; the Body of such, as Traffick in Stocks; and lastly, that Set of Factious Politicians, who were so violently bent, at least, upon *Clipping* our Constitution in Church and State. Therefore I shall not apply my self to any of those, but to all others indifferently, whether *Whig* or *Tory*, whose private Interest is best answered by the Welfare of their Country. And if among these there be any, who think we ought to fight on till King *Charles* is quietly settled in the Monarchy of *Spain*, I believe there are several Points, which they have not thoroughly considered.

For, First, It is to be observed, that this Resolution against any Peace without *Spain*, is a new Incident, grafted upon the Original Quarrel, by the Intrigues of a Faction among us, who prevailed to give it the Sanction of a Vote in both Houses of Parliament,[73] to justifie those, whose Interest lay in perpetuating the War. And, as this Proceeding was against the Practice of all Princes and States, whose Intentions were fair and honourable; so is it contrary to common Prudence, as well as Justice. I might add, that it was impious too, by presuming to controul Events, which are only in the Hands of God. Ours and the *States* Complaint against *France* and *Spain*, are deduced in each of our Declarations of War, and our Pretensions specified in the *Eighth Article* of the Grand Alliance; but there is not in any of these, the least mention of demanding *Spain* for the House of *Austria*, or of refusing any Peace without that Condition. Having already made an Extract from both Declarations of War, I shall here give a Translation of the Eighth Article in the Grand Alliance, which will put this Matter out of Dispute.

---

73 *Vote . . . Parliament*: on 22 December 1707, both Houses of Parliament passed resolutions that 'nothing could restore a just balance of power in Europe, but the reducing the whole Spanish monarchy to the obedience of the House of Austria' after the Lords resolved that 'No Peace can be honourable or safe, for her majesty and her allies, if Spain and the Spanish West Indies be suffered to continue in the House of Bourbon' (*Parliamentary History*, vol. VI, pp. 608–9). Swift's point about presuming to control events which are still in the hands of God was made by Scarborough, who argued that if the allies wanted a peace by partition, Great Britain would have to go along with it (HMC *Egmont*, vol. II, p. 221).

The Eighth ARTICLE of the GRAND ALLIANCE.[74]

When the War is once undertaken, none of the Parties shall have the Liberty to enter upon a Treaty of Peace with the Enemy, but jointly, and in concert with the others. Nor is Peace to be made, without having first obtained a just and reasonable Satisfaction for his Cesarean *Majesty, and for his Royal Majesty of* Great Britain, *and a particular Security to the Lords the* States-General, *of their Dominions, Provinces, Titles, Navigation, and Commerce, and a sufficient Provision, that the Kingdoms of* France *and* Spain *be never united, or come under the Government of the same Person, or that the same Man may never be King of both Kingdoms; and particularly, that the* French *may never be in Possession of the* Spanish West-Indies; *and that they may not have the liberty of Navigation, for conveniency of Trade, under any Pretence whatsoever, neither directly nor indirectly; except it is agreed, that the Subjects of* Great Britain *and* Holland, *may have full Power to use and enjoy all the same Privileges, Rights, Immunities and Liberties of Commerce, by Land and Sea, in* Spain, *in the* Mediterranean, *and in all the Places and Countries, which the late King of* Spain, *at the time of his Death, was in Possession of, as well in* Europe, *as elsewhere, as they did then use and enjoy; or which the Subjects of both, or each Nation, could use and enjoy, by virtue of any Right, obtained before the Death of the said King of* Spain, *either by Treaties, Conventions, Custom, or any other way whatsoever.*

Here, we see the Demands intended to be insisted on by the Allies upon any Treaty of Peace, are, a just and reasonable Satisfaction for the Emperor and King of *Great Britain*, a Security to the *States-General* for their Dominions, *&c.* and a sufficient Provision, that *France* and *Spain* be never united under the same Man, as King of both Kingdoms. The rest relates to the Liberty of Trade and Commerce for Us and the *Dutch*; but not a Syllable of engaging to dispossess the Duke of *Anjou*.[75]

74 *Eighth . . . Alliance*: Swift's translation of this article was attacked by Francis Hare, who claimed (correctly) that in the treaty the Eighth Article excludes the French completely from the Spanish trade in the West Indies and that Swift deliberately glossed over that fact; see Hare, *The Allies and the Late Ministry Defended*, Part I, 3rd edn corr. (1712), p. 44. Swift did in fact omit the following phrase: 'neither shall they [the French] be permitted to sail thither on the accont of Traffick directly or indirectly on any pretence whatsoever' (*A General Collection of Treatys*, vol. I, p. 419; it is this four-volume collection which Hare attacks Swift for failing to use).

75 *Duke of Anjou*: i.e., Philip V, Bourbon King of Spain, grandson of Louis XIV.

But to know how this new Language of *No Peace without Spain*, was first introduced, and at last prevailed among us, we must begin a great deal higher.

It was the Partition Treaty,[76] which begot the Will in favour of the Duke of *Anjou*: For this naturally led the *Spaniards* to receive a Prince supported by a great Power, whose Interest, as well as Affection, engaged them to preserve that Monarchy entire, rather than to oppose him in favour of another Family, who must expect Assistance from a Number of Confederates, whose principal Members had already disposed of what did not belong to them, and by a previous Treaty parcelled out the Monarchy of *Spain*.

Thus the Duke of *Anjou* got into the full Possession of all the Kingdoms and States belonging to that Monarchy, as well in the old World, as the new. And whatever the House of *Austria* pretended from their Memorials to Us and the *States*, it was at that time but too apparent, that the Inclinations of the *Spaniards* were on the Duke's side.

However, a War was resolved, and in order to carry it on with greater Vigor, a Grand Alliance formed, wherein the Ends proposed to be obtained, are plainly and distinctly laid down, as I have already quoted them. It pleased God in the Course of this War, to bless the Armies of the Allies with remarkable Successes; by which we were soon put into a Condition of demanding and expecting such Terms of a Peace, as we proposed to our selves when we began the War. But instead of this, our Victories only served to lead us on to further visionary Prospects; Advantage was taken of the Sanguin Temper, which so many Successes had wrought the Nation up to; new Romantick Views were proposed, and the old, reasonable, sober Design, was forgot.

This was the Artifice of those here, who were sure to grow Richer, as the Publick became poorer, and who after the Resolutions, which the two Houses were prevailed upon to make, might have carried on the War with Safety to themselves, till Malt and Land were Mortgaged, till a general Excise were established; and the *dizieme denier*[77] raised, by *Collectors in Red*

---

76 *Partition Treaty*: see above (pp. 52–3) and note.

77 *Malt and Land . . . dizieme denier*: 'scare' phrases; 'mortgaging the Malt Tax' and 'pawning' the Land Tax are cited further on by Swift as measures of desperation; the threat of a 'general excise' was almost enough to bring down Walpole in 1733; and a French-style 'tenth penny' tax (imposed on rare occasions in France as an extraordinary measure to meet war expenses) collected by British soldiers was a timely spectre: the French had just re-instituted the 'dixième'

THE CONDUCT OF THE ALLIES 91

Coats. And this was just the Circumstance which it suited their Interests to be in.

The House of *Austria* approved this Scheme with Reason, since whatever would be obtained by the Blood and Treasure of others, was to accrue to that Family, and they only lent their Name to the Cause.

The *Dutch* might, perhaps, have grown resty under their Burthen; but Care was likewise taken of That by a *Barrier-Treaty* made with the *States*, which deserveth such Epithets as I care not to bestow: But may perhaps consider it, at a proper Occasion, in a *Discourse* by it self.

By this Treaty, the Condition of the War, with respect to the *Dutch*, was widely altered: They fought no longer for Security, but for Grandeur; and we, instead of labouring to make them *safe*, must beggar our selves to render them *Formidable*.

Will any one contend, that if in the Treaty at *Gertruydenburg*,[78] we could have been satisfied with such Terms of a Peace, as we proposed to our selves by the Grand Alliance, the *French* would not have allowed them? 'Tis plain, they offered many more, and much greater, than ever we thought to insist on, when the War began: And they had reason to grant, as well as we to demand them, since Conditions of Peace do certainly turn upon Events of War. But surely there is some Measure to be observed in this: Those who have defended the Proceedings of our Negotiators at *Gertruydenburg*, dwell very much upon their Zeal and Patience, in endeavouring to work the *French* up to their Demands, but say nothing to justify those Demands, or the Probability, that *France* would ever accept them. Some of the Preliminary Articles were so very Extravagant, that in all Human Probability we could not have obtained them by a successful War of forty Years. One of them was inconsistent with common Reason; wherein the Confederates reserved to themselves full Liberty of demanding, what further Conditions they should think fit; and in the mean time, *France* was to deliver up several of their strongest Towns in a Month. These Articles were very gravely Signed by our Plenipotentiaries, and those of *Holland*, but not by the *French*, though it ought to have been done interchangeably; nay they were brought over by the Secretary of the Ambassy; and the Ministers here prevailed on the Queen to execute a Ratification of Articles, which only one Party had

on 14 October 1710, for the first time since 1529; see *Encyclopédie de Diderot et d'Alembert* (1751), s. v.

78 *Treaty at Gertruydenberg*: see note on p. 48.

Signed: This was an Absurdity in Form, as well as in Reason, because the usual Form of a Ratification is, with a Preamble, shewing, That *whereas Our Ministers and those of the Allies, and of the Enemy, have Signed*, &c. *We Ratify*, &c. The Person who brought over the Articles,[79] said in all Companies, (and perhaps believed) that it was a Pity, we had not demanded more, for the *French* were in a Disposition to refuse us nothing we would ask. One of our Plenipotentiaries affected to have the same Concern, and particularly, that we had not obtained some further Security for the Empire on the *Upper Rhine*.

What could be the Design of all this Grimace,[80] but to amuse the People, and raise Stocks for their Friends in the Secret, to Sell to Advantage? I have too great a Respect for the Abilities of those, who acted in this Negotiation, to believe they hoped for any other Issue from it, than what we found by the Event. Give me leave to suppose the continuance of the War was the Thing at Heart, among those in Power, both Abroad, and at Home, and then I can easily shew the Consistency of their Proceedings; otherwise they are wholly unaccountable and absurd. Did those, who insisted on such wild Demands, ever sincerely intend a Peace? Did they really think that going on with the War was more eligible[81] for their Country, than the least Abatement of those Conditions? Was the smallest of them worth Six Millions a Year, and an Hundred thousand Men's Lives? Was there no way to provide for the Safety of *Britain*, or the Security of its Trade, but by the *French* Kings turning his own Arms to beat his Grandson out of *Spain*? If these able Statesmen were so truly concerned for our Trade, which they made the Pretence of the War's Beginning, as well as Continuance, why did they so neglect it in those very Preliminaries, where the Enemy made so many Concessions, and where all that related to the Advantage of *Holland*, or the other Confederates, was expresly settled? But whatever concerned us, was to be left to a general Treaty; no Tariff agreed on with *France* or the *Low Countries*, only the *Schelde* was to remain shut, which ruins our Commerce with *Antwerp*. Our Trade with *Spain* was referred the same way; but this they will pretend to be of no Consequence, because that Kingdom was to be under the House of *Austria*; and we had already made a Treaty with

---

79 *Person…Articles*: Horatio Walpole, Secretary of the Embassy, according to a note in Faulkner's edition.

80 *Grimace*: in the now rare sense of 'pretence, sham' (*OED*).

81 *eligible*: i.e., 'suitable', 'more the preferred choice' (*OED*, but without a citation this early).

King *Charles*. I have indeed heard of a Treaty made by Mr. *Stanhope*,[82] with that Prince, for settling our Commerce with *Spain*: But whatever it were, there was another between Us and *Holland*, which went Hand in Hand with it, I mean that of *Barrier*, wherein a Clause was inserted,[83] by which all Advantages proposed for *Britain*, are to be in common with *Holland*.

Another Point which, I doubt, those have not considered, who are against any Peace without *Spain*, is, that the Face of Affairs in *Christendom*, since the Emperor's Death, hath been very much changed.[84] By this Accident the Views and Interests of several Princes and States in the Alliance, have taken a new Turn, and I believe, it will be found that Ours ought to do so too. We have sufficiently blundered once already, by changing our Measures with regard to a Peace, while our Affairs continued in the same Posture; and it will be too much in Conscience to blunder again by *not* changing the first, when the others are so much altered.

To have a Prince of the *Austrian* Family on the Throne of *Spain*, is undoubtedly more desirable than one of the House of *Bourbon*; but to have the Empire and *Spanish* Monarchy united in the same Person, is a dreadful Consideration, and directly opposite to that wise Principle, on which the Eighth Article of the Grand Alliance is founded.[85]

To this perhaps it will be objected, that the indolent Character of the *Austrian* Princes, the wretched Oeconomy of that Government, the want of a Naval Force, the remote distance of their several Territories from each other, would never suffer an Emperor, though at the same time King of *Spain*, to become Formidable: On the contrary, that his Dependance must continually be on *Great Britain*; and the Advantages of Trade, by a Peace founded upon that Condition, would soon make us Amends for all the Expences of the War.

82 *Treaty . . . Stanhope*: General James Stanhope (later Lord Mahon) negotiated a secret treaty in 1707 with Charles III whereby England and Austria would monopolize the trade of Spanish America, but, as Swift says, it was annulled by the Barrier Treaty of 1709. See Trevelyan, vol. III, p. 30.
83 *Clause . . . inserted*: Article XV of the Barrier Treaty; see below pp. 141–2.
84 *Face of Affairs . . . changed*: Emperor Joseph I (first son of Leopold I) had died on 17 April 1711; cf. Defoe, 'The Death of the Emperor is now the Surprize of *Europe*, and all our Eyes are upon the Consequences' (*Review*, 28 April 1711).
85 *We and* Holland, *as well as* Portugal, *were so apprehensive of this, that, by the 25th Article of the Offensive Alliance, his Portugueze Majesty was not to acknowledge the Arch-Duke for King of Spain, till the two late Emperors had made a Cession to* Charles *of the said Monarchy* [Swift's note].

In Answer to this, Let us consider the Circumstances we must be in, before such a Peace could be obtained, if it were at all practicable. We must become not only Poor for the present, but reduced by further Mortgages to a state of Beggary, for endless Years to come. Compare such a weak Condition as this with so great an Accession of Strength to *Austria*, and then determine how much an Emperor, in such a State of Affairs, would either fear or need *Britain*.

Consider, that the Comparison is not formed between a Prince of the House of *Austria*, Emperor and King of *Spain*, and between a Prince of the *Bourbon* Family, King of *France* and *Spain*; but between a Prince of the latter only King of *Spain*, and one of the former uniting both Crowns in his own Person.

What Returns of Gratitude can we expect, when we are no longer wanted? Has all that we have hitherto done for the Imperial Family been taken as a Favour, or only received as the Due of the *Augustissima Casa?*[86]

Will the House of *Austria* yield the least Acre of Land, the least Article of strained and even usurped Prerogative, to resettle the Minds of those Princes in the Alliance, who are alarmed at the Consequences of this Turn of Affairs, occasioned by the Emperor's Death? We are assured it never will. Do we then imagine, that those Princes, who dread the overgrown Power of the *Austrian*, as much as that of the *Bourbon* Family, will continue in our Alliance, upon a System contrary to that which they engaged with us upon? For instance; What can the Duke of *Savoy* expect in such a Case? Will he have any Choice left him but that of being a Slave and a Frontier[87] to *France*; or a *Vassal*, in the utmost Extent of the Word, to the Imperial Court? Will he not therefore, of the two Evils choose the least; by submitting to a Master, who has no immediate Claim upon Him, and to whose Family he is nearly allied; rather than to another, who hath already revived several Claims upon him, and threatens to revive more?[88]

Nor are the *Dutch* more inclined than the rest of *Europe*, that the *Empire* and *Spain* should be united in King *Charles*, whatever they may now pretend. *On the contrary, 'tis known to several Persons, that upon the Death of*

---

86 *Augustissima Casa*: 'most august house', i.e., the Imperial line, the Hapsburgs.
87 *Frontier*: in the obsolete sense of 'a barrier against attack' (*OED*).
88 *Will he not . . . revive more*: Victor Amadeus II, Duke of Savoy, was married to Anna Maria of Orleans, niece of Louis XIV; he had constant quarrels with the Imperial court arising from the Austrians' acquisitions in Italy of Naples, Sicily and Milan.

the late Emperor Joseph, *the* States *resolved, that those two Powers should not be joined in the same Person;* And this they determined as a fundamental Maxim, by which they intended to proceed. So that *Spain* was first given up by *Them*; and since they maintain no Troops in that Kingdom, it should seem, that they understand the Duke of *Anjou* to be lawful Monarch.

Thirdly, Those who are against any Peace without *Spain*, if they be such as no way find their private Account by the War, may perhaps change their Sentiments, if they will reflect a little upon our present Condition.

I had two Reasons for not sooner publishing this Discourse: The first was, Because I would give way to others, who might argue very well upon the same Subject, from general Topicks and Reason, though they might be ignorant of several Facts, which I had the Opportunity to know. The Second was, Because I found it would be necessary, in the course of this Argument, to say something of the State to which this War hath reduced us: At the same time I knew, that such a Discovery ought to be made as late as possible, and at another Juncture would not only be very indiscreet, but might perhaps be dangerous.

It is the Folly of too many, to mistake the Eccho of a *London* Coffee-house for the Voice of the Kingdom. The City Coffee-houses have been for some Years filled with People, whose Fortunes depend upon the *Bank, East-India*, or some other Stock: Every new Fund to these, is like a new Mortgage to an Usurer, whose Compassion for a young Heir is exactly the same with that of a Stockjobber to the Landed Gentry. At the Court-End of the Town, the like Places of Resort are frequented either by Men out of Place, and consequently Enemies to the Present Ministry, or by Officers of the Army: No wonder then, if the general Cry, in all such Meetings, be against any Peace either *with* Spain, or *without*; which, in other Words, is no more than this, That discontented Men desire another Change of Ministry; that Soldiers would be glad to keep their Commissions; and, that the Creditors have Mony still, and would have the Debtors borrow on at the old extorting Rates, while they have any Security to give.

Now, to give the most ignorant Reader some Idea of our present Circumstances, without troubling him or my self with Computations in form: Every body knows, that our Land and Malt Tax amount annually to about Two Millions and an half. All other Branches of the Revenue are mortgaged to pay Interest, for what we have already borrowed. The yearly Charge of the War is usually about Six Millions; to make up which Sum, we are forced to take up, on the Credit of new Funds, about Three Millions and an half. This last Year the computed Charge of the War came to above a Million more, than all the Funds the Parliament could contrive would pay Interest for; and so we have been forced to divide a Deficiency of Twelve hundred thousand Pounds among the several Branches of our Expence. This is a Demonstration, that if the War lasts another Campaign, it will be impossible to find Funds for supplying it, without mortgaging the Malt Tax, or by some other Method equally desperate.

If the Peace be made this Winter, we are then to consider, what Circumstances we shall be in towards paying a Debt of about Fifty Millions, which is a fourth Part of the Purchase of the whole Island, if it were to be Sold.

Towards clearing our selves of this monstrous Incumbrance, some of these Annuities will expire or pay off the Principal in Thirty, Forty, or an Hundred Years; the Bulk of the Debt must be lessened gradually by the best Management we can, out of what will remain of the Land and Malt Taxes, after paying Guards and Garrisons, and maintaining and supplying our Fleet in the time of Peace. I have not Skill enough to compute what will be left, after these necessary Charges, towards annually clearing so vast a Debt; but believe it must be very little: However, it is plain that both these Taxes must be continued, as well for supporting the Government, as because we have no other Means for paying off the Principal. And so likewise must all the other Funds remain for paying the Interest. How long a time this must require, how steddy an Administration, and how undisturbed a state of Affairs, both at Home and Abroad, let others determine.

However, some People think all this very reasonable; and that since the Struggle hath been for Peace and Safety, Posterity, who is to partake the Benefit, ought to share in the Expence: As if at the breaking out of this War there had been such a Conjuncture of Affairs, as never happened before, nor would ever happen again. 'Tis wonderful, that our Ancestors, in all their Wars, should never fall under such a Necessity; that we meet no Examples of it, in *Greece* and *Rome*; that no other Nation in *Europe* ever knew any thing like it, except *Spain*, about an Hundred and twenty Years ago; which they drew upon themselves, by their own Folly, and have suffered for it ever since: No doubt, we shall teach Posterity Wisdom, but they will be apt to think the Purchase too dear; and I wish they may stand to the Bargain we have made in their Names.

'Tis easy to entail Debts on succeeding Ages, and to hope they will be able and willing to pay them; but how to insure Peace for any Term of Years, is difficult enough to apprehend. Will Human Nature ever cease to have the same Passions? Princes to entertain Designs of Interest or Ambition, and Occasions of Quarrel to arise? May not we Ourselves, by the variety of Events and Incidents which happen in the World, be under a necessity of recovering Towns out of the very Hands of those, for whom we are now ruining Our Country to Take them? Neither can it be said, that those *States*,[89] with whom we may probably differ, will be in as bad a Condition as Ourselves; for, by the Circumstances of our Situation, and the Impositions of our Allies, we are more exhausted, than either they or the Enemy; and by the Nature of our Government, the Corruption of our Manners, and the Opposition of Factions, we shall be more slow in recovering.

It will, no doubt, be a mighty Comfort to our Grandchildren, when they see a few Rags hang up in *Westminster-Hall*,[90] which cost an hundred Millions, whereof they are paying the Arrears, and boasting, as Beggars do, that their Grandfathers were Rich and Great.

I have often reflected on that mistaken Notion of Credit, so boasted of by the Advocates of the late Ministry: Was not all that Credit built upon Funds, raised by the Landed Men, whom they so much hate and despise? Are not the greatest part of those Funds raised from the Growth and Product of Land? Must not the whole Debt be entirely paid, and our Fleets and Garrisons be maintained, by the Land and Malt-Tax, after a Peace? If they call it Credit to run Ten Millions in Debt, without Parliamentary Security, by which the Publick is defrauded of almost half, I must think such Credit to be dangerous, illegal, and perhaps treasonable. Neither hath any thing gone further to ruin the Nation, than their boasted Credit. For my own part, when I saw this false Credit sink, upon the Change of the Ministry,[91] I was singular enough to conceive it a good Omen. It seemed, as if the young extravagant Heir had got a new Steward, and was resolved to

---

89 *those States*: an innuendo by italics; Swift doubtless wants his readers to think of the *States-General* as a prime example.

90 *Rags . . . Westminster-Hall*: an allusion to the colours and standards captured at Blenheim, which in 1705 were taken in a great procession from the Tower and displayed in Westminster Hall (Marlborough–Godolphin, p. 406 n.).

91 *Change of the Ministry*: alluding to the fall of credit after the dismissal of Sunderland in 1710; see above, p. 86.

look into his Estate before things grew desperate, which made the Usurers forbear feeding him with Mony, as they used to do.

Since the Monied Men are so fond of War, I should be glad, they would furnish out one Campaign at their own Charge: It is not above six or seven Millions; and I dare engage to make it out, that when they have done this, instead of contributing equal to the Landed Men, they will have their full Principal and Interest, at 6 *per Cent.* remaining of all the Money they ever lent to the Government.

Without this Resource, or some other equally miraculous, it is impossible for us to continue the War upon the same Foot. I have already observed, that the last Funds of Interest[92] fell short above a Million, though the Persons most conversant in Ways and Means employed their utmost Invention; so that of necessity we must be still more defective next Campaign. But, perhaps our Allies will make up this Deficiency on our side, by greater Efforts on their own. Quite the contrary; both the Emperor and *Holland* failed this Year in several Articles; and signified to us, some time ago, that they cannot keep up to the same Proportions in the next. We have gained a noble Barrier for the latter, and they have nothing more to demand or desire: The Emperor, however sanguin he may now affect to appear, will, I suppose, be satisfied with *Naples, Sicily, Milan,* and his other Acquisitions, rather than engage in a long hopeless War, for the Recovery of *Spain,* to which his Allies the *Dutch* will neither give their Assistance nor Consent. So that since we have done their Business; since they have no further Service for our Arms, and we have no more Money to give them: And lastly, since we neither desire any Recompence, nor expect any Thanks, we ought, in pity, to be dismissed, and have leave to shift for ourselves. They are ripe for a Peace, to enjoy and cultivate what we have conquered for them; and so are we, to recover, if possible, the Effects of their Hardships upon Us. The first Overtures from *France,*[93] are made to *England,* upon safe and honourable Terms: We who bore the Burthen of the War, ought, in reason, to have the greatest share in making the Peace. If we do not hearken to a Peace, others certainly will; and get the Advantage of us there, as they have done

92 *Funds of Interest*: i.e., funds available for paying interest on loans.
93 *first Overtures from France*: alluding to the Preliminaries signed on 8 October 1711, though the negotiations were begun privately much earlier than this. On 28 September Swift wrote to Stella from Windsor, 'We have already settled all things with France, and very much to the honour and advantage of England' (Williams, *JSt,* p. 372).

in the War. We know the *Dutch* have perpetually threatned us, that they would enter into separate Measures of a Peace; and by the Strength of that Argument, as well as by *other Powerful Motives*,[94] prevailed on those, who were then at the Helm, to comply with them on any Terms, rather than put an end to a War, which every Year brought them such great Accessions to their Wealth and Power. Whoever falls off, a Peace will follow; and then we must be content with such Conditions, as our Allies, out of their great Concern for our Safety and Interest, will please to choose. They have no further occasion for Fighting; they have gained their Point, and they now tell us, it is *our War*; so that in common Justice, it ought to be *our Peace*.

All we can propose, by the desperate Steps of pawning our Land or Malt-Tax, or erecting a General Excise, is only to raise a Fund of Interest, for running us annually four Millions further in Debt, without any Prospect of ending the War so well, as we can do at present: And when we have sunk the only un-engaged Revenues we had left, our Incumbrances must of necessity remain perpetual.

We have hitherto lived upon *Expedients*, which in time will certainly destroy any Constitution, whether Civil or Natural, and there was no Country in *Christendom* had less Occasion for them, than ours. We have dieted a Healthy Body into a Consumption, by plying it with Physick, instead of Food; Art will help us no longer; and if we cannot recover by letting the Remains of Nature work, we must inevitably die.

What Arts have been used to possess the People with a *strong Delusion*,[95] that *Britain* must infallibly be ruined, without the Recovery of *Spain* to the House of *Austria*? Making the Safety of a great and powerful Kingdom, as ours was then, to depend upon an Event, which, even after a War of miraculous Successes, proves impracticable. As if Princes and Great Ministers could find no way of settling the Publick Tranquility, without changing the Possessions of Kingdoms, and forcing Sovereigns upon a People against their Inclinations. Is there no Security for the Island of *Britain*, unless a King of *Spain* be Dethroned by the Hands of his Grandfather? Has the

---

94 *Powerful Motives*: i.e., 'external influences' (see *OED*), in context probably an innuendo suggesting 'bribes'.

95 *strong Delusion*: cf. II *Thessalonians* 2:11, 'And for this cause God shall send them strong delusion, that they should believe a lie'; cf. Swift's use of this phrase at a climactic point in the 'Digression concerning Madness' in his *Tale*.

Enemy no Cautionary Towns and Sea-Ports, to give us for securing Trade? Can he not deliver us Possession of such Places, as would put him in a worse Condition, whenever he should perfidiously renew the War? The present King of *France* has but few Years to live, by the Course of Nature, and, doubtless, would desire to end his Days in Peace: Grandfathers in private Families are not observed to have great Influence on their Grandsons, and I believe they have much less among Princes. However, when the Authority of a Parent is gone, is it likely that *Philip* will be directed by a Brother, against his own Interest, and that of his Subjects? Have not those two Realms their separate Maxims of Policy, which must operate in Times of Peace? These at least are Probabilities, and cheaper by six Millions a Year than recovering *Spain*, or continuing the War, both which seem absolutely impossible.

But the common Question is, If we must now Surrender *Spain*, what have we been Fighting for all this while? The Answer is ready; We have been Fighting for the Ruin of the Publick Interest, and the Advancement of a Private. We have been fighting to raise the Wealth and Grandeur of a particular Family; to enrich Usurers and Stock-jobbers; and to cultivate the pernicious Designs of a Faction, by destroying the Landed-Interest. The Nation begins now to think these *Blessings* are not worth Fighting for any longer, and therefore desires a Peace.

But the Advocates on the other side cry out, that we might have had a better Peace, than is now in Agitation, above two Years ago. Supposing this to be true, I do assert, that by parity of Reason we must expect one just so much worse, about two Years hence. If those in Power could then have given us a better Peace, more is their Infamy and Guilt, that they did it not; why did they insist upon Conditions, which they were certain would never be granted? We allow it was in their Power to have put a good End to the War, and left the Nation in some hope of recovering it self. And this is what we charge them with as answerable to God, their Country, and Posterity, that the bleeding Condition of their Fellow-Subjects, was a Feather in the Balance with their private Ends.

When we offer to lament the heavy Debts and Poverty of the Nation, 'tis pleasant to hear some Men answer all that can be said, by crying up the Power of *England*, the Courage of *England*, the inexhaustible Riches of *England*. I have heard a Man very sanguine upon this Subject, with a good Employment for Life, and a Hundred thousand Pounds in the Funds, bidding us *Take Courage*, and *Warranting, that all would go well.*[96] This is the Style of Men at Ease, *who lay the heavy Burthens upon others, which they will not touch with one of their Fingers.*[97] I have known some People such ill Computers, as to imagine the many Millions in Stocks and Annuities, are so much real Wealth in the Nation; whereas every Farthing of it is entirely lost to us, scattered in *Holland, Germany*, and *Spain*; and the Landed-Men, who now pay the Interest, must at last pay the Principal.

Fourthly, Those who are against any Peace without *Spain*, have, I doubt, been ill informed, as to the low Condition of *France*, and the mighty Consequences of our Successes. As to the first, it must be confessed, that after the Battle of *Ramellies* the *French* were so discouraged with their frequent Losses, and so impatient for a Peace, that their King was resolved to comply on any reasonable Terms. But when his Subjects were informed of our exorbitant Demands,[98] they grew jealous of his Honour, and were unanimous to assist him in continuing the War at any hazard, rather than submit. This fully restored his Authority; and the Supplies he hath received from the *Spanish West-Indies*, which in all are computed, since the War, to amount to Four hundred Millions of Livres, (and all in *Specie*) have enabled him to pay his Troops. Besides, the Money is spent in his own Country; and he hath since waged War in the most thrifty manner, by acting on the Defensive, compounding with us every Campaign for a Town,[99] which costs us fifty times more than it is worth, either as to the Value, or the Consequences. Then he is at no Charge of a Fleet, further than providing

96 *a Man . . . go well*: probably a reference to the Earl of Halifax. Although Halifax was out of office during the whole of Anne's reign, he was 'Auditor of the Receipt', which was an 'office for life' (Holmes, p. 438.). Moreover, Halifax was noted for his expertise in fiscal matters and was not on good terms with the other Junto lords (Holmes, p. 239). Oldmixon (attrib.) comments on the passage without making the identification specific: 'the Person who is reported to have that Saying often in his Mouth, has indeed a good Employment, but little in the Funds, except in the *South-Sea*, and he has always said it *for* the *Peace*; the *War* is not so much in his Favour' (*Remarks on a False, Scandalous, and Seditious Libel, Intituled, The Conduct of the Allies, and of the Late Ministry* (1711), p. 29).
97 *who lay . . . Fingers*: adapted from Matthew 23: 4, Jesus' reproof of the Scribes and Pharisees: 'For they bind heavy burdens and grievous to be borne, and lay them on men's shoulders; but they themselves will not move them with one of their fingers.'
98 *exorbitant Demands*: the most exorbitant demand in these negotiations of 1709 was that Louis must help drive his grandson off the throne of Spain. See note on the Treaty of Gertruydenberg, above, p. 48.
99 *compounding . . . Town*: i.e., negotiating a settlement in which money changed hands.

Privateers, wherewith his Subjects carry on a Piratical War at their own Expence, and he shares in the Profit; which hath been very considerable to *France*, and of infinite Disadvantage to us, not only by the perpetual Losses we have suffered to an immense Value, but by the general Discouragement of Trade, on which we so much depend. All this considered, with the Circumstances of that Government, where the Prince is Master of the Lives and Fortunes of so mighty a Kingdom, shews that Monarch to be not so sunk in his Affairs, as we have imagined, and have long flattered Our selves with the Hopes of. For an absolute Government may endure a long War, but it hath generally been ruinous to Free Countries.

Those who are against *any Peace without Spain*, seem likewise to have been mistaken in judging our Victories, and other Successes, to have been of greater Consequence, than they really were.

When our Armies take a Town in *Flanders*, the *Dutch* are immediately put into *Possession*, and we at home make *Bonfires*. I have sometimes pitied the deluded People, to see them squandring away their Fewel to so little purpose. For Example, What is it to Us that *Bouchain* is taken, about which the Warlike Politicians of the Coffee-House make such a Clutter? What though the Garrison surrendered Prisoners of War, and in sight of the Enemy? We are not now in a Condition to be fed with Points of Honour. What Advantage have We, but that of spending three or four Millions more to get another Town for the States, which may open them a new Country for *Contributions*,[100] and encrease the Perquisites of the G——l?

In that War of Ten Years, under the late King, when our Commanders and Soldiers were raw and unexperienced, in comparison of what they are at present, we lost Battles and Towns, as well as we gained them of late, since those Gentlemen have better learned their Trade; yet we bore up then, as the *French* do now: Nor was there any thing decisive in their Successes: They grew weary, as well as we, and at last consented to a Peace, under which we might have been happy enough, if it had not been followed by that wise *Treaty* of *Partition*, which revived the Flame, that hath lasted ever since. I see nothing else in the modern way of making War, but that the Side, which can hold out longest, will end it with most Advantage. In such a close Country as *Flanders*, where it is carried on by Sieges, the Army, that acts offensively, is at a much greater Expence of Men and Mony; and there is hardly a Town taken in the common Forms, where the Besiegers have

100 *Contributions*: see above, p. 73, note 43.

not the worse of the Bargain. I never yet knew a Soldier, who would not affirm, That any Town might be Taken, if you were content to be at the Charge. If you will count upon sacrificing so much Blood and Treasure, the rest is all a regular, established Method, which cannot fail. When the King of *France*, in the Times of his Grandeur, sat down before a Town, his Generals and Engineers would often fix the Day when it should Surrender. The Enemy, sensible of all this, hath for some Years past avoided a Battle, where he hath so ill succeeded, and taken a surer way to consume us, by letting our Courage evaporate against Stones and Rubbish, and sacrificing a single Town to a Campaign, which he can so much better afford to Lose, than we to Take.

Lastly, Those who are so violent against *any Peace*, without *Spain* being restored to the House of *Austria*, have not, I believe, cast their Eye upon a Cloud gathering in the North,[101] which we have helped to raise, and may quickly break in a Storm upon our Heads.

The Northern War hath been on Foot, almost ever since our Breach with *France*: The Success of it various; but one Effect to be apprehended was always the same, that sooner or later it would involve us in its Consequences, and that, whenever this happened, let our Success be never so great against *France*, from that Moment *France* would have the Advantage.

By our Guaranty of the Treaty of *Travendall*,[102] we were obliged to hinder the King of *Denmark* from engaging in a War with *Sueden*. It was at that time understood by all Parties, and so declared, even by the *British* Ministers, that this Engagement especially regarded *Denmark*'s not assisting King *Augustus*. But, however, if this had not been so, yet our Obligation to *Sueden* stood in Force, by virtue of former Treaties with that Crown, which were all revived and confirmed by a subsequent one, concluded at the *Hague* by Sir *Joseph Williamson* and Monsieur *Lilienroot*, about the latter end of the late King's Reign.[103]

101 *gathering in the North*: after Russia defeated the Swedish armies of Charles XII at Poltava in 1709, Swedish dominions were open to attack by those neighbours (Poland, Denmark, Prussia, Hanover) who had claims on whatever Charles had previously conquered.
102 *Treaty of Travendall*: early in the Northern War (4 August 1700) the Swedes landed in Sjeland (Zealand) and threatened to take Copenhagen. In a few weeks Denmark withdrew from the hostilities and signed the Treaty of Travendal (18 August), the terms of which were guaranteed by England and Holland, who reaffirmed their guarantees in 1703. On 'King Augustus' see note on p. 58, above.
103 *Hague . . . King's Reign*: this treaty was agreed to at the Hague on 11 January 1700, by representatives of England, Charles XII and the States-General. Signatories included Nils

However, the War in the North proceeded, and our not assisting *Sueden*, was at least as well excused by the War, which we were entangled in, as his not contributing his Contingent to the Empire, whereof he is a Member, was excused by the Pressures he lay under, having a Confederacy to deal with.

In this War the King of *Sueden* was Victorious; and what Dangers were we not then exposed to? What Fears were we not in? He Marched into *Saxony*, and if he had really been in the *French* Interest, might at once have put us under the greatest Difficulties. But the Torrent turned another way, and he contented himself with imposing on his Enemy the Treaty of *Alt Rastadt*; by which King *Augustus* makes an absolute Cession of the Crown of *Poland*, renounces any Title to it, acknowledges *Stanislaus*; and then, both he and the King of *Sueden*, join in desiring the Guaranty of *England* and *Holland*. The Q——n did, indeed, not give this Guaranty in Form;[104] but, as a Step towards it, the Title of *King* was given to *Stanislaus*, by a Letter from Her Majesty; and the strongest Assurances were made to the *Suedish* Minister, in Her Majesty's Name and in a Committee of Council, that the Guaranty should speedily be granted; and that in the mean while, it was the same thing as if the Forms were passed.

In 1708, King *Augustus* made the Campaign in *Flanders*; what Measures he might at that time take, or of *what Nature* the Arguments might be that he made use of, is not known: But immediately after he breaks through all he had done, marches into *Poland*, and re-assumes the Crown.

After this we apprehended, that the Peace of the Empire might be endangered; and therefore entered into an Act of Guaranty for the Neutrality of it.[105] The King of *Sueden* refused, upon several Accounts, to submit to the Terms of this Treaty; particularly, because we went out of the Empire

---

Eosander, Baron Lillieroot, for the King of Sweden; and Sir Joseph Williamson (1633–1701), diplomatic agent for William III.

104 *Alt Rastadt . . . Form*: i.e., Altranstadt, a castle outside Leipzig; the treaty was signed 24 September 1706, with the terms Swift goes on to enumerate, whereby Augustus II, though keeping a courtesy title of King of Poland, in fact renounced the throne in favour of Stanislaus Leszczynski. 'In Form' means 'according to the rules or prescribed methods' (*OED*).

105 *Guaranty . . . Neutrality of it*: the Hague Convention of March 1710 for the Neutrality of the Empire. Signed by the Emperor, England, Holland, Hanover, Denmark, Prussia, Russia and Saxony, this agreed to neutrality in the Empire and protected Swedish possessions within the Empire; a second Convention signed in August created a 'corps' of 21,000 men to keep the peace (R. M. Hatton, *Charles XII of Sweden* (New York: Weybright and Talley, 1968), pp. 327–8).

to cover *Poland* and *Jutland*, but did not go out of it to cover the Territories of *Sueden*.

Let us therefore consider, what is our Case at present. If the King of *Sueden* returns,[106] and gets the better, he will think himself under no Obligation of having any Regard to the Interests of the Allies; but will naturally pursue, according to his own Expression, *His Enemy, wherever he finds him*. In this Case the *Corps* of the Neutrality is obliged to oppose him, and so we are engaged in a second War, before the first is ended.

If the Northern Confederates succeed against *Sueden*, how shall we be able to preserve the Balance of Power in the North, so essential to our Trade, as well as in many other Respects? What will become of that great Support of the *Protestant Interest* in *Germany*, which is the Footing that the *Suedes* now have in the Empire? Or, who shall answer that these Princes, after they have settled the North to their Minds, may not take a fancy to look Southward, and make our Peace with *France* according to their own Schemes?

And lastly, if the King of *Prussia*, the Elector of *Hanover*, and other Princes whose Dominions lie contiguous, are forced to draw from those Armies which act against *France*; we must live in hourly Expectation of having those Troops recalled, which they now leave with us; and this Recal may happen in the midst of a Siege, or on the Eve of a Battel. Is it therefore our Interest, to toil on in a ruinous War, for an impracticable End, till one of these Cases shall happen, or to get under shelter before the Storm?

There is no doubt, but the present Ministry (provided they could get over the Obligations of Honour and Conscience) might find their Advantage in advising the Continuance of the War, as well as the last did, though not in the same Degree, after the Kingdom has been so much exhausted. They might prolong it till the Parliament would desire a Peace; and in the mean time leave them in full Possession of Power. Therefore it is plain, that their Proceedings at present, are meant to serve their Country, directly against their private Interest; whatever Clamor may be raised by those, who for the vilest Ends, would remove Heaven and Earth to oppose their Measures. But they think it infinitely better, to accept such Terms as will secure our

---

106 *King of Sueden returns*: a genuine fear and consistent rumour; see Marlborough to Godolphin on 25 September 1710, Marlborough–Godolphin, p. 1641 and note. In fact, Charles XII did not return from Turkey to Europe until 1714 and was killed in combat in Norway in 1718.

Trade, find a sufficient Barrier for the *States*, give *Reasonable Satisfaction* to the Emperor, and restore the Tranquility of *Europe*, though without adding *Spain* to the Empire: Rather than go on in a languishing way, upon the vain Expectation of some improbable Turn, for the Recovery of that Monarchy out of the *Bourbon* Family; and at last be forced to a worse Peace, by some of the Allies falling off, upon our utter Inability to continue the War.

POSTSCRIPT

I have in this Edition explained three or four Lines in the 38th Page,[107] which mentions the *Succession*, to take off, if possible, all manner of Cavil; though, at the same time, I cannot but observe, how ready the Adverse Party is to make use of any Objections, even such as destroy their own Principles. I put a distant Case of the possibility that our *Succession*, through extream Necessity, might be changed by the Legislature, in future Ages; and it is pleasant to hear those People quarrelling at this, who profess themselves for changing it as often as they please, and that even without the Consent of the entire Legislature.

I have just seen a Paper, called, *An Answer to the Conduct*, &c. I am told several Others are preparing: I faithfully promise, that whatever Objections of Moment I can find in any of them, shall be fully answered in a Paragraph at the end of the Preface, in the next Edition of this Discourse.

107 *38th Page:* pp. 68–9 of this edition.

SOME ADVICE HUMBLY OFFER'D TO THE MEMBERS OF THE OCTOBER CLUB

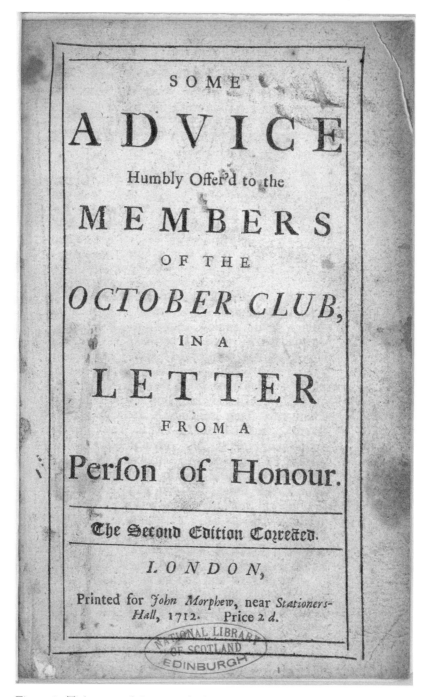

SOME

ADVICE

Humbly Offer'd to the

MEMBERS

OF THE

OCTOBER CLUB,

IN A

LETTER

FROM A

Perſon of Honour.

The Second Edition Corrected.

LONDON,

Printed for *John Morphew*, near *Stationers-Hall*, 1712.   Price 2 *d*.

Figure 2. Title page of the second edition: NLS, L.C.3339(6). Reproduction courtesy of the Trustees of the National Library of Scotland.

SOME
ADVICE, &c.

Gentlemen,

Since the first Institution of your Society, I have always thought you capable of the greatest Things. Such a number of Persons, Members of Parliament, true Lovers of our Constitution in Church and State, meeting at certain times,[1] and mixing Business and Conversation together, without the Forms and Constraint necessary to be observed in Publick Assemblies, must very much improve each others Understanding, correct and fix your Judgment, and prepare your selves against any Designs of the opposite Party. Upon the opening of this Session, an Incident hath happen'd,[2] to provide against the Consequences whereof will require your utmost Vigilance and Application. All this last Summer the Enemy was working under Ground, and laying their Train; they gradually become more frequent and bold in their Pamphlets and Papers, while those on our side were drop'd, as if we had no farther occasion for them. Some time before an Opportunity fell into their Hands, which they have cultivated ever since;[3] and thereby

---

1 *meeting at certain times*: the club met at the Bell Tavern, King Street, Westminster, daily when Parliament was in session.
2 *Incident hath happened*: the vote of the Lords on the first day of the Christmas session of Parliament for an amendment to the Queen's Address pledging no peace without Spain. The motion was made by the Earl of Nottingham, who in return got the vote of the Whig lords in favour of the Occasional Conformity bill. See Introduction, pp. 4–5.
3 *cultivated ever since*: Swift's letter to Archbishop King of 8 January 1712 tells the story as follows:

> Last September, at Windsor, the Duke of Somerset who had not been at Cabinet-Council for many Months, was advised by his Friends of the late Ministry to appear there, but the rest refused to sit with him; and the Council was put off until next Day, when the Duke went to a Horse Race. This was declaring open War, and ever since, both he and his Dutchess (who is in great Favour) have been using all Sorts of Means to break the present Ministry. Mrs. Masham was absent two Months from Windsor, with Lying-in at Kensington, and my Lord Treasurer six Weeks by Indisposition. Some Time before the Session, the Duke . . . went to all those Lords, who, by the Narrowness of their Fortunes, have depended on the Court, and engaged them to vote against the Ministry, by assuring them it was the Queen's Pleasure. He

have endeavoured, in some sort, to turn those Arts against us, which had been so effectually employ'd to their Ruin: A plain Demonstration of their superior Skill at Intrigue; to make a Stratagem succeed a second time, and this even against those who first try'd it upon Them. I know not whether this Opportunity I have mentioned could have been prevented by any Care, without straining a very *tender Point*, which those chiefly concern'd avoided by all means, because it might seem a Counterpart of what they had so much condemn'd in their *Predecessors.* Though it is certain the two Cases were widely different; and if Policy had once got the better of good Nature, all had been safe, for there was no other Danger in view: But the Consequences of this were foreseen from the beginning, and those who *kept the Watch* had early warning of it. It would have been a Master-Piece of Prudence, in this Case, to have made a *Friend* of an *Enemy.*[4] But whether that were possible to be compass'd, or whether it were ever attempted, is now too late to enquire. All Accommodation was render'd desperate, by an unlucky Proceeding some Months ago at *W—nds—r*, which was a Declaration of War too frank and generous for that Situation of Affairs, and, I am told, was not approved by a certain great *M——r.*[5] It was obvious to suppose, that in a Particular where the Honour and Interest of a *Husband* were so closely united with those of a *Wife*, he might be sure of her utmost Endeavours for his Protection, though she neither lov'd nor esteem'd him. The Danger of losing Power, Favour, Profit, and a Shelter from *Domestick Tyranny*, were strong Incitements to stir up a working Brain, *early* practis'd in all the Arts of Intriguing. Neither is it safe to count upon the Weakness of any Man's Understanding, who is thoroughly possess'd with the Spirit of Revenge to sharpen his Invention: Nothing else is required besides *Obsequiousness* and

---

is said to have added other powerful Motives. Bothmar's Memorial was published just at that Juncture . . . It is confidently affirmed by those, who should know, that Money was plentifully scattered. By these, and some other Accidents, the Vote was carried against the Ministry; and every Body of either Party, understood the Thing as intended directly against my Lord Treasurer's Head.   (Woolley, *Corr.*, vol. I, p. 410.)
 Cf. Swift's account in *History*, Davis, vol. VII, pp. 14–15.
4 *Friend of an Enemy*: i.e., to have reached accord with the Duke of Somerset.
5 *Declaration of War . . . M—r*: the Declaration was St John's refusing to sit at Cabinet Council while Somerset was there; see the note above and Swift's letter to King of 26 August 1711 (Woolley, *Corr.*, vol. I, p. 371); Swift goes on to say Somerset 'was advised by his Friends of the other Party, to take this Step'. The disapproving great minister was of course Oxford.

Assiduity, which as they are often the Talents of those who have no better, so they are apt to make Impressions upon the *best and greatest Minds*.

It was no small Advantage to the *designing Party*, that since the Adventure at *W—nds—r*, the *Person on whom we so much depend*,[6] was long absent by Sickness; which hinder'd him from pursuing those Measures, that Ministers are in Prudence forc'd to take, to defend their Country and themselves against an irritated Faction. The *Negotiators* on the other side, improv'd this favourable Conjuncture to the utmost; and by an unparallel'd Boldness, accompany'd with many Falshoods, persuaded certain L—ds, who were already in the same Principle, but were afraid of making a wrong Step, lest it should *lead them out of their Coaches into the Dirt*, that Voting, in appearance, against the C——rt, would be the safest Course, to avoid the danger they most apprehended, which was that of losing their P—ns—ns; and their Opinions, when produced, would, by seemingly contradicting their Interest, have an appearance of Virtue into the bargain. This, with some Arguments of more *immediate Power*, went far in producing that strange unexpected Turn we have so lately seen, and from which our Adversaries reckon'd upon such wonderful Effects: and some of them, particularly my Lord C—— J——,[7] began to act as if all were already in their Power.

But, though the more immediate Causes of this Desertion were what I have above related, yet I am apt to think, it would hardly have been attempted, or at least not have succeeded, but for a prevailing Opinion, that the Church Party, and the Ministers, had different Views, or at least were not so firmly united as they ought to have been. It was commonly said, and I suppose not without some Ground of Truth, that many Gentlemen of your Club were discontented to find so *little done*; that they thought it look'd as if People were *not in earnest*; that they expected to see a *thorough Change*, with respect to Employments; and though every Man could not be provided for, yet when all Places were filled with Persons of good Principles, there would be fewer Complaints, and less danger from the other Party;

---

6 *Person on whom . . . depend*: Oxford.
7 *Lord C—J—*: Sir Thomas Parker, Lord Chief Justice. By saying he acts as though already in power, Swift refers to the fact that Parker had recently sent for Swift's publisher Morphew, demanded to know the author of *The Conduct of the Allies* and bound him over for court next term. Swift remarked to Stella, 'He would not have the impudence to do this, if he did not foresee what was coming at court' (Williams, *JSt*, 13 December 1711, p. 438). See Swift's comment on the passage which so offended Parker, *Some Remarks*, below, pp. 129–30.

that this Change was hop'd for all last Summer, and even to the Opening of the Session, yet nothing done. On the other Hand, it was urged by some in favour of the Ministry, that it was impossible to find Employments for one *Pretender* in twenty, and therefore, in gratifying one, nineteen would be disoblig'd; but while all had leave to hope, they would all endeavour to deserve: But this again was esteem'd a very shallow Policy, which was too easily seen through, must soon come to an end, and would cause a general Discontent; with twenty other Objections, to which it was liable: And indeed, considering the short Life of M—n—ys in our Climate, it was with some Reason thought a little hard, that those for whom any Employment was intended, should, by such a Delay, be probably deprived of half their Benefit; not to mention, that a M———ry is best confirm'd, when all inferior Officers are in its Interest.

I have set this Cause of Complaint in the strongest Light, tho' my Design is to endeavour that it should have no manner of Weight with you, as I am confident our Adversaries counted upon, and do still expect to find mighty Advantages by it.

But it is necessary to say something to this Objection, which in all Appearance lies so hard upon the present M———ry. What shall I offer upon so tender a Point? How shall I convey an Answer that none will apprehend except those for whom I intend it? I have often pitied the Condition of great M———rs upon several Accounts, but never so much upon any, as when their Duty obliges them to bear the Blame and Envy of Actions, for which they will not be answerable in the next World, tho' they dare not convince the present, 'till it is too late. This Letter is sent you, *Gentlemen*, from no mean Hand, nor from a Person uninformed, though for the rest as little concerned in Point of Interest for any change of Ministry, as most others of his Fellow-Subjects. I may therefore assume so much to my self, as to desire you will depend upon it, that a short time will make manifest, how little the Defect you complain of, ought to lye at *that Door*, where your Enemies would be glad to see you place it. The wisest Man, who is not very near the Spring of Affairs, but views them only in their Issues and Events, will be apt to fix Applauses and Reproaches in the wrong Place; which is the true Cause of a Weakness that I never yet knew Great Ministers without, I mean their being deaf to all Advice; for if a Person of the best Understanding offers his Opinion in a Point where he is not Master of all the Circumstances, (which perhaps are not to be told) 'tis an hundred to one, that he runs into an Absurdity: From whence it is that Ministers falsly conclude themselves to be equally Wiser than others in general Things, where the common Reason of Mankind ought to be the Judge; and is probably less byassed than theirs. I have known a Great Man of excellent Parts, blindly pursue a Point of no Importance, against the Advice of every Friend he had, 'till it ended in his Ruin.[8] I have seen great Abilities rendred utterly useless, by unacountable and unnecessary Delay, and by difficulty of Access, by which a thousand Opportunities are suffered to escape. I have observed the *strongest Shoulders* to sink under too great a load of Business, for want of dividing a due Proportion among others: These and more that might be named, are obvious Failings, which every rational Man may be allowed to discern as well as lament, and wherein the wisest Minister may receive Advice from others of inferior Understanding: But in those Actions where we are not throughly inform'd of all the Motives and Circumstances, 'tis hardly possible, that our Judgment should not be mistaken. I have often been one of the Company, where we have all blamed a Measure taken, which has afterward proved the only one that could possibly have succeeded. Nay I have known those very Men who have formerly been in the Secret of Affairs, when a new Set of People hath come in, offering their Refinements and Conjectures in a very plausible manner upon what was passing, and widely err in all they advanced.

Whatever Occasions may have been given for Complaints that *enough hath not been done*, those Complaints should not be carried so far as to make us *forget what hath been done*, which at first was a great deal more than we hoped or thought practicable; and you may be assured, that so much Courage and Address, were not employ'd in the beginning of so great a Work, without a Resolution of carrying it through, as fast as Opportunities would offer. Any of the most sanguine Gentlemen in your Club, would gladly have compounded two Years ago, to have been assured of seeing Affairs in the present Situation: It is principally to the Abilities of *one great Person*,[9] that you, *Gentlemen*, owe the Happiness of meeting together, to cultivate good Principles, and form your selves into a Body for defending your Country against a restless and dangerous Faction. It is to the *Same* we

---

8 *Great Man . . . Ruin*: Temple Scott suggests, plausibly enough, that this refers to Godolphin's excessive reaction to being called 'Volpone' during the Sacheverell trial. See Swift's comment in *History* (Davis, vol. VII, p. 9).

9 *one great Person*: Oxford.

all owe that mighty Change in the most important Posts of the Kingdom; that we see the sacred Person of our *Prince*, encompassed by those whom we ourselves would have chosen, if it had been left to our Power: And if every thing besides, that you could wish, has not been hitherto done, you will be but just to impute it to some powerful though *unknown Impediments*,[10] wherein the Ministry is more to be lamented than blamed: But there is good Reason to hope from the vigorous Proceedings of the Court, that these *Impediments* will in a short time be effectually removed. And one great Motive to hasten the Removal of them, will doubtless be the Reflection upon those dangerous Consequences which had like to have ensued upon not removing them before. Besides, after so plain and formidable a Conviction, that mild and moderate Methods meet with no other Reception or Return, than to serve as Opportunities to the insatiable Malice of an Enemy; Power will awake to vindicate it self, and disarm its Opposers, at least, of all *offensive Weapons*.

Consider, if you please, how hard beset the present Ministry hath been on every side: By the impossibility of carrying on the War any longer, without taking the most desperate Courses; or of recovering *Spain* from the House of *Bourbon*, though we could continue it many Years longer: By the Clamors of a Faction against any Peace without that Condition, which the most knowing among themselves allowed to be impracticable: by the secret Cabals of Foreign Ministers, who have endeavoured to inflame our People, and Spirited up a sinking Faction to blast all our Endeavours for Peace, with those Popular Reproaches of *France* and the *Pretender*: Not to mention the Danger they have been in from *private Insinuations of such a Nature*, as it was almost impossible to fence against. These Clouds now begin to blow over, and those *who are at the Helm*, will have Leisure to look about them; and compleat what yet remains to be done.

That Confederate Body which now makes up the Adverse Party consists of an Union so monstrous and unnatural, that in a little time it must of necessity fall to Pieces. The *Dissenters* with Reason think themselves betray'd and sold by their *Brethren*. What they have been told, that the

10 *unknown Impediments*: the Duke and Duchess of Somerset. The Duke was dismissed on 19 January, a few days before this pamphlet appeared; the Duchess retained her position and remained in the Queen's favour.

present *Bill* against *Occasional Conformity*, was to prevent a greater Evil,[11] is an Excuse too gross to pass; and if any other profound Refinement were meant, it is now come to nothing. The remaining Sections of the Party, have no other Tye but that of an inveterate Hatred and Rancour against those in Power, without agreeing in any other common Interest; not cemented by Principle or Personal Friendship, I speak particularly of their Leaders; and though I know that Court-Enmities are as inconstant as its Friendships, yet from the difference of Temper and Principle, as well as the Scars remaining of former Animosities, I am persuaded their League will not be of long continuance; I know several of them who will never pardon those with whom they are now in Confederacy; and when once they see the present Ministry throughly fixed, they will grow weary of *Hunting upon a cold Scent*,[12] or playing a *desperate Game*, and crumble away.

On the other side, while the Malice of that Party continues in Vigour; while they yet feel the Bruises of their Fall, which pain them afresh since their late *Disappointment*; they will leave no Arts untried, to recover themselves; and it behoves all who have any regard for the Safety of the Qu——n or her Kingdom, to join unanimously against an Adversary who will return full fraught with Vengeance upon the first Opportunity that shall offer: and this perhaps is more to be regarded, because that Party seem yet to have a Reserve of Hope, in the *same Quarter from whence their last Reinforcement came.*[13] Neither can any thing cultivate this Hope of theirs so much, as a Disagreement among ourselves, founded upon a Jealousy of the Ministry, who I think need no better a Testimony of their good Intentions, than the incessant *Rage* of the *Party Leaders* against them.

There is one Fault which both Sides are apt to charge upon themselves, and very generously commend their Adversaries for the contrary Virtue. The *Tories* acknowledge, that the *Whigs* outdid them in rewarding their

---

11 *Bill . . . greater Evil*: Defoe, writing in fury at his fellow-dissenters in the *Review*, ridiculed their acting on the notion 'That is [*sic*] was done to prevent a worse Bill being brought in – But what was to bring it in? . . . Not one Word of this can be told us; so I heard of a Man that pull'd down his House before-hand, that is [*sic*] might not be burnt, but saw no Danger of any Body's setting it on Fire' (22 December 1711). In *History* Swift wrote that the Dissenters were satisfied 'upon Promises that this Law should soon be repealed, and Others more in their Favour enacted' once the Whigs came back to power (Davis, vol. VII, p. 21).

12 *Hunting . . . Scent*: said of a scent that is faint or weak (*OED*).

13 *Adversary . . . Reinforcement came*: i.e., the Whigs will be counting on the Somerset family to turn the Queen against the Ministry.

Friends, and adhering to each other. The *Whigs* allow the same to the *Tories*. I am apt to think, that the former may a little excell the latter in this Point; for doubtless the *Tories* are less vindicative of the two; and whoever is remiss in *Punishing*, will probably be so in *Rewarding*; tho' at the same time I well remember the Clamors often raised during the Reign of that Party against the Leaders, by those who thought their Merits were not rewarded; and they had Reason on their side; because it is, no doubt, a Misfortune, to forfeit *Honour* and *Conscience* for nothing: But surely the Case is very different at this time, when whoever adheres to the Administration, does Service to God, his Prince, and his Country, as well as contributes to his own private Interest and Safety.

But if the *Whig* Leaders were more grateful in rewarding their Friends, it must be avowed likewise, that the Bulk of them was in general more zealous for the Service of their Party, even when abstracted from any private Advantage, as might be observed in a thousand Instances; for which I would likewise commend them, if it were not natural to Mankind to be more *violent in an ill Cause* than a good one.

The perpetual Discord of Factions, with several Changes of late Years in the very nature of our Government, have controuled[14] many Maxims among us. The *Court* and *Country Party* which used to be the old Division, seems now to be ceased, or suspended for *better Times* and *worse Princes*. The Qu—n and Ministry are at this time fully in the true Interest of the Kingdom; and therefore the *Court* and *Country* are of a side; and the *Whigs*, who originally were of the latter, are now of neither, but an independent Faction, nursed up by the *Necessities* or *Mistakes* of a late *good, tho' unexperi-enc'd Prince. Court* and *Country* ought therefore to join their Forces against these Common Enemies, till they are entirely dispersed and disabled. It is enough to arm Ourselves against them, when we consider that the greatest Misfortunes which can befall the Nation, are what would most answer their *Interest* and their *Wishes*; a perpetual War encreases their Mony, breaks and beggars their *Landed Enemies*. The Ruin of the Church would please the Dissenters, Deists, and Socinians, whereof the Body of their Party consists. A *Commonwealth*, or a *Protector*, would gratify the *Republican Principles* of some, and the Ambition of others among them.

---

14 *controuled*: 'challenged' (*OED*).

I would infer from hence, that no Discontents of an inferior nature, such I mean as I have already mentioned, should be carried so far as to give any ill Impression of the present Ministry. If all Things have not been hitherto done as you, *Gentlemen*, could reasonably wish, it can be imputed only to the *secret Instruments*[15] of that Faction. The Truth of this hath appeared from some late Incidents more visible than formerly. Neither do I believe, that any one will now make a Doubt whether a *certain Person*[16] be *in earnest*, after the united and avow'd Endeavours of a whole Party to strike directly at his Head.

When it happens, by some private cross Intrigues, that a great Man has not that Power which is thought due to his Station, he will however probably desire the Reputation of it, without which he neither can preserve the Dignity, nor hardly go through the common Business of his Place; yet is it that Reputation to which he owes all the Envy and Hatred of others, as well as his own Disquiets. Mean time, his expecting Friends impute all their Disappointments to some deep Design, or to his Defect of Good-will, and his Enemies are sure to cry up his Excess of Power; especially in those Points where they are confident it is most shortned. A Minister, in this difficult Case, is sometimes forced to preserve his Credit, by forbearing what *is* in his Power, for fear of discovering how far the Limits extend of what *is not*; or perhaps for fear of shewing an Inclination contrary to that of his Master. Yet all this while he lies under the Reproach of *Delay, Unsteddiness*, or *Want of Sincerity*. So that there are many Inconveniences and Dangers, either in discovering or concealing the want of Power. Neither is it hard to conceive, that Ministers may happen to suffer for the *Sins of their Predecessors*, who by their great Abuses and Monopolies of Power and Favour, have taught Princes to be more thrifty for the future in the Distribution of both. And as in common Life, whoever hath been long confined, is very fond of his Liberty, and will not easily endure the very Appearance of Restraint even from those who have been the Instruments of setting him free; so it is with the Recovery of Power; which is usually attended with an undistinguish'd Jealousy, lest it should be *again* invaded. In such a Juncture, I cannot discover why a wise and honest Man should venture to place himself at the Head of Affairs upon any other Regard than

15 *secret Instruments*: again the allusion is to the Duke and Duchess of Somerset.
16 *certain Person*: Oxford.

the Safety of his Country, and the Advice of *Socrates*,[17] to *prevent an ill Man from coming in.*

Upon the whole, I do not see any one ground of Suspicion or Dislike, which you, *Gentlemen*, or others who wish well to their Country may have entertained about Persons or Proceedings, but what may probably be misapprehended even by those who think they have the best Information. Nay, I will venture to go one Step farther, by adding, that although it may not be prudent to speak out upon this Occasion, yet whoever will reason impartially upon the whole State of Affairs, must entirely acquit the M———ry of that Delay and Neutrality which have been laid to their Charge. Or suppose some small part of this Accusation were true, (which I positively know to be otherwise, whereof the World will soon be convinced) yet the Consequences of any Resentment at this time, must either be none at all, or the most fatal that can be imagined; For if the present Ministry be made so uneasy that a Change be thought necessary, Things will return of course into the old Hands of those whose *Little-Fingers will be found heavier than their Predecessors Loins.*[18] The *Whig-Faction* is so dextrous at Corrupting, and the People so susceptible of it, that you cannot be ignorant how easy it will be, after such a Turn of Affairs, upon a new Election, to procure a Majority against you. They will resume their Power with a Spirit like that of *Marius* or *Sylla*, or the last Triumvirate;[19] and those Ministers who have been most censured for too much Hesitation, will fall the first Sacrifices to their Vengeance. But these are the smallest Mischiefs to be apprehended from such returning Exiles. What Security can a Prince hope for his Person

17 *Advice of Socrates*: alluding to Plato's *Republic*, I.347, where Socrates explains that the main motive for decent people to accept power is the fear of being ruled by someone inferior.

18 *Little-Fingers . . . Loins*: Adapted from 1 Kings 12, in which Rehoboam, after the death of his father Solomon, is advised by his friends to tell the people who had asked him to make their yoke lighter, 'thus shalt thou say unto them, My little finger shall be thicker than my father's loins'.

19 *Marius . . . last Triumvirate*: referring to the bitter rivals Gaius Marius (137–88 BC), six times consul, and his ex-quaestor L. Cornelius Sulla (138–78 BC), whose personal hatred and differences in family backgrounds provoked civil war. Swift emphasizes the extent to which both men on their returns to power during their careers exacted vengeance on their rivals. Marius, seeking consulship a sixth time, turned against his former associates, and much later began a reign of terror against senators before seeking the consulship a seventh time; Sulla, at the end of the civil war and after Marius' death, initiated a 'proscription' in which his political enemies were executed. (See Plutarch's *Lives of Sylla* and *Gaius Marius*.) By 'Last triumvirate' Swift means 'the Second Triumvirate', established in 43 BC and renewed in 37 BC, who also engaged in proscriptions. Its members were Octavian (Augustus), Marc Antony (defeated at Actium in 31 BC) and Marcus Aemilius Lepidus (deposed in 36 BC).

or his Crown, or even for the Monarchy itself? He must expect to see his best Friends brought to the Scaffold, for *Asserting his Rights*; to see his *Prerogative* trampled on, and his *Treasures* applied to *feed the Avarice of those who make themselves his Keepers*: To hear himself treated with Insolence and Contempt; to have his *Family purged at Pleasure* by their Humour and Malice; and to retain even the Name and Shadow of a King, no longer than his *Ephori*[20] shall think fit.

These are the inevitable Consequences of such a Change of Affairs, as that envenom'd Party is now projecting; which will best be prevented by your firmly adhering to the present Ministry, till this *Domestick Enemy* is out of all possibility of making Head any more.

---

20 *Ephori*: In ancient Sparta, the five magistrates, appointed annually by popular election, who exercised a controlling power over the kings.

SOME REMARKS ON THE BARRIER TREATY

SOME
REMARKS
ON THE
Barrier Treaty,
BETWEEN
HER MAJESTY
AND THE
States-General.

By the AUTHOR of
The Conduct of the ALLIES.

To which are added,

The said BARRIER-TREATY,
with the Two Separate Articles;
Part of the Counter-Project; The
Sentiments of Prince *Eugene* and
Count *Sinzendorf*, upon the said
Treaty; And a Representation of
the *English* Merchants at *Bruges*.

LONDON,
Printed for *John Morphew*, near *Stationers-Hall*, 1712. Price 6 d.

Figure 3. Title page: CUL, Williams 358.

THE PREFACE

When I Published the Discourse called, The Conduct of the Allies, *I had Thoughts either of inserting or annexing the* Barrier-Treaty *at length, with such Observations, as I conceived might be useful for publick Information: But that Discourse taking up more room than I designed, after my utmost Endeavours to abbreviate it, I contented my self only with making some few Reflections upon that* famous *Treaty, sufficient, as I thought, to answer the Design of my Book. I have since heard that my Readers in general seemed to wish I had been more particular, and have discovered an Impatience to have that Treaty made publick, especially since it hath been laid before the House of Commons.*[1]

    That I may give some Light to the Reader, who is not well vers'd in these Affairs, he may please to know, that a Project for a Treaty of Barrier with the States, *was transmitted hither from* Holland; *but being disapproved of by our Court in several Parts, a new Project, or Scheme of a Treaty, was drawn up here, with many Additions and Alterations. This last was called the* Counter-Project; *and was the Measure whereby the Duke of* M———h *and my Lord* T———d *were Commanded and Instructed to proceed, in Negotiating a* Treaty of Barrier *with the* States. *I have added a Translation of this* Counter-Project, *in those Articles where it differs from the* Barrier-Treaty, *that the Reader, by comparing them together, may judge how punctually those Negotiators observed their Instructions. I have likewise subjoined the Sentiments of Prince* Eugene *of* Savoy *and the Count* de Sinzendorf,[2] *relating to this Treaty, written (I suppose) while it was negotiating. And lastly, I have added a Copy of the Representation of the* British Merchants *at* Bruges, *signifying what Inconveniencies they already felt, and further apprehended, from this* Barrier-Treaty.

---

1 *House of Commons*: on 29 January 1712 the Barrier Treaty was laid before the House of Commons, and two weeks later resolutions were passed condemning the treaty and those who had been active in making it. On 14 February, about a week before his pamphlet was published, Swift reported to Stella that the Commons 'have been very severe on the Barrier Treaty; as you will find by their Votes' (Williams, *JSt*, p. 488).
2 *Count de Sinzendorf*: Count Philip Ludwig von Zinzendorf, representative of the Emperor in the negotiations with the Dutch in 1709. In July 1712 Abel Boyer called him 'the first Imperial Plenipotentiary, who was indefatigable in the Discharge of his Office' (*State*, vol. IV (1712), p. 11).

SOME REMARKS ON THE
BARRIER-TREATY

Imagine a reasonable Person in *China*, were reading the following Treaty, and one who was ignorant of our Affairs, or our Geography; He would conceive their High Mightinesses the States-General, to be some vast powerful Common-wealth, like that of *Rome*, and Her Majesty to be a Petty Prince, like one of those to whom that Republick would sometimes send a *Diadem* for a Present, when they behaved themselves well; otherwise could depose at pleasure, and place whom they thought fit in their stead. Such a Man would think, that the States had taken our Prince and Us into their *Protection*; and in return honoured us so far, as to make use of our Troops as some small Assistance in their Conquests, and the enlargement of their Empire, or to prevent the Incursions of *Barbarians* upon some of their out-lying Provinces. But how must it sound in an *European* Ear, that *Great Britain*, after maintaining a War for so many Years, with so much Glory and Success, and such prodigious Expence; After saving the Empire, *Holland*, and *Portugal*, and almost recovering *Spain*, should, towards the close of a War, enter into a Treaty with Seven *Dutch* Provinces, to secure to them a Dominion larger than their own, which She had conquered for them; to undertake for a great deal more, without stipulating the least Advantage for Her self; and accept as an Equivalent, the mean Condition of those *States* assisting to preserve her Queen on the Throne, whom, by God's Assistance, she is able to defend against all Her Majesty's *Enemies* and *Allies* put together?

Such a wild Bargain could never have been made for Us, if the *States* had not found it their Interest to use very *powerful Motives*[3] to the chief Advisers, (I say nothing of the Person immediately employ'd); and if a Party here at Home had not been resolved, for Ends and Purposes very well known, to continue the War as long as they had any occasion for it.

---

3 *powerful Motives*: as Swift uses this phrase, the 'Motives' may include bribes; cf. *Conduct*, pp. 98–9.

The *Counter-Project*[4] of this Treaty, made here at *London*, was bad enough in all Conscience: I have said something of it in the *Preface*: Her Majesty's Ministers were instructed to proceed by it in their Negotiation. There was one Point in that Project which would have been of Consequence to *Britain*, and one or two more, where the Advantages of the *States* were not so very exorbitant, and where some Care was taken of the House of *Austria*. Is it possible that *our good Allies and Friends*[5] could not be brought to any Terms with us, unless by striking out every Particular that might do Us any good, and adding still more to Them, where so much was already granted? For instance, the Article about demolishing of *Dunkirk*, surely might have remained, which was of some Benefit to the *States*, as well as of mighty Advantage to Us, and which the *French* King has lately yielded in one of his Preliminaries, tho' clogged with the Demand of an Equivalent, which will owe its difficulty only to this Treaty.

But let me now consider the Treaty it self: Among the one and twenty Articles of which it consists, only two have any relation to Us, importing that the *Dutch* are to be Guarantees[6] of our Succession, and are not to enter into any Treaty till the Queen is acknowledged by *France*. We know very well, that it is in Consequence the Interest of the *States*, as much as ours, that *Britain* should be governed by a Protestant Prince. Besides, what is there more in this Guarantee, than in all common Leagues Offensive and Defensive between two Powers, where each is obliged to defend the other against any Invader with all their Strength? Such was the Grand Alliance between the Emperor, *Britain* and *Holland*, which was, or ought to have been, as good a Guarantee of our Succession, to all Intents and Purposes, as this in the *Barrier-Treaty*; and the mutual Engagements in such Alliances

---

4 *Counter-Project*: see Swift's Preface; this 'Project' contained the alternative proposals Britain gave to her negotiators in reaction to the first version offered by Holland. Swift had apparently been furnished with these by the ministry, enabling him to offer his readers damning contrasts between the instructions given Marlborough and Townshend and the terms of the treaty they actually negotiated.

5 *our good... Friends*: Swift points up this phrase several times as a sarcastic echo of a diplomatic cliché. Although the wording does not appear in the Barrier Treaty itself, it was a common formula. Moreover, Francis Hare in his response to Swift's *Conduct* had quoted the addresses of both Houses of Parliament in 1708 asking the Queen to establish 'a good and firm Friendship among all the Allies'; according to Hare, the Barrier Treaty had effected such a friendship (*The Allies and the Late Ministry Defended*, Part II, 2nd edn (1711), p. 6).

6 *Guarantees*: see *Conduct*, p. 69 note.

have been always reckoned sufficient, without any separate Benefit to either Party.

It is, no doubt, for the Interest of *Britain*, that the *States* should have a sufficient Barrier against *France*: But their High Mightinesses, for some few Years past, have put a different Meaning upon the word *Barrier*, from what it formerly used to bear, when applied to Them. When the late King was Prince of *Orange*, and commanded their Armies against *France*, it was never once imagined that any of the Towns taken, should belong to the *Dutch*; they were all immediately delivered up to their lawful Monarch; and *Flanders* was only a Barrier to *Holland*, as it was in the Hands of *Spain* rather than *France*. So in the Grand Alliance of 1701, the several Powers promising to endeavour to recover *Flanders* for a Barrier, was understood to be the recovering those Provinces to the King of *Spain*: But in this Treaty, the Style is wholly changed: Here are about twenty Towns and Forts of great Importance,[7] with their Chatellanies[8] and Dependencies (which Dependencies are likewise to be enlarged as much as possible) and the whole Revenues of them, to be under the perpetual Military Government of the *Dutch*, by which that Republick will be entirely Masters of the richest Part of all *Flanders*. And upon any Appearance of War, they may put their Garrisons into any other Place of the *Low-Countries*; and further, the King of *Spain* is to give them a Revenue of four hundred thousand Crowns a Year, to enable them to maintain those Garrisons.

Why should we wonder, that the *Dutch* are inclined to perpetuate the War, when, by an Article in this Treaty, the King of *Spain* is *not to possess one single Town in the* Low-Countries, *till a Peace is made*. The Duke of *Anjou* at the beginning of this War, maintained six and thirty Thousand Men out of those *Spanish* Provinces he then possessed; To which if we add the many Towns since taken, which were not in the late King of *Spain*'s Possession at the Time of his Death, with all their Territories and Dependencies, it is visible what Forces the *States* may be able to keep, even without any Charge to their peculiar Dominions.

The Towns and Chatellanies of this Barrier always maintained their Garrisons when they were in the Hands of *France*, and, as it is reported, returned a considerable Sum of Mony into the King's Coffers; yet the King

---

7 *Towns . . . Importance*: see Article VI, below, pp. 138–9, and for what Swift next says, Article XI, p. 140.

8 *Chatellanies*: i.e., 'castellanies', districts or offices belonging to a castle (*OED*).

of *Spain* is obliged by this Treaty (as we have already observed) to add, over and above, a Revenue of Four hundred thousand Crowns a Year. We know likewise, that a great part of the Revenue of the *Spanish Netherlands* is already pawned to the *States*; so that after a Peace, nothing will be left to the Sovereign, nor will the People be much eased of the Taxes they at present labour under.

Thus the *States*, by vertue of this *Barrier-Treaty*, will, in effect, be absolute Sovereigns of all *Flanders*, and of the whole Revenues in the utmost Extent.

And here I cannot, without some Contempt, take notice of a sort of Reasoning offered by several People, that the many Towns we have taken for the *Dutch* are of no Advantage, because the whole Revenues of those Towns are spent in maintaining them. For First, The Fact is manifestly false, particularly as to *Lisle* and some others: Secondly, The *States*, after a Peace, are to have Four hundred thousand Crowns a Year out of the remainder of *Flanders*, which is then to be left to *Spain*: And lastly, Suppose all these acquired Dominions will not bring a Penny into their Treasury; What can be of greater Consequence, than to be able to maintain a mighty Army out of their new Conquests, which before they always did by taxing their natural Subjects?

How shall we be able to answer it to King *Charles* the Third,[9] that while we pretend to endeavour restoring him to the entire Monarchy of *Spain*, we join at the same time with the *Dutch* to deprive him of his natural Right to the *Low-Countries*?

But suppose by a *Dutch Barrier* must now be understood only what is to be in Possession of the *States*; yet even under this Acceptation of the Word, nothing was originally meant except a *Barrier* against *France*; whereas several Towns demanded by the *Dutch* in this Treaty, can be of no use at all in such a *Barrier*. And this is the Sentiment even of Prince *Eugene* himself (the present Oracle and Idol of the Party here)[10] who says, *That* Dendermond, Ostend, *and the Castle of* Gand, *do in no sort belong to the Barrier, nor can be of other use than to make the States-General Masters*

---

9 *Charles the Third*: the Archduke Charles of Austria, now Emperor Charles VI as well as claimant of the title Charles III of Spain.

10 *Oracle . . . Party here*: Prince Eugene of Savoy, general of Imperial troops and friend of Marlborough, was currently on a visit to England, where he was idolized by both sides but especially of course by the Whigs. Swift wrote on 27 January, 'I could not see prince Eugene

of the Low-Countries, and hinder their Trade with England. And further,
That those who are acquainted with the Country know very well, that Lier,
and Hale *to* fortifie, *can give no Security to the* States *as a Barrier, but only
raise a Jealousie in the People, that these Places are only fortified in order to block
up* Brussels, *and the other great Towns of* Brabant.

In those Towns of *Flanders* where the *Dutch* are to have Garrisons, but
the Ecclesiastical and Civil Power to remain to the King of *Spain* after
a Peace; the *States* have Power to send Arms, Ammunition and Victuals
without paying Customs; under which Pretence they will engross the whole
Trade of those Towns, exclusive to all other Nations. This, Prince *Eugene*
likewise foresaw, and, in his Observations upon this Treaty here annexed,
proposed a Remedy for it.

And if the *Dutch* shall please to think, that the whole *Spanish Netherlands*
are not a sufficient Barrier for them, I know no Remedy from the Words
of this Treaty, but that we must still go on, and Conquer for them as long
as they please. For the Qu—— is obliged, whenever a Peace is treated, to
procure for them *whatever shall be thought necessary*[11] besides; and where
their *Necessity* will terminate, is not very easie to foresee.

Could any of Her Majesty's Subjects conceive, that in the Towns we have
taken for the *Dutch*, and given into their Possession as a Barrier, either the
States should demand, or our Ministers allow, that the Subjects of *Britain*
should, in respect to their Trade, be used worse in those very Towns, than
they were under the late King of *Spain*? Yet this is the Fact, as monstrous
as it appears: All Goods going to, or coming from *Newport* or *Ostend*, are
to pay the same Duties as those that pass by the *Scheld* under the *Dutch*
Forts; And this, in effect, is to shut out all other Nations from Trading
to *Flanders*.[12] The *English* Merchants at *Bruges* complain, That *after they
have paid the King of* Spain's *Duty for Goods imported at* Ostend, *the same
Goods are made liable to further Duties, when they are carried from thence into
the Towns of the* Dutch *new Conquests*; and desire only *the same Privileges
of Trade they had before the Death of the late King of* Spain, Charles *II.* And

at Court to-day, the crowd was so great. The Whigs contrive to have a crowd always about
him, and employ the rabble to give the word, when he sets out from any place' (Williams, *JSt*,
p. 473). For Eugene's remarks on the Barrier towns, which Swift paraphrases and partially
quotes at the end of this paragraph, see below, p. 150.
11 *whatever . . . necessary*: quoted from Article V, below, p. 138.
12 *Trading to Flanders*: see the 'Representation of the English Merchants', below, pp. 152–3.

in consequence of this Treaty, the *Dutch* have already taken off 8 *per Cent.* from all Goods they send to the *Spanish Flanders*, but left it still upon Us.

But what is very surprising; in the very same Article where *our good Friends and Allies* are wholly shutting us out from Trading in those Towns we have Conquered for them with so much Blood and Treasure, the Qu——— is obliged to procure that the *States* shall be used as favourably in their Trade over all the King of *Spain*'s Dominions, as Her own Subjects, or *as the People most favoured.* This I humbly conceive to be perfect Boys Play, *Cross I win*, and *Pile you lose*;[13] or, *What's yours is mine*, and *What's mine is my own.* Now if it should happen that in a Treaty of Peace, some Ports or Towns should be yielded us for the Security of our Trade in any Part of the *Spanish* Dominions, at how great a distance soever; I suppose the *Dutch* would go on with their Boys Play, and *challenge Half* by Virtue of that Article: Or would they be content with the Military Government and the Revenues, and reckon them among *what shall be thought necessary* for their Barrier?

This prodigious Article is introduced as subsequent to the Treaty of *Munster*,[14] made about the Year 1648, at a time when *England* was in the utmost Confusion, and very much to our Disadvantage. Those Parts in that Treaty, so unjust in themselves, and so prejudicial to our Trade, ought in reason to have been remitted, rather than confirmed upon us for the Time to come: But this is *Dutch* Partnership, to share in all our beneficial Bargains, and exclude us wholly from theirs, even from those which we have got for them.

In one Part of *The Conduct of the Allies*, &c. among other Remarks upon this Treaty, I make it a Question, whether it were right in point of Policy or Prudence to call in a Foreign Power to be Guarantee to our Succession; because by that means *we put it out of the Power of our own Legislature to alter the Succession, how much soever the Necessity of the Kingdom may require it?* To comply with the Cautions of some People, I explained my Meaning

---

13 *Cross I win . . . you lose*: i.e., 'Heads I win, tails you lose'; cf. French '*pile ou face*' (Brewer, *Dictionary of Phrase and Fable*).

14 *Treaty of Munster*: signed on 30 January 1648, this treaty recognized the independence of the Netherlands from Spain and among other provisions agreed that the States General were to remain in possession and enjoyment of whatever towns, castles, fortresses, commerce and country in the East and West Indies and Brazil and on the coasts of Africa, Asia and America as they then possessed.

in the following Editions.[15] I was assured that my L—d Ch——f J——ce affirmed that Passage was Treason; one of my Answerers, I think, decides as favourably; and I am told, that Paragraph was read very lately during a Debate, with a Comment in very injurious Terms, which, perhaps, might have been spared.[16] That the Legislature should have Power to change the Succession, whenever the Necessities of the Kingdom require, is so very useful towards preserving our Religion and Liberty, that I know not how to recant. The worst of this Opinion is, that at first sight it appears to be *Whiggish*; but the Distinction is thus, The *Whigs* are for changing the Succession when they think fit, though the entire Legislature do not consent; I think it ought never to be done but upon great Necessity, and that with the Sanction of the whole Legislature. Do these Gentlemen of *Revolution-Principles* think it impossible that we should ever have occasion *again* to change our Succession? And if such an Accident should fall out, must we have no Remedy, 'till the Seven Provinces will give their Consent? Suppose that this Virulent Party among us were as able, as some are willing, to raise a *Rebellion* for reinstating them in Power, and would apply themselves to the *Dutch*, as Guarantees of our Succession, to assist them with all their Force, under pretence that the Q—— and M——ry, a great Majority of both Houses, and the Bulk of the People were for bringing over *France, Popery*, and the *Pretender*? Their High-Mightinesses would, as I take it, be sole Judges of the Controversie, and probably decide it so well, that in some time we might have the Happiness of becoming a Province to *Holland*. I am humbly of Opinion, that there are two Qualities necessary to a Reader, before his Judgment should be allowed; these are, *common Honesty*, and *common Sense*; and that no Man could have misrepresented that Paragraph in my Discourse, unless he were utterly destitute of one or both.

15 *Meaning . . . Editions*: see *Conduct*, pp. 68–9, and Postscript to *Conduct*, p. 106. On Lord Chief Justice Parker see p. 111 of *Some Advice to the October Club* and note.

16 *Debate . . . spared*: cf. Swift's remark to Stella, 'A Whig Membr took out the Conduct of the Allyes, and read that Passage about the Succession, with great Resentmt, but none seconded him' (Williams, *JSt*, p. 488, 14 February 1712). The Whig member's injurious remarks are not in *CJ*, and he has not been certainly identified; Swift's description and the failure to obtain a second suggest a particularly outspoken and quarrelsome Whig, like Nicholas Lechmere, who had been one of the managers of Sacheverell's impeachment and whom Swift had ridiculed in the *Examiner* for 25 January 1711; see *HP 1690–1715*, vol. IV, pp. 601–6. The debate on the treaty began on 13 February, and a few days later Townshend and his associates were voted to be 'Enemies to the Queen and Kingdom' (*CJ*, vol. XVII, p. 86).

The Presumptive Successor, and her immediate Heirs,[17] have so established a Reputation in the World, for their Piety, Wisdom, and Humanity,
that no Necessity of this kind, is like to appear in their Days; but I must still
insist, that it is a diminution to the Independency of the Imperial Crown of
Great Britain, to call at every Door for Help to put our Laws in execution:
And we ought to consider, that if in Ages to come, such a Prince should
happen to be in Succession to our Throne, who should be entirely unable to
Govern; That very Motive might encline our Guarantees to support him,
the more effectually to bring the Rivals of their Trade into Confusion and
Disorder.

But to return: The Qu—— is here put under the unreasonable
Obligation of being Guarantee of the whole *Barrier-Treaty*, of the *Dutch*
having Possession of the said Barrier and the Revenues thereof, before a
Peace; of the Payment of Four hundred thousand Crowns by the King of
Spain; that the *States* shall possess their Barrier even before King *Charles* is
in Possession of the *Spanish Netherlands*: Although by the Fifth Article of
the Grand Alliance, Her Majesty is under no Obligation to do any thing
of this Nature; *except in a General Treaty*.

All Kings, Princes, and States are invited to enter into this Treaty, and
to be Guarantees of its Execution. This Article, though very frequent in
Treaties, seems to look very odly in that of the Barrier: *Popish Princes*
are here invited among others, to become Guarantees of our *Protestant
Succession*: Every Petty Prince in *Germany* must be intreated to preserve the
Q—— of *Great Britain* upon Her Throne: The King of *Spain* is invited
particularly and by Name, to become Guarantee of the Execution of a
Treaty, by which his Allies, who pretend to fight his Battles, and recover
his Dominions, strip him in effect of all his Ten Provinces: A clear Reason
why they never sent any Forces to *Spain*, and why the Obligation not
to enter into a Treaty of Peace with *France*, 'till that entire Monarchy
were yielded as a Preliminary, was struck out of the *Counter-Project* by the
Dutch. They fought only in *Flanders*, because there they only fought for
themselves. King *Charles* must needs accept this Invitation very kindly, and
stand by with great Satisfaction, while the *Belgick* Lion[18] divides the Prey,
and assigns it all to himself. I remember there was a parcel of Soldiers who

17 *Presumptive . . . Heirs*: the Electress Sophia, granddaughter of James I, mother of George the
    Elector of Hanover (later George I).
18 *Belgick Lion*: i.e., the Dutch.

robbed a Farmer of his Poultry, and then made him wait at Table while they devoured his Victuals, without giving him a Morsel; and upon his Expostulating, had only for Answer; *Why, Sirrah, are not we come here to protect you?* And thus much for this generous Invitation to all Kings and Princes, to lend their Assistance, and become Guarantees, out of pure good Nature, for securing *Flanders* to the *Dutch.*

In the Treaty of *Ryswick*,[19] no care was taken to oblige the *French* King to acknowledge the Right of Succession in Her present Majesty; for want of which Point being then settled, *France* refused to Acknowledge Her for Queen of *Great Britain*, after the late King's Death. This unaccountable Neglect (if it were a Neglect) is here called an *Omission*, and Care is taken to supply it in the next General Treaty of Peace. I mention this occasionally,[20] because I have some stubborn Doubts within me, whether it were a *wilful Omission* or no. Neither do I herein reflect in the least upon the Memory of His late Majesty, whom I entirely acquit of any Imputation upon this Matter. But when I recollect the Behaviour, the Language, and the Principles of *some certain Persons*[21] in those Days, and compare them with that *Omission*; I am tempted to draw some Conclusions, which a certain Party would be more ready to call False and Malicious, than to prove them so.

I must here take leave (because it will not otherwise fall in my way) to say a few Words in return to a Gentleman, I know not of what Character or Calling, who has done me the Honour to write Three Discourses against that Treatise of the *Conduct of the Allies*,[22] &c. and promises, for my Comfort, to conclude all in a Fourth. I pity Answerers with all my Heart, for

---

19 *Treaty of Ryswick*: the omission mentioned here is the subject of Article XX of the Barrier Treaty; see below, p. 143.
20 *occasionally*: i.e., 'incidentally' (*OED*).
21 *some certain Persons*: by these dark hints Swift means Whig leaders in the circle around William III, some of whom (most importantly Godolphin and Shrewsbury) had been named in 1696 by the Jacobite conspirator Sir John Fenwick (himself accused in a plot to assassinate the King) as having had treasonable correspondence with the Jacobite court. Swift suggests that they deliberately saw to it that the Treaty of Ryswick a year later (1697) omitted acknowledgement of the right of Succession to Queen Anne, presumably as a way of hedging their bets in case of successful Jacobite intrigues after William's death.
22 *Gentleman . . . Allies*: Francis Hare, whose *Management of the War* Swift had attacked in the *Examiner* (15 February 1711); Swift had also furnished hints for Mrs Manley's response to a pro-war sermon by Hare in September 1711. But as St John wrote, 'Lord Marlborough's stupid Chaplain continues to spoil paper', and, as Swift indicates here, Hare answered *Conduct of the Allies* in *The Allies and the Late Ministry Defended*, in four parts, identifying Swift as the author; see the Introduction. Hare has often erroneously been said to respond to the present tract with *The Barrier Treaty Vindicated* (1712), actually by Stephen Poyntz.

the many Disadvantages they lie under. My Book did a World of Mischief (as he calls it) before his First Part could possibly come out; and so went on through the Kingdom, while his limped slowly after, and if it arrived at all, it was too late; for Peoples Opinions were already fixed. His manner of answering me is thus: Of those Facts which he pretends to examine, some he resolutely denies, others he endeavours to extenuate, and the rest he distorts with such unnatural Turns, that I would engage, by the same Method, to disprove any History, either Ancient or Modern. Then the whole is Interlarded with a thousand injurious Epithets and Appellations, which heavy Writers are forced to make use of, as a supply for that want of Spirit and Genius they are not born to: Yet, after all, he allows a very great Point for which I contend, confessing in plain Words, that the Burthen of the War has chiefly lain upon Us; and thinks it sufficient for the *Dutch*, that, next to *England*, they have born the greatest Share. And is not this the great Grievance of which the whole Kingdom complains? I am inclined to think that my Intelligence was at least as good as his; and some of it, I can assure him, came from Persons of his own Party, though perhaps not altogether so inflamed. Hitherto therefore, the Matter is pretty equal, and the World may believe Him or Me, as they please. But, I think, the great Point of Controversie between us, is, whether the Effects and Consequences of Things follow better from His Premises or mine: And there I will not be satisfied, unless he will allow the whole Advantage to be on my side. Here is a flourishing Kingdom brought to the Brink of Ruin, by a *most Successful and Glorious War* of Ten Years, under an *Able, Diligent, Loyal Ministry*; a *most Faithful, Just, and Generous Commander* ; and in Conjunction with the most Hearty, Reasonable, and Sincere Allies: This is the Case, as that Author represents it. I have heard a Story, I think it was of the Duke of ———[23] who playing at Hazard at the Groom-Porters in much Company, held in a great many Hands together, and drew a huge Heap of Gold; but, in the heat of Play, never observed a Sharper, who came once or twice under his Arm, and swept a great deal of it into his Hat: The Company thought it had been one of his *Servants*: When the Duke's Hand was out, they were talking how much he had won: Yes, said he, I held in very long;

---

23 *Duke of* ———: the Duke cannot be specifically identified, if the story is to be taken as factual. Swift means it of course mainly as a comment on the Dutch, but contemporary readers might also see an application to the Queen's 'servant', Marlborough.

yet, methinks, I have won but very little: They told him, his SERVANT had got the rest in his Hat; and then he found he was cheated.

It hath been my good Fortune to see the most important Facts that I have advanced, justify'd by the Publick Voice; which let this Author do what he can, will incline the World to believe, that I may be right in the rest: And I solemnly declare, that I have not wilfully committed the least Mistake. I stopt the Second Edition, and made all possible Enquiries among those who I thought could best inform me, in order to correct any Error I could hear of: I did the same to the Third and Fourth Editions, and then left the Printer to his liberty. This I take for a more effectual Answer to all Cavils, than an hundred Pages of Controversy.

But what disgusts me from having any thing to do with this Race of *Answer-jobbers*, is, that they have no sort of Conscience in their Dealings: To give one Instance in this Gentleman's Third Part, which I have been lately looking into. When I talk of the *most Petty Princes*, he says, I mean *Crowned Heads*: When I say, *the Soldiers of those Petty Princes are ready to rob or starve at Home*: He says I call *Kings* and *Crowned Heads, Robbers* and *Highwaymen*. This is what the *Whigs* call answering a Book.

I cannot omit one Particular, concerning this Author, who is so positive in asserting his own Facts, and contradicting mine: He affirms, *That the Business of* Thoulon *was discovered by the Clerk of a certain Great Man, who was then Secretary of State.*[24] It is neither wise, nor for the Credit of his Party, to put us in mind either of *that Secretary*, or of *that Clerk*; however, so it happens, that nothing relating to the Affair of *Thoulon* did ever pass through that Secretary's Office: Which I here affirm, with great Phlegm, leaving the Epithets of *False, Scandalous, Villainous*, and the rest, to the Author and his Fellows.

---

24 *Business . . . State*: see note to *Conduct of the Allies*, above, pp. 76–7. Swift writes disingenuously as though Hare had claimed the comment in the *Conduct* alluded to the affair of William Greg, Harley's clerk in the Secretary's office executed for treason in April 1708. But Hare in response vigorously denied he had intended Greg, saying 'no, I meant a Person now alive' who committed 'a Folly which the Person hinted at has paid dearly for' (Hare, *Allies and the Late Ministry Defended*, Part IV (1712), p. 79.) In fact Hare thought that 'common justice' had been violated by the furious pursuit of Greg as a weapon against Harley (*Private Corr. of Sarah, Duchess of Marlborough* (1838), vol. II, p. 64). Finally, as though tired of the game, or perhaps merely to score the same point again, Hare in another tract argues that the 'Creature' is known to very few people in England, but everyone can remember Greg, who was deservedly hanged (*A Full Answer to the Conduct of the Allies* (1712), p. 58).

But to leave this Author; let us consider the Consequence of our Tri-umphs, upon which some set so great a Value, as to think that nothing less than the Crown can be a sufficient Reward for the Merit of the G——l:[25] We have not enlarged our Dominions by one Foot of Land: Our Trade, which made us considerable in the World, is either given up by Treaties, or clogged with Duties, which interrupt and daily lessen it: We see the whole Nation groaning under excessive Taxes of all sorts, to raise three Millions of Money for payment of the Interest of those Debts we have contracted. Let us look upon the reverse of the Medal, we shall see our Neighbours, who in their utmost Distress, called for our Assistance, become, by this Treaty, even in time of Peace, Masters of a more considerable Country than their own;[26] in a condition to strike Terror into Us, with fifty thousand *Veterans* ready to invade us, from that Country which we have conquered for them; and to commit insolent Hostilities upon us, in all other Parts, as they have lately done in the *East-Indies*.[27]

25 *Crown . . . General*: alluding to Marlborough, who had wished to be made general for life, a request which the Tories manipulated into a wish to be King; cf. *Conduct*, p. 87 and note.

26 *Masters . . . their own*: The Spanish low countries.

27 *Neighbours . . . East-Indies*: alluding first to recent conflicts between English merchants and the Dutch in the East Indies. On 19 April 1711, St John suggested that Lord Raby in the planning for a peace conference make the most of this: 'It may not improperly be let fall, that we have great grounds to complain of the conduct of the subjects of Holland, both on the coast of Africa, and in the East-Indies; and that there is no small difficulty in keeping our merchants from making very loud remonstrances upon these heads'; and he repeated the charge a month later, 'The Dutch encroach daily upon us . . . in the East-Indies.' (Bolingbroke, *Letters*, vol. I, pp. 156–7, 193). But though the diplomatic issue was clearly Swift's immediate meaning, his readers would also know of a long history of such conflicts, starting with the notorious massacre in 1623 of English settlers by the Dutch in Amboyna, an event revived over and over as an archetype of Dutch villainy in the spate of anti-Dutch writings in England erupting in 1712–13. Thus Robert Ferguson's *Account of the Obligations the States of Holland have to Great-Britain* (1711), builds on the Amboyna incident to indict the Dutch for a whole series of attacks on English ships and settlements throughout the East Indies in the first half of the seventeenth century (pp. 36–40). For other examples of the current exploitation of this anti-Dutch theme, see Bevil Higgons, *A Poem on the Peace* (1713), p. 12; see also *The History of the Dutch Usurpations* (1712); *Dutch Alliances* (1712); *The Dutch Won't Let us Have Dunkirk* (1712); Defoe's *Memoirs of Count Tariff* (1713); and the *Examiner* of 13 July 1713.

The *Barrier-Treaty* between Her Majesty and the *States-General.*

Her Majesty, the Queen of Great Britain, *and the Lords the States-General of the United Provinces, having considered how much it concerns the Quiet and the Security of their Kingdoms and States, and the publick Tranquility, to maintain and to secure on one side the Succession to the Crown of* Great Britain, *in such manner as it is now established by the Laws of the Kingdom; and on the other side, That the said States-General of the* United Provinces *should have a strong and sufficient Barrier against* France, *and others, who would surprise or attack them: And Her Majesty and the said States-General apprehending, with just reason, the Troubles and the Mischiefs which may happen, in relation to this Succession, if at any time there should be any Person or any Power who should call it in Question; and, That the Countries and States of the said Lords the States-General, were not furnished with such a Barrier. For these said Reasons, Her said Majesty the Queen of* Great Britain, *tho' in the vigour of Her Age, and enjoying perfect Health, (which may God preserve Her in many Years) out of an effect of Her usual Prudence and Piety, has thought fit to enter, with the Lords the States-General of the* United Provinces, *into a particular Alliance and Confederacy, the principal End and only Aim of which, shall be the publick Quiet and Tranquility; and to prevent, by Measures taken in time, all the Events which might one day excite new Wars. It is with this View that Her* British *Majesty has given Her full Power to agree upon some Articles of a Treaty, in addition to the Treaties and Alliances that She has already with the Lords the States-General of the* United Provinces, *to Her Ambassador Extraordinary and Plenipotentiary,* Charles *Viscount* Townshend, *Baron of* Lyn-Regis, *Privy-Councellor of Her* British *Majesty, Captain of Her said Majesty's Yeomen of the Guard, and Her Lieutenant in the County of* Norfolk: *And the Lords the States-General of the* United Provinces, *the* Sieurs John de Welderen, *Lord of* Valburgh, *Great Bayliff of the* Lower Betuwe, *of the Body of the Nobility of the Province of* Guelder; Frederick *Baron of* Reede, *Lord of* Lier, St. Anthony *and* T'er Lee, *of the Order of the Nobility of the Province of* Holland *and*

West Frizeland; Anthony Heinsius, *Counsellor Pensionary of the Province of* Holland *and* West-Frizeland, *Keeper of the Great Seal, and Super-Intendant of the Fiefs of the same Province;* Cornelius Van Gheel, *Lord of* Spanbroek Bulkesteyn, *&c.* Gedeon Hoeuft, *Canon of the Chapter of the Church of St.* Peter *at* Utrecht, *and elected Counsellor in the States of the Province of* Utrecht; Hessel van Sminia, *Secretary of the Chamber of Accounts of the Province of* Frizeland; Ernest Ittersum, *Lord of* Osterhof, *of the Body of the Nobility of the Province of* Overyssel; *and* Wicher Wichers, *Senator of the City of* Groningen; *all Deputies to the Assembly of the said Lords the States-General on the part, respectively, of the Provinces of* Guelder, Holland, West-Friezeland, Zeeland, Utrecht, Frizeland, Overyssell, *and* Groninguen, *and* Omme-lands, *who, by Vertue of their full Powers, are agreed upon the following Articles.*

Article I.

The Treaties of Peace, Friendship, Alliance and Confederacy between Her *Britannick Majesty* and the *States-General* of the *United Provinces*, shall be approved and confirmed by the present Treaty, and shall remain in their former Force and Vigour, as if they were inserted Word for Word.

II.

The Succession to the Crown of *England* having been Setled by an Act of Parliament passed the Twelfth Year of the Reign of His late Majesty King *William* the Third; the Title of which is, *An Act for the further Limitation of the Crown, and better Securing the Rights and Liberties of the Subject* : And lately, in the Sixth Year of the Reign of Her present Majesty, this Succession having been again Established and Confirmed by another Act made for the *greater Security of Her Majesty's Person and Government, and the Succession to the Crown of* Great Britain, &c. *in the Line of the most Serene House of* Hanover, *and in the Person of the Princess* Sophia, *and of Her Heirs, Successors and Descendants, Male and Female, already Born or to be Born*: And though no Power has any Right to Oppose the Laws made upon this Subject, by the Crown and Parliament of *Great Britain*, if it should happen, nevertheless, that under any Pretence, or by any Cause whatever, any Person, or any Power or State may pretend to dispute the Establishment which the Parliament has made of the aforesaid Succession, in the most Serene House of *Hanover*, to Oppose the said Succession, to Assist or Favour those who may Oppose it, whether directly or indirectly, by open War, or by fomenting Seditions and Conspiracies against Her or Him to whom the Crown of *Great Britain* shall descend, according to the Acts aforesaid; The *States-General* engage and promise to Assist and Maintain, in the said Succession, Her or Him to whom it shall belong, by Vertue of the said Acts of Parliament, to assist them in taking Possession, if they should not be in actual Possession, and to Oppose those who would disturb them in the taking such Possession, or in the actual Possession of the aforesaid Succession.

III.

Her said Majesty and the *States-General*, in Consequence of the Fifth Article of the Alliance concluded between the Emperor, the late King of *Great Britain*, and the *States-General*, the 7th of *September*, 1701, will employ all their Force to recover the rest of the *Spanish Low-Countries*.

IV.

And further, they will endeavour to Conquer as many Towns and Forts as they can, in order to their being a Barrier and Security to the said *States*.

V.

And whereas, according to the Ninth Article of the said Alliance, it is to be agreed, amongst other Matters, how and in what manner the *States* shall be made Safe by means of this Barrier, the Queen of *Great Britain* will use Her Endeavours to procure, that in the Treaty of Peace it may be agreed, that all the *Spanish Low-Countries*, and what else may be found necessary, whether Conquered or Unconquered Places, shall serve as a Barrier to the *States*.

VI.

That to this end their High Mightinesses shall have the Liberty to put and keep Garrison, to change, augment and diminish it as they shall judge proper, in the Places following: Namely, *Newport, Furnes*, with the Fort of *Knocke, Ipres, Menin*, the Town and Cittadel of *Lisle, Tournay* and its Cittadel, *Condé, Valenciennes*; and the Places which shall from hence-forward be Conquered from *France*. *Maubeuge, Charleroy, Namur* and its Cittadel, *Liere, Hale* to Fortifie, the Ports of *Perle, Philippe, Damme*, the Castle of *Gand*, and *Dendermonde*; the Fort of St. *Donas* being joined to the Fortifications of the Sluice, and being entirely incorporated with it, shall remain and be yielded in Property to the *States*. The Fort of *Rodenhuysen*, on this side *Gand*, shall be Demolished.

VII.

The said *States-General* may, in case of an apparent Attack, or War, put as many Troops as they shall think necessary in all the Towns, Places and Forts in the *Spanish Low-Countries*, where the Reason of War shall require it.

VIII.

They may likewise send into the Towns, Forts and Places, where they shall have their Garrisons, without any Hindrance, and without paying any Duties, Provisions, Ammunitions of War, Arms and Artillery, Materials for the Fortifications, and all that shall be found convenient and necessary for the said Garrisons and Fortifications.

IX.

The said *States-General* shall also have Liberty to Appoint in the Towns, Forts and Places of their Barrier, mentioned in the foregoing Sixth Article, where they may have Garrisons, such Governors and Commanders, Majors and other Officers, as they shall find proper, who shall not be subject to any other Orders, whatsoever they may be, or from whence soever they may come, relating to the Security and Military Government of the said Places, but only to those of their High Mightinesses (exclusively of all others); still preserving the Rights and Privileges, as well Ecclesiastical as Political, of King *Charles* the Third.

X.

That, besides, the said *States* shall have Liberty to Fortifie the said Towns, Places and Forts which belong to them, and Repair the Fortifications of them, in such manner as they shall judge necessary; and further to do whatever shall be useful for their Defence.

XI.

It is agreed, That the *States-General* shall have all the Revenues of the Towns, Places, Jurisdictions, and their Dependencies, which they shall have for their Barrier from *France*, which were not in the Possession of the Crown of *Spain*, at the time of the Death of the late King *Charles* the Second; and besides, a Million of Livres shall be settled for the Payment of One hundred thousand Crowns every three Months, out of the clearest Revenues of the *Spanish Low-Countries*, which the said King was then in Possession of; both which are for maintaining the Garrisons of the *States*, and for supplying the Fortifications, as also the Magazines, and other necessary Expences, in the Towns and Places above-mentioned. And that the said Revenues may be sufficient to support these Expences, Endeavours shall be used for enlarging the Dependencies and Jurisdictions aforesaid, as much as possible; and particularly for including with the Jurisdiction of *Ipres*, that of *Cassel*, and the Forest of *Niepe*; and with the Jurisdiction of *Lisle*, the Jurisdiction of *Douay*, both having been so joined before the present War.

XII.

That no Town, Fort, Place, or Country of the *Spanish Low-Countries*, shall be granted, transferred, or given, or descend to the Crown of *France*, or any one of the Line of *France*, neither by vertue of any Gift, Sale, Exchange, Marriage, Agreement, Inheritance, Succession by Will, or through want of Will, from no Title whatsoever, nor in any other manner whatever, nor be put into the Power or under the Authority of the most Christian King, or any one of the Line of *France*.

XIII.

And whereas the said *States-General*, in Consequence of the Ninth Article of the said Alliance, are to make a Convention or Treaty with King *Charles* the Third, for putting the *States* in a Condition of Safety, by means of the said Barrier, the Queen of *Great Britain* will do what depends upon Her, that all the foregoing Particulars, relating to the Barrier of the *States*, may be inserted in the aforesaid Treaty or Convention; and that Her said Majesty will continue Her good Offices, 'till the above-mentioned Convention, between the *States* and the said King *Charles* the Third, be concluded, agreeably to what is before-mentioned; and that Her Majesty will be Guarantee of the said Treaty or Convention.

XIV.

And that the said *States* may enjoy from henceforward, as much as possible, a Barrier for the *Spanish Low-Countries*, they shall be permitted to put their Garrisons in the Towns already taken, and which may hereafter be so, before the Peace be concluded and ratified. And in the mean time the said King *Charles* the Third shall not be allowed to enter into Possession of the said *Spanish Low-Countries*, neither entirely nor in part; and during that time the Queen shall assist their High Mightinesses to maintain them in the Enjoyment of the Revenues, and to find the Million of Livres a Year above-mentioned.

XV.

And whereas their High Mightinesses have Stipulated by the Treaty of *Munster*, in the Fourteenth Article, That the River *Schelde*, as also the Canals of *Sas*, *Swyn*, and other Mouths of the Sea bordering thereupon, should be kept shut on the Side of the *States*:

And in the Fifteenth Article, That the Ships and Commodities going in and coming out of the Harbours of *Flanders*, shall be and remain charged with all such Imposts and other Duties, as are raised upon Commodities going and coming along the *Schelde*, and the other Canals above-mentioned:

The Queen of *Great Britain* promises and engages, That their High Mightinesses shall never be disturbed in their Right and Possession, in that respect, neither directly nor indirectly; as also that the Commerce shall not, in prejudice of the said Treaty, be made more easy by the Sea-Ports, than by the Rivers, Canals and Mouths of the Sea, on the side of the States of the *United Provinces*, neither directly nor indirectly.

And whereas by the 16th and 17th Articles of the same Treaty of *Munster*, his Majesty the King of *Spain*, is obliged to treat the Subjects of their High Mightinesses as favourably as the Subjects of *Great Britain* and the *Hans Towns*,[28] who were then the People the most favourably treated; Her

---

28 *Hans Towns*: the towns of the Hanseatic League.

Britanick Majesty and their High Mightinesses promise likewise, to take care that the Subjects of *Great Britain*, and of their High Mightinesses, shall be treated in the *Spanish Low-Countries*, as well as in all *Spain*, the Kingdoms and States belonging to it, equally, and as well the one as the other, as favourably as the People the most favoured.

XVI.

The said Queen and States-General oblige themselves to furnish, by Sea and Land, the Succours and Assistance necessary to maintain, by force, Her said Majesty in the quiet possession of Her Kingdoms; and the most Serene House of *Hanover* in the said Succession, in the manner it is settled by the Acts of Parliament before-mentioned; and to maintain the said States-General in the possession of the said Barrier.

XVII.

After the Ratifications of this Treaty, a particular Convention shall be made of the Conditions by which the said Queen, and the said Lords, the States-General, will engage themselves to furnish the Succours which shall be thought necessary, as well by Sea as by Land.

XVIII.

If Her *British* Majesty, or the States-General of the *United Provinces*, be attacked by any Body whatsoever, by reason of this Convention, they shall mutually assist one another with all their Forces, and become Guarantees of the Execution of the said Convention.

XIX.

There shall be invited and admitted into the present Treaty, as soon as possible, all the Kings, Princes and States, who shall be willing to enter into the same, particularly his Imperial Majesty, the Kings of *Spain* and *Prussia*, and the Elector of *Hanover*. And Her *British* Majesty, and the States-General of the *United Provinces*, and each of them in particular, shall be permitted to require and invite those whom they shall think fit to require and invite, to enter into this Treaty, and to be Guarantees of its Execution.

XX.

And as Time has shewn the Omission which was made in the Treaty signed at *Ryswick* in the Year 1697, between *England* and *France*, in respect of the Right of the Succession of *England*, in the Person of Her Majesty the Queen of *Great Britain* now reigning; and that for want of having settled in that Treaty this indisputable Right of Her Majesty, *France* refused to acknowledge Her for Queen of *Great Britain*, after the Death of the late King *William* the Third, of glorious Memory: Her Majesty, the Queen of *Great Britain*, and the Lords, the States-General of the *United Provinces*, do agree and engage themselves likewise, not to enter into any Negociation or Treaty of Peace with *France*, before the Title of Her Majesty to the Crown of *Great Britain*, as also the Right of Succession of the most Serene House of *Hanover*, to the aforesaid Crown, in the manner it is settled and established by the before-mentioned Acts of Parliament, be fully acknowledged, as a Preliminary by *France*, and that *France* has promised at the same time to remove out of its Dominions the Person who pretends to be King of *Great Britain*; and that no Negociation nor formal discussion of the Articles of the said Treaty of Peace shall be entered into, but jointly and at the same time with the said Queen, or with Her Ministers.

XXI.

Her *British* Majesty, and the Lords the *States-General* of the *United Provinces,* shall ratify and confirm all that is contained in the present Treaty, within the space of four Weeks, to be reckoned from the Day of the Signing. In Testimony whereof, the underwritten Ambassador Extraordinary and Plenipotentiary of Her *British* Majesty, and the Deputies of the Lords the *States-General* have signed this present Treaty, and have affixed their Seals thereunto.

At the Hague, *the* 29*th of* October, *in the Year* 1709.

(L. S.)[29] *Townshend.*   (L. S.) *J. V. Welderen.*
　　　　　　　　　　　(L. S.) *J. B. Van Reede.*
　　　　　　　　　　　(L. S.) *A. Heinsius.*
　　　　　　　　　　　(L. S.) *G. Hoeuft.*

29 *L. S.*: *locus sigilli*, the place of the seal.

(L. S.) *H. Sminia.*
(L. S.) *E. V. Ittersum.*
(L. S.) *W. Wichers.*

The Separate Article.

As in the Preliminary Articles Signed here at the *Hague* the 28th of *May*,
1709, by the Plenipotentiaries of his Imperial Majesty, of Her Majesty
the Queen of *Great Britain*, and of the Lords the States-General of the
United Provinces, it is Stipulated, amongst other Things, that the Lords the
States-General shall have, with entire Property and Sovereignty, the Upper
Quarter of *Guelder*, according to the Fifty-second Article of the Treaty of
Munster of the Year 1648; as also that the Garrisons which are or hereafter
shall be on the Part of the Lords the States-General in the Town of *Huy*,
the Cittadel of *Liege*, and in the Town of *Bonne*, shall remain there, 'till it
shall be otherwise agreed upon with his Imperial Majesty and the Empire.
And as the Barrier which is this Day agreed upon in the principal Treaty,
for the mutual Guaranty between Her *British* Majesty and the Lords the
States-General, cannot give to the *United Provinces* the Safety for which
it is Established, unless it be well secured from one end to the other, and
that the Communication of it be well joined together; for which the Upper
Quarter of *Guelder*, and the Garrisons in the Cittadel of *Liege, Huy* and
Bonne are absolutely necessary: Experience having thrice shewn, that *France*
having a design to attack the *United Provinces*, has made use of the Places
above-mentioned in order to come at them, and to penetrate into the said
Provinces. That further, in respect to the Equivalent for which the Upper
Quarter of *Guelder* is to be yielded to the *United Provinces*, according to
the Fifty-second Article of the Treaty of *Munster* above-mentioned, His
Majesty King *Charles* the Third will be much more gratified and advantaged
in other Places, than that Equivalent can avail. So that to the end the Lords
the States-General may have the Upper Quarter of *Guelder*, with entire
Property and Sovereignty, and that the said Upper Quarter of *Guelder*
may be yielded in this manner to the said Lords the States-General, in
the Convention, or the Treaty that they are to make with His Majesty
King *Charles* the Third, according to the Thirteenth Article of the Treaty
concluded this Day; as also that their Garrisons in the Cittadel of *Liege*, in

that of *Huy* and in *Bonne*, may remain there, until it be otherwise agreed upon with his Imperial Majesty and the Empire, Her Majesty, the Queen of *Great Britain*, engages Herself and promises by this separate Article, which shall have the same Force as if it was inserted in the principal Treaty, to make the same Efforts for all this as She has engaged Herself to make, for their obtaining the Barrier in the *Spanish Low-Countries.* In Testimony whereof the Underwritten Ambassador-Extraordinary and Plenipotentiary of Her *British* Majesty, and Deputies of the Lords the States-General, have Signed the present Separate Article, and have affixed their Seals thereunto. *At the* Hague, *the* 29*th of* October, 1709.

(L. S.) *Townshend.*   (L. S.) *J. V. Welderen.*
                 (L. S.) *J. B. van Reede.*
                 (L. S.) *A. Heinsius.*
                 (L. S.) *G. Hoeuft.*
                 (L. S.) *H. Sminia.*
                 (L. S.) *E. V. Ittersum.*
                 (L. S.) *W. Wichers.*

The Second Separate Article.

As the Lords the States-General have represented, That in *Flanders*, the Limits between *Spanish Flanders*, and that of the *States*, are settled in such a manner, as that the Land belonging to the *States* is extreamly narrow there; so that in some Places the Territory of *Spanish Flanders* extends it self to the Fortifications, and under the Cannon of the Places, Towns, and Forts of the *States*, which occasions many Inconveniencies, as has been seen by an Example a little before the beginning of the present War, when a Fort was designed to have been built under the Cannon of the *Sas van Gand*, under pretence, that it was upon the Territory of *Spain*. And as it is necessary for avoiding these and other sorts of Inconveniencies, that the Land of the *States*, upon the Confines of *Flanders* should be enlarged, and that the Places, Towns and Forts should, by that means, be better covered; Her *British* Majesty entring into the just Motives of the said Lords the States-General in this respect, promises and engages Herself by this *Separate Article*, That in the Convention that the said Lords, the States-General, are to make with His Majesty, King *Charles* the Third, She will so assist them, as that it may be agreed, That by the Cession to the said Lords, the States-General, of the Property of an Extent of Land necessary to obviate such like and other Inconveniencies, their Limits in *Flanders* shall be enlarged more conveniently for their Security, and those of the *Spanish Flanders* removed farther from their Towns, Places and Forts, to the End that these may not be so exposed any more. In Testimony whereof, the underwritten Ambassador Extraordinary and Plenipotentiary of Her *British* Majesty, and Deputies of the Lords the States-General, have Signed the present *Separate Article*, and have affixed their Seals thereunto. *At the* Hague, *the* 29*th of October*, 1709.

(L. S.) *Townshend.*   (L. S.) *J. B. van Reede.*
(L. S.) *A. Heinsius.*
(L. S.) *G. Hoeuft.*
(L. S.) *H. Sminia.*
(L. S.) *E. V. Ittersum.*

The Articles *of the* Counter-Project, *which were struck out or altered by the* Dutch, *in the* Barrier-Treaty: *With some* Remarks.

Article VI.

To this End, their High Mightinesses shall have Power to put and keep Garrisons in the following Places, *viz. Newport, Knock, Menin*, the Cittadel of *Lisle, Tournay, Conde, Valenciennes, Namur* and its Cittadel, *Liere, Hale* to *fortifie*, the Fort of *Perle, Damme*, and the Castle of *Gand.*

REMARKS.

In the Barrier-Treaty, *the* States *added the following Places to those mentioned in this Article,* viz. Furnes, Ipres, *Town of* Lisle, Maubeuge, Charleroy, Philippe, *Fort of* St. Donas *(which is to be in Property to the* States*) and the Fort of* Rodenhuysen, *to be Demolished. To say nothing of the other Places,* Dendermond *is the Key of all* Brabant; *and the Demolishing of the Fort of* Rodenhuysen, *situate between* Gand *and* Sas van Gand, *can only serve to Defraud the King of* Spain *of the Duties upon Goods Imported and Exported there.*

Article VII.

The said *States* may put into the said Towns, Forts and Places, and in case of open War with *France*, into all the other Towns, Places and Forts, whatever Troops the Reasons of War shall require.

    Remarks. *But in the* Barrier-Treaty *it is said*, in case of an apparent Tack or War, *without specifying against* France: *Neither is the Number of Troops limited to what the Reason of War shall require, but what the* States *shall think necessary.*

    Article IX. *Besides some smaller Differences, ends with a* Salvo, *not only for the Ecclesiastical and Civil Rights of the King of* Spain, *but likewise for his Revenues in the said Towns; which* Revenues, *in the* Barrier-Treaty, *are all given to the* States.

Article XI.

The Revenues of the Chattellanies and Dependencies of the Towns and Places, which the *States* shall have for their Barrier against *France*, and which were not in possession of the Crown of *Spain*, at the late King of *Spain*'s Death, shall be settled to be a Fund for maintaining Garrisons, and providing for the Fortifications and Magazines, and other necessary Charges of the said Towns of the Barrier.

    Remarks. *I desire the Reader to compare this with the Eleventh Article of the* Barrier-Treaty, *where he will see how prodigiously it is enlarged.*

Article XIV.

All this is to be without Prejudice to such other Treaties and Conventions as the Queen of *Great Britain*, and their High Mightinesses, may think fit to make for the future with the said King *Charles* the Third, relating to the said *Spanish Netherlands*, or to the said *Barrier*.

Article XV.

And to the End that the said *States* may enjoy, at present, as much as it is possible, a *Barrier* in the *Spanish Netherlands*, they shall be permitted to put their Garrisons in the chief Towns already taken, or that may be taken, before a Peace be made.

Remarks. *These Two Articles are not in the* Barrier-Treaty, *but Two others in their stead; to which I refer the Reader. And indeed it was highly necessary for the* Dutch *to strike out the former of these Articles, when so great a part of the Treaty is so highly and manifestly prejudicial to* Great Britain, *as well as to the King of* Spain; *especially the Two Articles inserted in the place of these, which I desire the Reader will Examine.*

Article XX.

And whereas by the 5th and 9th Articles of the Alliance between the Emperor, the late King of *Great Britain*, and the States-General, concluded the 7th of *September* 1701, it is agreed and stipulated, That the Kingdoms of *Naples* and *Sicily*, with all the Dependencies of the Crown of *Spain* in *Italy*, shall be recovered from the Possession of *France*, as being of the last Consequence to the Trade of both Nations, as well as the *Spanish Netherlands*, for a Barrier for the *States-General*; therefore the said Queen of *Great Britain*, and the *States-General*, agree and oblige themselves, not to enter into any Negociation or Treaty of Peace with *France*, before the Restitution of the said Kingdoms of *Naples* and *Sicily*, with all the Dependencies of the Crown of *Spain* in *Italy*, as well as the *Spanish Low-Countries*, with the other Towns and Places in the Possession of *France*, above-mentioned in this Treaty; and also after the manner specified in this Treaty; as likewise all the rest of the entire Monarchy of *Spain*, be yielded by *France* as a Preliminary.

Article XXII.

And whereas Experience hath shewn of what Importance it is to *Great Britain* and the *United Provinces*, that the Fortress and Port of *Dunkirk* should not be in the Possession of *France*, in the Condition they are at present; the Subjects of both Nations having undergone such great Losses, and suffered so much in their Trade, by the Prizes taken from them by Privateers set out in that Port; insomuch that *France*, by her unmeasurable Ambition, may be always tempted to make some Enterprizes upon the Territories of the Queen of *Great Britain* and their High Mightinesses, and interrupt the Publick Repose and Tranquility; for the Preservation of which, and the Balance of *Europe* against the exorbitant Power of *France*, the Allies engaged themselves in this long and burthensome War; therefore the said Queen of *Great Britain*, and their High Mightinesses agree and oblige themselves, not to enter into any Negotiation or Treaty of Peace with *France*, before it shall be yielded and stipulated by *France* as a Preliminary, that all the Fortifications of the said Town of *Dunkirk*, and the Forts that depend upon it, be entirely demolished and razed, and that the Port be entirely ruined, and rendred impracticable.

    Remarks. *These two Articles are likewise omitted in the* Barrier-Treaty; *whereof the first regards particularly the Interests of the House of* Austria; *and the other about Demolishing of* Dunkirk, *those of* Great Britain. *It is something strange, that the late Ministry, whose Advocates raise such a Clamour about the Necessity of Recovering* Spain *from the House of* Bourbon, *should suffer the* Dutch *to strike out this Article; which, I think, clearly shows, the Reason why the* States *never troubled themselves with the Thoughts of Reducing* Spain, *or even Recovering* Milan, Naples, *and* Sicily, *to the Emperor; but were wholly fix'd upon the Conquest of* Flanders, *because they had determined those Provinces as a Property for themselves.*

    As for the Article about Demolishing of Dunkirk, *I am not at all surprized to find it struck out; the Destruction of that Place, though it would be useful to the* States, *doth more nearly import* Britain, *and was therefore a Point that such Ministers could more easily get over.*

> *The Sentiments of Prince* Eugene *of* Savoy, *and of the Count* de Sinzendorf, *relating to the* Barrier *of the* States-General, *to the Upper-Quarter of* Guelder, *and to the Towns of the Electorate of* Cologn, *and of the Bishoprick of* Liege.

Altho' the Orders and Instructions of the Courts of *Vienna* and *Barcelona*, upon the Matters above-mentioned, do not go so far, as to give Directions for what follows; notwithstanding, the Prince and Count above-mentioned, considering the present State of Affairs, are of the following Opinion:

First, That the Counter-Project of *England*, relating to the Places where the States-General may put and keep Garrisons, ought to be followed, except *Lier, Halle to fortify*, and the Castle of *Gand*: Provided likewise, that the Sentiments of *England* be particularly conformed to, relating to *Dendermond* and *Ostend*, as Places in no wise belonging to the Barrier; and which, as well as the Castle of *Gand*, can only serve to make the States-General Masters of the *Low-Countries*, and hinder Trade with *England*. And as to *Lier* and *Halle*, those who are acquainted with the Country, know, that these Towns cannot give any Security to the States-General, but can only make People believe that these Places being fortified, would rather serve to block up *Brussels*, and the other great Cities of *Brabant*.

Secondly, As to what is said in the Seventh Article of the *Counter-Project* of *England*, relating to the Augmentation of Garrisons, in the Towns of the Barrier, in case of an open War; this is agreeable to the Opinions of the said Prince and Count; who think likewise, that there ought to be added to the Eighth Article, That no Goods or Merchandise should be sent into the Towns where the States-General shall have Garrisons, nor be comprehended under the Names of *such Things, as the said Garrisons and Fortifications shall have need of*: And that to this End, the said Things shall be inspected in those Places where they are to pass; as likewise, the Quantity shall be settled that the Garrisons may want.

Thirdly, As to the Ninth Article, relating to the Governours and Commanders of those Towns, Forts and Places, where the States-General shall have their Garrisons, the said *Prince* and *Count* are of Opinion, That the said Governours and Commanders ought to take an Oath, as well to the King of *Spain*, as to the States-General: But they may take a particular Oath to the Latter, That they will not admit Foreign Troops without their Consent, and that they will depend exclusively upon the said States, in whatever regards the Military Power. But at the same time they ought exclusively to promise the King of *Spain*, That they will not intermeddle in the Affairs of Law, Civil Power, Revenues, or any other Matters, Ecclesiastical or Civil, unless at the desire of the King's Officers, to assist them in the Execution: In which case the said Commanders should be obliged not to refuse them.

Fourthly, As to the Tenth Article, there is nothing to be added, unless that the States-General, may repair and encrease the Fortifications of the Towns, Places and Forts, where they shall have their Garrisons; but this at their own Expence. Otherwise, under that Pretext, they might seize all the Revenues of the Country.

Fifthly, As to the Eleventh Article, they think the States ought not to have the Revenues of the Chattellanies and Dependencies of these Towns and Places which are to be their Barrier against *France*; this being a sort of Sovereignty, and very prejudicial to the Ecclesiastical and Civil Oeconomy of the Country. But the said Prince and Count are of Opinion, That the States-General ought to have, for the Maintenance of their Garrisons and Fortifications, a Sum of Money of a Million and half, or two Millions of Florins, which they ought to receive from the King's Officers, who shall be ordered to pay that Sum, before any other Payment.

Sixthly, And the Convention which shall be made, on this Affair, between his Catholick Majesty and the States-General, shall be for a limited Time.

These are the utmost Conditions to which the said Prince and Count think it possible for his Catholick Majesty to be brought; and they declare at the same time, that their Imperial and Catholick Majesties will sooner abandon the *Low-Countries*, than take them upon other Conditions, which would be equally Expensive, Shameful, and Unacceptable to them.

On the other side, the said Prince and Count are persuaded, That the Advantages at this time yielded to the States-General, may hereafter be very prejudicial to themselves, forasmuch as they may put the People of the *Spanish Netherlands* to some dangerous Extremity, considering the Antipathy between the Two Nations; and that extending of Frontiers, is entirely contrary to the Maxims of their Government.

As to the Upper-Quarter of *Guelder*, the said Prince and Count are of Opinion, That the States-General may be allowed the Power of putting in Garrisons into *Venlo, Ruremond*, and *Stessenswaert*, with Orders to furnish the said *States*, with the Revenues of the Country, which amount to One hundred thousand Florins.

As to *Bonn*, belonging to the Electorate of *Cologn*; and *Liege* and *Huy*, to the Bishoprick of *Liege*; it is to be understood that these being Imperial Towns, it doth not depend upon the Emperor to consent, that Foreign Garrisons should be placed in them, upon any Pretence whatsoever. But whereas the States-General demand them only for their Security, it is proposed, to place in those Towns a Garrison of Imperial Troops, of whom the *States* may be in no suspicion, as they might be of a Garrison of an Elector, who might possibly have Views opposite to their Interests: But this is propos'd only in case that it shall not be thought more proper to raze one or other of the said Towns.

The Representation *of the* English *Merchants at* Bruges, *relating
to the* Barrier-Treaty.

David White, *and other Merchants, Her Majesty's Subjects residing at
Bruges, and other Towns in Flanders, crave Leave humbly to represent,*
That whereas the Cities of *Lisle, Tournay, Menin, Douay*, and other new
Conquests in *Flanders* and *Artois*, taken from the *French* this War, by the
united Forces of Her Majesty and Her Allies, are now become entirely
under the Government of the States-General; and that we Her Majesty's
Subjects may be made liable to such Duties and Impositions on Trade, as
the said States-General shall think fit to Impose on us: We humbly hope
and conceive, That it is Her Majesty's Intention and Design that the Trade
of Her Dominions and Subjects, which is carried on with these new Conquests, may be on an equal Foot with that of the Subjects and Dominions
of the States-General, and not be liable to any new Duty, when transported
from the *Spanish Netherlands*, to the said new Conquests, as to our great
Surprize is exacted from us on the following Goods, *viz.* Butter, Tallow,
Salmon, Hides, Beef, and all other Product of Her Majesty's Dominions,
which we import at *Ostend*, and there pay the Duty of Entry to the King of
Spain, and consequently ought not to be liable to any new Duty, when they
carry the same Goods, and all others from their Dominions, by a Free Pass
or *Transire*, to the said new Conquests: And we are under apprehension
that if the said new Conquests be settled or given entirely into the Possession of the States-General for their Barrier, (as we are made believe by a
Treaty lately made by Her Majesty's Ambassador, the Lord Viscount *Townshend*, at the *Hague*) that the said States-General may also soon declare all
Goods and Merchandises which are Contraband in their Provinces, to be
also Contraband or Prohibited in these new Conquests, or new Barrier, by
which Her Majesty's Subjects will be deprived of the Sale and Consumption of the following Products of Her Majesty's Dominions, which are,
and have long been, declared Contraband in the *United Provinces*, such as
English and *Scotch* Salt, Malt Spirits or Corn Brandy, and all other Sorts of
Distilled *English* Spirits, Whale and Rape Oil, *&c.* It is therefore humbly
conceived, That Her Majesty, out of Her great Care and gracious Concern
for the Benefit of Her Subjects and Dominions, may be pleased to direct,
by a Treaty of Commerce or some other way, that their Trade may be put
on an equal Foot in all the *Spanish Netherlands*, and the new Conquests or

Barrier, with the Subjects of *Holland*, by paying no other Duty than that of Importation to the King of *Spain*; and by a Provision, that no Product of Her Majesty's Dominions shall ever be declared Contraband in these new Conquests, except such Goods as were esteemed Contraband before the Death of *Charles* II. King of *Spain*. And it is also humbly prayed, That the Product and Manufacture of the New Conquests may also be Exported without paying any new Duty, besides that of Exportation at *Ostend*, which was always paid to the King of *Spain*; it being impossible for any Nation in *Europe* to Assort an entire Cargo for the *Spanish West-Indies*, without a considerable quantity of several of the Manufactures of *Lisle*, such as Caradoros, Cajant, Picoses, Boratten, and many other Goods, *&c.*

   The chief Things to be demanded of *France* are, To be exempted from Tonnage, to have a Liberty of Importing Herrings and all other Fish to *France*, on the same Terms as the *Dutch* do, and as was agreed by them at the Treaty of Commerce immediately after the Treaty of Peace at *Ryswick*. The enlarging Her Majesty's Plantations in *America*, *&c.* is naturally recommended.

THE NEW WAY OF SELLING PLACES AT COURT

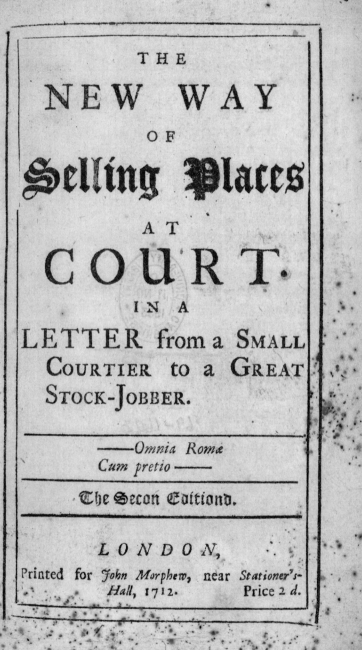

THE
NEW WAY
OF
𝕾𝖊𝖑𝖑𝖎𝖓𝖌 𝕻𝖑𝖆𝖈𝖊𝖘
AT
COURT.
IN A

LETTER from a SMALL COURTIER to a GREAT STOCK-JOBBER.

——*Omnia Romæ*
Cum pretio ——

𝕿𝖍𝖊 𝕾𝖊𝖈𝖔𝖓 𝕰𝖉𝖎𝖙𝖎𝖔𝖓𝖉.

LONDON,
Printed for *John Morphew,* near *Stationer's-*
Hall, 1712.   Price 2 *d.*

Figure 4. Title page: CUL, 7540.d.45 (8).

A
LETTER
FROM A
SMALL COURTIER
TO A
GREAT STOCK-JOBBER

SIR,

In that friendly Dispute which happen'd between us some time ago, wherein you endeavour'd to prove, that the City-Politicks out-did those of the Court, I remember there was nothing upon which you seemed to Pride your self more, than that Mystery of your Brethren in *Exchange-Alley*,[1] which is usually called, *Selling the Bear-Skin*;[2] whereby a very beneficial Trade was daily driven with imaginary Stocks, and many Thousands bought and sold, to great Advantage, by those who were not worth a Groat. This you challeng'd me to match, with all my Knowledge, in the lower Arts of the Court. I confess, you had then the better of the Argument, and I was forc'd to yield; which I would hardly do at present, if the Controversie were to be resumed: I could now make you acknowledge, that what you in the City call *Selling the Bear-Skin*, does not deserve the Name, when compar'd with the Dexterity of one of our Artists. I shall leave the Decision of this Matter to your self, after you have receiv'd the following Story, which I shall most faithfully relate.

There is a certain petty Retainer to the Court, who has no Employment at all himself, but is a Partner for Life to one that has: This Gentleman resides constantly with his Family among us, where being wholly at Leisure,

---

Title page motto] *Omnia Romae / Cum pretio*: Juvenal, *Satires*, iii.183–4: 'all things here / Are sold, and sold unconscionably dear' (John Dryden (trans.), *The satires of Decimus Junius Juvenalis* (1697), p. 59).

1 *Exchange-Alley*: near the Royal Exchange, Cornhill, the Alley was the haunt of brokers, stock-jobbers, gamblers and the like. Woolley notes ('Canon', p. 116) that the compositor's slip once of spelling it 'Ally' reflects what was actually Swift's preferred spelling.

2 *Selling the Bear-Skin*: the full proverb is 'to sell the bear's skin before one has caught the bear', according to the *OED*, which suggests that the stock-market term 'bear' originated in this saying in the early eighteenth century (*OED*, s. v. 'bear').

he is consequently very Speculative, perpetually turning his Thoughts to improve those happy Talents that Nature hath given him. He hath maturely consider'd with himself the strange Opinions that People at distance have of Courts: Strangers are apt to think, that whoever hath an Apartment in the Royal Palace, can go through the Lodgings, as if he were at Home, and talk familiarly with every one he meets, must needs have at any time a Dozen or two of Employments in his Power. The least Word from him to a Great Man, or, upon extraordinary Occasions, to the Q——n Her self, would certainly do the Business. This Ignorance hath often been made very good use of by dextrous Men among us. Old Courtiers will tell you Twenty Stories of *Harry Killigrew, Fleet. Shepherd,*[3] and others, who would often sell Places that were never in Being, and dispose of others a good Pennyworth before they were Vacant. How the Privy-Garden at Whitehall was actually Sold, and an Artist sent to Measure it. How one Man was made Curtain-lifter to the King, and another His Majesty's Gold-finder.[4] So that our Predecessors must be allowed their due Honour. Neither do I at all pretend, that the Hero I am now celebrating, was the first Inventor of that Art; wherein it must however be granted, that he hath made most wonderful Improvements.

This Gentleman, whom I take leave to call by the Name of *Guzman,*[5] in Imitation of a Famous *Spanish* Deceiver of that Name, having been formerly turned out of one or two Employments, for no other Crime than that of endeavouring to raise their Value, has ever since employed his Credit and Power for the Service of others; and where he could not secure them in reality, has been content to feed their Imaginations, which to a great part of Mankind is full as well. 'Tis true, he hath done all this with a prudent Regard to his own Interest; yet whoever has Traffick'd with him, cannot but own, that he sells at reasonable Rates; and is so Modest withal, that he is content the Credit of taking your Money should rest on the greatest

3 *Harry Killigrew, Fleet. Shepherd*: Henry Killigrew was groom of the bedchamber in the court of Charles II, and his friend Sir Fleetwood Sheppard (1634–98) was a celebrated figure and minor poet at the same court; Sheppard was also involved in the sale of offices at court as agent for the Earl of Dorset. See *ODNB* article on Sheppard by Frank Ellis for comment on both courtiers.

4 *Gold-finder*: scavenger (*OED*).

5 *Guzman*: from Mateo Aleman's *The Rogue: Or, the Life of Guzman de Alfarache* (Oxford, 1630), a work Swift owned (see Woolley, 'Canon', p. 115 n.). Swift uses the name for the real-life figure who tried to sell the Vice-Chamberlain's place, one Israel Fielding; see Introduction, pp. 16–17.

Men in *England*, rather than himself. He begg'd a small Employment for one of his Customers, from a Lord of the Admiralty, then told his Client, that the Great Man must have a Hundred Guineas presented him in a handsome manner. Our Place-Jobber brought an old lame Horse of his own, said the Admiral ask'd an Hundred Guineas for it, the other bought the Horse, without offering to cheapen him, or look in his Mouth.

Two or three such Atchievements as these, gave our Adventurer the Courage for some time past to deal by the Great, and to take all Employments at Court into his own Hands. And though he and his Family are firm Adherents to the honest Party,[6] and furious against the present Ministry (as I speak it to our Honour no small Number of us are) yet in the disposal of Places he was very Impartial, and gave every one their Choice. He had a standing Agent, to whom all People applied themselves that wanted any Employment, who had them ready of all Sizes, to fit whatever Customer came, from Twenty to a Thousand Pounds a Year.

If the Question be ask'd, Why he takes no Employment himself? he readily Answers, That he might, whenever he pleased, be in the Commission of the Customs, the Excise, or of Trade, but does not think it worth his while; because, without stirring from Court, or giving himself any Trouble, he can by his Credit oblige honest Gentlemen with Employments, and at the same time make better Advantage to himself. He hath several ways to establish a Reputation of his Interest at Court; sometimes, as I have already observed, he hath actually begg'd small Offices, and disposed of them to his Clients. Besides, by living in Her Majesty's Palace, and being Industrious at picking out Secrets, he often finds where Preferment is likely to go, even before those who are to be preferred can have any Notice of it themselves; then he immediately searches out for them, tells them of their Merits, asks them how they would like of such an Employment, and promises, by his Power at Court, to get it for them; but withal gives them a hint, that Great Men will take Money, though they will not be known to do it; that it therefore must be done by a second Hand, for which he profers his Service, tells them what Sum will be convenient, and then sinks it in his own Pocket; besides what is given to him, in Gratitude for his Sollicitations and good Will: This gives him Credit to pursue his Trade of Place-Jobbing. Whoever hath a mind for an Employment at Court, or any

---

6 *the honest Party*: alluding ironically to the Whigs.

where else, goes to *Guzman's* Agent, and he reads over to the Candidate a List of Places, with their Profit and Salaries. When one is fix'd upon, the Agent names the known Don *Guzman*, as a Person to be depended upon; tells the Client he must send his Honour a Hamper of Wine, if the Place they are in Treaty for be considerable, a Hogshead: At next Meeting the Price is agreed on, but unfortunately this Employment is half promised to another: However he believes that that Difficulty may be removed for Twenty or Thirty Guineas, which being but a Trifle, is immediately given. After two or three Meetings more, perhaps, the Bubble[7] hath Access to the Don himself, who assumes great Airs, says the thing shall be done, he hath already spoke to the Q——n or Lord T————.[8] At parting the Agent tells the Officer Elect, there is immediate Occasion for Forty or Fifty Guineas to be given among Clerks, or Servants of some Great Minister. Thus the poor Place-Hunter is drill'd on, from one Month to another, perpetually squeezed of ready Money, and nothing done. This Trade Don *Guzman* hath carried on for many Years, and frequently with five or six Cullies[9] in hand at a time, and perhaps all of them for one Place. I know it will be the Wonder of many People, as it hath been mine, how such Impostures as these, could be so frequently repeated, and how so many disappointed People could be kept from making a Noise and Clamour, that may ruin the Trade and Credit of this bold Projecter; but it is with him as with Almanack-makers, who gain more Reputation by one right Guess, than they lose by a Thousand wrong ones. Besides I have already observed, that once or twice in his Life, he did actually provide for one or two Persons; further, it was his constant Rule, whatever Employment was given away, to assure his Clients that he had the chief Hand in disposing of it. When a Man had no more to give, or was weary of attending, the Excuse was, either that he had some private Enemies, or the Q——n was engaged for that Turn, or that he must think of something else: And then it was a new Business, required new Fees, and new Hampers of Wine; or, lastly, Don *Guzman* was not to be seen, or talk'd cold and dry, or in very great haste, and so the Matter dwindled to nothing; the poor Pretender to an Employment discover'd the Cheat too late, was often asham'd to complain, and was only laugh'd at when he did.

---

7 *the Bubble*: dupe, gull (*OED*).   8 *Lord T*————: Lord Treasurer.
9 *Cullies*: those who are cheated or imposed upon (*OED*).

Having thus described some few of the Qualifications which have so much distinguish'd this worthy *Manager*, I shall crown all with informing you in the Particulars of a late Atchievement, that will give him an ever-lasting Renown: About two Months ago, a Gentleman of a good Fortune had a mind to buy some considerable Employment in the Court, and sent a Sollicitor, to Negociate this Affair with Don *Guzman*'s Agent, who, after one or two Meetings, told him the Vice-Chamberlain's Employment was to be disposed of, the Person who now enjoy'd it was wholly out of Favour with the Q——n; that the Choice of his Successor was in Don *Guzman*'s Power; that Seven thousand Pounds was the Price, whereof Four thousand was to be given to a Lady who was Foster-Sister to the Q——n,[10] Two thousand to the present Vice-Chamberlain,[11] in consideration of his being turned out, and the remaining Thousand to be divided between the great Don and the two small Agents: This was the result, after several Meetings, after two or three Hampers of Wine had been sent to Saint *James*'s, and some Guineas given to facilitate the putting off a Bargain, which, as pretended, was begun for the Employment, to another Person. This Matter went so far, that Notes were interchangeably given between the two Agents and their Principal, as well relating to the Thousand Pound which was to be divided among them, as to the main Sum; our Projector was likewise very curious to know, whether the new Vice-Chamberlain could speak *French*, which, he said, was absolutely necessary to his Office; whether he was well-fashion'd, had a genteel Manner, and polite Conversation; and directed, that the Person himself should, upon an appointed Day, be seen walking in the Garden before St. *James*'s House, that the Lady, the Q——n's Foster-Sister, might judge of his Mein, whether he were a sightly Man, and by his Appearance, qualified for so great an Employment. To carry the Imposture further, one *Sunday*, when in the Lord-Chamberlain's Absence,[12] Mr. Vice-Chamberlain lead Her Majesty to Chapel, Don *Guzman* being there with his Cully-Sollicitor, said to him, with an expressive Sneer, and a sort of Rapture, *Ah, Sir, what Happiness! I am ravished to think*

10 *Lady . . . to the Q*——*n*: Margery Fielding, the wife of the model for 'Guzman', Israel Fielding, and a domestic in the household of Queen Anne. See the Introduction, p. 17.
11 *Vice-Chamberlain*: Thomas Coke, MP, one of Swift's friends at Court; he himself apparently told Swift of this incident (Williams, *JSt*, p. 522).
12 *Lord-Chamberlain's Absence*: Charles Talbot, Duke of Shrewsbury.

of it; I wish your Friend was here now, to see the Vice-Chamberlain handing the
Q——n, I would make him give t'other Thousand Pound for his Employment.

These are the Circumstances of this Story, as near as I can remember. How the ingenious Don could have got off clean from this Business, I cannot possibly imagine, but it unfortunately happened, that he was not put to the Trial of shewing his Dexterity, for the Vice-Chamberlain, by what means I could never yet learn, got a little light into the Matter; He was told that some Body had been Treating for his Place, and had Information given him where to find the Sollicitor of the Person who was to succeed him; He immediately sent for the Man, who not conceiving himself to be engaged in a dishonest Action (and therefore conscious of no Guilt) very freely told him all that he knew; and, as he had good Reason, was as angry at the Cheat put upon him, and his Friend, as the Vice-Chamberlain himself; whereupon poor Don *Guzman* and his two Agents, were, at Mr. Vice-Chamberlain's Request, examined before a Principal Secretary of State,[13] and their Examinations taken in Writing. But here I must with Shame confess, that our Hero's Behaviour was much below his Character; he shuffled and dodged, denied and affirmed, contradicted himself every Moment, own'd the Fact, yet insisted on his Honour and Innocency: In short, his whole Demeanour was such, that the rawest Stock-Jobber in *Exchange-Ally* would blush to see it. 'Tis true, he hath since, in some manner, recovered his Reputation; he talks boldly where-ever he comes, as if he were the Party injur'd, and as if he expected Satisfaction; and, what is still more Heroical, goes on in his old Trade of disposing Places, tho' not of such great Consideration.

How the Affair will end, I cannot tell; the Vice-Chamberlain, between Generosity and Contempt, not being hitherto very forward in carrying it to a formal Prosecution; and the rest of the Court contenting themselves, some with laughing, and some in lifting up their Eyes with Admiration.

However, I think the Matter well deserves to be Recorded, both for the Honour of the *Manager*, and to let you and the World know, that great Abilities and Dexterity are not confined to *Exchange-Alley*. I am,

SIR,

Yours, &c.

---

13 *Principal Secretary of State*: William Legge, Earl of Dartmouth.

SOME REASONS TO PROVE . . . IN A LETTER TO A WHIG-LORD

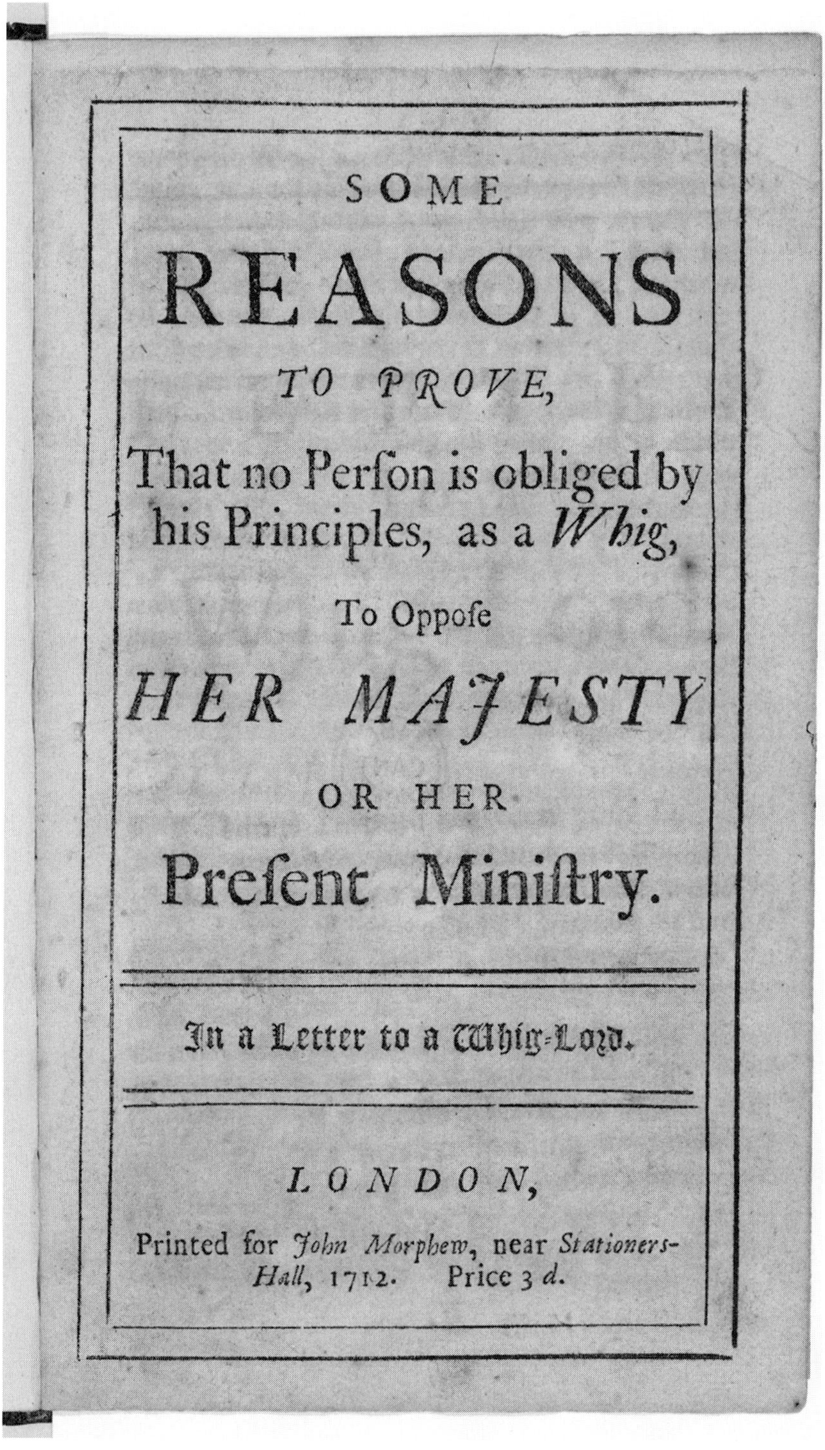

SOME

REASONS

TO PROVE,

That no Person is obliged by
his Principles, as a *Whig,*

To Oppose

HER MAJESTY

OR HER

Prefent Miniſtry.

In a Letter to a Whig-Lord.

LONDON,

Printed for *John Morphew,* near *Stationers-
Hall,* 1712.   Price 3 *d.*

Figure 5. Title page: CUL, Williams 357.

A
LETTER
TO A
WHIG-LORD [1]

MY LORD,

The Dispute between your Lordship and Me, hath, I think, no manner of
Relation to what, in the common Style of these Times, are called *Principles*;
wherein both Parties seem well enough to agree, if we will but allow their
Professions. I can truly affirm, That none of the reasonable sober *Whigs*
I have conversed with, did ever avow any Opinion concerning Religion
or Government, which I was not willing to subscribe; so that, according
to my Judgment, those Terms of Distinction ought to be dropped, and
others introduced in their stead, to denominate Men, as they are inclined
to *Peace* or *War*, to the *Last*, or the *Present Ministry*: For whoever thoroughly
considers the matter, will find these to be the only Differences that divide
the Nation at present. I am apt to think your Lordship would readily allow
this, if you were not aware of the Consiquence I intend to draw: For it is
plain that the making Peace and War, as well as the Choice of Ministers, is
wholly in the Crown; and therefore the Dispute at present lies altogether
between those who would support, and those who would violate the Royal
Prerogative. This Decision may seem perhaps too sudden and severe, but
I do not see how it can be contested. Give me leave to ask your Lordship,
whether you are not resolved to oppose the present Ministry to the utmost?
and whether it was not chiefly with this design, that upon the opening of
the present Session,[2] you gave your Vote against any Peace, till *Spain* and
the *West-Indies* were recovered from the *Bourbon* Family? I am confident
your Lordship then believed, what several of your House and Party have
acknowledged, that the Recovery of *Spain* was grown impracticable by
several Incidents, as well as by our utter Inability to continue the War upon
the former foot. But you reasoned right, that such a Vote, in such a Juncture,

---

1 *Whig-Lord*: on the figures who have been suggested as possible models for this lord, see the
   Introduction.
2 *opening of the present Session*: see *Some Advice* note on pp. 109–10.

was the most probable way of ruining the present Ministry. For as Her M——y would certainly lay much weight upon a Vote of either House, so it was judged that her Ministers would hardly venture to act directly against it; the natural Consequence of which must be, a Dissolution of the Parliament, and a return of all your Friends into a full Possession of Power. This Advantage the Lords have over the Commons, by being a fix'd Body of Men, where a Majority is not to be obtained, but by Time and Mortality, or new Creations, or other Methods, which I will suppose the present Age too virtuous to admit. Several Noble Lords who join'd with you in that Vote, were but little inclined to disoblige the Court, because it suited ill with their Circumstances; but the poor Gentlemen were told it was the safest Part they could act: For it was boldly alledged, that the Qu——n her self was at the bottom of this Affair; and one of your Neighbours,[3] whom the dread of losing a great Employment often puts into Agonies, was growing fast into a very good Courtier, began to cultivate the chief M——r, and often expressed his Approbation of present Proceedings, till that unfortunate Day of Trial came, when the mighty Hopes of a Change revived his Constancy, and encouraged him to adhere to his old Friends. But the Event, as your Lordship saw, was directly contrary to what your great Undertaker had flatter'd you with. The Q——n was so far from approving what you had done, that to shew she was in Earnest, and to remove all future Apprehensions from that Quarter, she took a resolute necessary Step,[4] which is like to make her easy for the rest of her Reign; and which I am confident your Lordship would not have been one of those to have put Her upon, if you had not been most shamefully misinformed. After this your Party had nothing to do, but sit down and murmur at so extraordinary an Exertion of the Prerogative, and quarrel at a Necessity which their own Violence, enflamed by the Treachery of others, had created. Now, my Lord, if an Action so indisputably in Her M——y's Power requires any Excuse, we have a very good one at hand: We alledge, that the Majority you *hardly*

---

3 *one of your Neighbours*: the Duke of Somerset, who was 'louder than any in the house for the clause against Peace' (Williams, *JSt*, p. 433). Cf. Swift's report a few days later of his conversation with Oxford: 'I could not forbear hinting, that he was not sure of the queen; and that those scoundrel, starving lords would never have dared to vote against the Court, if Somerset had not assured them, that it would please the queen. He said, That was true, and Somerset did so' (Williams, *JSt*, p. 436).

4 *resolute necessary Step*: the creation of twelve new peers to give the Tories a majority in the House of Lords.

acquired, with so much Art and Management, partly made up from a *certain transitory Bench*,[5] and partly of those, whose Nobility began with themselves; was wholly formed during the long Power of your Friends, so that it became necessary to turn the Balance, by new Creations; wherein, however, great Care was taken to encrease the Peerage as little as possible, and to make a Choice against which no Objection could be raised, with relation to Birth or Fortune, or other Qualifications requisite for so high an Honour.[6]

There is no Man hath a greater Veneration than I, for that Noble Part of our Legislature, whereof your Lordship is a Member; and I will venture to assert, that, supposing it possible for Corruptions to go far in either Assembly, yours is less liable to them than a House of Commons: A standing Senate of Persons, nobly born of great Patrimonial Estates, and of pious learned Prelates, is not easily perverted from intending the true Interest of their Prince and Country; whereas we have found by Experience, that a corrupt Ministry, at the Head of a monied Faction, is able to procure a Majority of whom they please, to represent the People: But then, my Lord, on the other side, if it hath been so contrived by Time and Management, that the Majority of a standing Senate is made up of those who wilfully, or otherwise, mistake the Publick Good; the Cure, by common Remedies, is as slow as the Disease; whereas a good Prince, in the Hearts of his People, and at the Head of a Ministry who leaves them to their free choice, cannot miss a good Assembly of Commons. Now, my Lord, we do assert, that this Majority of yours hath been the Workmanship of above twenty Years: During which time, considering the Choice of Persons, in the several Creations; considering the many Arts used in making Proselites among the young Nobility, who have since grown up; and the wise Methods to prevent their being tainted by University-Principles: Lastly, considering the Age of those who fill up a certain Bench,[7] and with what Views their Successions have been supply'd; I am surprized to find your Majority so bare and weak, that it is not possible for you to keep it much longer, unless old Men be

---

5 *certain transitory Bench*: the bishops, 'transitory' because not hereditary peers.
6 *Care was taken . . . Honour*: cf. Swift in *History*: 'This Promotion was so ordered, that a Third Part were of those to whom or their Posterity Peerage would naturally devolve; and the rest were such whose Merit, Birth, and Fortune could admitt of no Exception' (Davis, vol. VII, p. 20).
7 *a certain Bench*: i.e., the bishops, predominantly Whigs.

immortal: Neither perhaps would there be any Necessity to wait so long, if *certain Methods*[8] were put in Practice, which your Friends have often tried with Success. Your Lordship plainly sees by the Event, that neither Threats nor Promises are made use of, where it is pretty well agreed, that they would not be ineffectual; Voting against the Court, and indeed against the Kingdom, in the most important Cases, hath not been followed by the Loss of Places or Pensions, unless in very few Particulars, where the Circumstances have been so extreamly aggravating, that to have been passive would have argued the lowest Weakness or Fear: To instance only in the D. of *M.* who against the wholsome Advice of those who consulted his true Interest, much better than his Flatterers, would needs put all upon that desperate Issue, of destroying the present M——ry, or falling himself.[9]

I believe, my Lord, you are now fully convinced, that the Q—— is altogether averse from the Thoughts of ever employing your Party in Her Councils or Her Court. You see a prodigious Majority in the House of Commons of the same Sentiments: And the only Quarrel against the Tr——r, is an Opinion of more Mildness towards your Friends, than it is thought they deserve; neither can you hope for better Success in the next Election, while Her M——y continues her present Servants, although the Bulk of the People were better disposed to you than it is manifest they are. With all the Advantages I lately mentioned, which a H—— of L——ds has over the C————s, it is agreed, That the Pulse of the Nation is much better felt by the latter, than the former, because those represent the whole People: But your Lordships (whatever some may pretend) do represent only your own Persons. Now it has been the old Complaint of your Party, that the Body of Country Gentlemen always leaned too much (since the *Revolution*) to the Tory-side: And as your Numbers were much lessened, about two Years ago, by a very unpopular Quarrel,[10] wherein the Church thought it self deeply concerned; so you daily diminish by your Zeal against

---

8 *certain Methods*: i.e., ministerial threats and promises, which Swift goes on to claim have not been employed by the present ministry.

9 *D. of M. . . . falling himself*: cf. Swift's expanded comments on this theme in *History*, Davis, vol. VII, pp. 27–30.

10 *unpopular Quarrel*: the impeachment and trial of Dr Henry Sacheverell in February–March 1710 after a sermon in November which attacked Godolphin and seemed to impugn the Revolution Settlement. The affair, Swift said later, gave the people a chance to 'discover and exert their Dispositions, very opposite to the Designs of those who were then in Power', and resulted in the summer of 1710 in a 'gradual Change of the Ministry' (*History*, Davis, vol. VII, p. 34).

Peace, which the Landed-Men, half ruined by the War, do so extreamly want, and desire.

'Tis probable, my Lord, that some Persons may, upon occasion, have endeavoured to bring you over to the present Measures: If so, I desire to know whether such Persons required of you to change any Principles relating to Government, either in Church or State, to which you have been educated? Or did you ever hear that such a Thing was offered to any other of your Party? I am sure neither can be affirmed; and then it is plain, that *Principles* are not concerned in the Dispute. The two chief, or indeed the only Topicks of Quarrel, are, whether the Q—— shall chuse Her own Servants? and, whether She shall keep Her Prerogative of making Peace? And I believe there is no Whig in *England* that will openly deny Her Power in either: As to the latter, which is the more avowed, Her M—— has promised that the Treaty shall be laid before Her Parliament; after which, if it be made without their Approbation, and proves to be against the Interest of the Kingdom, the Ministers must answer for it at their extreamest Peril. What is there in all this that can possibly affect your Principles, as a Whig? Or rather, my Lord, are you not, by all sorts of Principles lawful to own, obliged to acquiesce and submit to Her M—— upon this Article? But I suppose, my Lord, you will not make a Difficulty of confessing the true genuine Cause of Animosity to be, that those who are *out of Place* would fain be *in*; and that the Bulk of your Party are the *Dupes* of *half a dozen*, who are impatient at their Loss of Power. 'Tis true, they would fain infuse into your Lordship such strange Opinions of the present Ministry,[11] and their Intentions, as none of themselves at all believe. Has your Lordship observed the least Step made towards giving any suspicion of a Design to alter the Succession, to introduce Arbitrary Power, or to hurt the Toleration? unless you will reckon the last to have been damaged by the Bill lately obtained against *Occasional Conformity*, which was your own Act and Deed, by a strain of such profound Policy, and the Contrivance of so profound a Politician, that I cannot unravel it to the Bottom.[12]

11 *strange Opinions . . . Ministry*: i.e., that they are Jacobites who intend to alter the Protestant Succession.
12 *Bill . . . Bottom*: the Bill against occasional conformity, passed on 15 December 1711; support for that Bill gained for the Whigs the alliance of Daniel Finch, 2nd Earl of Nottingham, who in exchange moved an Amendment to the Queen's Address pledging the Lords against any Peace without Spain. See *Some Advice*, p. 109 and note. Nottingham is presumably the 'profound . . . Politician' referred to in this passage.

Pray, my Lord, give your self leave to consider whence this indefatigable
Zeal is derived, that makes the Heads of your Party send you an hundred Messages, accost you in all Places, and remove Heaven and Earth
to procure your Vote upon a Pinch, whenever they think it lies in their
way to distress the Q—— and Ministry. Those who have already rendred
themselves desperate, have no other resource than in an utter Change:
But this is by no means your Lordship's Case. While others were at the
Head of Affairs, you serv'd the Q——n with no more Share in them,
than what belonged to you as a Peer, although perhaps you were inclined
to their Persons or Proceedings, more than to those of the present Sett:
Those who are now in Power, cannot justly blame you for doing so; neither can your Friends out of Place reproach you, if you go on to serve Her
M—— and make Her easy in Her Government, unless they can prove,
that unlawful or unreasonable Things are demanded of you. I cannot see
how your Conscience or Honour are here concerned; or why People who
have cast off all Hopes, should desire you to embark with them against
your Prince, whom you have never directly offended. 'Tis just as if a Man
who had committed a Murder, and was flying his Country, should desire
all his Friends and Acquaintance to bear him Company in his Flight and
Banishment. Neither do I see how this will any way answer your Interest;
for tho' it should possibly happen that your Friends would be again taken
into Power, your Lordship cannot expect they will admit You to the Head
of Affairs, or even into the *Secret*. Every thing of Consequence is already
bespoke. I can tell you who is to be *Treasurer*, who *Chamberlain*, and who to
be *Secretaries*: These Offices, and many others, have been some time fixed;
and all your Lordship can hope for, is only the Lieutenancy of a County,
or some other honorary Employment, or an Addition to your Title; or, if
you were poor, perhaps a Pension. And is not the Way to any of these as
fully open at present? And will you declare you cannot Serve your Q——
unless you chuse her M——ry? Is this *Forsaking your Principles*? But that
Phrase is dropt of late, and they call it *Forsaking your Friends*. To serve
your Q—— and Country, while any but They are at the Helm, is to *Forsake your Friends*. This is a new Party-figure of Speech, which I cannot
comprehend. I grant, my Lord, that this way of Reasoning is very just,
while it extends no farther than to the several Members of their Junto's
and Cabals; and I could point out half a score Persons, for each of whom
I should have the utmost Contempt, if I saw them making any Overtures

to be received into Trust. Wise Men will never be persuaded, that such violent Turns can proceed from Virtue or Conviction: And I believe you and your Friends do in your own Thoughts most heartily despise *that igno-minious Example of Apostacy*,[13] whom you outwardly so much caress. But You, my Lord, who have shared no farther in the Favour and Confidence of your Leaders, than barely to be listed of the Party, cannot honorably refuse Serving Her M---y, and contributing, in your Power, to make her Government easy, though her weighty Affairs be not trusted to the Hands where you would be glad to see them. One Advantage your Lordship may count upon, by acting with the present Ministry, is, that you shall not undergo a State-Inquisition into your Principles, but may believe as you please, in those Points of Government, wherein so many Writers perplex the World with their Explanations. Provided you heartily renounce the Pretender, you may suppose what you please of his Birth;[14] and if you allow Her M——y's undoubted Right, you may call it Hereditary or Parliamentary, as you think fit. The Ministers will second your utmost Zeal for securing the Indulgence to Protestant Dissenters. They abhor Arbitrary Power as much as You: In short, there is no Opinion properly belonging to you, as a *Whig*, wherein you may not still continue, and yet deserve the Favour and Countenance of the Court; provided you offer nothing in Violation of the Royal Prerogative, nor take the Advantage in critical Junctures to bring Difficulties upon the Administration, with no other View, but that of putting the Q—— under the necessity of changing it. But your own Party, my Lord, whenever they return into play, will not receive you upon such easy Terms, although they will have much more need of your Assistance: They will vary their political Catechism as often as they please; and you must answer directly to every Article, as it serves the present Turn. This is a Truth too visible for you to call in doubt. How unanimous are you to a Man in every Point, whether of moment or no! whereas upon Our Side, many Stragglers have appeared in all Divisions, even among those who believed the Consequence of their Dissent would be the worst we could

13 *Example of Apostasy*: Nottingham, who moved from his role as a high-Church Tory to support of the Whigs; see last note. See also Swift's poem 'An Excellent New Song, Being the Intended Speech of a famous Orator against the Peace', Williams, *Poems*, pp. 141–5. Given the Earl's strong religious feelings, Swift's use of the word 'Apostasy' is meant to be galling.
14 *what you please of his Birth*: i.e., whether you believe that 'James III' is only a changeling and not in fact the son of James II, or that he is the Stuart heir but excluded by Act of Parliament; hence the terms 'Hereditary' and 'Parliamentary' in the next clause.

fear: For which, the Courage, Integrity, and Moderation of those at the Helm, cannot be sufficiently admired; though I question whether, in good Politicks, the last ought always to be imitated.[15]

If your Lordship will please to consider the Behaviour of the *Tories* during the long Period of this Reign, while their Adversaries were in Power, you will find it very different from that of your Party at present. We opposed the Grant to the D. of *M.*[16] till he had done something to deserve so great a Reward; and then it was granted, *nemine contradicente*. We opposed Repealing the *Test*, which would level the Church Established, with every sniveling Sect in the Nation. We opposed the Bill of General Naturalization, by which we were in danger to be over-run by Schismaticks and Beggars: The Scheme of breaking into the Statutes of Colleges, which obliged the Fellows to take holy Orders; the Impeachment of Dr. *Sacheverill*; the hopeful Project of limiting Clergymen what to Preach; with several others of the same Stamp, were strenuously opposed, as manifestly tending to the Ruin of the Church.[17] But you cannot give a single Instance, where the least Violation hath been offered to Her Majesty's undoubted Prerogative, in either House, by the Lords or Commons of Our Side. We should have been glad indeed to have seen Affairs in other Management; yet, we never attempted

15 *last . . . imitated*: another expression of Swift's concern over Oxford's 'Moderation'.
16 *Grant to the D. of M.*: referring to the effort by Queen Anne in December 1702 to give Marlborough an annual grant of £5,000 *'antecedent to any visible Merit '*, as Swift says in *Examiner* for 22 February 1711. The measure was defeated by the Tories. For the grants which he received after he had 'done something', see Swift's catalogue in *The Examiner* for 23 November 1710.
17 *Repealing the Test . . . Ruin of the Church*: Swift's persistent concern over Whig efforts to repeal the Sacramental Test had been voiced in his *Letter . . . concerning the Sacramental Test* of 1708 and has been supposed as the spark for his *Argument* (written 1708, published 1711), though not its main focus. See also his *Examiners* of 4 and 25 January, 5 May 1711. 'Bill of general naturalization' refers to the Act for naturalizing foreign Protestants (7 Ann. c. 5) of 1709, opposed by Tories, an act which led to a great influx of Palatine refugees in the spring of 1709, itself becoming a party issue; see Swift's *Examiner* for 7 June 1711 and *History* (Davis, vol. VII, pp. 94–5). The 'Scheme of breaking into the Statutes of Colleges' refers to a rejected clause in the Act in 1710 for the encouragement of learning (8 Anne c. 21). If it had passed, it would have removed the obligation of Fellows of Colleges to take holy orders; see Ellis, *Examiner* for 14 December 1710, and the notes by Ellis on p. 98. The impeachment and trial of the high-Church clergyman Dr Henry Sacheverell in 1710, mentioned next in Swift's list, was of course the most important single event that made the change of ministries inevitable; and it was a short step from that trial to the general fear that 'Republican Politicks' would have the clergy '*prescrib'd* what to teach, by those who are to learn from them' (Swift, *Examiner*, 28 December 1710).

to bring it about by stirring up the City, or inviting Foreign Ministers to direct the Q——n in the Choice of Her Servants, much less by infusing Jealousies into the next Heir:[18] Endeavours were not publickly used to blast the Credit of the Nation, and discourage Foreigners from Trusting their Money in our Funds:[19] Nor were Writers suffered openly, and in Weekly Papers, to revile Persons in the highest Employments. In short, if you can prove where the Course of Affairs, under the late Ministry, was any way clogged by the Church-Party, I will freely own the latter to have so far acted against Reason and Duty. Your Lordship finds I would argue from hence, that even the warmest Heads on your Side, and those who are deepest engaged, have no tolerable Excuse for thwarting the Q——n upon all Occasions; much less You, my Lord, who are not involved in their Guilt or Misfortunes, nor ought to involve your self in their Resentments.

I have often wondered with what Countenance these Gentlemen, who have so long engrossed the greatest Employments, have shared among them the Bounties of the Crown and the Spoils of the Nation, and are now thrown aside with universal Odium, can accost others, who either never received the Favours of the Court, or who must depend upon it for their daily Support; with what Countenance, I say, these Gentlemen can accost such Persons in their usual Style, *My Lord, you were always with us; you will not forsake your Friends: You have been still right in your Principles: Let us join to a Man, and the Court will not be able to carry it.* And this frequently in Points where *Whig* and *Tory* are no more concerned, than in the length or colour of your Perriwigs? Why all this Industry to ply you with Letters, Messages and Visits, for carrying some peevish Vote, which only serves to display inveterate Pride, ill Nature and Disobedience, without effect? Though you are flattered it must possibly make the Crown and Ministry so uneasy, as to bring on the necessity of a Change: Which however is at

18 *Jealousies into the next Heir*: in *History*, Swift complains that the Elector of Hanover was so deceived by misrepresentations on the part of the States that he allowed his envoy, Bothmar, to publish a memorial against the peace 'drawn up . . . by some Party-Pen' in England directly disapproving all of the Queen's proceedings (Davis, vol. VII, p. 24, and see Williams, *JSt*, p. 430). The Elector soon became the key figure in an alliance of Whigs and the Allies against the Tory peace initiatives.
19 *stirring up the City . . . our Funds*: in making many of these charges against the Whigs, Swift has in mind especially their tactics in reaction to the dismissal of Sunderland in June 1710; see note on *Conduct*, above, p. 86.

best a Design but ill becoming a good Subject, or a Man of Honour. I shall say nothing of those who are fallen from their heights of Power and Profit, who then think all claim of Gratitude for past Favours is cancelled: But you, my Lord, upon whom the Crown has never cast any peculiar Marks of Favour or Displeasure, ought better to consider the Duty you owe your Sovereign, not only as a Subject in general, but as a Member of the Peerage, who have been always the strenuous Asserters of just Prerogative, against popular Encroachments, as well as of Liberty, against Arbitrary Power: So that it is something unnatural, as well as unjust, for one of your Order, to oppose the most Mild and Gracious Prince that ever reigned, upon a Party-Picque, and in Points where Prerogative was never disputed.

But after all, if there were any probable Hopes of bringing Things to another Turn by these violent Methods of your Friends, it might then perhaps be granted, that you acted at least a politick Part: But surely the most Sanguine among them could hardly have the Confidence to insinuate to your Lordship, the Probability of such an Event, during Her M——y's Life. Will any Man of common Understanding, when he has recovered his Liberty, after being kept long in the strictest Bondage, return of his own Accord to Goal, where he is sure of being confined for ever? This Her Majesty and Millions of her Subjects, firmly believe to be exactly the Case; and whether it be so or no, 'tis enough that it is so believed: And this Belief is attended with as great an Aversion for those Keepers, as a good Christian can be allowed to entertain, as well as with a Dread of ever being again in their Power: So that whenever the Ministry may be changed, it will certainly not be to the Advantage of your Party, except under the next Successor, which I hope is too remote a View for your Lordship to proceed by; though I know some of your Chiefs, who build all their Expectations upon it.

For indeed, my Lord, your Party is much deceived, when they think to distress a Ministry for any long Time, or to any great Purpose, while those Ministers act under a Q——n who is so firmly convinced of their Zeal and Ability for Her Service, and who is at the same time so thoroughly possessed of Her Peoples Hearts. Such a Weight will infallibly at length bear down the Balance: And, according to the Nature of our Constitution, it ought to be so; because, when any one of the Three Powers whereof our Government is composed, proves too strong for the other Two, there is an End of our Monarchy. So little are you to regard the crude Politicks of those who cried out, *The Constitution was in Danger*, when Her M———sty lately encreased the Peerage;[20] without which it was impossible the two Houses could have proceeded, with any Concert, upon the most weighty Affairs of the Kingdom.

I know not any Quarrels your Lordship, as a Member of the *Whig*-Party, can have against the Court, except those which I have already mentioned; I mean, the Removal of the late Ministry, the Dismission of the D. of *M.* and the present Negotiations of Peace. I shall not say any thing farther upon these Heads; only, as to the second, which concerns the D. of *M.* give me leave to observe, that there is no Kingdom or State in *Christendom*, where a Person in such Circumstances, would have been so gently treated. But it is the Misfortune of Princes, that the Effects of their Displeasure, are frequently much more publick than the Cause: The Punishments are in the Face of the World, when the Crimes are in the Dark: And Posterity, without knowing the Truth of Things, may perhaps number us among the ungrateful Populace of *Greece* and *Rome*, for discarding a General, under whose Conduct our Troops have been so many Years Victorious: Whereas it is most certain, that this great Lord's Resolution against Peace upon any Terms whatsoever, did reach the Ministry at home as much as the Enemy abroad: Nay, his Rage against the former was so much the more violent of the two, that, as it is affirmed by skilful Computors, he spent more Money here upon *Secret Service*,[21] in a few Months, than he did for many Years in *Flanders*. But whether that be true or false, your Lordship knows very well, that he resolved to give no Quarter, whatever he might be content to take, when he should find himself at Mercy. And the Question was brought to this Issue, Whether the Q———n should dissolve the present Parliament, procure a new one of the *Whig*-Stamp, turn out those who had ventured so far to rescue her from Insolence and ill Usage, and invite her old Controllers to resume their Tyranny, with a recruited Spirit of Vengeance? Or, Whether she should save all this Trouble, Danger, and Vexation, by only changing one General for another?

---

20 *encreased the Peerage*: Anne's creation of twelve new lords to save the Oxford ministry in the last days of 1711.

21 *Secret Service*: Swift alludes sarcastically to Marlborough's explanation when he was charged in December 1711 with taking commissions on bread contracts for his army; he claimed that he had spent the money on secret service, and that therefore no exact accounting of the funds was possible.

Whatever good Opinion I may have of the Present Ministry, I do not pretend, by any thing I have said, to make your Lordship believe that they are Persons of sublime abstracted *Roman* Virtue: But, where two Parties divide a Nation, it so usually happens, that although the Virtues and Vices may be pretty equal on both sides, yet the publick Good of the Country may suit better with the private Interest of one Side than of the other. Perhaps there may be nothing in it but Chance; and it might so have happened if Things were to begin again, that the *Junto*[22] and their Adherents would have found it their Advantage to be obedient Subjects, faithful Servants, and good Church-men. However, since these Parts happen to be acted by another Sett of Men, I am not very speculative, to enquire into the Motives; but having no Ambition at Heart, to mislead me, I naturally side with those who proceed most by the Maxims wherein I was educated. There was something like this in the Quarrel between *Cæsar* and *Pompey*: *Cato* and *Brutus* were the two most virtuous Men in *Rome*; the former did not much approve the Intentions of the Heads on either side; and the latter, by Inclination, was more a Friend to *Cæsar*: But, because the Senate and People generally followed *Pompey*, and that *Cæsar*'s Party was only made up of the Troops with which he Conquered *Gaul*, with the Addition of some profligate Deserters from *Rome*; those two excellent Men, who thought it base to stand Neuter where the Liberties of their Country was at stake, joined heartily on that side which undertook to preserve the Laws and Constitution, against the Usurpations of a victorious General, whose Ambition was bent to overthrow them.[23]

I cannot dismiss your Lordship, without a Remark or two upon the Bill for appointing Commissioners to enquire into the Grants, since 1688. which was lately thrown out of your House, for no other Reason, than

22 *Junto*: the Whig leaders (Halifax, Orford, Somers, Sunderland and Wharton).
23 *Quarrel between . . . overthrow them*: the conflict between Caesar and Pompey, which came to a head in the battle at Pharsalus in 48 BC, is recounted in Plutarch's *Pompey*, chapters xlvi–lxxx, among many other ancient sources. Plutarch also explains that Brutus, though expected to choose Caesar's side because his father's death had been instigated by Pompey, put the public good above his own ties and attached himself to Pompey (*Brutus*, chapter iv). On Pompey's successful effort to win over Cato, see Plutarch, *Pompey*, chapter liv, and *Cato the Younger*, chapters xiv and l–lvii. Swift cites Plutarch in his comments on Caesar and Pompey in his *Discourse*, chapter iii, where they are called 'Two of the greatest Spirits that *Rome* ever produced' (Ellis, *Discourse*, pp. 108–9).

the hopes of putting the Ministry to a Plunge.[24] It was universally known that the Lord T——r had prevailed to wave the Tack[25] in the House of C——— and promised his Endeavours to make the Bill pass by it self in the House of L——. I could name at least, five or six of your Noble Friends, who, if left to the Guidance of their own Opinion, would heartily concur to an entire Resumption of those Grants; others assure me they could name a dozen; yet, upon the hope of weakening the Court, perplexing the Ministry, and shaking the Lord T——r's Credit in the H—— of C———, You went on so unanimously, that I do not hear there was one single Negative, in your whole List, nor above one *Whig*-Lord guilty of a *Suspicious Absence*; who, being much in your Lordships Circumstances, of a great Patrimonial Estate, and under no Obligations to either side, did not think himself bound to forward a Point, driven on meerly to make the Crown uneasy at this Juncture, while it no way affected his Principles as a *Whig*, and which I am told was directly against His private Judgment.[26] How he hath

---

24 *Bill . . . Plunge*: to 'put to a plunge' is to force into a crisis (*OED*). William III had made lavish grants of lands forfeited by Irish rebels and of Crown lands as well to Dutch friends and others; he was forced by the largely Tory Parliament into the 1700 Act of Resumption, whereby the Crown repossessed these grants and added the value of the estates to the public treasury. In 1702 another bill resuming all of William's grants, of English as well as Irish lands, was defeated. Now in 1712 the strong Tory element in the House, believing the Court was opposed to resuming the grants, was set on passing another Resumption Bill by the device of a 'tack' (see next note). Oxford convinced the leaders that he and the other ministers favoured the Bill, and it was allowed to go forward into the House of Lords. Swift reported to Stella, 'We were like to be undone some days ago with a Tack, but we carried it bravely, and the Whigs came in to help us' (Williams, *JSt*, p. 532; cf. Defoe exulting on the same theme, *Review*, 15 May 1712). In the Lords, however, on 20 May it was thrown out on a tie vote, which, Swift wrote to Archbishop King, was 'a great Disappointment to the Court, and Matter of Triumph to the other Party' (Woolley, *Corr.*, vol. I, p. 423). See Swift's detailed account in his *History*, Davis, vol. VII, pp. 100–3.

25 *Tack*: 'Something tacked on or attached as an addition or rider; an addendum, supplement, appendix; . . . in parliamentary usage, a clause relating to some extraneous matter, appended, in order to secure its passing, to a bill, esp. a bill of supply' (*OED*). Swift discusses the origin and arguments pro and con of the practice of tacks in *History*, Davis, vol. VII, pp. 102–3.

26 *one Whig-Lord . . . private Judgment*: it is difficult to identify this suspiciously absent lord, of a great patrimonial estate, who is under no obligations to either side and who since the vote has been treated as an apostate and betrayer. Temple Scott is surely incorrect in suggesting Sunderland (though he was indisposed that day) as the absent lord, but the specific reference is elusive. The division ended in a tie, the division list is lost, and the *LJ*, which lists only those present, is not a reliable guide for identifying those who were absent. For further light on this vote, see the letter by Ralph Bridges quoted by Clyve Jones, in '"Party Rage and Faction"– the View from Fulham, Scotland Yard, and the Temple: Parliament in the Letters

since been treated as an Apostate and Betrayer of his Friends, by some of the Leaders and their Deputies among you, I hope your Lordship is ashamed to reflect on; nor do I take such open and sudden Declarations to be very wise, unless you already despair of his Return, which, I think, after such Usage, you justly may. For the rest, I doubt your Lordship's Friends have missed every End they proposed to themselves in rejecting that Bill: My Lord Tr——rs Credit is not any way lessened in the H—— of C----m----s. In your own House you have been very far from making a Division among the Qu---'s Friends, as appeared manifestly a few days ago, when you lost your Vote by so great a Majority, and disappointed those who had been encouraged to hire Places, upon certain Expectations of seeing a Parade to the *Tower*.[27] Lastly, it may probably happen, that those who opposed an Inquisition into the Grants, will be found to have hardly done any very great Service to the present Possessors: To charge those Grants with six Years Purchase to the Publick, and then to confirm the Title by Parliament, would in effect be no real Loss to the Owners, because by such a Confirmation, they would rise in value proportionably, and differ as much as the best Title can from the worst. The adverse Party knew very well that nothing beyond this was intended; but they cannot be sure, what may be the Event of a second Inspection, which the Resentment of the H--- of C————s will probably render more severe, and which you will never be able to avert, when your Number lessens, as it certainly must; and when the Expedient is put in Practice, without a Tack, of making those Grants part of a Supply. From whence it is plain that the Zeal against that Bill, arose in a great measure from some other Cause, than a Tenderness to those who were to suffer by it.

I shall conclude, my Lord, with putting you in mind, that you are a Subject of the Q----, a Peer of the Realm, and a Servant of your Country; and in any of these Capacities, you are not to consider what you dislike,

---

of Thomas Bateman and John and Ralph Bridges to Sir William Trumbull, 1710–14', *BLJ* 19 (1993), 162–3.

27 *lost your Vote . . . Parade to the Tower*: cf. Swift's report to Stella, 31 May 1712: 'We got a great Victory last Wednesday in the H. of Lds by a Majority I think of 28, And the Whigs had desired their Friends to bespeak Places to see Ld Treasr carryed to the Tower' (Williams, *JSt*, pp. 535–6). As the note by Harold Williams explains, the debate (on 28 May) had focused on the Duke of Ormond's secret orders not to prosecute the war while the peace negotiations were at a delicate stage, orders which were revealed when he refused assistance to Prince Eugene in attacking Marshall Villars.

in the Persons of those who are in the Administration, but the manner of conducting themselves while they are in. And then I do not despair, but your own good Sense will fully convince you, that the Prerogative of your Prince, without which Her Government cannot subsist; the Honour of your House, which hath been always the great Asserter of that Prerogative; and the Welfare of your Country, are too precious to be made a Sacrifice to the Malice, the Interest, and the Ambition of a few Party-Leaders.

IT'S OUT AT LAST:
OR
FRENCH CORRESPONDENCE
CLEAR AS THE SUN

IT'S OUT AT LAST:
OR,
FRENCH CORRESPONDENCE
CLEAR AS THE SUN

There is a Story goes of an old Prophetess,[1] that Prophesied always true to no purpose; for her Fate was, never to be *believ'd*: The same thing has happen'd, to a worthy Patriot and Member of the House of *Commons*,[2] who has openly in his Speeches declar'd that he was sure that the M——stry *Coresponded* with *France*, and that in a little time there would appear manifest Proofs of it; but such is the Stupidity or rather Malignancy of the *Tory*-Party, that they took no manner of notice of what this Eloquent Gentleman warn'd them of, in his pathetick Harangues, 'till now that they have a convincing Proof of it, with a witness, in this treacherous Surrender of *Dunkirk*.

It is judiciously observed by a learned Author, that the Fate of Princes and States is very hard; for Plots against them are never believ'd 'till they are executed, and consequently without the possibility of being prevented, for every-body will allow me, that what is already executed, is so. I am afraid this will be soon verify'd upon this Nation, by the Clandestine giving up of that Important Place.

---

1 *an old Prophetess*: Cassandra, the Trojan prophetess.
2 *Member of the House of Commons*: Not identified, but if Swift has in mind an actual MP a good possibility is Richard Hampden, whom just a week or so earlier (26 June 1712) he had included in his poem, 'Toland's Invitation to Dismal to Dine with the Calves-Head Club': '*Sunderland, Orford, Boyl*, and *Richmond*'s Grace / Will come; and *Hampden* shall have *Walpool*'s Place' (*POAS*, vol. VII, p. 569). Hampden was a kinsman of the Earl of Wharton and a 'virulent' Whig who on 22 May had been threatened with the Tower by St John for saying England was pursuing 'an inactive and lazy campaign and a trifling negociation of peace; so that we are amused by our ministers at home, and tricked by our enemies abroad' (*Parliamentary History*, vol. VI, p. 1134); then on 17 June he had moved for the Allies to be guarantees of the Protestant Succession. See his sketch in *HP 1690–1715*, vol. IV, pp. 182–3. By the end of the year Hampden was said to be ready to turn Tory because of the peace issue, but then contributed to a collection for George Ridpath, writer of the *Flying Post*, to prove he was still a good Whig (*Wentworth Papers*, p. 310).

I take it, that the Surrender of *Dunkirk* is so plain a proof of our M——stry's Corresponding with *France*, that I should pity any Man, as oppressed with a political Lethargy, should he doubt of it any more: I say this as well to vindicate the Honour of that worthy Gentleman, as to awaken this insensible drousy Nation, who cannot perceive that it is Day when the Sun shines.

It was pleasantly said by a *Swedish* Poet,

Timeo Danos Dona ferentes.[3]

I am afraid of the *Danes* when they bring Presents.

Let us only consider the value of this Present of the *French* Monsieur; the many Millions it has cost him; the many more it has cost us: It is not only giving us a strong Fortification, but Fleets of Frigats and Privateers, and all Pretences[4] afterwards to disturb our Trade in the Channel, and all this is still doubted when it is taken from him, and given to us: And can any Man imagine he does all this for nought? If any Man can show me that ever he did the like before, I will yield the point; but if no such Instance can be given, it must follow demonstratively, that he reckons the present M——stry his Friends: for give me leave to say, no Man would make such a valuable Present but to a Friend, and it were very unbecoming for any but a Friend to accept of it: Therefore I wish the Pa————ent[5] would make the M——stry give an account if they came honestly by it.

I have often ruminated in my Mind, of the Reasons that have induc'd the F——h Monsieur[6] to make this Surrender; and I will give you my Conjectures in short. I think, in the first place, it is not altogether improbable that he has Sold it now, as he Bought it before; and I wish that may not be the chief Reason of the Scarcity of Species[7] at this time. 2*dly*, I believe he has done it out of pure spight to the *Whigs*, whom he knows to be his irreconcileable Enemies; and I will be bold to say, if he had been studying for it, he could not have serv'd them a more malicious spightful Trick. 3*dly*, Why may it not be a Token of Love to the *Tories*, and particularly to my

---

3 *Timeo . . . ferentes*: comic distortion of the famous line in Virgil, *Aeneid*, II.49: *timeo danaos et dona ferentes*, 'I fear the Greeks, even when bringing gifts' (trans. H. Fairclough).
4 *Pretences*: i.e., pretexts, grounds for (*OED*).   5 *Pa———ent*: Parliament.
6 *F——h Monsieur*: i.e., Louis XIV.   7 *Species*: coined money, cash.

Lady *M——sham*[8] for the great Service she has done him: and I am the more confirm'd in my Opinion, since the Governor has been nam'd.

Let us now consider the Difference between the Old and the New M——stry: They scorn'd to accept of *Dunkirk* and a dozen more strong Towns of the *French* King, when they were offer'd; a plain and convincing Proof that they had no secret Dealings with *France*. The D. of *M——gh* scorn'd that modern Frenchify'd way of taking of Towns; he scorn'd so pitiful a Conquest, without Powder and Bullets, Blood and Wounds. By the same uncorrupt and generous Temper, they refus'd a Sum of Money which the *F——h* King offer'd them to help to drive the D. of *Anjou*[9] out of *Spain. It shall never be said that* England *took* French *Money*, was the Saying of a Great and a Wise Minister; a Saying which ought to be Engrav'd in Letters of Gold upon his Tomb-stone. O the miserable Condition of the Nation, that has been forc'd to part with so uncorrupt, so wise, and so truly an *English* M——ry! Men that, for their own Ends, are carrying on private Bargains with our Enemies; in pursuance of which, they have not only accepted of *Dunkirk*, but would, without any manner of Hesitation, take *Toulon*[10] and St. *Malo* too, if they were offer'd.

Thus I think it is plain, from what has been said, that our M——ry are in a close Correspondence with *France*; and, that the *F——h* Monsieur expects Justice from them, not to say some little Favour to boot. I wish the Nation had open'd their Eyes before it was too late, and consider'd well before they had any Dealings with the Devil; for it is well known, that when once he has drawn them in to accept of the least Trifle as a Present, they are his for ever after.

---

8 *Lady M——sham . . . has been nam'd*: Lady Abigail Masham, first cousin to Duchess of Marlborough, favourite of Queen Anne, confidante of Robert Harley, and at this time in charge of the Privy Purse; her brother, General John Hill, was the new Governor of Dunkirk.
9 *D. of Anjou*: Duke of Anjou, grandson of Louis XIV and King of Spain; see *Conduct*, above, p. 56.
10 *Toulon*: under the 'old Ministry' the Allies had failed to take Toulon in a major effort in 1707. See *Conduct*, pp. 76–7.

A DIALOGUE UPON DUNKIRK, BETWEEN A WHIG AND A TORY

A DIALOGUE UPON DUNKIRK

Between a *Whig* and a *Tory*,
on *Sunday* Morning the 6th Instant.[1]

Whig.] Well, Mr. *Tory*, What do you think of the Expedition to *Dunkirk*? We were told, the Town was to be Delivered a Week ago, the Troops Embark'd, and the new Governor just ready to take Horse. What! Has Old *Lewis* outwitted you? I observe your Faction are damnably down in the Mouth: If it ben't a Secret, prithee tell us where it sticks.

Tory.] Where hast thou liv'd! Has no Body told you, that an Express came last Night from *France*, to let us know that the *French* are ready to Surrender *Dunkirk* at a Minute's Warning? and that General *Hill* is, for ought I know, some Miles on his Journey, in order to take Possession of it?

Whig.] Pshaw, Pox, this is a Bamboozle; I know you well enough: But confess ingenuously, What do you think will become of You and your Party, if, after all, this Promise of *Dunkirk* should prove a Bite?[2] For, between Friends, Can you imagine, that the *French* King, who has laid out some Millions on that Town, would give it up in a Whim to You, who have not Command over your own Troops, and cannot procure him a Cessation of Arms?[3] Come, come, our Friends the *Dutch* are better Politicians than you take them for, and, to my Knowledge, have offered better Terms to the *French* than you are able to give them; therefore I cannot imagine how you will get over this scurvy Business of *Dunkirk*, nor what Countenances you will put on when you find your selves disappointed.[4]

---

1 *6th Instant*: General Hill departed on 6 July 1712 for Dunkirk, arriving on 7 July. Woolley conjectures that Swift began the piece on 6 July and completed it on 7 July (Woolley, '*Dialogue*', p. 220 n.).

2 *a Bite*: a hoax (*OED*).

3 *cannot procure him a Cessation of Arms*: the cessation of arms could occur only after the handing over of Dunkirk, so this is a circular argument.

4 *the Dutch . . . disappointed*: cf. Swift, writing on 1 July to Stella, 'We rayl now all against the Dutch, who indeed have acted like Knaves Fools and Madmen' (Williams, *JSt*, pp. 544–5).

Tory.] Look ye, I am very Serious: What I told you at first is true, and Mr. *Hill*, bar Accidents, will certainly be at *Dunkirk* in Forty-eight hours.

Whig.] And are you really so silly to believe, that because the *French* have invited you over to *Dunkirk*, that they will let you in when you come there? Have the *French* ever kept their Word in any one thing this Fifty Years?

Tory.] Why the Devil shou'd we not take their Words as well as the *Dutch* do? You confess, and we know, they have lately made several Offers to *France*; and as for Breach of Faith, perhaps it is not so particular to that Kingdom: What do you think of publickly Acknowledging a Prince for Lawful Monarch, and then, for ten Years, allowing him only the Title of Duke?[5]

Whig.] No Reflections upon the late Ministry: You know, Reasons of State often make such Steps as these necessary.

Tory.] I allow it; and perhaps a political Casuist would find as good Evasion for the *French:* but this is not to the Matter. Suppose, for Argument sake, that the Gates of *Dunkirk* were immediately open'd to our Troops, what Objections will you have left then?

Whig.] A pretty Question that, Perhaps they may let you in: But what will the Town signify in your Hands, when they are Masters of the Citadel?

Tory.] Why Man, the Conditions are, that we are to be entire Masters of Town and Citadel; and if they give us only the former, we shall reckon they give us nothing at all. And can you imagine they will give themselves, as well as us, so much Trouble to no manner of purpose? But to cut this Matter short, I can assure you, the Town and Citadel are to be absolutely in our Power.

Whig.] Why, Lord, after all, what signifies *Dunkirk*? They can take it from you when they please: And besides, you are oblig'd to surrender it on course, if you can't obtain a Cessation of Arms, which, I hope, neither the *Dutch*, nor the Foreign Troops in our Pay, will ever give way to, 'till they make better Conditions for themselves.

Tory.] The *Dutch!* Why, I thought they had been utterly exhausted by the War, not able to pay their own Quota's, much less to maintain Forty Thousand Auxiliaries more? And at the same time dispute a Point with us, who will be just so much the stronger by what we paid to those Forty

---

5 *allowing him only the Title of Duke*: alluding to the Duke of Anjou, Philip V, King of Spain and grandson of Louis XIV. Cf. *Conduct*, p. 53.

Thousand Men, which, whenever our good Allies begin to be *Declaratory*,[6] will be a pretty good Argument to convince them into a Cessation; for if you please to consider, it is just Eighty Thousand Men upon the Ballance.

Whig.] But, sure, you will never be so infamous as to declare yourselves in conjunction with the *French*, against your Allies the *Dutch*? What do you make of that Article of the Grand Alliance,[7] by which no Peace is to be made without the Consent of the Three principal parties?

Tory.] After what you and your *Dutch* Friends have done in Concert with one another, you come in a good time to mention the Grand Alliance. I hope it will be one day prov'd, that you and your Friends have manag'd a Treasonable Correspondence with their High and Mightinesses, or else their sober Burgerships would have hardly acted at this wide, frolicksome rate, refusing to let our General[8] pass through their Towns, corrupting the Troops[9] we have paid to protect them; and some other Tricks that I don't care to mention.

Whig.] This is *France* and Popery all over. Tell me sincerely, don't you think the Ministry are privy to this Journey of the *Pretender*, and to his *pretended* Conversion?

Tory.] In my Conscience, I believe not; for they have held no manner of Correspondence that I can find, with L—d *Wh———n*, or his new Brother **Dismal**, nor any other of those *Whigs*, who got their Pardons for endeavouring to bring in the young Squire's Father.[10] But I shall defer this farther Discourse, 'till to Morrow, when I hope to hear that Her MAJESTY's Standard is set up in *Dunkirk*. In the mean time I am going to drink to General *Hill*'s good Success.

---

6 *Declaratory*: cf. *Conduct*, on the condition that Holland in 1702 would stop all trade with France in return for raising fewer men than first stipulated, 'But this Condition was never executed, the *Dutch* only amusing us with a specious Declaration till our Session of Parliament was ended' (pp. 71–2).

7 *Article of the Grand Alliance*: the Eighth Article, given by Swift in a somewhat edited translation in *Conduct*, p. 89.

8 *refusing to let our General . . . Towns*: referring to the forces of the Duke of Ormond; see *History*, Davis, vol. VII, pp. 140–1.

9 *corrupting the Troops . . . them*: see *History*, Davis, vol. VII, p. 136.

10 *Wh———n . . . Squire's Father*: cf. Swift's joke in his *Letter from the Pretender* that both the Whig leader Wharton and the recent Whig convert Nottingham ('Dismal') were loyal to the Pretender, below, pp. 201–2. His comment about other Whigs trying to restore James II after the Revolution refers to events of 1692, when 'several Leaders of that Party had their Pardons sent them' by James 'and had entered upon Measures to restore him, on account of some Disobligations they receiv'd from King *William*' (*The Examiner* No. 40, 3 May 1711).

A HUE AND CRY AFTER DISMAL

A Hue and cry after Dismal;

Being a full and true Account, how a Whig L--d
was taken at Dunkirk, *in the Habit of a Chimney-*
sweeper, and carryed before General Hill.

WE have an old Saying, *That it is better to play at small Game than to stand out:* And it seems, the Whigs practice accordingly, there being nothing so little or so base, that they will not attempt, to recover their Power. On Wednesday Morning the 9th Instant, we are certainly informed, that Collonell K-le-gr-w (who went to France with Generall Hill) walking in Dunkirk Streets met a tall Chimney-Sweeper with his Brooms and Poles, and Bunch of Holly upon his Shoulders, who was followed by another of a shorter Size. The Tall Fellow cry'd in the French Language (which the Collonel understands) Sweep, Sweep; The Collonell thought he knew the Voice, and that the Tone of it was like one of your fine Speakers. This made him follow the Chimney-Sweeper, and examine nicely his Shape and Countenance. Besides, he conceived also that the Chimney-Sweeper's Man was not altogether unknown to him, so the Collonel went to wait on the Generall who is Governor of Dunkirk for Her Majesty, and told his Honor, that he had a strong Suspicion that he had seen Dismal in the Streets of Dunkirk. (Now you must know, that our Courtiers call a certain great Whig L——d by the Name of Dismal; belike, by reason of his back and dismal Countenance). That is impossible sure, said the Governor. I am confident of it said the Collonel; nay, and what is more, the Fellow that followed him was Mr Squash, tho' the Master was as black as his Man; and if your Honor pleases, I will bring them both to you immediately, for I observed the House they went in. So, away went the Collonel with a File of Musquiteers, and found them both in an Ale-house, that was kept by a Dutch-man. He could see nothing of the Master, but a Leg upon each Stobb, the rest of the Body being out of sight, the Collonel ordered him to come down, which he did, with a great heap of Soot after him. Master and Man were immediately conducted through the Town, with a great Mob at their Heels to the Governor's Castle, where his Honor was sitting in a Chair with his English and French Nobles about him. The Governor with a stern Countenance asked the tall Man who he was! He answered he was a Savoyard, (for beyond Sea, all the Chimney-Sweepers come from Savoy, a great Town in Italy) and he spoke a sort of Gibberish like broken French. But the French Mounseers that were by, assured the Governor, he could be no French-man, no nor Savoyard neither. So then the Governor spoke to him in English, said there was Witnesses ready to prove, that under pretence of sweeping Chimnyes cheaper than other People, he endeavored to persuade the Townsfolks not to let the English come into the Town, and how as that he should say, that the English would cut all the French-mens Throats, and that his Honor believed he was no Chimny-Sweeper (though that was too good a Trade for him) but some Whiggish English Traitor. The Governor then gave Command, that both of them should be washed in his Presence by two of his Guards. And first they began with the Man, and spent a whole Pail full of Water in vain: Then they used Soap and Suds, but all to no Purpose; at last they found he was a Black-a-more, and that they had been acting the Labor-in-vain. Then the Collonel whispered the Governor, your Honor may planly see that this is Squash. (Now you must know, that Squash is the Name of a Blacka-more that waits upon the L——d whom the Courtiers call Dismal). Then with a fresh Pail they began to wash the Master; but for a while, all their Scrubbing did no good; so that they thought he was a Black-amoor too. At last they perceived some dawning of a dark sallow Brown; and the Governor immediately knew it was the L——d Dismal, which the other, after some shuffling Excuses, confessed. The Governor then said, I am sorry to see your L——dship in such a Condition, but you are Her Majesty's Prisoner, and I will send you immediately to England, where the Queen my Liege may dispose of you according to Her Royal Pleasure. Then his Honor ordered new Cloaths to be made both for Master and Man, and sent them on Shipboard: From whence in a few Hours they landed in England.

It is observed, that the L——d's Face, which at best is very Black and Swarthy, hath been much darker ever since, and all the Beauty-washes he uses, it is thought will never be able to restore it. Which wise Men reckon to be a just Judgment on him for his late Apostacy.

London, Printed in the Year, 1712.

Figure 6. Title page: CUL, Williams 389.

𝕬 𝕳𝖚𝖊 𝖆𝖓𝖉 𝖈𝖗𝖞 𝖆𝖋𝖙𝖊𝖗 𝕯𝖎𝖘𝖒𝖆𝖑; [1]

Being a full and true Account, how a Whig L--d
was taken at Dunkirk, in the Habit of a Chimney-
sweeper, and carryed before General Hill. [2]

We have an old Saying, *That it is better to play at small Game than to stand out:*[3] And it seems, the Whigs practice accordingly, there being nothing so little or so base, that they will not attempt, to recover their Power. On Wednesday Morning the 9th Instant, we are certainly informed, that Collonell K-le-gr-w[4] (who went to France with Generall Hill) walking in Dunkirk Streets met a tall Chimney-Sweeper with his Brooms and Poles, and Bunch of Holly[5] upon his Shoulders, who was followed by another of a shorter Size. The Tall Fellow cry'd in the French Language (which the Collonel understands) Sweep, Sweep; The Collonell thought he knew the Voice, and that the Tone of it was like one of your fine Speakers. This

---

1 *Dismal*: the nickname 'Dismal' for Daniel Finch, 2nd Earl of Nottingham, had been around at least since Steele's *The Tatler* of 28 May 1709, which presented a character named 'Don Diego Dismallo'. However, Steele later denied that he had intended Nottingham, and Swift's audience was more likely to remember the recent 'Don Diego Dismallo, the Conjurer' from Arbuthnot's first *John Bull* pamphlet (4 March 1712), where the Earl was unmistakably being satirized.

2 *General Hill*: Brigadier-General John Hill, brother of Lady Masham, had been given command of the occupying force and governorship of Dunkirk on 27 June 1712. He and Swift were on friendly terms; see Swift's letter to him of 12 August 1712 (Woolley, *Corr.*, vol. I, pp. 434–6) and the reference in Williams, *JSt* (p. 544) for 1 July as Hill was about to depart.

3 *stand out*: collected by Tilley (*Proverbs*, G21), with examples throughout the seventeenth century, as 'He (the devil) will play at small game rather than sit out (before he will stand out).' By Swift's period the devil no longer seems involved; cf. Nathan Bailey in 1721, 'The meaning of this Proverb is, that Persons should not indolently sit down in Indifference, leave off all Honest Endeavours, and not do any Thing at all, because they can't presently attain to do what they wou'd' (*Divers Proverbs* (New Haven: Yale University Press, 1917), from Bailey's *Universal Etymological Dictionary*).

4 *Collonell K-le-gr-w*: also referred to by Swift in a joking letter to Hill on 12 August, identified by Woolley as Henry Killigrew, a Lt Colonel of Dragoons who went to France with General Hill (Woolley, *Corr.* vol. I, p. 436 n.).

5 *Bunch of Holly*: common among chimney-sweeps at this time, who used holly branches not for decoration but as cleaning tools.

made him follow the Chimney-Sweeper, and examine nicely his Shape and Countenance. Besides, he conceived also that the Chimney-Sweeper's Man was not altogether unknown to him, so the Collonel went to wait on the Generall who is Governor of Dunkirk for Her Majesty, and told his Honor, that he had a strong Suspicion that he had seen 𝕯𝖎𝖘𝖒𝖆𝖑 in the Streets of Dunkirk. (Now you must know, that our Courtiers call a certain great Whig L——d by the Name of 𝕯𝖎𝖘𝖒𝖆𝖑; belike, by reason of his 𝖉𝖆𝖗𝖐 and 𝖉𝖎𝖘𝖒𝖆𝖑 Countenance). That is impossible sure, said the Governor. I am confident of it said the Collonel; nay, and what is more, the Fellow that followed him was Mr Squash,[6] tho' the Master was as black as his Man; and if your Honor pleases, I will bring them both to you immediately, for I observed the House they went in. So, away went the Collonel with a File of Musquiteers, and found them both in an Ale-house, that was kept by a Dutch-man.[7] He could see nothing of the Master, but a Leg upon each Stobb, the rest of the Body being out of sight, the Collonel ordered him to come down, which he did, with a great heap of Soot after him. Master and Man were immediately conducted through the Town, with a great Mob at their Heels to the Governor's Castle, where his Honor was sitting in a Chair with his English and French Nobles about him. The Governor with a stern Countenance asked the tall Man who he was! He answered he was a Savoyard,[8] (for beyond Sea, all the Chimney-Sweepers come from Savoy, a great Town in Italy) and he spoke a sort of Gibberish like broken French. But the French Mounseers that were by, assured the Governor, he could

6 *Mr Squash*: cf. a marginal note in a MS poem of 1703 glossing the phrase '*Dicky* the black' as 'Dick Squash, the Ld. Nottingham's Black [page]', *POAS*, vol. VI, p. 543 n. Mention of him was common in satires on Nottingham. See e. g. the *Examiner* for 3–6 April, attacking Nottingham for his 'Observations upon the State of the Nation', which has a dialogue featuring 'Mr Squash', 'Mrs Eleanor James', and 'Don Dismallo'. Squash says that in his country, where he lived before he was 'caught', they never ate people raw unless they were very hungry, and so on. Again, the last line of Swift's poem 'Toland's Invitation to Dismal' is 'Then order *Squash* to call a Hackney Chair.'

7 *kept by a Dutch-man*: Swift's innuendo is that Nottingham, by opposing the Peace, was allying himself with the interests of the Dutch, who were not only continuing the war but might soon be at war with Britain, or so the fear was this summer; cf. Defoe in the *Review* of 17 July, the same day this piece was published, 'If it be as some pretend . . . we are now running Headlong into a War with the *Dutch*.'

8 *Savoyard*: most likely referring simply to the fact that the art of the 'climbing boys' was learned from the children of Piedmont and Savoy, who emigrated to London in the late seventeenth century (Benita Cullingford, *British Chimney Sweeps* (Lewes: Book Guild, 2000), p. 73). In Arbuthnot's first 'John Bull' pamphlet, *Law is a Bottomless Pit* (1712), Victor Amadeus, the Duke of Savoy, is represented by 'Lying Ned the Chimney-sweeper'.

be no French-man, no nor Savoyard neither. So then the Governor spoke to him in English, said there was Witnesses ready to prove, that under pretence of sweeping Chimnyes cheaper than other People, he endeavored to persuade the Townsfolks not to let the English come into the Town, and how as that he should say, that the English would cut all the French-mens Throats, and that his Honor believed he was no Chimny-Sweeper (though that was too good a Trade for him) but some Whiggish English Traitor. The Governor then gave Command, that both of them should be washed in his Presence by two of his Guards. And first they began with the Man, and spent a whole Pail full of Water in vain: Then they used Soap and Suds, but all to no Purpose; at last they found he was a Black-a-more, and that they had been acting the Labor-in-vain.[9] Then the Collonel whispered the Governor, your Honor may plainly see that this is Squash. (Now you must know, that Squash is the Name of a Blacka-more that waits upon the L—d whom the Courtiers call Dismal). Then with a fresh Pail they began to wash the Master; but for a while, all their Scrubbing did no good; so that they thought he was a Black-amoor too. At last they perceived some dawning of a dark sallow Brown; and the Governor immediately knew it was the L—d Dismal, which the other, after some shuffling Excuses, confessed. The Governor then said, I am sorry to see your L—dship in such a Condition, but you are Her Majesty's Prisoner, and I will send you immediately to England, where the Queen my Liege may dispose of you according to Her Royal Pleasure. Then his Honor ordered new Cloaths to be made both for Master and Man, and sent them on Shipboard: From whence in a few Hours they landed in England.

It is observed, that the L——d's Face, which at best is very Black and Swarthy, hath been much darker ever since, and all the Beauty-washes he uses, it is thought will never be able to restore it. Which wise Men reckon to be a just Judgment on him for his late Apostacy.

---

9 *Labor-in-vain*: cf. a citation in *OED* from 1670 using this phrase: 'That Commission ended at Labour in vain; not, as the old Emblem is, to go about to make a Black-moor white, but to make him that was White to appear like a Black-moor.'

A LETTER FROM THE
PRETENDER,
TO A WHIG-LORD

A LETTER FROM THE
PRETENDER,
TO A WHIG-LORD

S. Germain, July 8, 1712.[1]

My Lord W------[2]

I thank you heartily for your Letter; and you may be firmly assured of my Friendship. In Answer to what you hint that some of our Friends suspect; I protest to you, upon the Word of a King, and my Lord M---ton[3] will be my Witness, that I never held the least Corresponddence with any one Person of the Tory Party: I observe, as near as I can, the Instructions of the King my Father, among whose Papers there is not one Letter, as I remember, from any Tory, except two Lords and a Lady,[4] who, as you know, have been for some Years past devoted to Me and the Whigs. I approve of the Scheme you sent me, sign'd by our Friends. I do not find 24's Name to it: Perhaps he may be sick, or in the Country. Mid---ton will be satisfied to be Groom of the Stole; and if you have Ireland, 11 may have the Staff, provided 15 resigns his Pretensions; in which Case, he shall have 6000l. a Year for Life, and a Dukedom. I am content 13 should be Secretary, and Lord; and I will pay his Debts when I am able. I confess I am sorry your General Pardon has so many Exceptions; but you, and my other Friends, are better Judges of that. It was with great Difficulty I prevailed on the Queen to let me

---

1 *S. Germain . . . 1712*: St Germain-en-Laye, near Paris, seat of the Court of the Pretender, 'James III'. The date is the same date, old style, as General Hill's move into Dunkirk; see the extended note by Woolley, 'Canon', p. 108. n. 67, for speculation on the reason Swift chose that date for this piece.

2 *Lord W------*: Swift is alluding to his old enemy Thomas, 1st Earl of Wharton, whom he considered a dissolute man but an expert politician, skilled in managing elections and in parliamentary affairs; see the 'Character' of him in *History* (Davis, vol. VII, pp. 9–10). Cf. his *Letter of Thanks* from Wharton to the Bishop of St Asaph (Davis, vol. VI) also printed in July 1712.

3 *M---ton*: Charles Middleton, 2nd Earl of Middleton, leading Jacobite, Secretary of State at the Pretender's Court at St Germain.

4 *two Lords and a Lady*: Temple Scott reasonably conjectures that Swift intends Marlborough, his Duchess and Godolphin.

Sign that Commission for Life,[5] tho' her Majesty is entirely reconciled. If 2 will accept the Privy-Seal, which you tell me is what will please him,[6] the Salary shall be doubled. I am obliged to his good Intentions how ill soever they have succeeded. All other parts of your Plan I entirely agree with; only as to the Party that oposeth us, Your Proposal about Z may bring an Odium upon my Government: He stands the first Excepted; and we shall have enough against him in a legal way. I wish you would allow me twelve more Domesticks of my own Religion, and I will give you what Security you please, not to hinder any Designs you have of altering the present Establish'd Worship. Since I have so few Employments left me to dispose of, and that most of our Friends are to hold theirs for Life; I hope you will all be satisfied with so great a share of Power. I bid you heartily Farewel and am Your assured Friend.

JAMES R.

5 *Commission for Life*: alluding to Marlborough's effort to be appointed 'General for Life'; see *Conduct*, p. 87, and note.
6 *If 2 . . . please him*: the Earl of Nottingham; Swift says in his *History* that when he found himself passed over for Lord Privy Seal in 1711, Nottingham, realizing that the Queen was not going to give him any role in directing affairs, turned against the ministry and began to negotiate with the Whigs (*History*, Davis, vol. VII, p. 16).

A DEFENCE OF
ERASMUS LEWIS,
OR
THE EXAMINER
(2 FEBRUARY 1713)

THE EXAMINER

From 𝔉𝔯𝔦𝔡𝔞𝔶 *January 30, to* 𝔐𝔬𝔫𝔡𝔞𝔶 *February 2, 1712.*

Beware of Counterfeits, for such are abroad.	Saffold's *Quack-Bill.*
Quin, quæ dixisti modo,	
Omnia ementitus equidem Sosia Amphytrionis sum.	Plaut.
Parva motu primo, mox sese attollit in auras.	Virg.

I intend this Paper for the Service of a particular Person; but herein, I hope, at the same time, to do some Service to the Publick. A Monstrous Story hath been for a while most industriously handed about, reflecting upon a Gentleman in great Trust, under the Principal Secretary of State; who hath Conducted himself with so much Prudence, that, before this Incident, neither the most virulent Pens nor Tongues have been so bold to attack him. The Reader easily understands, that the Person here meant is Mr. *Lewis*,[1] Secretary to the Earl of *Dartmouth*, concerning whom a Story hath run, for about Ten Days past, which makes a mighty Noise in this Town, is no doubt with very ample Additions transmitted to every Part of the Kingdom, and probably will be return'd to us by the *Dutch Gazetteer*,[2] with the Judicious Comments peculiar to that Political Author: Wherefore having received the Fact and the Circumstances from the best Hands, I

Mottos] *Saffold*: Thomas Saffold, quack doctor and astrologer, died in 1691 but his name continued to appear on his almanac, a custom Swift exploits in *Vindication*, his final 'Bickerstaff' paper. Saffold's nostrums continued to be a subject of ridicule in the first half of the eighteenth century; see *ODNB*.

    Quin, quae dixisti modo . . . sum: Plautus, *Amphytrion*, 410–11: 'You lie, I tell you; your every word has been a lie. I am Amphytrion's Sosia, beyond dispute' (trans. P. Nixon).

    Parva metu primo: Virgil, *Aeneid*, IV.176: 'small at first through fear, soon she mounts up to heaven' (describing Rumour; trans. H. Fairclough).

1 *Lewis*: Erasmus Lewis (1670–1754), Under-Secretary to the Earl of Dartmouth, Secretary of State, and a close friend of Swift's.

2 *Dutch Gazetteer*: i. e., the *Gazette d'Amsterdam*; actually that paper gave the story itself in a straightforward fashion, but it showed its bias by quoting the depositions only of Henry Lewis and Skelton, not those of Erasmus Lewis or Charles Ford.

shall here set them down before the Reader, who will easily pardon the Style, which is made up of Extracts from the Depositions and Assertions of the several Persons concerned.

On *Sunday* last was Month, Mr. *Lewis*, Secretary to the *Earl* of *Dartmouth*, and Mr. *Skelton*,[3] met by Accident at Mr. *Scarborough*'s[4] Lodgings in St. *James*'s, among Seven other Persons, *viz.* the Earls of *Sussex*[5] and *Finlatter*,[6] the Lady *Barbara Skelton*,[7] Lady *Walter*,[8] Mrs. *Vernon*,[9] Mrs. *Scarborough*, and Miss *Scarborough*[10] her Daughter; who all declar'd, that Mr. *Lewis* and Mr. *Skelton* were half an Hour in Company together. There Mrs. *Scarborough* made Mr. *Skelton* and Mr. *Lewis* known to each other; and told the former, that he ought to thank Mr. *Lewis* for the Trouble he had given himself in the dispatch of a Licence,[11] under the *Privy Seal*, by which Mr. *Skelton* was permitted to come from *France* to *England.* Hereupon Mr. *Skelton* saluted Mr. *Lewis*, and told him, he would wait on him at his House to return him his Thanks. Two or three Days after, Mr. *Skelton*, in Company with the Earl of *Sussex*, his Lady's Father, went to a House in *Marlborough-street*, where he was inform'd Mr. *Lewis* liv'd; and as soon as the supposed Mr. *Lewis* appear'd, Mr. *Skelton* express'd himself in these Words; *Sir, I beg your Pardon; I find I am mistaken: I came to visit Mr.* Lewis *of my Lord* Dartmouth's *Office, to thank him for the Service he did me in passing my* Privy Seal, Mr. *Levi* alias *Lewis* answer'd, *Sir, There is no Harm done*: Upon which Mr. *Skelton* immediately withdrew to my Lord *Sussex*, who stay'd for him in the Coach, and drove away. Mr. *Skelton*, who was a Stranger to the Town, order'd the *Coachman* to drive to Mr. *Lewis*'s without more particular Directions, and this was the occasion of the Mistake.

---

3 *Mr Skelton*: Charles Skelton, son-in-law of the Earl of Sussex, and a lieutenant-general in French service.
4 *Mr Scarborough*: Charles Scarborough, Clerk of the Board of the Green Cloth.
5 *Sussex*: Thomas Lennard, Lord Dacre, Earl of Sussex (1654–1715).
6 *Finlatter*: James Ogilvy, 4th Earl of Findlatter (1663–1730).
7 *Barbara Skelton*: Lady Barbara Skelton, d. 1741, wife of Charles Skelton and daughter of the Earl of Sussex.
8 *Lady Walter*: wife of Sir John Walter, Bart.
9 *Mrs Vernon*: probably wife of James Vernon (1646–1727), formerly Secretary of State (1697–1700).
10 *Miss Scarborough*: daughter of Charles Scarborough and Maid of Honour.
11 *Licence*: a licence was needed for Skelton to enter the country because he was in the service of the French.

For above a Fortnight nothing was said of this Matter; but on *Saturday* the 24th of *January* last, a Report began to spread, that Mr. *Skelton*, going by Mistake to Mr. *Henry Levi* alias *Lewis*, instead of Mr. *Lewis* of the *Secretary's Office*, had told him, *That he had Services for him* [12] *from the* Earls *of* Perth, Middleton, Melfort, *and about Twelve Persons more of the* Court of St. Germains.[13] When Mr. *Lewis* heard of this, he writ to the above-mentioned *Henry Levi* alias *Lewis*, desiring to be inform'd, what ground there was for this Report; and receiv'd for Answer, *That his Friend* Skelton *could best inform him.* Mr. *Lewis* writ a second Letter, insisting on an Account of this Matter, and that he would come and demand it in Person. Accordingly he and *Charles Ford*,[14] Esq; went the next Morning, and found the said *Levi* in a great Surprise at the Report, who declared, *He had never given the least occasion for it; and that he would go to all the* Coffee-houses *in Town, to do Mr.* Lewis *Justice.* He was ask'd by Mr. *Lewis*, whether Mr. *Skelton* had named from what Places and Persons he had brought those Services? Mr. *Levi* alias *Lewis* answered, *He was positive Mr.* Skelton *had neither nam'd Person nor Place.* Here Mr. *Skelton* was call'd in, and Mr. *Levi* alias *Lewis* confirm'd what he had said in his Hearing. Mr. *Lewis* then desir'd, he would give him in Writing what he had declar'd before the Company; but Mr. *Levi* alias *Lewis* excus'd it as unnecessary, because he had already said, *He would do him Justice in all the* Coffee-houses *in* Town. On the other Hand, Mr. *Lewis* insisted to have it in Writing, as being less troublesome; and to this Mr. *Levi* alias *Lewis* reply'd, *That he would give his* Answer *by* Three a Clock *in the Afternoon.* Accordingly Mr. *Ford* went to his House at the Time appointed, but did not find him at home; and in the mean time the said *Levi* went to *White's Chocolate-House*, where notwithstanding all he had before denied, he spread the above-mentioned Report afresh, with several additional Circumstances, as that when Mr. *Skelton* and the Earl of *Sussex* came to his House, they stay'd with him a considerable time, and drank Tea.

---

12 *Services for him*: i.e., respects to be paid, 'Complements from some Persons', as Swift puts it in the next to last paragraph.

13 *Earls of Perth . . . St Germains*: James Drummond (1648–1716), 4th Earl of Perth; and his brother John Drummond (1650–1715), made Earl of Melfort by James II, both Jacobites at one time serving at the Pretender's Court at St Germain; 'The fact that Melfort had not been allowed near the Jacobite Court since before 1702 seems to have bothered no-one' (Szechi, p. 145, commenting on the stories about the Lewises). On Middleton, see *Letter from the Pretender*, above, p. 201 and note.

14 *Ford*: Charles Ford (1682–1741), a close friend of Swift, appointed Gazetteer in 1712 by Swift's influence.

The Earl of *Peterborough*,[15] Uncle to the said Mr. *Skelton*, thought himself oblig'd to enquire into the Truth of this Matter; and after some search, found Mr. *Levi* alias *Lewis* at the *Thatch'd-House Tavern*, where he deny'd every thing again to *his Lordship*, as he had done in the Morning to Mr. *Ford*, Mr. *Lewis*, and Mr. *Skelton*.

This Affair coming to the Knowledge of the *Queen*, Her *Majesty* was pleas'd to order an Examination of it by some *Lords* of the *Council*. Their *Lordships* appointed *Wednesday* the 28th of *January* last for this Enquiry; and gave notice for Attendance to the said *Levi* alias *Lewis*, and several other Persons who had knowledge of the Matter. When Mr. *Levi* alias *Lewis* was call'd in, he declar'd, *That Mr.* Skelton *told him he had Services for him from* France, *but did not name any Persons. William Pulteney*,[16] Esq; who was summoned, affirmed, *That he had told him, Mr.* Skelton *nam'd the Earl of* Perth *and* Melfort. *Levi* alias *Lewis* appear'd in some Confusion; for he had intreated Mr. *Pulteney*, not to say he had named any Names, *For he would not stand to it*; but Mr. *Pulteney* answer'd, *You may give your self the Lie; I won't.* The Earl of *Sussex* declar'd, he did not go out of his Coach, and that his Son-in-Law, Mr. *Skelton*, had not been gone half a Minute before he return'd to the Coach. Mr. *Skelton* declar'd, That he knew Mr. *Lewis* by sight perfectly well; that he immediately saw his mistake; that he said nothing to him but the Words first mentioned; and that he had not brought Mr. *Lewis* any Service from any Person whatsoever. The Earl of *Finlatter*, and other Persons summon'd, declar'd, That Mr. *Lewis* and Mr. *Skelton* were Personally known to each other, which render'd it wholly Improbable that Mr. *Skelton* should mistake him: So that the whole Matter appear'd to be only a foolish and malicious Invention of the said *Levi* alias *Lewis*, who, when called to an Account, utterly disown'd it.

If Mr. *Levi*'s View, in broaching this incoherent Slander, was to make his Court to any particular Persons, he has been extreamly disappointed, since all Men of Principle, laying aside the Distinction of Opinions in Politicks, have entirely agreed in abandoning him; which I observe with a great deal of Pleasure, as it is for the Honour of Humane-kind. But as neither Virtue nor Vice are wholly engross'd by either Party, the good Qualities of the Mind, whatever Byass they may receive by mistaken Principles, or mistaken

---

15 *Peterborough*: Charles Mordaunt, 3rd Earl of Peterborough (?1658–1735); see *Conduct*, p. 63 and note.
16 *Pulteney*: William Pulteney (1684–1764), Whig MP, later Earl of Bath and leader of the opposition to Walpole.

Politicks, will not be extinguish'd. When I reflect on this, I cannot, without being a very partial Writer, forbear doing Justice to *William Pulteney*, Esq; who being desired by this same Mr. *Levi*, to drop one part of what he knew, refused it with Disdain. Men of Honour will always side with the Truth; of which the Behaviour of Mr. *Pulteney*, and of a great number of Gentlemen of Worth and Quality, are undeniable Instances.

I am only sorry, that the unhappy Author of this Report, seems left so entirely Desolate of all his Acquaintance, that he hath nothing but his own Conduct to direct him; and consequently is so far from acknowledging his Iniquity and Repentance to the World, that in the *Daily Courant* of *Saturday* last, he hath Publish'd a *Narrative*, as he calls it, of what pass'd between him and Mr. *Skelton*, wherein he recedes from some part of his former Confession. This *Narrative* is drawn up by way of Answer to an Advertisement in the same Paper two Days before: Which Advertisement was couch'd in very moderate Terms, and such as Mr. *Levi* ought, in all Prudence, to have acquiesced in. I freely acquit every Body but himself from any Share in this miserable Proceeding, and can foretel him, that as his prevaricating Manner of adhering to some part of the Story, will not convince one Rational Person of his Veracity; so neither will any Body interpret it, otherwise than as a Blunder of a helpless Creature, left to it self; who endeavours to get out of one Difficulty, by plunging into a greater. It is therefore for the sake of this poor young Man, that I shall set before him, in the plainest manner I am able, some few Inconsistences in that *Narrative* of his; the Truth of which, he says, he is ready to attest upon Oath; which, whither he would avoid, by an Oath only upon the Gospels, himself can best determine.[17]

Mr. *Levi* says, in this aforesaid Narrative in the *Daily Courant, That Mr.* Skelton, *mistaking him for Mr.* Lewis, *told him he had several Services to him from* France, *and nam'd the Names of several Persons, which he* [Levi] *will not be positive to.* Is it possible, that among several Names, he cannot be positive so much as to *One*, after having nam'd the Earls of *Perth, Middleton* and *Melfort*, so often at *White*'s and the *Coffee-houses*? Again, He declar'd, that my Lord *Sussex* came in with Mr. *Skelton*; that both drank Tea with him, and therefore whatever Words pass'd, my Lord *Sussex* must be a Witness to:

17 *Oath . . . determine*: Swift insinuates that Levi, who is probably a Jew, may, by swearing on the Gospels and on nothing else, avoid actually making a meaningful oath, since he does not believe in them.

But his Lordship declares before the Council, That he never stirr'd out of the Coach; and that Mr. *Skelton*, in going, returning, and talking with *Levi*, was not absent half a Minute: Therefore, now in his printed Narrative, he contradicts that essential Circumstance of my Lord *Sussex* coming in along with Mr. *Skelton*, so that we are here to suppose that this Discourse past only between him and Mr. *Skelton*, without any Third for a Witness, and therefore he thought he might safely affirm what he pleas'd. Besides, the nature of their Discourse, as Mr. *Levi* reports it, makes this part of his Narrative impossible and absurd, because the Truth of it turns upon Mr. *Skelton's* mistaking him for the real Mr. *Lewis*; and it happens that seven Persons of Quality were by in a Room, where Mr. *Lewis* and Mr. *Skelton* were half an Hour in Company, and saw them talk together. It happens likewise, that the Real and Counterfeit *Lewis*, have no more resemblance to each other in their Persons, than they have in their Understandings, their Truth, their Reputation, or their Principles. Besides in this Narrative, Mr. *Levi* directly affirms what he directly deny'd to the Earl of *Peterborow*, Mr. *Ford*, and Mr. *Lewis* himself; to whom he twice or thrice expresly affirm'd, That Mr. *Skelton* had not nam'd either Place or Person.

There is one Circumstance in *Levi's* Narrative which may deceive the Reader. He says Mr. *Skelton* was taken into the Dining-Room; this Dining-Room is a Ground-Room next the Street, and Mr. *Skelton* never went further than the Door of it. His many Prevarications in this whole Affair, and the many thousand various ways of telling his Story, are too tedious to be related. I shall therefore conclude with one Remark. By the true Account given in this Paper it appears, that Mr. *Skelton*, finding his mistake before he spake a Word, begg'd Mr. *Levi's* Pardon, and by way of Apology told him, His Visit was intended to Mr. *Lewis* of my Lord *Dartmouth's* Office, to thank him for the *Service* he had done him, in passing the Privy Seal. It is probable that Mr. *Levi's* low Intellectuals were deluded by the Word *Service*, which he took as Complements from some Persons, and then it was easie to find Names: Thus, what his Ignorance and Simplicity misled him to begin, his Malice taught him to propagate.

I have been the more Sollicitous to set this Matter in a clear Light, because Mr. *Lewis* being employ'd and trusted in Publick Affairs, if this Report had prevail'd, Persons of the first Rank might possibly have been wounded through his Sides.

VOTE OF THANKS BY THE HOUSE OF LORDS
(9 APRIL 1713)

AND

THE HUMBLE ADDRESS OF THE LORDS
(11 APRIL 1713)

[VOTE OF THANKS]

Ordered by the Lords Spiritual and Temporal in Parliament Assembled, That an humble Address be presented to Her Majesty to Return the Thanks of this House for Her Most Gracious Speech from the Throne; and for Her Majesties Communicating to this House that a Peace is Concluded; and to Congratulate Her Majesty upon the Success of Her Endeavours for a General Peace; and for what Her Majesty has done to Secure the Protestant Succession; and to assure Her Matie that as She is pleased to express her Dependance next under God upon the Affection of Her People, This House will make all Returns due from obedient Subjects to an Indulgent Sovereign.

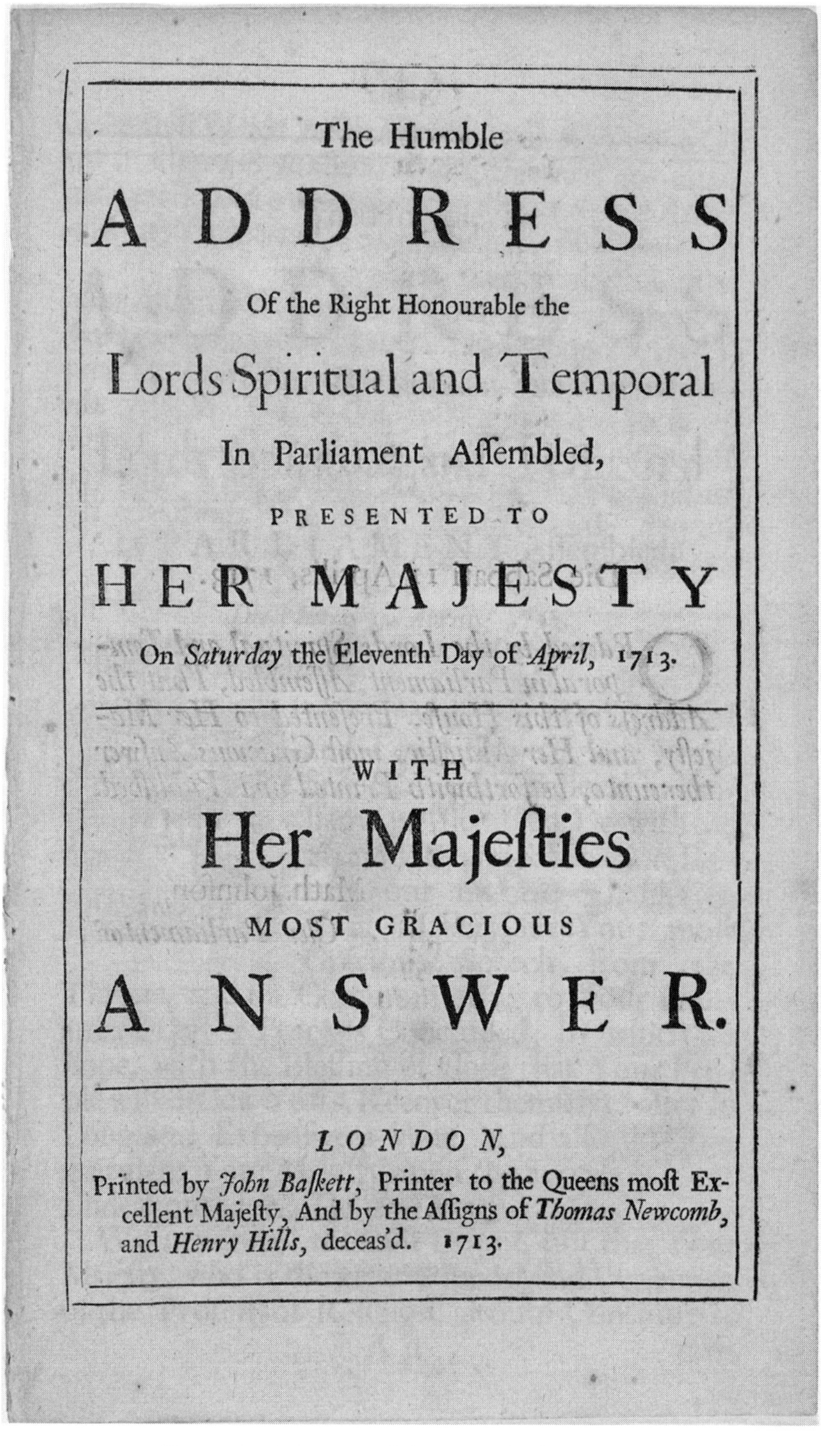

The Humble

ADDRESS

Of the Right Honourable the

Lords Spiritual and Temporal

In Parliament Assembled,

PRESENTED TO

HER MAJESTY

On *Saturday* the Eleventh Day of *April,* 1713.

WITH

Her Majesties

MOST GRACIOUS

ANSWER.

LONDON,

Printed by *John Baskett,* Printer to the Queens most Excellent Majesty, And by the Assigns of *Thomas Newcomb,* and *Henry Hills,* deceas'd. 1713.

Figure 7. Title page: CUL, Broadsides B.71.42.

THE HUMBLE
ADDRESS
OF THE RIGHT HONOURABLE THE
LORDS SPIRITUAL AND TEMPORAL
IN PARLIAMENT ASSEMBLED

Die Veneris 10 *Aprilis,* 1713.

Most Gracious Sovereign,

We your Majesties most Dutiful and Loyal Subjects, the Lords Spiritual and Temporal in Parliament Assembled, Do, with the greatest Joy and Satisfaction, Return our humble Thanks to Your Majesty for Your most Gracious Speech from the Throne, and for Communicating to Your Parliament that a Peace is Concluded; by which we hope, with the Blessing of God, that Your People will, in few Years, Recover themselves after so Long and Expensive a War; And also do Congratulate Your Majesty upon the Success of Your Endeavours for a General Peace.

We never had the least Doubt, but that Your Majesty, who is the great Support and Ornament of the Protestant Religion, would Continue to take, as You have always done, the Wisest Measures for Securing the Protestant Succession, towards which nothing can be more Necessary than the perfect Friendship there is between Your Majesty and the House of *Hanover.*

And we do humbly Assure Your Majesty, That as You Express Your Dependence, next under God, upon the Duty and Affection of Your People, we think our selves Bound, by the strictest Tyes of Religion, Loyalty, and Gratitude, to make all the Dutiful Returns that can be paid, by the most Obedient Subjects to the most Indulgent Sovereign.

Title] On 8 March Swift reported to Stella that he had been asked by Oxford, the Lord Treasurer, to write this: 'He shewd me some of the Qu—'s Speech, wch I corrected in sevrall Places and penned the vote of Address of thanks for the Speech' (Williams, *JSt*, p. 635); see also the entries for 15, 17 March and 7 April for Oxford's delays in looking over what Swift had written.

THE IMPORTANCE OF THE GUARDIAN CONSIDERED

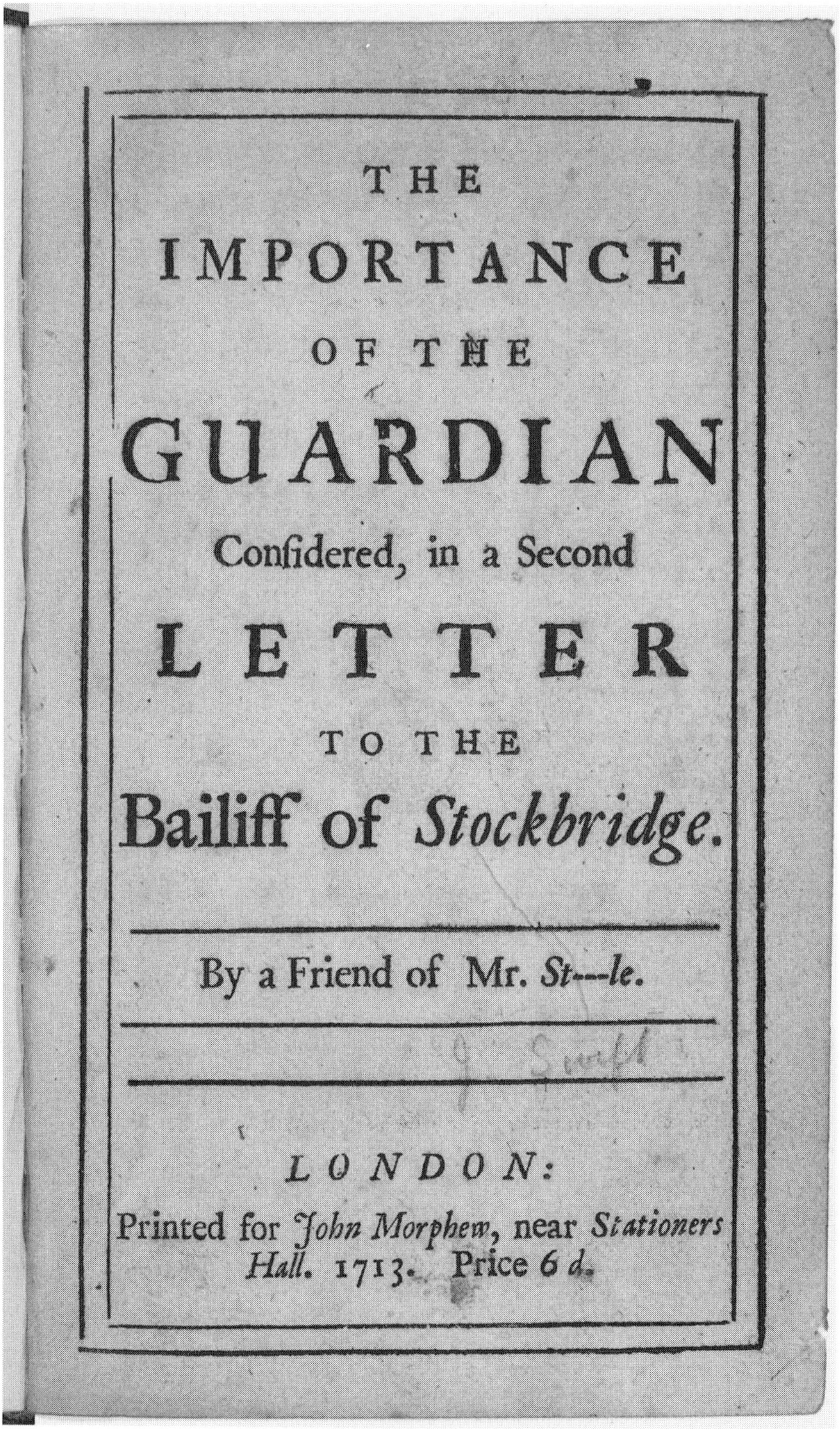

THE

IMPORTANCE

OF THE

GUARDIAN

Confidered, in a Second

LETTER

TO THE

Bailiff of *Stockbridge*.

By a Friend of Mr. *St---le.*

J. Swift

L O N D O N:

Printed for *John Morphew*, near *Stationers*
Hall. 1713. Price 6 *d.*

Figure 8. Title page: CUL, Williams 312.

THE PREFACE

Mr. S---le *in his Letter to the Bailiff of* Stockbridge *has given us leave to* treat him as we think fit, as he is our Brother-Scribler; but not to attack him as an honest Man. *That is to say, he allows us to be his* Criticks, *but not his* Answerers; *and he is altogether in the right, for there is in his Letter much to be* Criticised, *and little to be* Answered. *The Situation and Importance of* Dunkirk *are pretty well known, Mons.* Tugghe's *Memorial,*[1] *published and handed about by the Whigs,*[2] *is allowed to be a very Trifling Paper: And as to the immediate Demolishment of that Town, Mr.* St---- *pretends to offer no other Argument but the* Expectations *of the People, which is a figurative Speech, naming the tenth Part for the whole: As* Bradshaw *told King* Charles *I. that the People of* England Expected *Justice against him.*[3] *I have therefore entred very little into the Subject he pretends to Treat, but have considered his Pamphlet partly as a* Critick, *and partly as a* Commentator, *which, I think, is to treat him only as my Brother-Scribler,* according to the Permission he has graciously allowed me.

---

1 *Tugghe's Memorial*: i.e., *A most humble Address or Memorial presented to Her Majesty the Queen of Great Britain, by the Deputy of the Magistrates of Dunkirk to Her Majesty* (1713). Steele reprints this second memorial by Tugghe in the opening of his pamphlet, claiming it was handed out gratis in the streets. Tugghe says he was 'Thunderstruck' by the denunciation from Bolingbroke that followed his first memorial and asks only that the moles and dikes be spared, with the Queen's 'Thunderbolts' falling on only the 'Martial Works' of the harbour (as reprinted by Steele, *Tracts*, p. 93).
2 *by the Whigs*: Swift constantly claimed that the Whigs themselves were responsible for circulating the 'Memorials' from M. Tugghe which gave so much offence.
3 *Bradshaw . . . Justice against him*: John Bradshaw (1602–59) was Lord President of the court that tried and condemned Charles I in January 1649. The comment Swift cites is typical of his exchanges with the King. As reported in Gilbert Mabbot's *A Perfect Narrative of the Whole Proceedings of the High Court of Justice, In the Tryal of the King* (1649), when the King repeatedly refused to answer the charge or accept the authority of the court, Bradshaw, in the name of the court, told him 'The Court expects your Answer' (p. 5); and 'The Court expects you should give them a final Answer' (p. 7). Then, recapping the situation in the next day's proceedings, 22 January, Bradshaw said, 'Since that the Court hath taken into Consideration what you then said, they are fully satisfied with their owne authority; and they . . . do expect you should either confesse or deny it' (p. 10). When the King replied, he used the word 'expect' also: 'when that I came here, I did expect particular reasons to know by what Law, what Authority you did proceed against me here' (p. 11).

219

TO THE WORSHIPFUL
MR. JOHN SNOW,
BAILIFF OF STOCKBRIDGE

SIR,

I have just been reading a Twelve-peny Pamphlet about *Dunkirk*, addressed to your Worship from one of your intended Representatives; and I find several Passages in it which want Explanation, especially to You in the Country: For we in Town have a way of Talking and Writing, which is very little understood beyond the Bills of Mortality.[4] I have therefore made bold to send you here a second Letter, by way of Comment upon the former.

In order to this, *You Mr.* Bailiff, *and at the same time the whole Burrough*, may please to take Notice, that *London*-Writers often put Titles to their Papers and Pamphlets which have little or no Reference to the main Design of the Work: So, for Instance, you will observe in reading, that the Letter called, *The Importance of Dunkirk*, is chiefly taken up in shewing you the *Importance* of Mr. *St*——; wherein it was indeed reasonable your Burrough should be informed, which had chosen him to Represent them.

I would therefore place the *Importance* of this Gentleman before you in a clearer Light than he has given himself the Trouble to do; without running into his early History, because I owe him no Malice.

Mr. *St*—— is Author of two tolerable Plays,[5] (or at least of the greatest part of them) which, added to the Company he kept, and to the continual Conversation and Friendship of Mr. *Ad---son*, hath given him the Character of a Wit. To take the height of his Learning, you are to suppose a Lad just fit for the University, and sent early from thence into the wide World, where he followed every way of Life that might least improve or preserve the Rudiments he had got. He hath no Invention, nor is Master of a tolerable Style; his chief Talent is Humour,[6] which he sometimes

---

4 *Bills of Mortality*: i.e., the district covered by the official listings of deaths in London.
5 *Plays*: The Funeral (1702), The Lying Lover (1703) and The Tender Husband (1705) were Steele's plays to date; it is not clear whether Swift intended to omit one as 'intolerable.'
6 *Humour*: a quality which Swift was later to analyse and praise as an attribute of his friend Gay; see Woolley, *The Intelligencer*, no. 3 (May 1728), and Woolley's introductory note, pp. 59–60.

discovers both in Writing and Discourse; for after the first Bottle he is no disagreeable Companion. I never knew him taxed with Ill-nature, which hath made me wonder how Ingratitude came to be his prevailing Vice; and I am apt to think it proceeds more from some unaccountable sort of Instinct, than Premeditation. Being the most imprudent Man alive, he never follows the Advice of his Friends, but is wholly at the mercy of Fools or Knaves, or hurried away by his own Caprice; by which he hath committed more Absurdities in Oeconomy, Friendship, Love, Duty, good Manners, Politicks, Religion and Writing, than ever fell to one Man's share. He was appointed Gazetteer by Mr. *Harley* (then Secretary of State) at the Recommendation of Mr. *Mainwaring*, with a Salary of Three Hundred Pounds; was a Commissioner of Stampt-Paper of equal Profit, and had a Pension of a Hundred Pound *per Annum*, as a Servant to the late Prince *George*.[7]

This Gentleman, whom I have now described to you, began between four and five Years ago to publish a Paper thrice a Week, called the *Tatler*; It came out under the borrowed Name of *Isaac Bickerstaff*, and by Contribution of his ingenious Friends, grew to have a great Reputation, and was equally esteemed by both Parties, because it meddled with neither. But, sometime after *Sacheverell*'s Tryal, when Things began to change their Aspect; Mr. *St---*, whether by the Command of his Superiors, his own Inconstancy, or the Absence of his Assistants, would needs corrupt his Paper with Politicks; published one or two most virulent Libels, and chose for his Subject even that individual Mr. *Harley*, who had made him Gazetteer. But his Finger and Thumb not proving strong enough to stop the general Torrent, there was an universal Change made in the Ministry; and the Two new Secretaries, not thinking it decent to employ a Man in their Office who had acted so infamous a Part; Mr. *St——*, to avoid being discarded, thought fit to resign his Place of Gazetteer. Upon which occasion I cannot forbear relating a Passage *to You Mr. Bailiff, and the rest of the Burrough*, which discovers a very peculiar Turn of Thought in this Gentleman you have chosen to Represent you. When Mr. *Mainwaring*

---

7 *Prince George*: in 1706 Steele was made gentleman usher to George, Prince of Denmark (d. 1708), Prince Consort of Queen Anne. As Swift goes on to say, in 1710 he lost his position as Gazetteer (i.e., editor of the *London Gazette*), a position he had obtained with the help of the Whig writer Arthur Mainwaring (see pp. 76–7, note), because he had published *The Tatler*, no. 193 (4 July 1710) ridiculing Harley, just as (it was thought) he had done in the case of *Tatler*, no. 191. See Swift's comments in Williams, *JSt*, pp. 13, 67.

recommended him to the Employment of Gazetteer, Mr. *Harley* out of an Inclination to encourage Men of Parts, raised that Office from Fifty Pound to Three Hundred Pound a Year; Mr. *St*——— according to form, came to give his new Patron Thanks; but the Secretary, who had rather confer a hundred Favours than receive Acknowledgments for one, said to him in a most obliging manner: Pray Sir, do not thank me, but thank Mr. *Main-waring*. Soon after Mr. *St*———'s quitting that Employment, he complained to a Gentleman in Office, of the Hardship put upon him in being forced to quit his Place; that he knew Mr. *Harley* was the Cause; that he never had done Mr. *Harley* any Injury, nor received any Obligation from him. The Gentleman amazed at this Discourse, put him in mind of those Libels published in his *Tatlers*: Mr. *St*——— said, he was only the Publisher, for they had been sent him by other Hands. The Gentleman thinking this a very monstrous kind of Excuse, and not allowing it, Mr. *St*——— then said, Well, I have Libelled him, and he has turned me out, and so we are equal. But neither would this be granted: And he was asked whether the Place of Gazetteer were not an Obligation? No, said he, not from Mr. *Harley*; for when I went to thank him, he forbad me, and said, I must only thank Mr. *Mainwaring*.

But I return, Mr. Bailiff, to give you a further Account of this Gentleman's Importance. In less, I think, than Two Years, the Town and He grew weary of the *Tatler*: He was silent for some Months; and then a daily Paper came from him and his Friends under the Name of *Spectator*, with good Success: This being likewise dropt after a certain Period, he hath of late appeared under the Style of *Guardian*, which he hath now likewise quitted for that of *Englishman*; but having chosen other Assistance, or trusting more to himself, his Papers have been very coldly received, which hath made him fly for Relief to the never-failing Source of Faction.

On the ------- of *August* last, Mr. *St*——— writes a Letter to *Nestor Ironside*, Esq; and subscribes it with the Name of *English Tory*. On the 7th the said *Ironside* publishes this Letter in the *Guardian*. How shall I explain this Matter to you, Mr. Bailiff, and your Brethren of the Burrough? You must know then, that Mr. *St*——— and Mr. *Ironside* are the same Persons, because there is a great Relation between *Iron* and *Steel*; and *English Tory* and Mr. *St*——— are the same Persons, because there is no Relation at all between Mr. *St*——— and an *English Tory*; so that to render this Matter clear to the very meanest Capacities, Mr. *English Tory*, the very same Person with

Mr. *Steele*, writes a Letter to *Nestor Ironside*, Esq; who is the same Person with *English Tory*, who is the same Person with Mr. *Steele*: And Mr. *Ironside*, who is the same Person with *English Tory*, publishes the Letter written by *English Tory*, who is the same Person with Mr. *Steele*, who is the same Person with Mr. *Ironside*. This Letter written and published by these *Three* Gentlemen who are *One* of your Representatives, complains of a printed Paper in *French* and *English*, lately handed about the Town, and given *gratis* to Passengers in the Streets at Noon-day; the Title whereof is, *A most humble Address or Memorial presented to Her Majesty the Qu——* of Great Britain, *by the Deputy of the Magistrates of* Dunkirk. This Deputy, it seems, is called the Sieur *Tugghe*. Now, the Remarks made upon this Memorial by Mr. *English Tory*, in his Letter to Mr. *Ironside*, happening to provoke the *Examiner*, and another Pamphleteer, they both fell hard upon Mr. *St——*, charging him with Insolence and Ingratitude towards the Qu——. But Mr. *St——* nothing daunted, writes a long Letter *to you Mr. Bailiff, and at the same time to the whole Burrough*, in his own Vindication: But there being several difficult Passages in this Letter, which may want clearing up, I here send you and the Burrough my Annotations upon it.

Mr. *St——* in order to display his *Importance* to your Burrough, begins his Letter by letting you know *he is no small Man*; because in the Pamphlets he hath sent you down, you will *find*   P. 1. *him spoken of more than once in Print*. It is indeed a great Thing to be *spoken of in Print*, and must needs make a mighty Sound at *Stockbridge* among the Electors. However, if Mr. *St——* has really sent you down all the Pamphlets and Papers printed since the Dissolution, you will find he is not the only Person of Importance; I could Instance *Abel Roper*, Mr. *Marten* the Surgeon, Mr. *John Moor* the Apothecary at the Pestle and Mortar, Sir *William Read*, Her Majesty's Oculist, and of later Name and Fame, Mr. *John Smith* the Corncutter, with several others who are *spoken of more than once in Print*.[8] Then he recommends to your Perusal, and sends you a Copy of a printed Paper given *gratis* about the Streets, which is the Memorial of Monsieur *Tugghe* (above-mentioned) *Deputy of the Magistrates of Dunkirk*, to desire Her Majesty not to demolish the said Town. He tells you how insolent a Thing it is, that such a

---

8 *Abel Roper . . . Print*: a collection of minor writers, quacks, and purveyors of patent medicines who advertised in the newspapers; Roper, of course, was the author of the Tory *Post Boy*.

Paper should be publickly distributed, and he tells you true; but these Insolences are very frequent among the Whigs: One of their present Topicks for Clamour is *Dunkirk*: Here is a Memorial said to be presented to the Qu—— by an obscure *Frenchman*: One of your Party gets a Copy, and immediately Prints it by Contribution, and delivers it *gratis* to the People; which answers several Ends. *First*, It is meant to lay an Odium on the Ministry; *Secondly*, If the Town be soon demolished, Mr. *St——* and his Faction have the Merit, their Arguments and Threatnings have frighted my Lord Treasurer. *Thirdly*, If the Demolishing should be further deferred, the Nation will be fully convinced of his Lordship's Intention to bring over the *Pretender.*

Let us turn over fourteen Pages, which contain the Memorial it self, and which is indeed as idle a one as ever I read; we come now to Mr. *St——*'s Letter under the Name of *English Tory*, to Mr. *Ironside.*

In the Preface to this Letter, he hath these Words, *It is certain there is not much danger in delaying the Demolition of* Dunkirk *during* P. 15.   *the Life of his present most Christian Majesty, who is renowned for the most inviolable Regard to Treaties; but that pious Prince is Aged, and in case of his Decease,* &c. This Preface is in the Words of Mr. *Ironside* a professed Whig, and perhaps you in the Country will wonder to hear a Zealot of your own Party celebrating the *French* King for his Piety and his religious Performance of Treaties.[9] For this I can assure you is not spoken in jest, or to be understood by contrary; There is a wonderful resemblance between that Prince and the Party of Whigs among us. Is he for arbitrary Government? So are they: Hath he persecuted Protestants? So have the Whigs: Did he attempt to restore King *James* and his pretended Son? They did the same. Would he have *Dunkirk* surrendred to him? This is what they desire. Does he call himself the *Most Christian*? The Whigs assume the same Title, though their Leaders deny Christianity: Does he break his Promises? Did they ever keep theirs?

From the 16th to the 38th Page Mr. *St——*'s Pamphlet is taken up with a Copy of his Letter to Mr. *Ironside*, the Remarks of the *Examiner*, and another Author upon that Letter; the Hydrography of some *French* and *English* Ports, and his Answer to Mr. *Tugghe*'s Memorial. The

9 *Performance of Treaties*: Swift quotes Steele accurately but pretends to take seriously praise of Louis XIV which Steele obviously meant ironically.

Bent of his Discourse is in appearance to shew of what prodigious Consequence to the Welfare of *England*, the Surrendry of *Dunkirk* was. But here,
Mr. Bailiff, you must be careful; for all this is said in Raillery; for you may
easily remember, that when the Town was first yielded to the Qu————,
the Whigs declared it was of no Consequence at all, that the *French* could
easily repair it after the Demolition, or fortify another a few Miles off,
which would be of more Advantage to them. So that what Mr. *St——* tells
you of the prodigious Benefit that will accrue to *England* by destroying this
Port, is only suited to present Junctures and Circumstances. For if *Dunkirk*
should now be represented as insignificant as when it was first put into Her
Majesty's Hands, it would signify nothing whether it were demolished or
no, and consequently one principal Topick of Clamour would fall to the
Ground.

In Mr. *St——*'s Answer to Monsieur *Tugghe*'s Arguments against
the Demolishing of *Dunkirk*, I have not observed any thing that so
much deserves your peculiar Notice, as the great Eloquence of your
new Member, and his wonderful Faculty of varying his Style, which he
calls, *proceeding like a Man of great Gravity and Business*. He has   P. 31.
Ten Arguments of *Tugghe*'s to answer; and because he will not go in the
old beaten Road, like a Parson of a Parish, *First, Secondly, Thirdly*, &c. his
manner is this,

> In answer to the Sieur's *First.*
> As to the Sieur's *Second.*
> As to his *Third.*
> As to the Sieur's *Fourth.*
> As to Mr. Deputy's *Fifth.*
> As to the Sieur's *Sixth.*
> As to this Agent's *Seventh.*
> As to the Sieur's *Eighth.*
> As to his *Ninth.*
> As to the Memorialist's *Tenth.*

You see every Second Expression is more or less diversified to avoid the
Repetition of, *As to the Sieur's*, &c. and there is the Tenth into the Bargain: I
could heartily wish Monsieur *Tugghe* had been able to find Ten Arguments
more, and thereby given Mr. *St——* an Opportunity of shewing the utmost
Variations our Language would bear in so momentous a Tryal.

Mr. *St*—— tells you, That having now done *with his foreign Enemy Monsieur* Tugghe, *he must face about to his Domestick Foes, who accuse him of Ingratitude and insulting his Prince, while he is eating her Bread.*

To do him Justice, he acquits himself pretty tolerably of this last Charge: For he assures You, he gave up his Stampt-Paper-Office, and Pension as Gentleman-Usher, before he writ that Letter to himself in the *Guardian*,[10] so that he had already received his Salary, and spent the Money, and consequently the *Bread was eaten* at least a Week before he would offer to *insult his Prince*: So that the Folly of the Examiner's objecting Ingratitude to him upon this Article, is manifest to all the World.

But he tells you, he has quitted those Employments to render him more useful to his Qu—— and Country in the Station you have honoured him with. That, no doubt, was the principal Motive; however, I shall venture to add some others. *First*, The *Guardian* apprehended it impossible, that the Ministry would let him keep his Place much longer, after the Part he had acted for above two Years past. *Secondly*, Mr. *Ironside* said publickly, that he was ashamed to be obliged any longer to a Person (meaning Lord *Tr*——*r*) whom he had used so ill: For it seems, a Man ought not to use his Benefactors ill above two Years and a half. *Thirdly*, The *Sieur St*—— appeals for Protection to you, Mr. Bailiff, from *others* of your *Denomination*, who would have carried him *some where else*, if you had not removed him by your *Habeas Corpus* to St. *Stephen's* Chapel.[11] *Fourthly*, Mr. *English Tory* found, by calculating the Life of a Ministry, that it hath lasted above three Years, and is near expiring; he resolved therefore to *strip off the very Garments spotted with the Flesh*,[12] and be wholly regenerate against the Return of his old Masters.

In order to serve all these Ends, your Burrough hath honoured him (as he expresses it) with chusing him to represent you in Parliament, and it must be owned, he hath equally honoured you. Never was Burrough more happy

---

10 *Stampt-Paper-Office... Guardian*: Steele resigned his position as Commissioner of the Stamp Office in July in anticipation of his going into Parliament; and within a few weeks he gave up also his pension as gentleman-usher.

11 *St. Stephen's Chapel*: i.e., Steele would have been imprisoned for debt if he had not been elected a Member of Parliament, freeing him from fear of arrest during that session of the House of Commons.

12 *strip off... Flesh*: Jude 23: 'And others save with fear, pulling them out of the fire; hating even the garment spotted by the flesh.'

in suitable Representatives, than you are in Mr. *St*—— and his Collegue,[13] nor were ever Representatives more happy in a suitable Burrough.

When Mr. *St*—— talk'd of *laying before Her Majesty's Ministry, that the Nation has a strict Eye upon their Behaviour with*   P. 39. *relation to* Dunkirk, Did not you, Mr. Bailiff, and your Brethren of the Burrough presently imagine, he had drawn up a sort of Counter-Memorial to that of Monsieur *Tugghe's*, and presented it in form to my Lord *Tr*————*r*, or a Secretary of State? I am confident you did; but this comes by not understanding the Town: You are to know then, that Mr. *St*—— publishes every Day a Peny-paper to be read in Coffee-houses, and get him a little Money. This by a Figure of Speech, he calls, *laying Things before the Ministry*, who seem at present a little too busy to regard such Memorials; and, I dare say, never saw his Paper, unless he sent it them by the Peny-Post.

Well, but he tells you, he *cannot offer against the* Examiner *and his other Adversary, Reason and Argument without appearing*   Ibid. *void of both.* What a singular Situation of the Mind is this! How glad should I be to hear a Man *offer Reasons and Argument, and yet at the same time appear void of both!* But this whole Paragraph is of a peculiar Strain; the Consequences so Just and Natural, and such a Propriety in Thinking, as few Authors ever arrived to. *Since it has been the Fashion to run down Men of much greater Consequence than I am; I will*   Ibid. *not bear the Accusation.* This I suppose is, *to offer Reasons and Arguments, and yet appear void of both.* And in the next Lines; *These Writers shall treat me as they think fit, as I am their Brother-Scribler,*   P. 40. *but I shall not be so unconcerned when they attack me as an honest Man.* And how does he defend himself? *I shall therefore inform them that it is not in the Power of a private Man, to hurt the Prerogative,* &c. Well; I shall *treat* him *only as a Brother-Scribler*: And I guess he will hardly be attacked as an honest Man: But if his meaning be that his Honesty ought not to be attacked, because he *has no Power to hurt the Honour and Prerogative of the*

---

13 *his Collegue*: said lightly, but Thomas Broderick (1654–1730), the other new Member for Stockbridge, was all that Swift despised. A strong Whig and brother to the Speaker of the Irish House of Commons, he was noted for his anti-clerical views, to which Swift alluded in the *Short Character of the Earl of Wharton* (1710) and in his *Letter Concerning the Sacramental Test* (1709), where he says Broderick 'had the Impudence, some Years ago, in Parliament Time, to shake my Lord Bishop of *Killaloo* by his Lawn Sleeve, and tell him in a threatening Manner, *That he hoped to live to see the Day, where there should not be one of his Order in the Kingdom*' (Davis, vol. II, p. 117).

Crown without being punished; he will make an admirable Reasoner in the House of Commons.

But all this wise Argumentation was introduced, only to close the Paragraph by haling in a Fact, which he relates to you and your Burrough, in order to quiet the Minds of the People, and express his Duty and Gratitude to the Queen. The Fact is this; That *Her Majesty's Honour is in danger* of being lost *by Her Ministers tolerating Villains without Conscience to abuse the greatest Instruments of Honour and Glory to our Country, the most Wise and Faithful Managers, and the most Pious, disinterested, generous, and self-denying Patriots*; And the Instances he produces, are the Duke of *Marlborough*, the late Earl of *Godolphin*, and about two Thirds of the Bishops.

Mr. Bailiff, I cannot debate this Matter at length, without putting you and the rest of my Countrymen, who will be at the Expence, to Six-pence Charge extraordinary. The D—— and Earl were both removed from their Employments; and I hope you have too great a Respect for the Queen, to think it was done for nothing. The former was *at the Head* of many great Actions; and he has received plentiful Oblations of Praise and Profit: Yet having read all that ever was objected against him by the *Examiner*, I will undertake to prove every Syllable of it true, particularly that famous Attempt to be General for Life.[14] The Earl of *Godolphin* is dead, and his Faults may sojourn with him in the Grave, 'till some Historian shall think fit to revive part of them for Instruction and Warning to Posterity. But it grieved me to the Soul, to see so many good Epithets bestowed by Mr. *St*—— upon the Bishops: Nothing has done more hurt to that Sacred Order for some Years past, than to hear some Prelates extolled by Whigs, Dissenters, Republicans, Socinians, and in short by all who are Enemies to Episcopacy. God, in his Mercy, for ever keep our Prelates from deserving the Praises of such Panegyrists!

Mr. *St*—— is discontented that the Ministry have not

Ibid.   *called the* Examiner *to Account as well as the* Flying-Post. I will inform you, Mr. Bailiff, how that Matter stands. The Author of the Flying-Post[15] has thrice a Week, for above Two Years together, published the most impudent Reflections upon all the present Ministry, upon all their

14 *General for Life*: see *Conduct*, above, p. 87, note.
15 *Author of the Flying-Post*: George Ridpath; see *Publick Spirit of the Whigs*, below, p. 243, and note.

Proceedings, and upon the whole Body of *Tories*. The *Examiner* on the other side, writing in Defence of those whom Her Majesty employs in her greatest Affairs, and of the Cause they are engaged in, hath always borne hard upon the Whigs, and now and then upon some of their Leaders. Now, Sir, we reckon here, that supposing the Persons on both Sides to be of equal Intrinsick Worth, it is more Impudent, Immoral, and Criminal to reflect on a *Majority* in Power, than a *Minority* out of Power. Put the Case, that an odd Rascally Tory in your Borough should presume to abuse your Worship who, in the Language of Mr. *St——*, is first Minister, and the Majority of your Brethren, for sending Two such Whig-Representatives up to Parliament: And on the other side, that an honest Whig should stand in your Defence, and fall foul on the Tories; would you equally resent the Proceedings of both, and let your Friend and Enemy sit in the Stocks together? Hearken to another Case, Mr. Bailiff; suppose your Worship, during your Annual Administration, should happen to be kick'd and cuff'd by a parcel of Tories, would not the Circumstance of your being a Magistrate, make the Crime the greater, than if the like Insults were committed on an ordinary Tory Shopkeeper, by a Company of honest Whigs? What Bailiff would venture to Arrest Mr. *St——*, now he has the Honour to be your Representative? and what Bailiff ever scrupled it before?

You must know, Sir, that we have several Ways here of abusing one another, without incurring the Danger of the Law. First, we are careful never to print a Man's Name out at length; but as I do that of Mr. *St——le*: So that although every Body alive knows whom I mean, the Plaintiff can have no Redress in any Court of Justice. Secondly, by putting Cases; Thirdly, by Insinuations; Fourthly, by celebrating the Actions of others, who acted directly contrary to the Persons we would reflect on; Fifthly, by Nicknames, either commonly known or stamp'd for the purpose, which every Body can tell how to apply. Without going on further, it will be enough to inform you, that by some of the ways I have already mentioned, Mr. *St——* gives you to understand, that the Queen's Honour is blasted by the Actions of Her present Ministers; P. 43. that Her *Prerogative is disgraced by erecting a dozen Peers, who, by their Votes, turned a Point upon which Your All depended;* That *these Ministers made the Queen lay down Her conquering Arms, and deliver Her Self up to be vanquish'd; That they made Her Majesty betray Her Allies, by ordering*

Her Army to face about, and leave them in the Moment of Distress;

P. 44.   *That the present Ministers are Men of poor and narrow Concep-*
tions, Self-Interested, and without Benevolence to Mankind; and
were brought into Her Majesty's Favour for the Sins of the Nation, and only think
what they may do, not what they ought to do. This is the Character given by
Mr. *St——* of those Persons, whom Her Majesty has thought fit to
place in the highest Stations of the Kingdom, and to trust them
with the Management of Her most weighty Affairs: And this is the

P. 40.   Gentleman who cries out, *Where is Honour? Where is Government?*
Where is Prerogative? Because the *Examiner* has sometimes dealt
freely with those, whom the Qu—— has thought fit to *Discard*, and the
Parliament to *Censure.*

But Mr. *St——* thinks it highly dangerous to the Prince,
that any Man should be hindred from offering his Thoughts upon pub-

P. 45.   *lick Affairs*; and resolves to do it, *tho' with the Loss of Her Majesty's*
Favour. If a Clergy-man offers to preach Obedience to the higher
Powers, and proves it by Scripture,[16] Mr. *St——* and his Fraternity immediately cry out, What have Parsons to do with Politicks? I ask, What shadow
of a Pretence has he to offer his crude Thoughts in Matters of State? to
Print and Publish them? *to lay them before the Queen and Ministry?* and to
reprove Both for Male-Administration? How did he acquire these Abilities of directing in the Councils of Princes? Was it from 𝔓𝔲𝔟𝔩𝔦𝔰𝔥𝔦𝔫𝔤[17] *Tatlers*
and *Spectators*, and Writing now and then a *Guardian*? Was it from his
being a Soldier, Alchymist,[18] Gazetteer, Commissioner of Stampt Papers,
or Gentleman-Usher? No; but he insists it is every Man's Right to find
fault with the Administration in Print, whenever they please: And therefore you, Mr. Bailiff, and as many of your Brethren in the Borough as can

16 *Clergy-man . . . proves it by Scripture*: alluding to the Sacheverell affair.

17 *Publishing*: the emphasis in black letter is not intended to mock Steele's affectations in typography, as Temple Scott thought, since use of black-letter was actually not his characteristic
practice. Rather Swift is suggesting that 'publishing,' not 'writing,' was Steele's main role
in his two most famous periodicals; here he is credited with 'writing' only an occasional
Guardian, the paper in which after a neutral start he became openly political. Cf. the 'Examiner' speaking as a character in *The Examiner* for 9 November 1713, 'I wrote *Spectators* and
Tatlers, when he [Steele] only published them.' Years later, after Steele's death, Swift repeated
the charge in *A Libel on D-- D----- and a Certain Great Lord*, written in 1730: 'Thus, *Steel*
who own'd what others writ, / And flourish'd by imputed Wit'. That Steele's wit was mostly
due to Addison in particular became a standard Tory theme.

18 *Alchymist*: Steele's early experiments and dabbling in alchemy furnished his enemies with a
ready stock of topics for ridicule; for a quick summary of the tradition and the evidence, see
Steele, *Correspondence*, pp. 429–30.

Write and Read, may publish Pamphlets, and *lay them before the Queen and Ministry*, to shew your utter dislike of all their Proceedings; and for this Reason, because you *can certainly see and apprehend with your own Eyes and Understanding, those Dangers which the* Ministers *do not*.

One thing I am extreamly concerned about, that Mr. *St*—— resolves, as he tells you, when he comes into the House, *to follow no Leaders,* P. 46.
but Vote according to the Dictates of his Conscience; He must, at that rate, be a very useless Member to his Party, unless his Conscience be already cut out and shaped for their Service, which I am ready to believe it is, if I may have leave to judge from the whole Tenor of his Life. I would only have his Friends be cautious, not to reward him too liberally: For, as it was said of *Cranmer, Do the Archbishop an ill Turn, and he is your Friend for ever*:[19] So I do affirm of your Member, *Do Mr.* St—— *a good Turn, and he is your Enemy for ever.*

I had like to let slip a very trivial Matter (which I should be sorry to have done). In reading this Pamphlet, I observed several Mistakes, but knew not whether to impute them to the Author or Printer; till turning to the end, I found there was only one *Erratum*, thus set down *Pag*. 45. *Line* 28. *for* Admonition *read* Advertisement. This (to imitate Mr. *St*——'s Propriety of Speech) is a very *old* Practice among *new* Writers, to make a wilful Mistake, and then put it down as an *Erratum*. The Word is brought in upon this Occasion: To convince all the World that he was not guilty of Ingratitude, by reflecting on the Qu——, when he was actually under Sallary, as the *Examiner* affirms; he assures you, he *had resign'd and divested himself of all, before he would presume to write any thing which was so apparently an* ADMONITION *to those employed in* P. 45. *Her Majesty's Service*. In case the *Examiner* should find fault with this Word, he might Appeal to the *Erratum*; and having formerly been *Gazetteer*, he conceived he might very safely venture to *Advertise*.[20]

---

19 *Cranmer . . . for ever*: John Foxe, in discussing Cranmer's spirit of forgiveness, writes as follows: 'Insomuch that it came into a common proverbe: Doe unto my lord of Canturbury displeasure or a shrewd turne, and then you may bee sure to have him your friend whiles he liveth' (*The Seconde Volume of the Ecclesiasticall Historie Conteyning the Acts and Monuments of Martyrs* (1597), p. 691, col. 1).

20 *Advertise*: in all definitions given in the *OED*, 'admonition' has the sense of 'reproof' and 'censure'; whereas 'advertisement,' although in some obsolete senses it could have the same meaning, usually means merely a 'statement calling attention to anything; a notification' (*OED*).

You are to understand, Mr. Bailiff, that in the great Rebellion against King *Charles* I. there was a Distinction found out between the *Personal* and *Political* Capacity of the Prince; by the help of which, those Rebels professed to Fight for the *King*, while the great Guns were discharging against *Charles Stuart.* After the same manner Mr. *St*—— distinguishes between the *Personal* and *Political* Prerogative. He does not care to trust this Jewel

P. 48.   *to the Will, and Pleasure, and Passion of Her Majesty.*[21] If I am not mistaken, the Crown-Jewels cannot be alienated[22] by the Prince; but I always thought the Prince could *wear* them during his Reign, else they had as good be in the Hands of the Subject: So, I conceive, Her Majesty may and ought to *wear* the Prerogative; that it is Her's during Life; and She ought to be so much the more careful, neither to soil nor diminish it, for that very Reason, because it is by Law unalienable. But what must we do with this Prerogative, according to the Notion of Mr. *St*——? It must not be trusted with the Queen, because Providence has given Her *Will, Pleasure, and Passion.* Her Ministers must not act by the Authority of it; for then Mr. *St*—— will cry out,

P. 46.   What? *Are Majesty and Ministry consolidated? And must there be no Distinction between the one and the other?* He tells you, *The*

P. 48.   *Prerogative attends the Crown*; and therefore, I suppose, must lie in the *Tower* to be shewn for Twelve pence, but never produced, except at a Coronation, or passing an Act. Well; but says he, *A*

P. 46.   *whole Ministry may be Impeached and condemned by the House of Commons, without the Prince's suffering by it*: And what follows? Why, therefore a single Burgess of *Stockbridge*, before he gets into the House, may at any time Revile a whole Ministry in Print, before he knows whether they are guilty of any one Neglect of Duty, or Breach of Trust.

I am willing to join Issue with Mr. *St*—— in one Particular; which perhaps may give you some Diversion. He is taxed by the *Examiner* and others,

---

21 *Jewel . . . Majesty*: Steele wrote, more cautiously than Swift reports, that the Prerogative 'attends the Crown, Honour and Dignity, and not the Will and Pleasure, or, it may be Passion of the Prince' (*Tracts*, p. 115). The 'Jewel' image, which Swift uses to such good advantage, does not even appear in Steele's tract.
22 *alienated*: 'Transferred to other ownership' (*OED*).

for an insolent Expression, that the *British* Nation *Expects* the immediate Demolition of *Dunkirk*.[23] He says, the Word EXPECT, was meant to the *Ministry,* and not to the *Queen*; *but that however, for Argument sake, he will suppose those Words were addressed immediately to the*   P. 47. *Queen.* Let me then likewise for Argument sake, suppose a very ridiculous Thing, that Mr. *St——* were admitted to Her Majesty's Sacred Person, to tell his own Story, with his Letter to You, Mr. Bailiff, in his Hand to have recourse to upon Occasion. I think his Speech must be in these Terms.

Madam,

I R——d St— *Publisher of the* Tatler *and* Spectator, *late* Gazetteer, *Commissioner of Stampt Papers, and Pensioner to Your Majesty, now Burgess Elect of* Stockbridge, *do see and apprehend with my own Eyes and Understanding, the imminent Danger that attends the Delay of the*   P. 47. *Demolition of* Dunkirk, *which I believe Your Ministers, whose greater Concern it is, do not: For, Madam, the Thing is not done, My Lord* Treasurer *and Lord* Bolingbroke, *my Fellow-Subjects, under whose immediate Direction it is, are careless, and overlook it, or something worse; I mean, they design to sell it to* France, *or make use of it to bring in the* Pretender. *This is clear from their suffering Mr.* Tugghe's *Memorial to be published without punishing the* Printer. *Your Majesty has told us, that the Equivalent for* Dunkirk *is already in the* French *King's Hands; therefore all Obstacles are removed on the Part of* France; *and I, though a mean Fellow, give Your Majesty to understand in the best Method I can take, and from the Sincerity of my* GRATEFUL *Heart, that the* British *Nation* EXPECTS *the* IMMEDIATE *Demolition of* Dunkirk; *as you hope to preserve Your Person, Crown, and Dignity, and the Safety and Welfare of the People committed to Your Charge.*

I have contracted such a Habit of treating Princes familiarly, by reading the Pamphlets of Mr. *St——* and his Fellows, that I am tempted to suppose Her Majesty's Answer to this Speech might be as follows.

---

23 *Expects . . . Dunkirk*: said by Steele three times in his *Guardian* of 7 August (no. 128), an essay he signed as 'English Tory' and reprinted in the *Importance of Dunkirk*; the phrase was picked up and attacked in *The Examiner* of 24 August and in several separate Tory pamphlets, all portraying it as an insolent assault on the royal prerogative.

MR. R——d St—, late Gazetteer, &c. I do not conceive that any of your Titles empower you to be my Director, or to report to me the Expectations of my People. I know their Expectations better than you; they love me, and will trust me. My Ministers were of my own free Choice; I have found them Wise and Faithful; and whoever calls them Fools or Knaves, designs indirectly an Affront to my Self. I am under no Obligations to demolish Dunkirk, *but to the Most* Christian *King; if you come here as an* Orator *from that Prince to demand it in his Name, where are your Powers? If not, let it suffice you to know, that I have my Reasons for deferring it; and that the Clamours of a* Faction *shall not be a Rule by which I or my Servants are to proceed.*

Mr. *St——* tells you; his *Adversaries are so unjust, they will not take the least Notice of what led him into the Necessity of writing his Letter* P. 48. *to the* Guardian. And how is it possible, any Mortal should know all his *Necessities?* Who can guess, whether this *Necessity* were imposed on him by his *Superiours,* or by the Itch of Party, or by the meer want of other Matter to furnish out a *Guardian?*

But Mr. *St——* has *had a Liberal Education, and knows the World as well as the Ministry does, and will therefore speak on whether he* P. 50. *offends them or no, and though their Cloaths* be ever so *New; when he thinks his Queen and Country is,* (or as a Grammarian would express it, *are) ill treated.*

It would be good to hear Mr. *St——* explain himself upon this Phrase of *knowing the World;* because it is a Science which maintains abundance of Pretenders. Every idle young Rake, who understands how to pick up a Wench, or bilk a Hackney-Coachman, or can call the Players by their Names, and is acquainted with five or six Faces in the Chocolate-House, will needs pass for a Man that *knows the World.* In the like manner Mr. *St——* who from some few Sprinklings of rudimental Literature, proceeded a Gentleman of the Horse-Guards, thence by several Degrees to be an Ensign and an Alchymist, where he was wholly conversant with the lower Part of Mankind, thinks he *knows the World* as well as the Prime Minister; and upon the Strength of that Knowledge, will needs direct Her Majesty in the weightiest Matters of Government.

And now, Mr. Bailiff, give me Leave to inform you, that this long Letter of Mr. *St——* filled with Quotations and a Clutter about *Dunkirk,* was wholly written for the sake of the six last Pages, taken up in vindicating himself directly, and vilifying the Q—— and Ministry by Innuendo's. He apprehends, that *some Representations have been given of* him *in your Town, as, that a Man of so small a Fortune as he must have secret Views or Supports, which could move him to leave his Employments*, &c. He answers, by owning he *has indeed very particular Views; for he is animated in his Conduct by Justice and Truth, and Benevolence to Mankind*. He has given up his Employments, because he *values no Advantages above the Conveniencies of Life, but as they tend to the Service of the Publick*. It seems, he could not *serve the Publick* as a Pensioner, or Commissioner of Stamp'd Paper, and therefore gave them up to sit in Parliament out of *Charity to his Country*, and *to contend for Liberty*. He has transcribed the common Places of some canting Moralist *de contemptu mundi, & fuga seculi*,[24] and would put them upon you as Rules derived from his own Practice.

P. 56.

P. 57.

P. 58.

Here is a most miraculous and sudden Reformation, which I believe can hardly be match'd in History or *Legend*. And Mr. *St——*, not unaware how slow the World was of Belief, has thought fit to anticipate all Objections; he foresees that *prostituted Pens will entertain a Pretender to such Reformations with a Recital of his own Faults and Infirmities, but he is prepared for such Usage, and gives himself up to all nameless Authors, to be treated as they please.*

P. 59.

It is certain, Mr. Bailiff, that no Man breathing can pretend to have arrived at such a sublime pitch of Virtue as Mr. *St——* without some Tendency in the World, to suspend at least their Belief of the Fact, till Time and Observation shall determine. But I hope few Writers will be so *prostitute* as to trouble themselves with *the Faults and Infirmities* of Mr. *St——*'s past Life, with what he somewhere else calls *the Sins of his Youth*,[25] and in one of his late Paper's confesses to have been *numerous* enough. A

---

24 *de contemptu . . . seculi*: 'about the contempt of the world and fleeing from worldly things'. Swift is probably echoing the cynicism of Rabelais, one of his favourite authors: cf. the speech of the monk, Friar John, in *Gargantua and Pantagruel* (book I, chapter xlii), 'And therefore when I shall see them fallen into a river, and ready to be drowned, I shall make them a faire long sermon *de contemptu mundi & fuga seculi*; and when they are stark dead, shall then go to their aide and succour in fishing after them' (Thomas Urquhart (trans.), *The first book of the works of Mr Francis Rabelais* (1653), p. 189).

25 *the Sins of his Youth*: Swift alludes, finally, to his personal quarrel with Steele five months earlier and to the particular element in it which may have galled him most of all. In *The Guardian* No. 53 (12 May 1713), Steele, over his own name, had written about the identity of the

shifting scambling Scene of Youth, attended with Poverty and ill Company, may put a Man of no ill Inclinations upon many Extravagancies, which as soon as they are left off, are easily pardoned and forgot. Besides, I think Popish Writers tell us, that the greatest Sinners make the greatest Saints; but so very quick a Sanctification, and carried to so prodigious a Height, will be apt to rouze the Suspicion of Infidels, especially when they consider that this Pretence of his to so Romantick a Virtue, is only advanced by way of Solution to that difficult Problem, *Why he has given up his Employments?* And according to the new Philosophy, they will endeavour to solve it by some easier and shorter way. For Example, the Question is put, Why Mr. *St*—— gives up his Employment and Pension at this Juncture? I must here repeat with some Enlargement what I said before on this Head. These unbelieving Gentlemen will answer, First, That a new Commission was every day expected for the Stamp'd Paper, and he knew his Name would be left out; and therefore his Resignation would be an Appearance of Virtue cheaply bought.

Secondly, He dreaded the Violence of Creditors, against which his Employments were no manner of Security.

Thirdly, being a Person of great Sagacity, he hath some Foresight of a Change from the usual Age of a Ministry, which is now almost expired; from the little Misunderstandings that have been reported sometimes to happen among the Men in Power; from the Bill of Commerce being rejected,[26] and from some *HORRIBLE EXPECTATIONS*,[27] wherewith his Party have been deceiving themselves and their Friends *Abroad* for about two Years past.

Fourthly, He hopes to come into all the Perquisites of his Predecessor *RIDPATH*, and be the principal Writer of his Faction, where every thing

---

author of *The Examiner* as follows: 'tho' sometimes I have been told, by familiar Friends, that they saw me such a Time talking to the *Examiner*; others, who have rally'd me upon the Sins of my Youth, tell me it is credibly reported that I have formerly lain with the *Examiner*', adding, 'it is nothing to me, whether the *Examiner* writes against me in the Character of an estranged Friend, or *an exasperated Mistress*'. For Swift's furious letter to Addison in response and the bitter exchanges between him and Steele in the following weeks, in what was to be their last correspondence, see the Introduction, pp. 31–2.

26 *Bill of Commerce being rejected*: on 18 June 1713 the Commons, in a defeat for the Tory ministry, had rejected on its third reading the Bill to make effective the Eighth and Ninth Articles of the Treaty of Commerce with France.

27 *HORRIBLE EXPECTATIONS*: i.e., that the death of the Queen was imminent.

is printed by Subscription, which will amply make up the Loss of his Place.

But it may be still demanded, Why he affects those exalted Strains of Piety and Resignation? To this I answer, with great probability, That he hath resumed his old Pursuits after the *Philosopher's Stone*, towards which it is held by all *Adepts* for a most essential Ingredient, that a Man must seek it meerly for the Glory of God, and without the least Desire of being rich.[28]

Mr. *St*—— is angry that some of our Friends have been reflected on in a Pamphlet, because they left us in a Point of the great-   P. 60. est Consequence; and upon that Account he runs into their Panegyrick against his Conscience, and the Interest of his Cause, without considering that those Gentlemen have reverted to us again.[29] The Case is thus: He never would have praised them, if they had remained firm, nor should we have railed at them. The one is full as honest, and as natural as the other: However, Mr. *St*—— hopes (I beg you Mr. Bailiff to observe the Consequence) that notwithstanding this Pamphlets reflecting on some Tories who opposed the Treaty of Commerce, *the Ministry will*   Ibid. *see* Dunkirk *effectually demolished.*

Mr. *St*—— says something in Commendation of the Queen; but stops short, and tells you (if I take his meaning right) that he *shall leave what he has to say on this Topick; till he and Her Majesty are both*   P. 61. *dead.* Thus, he defers his *Praises* as he does his *Debts*, after the manner of the *Druids*, to be paid in another World. If I have ill interpreted him, it is his own Fault, for studying Cadence instead of Propriety, and

---

28   *least Desire of being rich*: cf., for example, Jonson's *The Alchemist*, 'he must be *homo frugi*, / A pious, holy, and religious man, / One free from mortal sin, a very virgin' (Ian Donaldson (ed.), *The Oxford Authors: Ben Jonson* (Oxford: Oxford University Press, 1985), II. ii. 97–9).

29   *reflected on in a Pamphlet . . . reverted to us again*: actually, since Steele says 'in one of the Papers I send you', he could be referring to the *Examiner* as well as to pamphlets like Defoe's *Memoirs of Count Tariff* (1713) or *A Letter from a Member of the House of Commons relating to the Bill of Commerce* (1713), both of which can be read as reproving the dissident Tories. The two pamphlets he expressly mentions have no such reflections on dissident Tories. Although he does not mention them by name, Steele professed to be particularly concerned over the attacks in the Tory press on Sir Thomas Hanmer, the leader of the 'Whimsicals' or 'Hanoverian Tories' in the Commons, and the Earls of Anglesey and Abingdon in the Lords, who had used their influence to affect the vote. See also Esther Vanhomrigh's letter to Swift on 23 June (Woolley, *Corr.*, vol. I, pp. 507–9). Despite Swift's confident tone here, the vote did represent a significant move away from the ministry; see Holmes, pp. 280–1 and Keith Feiling, *A History of the Tory Party, 1640–1714* (Oxford: Clarendon Press, 1924), pp. 450–1.

filling up Nitches with Words before he has adjusted his Conceptions to
them.[30] One part of the Queen's Character is this, *that all the*

Ibid.   *Hours of her Life, are divided between the Exercises of Devotion,
and taking Minutes of the Sublime Affairs of Her Government.*
Now, if the Business of *Dunkirk* be one of the *Sublime Affairs of Her* Majesty's
Government, I think we ought to be at ease, or else she *takes Her Minutes*

P. 61.   to little Purpose. No, says Mr. *St——*, the Queen is a *Lady*, and
unless a Prince will now and then get drunk with his Ministers,[31]
he cannot learn their Interests or Humours; but this being by no means proper
for a *Lady*, she can know nothing but what they think fit to tell her when
they are Sober. And therefore *all the Fellow-Subjects* of these Ministers

Ibid.   must watch their Motions and *be very solicitous for what passes
beyond the ordinary Rules of Government*; For while we are foolishly
relying upon Her Majesty's Virtues; These Ministers are *taking the Advantage
of encreasing the Power of* France.

There is a very good Maxim, I think it is neither *Whig* nor *Tory*, that the
Prince can do no wrong; which I doubt is often applied to very ill Purposes.
A Monarch of *Britain* is pleased to create *a Dozen Peers*, and to make a Peace;
both these Actions are, (for instance,) within the undisputed Prerogative
of the Crown, and are to be reputed and submitted to as the Actions of
the Prince: But as a King of *England* is supposed to be guided in Matters
of such Importance, by the Advice of those he employs in his Councils;
whenever a Parliament thinks fit to complain of such Proceedings, as a
publick Grievance, then this Maxim takes Place, that the Prince can do no
wrong, and the Advisers are called to Account. But shall this empower such
an Individual as Mr. *St——* in his *Tatling of Pamphleteering*

P. 62.   Capacity, to fix *the ordinary Rules of Government*, or to affirm
that *Her Ministers, upon the Security of Her Majesty's Goodness,
are labouring for the Grandeur of* France? What ordinary Rule of
Government is transgressed by the Queen's delaying the Demolition of
Dunkirk? Or what Addition is thereby made to the Grandeur of *France*?

---

30 *Conceptions to them*: Swift does not seem to be distorting Steele's meaning; here are his words:
   'But I shall leave what I have to say on this Topick, to the Time when the Consequence of
   it will be Insignificant to me, but which I hope will do her Honour, that is Justice, when I
   am no more, and the Remains of Her Sacred Person are as common Dust as mine' (*Tracts*,
   p. 123).
31 *get drunk . . . Ministers*: Steele, in fact, speaks only of a Lady being dependent on Ministers
   for reports of 'Conversation' among great men 'even in their unguarded Leisure'.

Every Taylor in your Corporation is as much a *Fellow-Subject* as Mr. *St*——, and do you think in your Conscience that every Taylor of *Stockbridge* is fit to direct Her Majesty and Her Ministers in *the sublime Affairs of her Government*?

But He *persists in it, that it is no manner of Diminution of the Wisdom of a Prince, that he is obliged to act by the Information of others.* The Sense is admirable; and the Interpretation is this, that what a Man is forced to *is no diminution of his Wisdom*: But if he would conclude from this Sage Maxim, that, because a Prince *acts by the Information of others*, therefore those Actions may lawfully be traduced in Print by every Fellow-Subject; I hope there is no Man in *England*, so much a *Whig*, as to be of his Opinion.
Ibid.

Mr. *St*—— concludes his Letter to you with a Story about King *William* and his *French Dog-keeper, who gave that Prince a Gun loaden only with Powder, and then pretended to wonder how his Majesty could miss his Aim: Which was no Argument against the King's Reputation for Shooting very finely.* This he would have you apply, by allowing Her Majesty to be a Wise Prince, but deceived by wicked Counsellors, who are in the Interest of *France*. Her Majesty's Aim was Peace, which, I think, She hath not miss'd; and, God be thanked, She hath got it, without any more Expence, either of SHOT or POWDER. Her *Dog-keepers*, for some Years past, had directed Her *Gun* against Her *Friends*, and at last *loaded* it so deep, that it was in danger to *burst* in Her Hands.
Ibid.

You may please to observe, that Mr. *St*——calls this *Dog-keeper* a *Minister*, which, with humble Submission, is a gross Impropriety of Speech. The Word is derived from *Latin*, where it properly signifies a *Servant*; but in *English* is never made use of otherwise, than to denominate those who are employ'd in the Service of Church or State: So that the Appellation, as he directs it, is no less absurd, than it would be for you, Mr. Bailiff, to send your Prentice for a Pot of Ale, and give him the Title of your *Envoy*; to call a Petty-Constable a *Magistrate*, or the Common Hangman a *Minister* of Justice. I confess, when I was choqued[32] at this Word in reading the Paragraph, a Gentleman offer'd his Conjecture, that it might possibly be intended for a Reflection or a Jest: But if there be any thing further

---

32 *choqued*: i.e. 'shocked.'

in it, than a want of Understanding our Language, I take it to be only a Refinement upon the old levelling Principle of the Whigs. Thus, in their Opinion, a *Dog-keeper* is as much a *Minister* as any Secretary of State: And thus Mr. *St——* and my Lord *Treasurer* are both *Fellow-Subjects*. I confess, I have known some *Ministers*, whose Birth, or Qualities, or both, were such that nothing but the Capriciousness of Fortune, and the Iniquity of the Times, could ever have raised them above the Station of *Dog-keepers*; and to whose Administration I should be loath to entrust a Dog I had any Value for: Because, by the Rule of Proportion, they who treated their *Prince* like a *Slave*, would have used their *Fellow-Subjects* like *Dogs*; and how they would treat a *Dog*, I can find no Similitude to express; yet I well remember, they maintained a large Number, whom they taught to *Fawn* upon themselves, and *Bark* at their Mistress. However, while they were in Service, I wish they had only kept Her Majesty's DOGS, and not been trusted with Her GUNS. And thus much by way of Comment upon this worthy Story of King *William* and his *Dog-keeper*.

I have now, Mr. Bailiff, explained to you all the difficult Parts in Mr. *St——*'s Letter. As for the Importance of *Dunkirk*, and when it shall be Demolished, or whether it shall be Demolished or not, neither he, nor you, nor I, have any thing to do in the Matter. Let us all say what we please, Her Majesty will think Her self the best *Judge*, and Her Ministers the best *Advisers*; neither hath Mr. *St——* pretended to prove that any Law Ecclesiastical or Civil, Statute or Common, is broken, by keeping *Dunkirk* undemolished, as long as the Queen shall think best for the Service of Her Self and Her Kingdoms; and it is not altogether impossible, that there may be some few Reasons of State, which have not been yet communicated to Mr. *St——*. I am, with Respect to the Borough and Your self,

> SIR,
> *Your most Humble*
> *and most Obedient Servant,*
> &c.

THE PUBLICK SPIRIT OF
THE WHIGS

THE

PUBLICK SPIRIT

OF THE

WHIGS:

Set forth in their Generous

Encouragement of the Author

OF THE

CRISIS:

WITH SOME

OBSERVATIONS

ON THE

SEASONABLENESS, CANDOR, ERUDITION,
and STYLE of that Treatife.

LONDON:

Printed for *John Morphew*, near *Stationers-Hall*.
MDCCXIV.

Price One Shilling.

Figure 9. Title page of first unexpurgated edition: CUL, Syn. 5.71.21(11).

THE
PUBLICK SPIRIT
OF THE
WHIGS, &c.

I cannot without some Envy, and a just Resentment against the opposite Conduct of others, reflect upon that Generosity and Tenderness, wherewith the Heads and Principal Members of a struggling Faction treat those who will undertake to hold a Pen in their Defence. And the Behaviour of these Patrons is yet the more laudable, because the Benefits they confer are almost *gratis*: If any of their Labourers can scratch out a Pamphlet, they desire no more; There is no Question offered about the Wit, the Style, the Argument. Let a Pamphlet come out upon demand in a proper Juncture, you shall be well and certainly paid; you shall be paid before-hand, every one of the Party who is able to read and can spare a Shilling shall be a Subscriber: Several Thousands of each Production shall be sent among their Friends through the Kingdom: The Work shall be reported admirable, sublime, unanswerable, shall serve to raise the sinking Clamours, and confirm the Scandal of introducing Popery and the Pretender upon the QUEEN and Her Ministers.

Among the present Writers on that Side, I can recollect but Three of any great Distinction, which are the *Flying-Post*, Mr. *Dunton*, and the Author of the *Crisis*:[1] The first of these seems to have been much sunk in Reputation since the sudden Retreat of the *only true genuine Original Author Mr.* Ridpath, who is celebrated by the *Dutch* Gazeteer, as *One of the best Pens of* England. Mr. *Dunton* hath been longer and more conversant in Books than any of the Three, as well as more voluminous in his Productions: However, having employ'd his Studies in so great a Variety of other Subjects,

---

1 *Flying-Post . . . Crisis*: George Ridpath, whom Swift called a 'Scotch rogue' (Williams, *JSt*, p. 568), had been found guilty in February of writing libels, but by this time had fled to Holland, where he remained until after the accession of George I; cf. Swift's use of his name to ridicule Steele, above, p. 236. By the 'Dutch Gazeteer' Swift means the *Gazette d'Amsterdam*, also known in France as the *Gazette d'Hollande*; however, no such account of Ridpath has been found in that paper. John Dunton (1659–1753) was a bookseller and hack writer, whom Swift had sneered at in *Tale of a Tub*, though he had unwittingly published his second printed poem in Dunton's *Athenian Gazette*.

he hath I think but lately turned his Genius to Politicks. His famous Tract, Intituled, *Neck or Nothing*, must be allowed to be the shrewdest Piece, and written with the most Spirit of any which hath appeared from that Side since the Change of the Ministry: It is indeed a most cutting Satire upon the Lord Treasurer and Lord *Bolingbroke*, and I wonder none of our Friends ever undertook to Answer it. I confess I was at first of the same Opinion with several good Judges, who from the Style and Manner supposed it to have issued from the sharp Pen of the E. of *N-t-ng--m*; and I am still apt to think it might receive his L--dsh-p's last Hand.[2] The Third and Principal of this Triumvirate is the Author of the *Crisis*; who although he must yield to the *Flying-Post* in Knowledge of the World, and Skill in Politicks, and to Mr. *Dunton* in Keenness of Satire, and Variety of Reading, hath yet other Qualities enough to denominate him a Writer of a Superior Class to either, provided he would a little regard the Propriety and Disposition of his Words, consult the Grammatical Part, and get some Information in the Subject he intends to handle.

Omitting the generous Countenance and Encouragement that have been shewn to the Persons and Productions of the Two former Authors, I shall here only consider the great Favour conferred upon the last. It hath been advertised for several Months in the *Englishman* and other Papers, that a Pamphlet, called, *The Crisis*, should be published at a proper Time, in order to open the Eyes of the Nation.[3] It was proposed to be Printed by

2 *Neck or Nothing . . . last Hand*: *Neck or nothing: in a letter to the Right Honourable the Lord – being a supplement to the Short history of the Parliament* (1713), which Swift praises with such ironic extravagance, is indeed by Dunton and consists mostly of 'Calling The Ministry Vile Names' (Defoe to Oxford in G. H. Healey, *Letters of Daniel Defoe* (Oxford: Clarendon Press, 1955), p. 438). Swift pretends here that it might well be by Nottingham so as to associate Nottingham with extreme and in this case bizarre Whiggery and thus underscore the irony of the defection of that high-Church statesman from the Tories. Cf. Swift's broadside *Toland's Invitation to Dismal, to Dine with the Calves-Head Club* (1712), in which the deist John Toland invites Nottingham to join in exulting over the execution of Charles I. 'Last hand': i.e., his finishing touches (*OED*, s.v. 'last', 6b, citing *Tale of a Tub*, Bookseller to the Reader).

3 *Eyes of the Nation*: the publisher Samuel Buckley first advertised *The Crisis* in Steele's *The Englishman* for 22 October as an 'Antidote against the treasonable Insinuations which are licentiously handed about the Town', and the notices continued in that organ almost weekly for the next 10 weeks (*Englishman*, p. 411). Swift or more likely an imitator of his also ridiculed the heavy advertising in *The First Ode of the Second Book of Horace Paraphras'd: And Address'd to Richard St–le* (6 or 7 January 1713), predicting as well that despite the fanfare the new pamphlet will merely repeat the same old Whig themes: 'Thou pompously wilt let us know / What all the World knew long ago . . . / That we a *German* Prince must own / When *A–N* for Heav'n resigns Her Throne.' The writer was apparently unaware that the Whigs had sought money

Subscription, Price a Shilling. This was a little out of Form; For Subscriptions are usually begged only for Books of great Price, and such as are not likely to have a general Sale. Notice was likewise given of what this Pamphlet should contain; only an Extract from certain Acts of Parliament relating to the Succession, which at least must sink Nine-Pence in the Shilling, and leave but Three-Pence for the Authors Political Reflections; so that nothing very wonderful or decisive could be reasonably expected from this Performance. But a Work was to be done, a hearty Writer to be encouraged, and accordingly many Thousand Copies were bespoke: Neither could this be sufficient; for when we expected to have our Bundles delivered us, all was stopt; the Friends to the Cause sprang a new Project, and it was advertised that the *Crisis* could not appear till the Ladies had shewn their Zeal against the *Pretender* as well as the Men; against the *Pretender* in the Bloom of his Youth, reported to be Handsome, and endued with an Understanding exactly of a Size to please the Sex.[4] I should be glad to have seen a printed List of the fair Subscribers prefixed to this Pamphlet; by which the *Chevalier* might know he was so far from *pretending* to a Monarchy here, that he could not so much as *pretend* to a Mistrefs.

At the destined Period, the first News we hear, is of a huge Train of Dukes, Earls, Viscounts, Barons, Knights, Esquires, Gentlemen, and others, going to *Sam. Buckley's* the Publisher of the *Crisis*, to fetch home their Cargo's, in order to transmit them by Dozens, Scores, and Hundreds, into the several Counties, and thereby to prepare the Wills and Understandings of their Friends against the approaching Sessions. Ask any of them whether they have read it? they will answer, No; but they have sent it every where, and it will do a World of Good: It is a Pamphlet, and a Pamphlet they hear against the Ministry, talks of Slavery, *France*, and the Pretender; they Desire no more; It will settle the Wavering, confirm the Doubtful, instruct the Ignorant, inflame the Clamorous, though it never be once looked into. I am told by those who are expert in the Trade, That the Author and Bookseller of this Twelve-peny Treatise, will be greater Gainers, than from

---

from the Elector of Hanover himself to help finance *The Crisis*; see Steele, *Correspondence*, pp. 436–7.

4 *please the Sex*: the notice appeared in *The Englishman* No. 36 (26 December 1713): '*At the desire of several Ladies of Quality, the publication of the CRISIS is put off till the Female World have expressed their Zeal for the Publick, by a Subscription as large as that made by the other Sex*' (*Englishman*, p. 431)

one Edition of any Folio that hath been published these Twenty Years. What needy Writer would not sollicite to Work under such Masters, who will pay us before-hand, take off as much of our Ware as we please at our own Rates, and Trouble not themselves to examine either before or after they have bought it, whether it be Staple[5] or no?

But in order to illustrate the implicite Munificence of these Noble Patrons, I cannot take a more effectual Method than by examining the Production it self; by which we shall easily find that it was never intended, further than from the Noise, the Bulk, and the Title of *Crisis*, to do any Service to the factious Cause. The entire Piece consists of a Title Page, a Dedication to the Clergy, a Preface, an Extract from certain Acts of Parliament, and about Ten Pages of dry Reflections on the Proceedings of the QUEEN and Her Servants; which his Coadjutors, the E—— of *N--t--ng---m*, Mr. *Dunton*, and the *Flying-Post*, had long ago set before us in a much clearer Light.

In Popish Countries, when some Impostor cries out, A *Miracle!* A *Miracle!* it is not done with a Hope or Intention of converting Hereticks, but confirming the deluded Vulgar in their Errors; and so the Cry goes round without examining into the Cheat. Thus the Whigs among us give about the Cry, A *Pamphlet!* A *Pamphlet!* The *Crisis!* The *Crisis!* not with a View of convincing their Adversaries, but to raise the Spirits of their Friends, recall their Stragglers, and unite their Numbers by Sound and Impudence, as Bees assemble and cling together by the Noise of Brass.

That no other Effect could be imagined or hoped for, by the Publication of this timely Treatise, will be manifest, from some obvious Reflections upon the several Parts of it; wherein the Follies, the Falshoods, or the Absurdities, appear so frequent, that they may boldly contend for Number with the Lines.

When the Hawker holds this Pamphlet towards you, the first Words you perceive are, *The Crisis:* Or, *A Discourse,* &c. The Interpreter of *Suidas*[6] gives Four Translations of the Word *Crisis*; any of which may be as properly

---

5 *Staple*: i.e., holding a foremost place among products of its kind.
6 *Interpreter of Suidas*: Suidas or 'The Suda' is the name of a massive tenth-century lexicon or historical encyclopedia. Swift owned an edition of 1619 in Greek and Latin (no. 94 in his library list) and referred to the lexicon in his mock-scholarly parody *A Discourse to Prove the Antiquity of the English Tongue* (Davis, vol. IV, p. 238). Under the word *krisis* the Latin 'Interpreter' (translator) in the 1619 edition gives four terms, 'Iudicium. Examen. Suffragium. Quaestio', all fairly close in meaning, as Swift implies: 'judicium' (judicial investigation, a

applied to this Author's Letter to the Bayliff of *Stockbridge*. Next, what he calls *A Discourse*, consists only of Two Pages, prefixed to Twenty two more, which contain Extracts from Acts of Parliament; For as to the Twelve last Pages, they are provided for by themselves in the Title under the Name of *Some Seasonable Remarks on the Danger of a* Popish *Successor*. Another Circumstance worthy of our Information in the Title-Page, is, That the Crown hath been settled *by previous Acts*. I never heard of any Act of Parliament that was not *previous* to what it enacted, unless those Two by which the Earl of *Strafford* and Sir *John Fenwick*[7] lost their Heads, may pass for Exceptions. *A Discourse, representing from the most Authentick Records*. He hath borrowed this Expression from some Writer, who probably understood the Words, but this Gentleman hath altogether misapplied them; and under Favour,[8] he is wholly mistaken; for a Heap of Extracts, from several Acts of Parliament, cannot be called a Discourse: neither do I believe, he Copied them from the most Authentick Records, which as I take it are lodged in the *Tower*, but out of some common printed Copy. I grant there is nothing Material in all this, further than to shew the Generosity of our Adversaries in encouraging a Writer, who cannot furnish out so much as a Title-Page with Propriety or common Sense.

Next follows the Dedication to the Clergy of the Church of *England*, wherein the Modesty and the Meaning of the first Paragraphs are hardly to be matched. He tells them, he hath made *a Comment upon the Acts of* Settlement, which he *lays before them*, and *conjures them to recommend in their Writings and Discourses to their Fellow-Subjects*; and he does all this, *out of a just Deference to their great Power and Influence.* This is the right Whig-Scheme of directing the Clergy what to Preach. The Archbishop of *Canterbury*'s Jurisdiction extends no further than over his own Province; but the Author of the *Crisis*, constitutes himself Vicar-General over the whole

---

trial); 'examen', a weighing, a consideration; 'quaestio', inquiry, or the subject of inquiry; and 'suffragium', which literally has to do with voting, but in transferred meaning is a decision, a judgement, an opinion (Aemilius Portus (ed.), *Suidas*, 2 vols. (Geneva, 1619)).

7 *Strafford . . . Fenwick*: Thomas Wentworth (1593–1641), Earl of Strafford, chief advisor to Charles I, was executed after the Puritan House of Commons passed a Bill of attainder; Sir John Fenwick (1645–1697) was a Jacobite conspirator executed in 1697 for a plot in 1696 to kill William III, again with a Bill of attainder being used after a witness absconded (see *Some Remarks*, pp. 132). Swift cites this example of an *ex post facto* act to ridicule Steele's awkward phrasing on the title page of the *Crisis*, where 'previous Acts' comes five lines after 'Settlements'.

8 *under Favour*: i.e., 'by your leave' (*OED*).

Clergy of the Church of *England.* The Bishops in their Letters or Speeches to their own Clergy proceed no further than to *Exhortation*; but this Writer *conjures* the whole Clergy of the Church to *recommend* his *Comment upon the Laws* of the Land *in their Writings and Discourses.*[9] I would fain know, who made him a *Commentator upon the Laws* of the Land; after which it will be time enough to ask him, by what Authority he directs the Clergy *to recommend his* Comments from the Pulpit or the Press?

He tells the Clergy *there are two Circumstances which place the Minds of the People under their Direction*; the first Circumstance is their Education; the second Circumstance is the Tenths of our Lands. This last, according to the *Latin* Phrase, is spoken *ad invidiam*;[10] for he knows well enough, they have not a Twentieth: But if you take it his own way, the Landlord has nine Parts in ten of the People's Minds under his Direction. Upon this Rock the Author before us is perpetually splitting, as often as he ventures out beyond the narrow Bounds of his Literature. He has a confused Remembrance of Words since he left the University, but has lost half their Meaning, and puts them together with no Regard but to their Cadence; as I remember a Fellow nailed up Maps in a Gentleman's Closet, some sideling, others upside down, the better to adjust them to the Pannels.

I am sensible it is of little Consequence to their Cause, whether this Defender of it understands Grammar or no; And if what he would fain say, discovered him to be a Well-willer to Reason or Truth, I would be ready to make large Allowances. But when with great Difficulty I descry a Composition of Rancor and Falshood, intermixed with plausible Nonsense; I feel a struggle between Contempt and Indignation, at seeing the Character of a *Censor*, a *Guardian*, an *English-man*, a *Commentator* on the *Laws*, an *Instructor* of the *Clergy*, assumed by a Child of Obscurity, without one single Qualification to support them.

9 *Writings and Discourses*: Steele's sloppy grammar left him open to this sally. He writes that he will lay before his readers 'the following Comment upon the Laws which regard the Settlement of the Imperial Crown of *Great Britain*', and he continues, 'My Purpose in addressing these Matters to you, is to conjure you . . . to recommend them . . . to your Fellow-Subjects.' Obviously 'them' in the phrase 'recommend them' was intended to refer to the 'Laws which regard the Settlement', or perhaps to the 'Matters' he is addressing, but Swift easily interprets it to refer to the 'Comment' itself.

10 *ad invidiam*: i. e., '*argumentum ad invidiam*', an appeal to envy, i. e. to inflame the reader's envy of the clergy. In the next sentence Swift uses a *reductio*: if the clergy's right to direct our minds depends on their having one-tenth tithe, then the landlord, who has the rest of the land, must have nine-tenths of the minds under his direction.

This Writer, who either affects, or is commanded of late to Copy after the B——p of *S--r--m*,[11] hath, out of the Pregnancy of his Invention, found out an old Way of insinuating the grossest Reflections under the Appearances of Admonitions; and is so judicious a Follower of the Prelate, that he taxes the Clergy for *enflaming their People with Apprehensions of Danger to them and* THEIR *Constitution, from Men who are Innocent of such Designs.* When he must needs confess, the whole *Design* of his Pamphlet is *to enflame the People with Apprehensions of Danger* from the present Ministry, whom *we* believe to be at least as *innocent Men* as the last.

What shall I say to a Pamphlet, where the Malice and Falshood of every Line would require an Answer, and where the Dulness and Absurdities will not deserve one?

By his pretending to have always maintained an inviolable Respect to the Clergy, he would insinuate, that those Papers among the *Tatlers* and *Spectators*, where the whole Order is abused, were not his own: I will Appeal to all who know the Flatness of his Style, and the Barrenness of his Invention, whether he does not grosly prevaricate? Was he ever able to Walk without Leading-Strings, or Swim without Bladders,[12] without being discovered by his Hobbling and his Sinking? Has he adhered to this Character in his Paper called the *Englishman*, whereof he is allowed to be sole Author, without any Competition? What does he think of the Letter signed by himself, which relates to *Molesworth*, in whose Defence, he affronts the whole Convocation of *Ireland*?[13]

---

11 *B——p of S--r--m*: Gilbert Burnet, Bishop of Salisbury, whom Swift despised. The clear parallel drawn here between Burnet and Steele had been made plain earlier in Swift's *Preface to the B—p of Sarum's Introduction* (7 December 1713), where he says Burnet, in the Introduction to the third volume of his *History of the Reformation of the Church of England*, writes 'as if Destruction hung over us by single Hair'. Obviously, everything Swift says in his *Preface* about Burnet's alarmism is meant to apply also to Steele and his *Englishman*; he depicts both as agents in the 'grand Preparations' which the Whigs are making against the next parliamentary session and says their 'Notions' have been dictated 'by the same Masters' (Davis, vol. IV, p. 57).

12 *Leading-strings . . . Bladders*: 'strings with which children used to be guided and supported when learning to walk' (*OED*); bladders: prepared animal bladders, which are inflated and used as floats (*OED*).

13 *Molesworth . . . Ireland*: The *Englishman*, no. 46 (19 January 1714, the same day as the publication of *The Crisis*) was given over to a 'letter' signed by Steele in his own name defending Robert Molesworth, Whig leader and member of the Irish Privy Council, from the aspersions of *The Examiner*. Molesworth, whom Swift had coupled with Wharton when writing to Archbishop King on 31 December, had quoted aloud, upon recognizing at the castle a clergyman who had participated in election-day riots, Acts 17: 6, 'These that have turned the world upside down are come hither also.' The result was a complaint to the House

It is a wise Maxim, that because the Clergy are no Civil Lawyers, they ought not to preach Obedience to Governors; and therefore, they ought not to preach Temperance, because they are no Physicians: Examine all this Author's Writings, and then Point me out a Divine who knows less of the Constitution of *England* than he; witness those many egregious Blunders in his late Papers, where he pretended to dabble in the Subject.[14]

But the Clergy have it seems imbibed their Notions of Power and Obedience abhorrent from our Laws, *from the pompous Ideas of Imperial Greatness, and the Submission to absolute Emperors.*[15] This is gross Ignorance, below a School-Boy in his *Lucius Florus:*[16] The *Roman* History, wherein Lads are instructed, reaches little above Eight hundred Years, and the Authors do every where instil Republican Principles; and from the Account of Nine in Twelve of the first Emperors, we learn to have a Detestation for Tyranny. The *Greeks* carry this Point yet a great deal higher, which none can be ignorant of, who hath read or heard them quoted. This gave *Hobbes* the Occasion of advancing a Position directly contrary, That the Youth of *England* was corrupted in their Political Principles, by reading the Histories of *Rome* and *Greece*, which having been writ under Republicks, taught the Readers to have ill Notions of Monarchy:[17] In this Assertion there was something Specious, but that advanced by the *Crisis* could only issue from the profoundest Ignorance.

But would you know his Scheme of Education for young Gentlemen at the University? It is, That they should spend their Time in perusing those Acts of Parliament, whereof his Pamphlet is an Extract, which, *if it had been done, the Kingdom would not be in its present Condition, but every Member sent into the World thus instructed, since the Revolution, would have been an Advocate for our Rights and Liberties.*

---

of Lords by the lower House of Convocation and eventually Molesworth's dismissal from the Privy Council; see King's letter to Swift of 13 January (Woolley, *Corr.*, vol. I, p. 581).

14 *dabble in the Subject*: referring, presumably, to *The Englishman*, nos. 25, 28, 32 (1, 8, 17 December 1713), all, as Blanchard points out, dealing with the origin and nature of government.

15 *absolute Emperors*: Steele says the clergy have 'inadvertently uttered' these notions; otherwise Swift quotes him exactly and accurately.

16 *Lucius Florus*: Lucius Annaeus Florus (fl. AD 130) Roman historian of the second century AD, who, relying heavily on Livy, compiled a brief sketch or *Epitome* of the history of Rome from the foundation of the city to the closing of the temple of Janus by Augustus (25 BC). It was intended as a panegyric of the Roman people and was very popular in the Middle Ages.

17 *Hobbes . . . Monarchy*: Hobbes, *Leviathan*, part II, chapter 21, 'Of the Liberty of Subjects', par. 9. Swift is alluding to this passage:

Here now is a Project for getting more Money by the *Crisis*, to have it read by Tutors in the Universities. I thoroughly agree with him, that if our Students had been thus employ'd for Twenty Years past, *the Kingdom had not been in its* present *Condition.* But we have too many of such Proficients already among the young Nobility and Gentry, who have gathered up their Politicks from Chocolate Houses and Factious Clubs, and who if they had spent their Time in hard Study at *Oxford* or *Cambridge*, we might indeed have said, that the factious Part of this Kingdom *had not been in its present Condition*, or have suffered themselves to be taught, that a few Acts of Parliament relating to the Succession are preferable to all other *Civil Institutions* whatsoever: Neither did I ever before hear, that an Act of Parliament relating to one particular Point could be called a Civil Institution.

He spends almost a Quarto Page in telling the Clergy, that they will be certainly Perjured if they bring in the *Pretender* whom they have abjured; and he wisely reminds them, that they have Sworn without Equivocation or Mental-Reservation; otherwise the Clergy might think, that as soon as they received the *Pretender*, and turned *Papists*, they would be free from their Oath.

This honest, civil, ingenious Gentlemen, knows in his Conscience, that there are not Ten Clergymen in *England*, (except Non-Jurors) who do not abhor the Thoughts of the *Pretender* reigning over us, much more than himself. But this is the Spittle of the B——p of *S--r--m*, which our Author licks up, and Swallows, and then Coughs out again, with an Addition of his own Phlegm. I would fain suppose the Body of the Clergy were to return an Answer by one of their Members to these worthy Counsellors: I conceive it might be in the following Terms.

In these westerne parts of the world, we are made to receive our opinions concerning the Institution, and Rights of Common-wealths from *Aristotle, Cicero*, and other men, Greeks and Romanes, that, living under Popular States, derived those Rights, not from the Principles of Nature, but transcribed them into their books, out of the Practice of their own Common-wealths, which were popular . . . And as *Aristotle*; so *Cicero*, and other Writers have grounded their Civill doctrine, on the opinions of the Romans, who were taught to hate Monarchy . . . And by reading of these Greek, and Latine Authors, men from their childhood have gotten a habit . . . of favouring tumults, and of licentious controlling the actions of their Soveraigns; and again of controlling those controllers. (*Leviathan* (1651), pp. 110–11).

Swift had cited the same remark of Hobbes in his *Sentiments* (1708).

My L——d and Gentleman,

The Clergy Command me to give you Thanks for your Advice; and if they knew any Crimes from which either of you were as free, as they are from those which you so earnestly Exhort them to avoid, they would return your Favour as near as possible in the same Style and Manner. However, that your Advice may not be wholly lost, particularly that Part of it which relates to the *Pretender*, they desire you would apply it to more proper Persons. Look among your own Leaders; Examine which of them engaged in a Plot to restore the late K. *James*, and received Pardons under his Seal; Examine which of them have been since tampering with his pretended Son, and to gratify their Ambition, their Avarice, their Malice and Revenge, are now willing to Restore him at the Expence of the Religion and Liberty of their Country.[18] Retire, good my Lord, with your Pupil, and let us hear no more of these Hypocrital Insinuations, lest the Qu—— and Ministers, who have been hitherto content with only *disappointing* the lurking Villanies of your Faction, may be at last provoked to *expose* them.

But his Respect for the Clergy is such, that he does not *instinuate* as if they really had these evil Dispositions; He only *insinuates*, that they give *too much Cause* for such *Insinuations.*

I will upon Occasion, strip some of his *Insinuations* from their Generality and Solecisms, and drag them into the Light. This Dedication to the Clergy is full of them, because here he endeavours to mold up his Rancor and Civility together; by which constraint, he is obliged to shorten his Paragraphs and to place them in such a Light, that they obscure one another. Supposing therefore, that I have scraped off his good Manners, in order to come at his Meaning which lies under; He tells the Clergy, that the Favour of the QUEEN and Her Ministers, is but a *colour of Zeal towards them*:[19] That the People were deluded by a groundless Cry of the Churches Danger at *Sacheverell*'s Tryal;[20] That the Clergy, as they are *Men of Sense and Honour*, ought to Preach this Truth to their several Congregations; and let them know, that the true Design of the present Men in Power in that and all their Proceedings since, in favour of the Church, was to bring in

18 *Examine . . . Country*: a persistent theme for Swift; see *The Examiner* for 3 May 1711 as well as his *Letter from the Pretender to a Whig-Lord* (1712); see above, pp. 201–2 and notes.
19 *colour of Zeal . . . them*: this and the other italicized phrases in the paragraph are quoted verbatim from Steele's pamphlet.
20 *Sacheverell's Tryal*: see *Some Reasons*, p. 168 and note.

Popery, France, and the *Pretender*, and to enslave all *Europe*, contrary to the *Laws of our Country, the Powers of the Legislature, the Faith of Nations, and the Honour of God*.

I cannot see, why the Clergy, as *Men of Sense, and Men of Honour*, (for he appeals not to them as Men of Religion) should not be allowed to know when they are in Danger, and be able to Guess whence it comes, and who are their Protectors. The Design of their Destruction indeed may have been projected in the Dark; but when all was ripe, their Enemies proceeded to so many Overt-Acts in the Face of the Nation, that it was obvious to the meanest People, who wanted no other Motives to rouze them. On the other side, Can this Author, or the wisest of his Faction, assign one single Act of the present Ministry, any Way tending towards bringing in the *Pretender*, or to weaken the Succession in the House of *Hanover*? Observe then the Reasonableness of this Gentleman's Advice: The Clergy, the Gentry, and the common People, had the utmost Apprehensions of Danger to the Church under the late Ministry; yet then it was the greatest Impiety to *enflame the People with any such Apprehensions*. His Danger of a *Popish* Successor from any Steps of the present Ministry, is an artificial Calumny raised and spread against the Conviction of the Inventors, pretended to be believed only by those who abhor the Constitution in Church and State, an obdurate Faction, who compass Heaven and Earth to restore themselves upon the Ruin of their Country; Yet here our Author *exhorts the Clergy* to preach up this Imaginary Danger to their People, and disturb the publick Peace with his strained Seditious Comments.

But how comes this gracious Licence to the Clergy from the *Whigs*, to concern themselves with Politicks of any Sort, though it be only the Glosses and Comments of Mr. *S——le*? The Speeches of the Managers at *Sacheverell*'s Tryal, particularly those of *Stanhope, Lechmere, King, Parker*,[21] and some other, seemed to deliver a different Doctrine. Nay, this very Dedication complains of *some in Holy Orders who have made the Constitution of their Country*, (in which and the *Coptick* Mr. *S——le* is equally skilled)

---

21 *Stanhope . . . Parker*: these were the among the twenty Whig managers of the Sacheverell impeachment in the House of Commons: Lieutenant-General James Stanhope; Nicholas Lechmere; Sir Peter King; and Sir Thomas Parker (by the time of the verdict Lord Chief Justice). Steele had sent *The Crisis* to Lechmere for corrections before publication, and his *Englishman* collection was dedicated to Stanhope (*Tracts*, p. 286). See Geoffrey Holmes, *The Trial of Doctor Sacheverell* (London: Eyre Metheun, 1973).

a very little Part of their Study, and yet made Obedience and Government the frequent Subjects of their Discourses. This Difficulty is easily solved; for by *Politicks*, they mean *Obedience.* Mr. *Hoadley*, who is a Champion for Resistance, was never charged as medling out of his Function: *Hugh Peters*, and his Brethren, in the Times of Usurpation, had full Liberty to preach up Sedition and Rebellion;[22] and so here Mr. *St——le* issues out his Licence to the Clergy to preach up the *Danger of a Popish Pretender*, in Defiance of the QUEEN and Her Administration.

Every Whiffler[23] in a Laced Coat, who frequents the Chocolate-House, and is able to spell the Title of a Pamphlet, shall Talk of the Constitution with as much Plausibility as this very Solemn Writer, and with as good a Grace blame the Clergy for medling with Politicks which they do not understand. I have known many of these able Politicians, furnished before they were of Age, with all the necessary Topicks of their Faction, and by the help of about Twenty Polysyllables capable of maintaining an Argument that would shine in the *Crisis*, whose Author gathered up his little Stock from the same Schools, and has writ from no other Fund.

But after all, it is not clear to me, whether this Gentleman addresseth himself to the Clergy of *England* in general, or only to those very few, (hardly enough in Case of a Change to supply the Mortality of those *Self-denying Prelates*[24] he celebrates) who are in his Principles, and among these, only such as live in and about *London*, which probably will reduce the Number to about half a Dozen at most. I should incline to guess the latter; because he tells them, they *are surrounded by a learned, wealthy, knowing Gentry, who know with what Firmness, Self-denial, and Charity, the Bishops adhered to the publick Cause, and what Contumelies those Clergymen have undergone,* &c. *who adhered to the Cause of Truth*: By those Terms, *the publick Cause*, and *the Cause of Truth*, he understands the *Cause* of the Whigs in Opposition to the QUEEN and Her Servants: Therefore by the *learned, wealthy, and knowing Gentry*, he must understand the *Bank*

---

22 *Hoadley . . . Rebellion*: Benjamin Hoadley (1676–1761), later Bishop in succession of Bangor, Hereford, Salisbury, and Winchester, who by this time had acquired a considerable reputation as a champion of 'revolution principles' by attacking the doctrines of hereditary right and passive obedience. Hugh Peters (1598–1660) was a Puritan preacher and regicide during the 'Times of Usurpation', i.e. the Commonwealth.

23 *Whiffler*: 'A trifler; an insignificant or contemptible fellow' (*OED*).

24 *Self-denying Prelates*: Steele had praised the 'self-denial' of the bishops; the phrases later in the paragraph about the '*Gentry*' are also quoted from *The Crisis*.

and *East-India Company*, and those other Merchants or Citizens within the Bills of Mortality, who have been strenuous against the Church and Crown and whose Spirit of Faction hath lately got the better of their Interest. For let him search all the rest of the Kingdom, he will find the *surrounded* Clergy, and the *surrounding* Gentry, wholly Strangers to the Merits of those Prelates, and adhering to a very different *Cause of Truth*, as will soon I hope be manifest by a fair Appeal to the Representatives of both.

It was very unnecessary in this Writer to bespeak the Treatment of *Contempt and Derision*, which the Clergy are to expect from his Faction whenever they come into Power. I believe that venerable Body is in very little Concern after what Manner their most mortal Enemies intend to *treat* them, whenever it shall please God for our Sins to visit us with so fatal an Event, which I hope it will be the united Endeavours both of Clergy and Laiety to hinder. It would be some support to this Hope, if I could have any Opinion of his predicting Talent, (which some have ascribed to People of this Author's Character) where he tells us, That *Noise and Wrath will not always pass for Zeal.* What other Instances of Zeal has this Gentlemen or the rest of his Party been able to produce? If Clamour be *Noise*, it is but opening our Ears to know from what Side it comes: And if Sedition, Scurrility, Slander and Calumny, be the Fruits of *Wrath*, read the Pamphlets and Papers issuing from the *Zealots* of that Faction, or Visit their Clubs and Coffee-Houses in order to Form a Judgment of the Tree.

When Mr. *St——le* tells us, WE *have a Religion that wants no Support from the Enlargement of Secular Power, but is well supported by the Wisdom and Piety of it's Preachers, and it's own Native Truth*; it would be good to know what Religion he professeth: For, the Clergy to whom he speaks, will never allow him a Member of the Church of *England*; they cannot agree, that the *Truth* of the Gospel, and the *Piety* and *Wisdom* of it's Preachers, are a sufficient *Support* in an Evil Age, against Infidelity, Faction, and Vice, without the Assistance of *Secular Power*; unless God would please to confer the Gift of Miracles on those who wait at the Altar. I believe, they venture to go a little further, and think, That upon some Occasions, they want a little *Enlargement of Assistance from the Secular Power*, against *Atheists, Deists, Socinians*, and other Hereticks: Every first day in *Lent*, a Part of the Liturgy is read to the People; in the Preface to which, the Church declares her Wishes for the Restoring of that Discipline she formerly had, and which for some Years past hath been more wanted than ever. But of this no more, lest it might *insinuate Jealousies between the Clergy and Laity*, which, the Author tells us, is the *Policy of vain Ambitious Men among the former, in hopes to derive from their Order, a Veneration they cannot deserve from their Virtue.* If this be their Method for procuring Veneration, it is the most singular that ever was thought on; and the Clergy should then indeed have no more to do with Politicks of any Sort than Mr. *St——le* or his Faction will allow them.

Having thus toiled through his Dedication, I proceed to consider his Preface, which half consisting of Quotation, will be so much the sooner got through. It is a very unfair Thing in any Writer to employ his *Ignorance* and *Malice* together, because it gives his Answerer double Work: It is like the Sort of Sophistry that the Logicians call *Two Mediums*, which are never allowed in the same Syllogism. A Writer with a weak Head, and a corrupted Heart, is an over-match for any single Pen; like a hireling Jade, dull and vicious, hardly able to stir, yet offering at every turn to Kick.

He begins his Preface with such an Account of the Original of Power, and the Nature of Civil Institutions, as I am confident was never once imagin'd by any Writer upon Government from *Plato* to Mr. *Lock.* Give me leave to transcribe his first Paragraph. *I never saw an unruly Crowd of People cool by Degrees into Temper, but it gave me an Idea of the Original of Power, and the Nature of Civil Institutions. One particular Man has usually in those Cases, from the Dignity of his Appearance, or other Qualities known or imagined by the Multitude, been received into sudden Favour and Authority, the Occasion of their Difference has been represented to him, and the Matter referred to his Decision.*

I have known a Poet, who was never out of *England*, introduce a Fact by Way of Simile, which could probably no where happen nearer than in the Plains of *Lybia*; and begin with, *So have I seen.* Such a Fiction I suppose may be justified by Poetical Licence; Yet *Virgil* is much more Modest: This Paragraph of Mr. *St--le*'s, which he sets down as an Observation of his own, is a miserable mangled Translation of Six Verses out of that famous Poet, who speaks after this manner: *As when a Sedition arises in a great Multitude,* &c. *Then, if they see a wise grave Man,* &c.[25] *Virgil*, who liv'd but a little after the Ruin of the *Roman* Republick, where Seditions often happened, and the Force of Oratory was great among the People, made

25 *As when . . . Man, &*c: *Aeneid*, I.148–56; the simile uses the political image to describe

use of a Simile, which Mr. *St——le* turns into a Fact, after such a manner, as if he had seen it an hundred Times; and builds upon it a System of the Origin of Government. When the Vulgar here in *England* assemble in a riotous Manner, (which is not very frequent of late Years) the Prince takes a much more effectual Way than that of sending Orators to appease them: But Mr. *St——le* imagines such a Crowd of People as this, where there is no Government at all; their *unruliness* quell'd, and their Passions *cool'd* by a particular Man, whose great Qualities they had known before. Such an Assembly must have risen suddenly from the Earth, and the *Man of Authority* dropt from the Clouds; for without some previous Form of Government, no such *Crowd* did ever yet assemble, or could possibly be acquainted with the Merits and Dignity of any *particular Man* among them. But to pursue his Scheme. This Man of Authority who *cools* the *Crowd* by Degrees, and to whom they all Appeal, must of Necessity prove either an open or *clandestine Tyrant*: A *clandestine Tyrant* I take to be a King of *Brentford*,[26] who keeps his Army in Disguise; And whenever he happens either to Die naturally, be knockt on the Head, or Deposed, the People *calmly take further Measures, and improve upon what was begun under his unlimited Power.* All this, our Author tells us, with extreme Propriety, *is what seems reasonable to common Sense*; That is, in other Words, it seems *reasonable* to *Reason.* This is what he calls *giving an Idea of the Original of*

Neptune calming the seas.

> As when in Tumults rise th' ignoble Crowd,
> Mad are their Motions, and their Tongues are loud;
> And Stones and Brands in ratling Vollies fly,
> And all the Rustick Arms that Fury can supply:
> If then some Grave and Pious Man appear,
> They hush their Noise, and lend a list'ning Ear;
> He sooths with sober Words their angry Mood,
> And quenches their innate Desire of Blood:
> So when the Father of the Flood appears,
> And o're the Seas his Sov'raign Trident rears,
> Their Fury falls: He skims the liquid Plains,
> High on his Chariot, and, with loosen'd Reins,
> Majestick moves along, and awful Peace maintains.
> (John Dryden (trans.), *The works of Virgil
> containing his Pastorals, Georgics, and Æneis*
> (1697), pp. 257–8).

26 *King of Brentford*: one of the two 'Kings of Brentford' in Buckingham's *Rehearsal* (1671), who keep their 'Army in Disguise', hidden in Knightsbridge. Steele had opened the way to this allusion by using the phrase '*clandestine Tyrant*' in *The Crisis*.

Power, and the Nature of Civil Institutions. To which I Answer with great Phlegm, That I defie any Man alive to shew me in double the Number of Lines, though writ by the same Author, such a complicated Ignorance in History, Humane Nature, or Politicks, as well as in the ordinary Proprieties of Thought or of Style.

But it seems, these profound Speculations were only premised to introduce some Quotations in favour of *Resistance.* What hath *Resistance* to do with the Succession of the House of *Hanover,* that the Whig-Writers should perpetually affect to tag them together? I can conceive nothing else, but that their Hatred to the QUEEN and Ministry, puts them upon Thoughts of introducing the Successor by *another* Revolution. Are Cases of *extream NECESSITY* to be produced as common Maxims by which we are always to proceed? Should not these Gentlemen sometimes inculcate the general Rule of Obedience, and not always the Exception of Resistance? Since the former hath been the perpetual Dictates of all Laws both Divine and Civil, and the latter is still in Dispute.

I shall meddle with none of the Passages he cites, to prove the Lawfulness of resisting Princes, except that from the present Lord Chancellor's Speech, in Defence of Dr *Sacheverell*: That *there are extraordinary Cases, Cases of Necessity, which are implied though not expressed in the general Rule*[27] [of Obedience.] These Words, very clear in themselves, Mr. *St——le* explains into Nonsense; which in any other Author I should suspect to have been intended as a Reflection upon as great a Person as ever filled or adorned that high Station: But I am so well acquainted with his Pen, that I much more wonder how it can trace out a true Quotation than a false Comment. To see him treat my Lord *Harcourt* with so much Civility looks indeed a little Suspicious, and as if he had Malice in his Heart. He calls his Lordship *a very Great Man*, and *a great living Authority*, places him in Company with General *Stanhope* and Mr. *Hoadley*; and in short, takes the most effectual Method in his Power of ruining his Lordship in the Opinion of every Man who is wise or good: I can only tell my Lord *Harcourt*, for his Comfort, that these Praises are encumbred with the

---

27 *Lord Chancellor's . . . general Rule*: Simon Harcourt, Viscount Harcourt, was made Lord Chancellor in April 1713 (see Williams, *JSt*, p. 656). He had conducted Sacheverell's defence. In spite of Swift's barbs here, Steele quoted from Harcourt's speech again in his *Apology* (October 1714), published after his expulsion from the House of Commons. The final words of this sentence are Swift's own interpolation.

Doctrine of *Resistance*, and the true Revolution-Principles; and provided he will not allow Mr. *St——le* for his Commentator, he may hope to recover the Honour of being Libelled again, as well as his Sovereign and Fellow Servants.

We come now to the *Crisis*: Where we meet with Two Pages by Way of Introduction to those Extracts from Acts of Parliament that constitute the Body of his Pamphlet. This Introduction begins with a Definition of Liberty, and then proceeds in a Panegyrick upon that great Blessing; His Panegyrick is made up of Half a Dozen Shreds, like a School-Boy's Theme, beaten, general Topicks, where any other Man alive might wander securely; but this Politician, by venturing to vary the good old Phrases and give them a new Turn, commits an hundred Solecisms and Absurdities. The weighty Truths which he endeavours to press upon his Reader are such as these. That, *Liberty is a very good Thing*; That, *Without Liberty we cannot be Free*; That, *Health is good, and Strength is good, but Liberty is better than either*; That, *No Man can be Happy, without the Liberty of doing whatever his own Mind tells him is best*; That, *Men of Quality love Liberty, and common People love Liberty*; even Women and Children love Liberty; and you cannot please them better than by letting them do what they please. Had Mr. *St——le* contented himself to deliver these and the like Maxims in such intelligible Terms, I could have found where we agreed and where we differed. But let us hear some of these Axioms as he has involved them. *We cannot possess our Souls with Pleasure and Satisfaction except we preserve to our selves that inestimable Blessing which we call Liberty: By Liberty, I*   Pag. 1. *desire to be understood, to mean the Happiness of Men's living*, &c.---The true *Life of Man consists in conducting it according to his own just Sentiments and innocent Inclinations.—— Man's Being is degraded below that of a free Agent, when his Affections and Passions are no*   Pag. 1. *longer governed by the Dictates of his own Mind.-- Without Liberty, our Health* (among other Things) *may be at the Will of a Tyrant, employ'd to our own Ruin and that of our Fellow Creatures.* If there be any of these Maxims, which is not grosly defective in Truth, in Sense or in Grammar, I will allow them to pass for uncontroulable.[28] By the First, Omitting the

---

28 *uncontroulable* (i.e., 'uncontrollable'): 'Incontrovertible, indisputable, irrefutable' (*OED*, citing, among others, Swift's *Contests and Dissensions* and *Polite Conversation*).

Pedantry of the whole Expression, There are not above one or two Nations in the World, where any one Man can *possess his Soul with Pleasure and Satisfaction*. In the Second, He *desires to be understood to mean*; that is, he desires to be meant to mean, or to be understood to understand. In the Third, *The Life of Man consists in conducting* his Life. In the Fourth, he affirms, That *Men's Beings are degraded when their Passions are no longer governed by the Dictates of their own Mind*; directly contrary to the Lessons of all Moralists and Legislators, who agree unanimously, That the Passions of Men must be under the Government of Reason and Law; neither are Laws of any other Use than to Correct the Irregularity of our Affections. By the Last, *Our Health is ruinous to our selves and other Men, when a Tyrant pleases*; which I leave him to make out.

    I cannot sufficiently commend our Ancestors for transmitting to us the

Ibid. Blessing of Liberty; yet having *laid out their Blood and Treasure upon the Purchase*, I do not see how they *acted Parsimoniously*; because, I can conceive nothing more generous than that of employing our Blood and Treasure for the Service of others. But I am suddenly struck with the Thought, that I have found his Meaning: Our Ancestors acted Parsimoniously, because they only spent their own Treasure for the good of their Posterity; whereas we squandered away the Treasures of our Posterity too; but whether they will be Thankful, and think it was done for the Preservation of their Liberty, must be left to themselves for a Decision.[29]

    I verily believe, though I could not prove it in *Westminster-Hall*

Page. 2. before a *Lord Chief Justice*,[30] That by *Enemies to our Constitution*, and *Enemies to our present Establishment*, Mr. St——le *would desire to be understood to mean*, My Lord Treasurer, and the rest of the Ministry: By *those who are grown Supine in Proportion to the Danger to which our Liberty is every Day more exposed*, I should guess, he means the Tories: And, by *honest Men who ought to look up with a Spirit that becomes Honesty*, he understands the Whigs. I likewise believe, he would take it ill, or think me stupid, if I did not thus expound him. I say then, that according to this Exposition, The Four Great Officers of State, together with the rest of the

---

29 *Our Ancestors . . . Decision*: as Temple Scott points out, Swift here turns Steele's very general meaning into a comment on the costs of the war just ended by the Peace of Utrecht.

30 *Lord Chief Justice*: Swift reflects again on Lord Chief Justice Parker, who was offended by a passage in *Conduct*, see *Some Remarks*, above, pp. 129–30 and note; and *Some Advice*, above, p. 111.

Cabinet-Council, (except the Archbishop of *Canterbury*) are *Enemies to our Establishment, making artful and open Attacks upon our Constitution*, and are now *practising indirect Arts, and mean Subtilties, to weaken the Security of those Acts of Parliament* for Settling the Succession in the House of *Hannover*. The First, and most Notorious of these Criminals is, *Robert Harley*, Earl of *Oxford*, Lord High Treasurer, who is reputed to be Chief Minister: The Second is, *James Butler*, Duke of *Ormond*, who Commands the Army, and Designs to Employ it in bringing over the *Pretender*: The Third is, *Henry St. John*, Lord Viscount *Bolingbroke*, Secretary of State, who must be supposed to hold a constant Correspondence with the Court at *Bar le Duc*,[31] as the late E. of *G-d--ph-n* did with that of St. *Germains*: And to avoid Tediousness, Mr. *Bromley*[32] and the rest are employ'd in their several Districts to the same End. These are the Opinions which Mr. *St——le* and his Faction, under the Direction of their Leaders, are endeavouring with all their Might to propagate among the People of *England*, concerning the present Ministry; with what Reservation to the Honour, Wisdom, or Justice of the QUEEN, I cannot determine; who by Her own free Choice, after long Experience of their Abilities and Integrity, and in Compliance to the general Wishes of Her People, called them to Her Service. Such an Accusation, against Persons in so high Trust, should require, I think at least, one single Overt-Act to make it good. If there be no other Choice of Persons fit to serve the Crown without Danger from the *Pretender*, except among those who are called the Whig-Party, the *Hanover* Succession is then indeed in a very desperate State; that illustrious Family will have almost Nine in Ten of the Kingdom against it, and those principally of the Landed-Interest, which is most to be depended upon in such a Nation as ours.

I have now got as far as his Extracts, which I shall not be at the Pains of comparing with the Originals, but suppose he has got them fairly transcribed: I only think, That whoever is Patentee for Printing Acts of Parliament, may have a very fair Action against him, for Invasion of Property, but this is none of my Business to enquire into.

---

31 *Bar le Duc*: the Court of the Pretender in Lorraine, to which he went in 1713 after being expelled from France as a condition of the Treaty of Utrecht.
32 *Bromley*: William Bromley (1664–1732), MP for the University of Oxford, elected Speaker of the House in 1710 and made a Secretary of State in 1713.

After Two and twenty Pages spent in reciting Acts of Parliament,

Pag. 24.   *he desires leave to repeat the History and Progress of the Union*; upon which, I have some few Things to observe.

This Work, he tells us, *was unsuccessfully attempted by several of Her Majesty's Predecessors*; though I do not remember it was ever Thought on by any except King *James* the First, and the late King *William*. I have read indeed, That some small Overtures were made by the former of these Princes towards an Union between the Two Kingdoms, but rejected with Indignation and Contempt by the *English*. And the Historian[33] tells us, That how degenerate and corrupt soever the Court and Parliament then were, they would not give Ear to so infamous a Proposal. I do not find that any of the succeeding Princes before the Revolution ever resumed the Design;[34] because it was a Project for which there could not possibly be assigned the least Reason or Necessity: For I defy any Mortal to name one single Advantage that *England* could ever expect from such an Union.

But towards the End of the late King's Reign, upon Apprehension of the Want of Issue from him or the Princess *Anne*, a Proposition for Uniting both Kingdoms was begun, because *Scotland* had not settled their Crown upon the House of *Hanover*, but left themselves at Large, in Hopes to make their Advantage: And it was thought highly dangerous to leave that Part of the Island inhabited by a poor, fierce Northern People,[35] at Liberty to put themselves under a different King. However, the Opposition to this Work was so great, that it could not be overcome till some Time after Her present Majesty came to the Crown; when by the Weakness or Corruption

33 *the Historian*: Swift is probably alluding to volume II of *A Complete History of England*, a compilation published in 1706 and now best known for its third volume by White Kennett. Volume II incorporated in pp. 661–792 a reprint of *The History of King James I* by Arthur Wilson, first published in London in 1653; Wilson was hostile to the whole idea of the Union, a project which he discusses at length (pp. 676–86) and to which he at some points objects in strong language. Swift does not borrow his language, but of the histories of England available to him when he was writing, this is the best candidate and very much coloured to his taste.

34 *Princes . . . the Design*: Swift corrected this in *The Examiner* for 1 March, saying 'he hath been since told, That some Overtures were made to that End, in the Reigns of other Princes'. Though Swift is of course not thinking of him as one of the 'Princes', under Cromwell there were also such discussions in the period 1654–7; and in the reign of Charles II commissioners from both countries in 1668 explored an economic union, with an attempt at a complete Union in 1670 (see William Ferguson, *Scotland's Relations with England* (Edinburgh: Donald, 1977)). See also T. C. Smout, 'The Road to Union,' in Geoffrey Holmes (ed.), *Britain After the Glorious Revolution 1689–1714* (London: Macmillan, 1969), pp. 176–96.

35 *poor fierce . . . People*: on the serious trouble this phrase cost Swift, see the Introduction, pp. 37–9.

of a certain Minister since dead,[36] an Act of Parliament was obtain'd for the *Scots*, which gave them leave to Arm themselves, and so the Union became necessary, not for any actual Good it could possibly do us, but to avoid a probable Evil; and at the same time, save an obnoxious Minister's Head, who was so Wise, as to take the first Opportunity of procuring a general Pardon by Act of Parliament, because he could not with so much Decency or Safety desire a particular One for himself.[37] These Facts are well enough known to the whole Kingdom; And I remember, Discoursing above Six Years ago with the most considerable Person of the adverse Party,[38] and a great Promoter of the Union, he frankly own'd to me, That this Necessity, brought upon us by the wrong Management of the E—— of G——, was the only Cause of the Union.

Therefore I am ready to grant Two Points to the Author of the *Crisis*: First, That the Union became Necessary for the Cause above related; because it prevented the Island from being governed by Two Kings, which *England* would never have suffered; and it might probably have Cost us a War of a Year or two to reduce the *Scots*. Secondly, That it would be dangerous to break this Union, at least in this Juncture, while there is a *Pretender* abroad, who might probably lay hold of such an Opportunity. And this made me wonder a little at the Spirit of Faction last Summer among some People, who having been the great Promoters of the *Union*, and several of them the principal Gainers by it, could yet proceed so far, as to propose in the House of Lords, that it should be Dissolved; while at the same time, those Peers who had ever opposed it in the Beginning, were then for Preserving it, upon the Reason I have just assigned, and which the Author of the *Crisis* hath likewise taken Notice of.[39]

---

36 *Minister since dead*: Godolphin, who advised the Queen, after a year of delay, to consent to the Act of Security in August of 1704 (see Trevelyan, vol. II, p. 242). See Swift's earlier attack on this topic in his little allegorical 'Story' in *The Examiner* for 14 December 1710 and his further remarks in *Examiner* for 22 February 1711.

37 *general Pardon . . . himself*: 'An Act for the Queen's most gracious general and free Pardon' (7 Ann. c. 22) was enacted in 1709; cf. Swift's brief but scathing comments on it in *The Examiner* for 30 November 1710, where the context is his assault on Wharton.

38 *Person of the adverse Party*: Somers.

39 *Spirit of Faction . . . taken Notice of*: in June of 1713 Scottish peers, angry at the Malt Tax, which seemed to violate a stipulation of the Act of Union, brought in a Bill to dissolve the Union and were supported by Whig leaders like Wharton and Sunderland; see Holmes, p. 339. They were unsuccessful, but the behaviour of the Whigs, who wished to embarrass the government, had its ironies. Erasmus Lewis wryly reported to Swift on 2 June, ''twas very

Pag. 25

But when he tells us, *The* Englishmen *ought in Generosity to be more particularly Careful in preserving this Union*, he argues like himself. *The late Kingdom of* Scotland, (saith he) *had as numerous a Nobility as* England, *&c.* They had indeed; and to that we owe one of the great and necessary Evils of the Union upon the Foot it now stands. Their Nobility is indeed so numerous, that the whole Revenues of their Country would be hardly able to maintain them according to the Dignity of their Titles; and what is infinitely worse, they are never likely to be Extinct till the last Period of all Things, because the greatest Part of them Descend to Heirs general.[40] I imagine, a Person of Quality prevailed on to Marry a Woman much his Inferior, and without a Groat to her Fortune, and her Friends arguing, she was as good as her Husband, because she brought him as numerous a Family of Relations and Servants, as she found in his House. *Scotland* in the Taxes is obliged to contribute One Penny for every Forty pence laid upon *England*; and the Representatives they send to Parliament are about a Thirteenth: Every other *Scotch* Peer has all the Priviledges of an *English* one, except that of Sitting in Parliament, and even Precedence before all of the same Title that shall be created for the time to come. The Pensions and Employments possessed by the Natives of that Country now among us, do amount to more than the whole Body of their Nobility ever spent at Home; And all the Money they raise upon the Publick is hardly sufficient to defray their Civil and Military Lists. I could Point out some with great Titles, who affected to appear very vigorous for Dissolving the Union, though their whole Revenues before that Period would have ill maintained a *Welch* Justice of the Peace; and have since gathered more Money than ever any *Scotchmen*, who had not travell'd, could form an Idea of.[41]

---

comical to see the Tory's who voted with Ld Treasurer agt. the Dissolution of the Union, under all the perplexity's in the world least they sh'd be victorious, and the Scotch who voted for a bill of dissolution under agony's least they themselves sh'd carry the point they pretended to desire' (Woolley, *Corr.*, vol. I, p. 499).

40 *Heirs general*: 'heir-general' is a term 'used to include heirs female as well as heirs male' in the category 'heir-at-law', i.e. 'the person who succeeds another by right of blood in the enjoyment of his property; in English law confined to one who has such a right in real property, and distinguished from executors or administrators' (*OED*).

41 *great Titles . . . Idea of*: Swift alludes here, presumably, to John Campbell, 2nd Duke of Argyll, and his brother Archibald, Earl of Ilay; the Duke, formerly a Tory and on friendly terms with Swift, had recently abandoned his support of the ministry and joined with the Whigs. He was removed from all his places on 14 March 1714.

I have only one Thing more to say upon Occasion of the Union Act; which is, That the Author of the *Crisis* may be fairly proved from his own Citations to be guilty of HIGH TREASON. In a Paper of his called the *Englishman*, of *October* 29. there is an Advertisement about taking in Subscriptions for Printing the *Crisis*, where the Title is published at length, with the following Clause, which the Author thought fit to drop in the Publication: [*And that no Power on Earth can barr, alter, or make void the present Settlement of the Crown, &c. By R——d St——le.*] In his Extract of an Act of Parliament made since the Union, it appears to be *High Treason* for *any Person, by Writing or Printing, to maintain and affirm, That the Kings or Queens of this Realm, with and by the Authority of Parliament, are not able to make Laws and Statutes of sufficient Force and Validity to limit and bind the Crown, and the Descent, Limitation, Inheritance, and Government thereof.* This Act being subsequent to the Settlement of the Crown confirmed at the Union; it is probable, some Friend of the Author advis'd him to leave out those *Treasonable* Words in the printed Title Page, which he had before published in the *Advertisement*; and accordingly we find, that in the Treatise it self, he only *offers it to every good Subject's Consideration, whether this Article of the Settlement of the Crown is not as firm as the Union it self, and as the Settlement of Episcopacy in* England, &c. And he thinks the *Scots understood it so, that the Succession to the Crown was never to be controverted.* Pag. 25. Pag. 26.

These I take to be only *treasonable* Insinuations; but the Advertisement above-mentioned is actually *High-Treason*, for which the Author ought to be Prosecuted, if that would avail any Thing, under a Jurisdiction where Cursing the QUEEN is not above the Penalty of Twenty Marks.

Nothing is more Notorious, than that the Whigs of late Years, both in their Writings and Discourses, have affected upon all Occasions to allow the Legitimacy of the *Pretender*: This makes me a little wonder to see our Author labouring to prove the contrary, by producing all the popular Chat of those Times, and other solid Arguments from *Fuller's* Narrative:[42] But it must be suppos'd, that Pag. 27.

---

42 *Fuller's narrative*: William Fuller, a secret agent and informer, wrote *A brief discovery of the true mother of the pretended Prince of Wales known by the name of Mary Grey* (Edinburgh, 1696), one of the many efforts to prove the identity of the 'pretended' Prince of Wales. Swift's point here is that the Whigs generally were not prone to accept the view that the Pretender was a changeling, since if it were true his exclusion would be due to his birth and not only to an

this Gentleman acts by the Commands of his Superiors, who have thought fit at this Juncture to issue out new Orders, for Reasons best known to themselves. I wish they had been more clear in their Directions to him upon that weighty Point, whether the Settlement of the Succession in the House of *Hanover* be alterable or no: I have observ'd, where in his former Pages he gives it in the Negative; but in the turning of a Leaf he has wholly changed his Mind; tells us, *He wonders there can be found any* Briton *weak enough to contend against a Power in their own Nation, which is practiced in a much greater Degree in other States*: And, *how hard it is that* Britain *should be debarred the Priviledge of establishing it's own Security, by relinquishing only those Branches of the Royal Line which threaten it with Destruction; whilst other Nations never scruple upon less Occasions to go much greater Lengths*; of which he produces Instances in *France, Spain, Sicily,* and *Sardinia*; and then adds, *Can* Great Britain *help to advance Men to other Thrones, and have no Power in limiting it's Own?* How can a Senator, capable of **doing Honour to Sir* Thomas Hanmer, be guilty of such ridiculous Inconsistencies?[43] The Author of the *Conduct of the Allies* (says he) *has dared to drop Insinuations about altering the Succession.* The Author of the *Conduct of the Allies* writes Sense and English, neither of which the Author of the *Crisis* understands: The former thinks it *wrong in Point of Policy to call in a Foreign Power to be Guarantee of our Succession, because it puts it out of the Power of our own Legislature to change our Succession without the Consent of that Prince or State who is Guaranty, whatever Necessity may happen in future Times.*[44] Now if it be High Treason to affirm by Writing, that the Legislature has no such Power; and if Mr. *St——le* thinks it strange that *Britain* should be debarred this Priviledge, what could be the Crime of putting such a Case, that in future Ages, a Necessity might happen of Limiting the Succession, as well as it has happened already?

Pag. 28.

**Mr. St—le's speech at the Election of a speaker.*

Pag. 33.

Conduct, Pag. 38.

Act of Parliament. On the later Whig attitude see also Swift in *The Examiner* for 31 May 1711.

43 *doing Honour . . . Inconsistencies*: Swift here mocks Steele's use in the House of Commons of the idiomatic phrase 'doing honour to' on the election of Hanmer as Speaker; see Ehrenpreis, vol. II, p. 712.

44 *wrong . . . future Times*: Swift paraphrases and quotes from his *Conduct*, above, pp. 68–9.

When Mr. *St——le reflects upon the many Solemn strong*
Barriers (to our Succession) *of Laws and Oaths,* &c. he *thinks*   Pag. 29.
all Fear vanisheth before them. I think so too; provided the Epithet
Solemn goes for nothing: Because, although I have often heard of a *Solemn*
Day, a *Solemn* Feast, and a *Solemn* Coxcomb, yet I can conceive no Idea to
my self of a *Solemn Barrier.* However, be that as it will; His *Thoughts* it seems
will not let him rest, but before he is aware, he asks himself several Questions:
And since he cannot Resolve them, I will endeavour to give him what Satisfaction I am able. The First is, *What are the Marks of a Lasting Security?*
To which I Answer, That the Signs of it in a Kingdom or State are first,
good Laws, and secondly, those Laws well Executed: We are pretty well
provided with the former, but extremely defective in the latter. Secondly,
What are our Tempers and our Hearts at Home? If by *Ours* he means those of
himself and his Abettors, they are most damnably Wicked; impatient for
the Death of the QUEEN; ready to gratifie their Ambition and Revenge by
all desperate Methods; wholly alienate from Truth, Law, Religion, Mercy,
Conscience, or Honour. Thirdly, *In what Hands is Power lodg'd Abroad?* To
Answer the Question naturally, *Louis* XIV. is King of *France, Philip* V. (by
the Councils and Acknowledgments of the Whigs) is King of *Spain,* and
so on. If by Power he means Money; the D—— of *M*——— is thought
to have more ready Money than all the Kings of *Christendom* together; but
by the peculiar Disposition of Providence it is locked up in a Trunk, to
which his Ambition has no Key, and that is our Security. Fourthly, *Are our*
unnatural Divisions our Strength? I think not; but they are the Sign of it; for
being *unnatural,* they cannot last; and this shews, that Union, the Founda
tion of all *Strength,* is more agreeable to our Nature. Fifthly, *Is it nothing to*
us, which of the Princes of Europe *hath the longest Sword?* Not much; if we
can Tie up his Hands, or put a strong *Shield* into those of his Neighbours:
Or if our *Sword* be as *Sharp,* as his is *Long*: Or if it be necessary for him to
turn his own *Sword* into a Plow-sheer: Or if such a *Sword* happens to be in
the Hands of an *Infant,* or struggled for by two Competitors. Sixthly, *The*
powerful Hand that deals out Crowns and Kingdoms all around us, may it not
in time reach a King out to us too? If the *powerful Hand* he means, be that of
France, it may *reach out* as many Kings as it pleases, but we will not accept
them. Whence does this Man get his Intelligence? I should think, even
his Brother *Ridpath* might furnish him with better. What *Crowns* or *King-*
doms hath *France dealt* about? *Spain* was given by the Will of the former

King, in consequence of that infamous Treaty of Partition, the Advisers of which will I hope never be forgot in *England. Sicily* was disposed of by Her Majesty of *Great-Britain.*[45] So in effect was *Sardinia. France* indeed once *reached out* a King to *Poland*, but the People would not receive him.[46] This Question of Mr. *St——le*'s was therefore only put *in terrorem*, without any regard to Truth. Seventhly, *Are there no Pretensions to our Crown that can ever be revived?* There may for ought I know be about a Dozen: And those in time may possibly beget an Hundred. But we must do as well as we can: Captain *Bessus,*[47] when he had fifty Challenges to answer, protested he could not Fight above three Duels a Day. *If the Pretender should fail* (says this Writer) *the* French *King has in his Quiver a Succession of them, the Dutchess of* Savoy, *or her Sons, or the* Dauphin *her Grandson.* Let me suppose the *Chevalier* de *St. George* to be Dead; The Dutchess of *Savoy*[48] will then be a *Pretender*, and consequently must leave her Husband, because His Royal Highness (for Mr. *St——le* has not yet acknowledged him for a King) is in Allyance with Her *British* Majesty: Her Sons, when they grow *Pretenders*, must undergo the same Fate. But I am at a Loss how to dispose of the *Dauphin*, if he happens to be King of *France* before the *Pretendership* to *Britain* falls to his share; for I doubt he will never be persuaded to remove out of his own Kingdom, only because it is too near *England.*[49]

Pag. 33.

But *the Duke of* Savoy *did some Years ago put in his Claim to the Crown of* England *in right of his Wife; and he is a Prince of great Capacity; in strict Allyance with France, and may therefore very well add to our Fears of a Popish Successor.* Is it the fault of the present or of any Ministry, that this Prince put in his Claim? Must we give him Opium to destroy his *Capacity?* Or can we prevent his Allyance with any Prince who is in Peace with Her Majesty? Must we send to Stab or Poyson all the *Popish* Princes who have any pretended Title to our Crown by the

45 *Treaty of Partition . . . Britain*: see *Conduct*, pp. 52–3 and note.
46 *Poland . . . receive him*: in 1696, on the death of John III, there were numerous candidates for the vacant throne of Poland. France backed François Louis de Bourbon, Prince de Conti (1664–1709), but the successful candidate was Frederick Augustus I, the Elector of Saxony, who reigned as Augustus II, King of Poland from 1697 to 1704, and from 1709 to 1733.
47 *Captain Bessus*: Braggadocio figure in Beaumont and Fletcher's *A King and No King*, who makes this excuse in III. ii.
48 *Dutchess of Savoy*: Anna Maria (1669–1728), wife of Victor Amadeus II, granddaughter of Charles and grandmother of Louis XV (at this writing the Dauphin).
49 *too near England*: as the Pretender was required to do by the Treaty of Utrecht.

Proximity of Blood? What, in the Name of God, can these People drive at? What is it they demand? Suppose the present *Dauphin* were now a Man, and King of *France*, and next Popish Heir to the Crown of *England*; Is he not excluded by the Laws of the Land? But what Regard will he have to our Laws? I answer; Hath not the Queen as good a Title to the Crown of *France*? And how is she excluded but by their Law against the Succession of Females, which we are not bound to acknowledge? And is it not in our Power to exclude Female Successors as well as in theirs? If such a Pretence shall prove the Cause of a War, what Humane Power can prevent it? But our Cause must necessarily be good and righteous; for either the Kings of *England* have been unjustly kept out of the Possession of *France*, or the *Dauphin*, though nearest of Kin, can have no legal Title to *England*. And he must be an ill Prince indeed, who will not have the Hearts and Hands of Ninety nine in a Hundred among his Subjects against such a *Popish Pretender*.

I have been the longer in answering the Seventh Question, because it led me to consider all he had afterwards to say upon the Subject of the *Pretender*. Eighthly and lastly, He asks himself *whether Popery and Ambition are become tame and quiet Neighbours?* In this I can give him no Satisfaction, because I never was in that Street where they live; nor do I Converse with any of their Friends; only I find they are Persons of a very evil Reputation. But I am told for certain that *Ambition* has removed her Lodging, and lives the very next Door to *Faction*; where they keep such a Racket that the whole Parish is disturbed, and every Night in an uproar.

Thus much in answer to those Eight *uneasy Questions*, put by the Author to himself, in order *to satisfy every Briton*, and give him an Occasion of *taking an impartial View of the Affairs of* Europe *in general, as well as of* Great-Britain *in particular*.

After enumerating the great Actions of the *Confederate* Armies under the Command of Prince *Eugene* and the Duke of *Marlborough*, Mr. *St--le* observes in the bitterness of his Soul, that the *British General, however unaccountable it may be to Posterity, was not permitted to enjoy the Fruits of his glorious Labour*. Ten Years *Fruits* it seems were not sufficient, and yet they were the *fruitfullest* Campagns that ever any General cropt. However, I cannot but hope, that Posterity will not be left in the dark, but some Care taken both of Her Majesty's Glory, and of the Reputation of those

She employs. An impartial Historian[50] may tell the World (and the next Age will easily believe what it continues to feel) that the Avarice and Ambition of a few factious insolent Subjects, had almost destroyed their Country, by continuing a ruinous War, in conjunction with Allies, for whose sakes principally we fought who refused to bear their just Proportion of the Charge, and were connived at in their Refusal for private Ends. That these Factious People treated the best and kindest of Sovereigns with Insolence, Cruelty and Ingratitude (of which he will be able to produce several Instances.) That they encouraged Persons and Principles alien from our Religion and Government, in order to strengthen their Faction. He will tell the Reasons why the *General* and *first Minister* were seduced to be Heads of this Faction, contrary to the Opinions they had always professed. Such an Historian will shew many Reasons which made it necessary to remove the *General* and his Friends, who knowing the Bent of the Nation were against them, expected to lose their Power when the War was at an End. Particularly the Historian will discover the whole Intrigue of the Duke of M——h's endeavouring to procure a Commission to be *General for Life*; wherein Justice will be done to a Person at that time of high Station in the Law; who, (I mention it to his Honour) advised the D——, when he was consulted upon it, not to accept of such a *Commission*.[51] By these, and many other Instances which Time will bring to Light, it may perhaps appear not very unaccountable to Posterity, why this great Man was dismissed at last, but rather why he was Dismissed no sooner.

But this is entring into a wide Field. I shall therefore leave *Posterity* to the Information of better Historians than the Author of the *Crisis* or my self, and go on to inform the present Age in some Facts, which this great Orator and Politician thinks fit to misrepresent with the utmost degree either of natural or wilful Ignorance. He asserts that in the Duke of *Ormond's* Campagne, *after a Suspension of Arms between* Great-Britain *and* France, *proclaimed at the Head of the Armies, the* British, *in the midst of the Enemies Garrisons, withdrew themselves from their Confederates.* The Fact is directly otherwise; For the *British* Troops were most infamously deserted by the

---

50 *An impartial Historian*: Swift, of course, intended to be that historian; on the rumour at the time of this pamphlet that his *History* was about to be published, see Davis, vol. VIII, pp. xix–xx.

51 *Person . . . Commission*: the person was William, 1st Earl Cowper, then Lord Chancellor; Swift describes the episode in *Memoirs* (Davis, vol. VIII, p. 114).

Confederates, after all that could be urged by the Duke of *Ormond*, and the Earl of *Strafford*, to press the Confederate Generals not to forsake them.[52] The Duke was directed to avoid engaging in any Action till he had further Orders, because an Account of the King of *Spain*'s Renunciation was every Day expected: This the *imperialists* and *Dutch* knew well enough, and therefore proposed to the Duke in that very Juncture to engage the *French*, for no other Reason but to render Desperate all the QUEEN's Measures towards a Peace. Was not the certain Possession of *Dunkirk* of equal Advantage to the uncertainty of a Battle? A whole Campaign under the Duke of *Marlborough*, with such an Acquisition, tho' at the Cost of many Thousand Lives, and several Millions of Money, would have been thought very gloriously Ended. Neither after all, was it a new Thing, either in the *British* General or the *Dutch* Deputies, to refuse Fighting, when they did not approve it: When the Duke of *Marlborough* was going to invest[53] *Bouchain*, the Deputies of the *States* pressed him in Vain to engage the Enemy, and One of them was so far Discontented upon his Grace's Refusal, that he presently became a Partizan of the Peace,[54] yet I do not remember any Clamour then raised here against the Duke upon that Account. Again, when the *French* invaded *Doway*, after the Confederates had deserted the

52 *Confederates . . . forsake them*: the allusion is to the famous 'restraining orders' given on 19 May 1712 to Swift's friend the Duke of Ormond by the Queen, or at least by Bolingbroke, which prevented his taking action against the French in 1712. 'It is therefore the Queen's positive command to your Grace, that you avoid engaging in any siege, or hazarding a battle, till you have farther orders from her Majesty' (Bolingbroke, *Letters*, vol. II, p. 320). These were orders which he was compelled to keep secret from the Allies, i.e. Prince Eugene and the Dutch. For Swift's view of this crisis in the life of one who had 'every Quality that can accomplish or adorn a great Man', see *History* (Davis, vol. IV, pp. 126–8). For Swift's distress at his later impeachment, see *Enquiry into the Behaviour of the Queen's Last Ministry* (Davis, vol. VIII, pp. 132–3).

53 *invest*: i.e., 'besiege' (*OED*).

54 *Partizan of the Peace*: referring to Sicco van Goslinga (1664–1731), a Dutch 'field Deputy' who had been critical earlier of Marlborough's tactics. In August 1711, after the allied troops marched to Arleux near Bouchain but did not attack, Goslinga became highly disturbed, not knowing that crossing the Scheld and besieging Bouchain had been Marlborough's intention all along rather than fighting a fixed battle (see Trevelyan, vol. III, pp. 132–3). According to his *Mémoires*, Goslinga felt Marlborough's 'damnable' politics were at work, that by avoiding the battle the Duke thought he could keep his command and also ruin the new ministry (*Mémoires*, ed. U. A. Evertsz and G. H. M. Delprat (Leeuwarden: Worcum, 1857), p. 141). As Swift implies, Goslinga, though eager for battle at Bouchain, had pressed for peace with France in 1709 and was later given full powers by the States-General in the peace negotiations at Utrecht. He was also delegated by the Dutch to take their good wishes to Louis XIV on the occasion of the peace (*Nieuw Nederlandsch Biografisch Woordenboek VIII* (Leiden, 1930), col. 625).

Duke of *Ormond*, Prince *Eugene* was violently bent upon a Battle, and said they should never have another so good an Opportunity: But Monsieur ——, a private Deputy, rose up, and opposed it so far, that the Prince was forc'd to desist.[55] Was it then more Criminal in the Duke of *Ormond* to refuse Fighting, by express Commands of the QUEEN, and in order to get Possession of *Dunkirk*, than for the Duke of *Marlborough* to give the same Refusal, without any such Orders, or any such Advantage? Or shall a *Dutch* Deputy assume more Power than the QUEEN of *Great Britain*'s General, acting by the immediate Commands of his Sovereign?

Pag. 31   *The Emperor and the Empire* (says Mr. *St——le*, by Way of Admiration) *continue the War!* Is his Imperial Majesty able to continue it or no? If he be, then *Great Britain* has been strangely used for Ten Years past: Then how came it to pass, That of above Thirty thousand Men in his Service in *Italy*, at the Time of the Battle of *Turin*,[56] there were not above Four thousand paid by himself? If he be not able to continue it, Why does he go on? The Reasons are clear, because the War only Affects the Princes of the Empire, (whom he is willing enough to Expose,) but not his own Dominions. Besides, the *Imperial* Ministers are in daily Expectation of the QUEEN's Death, which they hope will give a new Turn to Affairs, and rekindle the War in *Europe* upon the old Foot; and we know that the Ministers of that Court publickly Assign it for a Reason of their Obstinacy against Peace, that they Hope for a sudden Revolution in *England*. In the mean Time, this Appearance of the *Emperor* being

---

55 *Eugene . . . desist*: Douai fell on 8 September 1712 (n.s.) after a short siege. In 1712 there were only three Dutch Field Deputies: Willem Hooft (Holland), Willem van Haersolte (Overijssel) and Philip Frederik Vegelin van Claerbergen (Council of State) (Marlborough–Godolphin, p. 1701). According to Dr Guus Veenendaal, editor of the correspondence of Heinsius, Swift probably refers either to the first or the third (personal correspondence). However, decades later one of Eugene's former officers claimed that in fact more than one Deputy objected to this particular battle: 'When he [Prince Eugene] arrived, he found the Avenues to the *French* Camp so well entrenched that the Deputies of the States could not be induced to consent to the attacking of them' (John Banks, *The History of Francis-Eugene Prince of Savoy, by an English Officer*, 2nd edn. (1742), p. 309).

56 *Battle of Turin*: in 1706. In a digest of his responses to Swift's *Conduct*, Francis Hare admits much of what Swift had there said about the Austrian court's contributions but also makes excuses for the Emperors and their inability to supply their quotas of troops since the beginning of the war. Although he does not refer specifically to the payment of Imperial troops, he does say that at the time of the Battle of Turin, and just after that 'Prodigious Success', 'their Affairs were in the most desperate Condition' and made worse by the 'great Interest they pay here in *England* for Mony borrow'd on the best Funds they have'. See *A Full Answer to the Conduct of the Allies* (1712), pp. 54–5.

forsaken by his Ally, will serve to encrease the Clamour both here and in *Holland*, against Her Majesty and those She Employs.

Mr. *St——le* says, *There can be no Crime in affirming, (if it be a Truth) That the House of* Bourbon *is at this Juncture become more*   Ibid. *formidable, and bids fairer for an Universal Monarchy, and to engross the whole Trade of* Europe, *than it did before the War*.

No Crime in affirming it, if it be a Truth. I will for once allow his Proposition. But if it be false, then I affirm, That whoever advances so Seditious a Falshood, deserves to be Hanged. Does he mean by the House of *Bourbon*, the Two Kings of *France* and *Spain*? If so, I rejects his Meaning, which would insinuate that the Interests and Designs of both those Princes will be the same, whereas they are more opposite than those of any Two other Monarchs in *Christendom*. This is the old foolish Slander so frequently flung upon the Peace, and as frequently refuted. These factious Undertakers of the Press write with great Advantage; they strenuously affirm a thousand Falshoods, without Fear, Wit, Conscience, or Knowledge; and we who Answer them, must be at the Expence of an Argument for each: After which, in the very next Pamphlet, we see the same Assertions produced again, without the least Notice of what has been said to disprove them. By the House of *Bourbon*, does he mean only the *French* King for the Time being? If so, and his Assertion be true, Then that Prince must either deal with the Devil, or else the Money and Blood spent in our Ten Years Victories against him, might as well have continued in the Purses and Veins of Her Majesty's Subjects.

But the *particular* Assertions of this Author are easier detected than his *general* ones; I shall therefore proceed upon examining the former. For Instance: I desire him to ask the *Dutch*, who can best inform him, *Why they delivered up* Traerbach *to the* Imperialists?[57] For as to   Ibid. the QUEEN, Her Majesty was never once consulted in it; whatever his

---

57 *Traerbach . . . Imperialists*: Steele had complained, 'the *Dutch* have been treated to deliver up *Traerbach* to the Imperialists, as an expedient for the *French* to besiege it; because, forsooth, it lay convenient for their Incursions upon the Empire'. Like other fortifications after the peace in 1713, Trarbach, on the Mosel, was the subject of continuing negotiations between the States-General, the Empire and the French. In August France agreed to let the Dutch give it to the Empire, but after the Dutch held on, the French considered the town an enemy, despite the presence of a Dutch garrison (*The Daily Courant*, 19 August, 21 September). In October and November the Dutch finally prepared to leave and made the post ready for Imperial troops (*The Flying Post*, 18 November). Both Steele's indignation and Swift's response, blaming the Dutch, reflect their contrasting attitudes about the postures of the

Preceptors the Politicians of *Button*'s Coffee-House[58] may have informed him to the contrary.

Ibid.   Mr. *St——le* affirms, That *the* French *have begun the Demo-lition of* Dunkirk *Contemptuously and Arbitrarily their own Way.* The Governor of the Town, and those Gentlemen entrusted with the Inspection of this Work, do assure me, that the Fact is altogether otherwise: That the Method prescribed by those whom Her Majesty employs, hath been exactly followed, and that the Works are already demolished. I will venture to tell him further, That the Demolition was so long deferred, in order to remove those Difficulties which the Barrier-Treaty has put us under; and the Event hath shewn, that it was Prudent to proceed no faster till those Difficulties were got over. The *Mole* and *Harbour* could not be destroyed till the Ships were got out, which by Reason of some profound Secrets of State, did not

Pag. 32.   happen till t'other Day. Who *gave him those just Suspicions that the Mole and Harbour will never be destroy'd*? What is it he would now insinuate? That the Ministry is bribed to leave the most important Part of the Work undone; Or, that the Pretender is to Invade us from thence; Or, that the QUEEN hath entered into a Conspiracy with Her Servants to prevent the good Effects of the Peace, for no other End but to lose the Affections of Her People, and endanger Her Self.

Instead of any further Information, which I could easily give, but which no honest Man can want; I venture to affirm, That the Mole and Harbour of *Dunkirk* will in a short Time be most effectually destroy'd; and at the same Time, I venture to Prophesie, that neither Mr. *St——le*, nor his Faction, will ever confess they believe it.

After all, it is a little hard, That the QUEEN cannot be allow'd to demolish this Town in whatever Manner She pleases to fancy: Mr. *St——le* must have it done his own Way, and is angry the *French* have pretended to do it Theirs; and yet he wrongs them into the Bargain. For my own Part,

---

various powers in the winter of 1713–14. The Emperor and the French were still at war (until the Treaty of Rastadt in March 1714), and Swift and his party claimed that the Empire was the greater threat to the stability of Europe (see below, p. 275). In contrast, Steele's view is close to that of a Whig pamphlet published in the autumn of 1713 called *Europe a Slave, when the Empire is in Chains*, which argues that the ruin of the Empire means the ruin of Europe.

58 *Button's Coffee-House*: on Russel Street, Covent Garden, Button's was known as the gathering place of the 'Whig Wits', especially Addison, who had set up the proprietor Daniel Button in the business.

I do seriously think, the Most *Christian* King to be a much better Friend of Her Majesty's than Mr. *St——le*, or any of his Faction; besides, it is to be considered, that he is a Monarch and a Relation; and therefore if I were a Privy-Councellor, and my Advice to be asked, which of those Two †GENTLEMEN BORN[59] should have the Direction in the Demolition of *Dunkirk*, I would give it for the former; because I look upon Mr. *St——le*, in Quality of a Member of his Party, to be much more Skillful in *demolishing at Home* than *Abroad.*

†*Close to the* Englishman, *Pag.* 2.

There is a Prospect of more Danger to the Balance of *Europe*, and to the Trade of *Britain*, from the *Emperor* over-running *Italy*, than from *France* over-running the *Empire*; That his *Imperial* Majesty entertains such Thoughts, is visible to the World: And though little can be said to justifie many Actions of the *French* King, yet the worst of them hath never equalled the Emperor's Arbitrary keeping the Possession of *Milan*, directly contrary to his Oath, and to the express Words of the *Golden Bull*; which oblige him to deliver up every *Fief* that falls; or else they must all in the Course of Time lapse into his own Hands.[60]

I was at a Loss who it was that Mr. *St——le* hinted at some Time ago by *the powerful Hand, that deals out Crowns and Kingdoms all around us*: I now plainly find, he meant no other Hand but his own. He hath dealt out the Crown of *Spain* to *France*; to *France* he hath given leave to invade the *Empire* next Spring with Two hundred thousand Men; And now at last, he deals to *France* the *Imperial Dignity; and so farewel Liberty*; Europe *will be* French. But in order to bring all this about, *the Capital of* Austria, *the Residence of his*

Pag. 32.

Ibid.

59 *GENTLEMEN BORN:* mocking Steele's claim in *The Englishman*, 'I assert and declare . . . whoever talks with me is speaking to a Gentleman born' (*The Englishman* no. 57, 15 February 1714, in *Tracts*, p. 188).

60 *Golden Bull . . . Hands*: the Golden Bull of the Empire in 1356 established rules for the Electors in choosing future emperors. Although the 'express Words' of the document do not make the specific points that Swift describes, the Bull did begin a process of ceding power from the Emperor to the electoral princes which culminated in the Treaty of Westphalia (1648) and also in the 'Oath' Swift refers to, that taken by Emperor Charles VI at his coronation in 1711. Coxe explains that by that oath the Emperor 'was bound to restore the possessions of which the members of the empire had been forcibly deprived'; Charles had been invested with Milan 'as a fief of the empire' by his brother Emperor Joseph after Prince Eugene conquered it in 1706 (William Coxe, *History of the House of Austria*, 3rd edn (London: Bell and Daldy, 1868), vol. III, pp. 21, 88). Cf. Swift's comments in *History* on the Emperor's refusal at Utrecht to 'restore . . . Territories in *Italy* which He had taken from the rightful Proprietors' (Davis, vol. VII, p. 164).

Imperial *Majesty* must continue to be *visited by the Plague*, of which the *Emperor* must Die, and so the Thing is done.[61] Why should not I venture to *deal out* one *Scepter* in my Turn as well as Mr. *St——le*? I therefore *deal out* the *Empire* to the *Elector* of *Saxony*, upon failure of Issue to this *Emperor* at his Death; provided the Whigs will prevail on the *Son* to turn *Papist* to get an *Empire*, as they did upon the *Father* to get a *Kingdom*.[62] Or if this Prince be not approved of, I *deal out* in his stead, the *Elector* of *Bavaria*.[63] And in one or t'other of these, I dare engage to have all *Christendom* to second me, whatever the Spleen, in the Shape of Politicks, may Dictate to the Author of the *Crisis*.

The Design of Mr. *St——le*, in *representing the Circumstances of the Affairs of* Europe, is to signifie to the World, that all *Europe* is put in the high Road to Slavery by the Corruption of Her Majesty's present Ministers; and so Ibid. he goes on to *Portugal*; which *having, during the War supplied us with Gold in exchange for our* Woollen Manufacture, *has only at present a Suspension of Arms for it's Protection, to last no longer than till the* Catalonians *are reduced; and then the old Pretensions of* Spain *to* Portugal *will be revived*: And *Portugal* when once enslaved by *Spain*, falls naturally with the rest of *Europe* into the Gulph of *France*. In the mean time, let us see what Relief a little Truth can give this unhappy Kingdom. That *Portugal* hath yet no more than a Suspension of Arms, they may Thank themselves, because they came so late into the Treaty; and that they came so late, they may Thank the Whigs, whose false Representations they were so weak to Believe. However, the QUEEN has voluntarily given them a Guarantee to defend them against *Spain* till the Peace shall be made; and such Terms after the Peace, are stipulated for them, as the *Portuguese* themselves are contented with.[64]

---

61 *so the Thing is done*: Swift, of course, in this passage is ironically transforming Steele's alarmist speculations into statements of fact; thus Steele had gloomily predicted, 'Two hundred thousand *French* may be ready', 'a Prince of the House of *Bourbon* would probably bid fair for the Imperial Dignity', etc.

62 *Elector of Saxony . . . Kingdom*: Frederick Augustus I (1670–1733), twice King of Poland (as Augustus II), had converted to Catholicism to help his first bid to be elected King of Poland in 1697. Swift fantasizes satirically that just as the Elector turned Catholic to become King, at the urging (he claims) of English Whigs, his son can become Emperor if the present Emperor, Charles VI, dies without issue and the Whigs can persuade the son to become Catholic.

63 *Elector of Bavaria*: Maximilian II Emmanuel (1662–1725), 'for whose Interests *France* appeared to be . . . much concerned' (*History*, Davis, vol. VII, p. 60).

64 *Portugal . . . contented with*: cf. Swift's disdain for the Portuguese contributions to the war in *Conduct*, p. 79.

Having mentioned the *Catalonians*,[65] he puts the Question, *Who can name the* Catalonians *without a Tear?* That can I; For he   Pag. 32. has told so many melancholy Stories without one Syllable of Truth, that he has blunted the Edge of my Fears, and I shall not be startled at the worst he can say. What he affirms concerning the *Catalonians* is included in the following Particulars: First, *That they were drawn into the War by the Encouragement of the Maritime Powers*; by which are understood *England* and *Holland*: But he is too good a Friend of the *Dutch*, to give them any Part of the Blame. Secondly, That *they are now abandoned and exposed to the Resentment of an enraged Prince.* Thirdly, That *they always opposed the Person and Interest of that Prince*, who is their present King. Lastly, That *the Doom is dreadful of those who shall in the Sight of God be esteemed their Destroyers.* And if we interpret the Insinuation he makes, according to his own Mind, the Destruction of those People, must be imputed to the present Ministry.

I am sometimes in Charity disposed to hope, That this Writer is not always sensible of the flagrant Falshoods he utters, but is either byassed by an Inclination to believe the worst, or a Want of Judgment to chuse his Informers. That the *Catalonians* were *drawn into the War by the Encouragement of Her Majesty*, should not in Decency have been affirmed till about Fifty Years hence; when it might be supposed there would be no living Witness left to disprove it. It was only upon the Assurances of a Revolt, given by the Prince of *Hesse* and others, and their Invitation, that the QUEEN was prevailed with to send her Forces upon that Expedition.[66] When *Barcelona* was taken by a most unexpected Accident, of a Bomb

---

65 *Catalonians*: although amnesty had been granted to the Catalans in accord with the Treaty of Utrecht, England's separate treaty with Spain (13 July 1713) did little for them, and their problems were by now a party issue. In contrast to Steele's emotional outburst, cf. *The Examiner* for 25 September 1713, which imagines Whigs transported to Spain, where they 'would certainly join the Faithful *Catalans* (whose Health is now the common Toast of their good Allies the *Kit-Cats*) and call fighting for Change of Masters, the Cause of Liberty'. Swift's passage here was wittily attacked in the Commons in April by John Aislabie, MP for Ripon, who referred to Swift as 'a Reverend Divine that was intimate with the Ministry' (*Wentworth Papers*, pp. 377–8). For what we may take as the ministerial point of view on this question, see [Defoe's] *Secret History of the White-Staff* Part I (1714), pp. 16–17. The italicized phrases in Swift's paragraph are quotations from Steele's *The Crisis*.

66 *It was only . . . Expedition*: the 'expedition' was the attack on Barcelona in September 1705 in support of Charles III, an attack led by the Earl of Peterborough and George, Prince of Hesse Darmstadt, commander of allied troops in Spain, who lost his life early in the battle. The conquest of the Citadel on 6 September (o.s.) was followed on 3 October by a riot of the Catalans attacking the captured Spanish commander and his forces as they were readying for transport in English ships. As Swift says, a shell exploded in a magazine of the Citadel, the explosion killing the Neapolitan commander and his main officers, but this

lighting on the Magazine, then indeed the *Catalonians* Revolted, having before submitted and sworn Allegiance to *Philip*, as much as any other Province of *Spain*. Upon the Peace between that Crown and *Britain*, the Queen, in order to ease the *Emperor*, and save his Troops, stipulated with King *Philip* for a Neutrality in *Italy*, and that his Imperial Majesty should have Liberty to evacuate *Catalonia*; upon Conditions of absolute Indemnity to the *Catalans*, with an entire Restitution to their Honours, Dignities, and Estates. As this Neutrality was never observed by the *Emperor*, so he never effectually evacuated *Catalonia*; for tho' he sent away the main Body, he left behind many Officers and private Men, who now spirit-up and assist those obstinate People to continue in their Rebellion. It is true indeed, that King *Philip* did not absolutely restore the *Catalans* to *all* their old Privileges, of which they never made other use than as an Encouragement to Rebel; but, to the same Privileges with his Subjects of *Castille*, particularly to the Liberty of Trading, and having Employments in the *West-Indies*, which they never enjoyed before. Besides, the QUEEN reserved to her self the Power of procuring farther Immunities for them, wherein the most *Christian* King was obliged to second Her: For, his *Catholick* Majesty intended no more, than to retrench those Privileges under the Pretext of which they now Rebel, as they had formerly done in favour of *France*. How dreadful then *must the Doom be of those* who hindred these People from submitting to the gentle Terms offered them by their Prince![67] and who, although they are conscious of their own Inability to furnish one single Ship for the Support of the *Catalans*, are at this Instant spurring them on to their Ruin, by Promises of Aid and Protection.

Thus much in Answer to Mr. *St——le*'s Account of the Affairs of *Europe*; from which he deduces the Universal Monarchy of *France*, and the Danger of I know not how many *Popish Successors* to *Britain*. His political Reflections are as good as his Facts. *We must observe* (says he) *that*

Pag. 32.   *the Person who seems to be the most favoured by the* French *King in the late Treaties, is the Duke of* Savoy. Extreamly right: For, whatever that Prince got by the Peace, he owes entirely to Her Majesty, as a just Reward for his having been so firm and useful an Ally; neither was *France*

---

event was apparently during the fighting on 17 September, well before the Catalan uprising on 14 October (Trevelyan, vol. II, pp. 73–6).
67 *How dreadful . . . Prince*: Swift mocks and turns around Steele's exclamation, 'Dreadful the Doom of those who shall be esteemed their Destroyers!'

brought with more Difficulty to yield any one Point, than that of allowing the Duke such a Barrier as the Queen insisted on. *He is become the most powerful Prince in* Italy. I had rather see *Him* so, than the *Emperor. He is supposed to have entred into a secret and strict Alliance with the House of* Bourbon. This is one of those Facts wherein I am most inclined to believe the Author, because it is what he must needs be utterly ignorant of, and therefore might possibly be true. Pag. 33.

I thought indeed we should be Safe from all Popish Successors as far as *Italy*, because of the prodigious Clutter about sending the *Pretender* thither. But they will never agree where to fix their *Longitude*. The Duke of *Savoy* is the more dangerous for removing to *Sicily*: He *adds to our Fears* for being *too far off*, and the *Chevalier de St. George* for being *too near*. So, *Whether* France *conquers* Germany, *or be in Peace and good Understanding with it;* either Event *will put us and* Holland *at Mercy of* France, who has a Quiver full of *Pretenders*, at his Back, whenever the *Chevalier* shall Die.[68] Pag. 33.

This was just the Logick of poor *Prince Butler*, a Splenatick Mad-Man, whom every Body may remember about the Town. Prince *Pamphilio* in *Italy* employ'd Emissaries to torment *Prince Butler* here. But what if Prince *Pamphilio* dies?[69] Why then, he has left in his Will for his Heirs and Executors to torment *Prince Butler* for ever.

I cannot think it a Misfortune, what Mr. *St——le* affirms, That *treasonable Books lately dispersed among us, striking apparently at the* Hanover *Succession, have passed almost without Observation from the Generality of the People*, because it seems a certain Sign that *the Generality of the People* are well disposed to that Illustrious Family: But I look upon it as a great Evil, to see Seditious Books *dispersed among us, apparently striking at the QUEEN* and her Administration, at the Constitution in Church and State, and at all Religion; yet *passing without Observation from the Generality of* those in Power: But whether this Remissness may be Ibid.

---

68 *the Chevalier shall Die*: in this paragraph the italicized portions are, of course, again Steele's phrases, which Swift is reassembling.

69 *Prince Pamphilio dies*: 'Prince Butler,' who also is mentioned in Swift's correspondence, believed he was persecuted by Cardinal Pamphili, and, just as Swift describes, suffered the delusion that after the cardinal's death, his heirs would continue to torment him. Butler, apparently with the help of Charles Davenant, also published numerous broadsides containing petitions and queries about the cloth trade. (F. Elrington Ball, 'Swift and Prince Butler,' *N&Q* 136 (1920), 404–5).

imputed to *White-Hall*, or *Westminster-Hall*,[70] is other Mens Business to enquire. Mr. *St——le* knows in his Conscience, that *the Queries concerning the* Pretender, issued from one of his own Party.[71] And as for the poor Nonjuring Clergyman, who was trusted with committing to the Press a late Book *on the Subject of Hereditary Right*, by a strain of the *Summum Jus*, he is now, as I am told, with half a score Children, starving and rotting among Thieves and Pick-pockets, in the common Room of a stinking Jail.[72] I have never seen either the Book or the Publisher; however, I would fain ask *one single Person* in the World a Question;[73] Why he who hath so often drank the Abdicated King's Health upon his Knees——But the Transition is natural and frequent, and I shall not trouble him for an Answer.

70 *White-Hall, or Westminster-Hall*: i.e., from the remissness of the government or of the law courts.
71 *Queries . . . Party*: *Queries Relating to the Birth and Birthright of a Certain Person*, by the non-juror and eminent antiquary George Hickes (1642–1715), titular 'Bishop of Thetford', first published in 1712 with the title, *Some queries proposed to civil, canon, and common lawyers in London, July 1712. In order to prove the legitimacy of the Pretender*. On the Whigs' recent acceptance of the Pretender's legitimacy, see above, note on p. 265. And on this and the next note, cf. Swift's comment in *The Examiner* for 22 March 1711, '*Dodwell, Hicks*, and *Lesley*, are gravely quoted, to prove that the *Tories* design to bring in the *Pretender*; and if I should quote Them to prove that the same Thing is intended by the *Whigs*, it would be full as reasonable, since I am sure they have at least as much to do with *Non-jurors* as we.'
72 *poor Nonjuring . . . Jail*: the work was entitled *The hereditary right of the Crown of England asserted; the history of the succession since the Conquest clear'd; and the true English constitution vindicated from the misrepresentations of Dr. Higden's View and Defence* (1713), and the poor non-juring clergyman wrongfully convicted of writing it was Hilkiah Bedford (1663–1724), later a non-juring bishop. The actual author was another non-juror, George Harbin, but Bedford confessed (in May 1714) that he had delivered the manuscript to the printer. He was pardoned in May 1718 for his part in this collaborative effort; see the *ODNB* essay by Christoph von Ehrenstein, to whom I am also indebted for additional details. The maxim Swift cites, *summum jus, summa injuria est*, 'The rigor of the law is the height of oppression', is from Cicero, *De officiis*, I.10.33. For the way this 'pernicious book' was decried by the Duke of Marlborough as a work written 'either by direction or connivance' of the Lord Treasurer, see Marlborough to Robethon, 30 November 1713, Macpherson, *Papers*, vol. II, p. 546, and for an example of the Whig use of this claim even after the Succession, see *A Detection of the Sophistry and Falsities of . . . the Secret History of the White Staff*, Part II (1714), p. 14.
73 *one single Person . . . Question*: on Sir Thomas Parker, Lord Chief Justice, see note on *Some Advice*, p. 111. The *ODNB* makes no mention of any Jacobite activities in Parker's early life, as Swift claims, but it does report that one of Parker's scholarly acquaintances was the non-juror George Hickes, and Hickes was himself a close friend and mentor of Hilkiah Bedford, imprisoned for writing the *Hereditary Right*; see the note above. Swift may have known of this irony, but there is no evidence that he did. He did express pleasure later (1734–6) that Parker (who had become Earl of Macclesfield in 1721) had been impeached and fined in 1725 (Davis, vol. V, p. 265).

It is the hardest Case in the World, that Mr. *St——le* should
take up the artificial Reports of his own Faction, and then put them   Ibid.
off upon the World, as *additional Fears of a Popish Successor.* I can
assure him, that no good Subject of the QUEEN is under the least Concern
whether the *Pretender* be Converted or no, farther than their Wishes that
all Men would embrace the true Religion. But, reporting backwards and
forwards upon this Point, helps to keep up the Noise, and is a Topick for Mr.
St——le to enlarge himself upon, by shewing how little we can depend on
such Conversions; by collecting a List of Popish Cruelties, and repeating,
after himself and the Bishop of *S——m*, the dismal Effects likely to follow
upon the Return of that Superstition among us.

But as this Writer is reported by those who know him, to be what the
French call *Journalier*, his Fear and Courage operating according to the
Weather in our uncertain Climate; I am apt to believe, the two last Pages
of his *Crisis* were written on a *Sunshiny Day.*[74] This I guess from the
general Tenor of them, and particularly from an unwary Assertion, which,
if he believes as firmly as I do, will at once overthrow all his foreign and
domestick *Fears of a Popish Successor. As divided a People as we are,*
those who are for the House of Hanover, *are INFINITELY superior*
in Number, Wealth, Courage, and all Arts Military and Civil, to those   Pag. 36.
in the contrary Interest; besides which, we have the Laws, I say, the
Laws on our side. The Laws, I say, the Laws. This elegant Repetition is, I
think, a little out of place;[75] for the Stress might better have been laid upon
so great a Majority of the Nation; without which, I doubt the Laws would
be of little weight; although they are very good additional Securities. And,
if what he here asserts be true, as it certainly is, though he asserts it; (for I
allow even the Majority of his own Party to be against the *Pretender*) there
can be no Danger of a Popish Successor, except from the unreasonable
Jealousies of the *best* among that Party, and from the Malice, the Avarice,
or Ambition of the *worst*; without which, *Britain* would be able to defend
her Succession against all her Enemies both at Home and Abroad. Most

---

74 *French . . . Day*: Swift is punning on the sense of '*journalier*' as someone who works by the day
(hence 'journalist') and an older sense as an 'inconstant or fickle-headed' and 'improvident'
person (Randle Cotgrave, *A dictionarie of the French and English tongues* (1611; facs. edn.,
Columbia: University of South Carolina Press, 1950); cf. E. Littré, *Dictionnaire de la langue
française* (Paris: Librarie Hachette, 1885), 'Qui est sujet à changer d'un jour à l'autre.'
75 *The Laws . . . place*: the repetition is only half as elegant as it appears here, since the last six
italicized words are Swift's repetition of Steele's repetition.

of the Dangers from Abroad which he enumerates as the Consequences of
this very bad Peace, made by the QUEEN, and approved by Parliament,
must have subsisted under any Peace at all; unless, among other Projects
equally feasible, we could have stipulated to cut the Throats of every *Popish*
Relation to the Royal Family.

Well; by this Author's own Confession, a number infinitely superior, and
the best circumstantiated imaginable, are for the *Succession* in the House of
Hanover. This *Succession* is established, confirmed, and secured by several
Laws; Her Majesty's repeated Declarations, and the Oaths of all Her Subjects, engage both Her and Them to preserve what those Laws have settled.
This is a *Security* indeed, a *Security* adequate at least to the Importance of
the Thing; and yet, according to the Whig-Scheme, as delivered to us by
Mr. *St——le* and his Coadjutors, is altogether insufficient; and the Succession will be defeated, the *Pretender* brought in, and *Popery* established
among us, without the farther Assistance of this Writer and his Faction.

And what Securities have our Adversaries substituted in the Place of
these? A Club of Politicians, where *Jenny Man* presides;[76] A *Crisis* written
by Mr. *St——le*; A Confederacy of knavish Stock-Jobbers to ruin Credit;
A Report of the QUEEN's Death; An *Effigies* of the *Pretender* run twice
through the Body by a valiant Peer: A Speech by the Author of the *Crisis*;
And to Sum up all, an unlimited Freedom of reviling Her Majesty, and
those She Employs.

I have now finished the most disgustful Task that ever I undertook: I
could with more ease have written *Three* dull Pamphlets, than remark'd
upon the Falshoods and Absurdities of *One*. But I was quite confounded
last *Wednesday* when the Printer came with another Pamphlet in his Hand,
written by the same Author, and entituled, *The Englishman, being the Close
of the Paper so called*, &c.[77] He desired I would read it over, and consider
it in a Paper by it self; which last I absolutely refused. Upon Perusal, I

---

76 *Jenny Man presides*: i.e, a group of coffee-house wits; Jenny Man was Proprietor of 'Jenny
    Man's Tilt-yard Coffee House', near the Palace of Whitehall, which Steele mentions in
    Spectator, no. 109, 5 July 1711. Donald Bond's note describes it as a popular meeting place
    for soldiers. Cf. *The Spectator*, no. 403 (12 June 1712), in which Swift's point is illustrated:
    Mr Spectator visits the 'politicians' at Jenny Man's and the other coffee houses to get their
    reactions to the supposed death of Louis XIV. On its heavily Whig ambience, see Holmes,
    p. 23. Cf. the Tory *Post Boy*'s mock lament as the peace of Utrecht was being worked out, 'In
    the mean time, we are inform'd that Jenny ----- Man is indispos'd' (3–5 January 1712).
77 *Englishman . . . &c.*: published as a separate quarto pamphlet serving as No. 57 of *The
    Englishman*, 15 February 1740.

found it chiefly an Invective against *Toby*,[78] the Ministry, the *Examiner*, the Clergy, the Qu--n, and the *Post-Boy*: Yet at the same time with great Justice exclaiming against those who presumed to offer the least Word against the Heads of that Faction whom Her Majesty discarded. The Author likewise proposes an *equal Division of Favour and Employments* between the Whigs and Tories: For, if the former *can have no Part or Portion in David, they desire no longer to be his Subjects.*[79] He insists, That Her Majesty *has exactly followed* Monsieur *Tughe's Memorial against Demolishing of* Dunkirk.[80] He reflects with *great Satisfaction on the good already done to his Country by the* Crisis. *Non nobis Domine, non nobis*, &c.--[81] He gives us hopes that he will leave off Writing, *and consult his own Quiet and Happiness*; And concludes with a *Letter to a Friend at Court.*[82] I suppose by the Style of *old Friend*, and the like, it must be somebody *there* of his own Level; among whom, his Party have indeed more *Friends* than I could wish. In this Letter, he asserts, That the present Ministers were not educated in the Church of *England*, but are *new Converts from Presbytery.*[83] Upon which I can only reflect, how blind the Malice of that Man must be, who invents a groundless Lye in order to Defame his Superiors, which would be no Disgrace, if it had been a Truth. And he concludes, with making Three Demands *for the Satisfaction of himself* and other *Malecontents.* First, *The Demolition of the Harbour of* Dunkirk: Secondly, *That Great Britain and* France *would heartily joyn against the Exorbitant Power of the Duke of* Lorrain, *and force the* Pretender *from his* Asylum *at* Bar le

Pag. 5.

Pag. 11.

Pag. 18.

Pag. 22.

---

78 *Toby*: referring to the abusive pamphlet *The Character of Richard St–le, Esq., with some remarks. By Toby, Abel's Kinsman . . . In a Letter to his Godfather* (1713), a piece Steele assumed to be by Swift but which was reprinted in the works of William Wagstaffe in 1726.

79 *Part . . . Subjects*: see I Kings 12: 16, 'So when all Israel saw that the king hearkened not unto them, the people answered the king, saying, What portion have we in David?' Steele had alluded to the passage when comparing those tribes alienated from David to *The Examiner* and 'his Abettors' (*Englishman*, no. 57, p. 230).

80 *He insists . . . Dunkirk*: but Steele's complaint was that she had, as Tugghe wished, demolished the 'Works' and left the harbour and its accesses intact.

81 *Non nobis . . . &c.*: 'non nobis, Domine, non nobis, sed nomini Tuo da gloriam' (Not unto us, Lord, not unto us, but unto thy name give glory.) The first line of Psalm 115 (line 9 of Psalm 113 in the Vulgate). The Latin verse was also common in vocal music in the seventeenth and eighteenth centuries, apparently first set by William Byrd.

82 *Friend at Court*: perhaps intended to represent Swift; see *Englishman*, p. 446.

83 *Converts from Presbytery*: an obvious hit at Oxford's early background as a Dissenter; this paragraph was among those singled out in Steele's trial in the House of Commons that led to his expulsion on 18 March.

Duc: Lastly, *That his* Electoral Highness *of* Hanover *would be so grateful to signifie to all the World, the perfect good Understanding he has with the Court of* England, *in as plain Terms, as Her Majesty was pleased to declare She had with that House on Her Part.*

As to the First of these Demands, I will venture to undertake it shall be granted; But then Mr. *St--le*, and his Brother *Malecontents*, must Promise to believe the Thing is done, after those employ'd have made their Report; or else bring Vouchers to disprove it. Upon the Second; I cannot tell, whether Her Majesty will engage in a War against the Duke of *Lorrain*, to *force him to remove the* Pretender; But I believe, if the Parliament should think it necessary to Address upon such an Occasion, the QUEEN will move that Prince to send Him away. His last Demand, offered under the Title of a *Wish*, is of so insolent and seditious a Strain, that I care not to touch it. Here he directly charges Her Majesty with delivering a Falshood to Her Parliament from the Throne; and declares he will not believe her, till the Elector of *Hanover* himself shall vouch for the Truth of what She hath so Solemnly affirmed.

I agree with this Writer that it is an idle Thing in his Antagonists to trouble themselves upon the *Articles of his Birth, Education, or* Pag. 2. *Fortune*; For whoever writes at this Rate of his Sovereign, to whom he owes so many Personal Obligations, I should never enquire whether he be a *GENTLEMAN BORN*, but whether he be a *HUMAN CREATURE*.

A DISCOURSE
CONCERNING THE FEARS
FROM THE PRETENDER

A
DISCOURSE CONCERNING THE FEARS FROM THE PRETENDER.

There are some disputes between the two contending Partyes now among us, which in reason ought no longer to subsist, because Time and Events have put an End to the Causes of them. For instance, Whether our Peace with France and Spain were safe and honorable; Whether the States Generall have a sufficient Barrier. Whether Spain ought to be governed by a Prince of the Bourbon Family. These Points are already determined, whether wisely or not; and reasonable Men of both sides will, I suppose allow, that the War can not be renewed at present to settle them better.

Other Differences there are, and of great Importance, which still depend, and cannot speedily be brought to an Issue without some degree of Correspondence between both Partyes. As, whether the Treaty of Commerce with France shall be confirmed by Parliament as beneficiall to our Trade, or rejected as pernicious. Whether the Princess Sophia of Hanover shall be invited to reside in England, as an Expedient for securing the Succession to Her Family upon the Qu—'s Demise. Whether the Pretender shall be forced to remove from Bar le duc, or permitted to reside any where on this side the Alpes.[1] There are some other Controversyes of lesser Moment

---

1 *Treaty of Commerce . . . the Alpes*: in June 1713, articles 8 and 9 of the commercial treaty with France negotiated at Utrecht (removing some duties from French imports) were rejected by the House, but the matter was not dead; as Steele said in *The Englishman*, no. 3 (10 October 1713), 'It is so far from a Secret, that it is a declared Circumstance, that the late *rejected Bill* will come before our Country in Parliament a second time.' Sophia, Dowager Electress of Hanover, resolved the conflict over her residence in England by dying on 8 June 1714, predeceasing Queen Anne by almost two months. But the question over the Pretender's residence was still pending. Both the Lords and the Commons had sent addresses to the Queen in July 1713 asking her to request Leopold, Duke of Lorraine, to expel him from Bar-le-Duc, where he had arrived on 22 February 1714. But neither Oxford nor the French wanted to force James from Lorraine when his likely alternative would be Rome, and both Oxford and Bolingbroke privately saw to it that the Duke of Lorraine would refuse the request (Gregg, p. 368). And there matters stood when Swift wrote this; James remained in Bar-le-Duc until 28 October 1715, when he escaped to lead his ill-fated invasion of that year (see Henry W. Wolf, 'The Pretender at Bar-le-Duc', *Blackwoods Edinburgh Magazine* 156 (1894), 220–46). See Szechi, pp. 184–9.

between the two contending Partyes; but the most popular Topick of Quarrell, is the Pretender. I have heard many significant Persons of the side which is against the Court, affirm with great appearance of Sincerity that if they could be perfectly satisfied upon this Article, they would leave it to Her Majesty to chuse her own Servants, and give her no further Uneasyness in any part of her Administration.

SOME FREE THOUGHTS UPON THE PRESENT STATE OF AFFAIRS

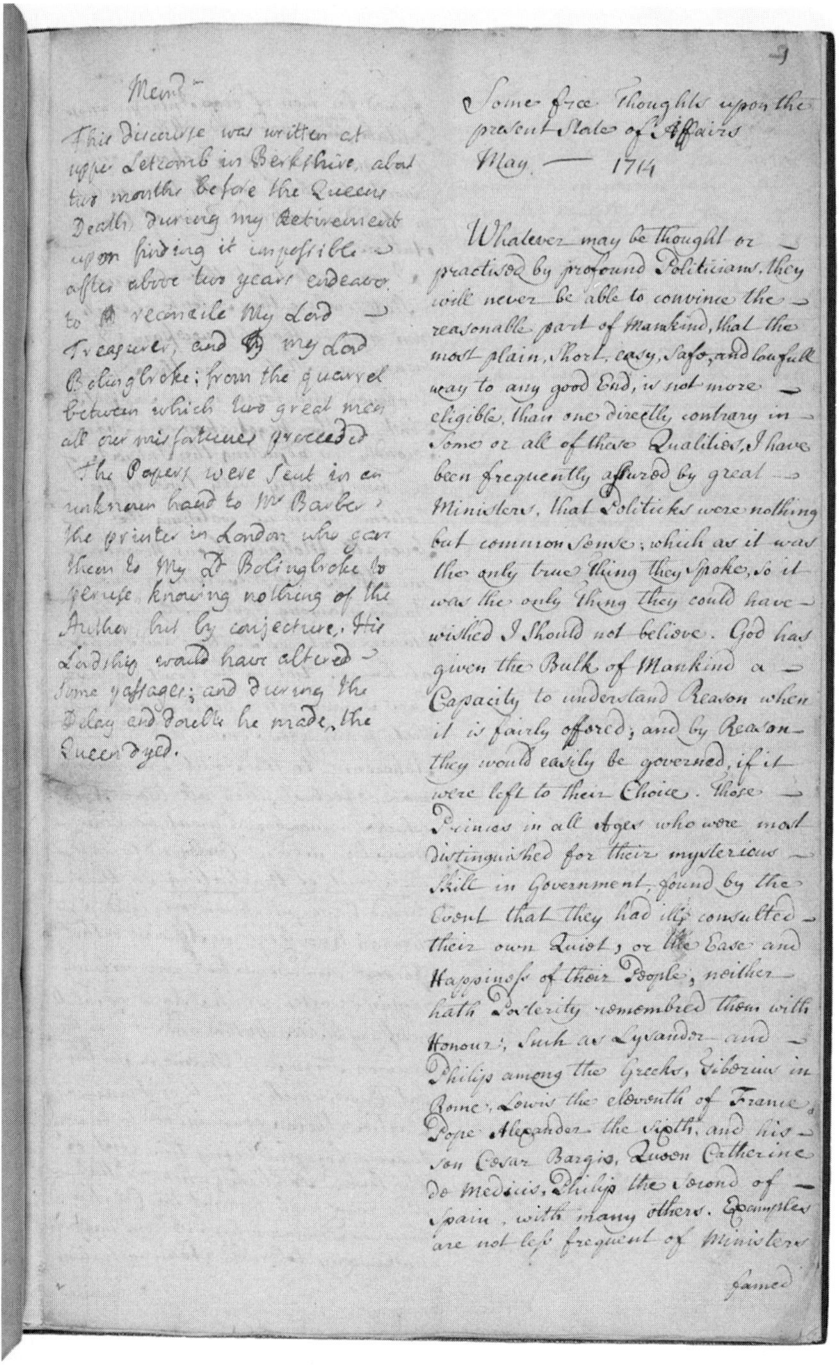

Mem.

This discourse was written at upper Letcomb in Berkshire, about two months before the Queens Death, during my Retirement, upon finding it impossible, after above two years endeavour, to reconcile My Lord Treasurer, and my Lord Bolingbroke; from the quarrel between which two great men all our misfortunes proceeded. The Papers were sent in an unknown hand to Mr Barber, the printer in London who gave them to My Ld Bolingbroke to peruse, knowing nothing of the Author but by conjecture. His Lordship would have altered some passages; and during the Delay and Bustle he made, the Queen dyed.

Some free Thoughts upon the present State of Affairs

May. —— 1714

Whatever may be thought or practised by profound Politicians, they will never be able to convince the reasonable part of mankind, that the most plain, short, easy, safe, and lawfull way to any good End, is not more eligible, than one directly contrary in some or all of those Qualities. I have been frequently assured by great Ministers, that Politicks were nothing but common Sense; which as it was the only true thing they spoke, so it was the only thing they could have wished I should not believe. God has given the Bulk of Mankind a Capacity to understand Reason when it is fairly offered; and by Reason they would easily be governed, if it were left to their Choice. Those Princes in all Ages who were most distinguished for their mysterious Skill in Government, found by the Event that they had illy consulted their own Quiet, or the Ease and Happiness of their People; neither hath Posterity remembred them with Honour; Such as Lysander and Philip among the Greeks, Tiberius in Rome; Lewis the eleventh of France, Pope Alexander the sixth, and his son Cæsar Borgia, Queen Catherine de Medicis, Philip the second of Spain, with many others. Examples are not less frequent of Ministers

famed

Figure 10. The second folio (recto) of TCC, A.5.10.

SOME FREE THOUGHTS UPON THE PRESENT STATE OF AFFAIRS MAY——1714.

Whatever may be thought or practised by profound Politicians, they will never be able to convince the reasonable part of Mankind, that the most plain, short, easy, safe, and lawfull way to any good End, is not more eligible, than one directly contrary in some or all of these Qualities. I have been frequently assured by great Ministers, that Politicks were nothing but common sense;[1] which as it was the only true Thing they spoke, so it was the only Thing they could have wished I should not believe. God has given the Bulk of Mankind a Capacity to understand Reason when it is fairly offered; and by Reason they would easily be governed, if it were left to their Choice. Those Princes in all Ages who were most distinguished for their mysterious Skill in Government, found by the Event that they had ill consulted their own Quiet, or the Ease and Happiness of their People; neither hath Posterity remembered them with Honour; such as Lysander and Philip among the Greeks, Tiberius in Rome, Lewis the eleventh of France, Pope Alexander the Sixth, and his son Cesar Borgia, Queen Catherine de Medicis, Philip the Second of Spain, with many others. Examples are not less frequent of Ministers famed for men of deep Intrigue whose Politicks have produced little more than Murmurings, Factions, and Discontents, which usually terminated in the Disgrace and Ruin of the Authors.

I can recollect but three Occasions in a State, where the Talents of such Men may be thought necessary, I mean in a State where the Prince is obeyed and loved by his Subjects: First, in the Negotiation of a Peace: Secondly, in adjusting the Interests of our own Country with those of the Nations round us; watching the severall Motions of our Neighbours and Allyes, and preserving a due Ballance among them: Lastly in the Management of Parties and Factions at home. Yet in the first of these Cases I have often

---

1 *Politicks . . . common sense*: an unnecessary air of 'mystery' in politics is a favourite topic for complaint by Swift; see, e.g., *Enquiry into the Behaviour* (Davis, vol. VIII, p. 138) and the King of Brobdingnag's comments on the topic in *Gulliver's Travels*, bk. 2, ch. 7 (Davis, vol. XI, p. 119).

heard it observed, that plain good Sense, and a firm Adherence to the Point, have proved more effectual, than all those Arts which I remember a great foreign Minister used in Contempt to call *the Spirit of Negotiating*.[2] In the Second Case, much wisdom, and a through Knowledge in Affairs both Foreign and Domestick are certainly required; after which I know no Talents necessary besides Method and Skill in the common Forms of Business. In the last Case, which is that of Managing Parties, there seems indeed to be more Occasion for practicing this Gift of the lower Politicks; whenever the Tide runs high against the Court and those in Power; which seldom happens under any tolerable Administration; while the true Interest of the Nation is pursued. But here in England (for I do not pretend to establish Maxims of Government in general) while the Prince and Ministry, the Clergy, the Majority of landed Men, and Bulk of the People appear to have the same Views, and the same Principles, it is not obvious to me, how those at the Helm can have many Opportunities of shewing their Skill in Mystery and Refinement, besides what themselves think fit to create.

I have been assured by Men long practiced in Business, that the Secrets of Court are much fewer than is generally supposed; and I hold it for the greatest Secret of Court that they are so: Because the first Springs of great Events like those of great Rivers, are often so mean and so little, that in point of Credit and Reputation they ought to be hid: And therefore Ministers are so wise to leave their Proceedings to be accounted for by Reasoners at a distance, who often mould them into Systems, that do not only go down very well in the Coffee-House, but are Supplies for Pamphlets in the present Age, and may probably furnish Materials for Memoirs and Histories in the next.

Tis true indeed, that even those who are very near the Court, and are supposed to have a large Share in the Management of publick matters, are apt to deduce wrong Consequences by reasoning upon the Causes and Motives of those Actions, wherein themselves are employed. A great Minister puts you a Case, and asks your opinion, but conceals an essential Circumstance, upon which the whole Weight of the Matter turns; then he despises your Understanding for counselling him no better, and concludes

2 *Spirit of Negotiating*: a note present in the manuscript attributes the remark to the Marquis de Torcy, the French diplomat who represented Louis XIV in the peace negotiations at Utrecht.

he ought to trust entirely to his own Wisdom. Thus he grows to abound in Secrets, and Reserves, even towards those with whom he ought to act in the greatest Confidence and Concert; and thus the world is brought to judge, that whatever be the Issue and Event, it was all foreseen, Contrived, and brought to pass by some Master-Stroke of his Politicks.

I could produce innumerable Instances from my own memory and Observation, of Events imputed to the profound Skill and Address of a Minister, which in reality were either the meer Effects of Negligence, Weakness, Humour, Passion or Pride; or at best, but the Natural Course of Things left to themselves.

During this very Sessions of Parliam^t, a most ingenious Gentleman, who has much Credit with those in Power, would needs have it, that in the late Dissensions at Court, which grew too high to be any longer a Secret; the whole Matter was carried with the utmost Dexterity on one Side, and with manifest ill Conduct on the other. To prove this he made use of the most plausible Topicks, drawn from the Nature and Dispositions of the several Persons concerned, as well as of Her Majesty, all which he knows as much of as any Man: And gave me a Detail of the whole with such an Appearance of Probability, as committed to writing would pass for an admirable Piece of secret History. Yet I am at the same time convinced by the strongest Reasons, that the Issue of those Dissensions as to the Effects they had in the Court and House of Lords, was partly owing to very different Causes, and partly to the Scituation of Affairs, from whence in that Conjuncture they could not easily terminate otherwise than they did, whatever unhappy Consequences they may have for the future.

In like manner I have heard a Physician pronounce with great Gravity, that he had cured so many Patients of malignant Fevers, and as many more of the Small-Pox; whereas in truth nine parts in ten of those who recovered, owed their Lives to the Strength of Nature and a good Constitution, while such a one happened to be their Doctor.

But while it is so difficult to learn the Springs and Motives of Some Facts, and so easy to forget the Circumstances of others, it is no wonder they should be so grossly misrepresented to the Publick by curious inquisitive heads, who proceed altogether upon Conjectures, and in reasoning upon Affairs of State, are sure to be mistaken by searching too deep.

And as I have known this to be the frequent Errour of many others, so I am sure it hath been perpetually mine; whenever I have attempted to discover the Causes of Political Events by Refinement & Conjecture; which I must acknowledge hath very much abated my Veneration for what they call Arcana Imperij,[3] whereof I dare pronounce, that the fewer there are in any Administration, it is just so much the better.

What I have hitherto said, hath by no means been intended to detract from the Qualities requisite in those who are trusted with the Management of publick Affairs; On the contrary, I know no Station of Life, where virtues of all kinds are as highly necessary, and where the want of any is so quickly or universally felt. A great Minister has no virtue for wch the Publick may not be the better, nor any Vice by which the Publick may not be a Sufferer. I have known more than once or twice within four years past, a very small Omission in Appearance, prove almost fatal to a whole Scheam, and very hardly retrieved. It is not always sufficient for the Person at the Helm, that he is intrepid in his Nature, free from any Tincture of Avarice or Corruption, that he hath great naturall and acquired Abilities, that he loves his Prince and Country, and the Constitution in Church and State. I have seen all these Accomplishments unable to bear up their owner by the mixture of a few trifling Defects too inconsiderable to mention, and almost as easy to be remedied as related.

I never thought the Reputation of much Secrecy was a Character of any Advantage to a Minister, because it put all other men upon their Guard to be as secret as he, and was consequently the Occasion that Persons and Things were always misrepresented to Him; And likewise because too great an Affectation of Secrecy, is usually thought to be attended with those little Intrigues and Refinements which among the Vulgar denominate a Man a great Politician, but among others is apt whether deservedly or no, to acquire the Opinion of Cunning; A Talent which differs as much from the true Knowledge of Government, as that of an Attorney from an able Lawyer. Neither indeed am I altogether convinced, that this Habit of multiplying Secrets may not be carried on so far as to stop that Communication which is necessary in some degree among all who have any considerable Part in the Management of Publick Affairs: Because I have observed the Inconveniencies arising from a want of Concert between those who were to give

---

3 *Arcana Imperij*: secrets of State. Throughout this section Swift is criticizing the secretiveness of Oxford and its effect on the ministry; this quality figures large in all the portraits of Oxford in Swift's posthumously published historical writing. Cf. especially his portrait of Oxford in *History*, Davis, vol. VII, pp. 74–5.

Directions, to have been of as ill Consequences, as any that could happen from the Discovery of Secrets. I suppose, when a Building is to be erected, the Model may be the Contrivance only of one Head; and it is sufficient that the under-workmen be ordered to cut Stones into certain Shapes, and place them in certain Positions; but the several Master-Builders must have some general Knowledge of the Design, without which they can give no Orders at all. And indeed I do not know a greater Mark of an able Minister, than that of rightly adapting the several Faculties of Men; nor is any thing more to be lamented than the Impracticableness of doing this in any great Degree under our present Circumstances, while so great a Number shut themselves out by adhering to a Faction, and while the Court is enslaved to the Impatience of others, who desire to sell their Vote or their Interest as dear as they can. But whether this hath not been submitted to more than was necessary, whether it hath not been dangerous in the Example, and pernicious in the Practice, I will leave to the Enquiry of Others.

It may be matter of no little Admiration to consider in some Lights the State of Affairs among us for four years past. The Queen finding her Self and the Majority of her Kingdom grown weary of the Avarice and Insolence, the mistaken Politicks, and destructive Principles of her former Ministers, calls to the Service of the Publick, another Sett of Men, who by Confession of their Enemies had equal Abilities at least with their Predecessors; Whose Interest made it necessary for them (although their Inclinations had been otherwise) to act upon those Maxims which were most agreeable to the Constitution in Church and State; Whose Birth and Patrimonies gave them weight in the Nation; And who (I speak of the chief Managers) had long lived under the strictest Bonds of Friendship. With all these Advantages supported by a vast Majority of the landed Interest, and the Inferiour Clergy almost to a Man, we have several times seen the present Administration in the greatest Distress, and very near the Brink of Ruin, together with the Cause of the Church and Monarchy committed to their Charge; neither doth it appear to me at the minute I am now writing, that their Power or Duration are upon any tolerable Foot of Security. The Cause of all which I do not so much impute to the Address and Industry of their Enemies, the uncertain timorous Nature of the Queen, as Obstructions from any private Remora[4] about the Court, as

4 *Remora*: i.e., obstacle, hindrance, impediment, obstruction (*OED*).

to some Failures which I think have been full as visible in their Causes as Effects.

Nothing has given me greater Indignation than to behold a Ministry, which came in with the Advantages I have represented, forced ever since to act upon the Defensive in the House of Lords with a Majority on their Sides, and instead of calling others to account, as it was reasonably expected, misspending their time and losing many Opportunities of doing good, because a Strugling Faction kept them continually in play. This Courage among the Adversaries of the Court, was inspired into them by various Incidents, for every one of which I think the Ministers alone are to answer.

For, first, that Race of Politicians, who in the Cant Phrase are called the Whimsicalls,[5] was never so numerous or at least so active, as it has been since the great Change at Court; Many of those who pretended wholly to be in with the Principles upon which Her Majesty and her new servants proceeded, either absenting themselves with the utmost Indifference, in those Conjunctures upon which the whole Cause depended, or siding directly with the Enemy. All which indeed arose from a very unjust, and perhaps an affected Diffidence towards those at the Helm.

I very well remember, when this Ministry was not above a year old, there was no little murmuring among such as are called the higher Tories or Churchmen (particularly some who have since affected great Fears of the Pretender, and quarrelled very much with the Treatise of Peace & Commerce with France) that a quicker Progress was not made in removing those of the discontented Party out of Employments;[6] I remember likewise, the Reasonings upon this matter were various, even among many who were allowed to know a good deal of the Inside of the Court: some supposed the Queen was at first prevailed on to make that great Change with no other View than that of acting for the future upon a moderating Scheam, in order to reconcile both Parties; And I believe there might possibly have been some Grounds for this Supposition. Others

---

5 *Whimsicalls*: the 'Hanoverian' wing of the Tory party in 1713–14, who reacted with alarm to the alienation of the Elector and who were increasingly concerned about the threat posed by Jacobites in their party and in the ministry. In the Commons in 1714 they were led by the Speaker, Sir Thomas Hanmer, in the Lords by the Earl of Anglesey. See Holmes, pp. 94, 280–4.

6 *Party . . . Employments*: on this part of Swift's discussion see the Introduction, and the notes to his earlier pamphlet, *Some Advice*, above, pp. 109–19.

conceived, the Employments were left undisposed of, in order to keep alive the Hopes of many more impatient Candidates than ever could be gratifyed. This hath since been looked on as a very high Strain of Politicks, and to have succeeded accordingly, because it is the opinion of many, that the numerous Pretenders to Places would never have been kept in order if all Expectation had been cut off. Others were yet more refined, and thought it neither wise nor safe wholly to extinguish all Opposition from the other Side; because in the Nature of Things it was absolutely necessary that there should be Parties in an English Parliament; and a Faction already odious to the People, might be suffered to continue with less Danger than any new one that could arise. To confirm this, it was said that the Majority in the House of Commons was too great on the side of the High Church, and began to form themselves into a Body by the Name of the October Club, in order to put the Ministry under Subjection. Lastly, the Danger of introducing too great a Number of unexperienced Men at once into Office, was urged as an irrefragable Reason for making Changes by slow Degrees: And that to discard an able Officer from an Employment or part of a Commission where the Revenue or Trade were concerned, for no other Reason but differing in some Principles of Government, might be of dangerous Consequence.

However, it is certain that none of these Excuses were able to pass among men who argued only from the Principles of generall Reason. For first, they looked upon all Scheams of Comprehension[7] to be as visionary and impossible in the State as in the Church: Secondly, while the Spirit raised by the Tryall of D^r. Sacheverel[8] continued in Motion, Men were not so keen upon coming in themselves as to see their Enemies out, and deprived of all Power to do Mischief: It was urged further, that this universall Ambition of hunting after Places, grew chiefly from seeing them so long undisposed of, and from too generall an Encouragem^t by Promises to all who were thought capable of doing either Good or Hurt. Thirdly, the fear of erecting another Party in case the present Faction were wholly subdued, was in the Opinion of plain Men, and in regard to the Scituation of our Affairs, too great a Sacrifice of the Nation's Safety, to the Genius of Politicks;

---

7 *Scheams of Comprehension*: in the Church, these were schemes to include 'Nonconformists within the Established Church by enlarging the terms of ecclesiastical communion' (*OED*); Swift suggests that political compromises in matters of the State are equally visionary.
8 *Spirit . . . Sacheverel*: see *Some Reasons to Prove*, above, p. 168.

considering how much is to be done, and how little Time may probably be allowed. Besides, the Division of a House of Commons into Court and Country Party, which was the Evil they seemed to apprehend, can be never dangerous to a good Ministry, who have the true Interest and Constitution of their Country at Heart: As for the Apprehension of too great a Majority in the House of Commons, it proved so vain, that upon some Points of Importance, the Court was hardly able to procure one: And the October Club which appeared so formidable at first to some Politicians, proved in the Sequel to be the chief Support of those who suspected them. It was likewise very well known that the greatest Part of those Men whom the former Ministry left in Possession of Employments, were loudly charged with Insufficiency or Corruption, over and above their obnoxious Tenets in Religion and Government; So that it would have been a Matter of some Difficulty to make a worse Choice: Besides, that Plea for keeping Men of factious Principles in Employment upon the Score of their Abilities, was thought to be extended a little too far, and construed to take in all Employments whatsoever tho' many of them required no more Abilities than would serve to qualify a Gentleman-Usher at Court.[9] So that this last Excuse for the very slow Steps made in disarming the Adversaries of the Crown was allowed indeed to have more Plausibility, but less Truth than any of the former.

I do not here pretend to condemn the Councils or Actions of the present Ministry. Their Safety and Interest are visibly united with those of the Publick, they are Persons of unquestionable Abilities, altogether unsuspected of Avarice or Corruption, and have the Advantage to be further recommended by the Dread and Hatred of the Opposite Faction. However, it is manifest, that the Zeal of their Friends hath been cooling towards them for above two Years past. They have been frequently deserted or distressed upon the most pressing Occasions, and very near giving up in Despair. Their Characters have been often treated with the utmost Barbarity and Injustice in both Houses, by scurrilous and enraged Orators, while their nearest Friends and even those who must have a Share in their Disgrace, never offered a word in their Vindication.

When I examine with my self what Occasions the Ministry may have given for this Coldness, Inconstancy, and Discontent among their Friends,

---

9 *Gentleman-Usher at Court*: this example was perhaps deliberately chosen, since Swift must have still felt the bitterness of his recent quarrel with Steele, who had held just such a post until the summer of 1713.

I at the same time recollect the various Conjectures, Reasonings, and Suspicions, which have run so freely for three years past concerning the Designs of the Court; I do not only mean such Conjectures as are born in a Coffeehouse, or invented by the Malice of a Party, but also the Conclusions, (however mistaken) of wise and good Men, whose Quality and Station fitted them to understand the Reason of publick Proceedings, and in whose Power it lay to recommend or disgrace an Administration to the People. I must therefore take the Boldness to assert, that all these Discontents, how ruinous soever they may prove in the Consequences, have most unnecessarily arisen from the want of a due Communication and Concert. Every Man must have a Light sufficient for the Length of the Way he is appointed to go; there is a Degree of Confidence due to all Stations; and a petty Constable will neither act chearfully or wisely without that Share of it which properly belongs to Him. Though the main Spring in a Watch be out of Sight, there is an intermediate Communication between it and the smallest Wheel, or else no usefull Motion could be performed. This reserved mysterious way of acting, upon Points where there appeared not the least Occasion for it, and towards Persons who in right of their Posts expected a more open Treatment, was imputed to some hidden Design, which every Man conjectured to be the very Evil he was most afraid of. Those who professed the Height of what is called the Church Principle, suspected that a Comprehension was intended, wherein the moderate Men on both Sides might be equally employed. Others went further, and dreaded such a Correspondence, as directly tended to bring the old exploded Principles and Persons once more into play. Again, some affected to be uneasy about the Succession, and seemed to think there was a View of introducing that Person, whatever he is,[10] who pretends to claim the Crown by Inheritance. Others, especially of late, surmised on the Contrary, that the Demands of the House of Hannover were industriously fomented by some in Power without the Privity of the Queen or —.[11] Now although these Accusations were too inconsistent to be all of them true, (and I have good reason to be confident that not one of them was so) yet they were maliciously suffered to pass, and thereby took off much of that Popularity, which those

10 *whatever he is*: i.e., whether the Pretender is legitimate or a 'changeling'; see note on *Publick Spirit*, p. 265.
11 *Queen or* —: presumably 'ministers' was intended for the blank. 'Privity' in this context means 'participation in the knowledge of something private or secret, usually implying concurrence or consent; private knowledge or cognizance' (*OED*).

at the Helm stood in need of, to support them under the Difficulties of a long perplexing Negotiation, a daily addition of publick Debts, and an exhausted Treasury.

But the Effects of this Mysticall manner of proceeding, did not end here; For the late Dissentions between the great Men at Court (which have been for some time past, the publick Entertainment of every Coffee-house) are said to have arisen from the same Fountain, while on one side too great a Reserve, and certainly too great a Resentment on the other, (if we may believe generall Report, for I pretend to know no further) have enflamed Animosities to such a Height as to make all Reconcilement impracticable: supposing this to be true, it may serve for a great Lesson of Humiliation to Mankind, to behold the Habits and Passions of Men otherwise highly accomplished, triumphing over Interest, Friendship, Honour, and their own Personall Safety as well as that of their Country, and probably of a most gracious Princess who hath entrusted it to them. A Ship's Crew quarrelling in a Storm, or while their Enemies are within Gun Shott is but a faint Idea of this fatal Infatuation; of which (although it be hard to say enough) some People may think perhaps I have already said too much.

Since this unhappy Incident, the Desertion of Friends, and loss of Reputation have been so great, that I do not see how the Ministers could have continued many Weeks in their Stations, if their Opposers of all kinds had agreed about the Methods by which they should be ruined; And their Preservation hitherto seems to resemble his, who had two Poisons given him together of contrary Operations: However, those incoherent Slanders which before were thrown without Distinction, are now fairly divided; and the Current Censure is, that one part of the Ministry is for restoring the old Faction, and the other for Introducing the Pretender.

Whether some have not insisted upon too implicite a Resignation to their Wisdom, Abilities and good Intentions, as well as to the Merit of having been the Sole Movers in that great Change at Court about four Years ago; Whether others have not contended for a greater Part in the Direction of Affairs than might possibly belong to them, and upon Refusal have not carried their Resentments further than private Friendship or the Safety of the Publick would admit;[12] Lastly, whether others at a greater

12 *Whether others . . . would admit*: Swift, writing to Ford on 18 July, predicted that this sentence in its original form would be cut by Bolingbroke: 'I fancy, one of L^d B's alterations will be to

distance, many of whom did equally share in the Advantages, though not in the Confidence of the Crown; have not been sometimes too medling and assuming, too craving and importunate; have not suffered those by whom they were preferred to be often distressed, and then taken Advantage of their Distresses; Whether some of them have not deserted their Friends and Principles upon the Prospect of those Dangers which their own Instability or Ambition created, and are now in hopes that their discontent will be a Foundation of Favour upon a Change they have in View. These with some other the like obvious Questions and Speculations may probably at this time of day be a little of the latest; Yet I am confident upon the whole, that a much inferiour Degree of Wisdom & Experience, joined with more unanimity and less Refinement, might have born us through all our Difficulties without any Suspicion of Magick. But it is an Observation as old as Tacitus, that some men have a Genius as much too high for publick Business, as others too low.[13]

It may seem very impertinent in one of my Level, to point out to those who sit at the Helm, what Course they ought to steer. I know enough of Courts to be sensible how mean an Opinion great Ministers have of most mens Understanding to a Degree that in any other Science would be called the grossest Pedantry. However, unless I offer my Sentiments in this Point, all I have hitherto said will be to no purpose.

The generall Wishes and Desires of a People are perhaps more obvious to other Men than to Ministers of State. There are two Points of the highest Importance, wherein a very great Majority of the Kingdom appear perfectly hearty and unanimous. First, that the Church of England should be preserved entire in all Her Rights, Powers and Priviledges; All Doctrines

---

soften a Particular that seems to fall hard upon him: *Whether others have not contended for a greater Part in the Direction of Affairs* &c., *than either Friendship, Gratitude*, or &c. The Word *Gratitude* seems hard there, and may be left out; but I will not have any thing harder on the Dragon than it is' (Woolley, *Corr.*, vol. II, p. 14). The word 'Gratitude' was duly removed by Ford and has not survived in any recovered text outside this passage in Swift's letter; the entire surrounding paragraph, critical of Bolingbroke, was omitted in the text printed in the edition of 1741. See Woolley's note to this passage.

13 *Tacitus . . . low*: perhaps alluding to the *Annals*, VI.39, about a modest official who for twenty-four years had been trusted to govern the greatest provinces, 'thanks to no shining ability but to the fact that he was adequate to his business, and no more' (trans. John Jackson). Cf. Swift: 'Men of great Parts are often unfortunate in the Management of publick Business; because they are apt to go out of the common Road, by the Quickness of their Imagination' (*Thoughts on Various Subjects*, Davis, vol. IV, p. 251).

relating to Government discouraged which She condemns; All Schisms, Sects and Heresies discountenanced and kept under due Subjection, as far as consists with the Lenity of our Constitution.[14] Her open Enemies (among whom I include at least Dissenters of all Denominations) not trusted with the smallest Degree of Civil or Military Power; and Her secret Adversaries under the Names of Whigs, Low-Church, Republicans, Moderation-Men, and the like, receive no Marks of Favour from the Crown, but what they should deserve by a sincere Reformation.

Had this Point been steddily pursued in all it's Parts for three Years past, and asserted as the avowed Resolution of the Court, there must probably have been an End of that Faction, which hath been able ever since with so much Vigour to disturb and insult the Administration. I know very well that some Refiners pretend to argue for the Usefullness of Parties in such a Government as ours; I have said Something of this already, and have heard a great many idle wise Topicks upon the Subject. But I shall not argue that Matter at present; I suppose if a Man thinks it necessary to play with a Serpent, he will chuse one of a kind that is least Mischievous; otherwise though it appears to be crushed, it may have Life enough to sting him to Death. So, I think it is not safe tampering with the present Faction, at least in this Juncture. First, because their Principles and Practices have been formerly ruinous, and since very often dangerous to the Constitution in Church and State: Secondly, because they are highly irritated, with the Loss of their Power, full of Venom and Vengeance, and prepared to execute every Thing that Rage or Malice can suggest. But principally because they have prevailed by Misrepresentations and other Artifices, to make the Successor look upon them as the only Persons he can trust. Upon which Account they cannot be too soon or too much disabled; Neither will England ever be safe from the Attempts of this wicked Confederacy, till their Strength and Interest shall be so far reduced, that for the future it shall not be in the

14 *All Schisms ... Constitution*: although this paragraph does not mention control of education as a means to repress dissenters, Bolingbroke's 'Schism Act' had that very goal and was being debated and passed in June as Swift was writing. It was intended to divert attention from the problem of the Succession and also to destroy Oxford by forcing him to support a Bill which the Queen favoured but which would alienate his moderate supporters (see Gregg, p. 386.) But despite these comments, Swift seemed undecided about the Schism Act; just before Oxford's (the 'Dragon's') dismissal, he wrote to Ford (25 July), 'I find y[ou] are not much displeased; nor I perhaps with the dragons being out; but with the manner of it; & the dispositions of those who come in; & perhaps their Crede Scheam', the last phrase an allusion to the Schism Act (Woolley, *Corr.*, vol. II, p. 28 and n. 3).

Power of the Crown, though in Conjunction with any rich and factious Body of Men, to chuse an ill Majority in a House of Commons.

One Step necessary to this great Work, will be to regulate the Army, and chiefly the Officers of those Troops which in their Turns have the Care of Her Majesties Person, who are many of them fitter to guard a Prince under an high Court of Justice, than seated on his Throne.[15] The peculiar Hand of Providence hath hitherto preserved Her Majesty encompassed, whether sleeping or travelling, by her Enemies; But since Religion teacheth us, that Providence ought not to be tempted, it is ill venturing to trust that precious Life any longer to those, who by their publick Behaviour and Discourse discover their Impatience to see it at an End; that they may have Liberty to be the Instruments of glutting at once the Revenge of their Patrons and their own. It should be well remembred, what a Satisfaction these Gentlemen (after the Example of their Betters) were so sanguine to express upon the Queen's last Illness at Windsor, and what threatnings they used of refusing to obey their General in Case that Illness had proved fatal. Nor do I think it a want of Charity to suspect, that in such an evil day, an enraged Faction would be highly pleased with the Power of the Sword, and with great Connivance leave it so long unsheathed till they were got rid of their most formidable Adversaries.[16] In the mean time it must be a very melancholly Prospect, that whenever it shall please God to visit us with this Calamity, those who are paid to be Defenders of the Civil Power will stand ready for any Acts of Violence, that a Junta composed of the greatest Enemies to the Constitution shall think fit to enjoin them.

15 *fitter . . . Throne*: i.e., better suited to guard a Prince accused of treason than one ruling peacefully; Swift uses language calculated to inflame Tory readers, since at this time the term 'High Court of Justice' would apply only to the 'revolutionary tribunal which sent Charles I to the scaffold' in 1649 (E. Jowitt, *Dictionary of English Law* (London: Sweet & Maxwell, 1959), vol. I, p. 908). Cf. Swift's implied comparison of Steele to the regicide Bradshaw in the Preface to *The Importance of the Guardian Considered*, above, p. 219.
16 *precious Life . . . Adversaries*: alluding to the behaviour of some officers of the 'Horse and Foot Guards' during the Queen's illness at Windsor during Christmas 1713; see Swift's description of their behaviour and of the unsuccessful efforts of their General (the Duke of Ormond) to obtain funds from Oxford to buy up their commissions and so dismiss them, *Enquiry into the Behaviour of the Queen's Last Ministry*, Davis, vol. VIII, pp. 155–6. On the joyful reaction of the Whigs to her illness and the dubious measures of the Tory ministers, see Gregg, pp. 374–5; see also *A Modest Enquiry into the Reasons of the Joy Expressed by a Certain Sett of People* (1714), written by Mrs Manley with help from Swift (ptd. as Appendix A, Davis, vol. VIII, pp. 183 ff.)

The other Point of great Importance is the Security of the Protestant Succession in the House of Hannover; not from any Partiality to that Illustrious House, further than as it hath had the Honour to mingle with the Blood Royal of England, and is the nearest Branch of our Regal Line reformed from Popery. This Point hath one Advantage over the former, that both Parties profess to desire the same Blessing for Posterity, but differ about the means of securing it. From whence it hath come to pass, that the Protestant Succession, in appearance the Desire of the whole Nation, hath proved the greatest Topick of Slander, Jealousy, Suspicion, and Discontent.

I have been so curious to ask severall Acquaintance among the opposite Party, whether they or their Leaders did really suspect there had been ever any Design in the Ministry to weaken the Succession in Favour of the Pretender or of any other Person whatsoever. Some of them freely answered in the Negative, Others were of the same Opinion, but added, they did not know what might be done in time, and upon farther Provocations. Others again pretended to believe the Affirmative, but could never produce any plausible Grounds for their Belief. I have likewise been assured by a Person of some Consequence, that during a very near and Constant Familiarity with the great Men at Court for four Years past, he never could observe even in those Hours of Conversation where there is usually least Restraint, that one Word ever passed among them to shew a Dislike of the present Settlement, although they would sometimes lament that the false Representations of their's and the Kingdom's Enemies had made some Impressions in the Mind of the Successor.[17] As to my own Circle of Acquaintance, I can safely affirm, that excepting those who are Non-jurers by Profession, I have not met with above two Persons who appeared to have any Scruples concerning the present Limitation of the Crown. I therefore think it may very impartially be pronounced, that the Number of those who wish to see the Son of the abdicated Prince[18] upon the Throne, is

17 *I have likewise . . . Successor:* cf. the same reflection in *Enquiry*, 'I never yet knew a Minister of State . . . so great a Master of Secrecy', etc. (Davis, vol. VIII, p. 165).
18 *abdicated Prince:* Swift's use of this term for James II in his *History* aroused the protest of Andrew Millar's London editor, Charles Lucas, who clearly thought Swift used the phrase to express the high Tory notion of non-resistance, i.e., to say that James departed by his own volition, not as the result of the forcible resistance of his people (Davis, vol. VII, p. 176). But *OED*, citing this very passage, recognizes the ambiguity of the term in the seventeenth century: 'Deposed from an office, function, or dignity. In 17th c. including deposition by others . . . but now, always, self-deposed, having formally laid down or divested himself of a

altogether inconsiderable. And further, I believe it will be found, that there are None who so much dread any Attempt he shall make for the Recovery of his imagined Rights, as the Roman-Catholicks of England, who love their Freedom and Properties too well, to desire his Entrance by a French Army, and a Field of Blood; who must continue upon the same Foot, if he changes his Religion, and must expect to be the first and greatest Sufferers if he should happen to fail.

As to the Person of this nominall Prince, he lyes under all Manner of Disadvantages: The Vulgar imagin him to have been a Child imposed upon the Nation by the fraudulent Zeal of his Parents and their bigotted Councellors; who took speciall Care, against all the Rules of Common Policy, to educate him in their hatefull Superstition, suckt in with his milk and confirmed in his Manhood, too strong to be now shaken by M^r. Lesley;[19] and, a counterfeit Conversion will be too gross to pass upon the Kingdom after what we have seen and suffered from the like Practice in his Father. He is likewise said to be of weak Intellectualls, and an unsound Constitution. He was treated contemptibly enough by the young Princes of France, even during the War; is now wholly neglected by that Crown, and driven to live in Exile upon a small Exhibition.[20] He is utterly unknown in England, which he left in the Cradle; His Father's Friends are most of them dead, the rest antiquated or poor; Six and twenty Years have almost passed since the Revolution, and the Bulk of those who are now in Action either at Court, in Parliament, or publick Offices, were then Boys at School or the Universities; and look upon that great Change to have happened during

---

dignity or trust. (See the ambiguity of its application to James II.)'. Cf. Swift's earlier treatment of the issue in the *Sentiments* (1708), where he says that whether James's 'Removal' was caused by 'his own *Fears*, or other Mens *Artifices*', since the throne was supposedly left vacant, the 'Body of the People was thereupon left at Liberty, to chuse what Form of Government they pleased' (Davis, vol. II, pp. 20–1). And in his marginal comments on Burnet's *History of His Own Time*, after Burnet disparages the dispute in the Convention Parliament over the word 'abdicate', Swift writes, 'It was a very material point' (vol. V, p. 291).

19 *Lesley*: Charles Leslie, a prolific non-juror and Jacobite, published in the spring of 1714 *A Letter from Mr Lesly to a Member of Parliament in London* reporting on his visit to Bar-le-Duc, where he tried to persuade the Pretender to change his religion; but the most he could get was the assertion that the Pretender felt 'obliged to do everything that is consistent with conscience and honour' (Andrew Browning (ed.), *English Historical Documents, 1660–1714* (London: Eyre & Spottiswoode, 1953) p. 911). On the views of the 'Vulgar' that the Pretender was a changeling, see above, p. 265, and Szechi, ch. 9.

20 *Exhibition*: 'an allowance of money for a person's support; a pension, salary' (*OED*, citing this example).

a Period of Time for which they are not accomptable. The Logick of the highest Tories is now, that this was the Establishment they found, as soon as they arrived to a Capacity of Judging; that they had no hand in turning out the late King, and therefore have no Crime to answer for, if it were any. That the Inheritance to the Crown is in pursuance of Laws made ever since their Remembrance, by which all Papists are excluded; and they have no other Rule to go by. That they will no more dispute King William the third's Title, than King William the first's; since they must have Recourse to History for both: That they have been instructed in the Doctrines of passive Obedience, Non-Resistance and Hereditary Right, and find them all necessary for preserving the present Establishment in Church and State, and for continuing the Succession in the House of Hannover, and must in their own Opinion renounce all those Doctrines by setting up any other Title to the Crown. This I say, seems to be the Politicall Creed of all the high-principled Men, I have for some time met with of forty Years old, and under; which although I am far from justifying in every part, yet I am sure it sets the Protestant Succession upon a much firmer Foundation, than all the indigested Scheams of those who profess to act upon what they call Revolution-Principles.[21] Neither should it perhaps be soon forgot, that during the greatest Licentiousness of the Press, while the sacred Character of the Queen was every day insulted in factious Papers and Ballads, not the least reflecting Insinuation ever appeared against the Hannover Family, whatever Occasion might have been laid hold on by intemperate Pens, from the Rashness or Indiscretion of one or two Ministers from thence.

From all these Considerations I must therefore lay it down as an uncontestible Truth, that the Succession to these Kingdoms in the Illustrious House of Hannover is as firmly secured as the Nature of the Thing can possibly admit; by the Oaths of all who are entrusted with any Office, by the very Principles of those who are termed the High-Church, by the generall Inclinations of the People, by the Insignificancy of that Person who claims it from Inheritance, and the little Assistance he can expect either from Princes abroad or Adherents at home.

---

21 *passive Obedience . . . Revolution-Principles*: as response to fears that the ministers and their adherents are Jacobites, Swift brings together in this passage the cornerstones of high Church and high Tory ideology with total acceptance of the Hanoverian Succession. On the place of this position in contemporary political thought, see Ian Higgins, *Swift's Politics: A Study in Disaffection* (Cambridge: Cambridge University Press, 1994), pp. 8–10.

However, since the virulent Opposers of the Queen and her Administration have so far prevailed by their Emissaries at the Court of Hannover,
and by their Practices upon one or two ignorant unmannerly Messengers
from thence, as to make the Elector desire some further Security, and send
over a Memoriall here to that End:[22] The great Question is how to give
reasonable Satisfaction to His Highness, and (what is infinitely of greater
Consequence) at the same time, consult the Honour and Safety of the
Queen, whose quiet Possession is of much more Consequence to us of the
present Age, than his Reversion: The Substance of his Memoriall, if I retain
it right, is to desire, that some one of his Family might live in England with
such a Maintainance as is usuall to those of the Royall Blood, and that certain Titles should be confered upon the rest, according to antient Custom.
The Memoriall doth not specify which of the Family should be invited
to reside here; and if it had, I believe however, Her Majesty would have
looked upon it as a Circumstance left to her own Choice: wherefore since
the old Electrice is lately dead, I am apt to think, that the Nation would
humbly submit to their Sovereign's Pleasure, if Her Majesty conceived it
proper upon certain Conditions to invite over the eldest Grandson of the
present Elector, have a Maintenance allotted him by Parliament, and give
him a Title.

But, as all this is most manifestly unnecessary in it self, and only in Com-
plyance with the mistaken Doubts of a presumptive Heir; so the Nation
would (to speak in the Language of M^{r}. Steele) *Expect* that Her Majesty
should be made perfectly easy from that Side for the future;[23] No more be

---

22 *Memoriall here to that End*: on 12 April Ludwig von Schütz, the Hanoverian agent in England,
   demanded that a writ be issued calling the Electoral Prince (later George II) to take his seat
   in Parliament as the Duke of Cambridge. Although the writ had to be issued, the Queen was
   furious, and the proposed visit became a pawn in the battle between Oxford and Bolingbroke
   (the *Examiner* of 21–4 May walked a careful line, but sneered at Schütz.) The Elector backed
   away from sending the Electoral Prince, but presented a Memorial to Thomas Harley, the
   British agent, asking only that 'some one in the Electoral family' be invited to reside in Great
   Britain, though he intimated that his younger brother might be a better candidate than his
   son. To this request the British responded with harsh letters from Oxford and the Queen
   herself, which arrived 25 May (o.s.). Three days later the Electress Sophia died, and the
   Elector, now heir apparent, renewed his demands (Gregg, pp. 383–4). It was against this
   background that Swift made the suggestion which follows here.

23 *Expect . . . future*: parodying Steele's insistent repetition of that word in the *Guardian* of
   7 August 1713 and in his *Importance of Dunkirk Consider'd* (1713); see Swift's *Importance of
   the Guardian*, above, pp. 232–3 and note. Four years later Steele was still pleased with himself
   over the furore aroused by his phrase; on 24 April 1717 he wrote in a letter to his wife, 'I

alarmed with Apprehensions of Visits or Demands of Writs, where She
hath not thought fit to give any Invitation. The Nation would likewise
expect that there should be an End of all private Commerce between that
Court and the Leaders of a Party here; And that His Electorall Highness
should declare Himself entirely satisfied with all Her Majesties Proceedings, Her Treatise of Peace and Commerce, Her Allyances abroad, Her
Choice of Ministers at Home, and particularly in her most gracious Con-
descensions to his Requests. That he would upon all proper Occasions,
and in the most publick Manner discover his utter Dislike of all Factious Persons and Principles, but especially of that Party which under
the pretence or Shelter of his Protection, hath so long disquieted the
Kingdom: And lastly that he would acknowledge the Goodness of the
Queen, and Justice of the Nation in so fully securing the Succession to his
Family.

It is indeed a Problem which I could never comprehend; why the Court
of Hannover, who have all along thought themselves so perfectly secure
in the Affections, the Principles, and the Professions of the Low-Church
Party, should not have endeavoured according to the usuall Politicks of
Princes, to gain over those who were represented as their Enemies; since
these supposed Enemies had made so many Advances, were in Possession
of all the Power, had framed the very Settlement to which that Illustrious
Family owes it's Claim; had all of them abjured the Pretender, were now
employed in the great Offices of State, and composed a Majority in both
Houses of Parliament, not to mention that the Queen her self with the
Bulk of the Landed Gentry and Commonalty throughout the Kingdom
were in the same Interest. This, one would think might be a Strength
sufficient not only to obstruct but to bestow a Succession; And since the
presumed Heir, could not but be perfectly secure of the other Party, whose
greatest avowed Grievance was the pretended Danger of his future Rights;
It might therefore surely have been worth his Thoughts to have made at
least one Step towards cultivating a fair Correspondence with the Power
in Possession. Neither could those who are called his Friends have blamed
him, or with the least Decency enter into any Engagement for defeating
his Title.

would not use so harsh a Phrase as *Expect*, tho I have formerly taken the liberty of that word
when it concerned a Queen' (Steele, *Correspondence*, p. 535).

But, why may not the Reasons of this Proceeding in the Elector be directly contrary to what is commonly imagined? Methinks, I could endeavour to believe, that His Highness is thorowly acquainted with both Parties; is convinced that no true Member of the Church of England, can easily be shaken in his Principles of Loyalty, or forget the Obligation of an Oath by any Provocation: That these are therefore the People he intends to rely upon, and keeps only fair[24] with the others from a true Notion he has of their Doctrines, which prompt them to forget their Duty upon every Motive of Interest or Ambition. If this Conjecture be right, His Highness cannot sure but entertain a very high Opinion of such Ministers who continue to act under the Dread and Appearance of a Successor's utmost Displeasure, and the Threats of an enraged Faction, whom he is supposed alone to favour, and to be guided entirely in his Judgment of British Affairs and Persons by their Opinions.

But, to return from this Digression; the Presence of that Infant Prince among us could not I think in any Sort be inconsistent with the Safety of the Queen. He would be in no Danger of being corrupted in his Principles, or exposed in his Person by vicious Companions; He could be at the Head of no factious Clubs and Cabals, nor be attended by a hired Rabble, which his Flatterers might represent as Popularity. He would have none of that Impatience which the Frailty of human Nature gives to expecting Heirs. There would be no Pretence for Men to make their Court by affecting German Modes and Refinements in Dress or Behaviour: Nor would there be any Occasion of insinuating to him how much more his Levee was frequented than the Anti-Chambers, at S^t. James's. Add to all this, the advantages of being educated in our Religion, Laws, Language, Manners, Nature of the Government, each so very different from those he would leave behind: By which likewise he might be highly usefull to His Father, if that Prince should happen to survive Her Majesty.

The late King William, who after his Marriage with the Lady Mary of England, could have no probable Expectation of the Crown, and very little even of being a Queen's Husband, (the Duke of York having then a young Wife) was no Stranger to our Language or Manners, and went often to the Chappel of His Princess; which I observe the rather, because I could heartily wish the like Disposition were in another Court, and because it

---

24 *keeps only fair*: i.e., 'only stays on good terms with' (*OED, s.v.* 'fair', adv. 2b).

may be disagreeable to a Prince to take up new Doctrines on a sudden, or speak to His Subjects by an Interpreter.

An illnatured or inquisitive Man may still perhaps desire to press the Question further, by asking what is to be done, in Case it should so happen that this Malevolent working Party at home may have Credit enough with the Court of Hannover, to continue the Suspicion, Jealousy, and Uneasiness there against the Queen and her Ministry; to make such Demands be still insisted on, as are by no means thought proper to be complyed with; and in the mean time to stand at arms Length with her Majesty, and in close Conjunction with those who oppose Her.

I take the Answer to be easy. In all Contests the safest way is to put those we dispute with, as much in the Wrong as we can. When Her Majesty shall have offered such or the like Concessions as I have above mentioned, in order to remove those Scruples artificially raised in the Mind of the expectant Heir, and to divide him from that Faction by which he is supposed to have been misled; She hath done as much as any Prince can do, and more than any other would probably do in her Case; and will be justified before God and Man, whatever be the Event. The equitable part of those who now side against the Court, will probably be more temperate, and if a due Dispatch be made in placing the Civil and Military Power in the Hands of such as wish well to the Constitution; It cannot be any way for the Quiet or Interest of a Successor to gratify so inconsiderable a Faction as will probably then remain, at the Expence of a much more numerous and considerable Part of his Subjects. Neither do I see how the Principles of such a Party either in Religion or Government, will prove very agreeable; because I think, Luther and Calvin seem to have differed as much as any two among the Reformers: And because a German Prince will probably be suspicious of those who think they can never depress the Prerogative enough.

But supposing once for all, as far as possible, that the Elector should utterly refuse to be upon any Terms of Confidence with the present Ministry, and all others of their Principles, as Enemies to him and the Succession; nor easy with the Queen her Self but upon such Conditions as will not be thought consistent with her Safety or Honour; and continue to place all his Hope and Trust in the discontented Party. In such an improbable Case, I think it were humbly to be wished, that whenever the Succession shall take place, the Alterations intended by the new Prince should be made by himself, and not by his Deputies. Because I am of Opinion, that the Clause empowering the Successor to appoint a latent unlimited Number additionall to the Seven Regents named in the Act, went upon a Supposition, that such a *Secret Committee* would not be of Persons whose Enmity and contrary Principles might dispose them to confound the rest. The late King William, whose Title was much more controverted than that of Her Majesty's Successor, can ever probably be, did for severall years leave the Administration of the Kingdom in the Hands of Lords Justices, during the Height of a War, and while the abdicated Prince himself was frequently attempting an Invasion. From whence we might imagine that the Regents appointed by Parliament upon the Demise of the Crown, would be able to keep the Peace during an Absence of a few Weeks, without any Colleagues. However, I am pretty confident, that the only Reason why a Power was given of chusing Dormant Viceroys, was to take away all Pretences of a necessity to invite over any of the Family here, during Her Majesty's Life. So that I do not well apprehend what Arguments the Elector can use to insist upon both.

To conclude; the only way of securing the Constitution in Church and State, and consequently this very Protestant Succession it self, will be by lessening the Power of our Domestick Adversaries as much as can possibly consist with the Lenity of our Government; and if this be not speedily done, it will be easy to point where the Nation is to fix the Blame. For we are very well assured, that since the Account Her Majesty received of the Cabals, the Triumphs, the insolent Behaviour of the whole Faction during her last Illness at Windsor, she hath been as willing to see them deprived of all Power to do Mischief, as any of her most Zealous and Loyall Subjects can desire.

SOME CONSIDERATIONS UPON THE CONSEQUENCES HOPED AND FEARED FROM THE DEATH OF THE QUEEN

.

SOME CONSIDERATIONS UPON THE CONSEQUENCES HOPED AND FEARED FROM THE DEATH OF THE QUEEN

In order to sett in a clear Light what I have to say upon this Subject, it will be convenient to examine the State of the Nation with reference to the two contending Partyes; this cannot well be done without some little Retrospection into the five last Years of her late Majesty's Reign.

I have it from unquestionable Authority, that the Dutchess of M—s Favor began to decline very soon after the Queen's Accession to the Throne, and that the E. of Godolphin's held not much above two years longer; although Her Majesty (no ill Concealer of her Affections) did not think fit to deprive them of their Power till a long time after.[1]

The D. of Marl. and the Earl of Godolophin having fallen early into the Interests of the lower Party, for certain Reasons not seasonable here to be mentioned, (but which may deserve a Place in the History of that Reign) they made larger steps that way upon the Death of the Prince of Denmark, taking in severall among the warmest Leaders of that Side, into the chief Employment[s] of the State.[2] M[r] Harley, then Secretary of State, who disliked their Proceedings, and had very near overthrown their whole Scheam was removed with utmost Indignation, and about the same time, S[r] Simon Harcourt, and M[r] S[t] John with some others voluntarily gave up their Employm[ts].

But the Queen, who had then a great Esteem for the Person and Abilityes of M[r] Harley (and in Proportion of the other two, though at that time not equally known to her) was deprived of his Service with some Regret, and

---

1 *Power . . . long time after*: Godolphin was dismissed from his post as Lord Treasurer on 7 August 1710; the Duchess, after a long estrangement from the Queen, finally resigned on 17 January 1711.

2 *Employment[s] of the State*: the Prince Consort, George of Denmark, died 28 October 1708; on the ascendancy of the Whig Junto's main figures following his death, see *Conduct*, pp. 85–6 note.

upon that and other Motives, well known at Court, began to think her self hardly used; and severall Storyes ran about, whether true or false, that Her Majesty was not allways treated with that Duty She might expect. Mean time the Church Party were loud in their Complaints, surmising from the Virulence of severall Pamphlets, from certain Bills projected to be brought into Parliam^t, from Endeavors to repeal the Sacramentall Test, from the avowed Principles, and free Speeches of some Persons in Power, and other Jealosyes needless to repeat, that ill-designs were forming against the Religion established.[3]

These Fears were all confirmed by the Tryall of Dr Sacheverill, which drew the Populace as one Man into the Party against the Ministry and Parliam^t.

The Ministry were very suspicious that the Queen had still a reserve of Favor for Mr Harley, which appeared by a Passage that happened some days after his Removal. For the E. of Godolophins Coach and his, happening to meet near Kensington: the Earl a few hours after reproached the Queen that She privately admitted Mr Harley, and was not without some difficulty undeceived by Her Majesty's Asseverations to the contrary.[4]

Soon after the Doctor's Tryall, this Gentleman by the Queen's Command, and the Intervention of M^{rs} M—m was brought up the Backstairs; and that Princess, Spirited by the Addresses from all Parts, which shewed the Inclinations of her Subjects to be very averse from the Proceedings in Court and Parliam^t, was resolved to break the united Power of the Marlborough and Godolphin Familyes, and to begin this Work, by taking the disposall of Employm^{ts} into her own Hands; for which an Opportunity happened by the Death of the Earl of Essex, Lieutenant of the Tower, whose Employm^t was given to the Earl Rivers, to the great discontent of the D. of Marl—, who intended it for the D. of Northumb— then Collonell of the Oxford Regim^t, to which the Earl of Hertford was to succeed. Some time after, the Chamberlain's Staff was disposed of to the D. of Shr— in the absence and without the Privity of the E. of Godolphin. The Earl of Sund—'s Removal followed, and lastly that of the High Treasurer himself,

---

3 *Church Party . . . established*: these lines form the background to Swift's writings on Church and State in 1708–9, such as the *Sentiments*, *Letter . . . Concerning the Sacramental Test*, the *Argument* and his unfinished *Remarks*; cf. Swift's comments on this phase of his life in *Memoirs* (Davis, vol. VIII, pp. 121–2).
4 *Asseverations to the contrary*: cf. the same story in Swift's *Memoirs* (pp. 115–16).

whose Office was put into Commission, whereof Mr Harley (made at the same time Chancellor of the Exchequer) was one; I need say nothing of other Removalls, which are well enough known and remember^d; let it suffice, that in 8 or nine Months time the whole Face of the Court was altered, and very few Friends of the former Ministry left in any great Stations there.

I have good Reasons to be assured, that when the Queen began this Change, She had no Intentions to carry it so far as the Church Party expected, and have since been so impatient to see. For altho' She were a true Professor of the Religion established Yet the first Motives to this Alteration did not arise from any Dangers She apprehended to that or the Government; but from a desire to get out of the Dominion of some who She thought had kept her too much and too long in Pupillage. She was in her own Nature extreamly dilatory and timorous; yet upon some Occasions, positive to a great degree: And when She had got rid of those who had as She thought given her the most uneasyness, she was inclined to stop, and entertain a fancy of acting upon a moderating Scheam, from whence it was very difficult to remove her. At the same time I must confess my Belief, that this Imagination was put into her Head, and made use of as an Encouragement to begin that work, after which her Advisers might think it easier to prevail with her to go as far as they thought fit. That these were Her Majesty's dispositions in that Conjuncture, may be confirmed by many Instances. In the very Height of the Change, She appeared very loth to part with two great Officers of State of the other Party,⁵ and some whose Absence the new Ministers most earnestly wished held in for above two years after.

Mr Harley who acted as first Minister before he had the Staff, as he was a Lover of gentle Measures, and inclined to Procrastination, so he could not with any decency press the Queen too much against her Nature, because it

5 *two great Officers . . . Party*: in *Memoirs* (p. 124) Swift mentions the Duke of Somerset and the Earl of Cholmondely as continuing their employments 'in great stations at court' despite the change of ministry in 1710. Somerset (Master of the Horse), who with his Duchess was greatly in the Queen's favour, is clearly one of the two intended here; Cholmondely (Treasurer of Her Majesty's Household) is less obvious as the intended second figure, but Swift in *History* includes him again with Somerset (along with Marlborough) as 'discontented Lords . . . still in possession of their Places' at the end of 1711. And in December 1711 he 'rallied' Oxford by saying that if he had the White Staff he would 'immediately turn lord Marlborough, his two daughters, the duke and duchess of Somerset, and lord Cholmondely out of all their employments' (Williams, *JSt*, p. 434).

would be like running upon the Rock where his Predecessors had Split. But violent Humors running both in the Kingdom and the new Parliam^t against the Principles and Persons of the low Church Party, gave this Minister a very difficult Part to play. The Warm Members in both Houses, especially among the Commons pressed for a thorow Change, and so did almost all the Queen's new Servants, especially after Mr Harley was made an Earl and High-Treasurer. He could not in good Policy own his want of Power nor fling the Blame upon his Mistress; And as too much Secrecy was one of his Faults, he would often upon these Occasions keep his nearest Friends in the dark. The Truth is, he had likewise other Views, which were better Suited to the Maxims of State in generall, than to that Scituation of Affairs. By leaving many Employm^{ts} in the Hands of the discontented Party, he fell in with the Queen's Humor, he hoped to acquire the Reputation of Lenity, and kept a great Number of Expectants in order, who had Liberty to hope, while any thing remained undisposed of. He seemed also to think, as other Ministers have done, that since Factions are necessary in such a Governm^t as ours it would be prudent not altogether to lay the present one prostrate, lest another more plausible, and therefore not so easy to grapple with might arise in it's Stead.

However, it is certain that a great Part of the Load he bore was unjustly laid on him. He had no Favorites among the Whig Party, whom he kept in upon the Score of old Friendship or Acquaintance, and he was a greater Object of their Hatred than all the rest of the Ministry together.

CONTRIBUTIONS
TO THE POST BOY
AND THE
EVENING POST

CONTRIBUTIONS
TO THE POST BOY
AND THE
EVENING POST

Post Boy *25–27 December 1711*

London, Dec. 27. On Saturday the 22d instant, about Four in the Morning, Mrs. Anne Long,[1] Sister of Sir James Long, Bart. died at Linn in Norfolk, after a Sickness but of Four Hours. She was a Lady very much celebrated here for her Beauty, Virtue, and good Sense; and is extremely lamented by all who knew her.

Evening Post *11–13 Nov 1712*

London, Nov. 13. We have received a more particular Account relating to the Box sent to the Lord Treasurer, as mention'd in our last, which is as follows.

On the Third Instant a tall, slender Boy, having on a Gray Coat and a brown bob Peruke, delivered a Band-box,[2] (directed to the Lord Treasurers Porter) at a Penny-Post House behind Ludgate, which the next Morning was carried to the Office in Chichesters Rents, Chancery Lane, and from thence to the Lord Treasurers by one Causon, a Penny Postman, in which, upon opening was found another Band-Box, directed to the Lord Treasurer. The Box was carry'd up to my Lord's Bed-Chamber, and deliver'd to his Lordship, who lifting up the Lid as far as the Pack-thread that ty'd it would give way, said, He saw a Pistol; whereupon, a Gentleman in the

---

1 *Anne Long*: since she was both a friend and a famous beauty fallen on hard times, Anne Long's problems were of much concern to Swift. See the references scattered through Williams, *JSt*, especially the character of her he draws after her death (p. 445), and see the Introduction, pp. 25–6.
2 *Band-box*: on this incident and Swift's role, see the Introduction (pp. 26–7). A band-box was 'a slight box of card-board or very thin chip covered with paper, for collars, caps, hats, and millinery; originally made for the "bands" or ruffs of the 17th c.' (*OED*).

Room desired the Box might be given to him; he took it to the Window, at some Distance from my Lord, and open'd it, by cutting with a Pen-knife the Pack-threads that fasten'd the Lid. The first Thing that appear'd was the Stock and Lock of a Pocket-Pistol, lying across the middle of the Band-Box, and fasten'd at each end with two Nails; on each side of the Fire-lock were laid the Middle-pieces of two large Ink-horns charg'd with Powder and Ball, and Touch-holes bored at the Butt-ends of 'em, to which were fasten'd two Linnen Bags of Gunpowder, and at the other end of the Bags were two Quils fill'd with Wildfire. These two artificial Barrels were plac'd with the Muzzels contrary-ways, and the Quil of one of 'em directed to the Pan of the Pistol, as the other probably was, tho' disorder'd by the Carriage. The Gentleman, who open'd the Box, apprehending some Mischief was intended, would not touch the Pistol-stock till he had remov'd all the other Machines; then gently widening the Box, the Nails which fastned the Stock at either end gave Way. He found the Firelock prim'd and cock'd, and a Piece of Thread fastned to the Trigger, which he conceiv'd he had cut in the opening. The small Nails which fasten'd the Stock at either end, were so contriv'd, That by taking it up at the first View, as it was natural to do with all the Implements about it, the Cock would have gone down and fir'd the whole Train, which would have immediately discharged both Barrels, different Ways; this could not have been avoided, had the Pistol stock been pull'd out with any Force, before the Nails were loosen'd, and the Thread cut which was tied to the Trigger.

Post Boy *15–18 November 1712*

On Saturday Morning last, about 7 of the Clock, the Duke of Hamilton and the Lord Mohun fought a Duel in Hide-Park; his Grace's Second was Col. Hamilton, and his Lordship's Major-Gen. Mackartney. The Ld Mohun died on the Spot; and my Ld Duke soon after he was brought home, who receiv'd the following Wounds, one on the Right side of his Leg, about 7 Inches long; another in his Right Arm; the third, in the upper part of his Left Breast, running downwards into his Body, which was lookt upon to be the immediate Occasion of his Death; the fourth Wound was on the outside of his Left Leg. My Ld Mohun receiv'd a very large Wound in his Groin; another on the Right Side through his Body, up to the Hilt of the Sword; and the third in his Arm; and other Wounds. As to the further Particulars, we shall refer them to our next.

Post Boy *18–20 November 1712*

London, Nov. 20. A farther Account of the Duel fought between his Grace the Duke of Hamilton[3] and the Lord Mohun, is as followeth.

Major-General Mackartney went Three times to the Duke's House with a Challenge from the Lord Mohun; on Friday last at Four in the Afternoon he deliver'd it to the Duke, and was at the Bagnio all Night with my Lord Mohun, who was observ'd to be seiz'd with Fear and Trembling at that time. They met at 7 the next Morning, with their Seconds, Col. Hamilton of the Foot-Guards for the Duke, and Mackartney for the Lord Mohun; there the Duke told Mackartney, That his Grace knew this was all of his Contrivance, but that he should have a Share in the Dance; for his Friend Hamilton resolv'd to entertain him. On Tuesday last, a Committee of Council sate at the Earl of Dartmouth's Office, and the Spectators of the Duel were examin'd, and we hear, that my Lord Duke and the Lord Mohun did not parry, but gave Thrusts at each other; and the latter shortening his Sword, stabb'd the Duke in the upper part of his Left Breast, running downwards into his Body, (which Wound, upon probing, was about 14 Inches long) who expired soon after he was put into the Coach. Col. Hamilton receiv'd a Wound in his Right Leg; and going afterwards to the Half-Moon Tavern in Cheapside, was dress'd by Mr. Woodward the Chirurgeon. His Grace is universally lamented by all Men of Honour and Honesty, or who have the least Regard for their Queen and Country; being a faithful Subject, a true Friend, a kind Master, and a loving Husband; And as a just Reward for his Services and Sufferings, was preferr'd to the greatest Honours and Employments of the Crown. His Grace is succeeded in Honour and Estate by his eldest Son, who is about 12 Years of Age. It is to be remembred, that the Lord Mohun was the Person who gave the Affront, which the Duke, observing him to be in Drink, disdain'd to regard. But the Faction, weary of him, resolv'd to employ him in some real Service to their Cause, and valu'd not what became of him, provided he did their Drudgery. For

3 *Duel . . . Duke of Hamilton*: see the Introduction (pp. 26–7) for the circumstances of this duel and Swift's anger at General Maccartney, the one he thought responsible for Hamilton's death.

the Dispute at Law between the Duke and his Lordship had continu'd many Years, without any personal Quarrel of Consequence. But this is the new Expedient of the Faction, Band-boxes and B——llies. Mackartney is absconded, but 'tis hoped a Proclamation will soon be issu'd out for apprehending him, in order to bring him to Justice.

N. B. This is the 4th Person that my Lord Mohun had the Misfortune to kill. His Lordship's Title is extinct.

Post Boy 27–29 November 1713

London, Jan. 29. A Report having been industriously spread, That Mr. Skelton,[4] a Gentleman lately come from France, by Licence from Her Majesty, under Her Privy-Seal, intending a Visit to Mr. Lewis, the Earl of Dartmouth's Secretary, to thank him for the Dispatch of the said Licence, went by mistake to one Mr. Henry Lewis in Marlborough-street, and told him he had Services to him from the Lords Perth and Melfort. These are to satisfy the Publick, That the said Mr. Henry Lewis declar'd yesterday before the Lords of the Cabinet Council, as he had likewise done before in Presence of the Earl of Peterborow, and several Gentlemen, That the said Report was utterly False.

4 *Skelton*: see the Introduction (pp. 27–8), and the *Defence of Erasmus Lewis*, above.

TEXTUAL INTRODUCTION
AND ACCOUNTS OF
INDIVIDUAL WORKS

TEXTUAL INTRODUCTION

In what remains the only article specifically focused on Swift's relationship with the London book trade during the reign of Anne, Michael Treadwell wryly noted that '[p]ast Swift scholars and editors . . . far from indulging in the excesses of compositor analysis . . . can hardly be accused of narrow bibliographical principles, or indeed, of many bibliographical principles at all' ('Swift's Relations', pp. 2–3). Treadwell was writing in 1983 and while, two decades later, there has been further bibliographical investigation of Swift's more well-known works, most notably *Gulliver's Travels*, the attention paid to Swift and the London book trade of the early eighteenth century has remained, with a few honourable exceptions, rather cursory. This, though, is not surprising. While *The Conduct of the Allies* probably ranks as Swift's most immediately influential and popular work, with 11,000 copies sold within two months, its bibliographical complexities – although much more tangled than previous scholars have acknowledged – are eclipsed by those presented by *A Tale of a Tub* and *Gulliver's Travels*. Similarly, given the account presented by Herbert Davis in his introductions to volumes six and eight of Swift's prose works (mentioning Barber by name only in the latter), it may seem that, apart from the success of *Conduct* and the inconclusive prosecutions following the publication of *The Publick Spirit of the Whigs*, the bibliographical story of Swift's output during those years is both straightforward and uninteresting. It is the aim of this introduction and the textual accounts provided for each work later in this volume to prove the case otherwise.

Swift, Barber and Morphew

As Treadwell observes, although Defoe and Pope both 'knew the trade far better than did Swift', Swift's relations with the London book trade were 'many and various' ('Swift's Relations', pp. 2, 1).[1] Between 1701–9, Swift's

---

1 Except where noted, the account of Barber presented here is derived from Michael Treadwell's article.

London publisher of choice was Benjamin Tooke, junior, but with the political ascendance of the Tories in late 1710 Swift's writings changed – and so did his printer and publisher. Of the eleven works included in this volume that were published between 1711 and 1714 (excluding the *Vote of Thanks, The Humble Address of the . . . Lords* (11 April 1713) and the contributions to periodicals), seven were definitely printed and published by John Barber. Born in 1675, Barber had established himself as a master printer in London in 1701, and by 1710 was one of the leading printers for the Tory party. He was one of perhaps seventy to eighty printers active in London between 1711 and 1714 but was clearly on the rise.[2] In 1709 he became printer to the City, in 1710 he became printer of *The Examiner*, in 1711 printer of *The Gazette*, and in 1713 he (and Tooke) gained the highly lucrative reversion for the patent for the Queen's Printer – the latter two achievements owed much to the intercession of Swift. While the death of Anne threw Barber into 'the political wilderness' (to use Nicholas Rogers's words), he combined his experience as a city politician (he had served as a common councilman since 1711) with some astute financial dealings in 1720 to become a city alderman in 1722, sheriff for 1729–30 and finally Lord Mayor for 1732–3 (*ODNB*).[3]

Swift may have met Barber before taking over the editorship of *The Examiner* in the autumn of 1710 but the first mention of Barber in Swift's letters to Stella comes on Boxing Day of that year. 'There is an intimacy between us,' Swift confided, 'built upon reasons that you shall know when I see you', suggesting that the two men shared more than mere political allegiance (Williams, *JSt*, pp. 140–1). Swift was a frequent visitor to Barber's printing house in Lambeth Hill over the next three and a half years, and not just when a work of his was in press.[4] Nonetheless, many of these meetings and dinners focused on Swift's own writings and, while the

---

2 Michael Treadwell, 'London Printers and Printing Houses in 1705', *Publishing History* 7 (1980), 5–44, and 'Lists of Master Printers: The Size of the London Printing Trade, 1637–1723', in Robin Myers and Michael Harris (eds.), *Aspects of Printing from 1600* (Oxford: Oxford Polytechnic Press, 1987), pp. 152–5, 163–6.

3 See also Rivington, which remains the fullest account of Barber's career.

4 Williams's index to *JSt* significantly under-represents the number of times Swift alludes to Barber, often misidentifying references to his 'printer' as John Morphew. Swift never seems to have mentioned Barber by name to Stella; as Paul V. Thompson and Dorothy Jay Thompson note, Swift wrote of meeting 'my printer' or 'a friend', or even 'I dined in the City' (*Account Books*, p. 1). Swift's account books also reveal many visits that went unrecorded in *JSt*. See also Treadwell, 'Swift's Relations', pp. 24–5.

publication of *Conduct* was exceptional, it showed exactly how closely the two men worked together on occasion: Swift visited Barber several times prior to publication, spent all afternoon on 30 November 1711 with him making changes, and remained in near-constant touch over the next week. Printing *Some Remarks on the Barrier Treaty* also involved several visits, including one explicitly to correct proof-sheets.[5] Such evidence reminds us that Swift took pains over the accuracy of his printed texts although, as both these works reveal, the exigencies of publication meant that they did not necessarily reach the public as free of mistakes as Swift's issues of the *Examiner* (Treadwell, 'Swift's Relations', p. 24, citing Ehrenpreis).[6] At times, though, Swift resorted to keeping his printer in the dark in order to prevent his identity as author being revealed – with mixed results. He was delighted in early 1712 when Barber asked for his comments about *Some Advice Humbly Offer'd to the Members of the October Club* 'which he said was sent him by an unknown hand . . . he never suspected me' (Williams, *JSt*, p. 468) but his publication plans were ultimately frustrated when he employed a similar tactic with *Some Free Thoughts upon the Present State of Affairs* in the weeks leading up to Anne's death.

Barber acted as Swift's printer and publisher; these works were printed in his printing house and he financed their publication. Several of the works were entered to him in the Stationers' Register, a sign that he was assuming financial responsibility for publication. He also arranged for wholesale distribution: the Earl of Oxford purchased from Barber 200 copies of *Conduct* and 100 of *Some Remarks* in December 1711 and February 1712 respectively.[7] However, Barber's name never appeared on any of these imprints, which means that, for those works where there is no evidence in the *Journal to Stella* or the Stationers' Register to link Barber with their production, it is not clear exactly who printed or published them. With *Some Reasons to Prove . . . In a Letter to a Whig-Lord,*

5 See the textual accounts given for each work in this volume.
6 Treadwell also quotes (p. 4) Swift's comment in 1693 – 'my Bookseller may be careless in the choice of the Copyes in which there is difference enough' – as evidence that Swift was well aware of the potential textual differences between copies of a single edition.
7 J. A. Downie, 'Swift and the Oxford Ministry: New Evidence', *SStud*, 1 (1986), 4–5. Oxford, who received Barber's bill while facing impeachment following Anne's death, was quoted trade prices; the bill was eventually settled in February 1716. Downie points out that, while Oxford purchased *Some Remarks* on publication day, the copies of *Conduct* were not bought until the fifth edition was published even though, as the price indicates, Oxford evidently purchased one of the first four one-shilling editions.

the likelihood is that Barber printed and published this as the name of John Morphew in the imprint indicates (for reasons that will be explained below); in addition, the type and format used are unremarkable but at least conform to the usual printing conventions of those pamphlets previously printed by Barber (octavo using english type). However, four of Swift's '7 penny Papers' (Williams, *JSt*, p. 553) of June and July 1712 are more difficult to assign with any confidence as their imprints name only London and the year of publication (and *A Letter from the Pretender, to a Whig-Lord* does not even have that). Three of them (*A Dialogue upon Dunkirk, between a Whig and a Tory; It's Out at Last;* and *A Hue and Cry after Dismal*) were advertised by Morphew which, perhaps, is an indication that Barber printed them; if nothing else, it would seem uncharacteristic for Swift to have gone elsewhere to print his political works, even if Barber was unaware of their authorship. The one exception to this is *Letter*, which is atrociously printed and was not advertised by Morphew; indeed, were the evidence for attribution to Swift less robust, it might be considered suspicious for bibliographical reasons alone.

Barber preferred octavo formats for Swift's works (*Publick Spirit* being the sole exception), and, aside from *Some Advice* (pica) and the later editions of *Conduct* (small pica), english type was used throughout. The single-sheet 'penny Papers' were set in pica, apart from *Letter* set in great primer. There was occasional use, principally on title pages, of black-letter. As one might expect from a leading London printer, printing is generally accurate and crisp. When Barber's workforce was called in for interrogation by the House of Lords in March 1714, it amounted to five journeymen, two apprentices and at least one 'smooter' or casual workman; exactly how many presses these men operated is not clear but, given the volume of periodicals and official city material that Barber printed, the printing house was unlikely to be small. This, along with the specialized nature of periodical printing, seems to account for Barber's striking use of standing type for reprinting subsequent editions of *Conduct* (even re-imposing when necessary) and may also explain the printing history of *Some Advice*. Three further works – *Some Remarks, The New Way of Selling Places at Court,* and *Publick Spirit* – were also re-issued as 'new' editions; it is possible, perhaps, that he kept standing type for these works as well.

John Morphew was publicly associated with nearly all of the works contained in this volume, either through imprints (invariably 'Printed for John

Morphew, near Stationers Hall'), advertisements, or both, but remains an under-researched and much misunderstood figure.[8] On at least two occasions, he was formally questioned by the authorities over the publication of these works and the identity of their anonymous author. He clearly knew Barber well, making entries in the Stationers' Register on the printer's behalf. Yet, as far as we can tell, Morphew was never involved in the printing or financing of Swift's works; indeed, aside from one specific reference to 'Morphew, the publisher' being called in for questioning following the publication of *Conduct*, Swift himself does not appear to mention him at all in his letters to Stella and it is possible that the two men never met (Williams, *JSt*, p. 437).[9]

Morphew was one of eighteenth-century London's 'trade publishers'. Between 1706 when he established himself at his premises near Stationers' Hall and his death in 1720, his name, according to Treadwell, 'must have appeared on well over a thousand works, excluding periodicals' ('Trade Publishers', 116–17). Trade publishers 'published' on behalf of others; in other words, they took on the burden of distribution without any of the other financial and legal obligations that publishing involved. Their names nearly always appeared on small topical works whose success depended upon a well-established, speedy and effective distribution network: the trade publishers 'supplied the mercuries, the mercuries supplied the hawkers, and the hawkers supplied the public' (123). Treadwell identifies three groups who had use for such individuals: self-publishing authors, printers who were otherwise financing publication, and 'proper' publishers who, for 'concealment [or] convenience', wished to use a trade publisher's distribution network (119–22). Barber's use of Morphew fell into the second category but the politically sensitive nature of the works meant that Morphew's name served two further purposes. On the one hand, it flagged the work as Tory (Morphew was the trade publisher of choice for Tory pamphleteers in this period) but it also acted as a means of frustrating unwelcome investigations. The trade publisher's 'plea of ignorance' might

8 No adequate biography is available; he has yet to be included in the *ODNB* and is curiously omitted from Michael Treadwell's otherwise copious and thorough unpublished notes (private communication with Michael Turner).
9 Williams erroneously believed Morphew to be Swift's printer; all the other references that Williams indexes as Morphew actually refer to Barber. The *Account Books*, which otherwise record Swift's visits to both Barber and Tooke, make no mention of Morphew.

seem ludicrous – Treadwell is sceptical of Morphew's 1714 claim that 'it is a very usual thing for persons to leave books & papers at his house . . . and a long time after to call for the value thereof, without making themselves known to the said publishers' – but it was surprisingly effective:

> It was simply one of the trade publisher's functions (and not the least important) to stand mute between the real proprietors and the authorities in time of any slight unpleasantness. . . . The rules of the game meant that the trade publisher was always the first to be pursued, but his known insignificance meant that he was rarely pursued for long.   (125)

Morphew was so pursued in connection with two of the works included here: *Conduct*, where he was called before the Lord Chief Justice, and *Publick Spirit* where both he and Barber were questioned by the House of Lords. In the former, nothing further seems to have happened; with the latter, he appears to have betrayed Barber's identity although, given that the Earl of Mar had already acted against Barber without even bothering with Morphew (a sign that Mar knew exactly who was responsible for publication), it would have been difficult for Morphew to have denied all knowledge.[10] For all intents and purposes, Morphew appeared to be the 'publisher' of Swift's works, something which not only misled the authorities in early eighteenth-century London but also generations of Swift's scholars. However, rather than use some tedious circumlocution to explain Morphew's role in relation to every work, I ask readers to understand that 'published by Morphew' in the individual textual accounts in this volume means what the eighteenth-century book trade meant by it: that Morphew received the work from Barber and began distribution to the public.[11]

One further name appears in the imprints of Swift's London editions and it is almost certainly false. Among the multiplicity of editions of *Publick Spirit* is one carrying the unexpurgated text ('According to the First Original Copy') and bearing the apparently innocuous imprint: 'Printed for *T. Cole*'. No address is given. No such individual is recorded in either of the Plomer dictionaries for this period; nor is any listed as an apprentice or master in the

---

10 See the textual accounts for these works for more detail about these prosecutions.
11 Swift's terminology, while confusing to modern eyes, is consistent: Barber was 'my printer', Tooke was 'my bookseller' and Morphew was 'the publisher'. See Treadwell, 'Trade Publishers', 99–101.

Stationers' Company apprentice registers.[12] The banality of the name does not militate against its probable falsity: Treadwell notes that 'commonplace names [account] for the largest number of [false] imprints'.[13] The purpose of 'T. Cole', here, was presumably to protect the piracy of a work that was, or had recently been, under investigation.

Dublin and Edinburgh reprints

Whether or not they or their readers knew the identity of the author, Dublin printers reprinted six of Swift's political works during this period. John Hyde and Edward Waters published editions of *Conduct* and *Barrier*, Cornelius Carter produced editions of *Some Advice*, *New Way* and *Some Reasons*, while editions of *Publick Spirit* appeared with John Henly's name in the imprint as well as anonymously.[14] In all cases, such reprinted editions appeared bearing the same or, in the case of *Conduct* which was printed late in the year, the following year in their imprints, indicating that their printers were seeking to capitalize on the topicality of the pamphlets. It is important to bear in mind that, in many cases, the London editions would have been available for sale in Dublin but cost and demand – as the multiple Dublin editions of *Conduct* and *Some Remarks* indicate – meant that reprinting often made commercial sense.[15] As Máire Kennedy observes: 'Books cost less in Dublin than in London. Dublin printers were

12 H. R. Plomer *et al. A Dictionary of the Printers and Booksellers who were at work in England, Scotland and Ireland from 1668 to 1725* (Oxford. Bibliographical Society, 1922); H. R. Plomer, G. H. Bushnell and E. R.McC. Dix, *A Dictionary of the Printers and Booksellers who were at work in England, Scotland and Ireland from 1725 to 1775* (Oxford: Bibliographical Society, 1932); McKenzie, *1641–1700* and *1701–1800*. A Timothy Cole and a Thomas Colls were freed Stationers in 1668 and 1678 respectively, but both would have required impressively long careers to have been still active in 1714.

13 Michael Treadwell, 'On False and Misleading Imprints in the London Book Trade, 1660–1750', in Robin Myers and Michael Harris (eds.), *Fakes and Frauds: Varieties of Deception in Print and Manuscript* (Winchester: St Paul's Bibliographies, 1989), p. 37. Cole, alas, is not among those that he lists.

14 For biographies of these men, see Pollard, pp. 92–3 (Carter, a Tory and Jacobite who was 'in continual trouble'), 283–4 (Henly), 304–6 (Hyde, who later published *Gulliver's Travels* and was described as Dublin's 'most Eminent and noted Bookseller' at his death in 1728), 589–91 (Waters).

15 Pollard notes that exports of books to Dublin remained high throughout the eighteenth century and that 'although the London trade occasionally complained volubly of their Irish neighbours, neither city could do without the other' – *Dublin's Trade in Books, 1550–1800* (Oxford: Clarendon Press, 1989), p. 90.

able to undercut their London rivals by reprinting in smaller formats, using cheaper paper, and not needing to purchase copyright.'[16] Poor quality paper, limited type-stock, missettings and untidy printing were characteristic of Waters and particularly Carter (whose standard of printing was described as 'deplorable' by Pollard), but Hyde's and Henly's editions took evident care over the quality and accuracy of their editions (Pollard, p. 93). In contrast to the situation in Dublin, only two of Swift's works were reprinted in Edinburgh, both by Robert Freebairn, the son of the Bishop of Edinburgh and Queen's Printer in Scotland: two editions of *Conduct* and one edition of *Some Remarks*.[17]

Faulkner to Davis

Given the editorial principles governing this volume of the Cambridge edition (see below), this volume is interested in the works at the time of their most relevance and influence rather than as revised over two decades later for inclusion in George Faulkner's collected editions. Consequently, while Faulkner's variant readings are of sufficient significance for them to be considered in the textual account of each work and to be included in the collation tables, the story of Faulkner's role in publishing these works is of much less relevance than for Swift's other works. Consequently, I do not intend here to dwell on Faulkner himself or his 'admirably conscientious' editions beyond noting that Swift's involvement in his edition is unquestioned ('Faulkner himself states that Swift had the proofs of both Vols. V and VI [of the 1738 edition] read to him, and himself made corrections' (Davis, vol. VI, p. 207)), that all of Swift's elisions were expanded, and that Swift's phraseology was 'improved' throughout: *though* became *although*, *'tis* became *it is* and so forth.[18] The interested reader is instead directed to the relevant textual accounts.

With the exception of *A Discourse concerning the Fears from the Pretender* which was first published in 1935, the *Vote of Thanks*, the contributions to

---

16 Máire Kennedy, 'Reading Print, 1700–1800', in Raymond Gillespie and Andrew Hadfield (eds.), *The Oxford History of the Irish Book: Volume III, The Irish Book in English 1550–1800* (Oxford: Oxford University Press, 2006), p. 151.

17 Plomer, *Dictionary . . . 1668 to 1725*, pp. 121–2.

18 Philip Gaskell, *From Writer to Reader: Studies in Editorial Method* (Winchester: St Paul's Bibliographies, 1978), p. 82. On Faulkner, see James E. Tierney, 'George Faulkner', *ODNB* and M. Pollard, 'George Faulkner', *SStud*, 7 (1992), 79–96.

the periodicals, and *It's Out at Last, Dialogue* and *Hue and Cry* (copies of which were only discovered in the twentieth century), all the works included in this volume were reprinted in eighteenth-century collected editions of Swift. Some (*Conduct, Some Remarks, Some Advice* and *Publick Spirit*) were available from 1738 (TS, nos. 25(7), 42 and 50); *Some Free Thoughts* first appeared in the 1742 *Miscellanies* (TS, no. 31(3)); *Some Reasons* in the 1752 *Supplement* (TS, no. 83); *Humble Address* and *Some Considerations* from 1765 (TS, nos. 47, 52, 53, 87, 90, 92); and *Importance, New Way, Letter,* and the account of Erasmus Lewis's misidentification in *The Examiner* (titled in this volume as *A Defence of Erasmus Lewis*) were all republished for the first time in John Nichols's 1776 *Supplement* (TS, no. 88). All twelve were included in Swift editions throughout the nineteenth and twentieth centuries but, although Nichols and Temple Scott in particular paid attention to the textual history of some of the works, it was not until Davis that these works were subject to detailed textual scrutiny.[19] Davis, with the exception of *Publick Spirit*, used first editions wherever possible; his transcriptions were highly accurate, with careful retention of capitalization, italics and punctuation, but were marred by reproducing Faulkner's habit of beginning paragraphs in small capitals and, less forgiveably, silently expanding all elisions (or 'emvowellings' to use Fielding's phrase). Philip Gaskell described Davis's edition as 'not entirely satisfactory': '[h]is textual notes, though comprehensive, are not easy to follow'.[20] Davis's appended textual apparatus provided relatively brief accounts of the textual history for each work and collation tables, although, particularly for longer works, these were not always comprehensive and, inexplicably, occasionally included selected accidental variants. While he acknowledged the existence of Scottish and Irish reprints, only once – with Hyde's edition of *Conduct* – were their variants included in the collations.

Attribution

None of the works included in this volume that were printed between 1711 and 1714 bore Swift's name on their title page; nonetheless, the attribution

---

19 C. B. Wheeler's 1916 edition of *Conduct* is an honourable exception although Davis seems to have not consulted this edition. On Nichols's editing of Swift, see Maner.
20 Gaskell, *From Writer to Reader*, pp. 95, 98n.

of most of them has long been unquestioned. As the very useful summary table given in David Woolley's article on Swift's pamphlets between 1710 and 1714 highlights, the *Journal to Stella* provides evidence in nearly all cases ('Canon', endpaper). In a few, however, attribution is more contentious and this edition has consequently had to consider the available evidence carefully, relying for the most part, but not uncritically, on Woolley's attributions. Thus, this edition includes *New Way*, *Dialogue*, *It's Out at Last*, *Hue and Cry*, *Letter*, *Importance* (the last three attributed primarily on the basis of Charles Ford's letter to Swift in November 1733 cataloguing Swift's political writings (Woolley, *Corr.*, vol. III, p. 699)),[21] *Defence* and the various contributions to The *Post Boy* and The *Evening Post* (all based on the evidence in the *Journal to Stella*), and the *Vote of Thanks* and *Humble Address*. Detailed explanations about the case for attributing each is given in the individual textual accounts.

We have also rejected two works previously attributed to Swift. While Swift notes on 15 January 1713 that he 'gave the Examiner a hint about this Prorogation, & to praise the Qu— for her tenderness to the Dutch in giving them still more time to submitt' (Williams, *JSt*, p. 603), Woolley dismisses the work in question, the 16 January 1713 issue of *The Examiner* (often described as an 'Appendix' to *Some Remarks*), out of hand: it is 'poor stuff, unworthy of a great author' ('Canon', 110). We have similar reasons for rejecting the Queen's speech to Parliament of April 1713; while Swift's hand in the *Vote of Thanks* and *Humble Address* is sufficient to warrant their inclusion here, his involvement in drafting the Queen's speech was confined only to correcting 'in sevrall Places' a version presented to him by Robert Harley at dinner, a full month before Parliament opened (Williams, *JSt*, p. 635).

Editorial principles

In drawing up editorial guidelines for the Cambridge edition of Swift's collected works, the general editors made an important exception to their stated policy of adopting 'the author's final intended version of a work': 'in the case of Swift's polemical tracts, the copy text will generally be the first

---

21 Swift did confess in his reply (vol. III, pp. 707–9) that he did not remember writing some of those Ford listed.

published text, because this is the text which is most closely addressed to the immediate circumstances, and which will have been read and responded to in the specific context of debate.'[22] In other words, the copy texts chosen for this volume represent Swift's intention at the moment of its most topicality and relevance. With the majority of these works, this presents little problem: the first or, in many cases, only contemporary London edition has been selected. In the case of *Conduct*, I have selected the fourth rather than first edition partly because the first four editions appeared in such rapid succession but mainly because Swift was closely involved in revising his text up to and including that fourth edition; however, with *Publick Spirit*, subject to hasty rewriting days after publication due to the unexpected attention of the authorities, the first unexpurgated edition has been used. Moreover, with the exception of these two works, Swift does not seem to have considered revising his political writings once they had been printed. *Dunkirk to be Let* – a different and probably later version of *Hue and Cry* – may seem to be an exception to this but, for reasons explained elsewhere in this volume, I do not believe this edition to have been revised by Swift.

In two cases, however, this policy has led to difficult editorial choices. The first concerns the *Vote of Thanks* and *Humble Address*, where I have chosen those texts with most immediate public currency (and hence not the initial drafts that survive in Swift's hand): this means that the text of the *Vote of Thanks* comes from the House of Lords' own journals and the *Humble Address* is based on the version that was printed by the Queen's Printer. The other involves *Some Free Thoughts* for which the surviving witnesses are a 1737 corrected manuscript copy and the text printed by Faulkner in 1741: here the *uncorrected* version of the 1737 manuscript has been chosen as more closely representing Swift's intentions in 1714.[23]

The texts

In reprinting Swift's works, ligatures, uses of the long-s, drop capitals, capitalization of opening words, and lineation have not been preserved. Otherwise, this edition presents the copy text's capitalization, punctuation,

---

22 *Cambridge Edition of the Works of Jonathan Swift: Editorial Guidelines*, privately circulated, July 2003.
23 In both cases, the reader is directed to the relevant textual accounts.

italicization, spelling, em-dashes, multiple hyphens and elisions. Spacing between sections has been retained, except for *New Way*, where it is used between every paragraph. Black letter (sometimes called Gothic or English) has been reproduced in headings and texts. Works printed from manuscript have been treated slightly differently, as, rather than presenting a full inclusive text (complete with alterations), we provide a clean-text critical edition – drawing on the system of transcription outlined by David L. Vander Meulen and G. Thomas Tanselle[24] – of what we believe to be the most authoritative version, with all manuscript alterations listed in appended notes. Spelling, punctuation, elisions and capitalization, however, have all been retained.

Each work is given its own separate textual account, detailing composition and, where appropriate, printing and publication, the textual relationship between editions, and the subsequent treatment of that text by later editors. (The only exception here are Swift's contributions to periodicals, which have been grouped together in a single textual account.) The copy text for each work is identified and all surviving contemporary editions (including Scottish and Irish reprints) have been examined, described and collated; wherever possible, multiple copies of the London editions have been examined and collated. In compiling the descriptions and collations, much more detail (e.g. the measurement of drop-capitals and the presence of watermarks) and many more variants were recorded than actually have been reproduced here; my textual accounts, however, have been informed, where relevant, by the fuller descriptions and collations. All measurements are in millimetres. For each edition, I have listed all the individual copies that I have consulted; these are keyed as follows: an asterisk indicates that the copy has been physically examined, ¶ indicates that the copy has been checked against the list of variants, † indicates that the copy has been manually collated, and § indicates that the copy has been collated using an optical collator. Tables of emendations (allowing readers to reconstruct the original copy-text readings), of historical collations of substantive variant readings (including all contemporary editions and at least the first republication of the work later in the eighteenth century) and of word divisions for compound words have been compiled.

---

24 David L. Vander Meulen and G. Thomas Tanselle, 'A System of Manuscript Transcription', *SB* 52 (1999), 201–12; for discussion of clean-text transcription, see 203–4.

Collation and error

The bibliographical investigation of works existing in multiple editions, most notably *Conduct* and *Publick Spirit*, has been much enhanced by the use of the McLeod portable collators at the Bodleian Library, Oxford, and the University Library, Cambridge. Thanks to Professor McLeod's copious instructions and patient encouragement by e-mail, optical collation has enabled me to identify not only variant readings but also, I believe, re-imposed and re-set pages where lineation has otherwise been preserved. This, coupled with the availability of texts on *ECCO*, has enabled me to collate many more copies than I would have otherwise been able to do within the project's timescale. However, towards the latter stages of the project, I encountered Joseph Dane's bracing critique of optical collation in which he questions both the accuracy and authority of optical collation, in particular its practice (shared with conventional collation) of collating against a single selected 'master'.[25] Not only does this prevent the possibility of identifying the relationship between variants, but Dane argues that it can never hope to identify all variants or indeed define exactly what constitutes a variant. This forms part of his wider criticism of how the very methodology of bibliographical and editorial practice seeks to efface textual singularity and to impose rigid orders and taxonomies upon the highly contingent and individual printed object.

I have much sympathy with Dane's argument: editorial principles which seem so neat and logical in theory can appear remarkably unsteady in the face of the evidence of actual printed books. Even simple tasks – such as establishing the precise size of type used – can be undermined by the material realities present in multiple copies of the same edition. Indeed, such is the nature of these works – anonymous, often printed in editions that were in fact re-issues, and 'published' by an individual who was not a publisher in the modern sense – that, like Celia's dressing-room, almost nothing is quite what it seems. I can, though, claim more success with optical collation than Dane but that is probably down to my tutor and to the fact that I was collating small well-printed books with relatively large type. My only defence to what seem to be Dane's counsels of editorial despair is, to pursue the optical metaphor, transparency. My textual accounts are as

25 Joseph A. Dane, *The Myth of Print Culture: Essays on Evidence, Textuality and Bibliographical Method* (Toronto: University of Toronto Press, 2003), pp. 88–97.

full and detailed as I hope readers can bear and I have attempted at all times to outline clearly my claims and the evidence for each, allowing readers to judge my interpretations without necessarily having to resort to the nearest rare books library. In collating the contemporary London editions, whether optically or manually, I have collated against the chosen copy text or, where this has not been possible, against another copy of the same edition that has already been collated against the copy text. Nonetheless, the opportunities for mistakes and misinterpretations here are legion. I have already been saved from many by previous editors, my co-editor and the edition's textual adviser but others will doubtless persist, awaiting the investigations of future scholars and editors. Towards the end of *Some Remarks*, Swift wrote: 'And I solemnly declare, that I have not wilfully committed the least Mistake.' It was, in fact, a disingenuous statement but, provided that considerable stress is placed upon the ninth word, I believe that I can claim this with much better faith than Swift.

THE CONDUCT OF THE ALLIES: TEXTUAL ACCOUNT

Swift probably began working on *Conduct of the Allies* in either August or September 1711. Allusions to 'some business' in his letters to Stella appear as early as 6 August; on 25 August, Swift wrote that '[t]here is now but one business the ministry wants me for' (Williams, *JSt*, pp. 327, 343; Ehrenpreis, vol. II, p. 483). There are similar cryptic references during September: 'something I am doing' (9 September), 'a plaguy deal of business' (21 September), 'something of weight I have upon my hands, and which must soon be done' (29 September) (Williams, *JSt*, pp. 356, 365, 373). By 13 October, Swift hoped that his busyness 'will be over' within a fortnight (p. 383). Five days later, Swift visited 'a printer' (presumably John Barber rather than, as Williams surmises, John Morphew) to settle 'some things'; on 30 October, he again visited 'a printer' and was to meet with Henry St John the following day 'about the same [matter]' (pp. 386, 397). By 10 November, this work – still unnamed and undescribed – was nearing publication:

> something is to be published of great moment, and three or four great people are to see there are no mistakes in point of fact: and 'tis so troublesome to send it among them, and get their corrections, that I am weary as a dog. I dined to-day with the printer, and was there all the afternoon; and it plagues me, and there's an end, and what would you have?
> (Williams, *JSt*, p. 408)

One of those 'great people' was St John, who on 17 November returned a sheet, 'which is I think very correct', to Swift; St John had initially written on 16 November but enclosed the wrong papers (Woolley, *Corr.*, vol. I, pp. 396–7). This was, as Woolley suggests, probably the corrected 'fifth sheet' – sheet E – that Swift gave to Barber on 21 November (Williams, *JSt*, p. 417). On 24 November, Swift finished 'my pamphlet' (the first time it was so styled), 'which has cost me so much time and trouble; it will be published in three or four days, when the parliament begins sitting' (p. 420).

The 'large' pamphlet, priced at a shilling, was published by Barber with Morphew's name in the imprint on 27 November, although copies had been sent to 'great men' the night before, including presumably Harley, whose copy was 'by him on the table' when Swift called upon him on the evening of publication day; the two men discussed the mottos on the title page, one of which Harley had supplied (pp. 421–2). Barber entered the work in SR on the same day.

The Conduct proved an immediate success. By 29 November, 1,000 copies – presumably all or nearly all of the first edition's run – had been sold; Barber visited Swift in the morning 'to tell me he must immediately print a second edition, and [that the] lord treasurer made one or two small additions: they must work day and night to have it out on Saturday [1 December]' (p. 423). This was the start of a frantic pattern of new editions and further corrections for the next week. Swift spent all afternoon on 30 November with the printer, presumably in the printing shop itself, 'adding something to the second edition' (p. 424). The most significant changes consisted of an expanded account of the number of troops that Britain was maintaining in Flanders, the addition of a footnote clarifying a point about the Spanish succession and a loaded comment about how 'an absolute Government may endure a long War, but it hath generally been ruinous to Free Countries'. Swift was also sufficiently bold to transform a reference to 'a certain *Great Man*' to 'my Lord G———n'.

On Saturday, Swift interpreted the fact that Barber had not sent him a copy of the second edition as a sign that the market was perhaps already 'glutted'; that same morning, two further 'small alterations' were received from Harley: 'I am going to be busy, &c' (p. 427). Early the following morning, however, Barber called on Swift to report that far from being saturated, the market was proving insatiable: the second edition had been sold out within five hours, 'they might have sold half another [edition]', and that ('though it be Sunday') his workers were already working on producing a third edition for the next day (pp. 427–8). The third edition consolidated the initial boldness of the second by changing references to 'a certain *Great Person*' and 'at the Head of the Treasury' to 'the Earl of G———n' and 'Lord High Treasurer' respectively. Swift also corrected his faulty recollection of the passage from Proverbs and appended a single erratum note.

By the evening of 3 December, half of the third edition had been sold; the further alterations proposed by Harley would now have to wait for the fourth edition 'which I believe will be soon' (p. 429). The following day, with 'above half' of the third edition now sold, Swift was evidently wearying: 'I have made some alterations in every edition, and it has cost me more trouble, for the time, since the printing than before' (pp. 429–30). On 5 December, eight days since publication of the first edition, a fourth edition was in press, 'which is reckoned very extraordinary, considering 'tis a dear twelve-penny book, and not bought up in numbers by the party to give away, as the Whigs do, but purely upon it's own strength', and the following day, Swift reports that Barber was to produce a 'small' fifth edition 'to be taken off by friends and sent into the country' (pp. 430–1).

Swift had heard on 3 December that the Whigs were seeking the condemnation of the work, and in particular its passing reference to the British Succession, in the House of Lords but Swift believed that Barber 'will stand to it, and not own the author; he must say, he had it from the penny-post' (p. 429). It seems that Barber's resolve was not tested on this occasion, but the unwelcome attention evidently prompted Swift to alter the offending passage in the fourth edition; a lofty postscript was also added, explaining that the rewording was intended 'to take off, if possible, all manner of Cavil'. The postscript also included an ultimately unfulfilled promise to answer other objections to *Conduct* in an extra prefatory paragraph in a future edition. On 12 December Morphew (on the strength of his name on the imprint) was called before Lord Chief Justice Parker and, having been pressed unsuccessfully for the identity of the pamphlet's author, was bound over to appear at the next legal term (pp. 437–8). Nothing further seems to have happened to Morphew; on 11 January 1712 Swift reassured Stella, who had expressed evident concern for Morphew's situation: 'all's safe there' (p. 462).

The 'small' fifth edition – it used smaller type, enabling Barber to use half the number of sheets per copy – was evidently on sale, for sixpence, by 18 December; the edition ran to 4,000 copies, 'as many as three editions, because they are to be sent in numbers into the country by great men, &c. who subscribe for hundreds' (pp. 459, 441). By 28 January 1712, a sixth edition, again using the smaller type, of 3,000 copies had been sold out, with a seventh mooted by the printer. Swift noted, with considerable pride, that 11,000 copies in total had been sold: 'a most prodigious run' (p. 474). Presuming Swift's figures to be accurate, we can surmise that the first four editions (rather than the 'three' that Swift claims) totalled 4,000 copies. At some point during 1712, a seventh edition did appear, and it was followed in 1713 by an eighth.

London editions, 1711–15

The first edition of *Conduct* bears a date of 1712, suggesting that Barber assumed the edition would suffice until the new year (in order to make the discussion and collation tables easier to follow, I have designated this edition as 1711a). Determining its format presents difficulties. It is similar in size to all the other editions printed by Barber but, in contrast to them, in all the copies I have examined, the chainlines are horizontal rather than vertical, as would be expected of an octavo. Moreover, the watermarks, where visible, come at the outer upper edges of the fifth, sixth, seventh and eighth leaves of the gathering, ruling out the possibility of a quarto. The duodecimo by cutting – where a third of the sheet is cut off, the remaining two-thirds folded as an octavo, and the cut-off portion folded and inserted within the rest of the gathering – could produce this pattern of chainlines and watermark position but in order to maintain the eight leaves per gathering found in 1711a, the 'third-of-a-sheet' would need to have formed part of separate gatherings (e.g., the cut-off parts of sheets A and B would form, together, sheet C). More likely is that Barber used sheets from large moulds that produced either twice-as-large sheets that could then be cut in half or two sheets side-by-side; both types of sheet (each bearing this particular combination of chainlines and watermarks) were in use in the eighteenth-century (Allen T. Hazen, 'Eighteenth-century Quartos with Vertical Chain-lines', *The Library*, 4th ser., 16 (1935), 337–42; G. Thomas Tanselle, 'The Concept of Format', *SB* 53 (2000), 82–91). The only way of distinguishing these sheets is through the identification of deckle edges on untrimmed copies but, as Tanselle argues, there is perhaps little to be gained from determining format based only on this. Thus, rather than claim that 1711a is effect a sextodecimo in half-sheets (as Williams wrote in the front of his copy), I have followed Tanselle's definition of format as 'a designation of the number of page-units . . . that the producers of a printed or manuscript item decided upon to fill each side of a sheet of paper or vellum of the selected size(s)' (112–13) in identifying this edition as an octavo.

Optical collation of the second, third and fourth editions (respectively 1711b, 1711c and 1711d), all of which are standard octavos, reveals that in order to meet the immense demand for copies, Barber seems to have kept much of the edition in standing type throughout the ten days or so that separated the first from the fourth editions. Individual corrections were made, lines were occasionally re-set and, in the case of the fourth edition, the type was re-imposed – but not significantly re-set – for about twenty pages in order to incorporate extra material; however, at least two formes-worth of type that had been set by 26 November were still being printed from on 5 December, while a further six formes-worth of type that had been set for the second edition were still being used to print the fourth edition. There are also several clear errors of setting made by the compositors who re-set from the first edition, reflecting the haste of production.

Table: Standing and reset type, 1711b–1711d

	1711b (2nd edition)	1711c (3rd edition)	1711d (4th edition)
A(o)	4^v, 5^r, 6^v, 7^r, 8^v re-set; title page re-set	As 2nd; variant on title page	As 2nd; variant on title page
A(i)	4^r, 5^v, 6^r, 7^v, 8^r re-set; variants on 2^r	Variants on 7^v	As 3rd; variant on 4^r, and pagination errors on 5^v and 6^r
B(o)	Re-set	As 2nd	As 2nd; line re-set on 1^r; variant on 2^v and 3^r, and pagination errors on 5^r and 6^v
B(i)	Re-set	As 2nd; with two variants on 1^v	As 3rd
C(o)	All but 8^v re-set; variant on 8^v	As 2nd, with variants on 5^r, 7^r, and 8^v	As 2nd; 3^r, 5^r, 6^v, 7^r, 8^v reimposed but not re-set
C(i)	Re-set	2^r, 3^r, 6^r re-set; variant on 8^r	As 3rd; 3^v, 4^r, 5^v, 6, 7^v, 8^r re-imposed but not re-set (6^r may have been re-set); two variants on 6^r, including addition of ten lines
D(o)	As 1st, with variants on 5^r, 6^v and 8^v; 3 lines re-set on 8^v	Re-set	As 3rd; 1^r, 2^v, 3^r, 4^v, 5^r re-imposed but not re-set

(Cont.)

	1711b (2nd edition)	1711c (3rd edition)	1711d (4th edition)
D(i)	As 1st; variants on 6^r and 7^v	Re-set	As 3rd; 1^v, 2^r, 3^v, 4^r, 5^v, 6^r re-imposed but not re-set
E(o)	As 1st, with substantial re-setting on 4^v	As 2nd, with variant on 1^r	As 3rd, with variant on 3^r
E(i)	As 1st although 6^r re-set/re-imposed due to footnote; variants on 3^v, 5^v and 6^r	As 2nd, with variant on 4^r	As 2nd
F(o)	As 1st; variants on 5^r and 7^r	Re-set	As 3rd, except postscript added on 8^v
F(i)	As 1st; variants on 3^v and 8^r	Re-set	As 3rd

NB. The table above only notes variants on pages that have not *otherwise been re-set. Not all variants are substantive. When a page has been re-set but lineation otherwise preserved, optical collating creates a rippling effect across the whole page that is markedly different from the 'flat' visual effect when two identical pages are collated.*

A single ninety-six-page 'sixth edition' (1712a) survives at the BL. However, Simon Pugh identifies this as 'the second edition [i.e. 1711b] reissued with a title page from the sixth edition [i.e. 1712b]' ('A Variant Second Edition of Jonathan Swift's *The Conduct of the Allies*', *N&Q* 229 (1984), 388–9). Although optical collation has not been possible, manual collation and careful examination of the copy support, but further complicate, his deduction. For the most part, the variants follow 1711b (including cases where 1711b has a unique variant, such 'the *Austrian*' on B1^v, the erroneously angled opening square brackets in the running title on C2^r and D3^v, and italicization on D5^r and D7^r), but a missing space on A2^v (which is also present in 1711a) and a missetting of A6^v suggest an earlier state of this forme. The setting (and wording) of the lower part of C8^r (inner forme) follows 1711c but non-italicization of 'single Person' on C8^v follows 1711b (outer forme). E1^r follows the 1711c setting and reading. Pugh notes that the title page is 'more discoloured than the rest and may be a later

addition' (p. 389). This seems plausible, not least in that, given the demand
for the work, Barber would presumably not have had any spare sheets of
1711a, 1711b or 1711c left by the time he was printing the sixth edition;
moreover, the fact that only one copy survives of such a ninety-six-page
sixth edition (Barber having moved to the smaller typeface) and the rather
mixed nature of the variants suggest that 1712a is probably a later made-up
copy. However, as 1712a provides – in sheet C at least – an interim state
between 1711b and 1711c, I have retained it in the list of editions and the
collation tables below.

For the fifth edition (1711e), Barber replaced the english type with small
pica, allowing him to increase the number of lines per page and so squeeze
the text on to six half-sheets. 1711e follows 1711d for the most part, with
some minor changes of punctuation, spelling and capitalization; there are a
good number of missettings but there are at least eleven plausible substantive variants (including two in the text of the eighth article of the Grand
Alliance) along with several where the word order is changed. It is possible
that these changes, all of which are stylistic or syntactic, were authorially
sanctioned but, for reasons given below, this edition takes 1711d as its
copy text rather than 1711e or its successors. 1711e is also more circum-
spect than 1711a–d, 'emvowelling' far more references to the 'Queen' and
'General'.

The sixth edition (1712b, not to be confused with the ninety-six-page
1712a) mixed existing sheets (D-F) with re-set sheets, introducing two
new substantive variants; in correcting most of 1711e's errors, 1712b may
well have looked back to a copy of 1711d, but it is clear from the lineation
alone of the re-set sheets that these were nonetheless set primarily from
1711e. The running title on E2^r for at least three copies of 1711e (BL
1093.c.120, CUL Williams 279, CUL Ddd.25.159(5)) reads erroneously
'53', while at least two of the 1712b copies (John Rylands and CUL) give
the correct pagination, suggesting at least two distinct states. Sheets A-C
and E-F of the seventh edition (1712c) are identical to 1712b (but for one
re-set line on C1^v and E3^r, and the re-set top half of F3^v); D, however, is
re-set, with one significant variant. Intriguingly, 1712c appears to restore
what I believe to be a corrected reading, replacing 'Part' with 'Party' in the
line: 'the Ministers here prevailed on the Queen to execute a Ratification
of Articles, which only one Party had signed'. It is unlikely that this is
the consequence of Swiftian intervention, but the reading is sufficiently

superior (*pace* Davis, who retains the reading) for me to emend the chosen copy text for this edition.

Davis (vol. VI, p. 205) claims the eighth and final London edition (1713) to be both an 'exact reprint of the seventh' and 'published in 1715'. Neither is true: the wholly re-set eighth edition bears 1713 on its title page and while it follows 1712c (and hence 1711e and 1712b) very closely, there are numerous minor variants.

Irish and Scottish reprints

On 2 December 1711, given the 'extraordinary' 'noise' that *Conduct* was making, Swift surmised that the pamphlet would be reprinted in Ireland, and on 4 December Swift reported that it had been sent over to Ireland (Williams, *JSt*, pp. 428, 430, 441). By early February, Stella was able to report that three editions had appeared, to Swift's considerable amazement: 'why really three editions of the *Conduct*, &c. is very much for Ireland; it is a sign you have some honest among you' (p. 483). Three Dublin editions survive, although two of them claim − perhaps falsely or to imply an erroneous relationship with the relevant London editions − to be the fourth and fifth editions. Of these, the edition published by John Hyde (1712e) is the most interesting.

In August 1711, Hyde was given permission by Dublin's Guild of St Luke the Evangelist (the city's book trade guild) to travel to England where, Woolley speculates, he gained access to a copy of *Conduct* 'with authorial revisions'; these revisions represent 'a stemma distinct from the series deriving from the successive London editions' and formed the basis for Faulkner's 1738 edition ('Swift's Copy of *Gulliver's Travels*: The Armagh *Gulliver*, Hyde's Edition, and Swift's Earliest Corrections', in Clive T. Probyn (ed.), *The Art of Jonathan Swift* (London: Vision, 1978), p. 142; Pollard, p. 305). 1712e is clearly set from 1711a but there are six occasions where it does indeed offer substantive readings that differ from all the other 1711−12 editions. Accounting for this apparent separate stemma, however, is difficult as the variants suggest that at some point between 27 November and 1 December (between the publication of 1711a and 1711b) Swift made *different* corrections to a copy of 1711a from those that appeared in 1711b. Moreover, given the speed with which the first four editions appeared, it would seem strange that Hyde, if he were indeed still in London, would prefer to follow 1711a when these later editions bore Swift's own revisions. Swift himself notes that the work had been 'sent over' to Ireland on 4 December while the fourth edition was in preparation (Williams, *JSt*, p. 430). Two alternative hypotheses present themselves. The first is that 1712e is based on a version of *Conduct* that pre-dates 1711a. If so, the absence of any mention of Hyde in *JSt* suggests that Hyde's source could have been proof-sheets rather than a manuscript, and it does seem more plausible for Hyde, a senior member of the Dublin guild, to have visited one of London's leading printers with an eye to what he might be able to reprint in Dublin. The second hypothesis is that Hyde himself made the changes, which is possible given the small number of changes made and the fact that only two ('not' for 'hardly' and 'are' for 'were') represent substitutions of wholly new words.

The two other surviving Dublin editions, 1712f and 1712g (described as 'fourth' and 'fifth' editions respectively), were printed by Edward Waters. Poorly printed, they evidently sorely tested Waters's stock of type: initial capitals, clauses, sentences, paragraphs and even whole pages are sometimes set in italic (and, even on occasion, in black-letter), and there are also several passages where 'vv' replaces every 'w', all presumably a consequence of depleted roman type. 1712f follows 1711b closely, including the misspelling 'Subsides' (B2^r) and the correctly set 'Allies' (B3^r); only in two places does it offer substantive variants: 'interest' for 'interests' (A3^v) and 'estate' for 'state' (B2^r). 1712g is a straightforward re-setting of 1712f, following for the most part 1712f's lineation and page breaks but using a greater abundance of italics. There are some minor differences in spelling, capitalization (although possibly linked to low levels of particular type) and punctuation; there are a handful of substantive differences, none of which suggest more than compositorial errors or corrections of 1712f's errors. Curiously, the mispagination in 1712f ('39', '40', '39', '40', '41' etc.) is repeated in 1712g. The two editions differ in their use of parentheses around the page numbers (1712f mixes regular and square parentheses; 1712g only uses regular) which would rule out shared skeleton formes; sheet F in both – the mispagination begins on F1^r – does just use regular parentheses but 1712g seems to have favoured italic parentheses more than 1712f. Nor is there any evidence that 1712g is anything other than a fully re-set reprint of 1712f. Instead, this may suggest that sheet F (and perhaps also G) was set and printed earlier than the other sheets – or perhaps even printed elsewhere in Dublin?

Two Edinburgh editions (1711f and 1712d) were printed by Robert Freebairn. 1711f was evidently set from 1711a, although in a few places its reading diverges; it also re-punctuates, re-capitalizes, is more consistent than 1711a in separating 'ourselves' into two words, and suffixes 'e' to 1711a's 'examin', 'human' and 'sanguin'. 1712d follows 1711f closely, including, for the most part, lineation (optical collation confirms that 1712d is wholly re-set), although on several occasions it does alter punctuation, spelling and capitalization. Its attempted correction ('but it is the Owner sure to be undone first', A3^v) of an erroneous reading in 1711f suggests that it did not have sight of any other London editions; however, on two occasions it manages to restore readings ('skreen' for 'Skrew' on E4^r, 'especially' for 'specially' on G3^v) present in the London editions. There are also a handful of substantive misreadings.

Later editions

Conduct was reprinted in 1738 by Faulkner in volume V of his octavo (hereafter 1738a) and duodecimo (hereafter 1738b) editions of Swift's *Works* (TS, nos. 42, 50); in the same year, it was included in the first volume of Charles Davis's London edition of Swift's *Political Tracts* (TS, no. 25(7); hereafter 1738c). 1738a has been fully collated against 1711d, with the variants cross-checked with 1738b−c. As Davis notes (vol. VI, p. 207), Faulkner takes Hyde's Dublin edition (1712e), itself based on 1711a, as its copy text. The choice is a strange one, given the significant differences between 1711a and the later London editions; however, as I have mentioned above, there is some, albeit slim, evidence that Hyde may have had access to a distinct authorially approved version. As when he reprinted Swift's other political works, Faulkner changed spelling, punctuation, italicization and capitalization and 'improved' some of Swift's word choices ('although' for 'though', 'It is' for ''Tis'); he also included footnotes identifying individuals alluded to in the work. The 1738 editions did also introduce some new variant readings (an interpolated 'I say' and the changing of 'hundred' to 'thousand' and a 'fourth' to a 'sixth' among others) that might, as Davis argues, indicate the hand of the author:

> Faulkner himself states that Swift had the proofs of both Vols. V and VI read to him, and himself made corrections. And this may well have been so. Swift clearly did not bother to see that the text used was the one he had finally approved, but it may still be as Faulkner claimed that he did take the trouble to make some improvements for the sake of greater clarity while the book was still in proof.   (vol. VI, p. 207)

However, if the source of these changes was Swift, he did not seek to incorporate, or recover, the amendments he had made in London in 1711; even if he had no copy of a London edition to hand, why did he not correct the potentially embarrassing misquotation from Proverbs? 1738c is a straightforward reprint of 1738a, correcting a few of 1738a's obvious errors. The relationship between 1738a and 1738b is more complicated. Both carry variants not present in 1712e, but 1738b retains more of 1712e's readings than 1738a; it may also have had sight of a London or one of Waters's Dublin editions in that it retained the unlikely reading of 'Hands' on B7^v over 1712e's more plausible 'Heads'.

Conduct also appeared in volume V of Faulkner's octavo edition of 1741 (TS, no. 44). This followed 1738a closely (including lineation, although it did change capitalization and punctuation at times); on one occasion it evidently attempted to correct 1738a's problematic reading 'in time vie' without reference to any other edition. It also introduced a few alternative readings (included in the collation table), none of which can be considered significant.

In 1748, 1712b was reprinted as *Good Queen Anne Vindicated, and the Ingratitude, Insolence &c of Her Whig Ministry and the Allies*. According to *ESTC*, five octavo editions survive: three were published by the London bookseller, William Owen (one of which claimed distribution in Oxford, Manchester, Edinburgh and Dublin), another was published by Thomas Cooper's widow, Mary, and another by Faulkner and others from Dublin. (TS only lists three: TS, nos. 543, 544 and 1660.) Only one cites Swift explicitly as the author, none use *The Conduct of the Allies* as their title, and all omit the preface and the postscript. The following have been collated: Owen's first edition (1748a), with its variants cross-checked with Owen's second edition (1748b), and Faulkner's (1748c), with the latter's variants cross-checked with Cooper's (1748d). Although I have not attempted a full optical collation of these editions, careful examination reveals that 1748b seems to be identical to 1748a, and hence possibly a re-issue; a similar relationship seems to be the case between 1748c and 1748d. There are several occasions where they all offer the same alternative reading, which suggests a direct relationship between these editions. The pattern of variants indicate that 1748c–d were derived from 1748a–b rather than earlier editions: in two places, Faulkner's and Cooper's editions provide different variants while the Owen editions preserve the original 1712b reading; in another instance, the Owen editions present what is probably a missetting ('got' for 'not') which the Faulkner and Cooper editions attempt to correct by omitting the problematic word, thus reversing the original meaning of the line.

Conduct remained a staple of Swift's collected works from 1738 onwards but its bibliographical complexity was only first fully appreciated by John Nichols in the 1770s. His *Supplement* of 1776 (TS, no. 88) included a note about Swift's postscript to 1711d, and the amended passage to which it referred, although Nichols claimed, imprecisely, that these changes had been made '[a]fter the first edition' (p. 610). An exchange followed in *The Gentleman's Magazine*. 'Mr Scrutator' responded to the review of the *Supplement* by observing that 'the *fourth* edition of [*Conduct*] . . . has been said to contain several passages not to be found in any other. If this be fact it may be adviseable to collate this *fourth* edition throughout' (*GM*, 47 (1777), 218). Nichols noted, with a certain testiness, that the alterations he had included in the *Supplement* had come from the fourth edition, but Scrutator, undaunted, persisted: 'There are surely many more alterations in [this edition] . . . than are noticed in . . . this *Supplement*' (which indeed, as the collations below indicate, is something of an understatement) (261, 381). In September, Nichols replied that he had obtained 'the *five first editions*' of *Conduct*, which he now proposed to collate for his own edition of Swift's complete works (420). His 1801 and 1808 editions, however, seemed to make little of these collations, only repeating the misleading claim about the postscript's first appearance. Walter Scott's editions of 1814 and 1824 compounded the issue by baldly describing the postscript as part of the second edition. It is only with Temple Scott in 1901 that an editor made it clear which *Conduct* he was reprinting. He used the first edition but indicated that it had been collated with 'the following editions issued in 1711' (vol. V, p. 58); in addition, he supplied half a dozen footnotes indicating significant variant passages, citing all the editions up to and including the seventh.

Clarendon Press published an edition of *Conduct*, edited by C. B. Wheeler, in 1916 (an inauspicious year, perhaps, to reprint a work criticizing a ruinous war). Wheeler quoted the relevant extracts from *JSt* without much elucidation, but his modest bibliographical note was very sound: he noted that the first, second, third, fourth and sixth editions (he evidently consulted the sixth 'made-up' edition in the BL) were printed 'largely from the same type-setting', and that this sixth edition 'follows edition 2 closely'. The fifth and seventh editions were also 'largely from the same type-setting' (p. lii). Wheeler took the seventh edition as his copy text and supplied a number of collations as footnotes, several of which Davis would later overlook in his edition.

John Hayward included selections of *Conduct* in the Nonesuch edition (1934) of *Gulliver's Travels and Selected Writings*. However, while acknowledging Wheeler's identification of the seventh edition as the 'definitive text', he reprints the first edition on the grounds that 'apart from a few revisions not affecting the present selection, the first seven editions are verbally almost identical' (p. 348).

Davis, citing Swift's account of his authorial interventions in *Some Remarks* (see below), took an uncut Yale Library copy of 1711d as his copy text. His two sets of collations (one for the London and Hyde editions, one for Faulkner's 1738 edition) are detailed but not comprehensive; he also made a point of including a selective handful of non-substantive variants such as changes of spelling and italicization. Although he was aware of the Edinburgh editions and the Waters's editions from Dublin, he did not collate these; he also seemed unaware of the existence of the BL 'sixth edition' (1712a). He changed capitalization on occasion and silently expanded all elided names. He only made one significant emendation which we have followed: 'became' on B2^r became 'become'.

Conduct is included in Angus Ross and David Woolley's Oxford Authors edition of Swift (1986). Obviously not intended as a full-scale scholarly edition, the textual information about *Conduct* is restricted to brief notes about the footnote and postscript (pp. 316, 326, 655). Ross and Woolley evidently took 1711a as their copy text and use square brackets to indicate later readings (although this is not explained and runs counter to the claim in the volume's 'Note on the text' that all such parenthetical material is editorial); the footnote and postscript are both glossed with notes of their source. On at least two occasions, readings from 1711b–d are incorporated

354 ENGLISH POLITICAL WRITINGS 1711–1714

without marking them as such (presumably considering them to be emendations rather than variants), while its conflation of 1711a's 'articles in that treaty' and 1711b–d's 'preliminary articles' as '[preliminary] articles in that treaty' does not seem helpful. The text, understandably, is thoroughly modernized in terms of spelling, capitalization, italicization and punctuation; elisions are sometimes expanded silently, sometimes in square brackets and sometimes not at all.

Choice of copy text

In *Some Remarks on the Barrier Treaty*, written in February 1712, by which time the printer was considering a seventh edition of *Conduct*, Swift replied at length to 'a Gentleman, I know not of what Character or Calling' who had written three 'Discourses' (see p. 132) in response to *Conduct* (Swift's quotations seem to indicate that he had Francis Hare's *Remarks upon Remarks* in mind). In particular, Swift 'solemnly' declared that he had 'not wilfully committed the least Mistake' in composing *Conduct*: 'I stopt the Second Edition, and made all possible Enquiries among those who I thought could best inform me, in order to correct any Error I could hear of: I did the same to the Third and Fourth Editions, and then left the Printer to his liberty' (see p. 134). Swift's claim is borne out by the pattern of variants; the substantive variants present in the London editions of 1711e and beyond, while they may be authoritative, could equally be explained by compositorial error or 'correction' of 1711d's copy. Moreover, Swift would seem unexpectedly modest if he had indeed intervened in those later editions. Also, this edition's policy of preferring texts that had the most immediate relevance to the political situation at hand means that we have discounted the editions of 1738 onwards. Consequently, this edition, like Davis, has chosen 1711d as its copy text, but has collated this against every other edition published between 1711 and 1713, and, whenever possible, multiple copies of 1711a–d; it has also collated 1738a (variants cross-checked with 1738b–c), 1741, 1748a and 1748c (cross-checked with 1748b and 1748d). The collation tables also include Davis. Given the complex textual history of 1711a–e, 1712a–c and 1713, I have retained for the information of the reader misprints and italicizations in these editions that would have been otherwise omitted from a table of historical collations.

I have emended with a light touch. The obvious missettings ('have of', 'Matetr' etc) have been corrected, and I have restored two superior 1711a readings ('become' and 'Heads'). This edition is also the first since Wheeler (himself following 1712c) to include the highly plausible reading of 'Party' instead of 'Part'. I have, however, rejected four emendations: the insertion of 'of' in *the loading the* Dutch *Inhabitants*' and '*the seizing the* Spanish Netherlands' (A8^r), the insertion of 'it' in 'which whoever introduced among us' (which 1711f and 1712d suggest), and the changing of 'Ausburg' for Augsburg. Although the first three make grammatical and the fourth geographical sense, these readings evidently did not sufficiently trouble those who reprinted the text in later eighteenth-century editions.

Copy text: CUL, Acton.d.25.1001 (6)

References: TS, nos. 539 (1711a–e, 1712b–c, 1713), 540 (1712e), 541 (1712f–g), 542 (1711f, 1712d). Davis, vol. VI, pp. 1–65, 205–9 (notes). Woolley, 'Canon', no. 10. *ESTC* T31146 (1711a, listing fifty-seven copies), T31147 (1711b, listing twenty-eight copies), T162401 (1711c, listing twenty-five copies), T31148 (1711d, listing thirty-six copies), T31149 (1711e, listing forty-seven copies), T153304 (1711f, listing eleven copies), T27320 (1712a, listing two copies), N14820 (1712b, listing twenty-seven copies), T31150 (1712c, listing thirty-five copies), N1498 (1714d, listing ten copies), T162402 (1712e, listing eight copies), N14815 (1712f, listing four copies), N14817 (1712g, listing four copies), N14821 (1713, listing eleven copies)

London edition, 1711a

Title: [within double rules, 149 × 86 mm] THE | *CONDUCT* | OF THE | ALLIES, | AND OF THE | 𝕷𝖆𝖙𝖊 𝕸𝖎𝖓𝖎𝖘𝖙𝖗𝖞, | IN | Beginning and Carrying on | THE | Present War. | [double rule] | —— *Partem tibi Gallia nostri* | *Eripuit: partem duris Hispania bellis*: | *Pars jacet Hesperia: totoq; exercitus orbe* | *Te vincente perit.* —— | *Odimus accipitrem quia semper vivit in armis.* | —— *Victrix Provincia plorat.* | [double rule] | *LONDON*, | Printed for *John Morphew*, near *Statio-* | *ners-Hall.* 1712.

Collation: 4°: A–F^8

Pagination: 1–6, 7–96

Contents: A1^r title page; A1^v blank; A2^r–A3^r preface; A3^v blank; A4^r–F8^v text (E2^v–E3^r Eighth Article of the Grand Alliance)

Typography: thirty-three lines per page (B4^r), type-page 151 (161) × 86 mm, twenty lines of roman type 93 mm; preface, twenty lines of italic type 92 mm

Failures of catchwords to catch:
B5^r gerous]~,
E6^v imagine] ~,
F6^r Lastly] LASTLY

Copies examined:
*§Bodl, G.Pamph. 825(1): 177 × 114 mm, trimmed, with occasional loss of running title and (on C3^r) part of top line; in volume of ten early eighteenth-century pamphlets, including *Some Remarks on the Barrier Treaty* (first edition); C3^r has been detached and tipped in
*§Bodl, 8° K.102(1) Linc: 189 × 122 mm, trimmed; in volume of seven 1711–12 items on the war, including *Some Remarks on the Barrier Treaty* (second edition); one of registration copies deposited at Stationers' Hall (Chalmers, p. 421)
*§CUL, Williams 278: 208 × 133 mm, untrimmed; re-bound; includes typewritten note by Williams claiming it to be 'a 16mo in half-sheets'
*TCC, RW.62.31: 204 × 140, untrimmed; disbound and stitched; Rothschild Library, no. 2025
*TCC, RW.68.14 (3): 185 × 114, trimmed; in volume of thirteen 1711–12 items; Poley collection, volume 14; front board detached; Rothschild Library, no. 2026
¶Humanities Research Center, University of Texas, D282.5 P35 1711 no. 1: copy not physically examined; reproduction used

London edition, 1711b

Title: [within double rules, 157 × 87 mm] THE | *CONDUCT* | OF THE | ALLIES, | AND OF THE | 𝕷𝖆𝖙𝖊 𝕸𝖎𝖓𝖎𝖘𝖙𝖗𝖞, | IN | Beginning and Carrying on | THE | Present War. | [rule] | —— *Partem tibi Gallia nostri* | *Eripuit: partem* | *duris Hispania bellis:* | *Pars jacet Hesperia: totoq; exercitus orbe* | *Te vincente* | *perit. Terris fudisse cruorem* | *Quid juvat Arctois, Rhodano, Rhenoq; subactis?* |

Odimus accipitrem quia semper vivit in armis. | ——— *Victrix Provincia plorat.* | [rule] | 𝕿𝖍𝖊 𝕾𝖊𝖈𝖔𝖓𝖉 𝕰𝖉𝖎𝖙𝖎𝖔𝖓, 𝕮𝖔𝖗𝖗𝖊𝖈𝖙𝖊𝖉. | [rule] | *LONDON,* | Printed for *John Morphew,* near *Statio-* | *ners-Hall.* 1711.

Collation: 8°: A–F⁸

Pagination: *1–6*, 7–96

Contents: A1ʳ title page; A1ᵛ blank; A2ʳ–A3ʳ preface; A3ᵛ blank; A4ʳ–F8ᵛ text (E2ᵛ–E3ʳ Eighth Article of the Grand Alliance)

Typography: thirty-three lines per page (A7ʳ), type-page 155 (164) × 87.5 mm, twenty lines of roman type 94.5 mm; preface, twenty lines of italic type 94 mm

Failures of catchwords to catch:
A5ᵛ extin] extinguished
C3ʳ or] our [TCC copy; BL copy: our | our]
E6ᵛ imagine] ~,
F6ʳ Lastly] LASTLY

Copies examined:
*§BL, 1093.c.119: 186 × 129 mm, trimmed, with partial or complete loss of page numbers on some leaves; re-bound 1947; *ECCO* copy
*¶Bodl, G.Pamph.1144 (20): 204 × 128 mm, trimmed; in volume of twenty-one political tracts from 1711
§CUL, Acton.d.25.1023(2): copy not physically examined; reproduction used
*TCC, RW.62.32: 206 × 134 mm, trimmed; disbound with gilt top edge; scorch marks upper right edge; Rothschild Library, no. 2027

London edition, 1711c

Title: [within double rules, 156 × 86 mm] THE | *CONDUCT* | OF THE | ALLIES, | AND OF THE | 𝕷𝖆𝖙𝖊 𝕸𝖎𝖓𝖎𝖘𝖙𝖗𝖞, | IN | Beginning and Carrying on | THE | Present War. | [rule] | ——— *Partem tibi Gallia nostri* | *Eripuit: partem duris Hispania bellis:* | *Pars jacet Hesperia: totoq; exercitus orbe* | *Te vincente perit. Terris fudisse cruorem* | *Quid juvat Arctois, Rhodano, Rhenoq;* | *subactis? | Odimus accipitrem quia semper vivit in armis.* | ——— *Victrix*

Provincia plorat. | [rule] | 𝕿𝖍𝖊 𝕿𝖍𝖎𝖗𝖉 𝕰𝖉𝖎𝖙𝖎𝖔𝖓, 𝕮𝖔𝖗𝖗𝖊𝖈𝖙𝖊𝖉. | [rule] | *LONDON,* | Printed for *John Morphew,* near *Statio-* | *ners-Hall.* 1711.

Collation: 8°: A–F⁸

Pagination: 1–6, 7–96

Contents: A1ʳ title page; A1ᵛ blank; A2ʳ–A3ʳ preface; A3ᵛ blank; A4ʳ–F8ᵛ text (E2ᵛ–E3ʳ Eighth article of the Grand Alliance); F8ᵛ Errata: 'ERRATA in the Second Edition of this Book, which the Reader is desired to Correct with his Pen. Page 20. l. 30 for *our Allies,* read *our Selves.*'

Typography: thirty-three lines per page (A7ʳ), type-page 155 (164) × 87 mm, twenty lines of roman type 93.5 mm; preface, twenty lines of italic type 94 mm

Failures of catchwords to catch:
C3ᵛ How] However
E6ᵛ imagine] ∼,
F8ʳ Em-] Empire

Copies examined:
*§Bodl, Pamph. 295 (10): 194 × 120 mm, trimmed; in volume of twenty-two 1711 pamphlets; binding split; crosses and numbers inked in margins; *ECCO* copy
*§CUL, Syn.7.71.49(1): 194 × 122 mm, trimmed; re-bound in paper binding; stitching holes visible; inked annotation on E2ᵛ: parentheses are placed around '*except it is agreed,*' (line 19, in Eighth Article) with note below: 'the words enclosᵈ false () & instead of yᵐ onely yᵉ | word [']and['] is to be incerted'

London edition, 1711d

Title: [within double rules, 155 × 88 mm] THE | *CONDUCT* | OF THE | ALLIES, | AND OF THE | 𝕷𝖆𝖙𝖊 𝕸𝖎𝖓𝖎𝖘𝖙𝖗𝖞, | IN | Beginning and Carrying on | THE | Present War. | [rule] | —— *Partem tibi Gallia nostri* | *Eripuit: partem duris Hispania bellis:* | *Pars jacet Hesperia: totoq, exercitus orbe* | *Te vincente perit. Terris fudisse cruorem* | *Quid juvat Arctois, Rhodano, Rhenoq, subactis?* | *Odimus accipitrem quia semper vivit in armis.* | —— *Victrix Provincia plorat*. | [rule] | 𝕿𝖍𝖊 𝕱𝖔𝖚𝖗𝖙𝖍 𝕰𝖉𝖎𝖙𝖎𝖔𝖓, 𝕮𝖔𝖗𝖗𝖊𝖈𝖙𝖊𝖉. | [rule] | *LONDON*, | Printed for *John Morphew*, near *Statio-* | *ners-Hall*. 1711.

Collation: 8°: A–F⁸

Pagination: *1–6*, 7–9, '11', '10', 12–24, '15', 26–7, '18', 29–96

Contents: A1ʳ title page; A1ᵛ blank; A2ʳ–A3ʳ preface; A3ᵛ blank; A4ʳ–F8ᵛ text (E2ᵛ–E3ʳ Eighth Article of the Grand Alliance); F8ᵛ postscript

Typography: thirty-three lines per page (A7ʳ), type-page 155.5 (165) × 87.5 mm, twenty lines of roman type 94 mm; preface, twenty lines of italic type 94 mm

Failures of catchwords to catch:
A4ʳ [*om.*]] it
D1ʳ on] no
E4ʳ greater[,]] ∼, [mis-inking?]
E6ᵛ imagine] ∼,
F5ʳ Our-] Our selves

Copies examined:
*§BL, 8132.a.4: 188 × 115 mm, trimmed; re-bound in 1949; *ECCO* copy
*§Bodl, Vet. A4e.2318: 206 × 128 mm, trimmed; re-bound
*§Bodl, Vet. A4e.759: 212 × 136 mm, untrimmed; marginal annotations and underlinings in ink
*§CUL, Acton.d.25.1001 (6): 185 × 115 mm, trimmed; in volume of fifteen printed pamphlets from 1711–18, including first edition of *Barrier Treaty*
*TCC, RW.62.57: 195 × 121 mm, trimmed; disbound and stitched; Rothschild Library, no. 2028

London edition, 1711e

Title: [within double rule, 153 × 86 mm] THE | *CONDUCT* | OF THE | ALLIES, | AND OF THE | 𝕷𝖆𝖙𝖊 𝕸𝖎𝖓𝖎𝖘𝖙𝖗𝖞, | IN | Beginning and Carrying on | THE | Present War. | [rule] | —— *Partem tibi Gallia nostri* | *Eripuit: partem duris Hispania bellis*: | *Pars jacet Hesperia: totoq; exercitus orbe* | *Te vincente perit. Terris fudisse cruorem* | *Quid juvat Arctois, Rhodano, Rhenoq; subactis?* | *Odimus accipitrem quia semper vivit in armis.* | —— *Victrix Provincia plorat.* | [rule] | 𝕿𝖍𝖊 𝕱𝖎𝖋𝖙𝖍 𝕰𝖉𝖎𝖙𝖎𝖔𝖓, 𝕮𝖔𝖗𝖗𝖊𝖈𝖙𝖊𝖉. | [rule] | *LONDON,* | Printed for *John Morphew,* near *Statio-* | *ners-Hall.* 1711.

Collation: 8°: A–F⁴ (F2 missigned 'F3')

Pagination: *1–4*, 5–34, '53', 36–48

Contents: A1ʳ title page; A1ᵛ blank; A2ʳ⁻ᵛ preface; A3ʳ–F4ᵛ text (E2ʳ⁻ᵛ text of Eighth Article of the Grand Alliance); F4ᵛ postscript

Typography: forty-seven lines per page (C1ʳ), but some pages have forty-six lines, type-page 166 (174) × 87 mm, twenty lines of roman type 70.5 mm; preface, twenty lines of italic type 80.5 mm

Failures of catchwords to catch:
A2ʳ *are*,] *ces*
B2ᵛ been] had
E1ᵛ [*om.*]] HAVING

Copies examined:
*†BL, 1093.c.120: 191 × 116 mm, trimmed; re-bound 1947; *ECCO* copy
*BL, T.1107(15): 190 × 113 mm, trimmed; in volume of thirteen early eighteenth-century volumes; re-bound 1978; stitching holes visible
*BL, T.1599(7): 197 × 120 mm, trimmed; in volume of fifteen eighteenth-century works; re-bound 1978
*BL, C.108.bbb.37(5): 205 × 127 mm, untrimmed; modern note: 'stitched as issued'
*Bodl, Bliss A92(15): 197 × 115 mm, trimmed; in volume of sixteen miscellaneous tracts, 1710–36
*¶CUL, Williams 279: copy not physically examined; reproduction used
*¶CUL, Ddd. 25.159(5): copy not physically examined; reproduction used
*TCC, RW.62.58: 203 × 133 mm, untrimmed; disbound, with gilt top-edge, and stitched; Rothschild Library, no. 2029

Edinburgh edition, 1711f

Title: THE | *CONDUCT* | OF THE | ALLIES, | AND OF THE | 𝕷𝖆𝖙𝖊 𝕸𝖎𝖓𝖎𝖘𝖙𝖗𝖞, | IN | Beginning and Carrying on | THE | Present War. | [rule] | ——— *Partem tibi Gallia nostri* | *Eripuit: partem duris Hispania* *bellis:* | *Pars jacet Hesperia: totoque exercitus orbe* | *Te vincente perit* ——— |

Odimus accipitrem quia semper vivit in armis. | ——— *Vistrix* [*sic*] *provincia plorat.* | [rule] | *EDINBVRGH*: | Re-printed by Mr. *Robert Freebairn,* and sold at his Shop in | the Parliament-Closs, 1711.

Collation: 8°: A–G⁴

Pagination: *1–3*, 4–56

Contents: A1ʳ title page; A1ᵛ blank; A2ʳ preface; A2ᵛ–G4ᵛ text (F1ᵛ text of Eighth Article of the Grand Alliance)

Typography:
A2ᵛ-F1ʳ thirty-nine lines per page (C1ᵛ), type-page 159 (168) × 99 mm, twenty lines of roman type 81 mm
F1ᵛ-G4ᵛ forty-three lines per page (F2ʳ), type-page 159 (168) × 99 mm, twenty lines of roman type 73 mm
preface, twenty lines of italic type 67 mm

Failures of catchwords to catch:
B3ʳ: *stria*] ~,
B4ᵛ: *Dutch*] ~,
D1ʳ: [*om.*]] | Let
D3ᵛ: Easiness] ~,
D4ᵛ: wers] ~.
E3ʳ: lence] ~,
F4ᵛ: [*om.*]] | of

Copy examined:
*†BL, 1608/3971: 183 × 112 mm, trimmed with some loss of text along outer edge; visible watermarks on top near spine of B2, C2, E1, G1, G2; de-acidified, laminated and re-bound 1993–4; *ECCO* copy

London edition, 1712a (mostly a reissue of 1711b with title page of 1712b)

Title: [within double rule, 153 × 89 mm] THE | *CONDUCT* | OF THE | ALLIES, | AND OF THE | 𝔏𝔞𝔱𝔢 𝔐𝔦𝔫𝔦𝔰𝔱𝔯𝔶, | IN | Beginning and Carrying on | THE | Present War. [rule] | ——— *Partem tibi Gallia nostri* | *Eripuit: partem* *duris Hispania bellis:* | *Pars jacet Hesperia: totoq; exercitus orbe* | *Te vincente* *perit. Terris fudisse cruorem* | *Quid juvat Arctois, Rhodano, Rhenoq; subactis?* |

Odimus accipitrem quia semper vivit in armis. | —— *Victrix Provincia plorat.* | [rule] | 𝕿𝖍𝖊 𝕾𝖎𝖝𝖙𝖍 𝕰𝖉𝖎𝖙𝖎𝖔𝖓, 𝕮𝖔𝖗𝖗𝖊𝖈𝖙𝖊𝖉. | [rule] | *LONDON,* | Printed for *John Morphew,* near *Statio-* | *ners-Hall.* 1712.

Collation: 8°: A–F⁸

Pagination: 1–6, 7–96

Contents: A1ʳ title page; A1ᵛ blank; A2ʳ–A3ʳ preface; A3ᵛ blank; A4ʳ–F8ᵛ text (E2ᵛ–E3ʳ Eighth Article of the Grand Alliance)

Typography: thirty-three lines per page (A7ʳ; some pages thirty-two or thirty-four lines), type-page 156 (166.5) × 88 mm, twenty lines of roman type 94 mm; preface, twenty lines of italic type 94 mm

Failures of catchwords to catch:
C3ʳ: or] our
E6ᵛ: imagine] ~,
F6ʳ: Lastly] LASTLY

Copy examined:
†*BL, T.1784(1): 188 × 116 mm, trimmed; in volume with five other early eighteenth-century works; re-bound

London edition, 1712b

Title: [within double rule, 154 × 88 mm] THE | *CONDUCT* | OF THE | ALLIES, | AND OF THE | 𝕷𝖆𝖙𝖊 𝕸𝖎𝖓𝖎𝖘𝖙𝖗𝖞, | IN | Beginning and Carrying on | THE | Present War. | [rule] | —— *Partem tibi Gallia nostri* | *Eripuit: partem duris Hispania bellis:* | *Pars jacet Hesperia: totoq̃, exercitus orbe* | *Te vincente perit. Terris fudisse cruorem* | *Quid juvat Arctois, Rhodano, Rhenoq; subactis?* | *Odimus accipitrem quia semper vivit in armis.* | —— *Victrix Provincia plorat.* | [rule] | 𝕿𝖍𝖊 𝕾𝖎𝖝𝖙𝖍 𝕰𝖉𝖎𝖙𝖎𝖔𝖓, 𝕮𝖔𝖗𝖗𝖊𝖈𝖙𝖊𝖉. | [rule] | *LONDON,* | Printed for *John Morphew,* near *Statio-* | *ners-Hall,* 1712.

Collation: 8°: A–F⁴ (F2 missigned 'F3')

Pagination: 1–4, 5–48

Contents: A1ʳ title page; A1ᵛ blank; A2ʳ⁻ᵛ preface; A3ʳ–F4ᵛ text (E2ʳ⁻ᵛ text of Eighth Article of the Grand Alliance); F4ᵛ postscript

Typography: forty-seven lines per page (C1^r), but some pages have forty-six lines, type-page 169 (178) × 91 mm, twenty lines of roman type 72 mm; preface, twenty lines of italic type 82 mm

Failures of catchwords to catch:
B2^v: been] had
E1^v: [*om.*]] HAVING

Copies examined:
*Bodl, Pamph. 302 (5): 194 × 118 mm, trimmed; in volume of thirty-one c.1712 pamphlets
§CUL, X.28.19(6): copy not physically examined; reproduction used
†§John Rylands University Library, Manchester, 1285.7: copy not physically examined; reproduction used; *ECCO* copy

London edition, 1712c

Title: [within double rules, 157 × 88 mm] THE | *CONDUCT* | OF THE | ALLIES, | AND OF THE | 𝕷ate 𝕸inistry, | IN | Beginning and Carrying on | THE | Present War. | [rule] | —— *Partem tibi Gallia nostri* | *Eripuit: partem duris Hispania bellis*: | *Pars jacet Hesperia: totoq; exercitus orbe* | *Te vincente perit. Terris fudisse cruorem* | *Quid juvat Arctois, Rhodano, Rhenoq; subactis?* | *Odimus accipitrem quia semper vivit in armis.* | —— *Victrix Provincia plorat.* | [rule] | 𝕿he 𝕾eventh 𝕰dition, 𝕮orrected. | [rule] | *LONDON,* | Printed for *John Morphew*, near *Statio-* | *ners-Hall*, 1712.

Collation: 8°: A–F^4 (F2 missigned 'F3')

Pagination: *1–4*, 5–48

Contents: A1^r title page; A1^v blank; A2^{r-v} preface; A3^r–F4^v text (E2^{r-v} text of Eighth Article of the Grand Alliance); F4^v postscript

Typography: forty-seven lines lines per page (C1^r), but some pages have forty-six lines, type-page 167 (176) × 89 mm, twenty lines of roman type 71.5 mm; preface, twenty lines of italic type 82 mm

Failures of catchwords to catch:
B2^v: been] had
E1^v: [*om.*]] HAVING

F3^r: Wha] What ['t' dropped sort?]
F3^v: *Den-*] *Denmark's*

Copies examined:
*§BL, 101.d.29: 187 × 116 mm, trimmed; re-bound 1932; type has shifted at top of D2^r 'losing' the first word of the line; *ECCO* copy
*Bodl, G. Pamph. 1145 (1): 180 × 118 mm, trimmed; in volume of thirty-four political tracts 1712–13; front board, with A1 and A2, detached; A3 damaged; one-third of F4 torn off
*CUL, Syn. 7.71.49(2): 190 × 118 mm, trimmed, with occasional loss of RT, and loss of final characters of lines towards bottom of B1^r; re-bound in paper binding; type has shifted at top of D2^r 'losing' the first word of the line

Edinburgh edition, 1712d

Title: THE | *CONDUCT* | OF THE | ALLIES, | AND OF THE | 𝕷𝖆𝖙𝖊 𝕸𝖎𝖓𝖎𝖘𝖙𝖗𝖞, | IN | Beginning and Carrying on | THE | Present War. | [rule] | – – – – *Partem tibi Gallia nostri* | *Eripuit: partem duris Hispania bellis:* | *Pars jacet Hesperia: totoque exercitus orbe,* | *Te vincente perit* – – – – | *Odimus accipitrem quia semper vivit in armis.* | – – – – *Victrix provincia plorat.* | [rule] | *EDINBVRGH*: | Re-printed by Mr. *Robert Freebairn*, and sold at his Shop in | the Parliament-Closs, 1712.

Collation: 8°: A–G^4

Pagination: *1–3*, 4–56

Contents: A1^r title page; A1^v blank; A2^r preface; A2^v–G4^v text (F1^v text of Eighth Article of the Grand Alliance)

Typography:
A2^v–F1^r thirty-nine lines per page (B3^r), type-page 160 (168) × 102 mm, twenty lines of roman type 82 mm
F1^v–G4^v fourty-three lines per page (F2^r), type-page 158 (165.5) × 101 mm, twenty lines of roman type 73 mm
preface, twenty lines of italic type 67 mm

Failures of catchwords to catch:
B3^r: *stria*] ∼,
B4^v: *Dutch*] ∼,

C1ʳ: Hou] House [there is a space for hyphen]
D3ᵛ: Easiness] ~,
D4ᵛ: wers] ~.
E3ʳ: lence] ~,

Copies examined:
*CUL, Ddd.25.159(5): 181 × 113 mm, trimmed with some loss of running title; in volume of thirteen items 1701–32, including fifth London edition of *Conduct*; front board detached
†Huntington Library, California, 83334: copy not physically examined; reproduction used; *ECCO* copy

Dublin edition (Hyde), 1712e

Title: [within double rules 160 × 83 mm] THE | CONDUCT | OF THE | ALLIES, | AND OF THE | 𝔏𝔞𝔱𝔢 𝔐𝔦𝔫𝔦𝔰𝔱𝔯𝔶, | IN | Beginning and Carrying on | THE | Present WAR. | [double rule] | *Partem tibi Gallia nostri* | *Eripuit:* *Partem duris Hispania bellis*: | ―― *Pars jacet Hesperia*: *totoq*, *exercitus orbe* | *Te vincente perit* ―― | *Odimus accipitrem quia semper vivit in armis.* | ―― *Victrix Provincia plorat.* | [double rule] | *DVBLIN*, | Re-Printed for *John Hyde* Bookseller | in *Dames-street.* 1712.

Collation: 8°: A–D⁸, E⁴ [TCC copy: B4ᵛ signed 'B4']

Pagination: *1–4*, 5–72

Contents: A1ʳ title page; A1ᵛ blank; A2ʳ⁻ᵛ Preface; A3ʳ–E4ᵛ text (D2ᵛ–D3ʳ text of Eighth Article of the Grand Alliance)

Typography:
A2ʳ–D8ᵛ thirty-seven lines per page (A5ᵛ), type-page 150 (161) × 86 mm, twenty lines of roman type 81 mm
E1ʳ–E3ᵛ thirty-eight lines per page (E1ʳ; E2ᵛ, 37 lines), type-page 155 (166) × 86 mm, twenty lines of roman type 81 mm
E4ʳ forty-six lines, type-page 155 (c.164) × 86 mm, twenty lines of roman type 67 mm
E4ᵛ 47 lines, type-page 158 (c.167) × 86 mm, twenty lines of roman type 67 mm
preface, twenty lines of italic type 81 mm

Failures of catchwords to catch:
C5ʳ ten] Ten

Copies examined:
*TCC, RW.62.59: 167 × 100 mm, trimmed very tightly, but with only very occasional loss of direction lines; rebound and edges rubricated; Rothschild Library, no. 2030
*†Honourable Society of King's Inn, Dublin, Pamphlets v.256: 185 × 114 mm, lower edge possibly untrimmed; penultimate item in volume of fourteen miscellaneous Dublin and London pamphlets 1708–29; eighteenth-century binding, boards detached, spine cracked, bookplate: 'John Hort, Esq. Dub: 1757'.

Dublin edition (Waters, fourth) 1712f

Title: [within double rules 139 × 82+ mm] The Conduct | OF THE | ALLIES, | AND OF THE | 𝕷𝖆𝖙𝖊 𝕸𝖎𝖓𝖎𝖘𝖙𝖗𝖞, | In Begining [*sic*] and Carrying on the | Present War. | [rule] | —— *Partem tibi Gallia nostri | Eripuit: Partem duris Hispania bellis: | Pars jacet Hesperia: totoq; exercitus orbe | Te vincente perit. Terris fudisse cruorem | Quid juvat Arctois, Rhodano, Rhenoq; subactis? | Odimus accipitrem quia semper vivit in armis. | —— Victrix Provincia plorat.* | [rule] | 𝕿𝖍𝖊 𝕱𝖔𝖚𝖗𝖙𝖍 𝕰𝖉𝖎𝖙𝖎𝖔𝖓, 𝕮𝖔𝖗𝖗𝖊𝖈𝖙𝖊𝖉. | [rule] | *LONDON*: Printed by 𝕵𝖔𝖍𝖓 𝕸𝖔𝖗𝖕𝖍𝖊𝖜: | And Re=printed by 𝕰𝖉𝖜𝖆𝖗𝖉 𝕎𝖆𝖙𝖊𝖗𝖘 in *Essex-street*, | at the Corner of *Sycamore-Alley*, Dublin, 1712.

Collation: 8°: *A*⁴, B–G⁴

Pagination: *1–4*, 5–40, 39–54

Contents: A1ʳ title page; A1ᵛ blank; A2ʳ⁻ᵛ preface; A3ʳ–G4ᵛ text (F1ʳ text of Eighth Article of the Grand Alliance)

Typography:
forty-three lines per page (B4ʳ; some pages have forty-two lines), type-page 141.5 (151.5) × 82.5 mm, twenty lines of roman type 66 mm
preface, twenty lines of italic type 67 mm
F1ᵛ(lower half)–F2ʳ, twenty lines of black-letter type 65 mm

following pages have been set in italic type: B2^r (except first two and last eight lines), C3^v (except first two and a half lines), C4^r (upper half), E1^v (except first six lines), E3^r, F1^r, F1^v (upper half), F2^v

Failures of catchwords to catch:
A2^v THE] The
C1^v And] *A*nd
C3^v *been*] *so*
C4^v vvith] with
E2^v ever] *ever*
E3^r *stipulations*] Stipulations
F2^v *sture*] sture
F3^r [*om.*]] Will
G1^r vention] ~;

Copies examined:
*†RIA, Haliday Pamph. 20, no. 1: 158 × 94 mm, trimmed; tightly bound in volume of twelve 1712 political pamphlets (including Irish editions of *Some Reasons to Prove* and *Some Remarks on the Barrier Treaty*); some damage to some leaves; G4^v very dirty
†Houghton Library, Harvard University, *EC7 Sw551 711cdb: copy not physically examined; reproduction used; contemporary marginalia throughout; *ECCO* copy

Dublin edition (Waters, fifth), 1712g

Title: [within double rules 137 × 80.5 mm] The Conduct | OF THE | ALLIES, | AND OF THE | 𝕷𝖆𝖙𝖊 𝕸𝖎𝖓𝖎𝖘𝖙𝖗𝖞, | In Beginning and Carrying on the | Present War. | [rule] | —— *Partem tibi Gallia nostri* | *Eripuit: Partem duris Hispania bellis*: | *Pars jacet Hesperia: totoq; exercitus orbe* | *Te vincente perit. Terris fudisse cruorem* | *Quid juvat Arctois, Rhodano, Rhenoq; subactis?* | *Odimus accipitrem quia semper vivit in armis.* | —— *Victrix Provincia plorat.* | [rule] | 𝕿𝖍𝖊 𝕱𝖎𝖋𝖙𝖍 𝕰𝖉𝖎𝖙𝖎𝖔𝖓, 𝕮𝖔𝖗𝖗𝖊𝖈𝖙𝖊𝖉. | [rule] | *LONDON*: Printed by 𝕵𝖔𝖍𝖓 𝕸𝖔𝖗𝖕𝖍𝖊𝖜: | And Re printed by 𝕰𝖉𝖜𝖆𝖗𝖉 𝖂𝖆𝖙𝖊𝖗𝖘 in *Essex-street* | at the Corner of *Sycamore-Alley*, Dublin, 1712.

Collation: 8°: *A*^{4}, B–G^4

Pagination: *1–4*, 5–40, 39–54 ['26' set upside down]

Contents: A1ʳ title page; A1ᵛ blank; A2ʳ⁻ᵛ Preface; A3ʳ–G4ᵛ text (F1ʳ Eighth Article of the Grand Alliance)

Typography:
forty-three lines per page (F1ᵛ; some pages have forty-two lines), type-page 139 (147.5) × 80.5 mm, twenty lines of roman type 65 mm
preface, twenty lines of italic type 66 mm
D2ʳ, D2ᵛ(first three lines), F4ʳ (lines 23–35), F4ᵛ (except last ten lines), twenty lines of black-letter 65 mm
following pages have been set in italic: B2ʳ (except first two and last eight lines), B3ᵛ, B4ʳ (first fourteen lines), C3ᵛ (except first two and a half lines), C4ʳ (upper half), D2ᵛ (all but first three lines and last two lines), D3ʳ (except first two lines), D4ᵛ (lower half), E1ᵛ (except first six lines), E2ʳ (first six lines), E3ʳ (first fifteen and a half lines), F1ʳ (upper half), F2ᵛ, G3ʳ (lines 25–40), G3ᵛ (lines 8–37) (and occasional lines here and there)

Failures of catchwords to catch:
A2ᵛ THE] The
A3ʳ Trade] ~,
B3ᵛ narchy] ~,
C3ᵛ *been*] *so*
C4ᵛ with] with
D1ᵛ The] 𝕿𝖍𝖊
E2ᵛ ever] *ever*
E3ʳ *stipulations*] Stipulations
F2ᵛ *sture*] ~;
F4ʳ Towards] 𝕿𝖔𝖜𝖆𝖗𝖉𝖘
G1ʳ vention] ~;

Copy examined:
*†CUL, Hib.8.712.5/1: 153 × 98 mm, trimmed with occasional loss of direction line; in volume of fifteen mostly Dublin reprints of pamphlets 1699–1714

London edition, 1713

Title: [within double rules, 155 × 91 mm] THE | *CONDUCT* | OF THE | ALLIES, | AND OF THE | 𝕷𝖆𝖙𝖊 𝕸𝖎𝖓𝖎𝖘𝖙𝖗𝖞, | IN | Beginning and Carrying on

| THE | Present War. | [rule] | —— *Partem tibi Gallia nostri* | *Eripuit: partem duris Hispania bellis*: | *Pars jacet Hesperia: totoq; exercitus orbe* | *Te vincente perit. Terris fudisse cruorem* | *Quid juvat Arctois, Rhodano, Rhenoq; subactis?* | *Odimus accipitrem quia semper vivit in armis.* | —— *Victrix Provincia plorat.* | [rule] | 𝕿𝖍𝖊 𝕰𝖎𝖌𝖍𝖙𝖍 𝕰𝖉𝖎𝖙𝖎𝖔𝖓, 𝕮𝖔𝖗𝖗𝖊𝖈𝖙𝖊𝖉. | [rule] | *LONDON*, | Printed for *John Morphew*, near *Statio-* | *ners-Hall*, 1713.

Collation: 8°: A–F⁴

Pagination: *1–4*, 5–48

Contents: A1ʳ title page; A1ᵛ blank; A2ʳ⁻ᵛ preface; A3ʳ–F4ᵛ text (E2ʳ⁻ᵛ text of Eighth Article of the Grand Alliance); F4ᵛ postscript

Typography: forty-seven lines per page (C1ʳ; some pages forty-six lines), 168 (177.5) × 90 mm, twenty lines of roman type 72 mm; preface, twenty lines of italic type 82 mm

Failures of catchwords to catch:
E1ᵛ [*om.*]] HAVING

Copy examined:
*†CUL, Syn.7.71.49/3: 192 × 115 mm, trimmed; re-bound in paper binding
¶Houghton Library, Harvard University, *EC7.Sw551.711ch: copy not physically examined; reproduction used; *ECCO* copy

Emendations

53.20 have] 1711a; have of
53.22 hands of] 1711a; hands
    1711b, while reset, follows 1711a's reading. However, 1711c reset several lines on A7ᵛ to incorporate variant readings; at some point the 'of' in line 18 became detached and was added to the start of the reset line 17.
55.33 Subsidies] 1711a; Subsides
56.24 become] 1711a; became
63.24 Heads] 1711a; Hands
    Davis is surely right to read 'Heads' as the correct reading rather than 'Hands'.
64.21 *Marlborough*] 1711a; *Marlborugh*

74.16 he] 1711a; he he
78.9 Matter] 1711a; Matetr
82.10 to] 1711a; to to
91.34 Party] 1712c; Part
   Only one edition bears what seems to be the most appropriate reading here.
93.12 Peace,] 1711a; ~-
   Due to the reimposition of the lines on this page, the comma here and the end-line hyphen in 'Po-sture' in the next line evidently became reversed as it seems extremely unlikely that a compositor could misset the end of both lines in his stick.
93.12 Posture] 1711a; Po,sture
102.25 unexperienced] 1711a; unexperiened

Historical collation

47.1 THE PREFACE . . . *of the War.*] om. 1748
47.5 Ballads.] ~, 1711f, 1712d; ~^1712g
   The omitted period in 1712g could be just a consequence of poor printing.
47.5 *Person*] Man 1711a, 1711f, 1712d–e, 1738
48.5 *were*] was 1712g
48.23 *War*] Wars 1738
48.26 *we*] that we 1738
49.3 Neighbour] bour 1741c
   There is sufficient space left at the beginning of the line in 1741c for 'Neigh', indicating either that type fell out or that it did not print correctly (which may have been something to do with its position under the opening drop capital).
49.7 undertaken] undertakes 1711d [Yale copy]
   Davis (6.205) records this as a variant but I have not seen any other copy of 1711a–d bearing this.
49.14 in a few] in few 1712d
49.20 maturely] maentely [*sic*] 1711e
50.15 Interests] Interest 1712f–g
50.24 you] ye 1712d
50.33 but the Owner is] but is the Owner 1711f; but it is the Owner 1712d
   The spacing in 1711f is irregular, suggesting that the missetting was the result of correction once the type had been set; the reading in 1712d indicates that it was set from 1711f without reference to any other London edition.

51.1 But] Put 1711e

51.5 transports] transport 1738, 1741

51.5 of] from 1738a, 1738c, 1741

51.15 both] both sides 1711a, 1711f, 1712b–e, 1713, 1738, 1741, 1748

51.24 own] *om.* 1738, 1741

51.27 latter] later 1738, 1741

52.4 an Alliance] Alliance 1738, 1741

52.14 Author] Anthor 1711e

52.19 were got] wereg ot 1712a

52.22 those] these 1711f, 1712d

52.23 might in time vie] in time vie 1738a; in time vied 1738; in Time might vie 1741
  This seems to be an error in 1738a as the attempted correction in 1738c indicates. 1738b gives the correct reading.

53.1 of a Peace] of Peace 1712e, 1738, 1741

53.3 by] with 1738a, 1738c, 1741

53.13 the present War] this War 1711a, 1711f, 1712d–e, 1738, 1741

53.15 the Earl of *G——n*] a certain *Great Person* 1711a–b, 1711f, 1712a, 1712d–g, 1738, 1741
  1738a adds a footnote to indicate that this refers to Godolphin.

53.20 Lord High Treasurer] at the Head of the Treasury 1711a-b, 1711f, 1712a, 1712d–g, 1738, 1741

53.20 have] have of 1711c–d

53.22 hands of] hands 1711c–d

54.12 *the* French *Troops*] French *Troops* 1712d

54.20 *Country*] *County* 1738a, 1738c, 1741

55.1 then willing] willing 1711a, 1711f, 1712d–e, 1738

55.5 the Danger] Danger 1712b–c, 1713

55.24 Royal] *om.* 1711a, 1711f, 1712d–e, 1738, 1741

55.29 State] *Estate* 1712f–g

55.33 Subsidies] Subsides 1711b–e, 1712a *subsides* 1712f
  1711e fails to correct the error in 1711b–d.

56.1 their] the 1738a, 1738c, 1741

56.9 for] from 1738, 1741

56.10 rightly] *om.* 1711a–b, 1711f, 1712a, 1712d–g, 1738, 1741

56.15 *Austrian*] the *Austrian* 1711b, 1712a, 1712f–g

56.15 if] that if 1711a, 1711f, 1712d–e, 1738, 1741

56.15 for] of 1712d

56.24 become] became 1711b–d, 1712a

56.33 the Year 1688?] 1688? 1711a, 1711f, 1712d–e, 1738; ~. 1712g

57.6 offering at] offering 1748

57.14 particularly] particular 1712b–c, 1713

57.19 manifest] manifested 1711f, 1712d

57.24 of it] it 1738a, 1738c, 1741

57.26 Selves] Allies 1711b–c, 1712a, 1712f–g

    A probable eye-skip error made by the compositor setting 1711b from 1711a where 'selves' is directly above 'Allies'. It was corrected in 1711d.

57.32 come] came 1712g

57.33 had been] had had been 1711e, 1712b–c

    This was a consequence of miscatching between pages: B2ᵛ of 1711e ends on 'had' with 'been' as the catchword; B3ʳ begins 'had been'. 1713 corrects this.

58.10 manifest] minifest 1711e

58.13 that] this 1738, 1741

58.20 great] greater 1711f, 1712d

59.6 them] *om.* 1711e, 1712b–c, 1713

59.11 each] *om.* 1711e

59.22 Principal] Parties 1738, 1741

60.1 *the Nation*] a Nation 1711a, 1711f, 1712d–e, 1738, 1741

60.5 annual] aunual 1711e

60.16 begun] began 1738, 1741

60.22 Suffering] Sufferings 1741

60.27 That] I say, that 1738, 1741

60.29 extensive] entensive 1711e

60.35 War] Wars 1738a–b, 1741

60.37 so easy] being so easy 1738, 1741

60.37 as it is] as it 1712f; as it is, is 1712g

    1712g's compositor evidently tried to correct 1712f's garbled reading.

61.15 go on with] continue 1711a, 1711f, 1712d–e, 1738, 1741

    Swift presumably revised this to avoid the repetition of 'continue' and 'continuing' in successive sentences.

61.21 Successes] Success 1738, 1741

62.1 the determining] determine 1738, 1741

62.7 no other End] no other in it 1712g

62.9 *General*] G—*l* 1711e, 1712b–c, 1713; *C—l* 1748

62.11 working out] working 1711e, 1712b–c, 1713, 1748

62.13 all] *om.* 1738, 1741

62.23 Market] Mercat 1711f, 1712d

63.3 the] that 1738, 1741

63.24 Heads] Hands 1711b–e, 1712a–c, 1712f, 1713, 1738b; hands 1712g

64.17 And if . . .] [*new paragraph*] 1712b–c, 1713, 1748

64.21 Duke of *Marlborough's*] D— of *M—h's* 1711e, 1712b–c, 1713

64.28 introduced] introduced it 1711f, 1712d

65.29 hardly] not 1712e, 1738, 1741

> *Evidence of a separate stemma for 1712e?*

65.30 maintain] maintained 1748

66.5 were] are 1711e, 1712b–c, 1713, 1748

66.13 Perpetual.] ~^ 1711f, 1712d

> *An error by 1711f, which 1712d follows, although it does not capitalize the following 'in'.*

66.17 allows] allow 1738, 1741

66.19 here] there 1738, 1741

66.27 beside] besides 1712d, 1738, 1741

67.2 also are] are also 1711a, 1711f, 1712d–e, 1738, 1741

67.8 thinks] think 1738, 1741

67.22 were] are 1712e, 1738, 1741

> *Evidence of a separate stemma for 1712e?*

67.28 Armies] Arms 1712e, 1738, 1741

> *Evidence of a separate stemma for 1712e?*

68.15 Queen] Q—n 1711e, 1713; Qu—n 1712b–c, 1748

68.16 acknowledges] hath acknowledged 1738, 1741

68.16 Queen] Q—n 1711e; Qu—n 1712b–c, 1713, 1748

68.17 promises] promised 1738, 1741

68.18 his] that King's 1738, 1741

68.21 apprehend] apprehended 1712e, 1738, 1741

> *Evidence of a separate stemma for 1712e?*

68.27 hundred] thousand 1738, 1741

68.29 be] by 1712e

> *'e' is inked over 'y' in King's Inn copy.*

69.1 Guarantee; however our . . . in force.] Guarantee, how much soever the Necessities of the Kingdom may require it. 1711a–c, 1711f, 1712a, 1712d–g, 1738, 1741

70.5 Manufacturers] Manufactures 1712b–c, 1748

70.12 greatest] greatell 1712e

An inexplicable error: 'll' is not ligatured and these letters do not seem to have been broken or inadequately inked.

70.19 it is] is is 1712b–c

71.2 the Water] of the Water 1711e, 1712b–c, 1713, 1748

71.2 then had] had then 1711e, 1712b–c, 1713, 1748

71.8 Favourites] Favourers 1712e

Evidence of a separate stemma for 1712e? 1738 does not follow 1712e here.

71.30 further additional] further and additional 1712b–c, 1713, 1748

72.12 *M——'s*] *Marlborough's* 1711a–c, 1711f, 1712a, 1712d–g, 1738, 1741; *M—h's* 1748

72.13 past. The Troops . . . of sixty thousand:] past. 1711a, 1711f, 1712d–e, 1738, 1741; past: 1711b–c, 1712a, 1712f; past; 1712g

72.19 And it is well known, that the Battles of *Hochstet* and *Ramellies* were fought with not above Fifty thousand Men on a side.] *om.* 1711a, 1711f, 1712d–e, 1738, 1741; And . . . *Remellies* . . . side. 1711c

72.22 *Marlborough*] *Marlburgh* 1711c–d

1712a does not follow 1711c here.

72.22 entered] entred 1711a–b, 1712a, 1711f, 1738b

72.31 of] for 1738, 1741

72.32 Queen] Q—n 1711e, 1712b–c, 1713; Qu—n 1748

73.1 in Justice] *om.* 1711e, 1712b–c, 1713, 1748

73.13 Importance?] ~. 1711a–c, 1711f, 1712a, 1712e, 1712f–g, 1738, 1741

The compositor of 1712d evidently noticed that this was *a question and so diverged from 1711f's reading.*

73.19 *Maritime Ally*] Maritime Ally 1711a–b, 1711f, 1712a, 1712d

73.24 *Guarantees of our Succession*] Guarantees of our Succession 1711a–b, 1711f, 1712a, 1712d

73.25 not] got 1748a–b; *om.* 1748c–d

1748c–d evidently attempted to emend 1748a–b's problematic reading.

74.5 lies] were 1738, 1741

74.14 K---g *C*——*s*] King *Charles* 1711a–c, 1711f, 1712a, 1712d–e, 1738a, 1741; King Charles 1712f; *King Charles* 1712g

74.16 he] he he 1711b–d

74.17 I shall add . . . K---g *C*——*s* . . . his Grant.] I shall add . . . King *Charles* . . . his Grant. 1711b–c, 1712a; I shall add . . . King Charles . . . his Grant. 1712f; *I shall add . . . King Charles . . . his Grant.* 1712g; *om.* 1711a, 1711f, 1712d–e, 1738, 1741

74.23 this] the 1712c, 1713

75.8 hundred thousand] hundred thousand Crowns 1748

75.18 at our] to our 1712c

75.22 grievous] *om.* 1711a–b, 1711f, 1712d–g, 1738, 1741

75.24 that War] the War 1712d

76.3 *single Person*] single Person 1711a–b, 1711f, 1712a, 1712d

77.3 Employment] Business 1711a–c, 1711f, 1712a, 1712d–g, 1738, 1741

77.8 yet] *om.* 1748

77.28 proposed to] proposed by 1748c–d

77.31 First,] *om.* 1738a, 1738c, 1741

78.2 whereof] thereof 1741

78.8 immediately] *om.* 1738, 1741

78.9 Matter] Matetr 1711c–d

79.7 invaded?] ∼. 1711e, 1712b–c, 1713

79.19 particular] particulars 1712c; *om.* 1738, 1741

Wheeler reported another 1712c variant on this page (the omission of 'time' in 'But in a short time') but I have been unable to locate a copy bearing this reading.

79.23 *G*——*y*] *Galway* 1738, 1741

79.25 on the] of the 1748

80.26 G——l] General 1738, 1741

81.3 G————n] *Godolphin* 1711a–c, 1711f, 1712a, 1712d–e, 1738, 1741; Godolphin 1712f–g

81.17 carry] carried 1738, 1741

81.28 Contingent] *Contingent* 1711b, 1712a

Strictly speaking, not a substantive variant but one of only a few variants present in 1711b but not in 1711a or 1711c–d.

81.30 spare] possibly spare 1711a–b, 1711f, 1712a, 1712d–g, 1738, 1741

81.31 be true] true 1711e, 1712b, 1713; is true 1748
1748, following 1712b, attempts to correct its erroneous reading here.
81.36 even] *om.* 1712g
82.10 to] to to 1711c–d
It is surely only a coincidence that 'the Stupidity arising from the coldness of our Climate' follows this compositorial error. It is not clear how cold early December 1711 actually was.
82.17 I] it 1738, 1741
82.19 the People] our People 1738, 1741
82.24 my Lord *G*————*n*] a certain *Great Man* 1711a, 1711f, 1712d–e, 1738, 1741
82.26 him] *om.* 1712c
83.2 so] some 1712d
83.2 an Alliance] in the Alliance 1712d
83.3 Q——n] Queen 1738, 1741
83.5 Her Majesty's] Her M—y's 1711e, 1712b–c, 1713, 1748
83.9 Ambition] Power 1738, 1741
83.11 *M.*] *Marlborough* 1738, 1741; *M—h* 1748
83.23 *Powers*] Princes 1711a, 1711f, 1712d–e, 1738, 1741
83.23 G——l] General 1738, 1741
83.25 unmeasurable] unanswerable 1711a, 1711f, 1712d–e
1738 diverges from 1712e here.
84.2 Winter Foraging] Winter–Foraging 1711a, 1711f, 1712d, 1712e, 1738a, 1738c, 1741; *Winter–Foraging* 1711b, 1712a
84.10 were] *om.* 1738, 1741
84.17 the sole] sole 1738, 1741
84.33 Quota's] Quotas 1711a, 1711f, 1712d–e
85.19 *W*————*n*] *Wharton* 1738, 1741
85.20 it was indeed] indeed it was 1711e, 1712b–c, 1713, 1748
85.22 General] G—l 1711e, 1712b–c, 1713, 1748
85.23 Ministry] M—y 1711e, 1712b–c, 1713, 1748
85.25 skreen] Skrew 1711f
Evidence that 1712d, which otherwise follows 1711f in substantive readings, had access to a London edition – or perhaps an adventurous compositor?
85.26 Opportunity] Opportunity that fell 1711a, 1711f, 1712d–e, 1738, 1741

86.1 So] THUS 1738, 1741

86.1 Queen] Q— 1711e, 1712b–c, 1713, 1748

86.2 *wexed*] *waxed* 1711a, 1711f, 1712d–e, 1712g, 1738, 1741
  'wexed' is recorded as an obsolete form of 'waxed'; it is possible that it represents
  an accidental change made in the setting of 1712b, although in quoting what
  appears to be a proverb, Swift may have wanted an archaic spelling.

86.4 immediate] immediately the 1711e, 1712b–c, 1713, 1748

86.5 Her] *om.* 1711e, 1712b–c, 1713, 1748

87.2 M——y] Majesty 1738, 1741

87.5 Q——n] Queen 1738, 1741

87.6 *It is better to dwell in a corner of the House–top, than with a brawling*
  Woman in a wide House.] *It is better to live on the House Tops, than with a*
  scolding Woman in a large House. 1711a–b, 1711f, 1712d–e, 1738, 1741
  Presumably Swift's initial memory of Proverbs 21:9 (or indeed 25:24) proved
  faulty.

87.10 Queen] Qu–n 1711e, 1712b–c, 1748; Q—n 1713

87.15 became] become 1711e, 1712b–c, 1713, 1748

87.15 *G——l*] *General* 1738, 1741

87.16 *General*] *G—l* 1711e, 1712b–c, 1713, 1748

87.16 *G——l*] *General* 1738, 1741

87.18 M——y] Majesty 1738, 1741

88.10 among] amongst 1712d

88.28 in] of 1748c–d

89.3 Treaty of Peace] Treaty 1711e, 1712b–c, 1713, 1748

89.7 Navigation] Navigations 1711e, 1712b–c, 1713, 1748

90.6 great] greater 1712g

90.6 to] *om.* 1712d

90.12 well] well as 1738a, 1741

90.23 on] out 1712d

90.25 and] while 1738, 1741

91.7 likewise] likeways 1712d

91.14 in] at 1711a–b, 1711f, 1712a, 1712d–g, 1738, 1741

91.21 at] at the Treaty of 1711a, 1711f, 1712d–e, 1738, 1741

91.23 but say nothing. . . . those Demands] *om.* 1712g
  Eye-skip from the first and second uses of 'Demands' by the compositor of
  1712g.

91.24 Preliminary Articles] 𝔓𝔯𝔢𝔩𝔦𝔪𝔦𝔫𝔞𝔯𝔶 𝔄𝔯𝔱𝔦𝔠𝔩𝔢𝔰 1712f; preliminary Articles 1712g; Articles in that Treaty 1711a, 1711f, 1712d–e, 1738, 1741

91.34 Party] Part 1711a–f, 1712a–b, 1712d–g, 1713, 1738, 1741

92.30 ruins] must have ruined 1738, 1741

92.33 had] have 1738, 1741

93.12 Peace,] ~– 1711b–d

93.12 Posture] Po,sture 1711b–d

93.19 Grand] *om.* 1711a

93.19 founded. [*footnote marker; asterisk in copy text*]] founded. 1711a, 1711f, 1712d–e, 1738, 1741

93.27 Expences] Expence 1711e, 1712b–c, 1713, 1748

93 [footnote]] *om.* 1711a, 1711f, 1712d–e, 1738, 1741

94.30 than] thar 1711e, 1712b–c

Evidence that 1712b–c used existing sheers from 1711e.

96.3 would pay Interest for] were sufficient to pay Interest 1738, 1741

96.6 lasts] lasted 1712e; be to last 1738, 1741

Evidence of a separate stemma for 1712e?

96.11 fourth] sixth 1738, 1741

96.30 ever] never 1711f, 1712d

96.32 any thing] anythink 1711e, 1712b–c

97.15 hang] hung 1738, 1741

97.21 Are] Is 1738, 1741

98.2 used] were wont 1738a, 1738c, 1741

98.3 they would . . . Peace; and] *om.* 1712g

A straightforward eye-skip of a single line by 1712g's compositor (proof, incidentally, that it was set from 1712f and not vice versa).

100.6 Grandsons,] ~. 1711a–b, 1712a [not in 1711f]

100.11 Millions] Million 1738a–b, 1741

100.12 *Spain,*] ~. 1712e

101.2 *the heavy*] heavy 1711a–b, 1711f, 1712a, 1712d–g, 1738, 1741

101.5 it is] its 1738a, 1738c, 1741

102.9 For an . . . Free Countries.] *om.* 1711a, 1711f, 1712d–e, 1738, 1741

102.20 not] not not 1712c

102.23 G—l] General 1738, 1741

102.25 unexperienced] unexperiened 1711c–d

103.24 especially] specially 1711a–b, 1711f, 1712a, 1712e–g, 1738, 1741
1712d reads 'especially'.

104.14 Q—n] Queen 1738, 1741

104.16 made] given 1711a, 1711f, 1712d–e, 1738, 1741

105.4 returns] return 1738, 1741

105.4 gets] get 1738, 1741

105.7 is] be 1738, 1741

105.8 are] be 1738, 1741

105.28 would] *om.* 1711a, 1711f, 1712d–e, 1738, 1741

106.7 *POSTSCRIPT* . . . 38th . . . entire Legislature.] *POSTCRIPT* . . .
21st . . . entire Legislature. 1711e, 1712b–c, 1713; ERRATA in the
Second Edition of the this Book, which the Reader is desired to Correct
with his Pen. Page 20. l. 30. for *our Allies,* read our *Selves.* 1711c; *om.*
1711a–b, 1711f, 1712a, 1712d–g, 1738, 1741, 1748
*1711e, 1712b–c, 1713 amend the page reference accordingly. The erratum in
1711c refers to the second edition but is as applicable to 1711c as 1711b.*

106.17 I have . . . this Discourse] *om.* 1711a–c, 1711e–f, 1712a–g, 1713,
1738, 1741, 1748

Word division (compounds only)

Copy text
50.1 over-pressed
50.26 Common-wealth
57.4 Grand-son
67.9 like-wise
69.24 when-ever
74.23 Re-coinage
85.12 *over-thrown*
87.7 *House-top*
91.7 like-wise
95.14 some-thing

Edited text
95.19 Coffee-house

SOME ADVICE HUMBLY OFFER'D TO THE MEMBERS OF THE OCTOBER CLUB: TEXTUAL ACCOUNT

On 18 January 1712, Swift wrote to Stella that 'I have made [Charles] Ford copy out a small pamphlet, and send it to the press, that I might not be known for author; 'tis *A Letter to the October Club*, if ever you heard of such a thing' (Williams, *JSt*, p. 466). Swift's subterfuge seems to have worked, much to his delight; at dinner on 21 January, his printer, John Barber, showed him a copy 'which he said was sent him by an unknown hand; I commended it mightily; he never suspected me; 'tis a twopenny pamphlet' (p. 468). The work, presumably printed by Barber (Rivington, p. 248), was advertised in the 20–2 January issue of *The Post Boy* and was published by Morphew on 22 January (hereafter 1712a). It is not recorded in the SR. Swift continued to revel in the mystery surrounding its authorship. On 23 January, he was present at a dinner where Henry St John read 'a great deal' of the work to Robert Harley: 'they all commended it to the skies . . . and they began a health to the author'. According to Swift, Harley declared it to be the work of Charles Davenant, 'which is his [Harley's] cant when he suspects me. But I carried the matter very well' (Williams, *JSt*, p. 470). Five days later, however, and Swift was beginning to rue his ruse. While *Conduct of the Allies* was proving an extraordinary runaway bestseller, *Some Advice to the October Club* was not selling:

> I know not the reason; for it is finely written, I assure you; and, like a true author, I grow fond of it, because it does not sell: you know that it is usual to writers, to condemn the judgment of the world: if I had hinted it to be mine, every body would have bought it, but it is a great secret.
>
> (pp. 474–5)

By 1 February, however, sales picked up but Swift feared that its 'fame will hardly reach Ireland' (Williams, *JSt*, p. 478).

At some point, perhaps as an attempt to promote sales or as demand began to pick up, Barber reissued the work bearing a slightly reset title page claiming itself to be a 'Second Edition Corrected' (hereafter 1712b). These 'corrections' amounted to two substantive emendations on A6^r and A7^v (the second of which is clearly a correction) and three changes of punctuation and one lower-casing on A7^v and A8^r; the erroneous 'he' on A2^v and 'Negoitators' on A3^r remained untouched. Optically collating the first and second 'editions' reveals that four pages from the inner forme (A2^r, A3^v, A7^v, A8^r) were re-set, although the original lineation was maintained throughout; the remaining pages from the inner forme were not re-set. This suggests one of three possible scenarios:

- the corrections and re-setting were made during the printing of the edition, at which point Barber added a new title page;
- the corrections and re-setting were made during the printing of the edition; however, not all the corrected sheets were sold as part of the 'first edition' and Barber reissued the work with a revised title page. (That none of the first editions examined bear any of the corrected readings and that Barber explicitly described the 'second edition' as corrected would seem to argue against such a possibility);
- Barber finished printing the first edition but kept standing type in formes; corrections were made and type re-set. (The size of Barber's printing house and the bibliographical evidence for the printing of *Conduct* suggests this is a feasible suggestion.)

The work was reprinted in Dublin the following year by Cornelius Carter, who produced, for him, a reasonably well-printed edition (hereafter 1713); it followed 1712a closely, correcting the most obvious errors but varying the italicization, capitalization, punctuation and spelling on numerous occasions. None of its substantive differences seem to be more than a misreading of 1712a.

'Advice to the October Club' is listed in the catalogue of Swift's political pamphlets compiled by Charles Ford in 1733 (Woolley, *Corr.*, vol. III, p. 699). The text was reprinted in 1738 by Faulkner in volume VI of his octavo (hereafter 1738a) and duodecimo (hereafter 1738b) editions of Swift's *Works* (TS, nos. 42, 50); Faulkner characteristically 'improved' Swift's words ('although' for 'though', 'it is' for ''tis') and expanded all elisions. In the same year, the work was included in the second volume of Charles Davis's London edition of Swift's *Political Tracts*, a near line-by-line reprint of Faulkner's octavo edition (TS, no. 25(7); hereafter 1738c). In his edition, Faulkner provided an explicatory 'Publisher's Preface' based on information provided by 'an Intimate of the supposed Author': '[t]his Discourse . . . would have not been generally understood without some Explanation, which we have now endeavoured to give' (1738a, p. 122). This preface was reproduced with all subsequent reprintings of the work, to the extent that Temple Scott described it erroneously as a preface to 'the second edition' (Temple Scott, vol. V, p. 213); Davis, however, relegated the preface to an appendix (vol. VI, pp. 187–8). We have not included this preface in this edition. The text also appeared in volume VI of Faulkner's octavo edition of 1741 (TS, no. 44); there are only a handful of accidental variants.

Some Advice was reprinted by Boyer in his 1718 edition of *Political State* (vol. III, pp. 122–31) where it was attributed to Lord Harcourt. This copy has not been collated.

As 1712b, notwithstanding its claim to be a 'second edition', is in fact a corrected reissue of 1712a, I have taken 1712b as copy text. 1712b has also been collated against 1713, 1738a, 1741 and Davis; the variants have been cross-checked with 1738b–c.

Copy text: NLS, L.C.3339 (6)

References: TS, no. 557. Davis, vol VI, pp. 67–80. Woolley, 'Canon', no. 12. *ESTC* T49240 (first edition, listing thirty-eight copies); T160155 (second edition, listing thirteen copies, including a 'contributor match' copy at TCC; however, this item (shelfmark RW.68.19 (14)) is in fact a first edition); N43969 (Dublin reprint, listing two copies; the NLI copy (LO. Swift.109) is wanting as of May 2005). Rothschild Library, nos. 2034–5.

London edition, 1712a

Title: [Within double-rules 169 × 86 mm] SOME | ADVICE | Humbly Offer'd to the | MEMBERS | OF THE | *OCTOBER CLUB*, | IN A | LETTER | FROM A | Person of Honour. | [double rule] | *LONDON*, | Printed for *John Morphew*, near *Stationers-* | *Hall*, 1712. Price 2 *d.*

Collation: 8°: A^8

Pagination: 1–2, 3–16

Contents: A1^r title page; A1^v blank; A2^r–A8^v text

Typography: thirty-six lines per page (A5^r), type-page 145.5 (157) × 78.5, twenty lines of roman type 80.5 mm

Failures of catchwords to catch:
none

Copies examined:
*†BL, T.1107(19): 185 × c.119 mm, trimmed; in volume of thirteen early eighteenth-century works; re-bound 1978
*†§Bodl, Pamph. 300 (21): 196 × 121 mm, trimmed; in volume of twenty-nine miscellaneous 1712 printed items [optically collated with NLS, L. C.3339 (6)]
*†CUL, Williams 353: 190 × 112 mm, trimmed; re-bound
*†NLS, 2.241(11): 163.5 × c.102 mm, trimmed with partial or complete loss of final full line of text on A3^{r-v}, A5^r, A6^{r-v}; in volume of eleven miscellaneous printed items 1712
* TCC, RW.62.62: 211 × 126 mm, unopened; disbound

Re-issue of London edition, 1712b

Title: [Within double rules, 166 × 88 mm] SOME | ADVICE | Humbly Offr'd to the | MEMBERS | OF THE | *OCTOBER CLUB*, | IN A | LETTER | FROM A | Person of Honour. | [rule] | 𝕿𝖍𝖊 𝕾𝖊𝖈𝖔𝖓𝖉 𝕰𝖉𝖎𝖙𝖎𝖔𝖓 𝕮𝖔𝖗𝖗𝖊𝖈𝖙𝖊𝖉. | [rule] | *LONDON*, | Printed for *John Morphew*, near *Stationers-* | *Hall*, 1712. Price 2 *d.*

Collation: 8°: A^8

Pagination: 1–2, 3–16

Contents: A1^r title page; A1^v blank; A2^r–A8^v text

Typography: thirty-six lines per page (A5^r), type-page 147.5 (157) × 80, twenty lines of roman type 82 mm

Failures of catchwords to catch:
none

Copy examined:
*†§NLS, L. C.3339 (6): 180 x116 mm, trimmed [optically collated with Bodl, Pamph. 300 (21)]

Dublin reprint, 1713

Title: [within single rule] | SOME | ADVICE | Humbly ofler'd[*sic*] to the | MEMBERS | OF THE | *OCTOBER CLUB*, | IN A | LETTER | FROM A | Person of Honour. | *LONDON* | Printed, and Re-printed in *Dublin* by | *C. Carter.* 1713.

Collation: 8°: A^4, B^4

Pagination: *1–2*, 3–16

Contents: $A1^r$ title page; $A1^v$ blank; $A2^r$-$B4^v$ text

Typography: thirty-three lines per page

Failures of catchwords to catch:
$A3^r$: Lord,] ~ˆ
$B3^r$: Ill] ill

Copy examined:
†University of Illinois at Urbana-Champaign, × 942.069 P7591 no. 17: copy not physically examined; reproduction used; collation has been inferred

Emendations

110.20 be] 1713; he
    Presumably an eye-skip, given the 'he' two words previously.
111.7 *Negotiators*] 1713; *Negoitators*
115.15 them;] 1712a; ~ˆ
    The semi-colon is already straying out into the margins of the copies of 1712a that I have examined, so it presumably simply failed to print in this particular

*copy of 1712b (the last letters of each of the lines below this line in this copy of
1712b have also failed to print fully).*

Historical collation

109.2 SOME ADVICE, &c.] SOME ADVICE Humbly offered to
the MEMBERS OF THE *OCTOBER* CLUB 1738

110.7 Counterpart] Counter Part 1738a, 1738c, 1741; Counter-Part
1738b

110.8 Though] Although 1738, 1741

110.16 *W—nds—r*] *Windsor* 1738, 1741

110.18 M———r] Minister 1738, 1741

110.20 be] he 1712a–b

111.4 *W—nds—r*] *Windsor* 1738, 1741

111.9 L—ds] Lords 1738, 1741

111.12 C———rt] Court 1738, 1741

111.13 P—ns—ns] Pensions 1738, 1741

111.19 C——— J ———] Chief Justice 1738, 1741

111.20 though] although 1738, 1741

111.28 though] although 1738, 1741

112.9 M—n—ys] Ministries 1738, 1741

112.12 M———ry] Ministry 1738, 1741

112.14 tho'] although 1738, 1741

112.19 M———ry] Ministry 1738, 1741

112.22 M———rs] Ministers 1738, 1741

112.24 tho'] although 1738, 1741

112.25 'till] until 1738, 1741

112.26 though] although 1738, 1741

112.37 'tis an] it is a 1738, 1741

113.6 'till] until 1738, 1741

113.15 'tis] it is 1738, 1741

113.25 hoped] hope 1713

113.32 your selves] yourselves 1738, 1741

114.3 ourselves would have] our selves have 1713

114.5 though] although 1738, 1741

114.8 time be effectually removed] Time effectually be removed 1738,
1741

114.19 though] although 1738, 1741
115.8 Scars] Fears 1712a; 1713
   Presumably a simple misreading of the manuscript.
115.18 Qu——n] Q----n 1713; QUEEN 1738, 1741
116.4 tho'] although 1738, 1741
116.22 Qu—n] Q--n 1713; QUEEN 1738, 1741
116.25 *tho'*] *although* 1738, 1741
116.28 Ourselves] our selves 1713
117.11 that Power] the Power 1738, 1741
117.25 it] at 1712a
117.33 should] would 1713
118.6 best Information] Information 1713
118.9 M———ry] Ministry 1738, 1741
119.3 trampled] trample 1713
119.3 *Treasures*] *Treasure* 1738, 1741
119.10 till] until 1738, 1741

Word division (compounds only)

Copy text
none

Edited text
none

SOME REMARKS ON THE BARRIER TREATY: TEXTUAL ACCOUNT

Towards the end of *The Conduct of the Allies*, Swift wrote that he might 'perhaps consider it [the Barrier Treaty], at a proper Occasion, in a *Discourse* by it self' (see p. 91). Ehrenpreis believes that Swift was at work on such a '*Discourse*' as early as 7 February 1712 (vol. II, p. 538, citing Williams, *JSt*, p. 484). On 12 February, Swift told Stella that he had dined with his printer, John Barber, 'to consult with him about some Pap[e]rs Ld Tr— gave me last night'; the following day, he dined with Erasmus Lewis 'to consult about some Observations on the Barrier Treaty' (Williams, *JSt*, pp. 486–7). By 16 February, Swift had dined again with Barber 'to finish something I am doing about the Barrier Treaty but it is not quite done' and it was this that probably kept him 'very busy' for six hours the following evening (pp. 489–90). By 19 February, the work was being printed and on 20 February, he visited Barber's printing house to correct sheets 'wch must be finished to morrow' (p. 492). That same day, Barber entered the work in the SR and it was published (hereafter 1712a) by Morphew (who signed the SR entry on Barber's behalf) two days later on 22 February (Woolley, 'Canon', endpaper). At some point, Barber reissued the work with a partially re-set title page declaring the work to be a second edition (hereafter 1712b); however, apart from altering the parentheses around the page numbers on B3^v–B4^v from square to round, all the examined copies of the re-issue are identical with the copies of 1712a. In fact, three clear typographical errors are present in all the copies examined ('odly' on B4^v is not an error but an obscure variant of 'oddly'; all the 1712 and 1738 editions retain it). It is also worth noting that what appears to be an error on B2^v ('ouly' for 'only') in the *ECCO* facsimile of BL, 8122.aaa.10(3) is in fact a consequence of damage to the surface of the paper.

The title page of the London edition of *Some Remarks on the Barrier Treaty* declared the work to be 'By the AUTHOR of *The Conduct of the*

ALLIES' and so it was not surprising that the work should be reprinted by the same Edinburgh and Dublin printers as had reprinted *Conduct of the Allies* a few months earlier. Robert Freebairn's Edinburgh edition (hereafter 1712c) followed 1712a–b in italicization and layout but altered capitalization, spellings and punctuation (principally adding extra commas); there were also a number of compositional and printing errors (missing words and spaces, letters fallen out or poorly inked) as well as some substantive variants, nearly all of which seem to be symptoms of haste or poor proofing rather than alternative readings. (The rendering of 1712a–b's 'Scotch' to 'Scots', however, is an honourable exception.) In contrast, John Hyde's Dublin edition (1712d) closely followed the italicization, layout, capitalization and punctuation of the London edition, although there were some differences in spelling – most notably: omitting the 'e' in 'money' and an 'r' in 'garrison' – which, as the same spellings appear in Hyde's edition of *Conduct*, perhaps indicate a 'house style'. There are a handful of substantive differences between 1712d and 1712a–b although I do not feel that these warrant a hypothesis of an alternative stemma from the London editions; Hyde also freely changed numerals into words and vice versa. Edward Waters's Dublin edition ('Re-printed by *E. Waters*'; hereafter 1712e) is a sloppy production, replete with poor inking, misaligned type, misspellings and missettings. It strays much further from the accidentals of the London edition but, as it includes certain accidental readings that were introduced in the Hyde edition (most notably the concluding of the first paragraph with a period rather than a question mark), it seems likely that it was set from Hyde's edition rather than the London one. (However, if this was the case, Waters may still have had a copy of the London edition to hand as he rejected Hyde's 'demolishing *Dunkirk*' in favour of the London edition's 'demolishing of *Dunkirk*'.) For some reason – possibly demand, possibly marketing, possibly embarrassment at the number of mistakes – Waters re-issued the work under a new imprint ('Printed for *J. Morphew*; And Re-printed and Sold by *E. Waters*'; hereafter 1712f), mixing a completely re-set sheet A, which corrected all the misprints on that sheet, with existing sheets of B (probably), C and D. (B is missing from the only copy that survives, but re-set A ends at the same point as the original A, suggesting that B was uncorrected.)

Ehrenpreis suggested that *Some Remarks* 'failed to enjoy a particularly wide sale' (vol. II, p. 538) but this would seem to run counter both to the number of copies that survive of the London edition and the three Dublin and one Edinburgh reprints. Moreover, Davis quotes one irate response to the work complaining how Swift's supporters were buying 'his Libels by Dozens, and Dispers[ing] them about the Country to Poyson the Minds of the People' (vol. VI, p. xv).

The work was reprinted in 1738 by Faulkner in volume VI of his octavo (hereafter 1738a) and duodecimo (hereafter 1738b) editions of Swift's *Works* (TS, nos. 42, 50); in the same year, it was included in the second volume of Charles Davis's London edition of Swift's *Political Tracts* (TS, no. 25(7); hereafter 1738c). The 1738 editions (which vary from one another in only a few substantive cases) made numerous changes to spelling, punctuation, italicization, and capitalization; they also 'improved' some of Swift's word choices ('although' for 'though', 'until' for 'till'). The text also appeared in volume VI of Faulkner's octavo edition of 1741 (TS, no. 44), following 1738a except for minor differences in spelling, punctuation, capitalization and hyphenation. Consequently, while it has been collated, it has not been included in the collation table below. This edition adopts 1712a as its copy text (although, as previously indicated, 1712b is effectively identical to 1712a); it has been collated with 1712c–f, 1738a (with the 1738a variants cross-checked with 1738b–c) and Davis (who, as usual, silently expanded all elisions). Obvious misspellings (i.e. when it is self-evident what the correct word should be) in 1712c–f and changes between numerals and letters (e.g. III for 'the third') in 1712c–f and 1738 have also not been included.

Copy text: CUL, Williams 358 (1712a)

References: TS, nos. 559 (London), 560 (Dublin, Hyde), 561 (Dublin, Morphew & Waters), 562 (Edinburgh). Davis, vol. VI, pp. 81–117. Woolley, 'Canon', no. 14. *ESTC* T49371 (London, listing 114 copies), T49372 (London 'second edition', listing thirty-eight copies), T160283 (Edinburgh, listing thirteen copies), T160282 (Dublin, Hyde, listing eight copies, although Bodl copy is currently missing), T160280 (Dublin, Morphew & Waters, listing four copies), T207973 (Dublin, Waters, listing one copy, and including erroneous reference to TS). Rothschild Library, no. 2036.

London edition, 1712a

Title: [within double rules, 169 × 89 mm] SOME | REMARKS | ON THE | 𝔅arrier 𝔗reaty, | BETWEEN | HER MAJESTY | AND THE | States-General. | [rule] | By the AUTHOR of | *The Conduct of the ALLIES.* | [rule] | To which are added, | The said BARRIER-TREATY, | with the Two Separate Articles; | Part of the Counter-Project; The | Sentiments of Prince *Eugene* and | Count *Sinzendorf,* upon the said | Treaty; And a Representation of | the *English* Merchants at *Bruges.* | [rule] | *LONDON,* | Printed for *John Morphew,* near *Stationers-* | *Hall,* 1712. Price 6 *d.*

Collation: 8°: A–F⁴

Pagination: *1–4,* 5–48

Contents: A1ʳ title page; A1ᵛ blank; A2ʳ⁻ᵛ preface; A3ʳ–C3ʳ text; C3ᵛ–E1ʳ Treaty; E1ᵛ–E2ᵛ Separate article; E2ᵛ–E3ʳ Second separate article; E3ᵛ–F1ʳ Articles of the Counter-Project; F1ᵛ–F3ᵛ Sentiments of Prince Eugene and Count Sinzendorf; F3ᵛ–F4ᵛ Representation of English Merchants.

Typography: thirty-three lines per page (C2ʳ), type-page 155 (165) × 87 mm, twenty lines of roman type 94 mm; preface, twenty lines of italic type 94 mm; Counter-Project, twenty lines of roman type 82.5 mm

Failures of catchwords to catch:
A2ᵛ SOME] *Some*
B3ʳ rably,] ∼;
C3ʳ *The*] The
D4ʳ [*om.*]] XIX. There
D4ᵛ Crown] ∼,

Copies examined:
*†§BL, 8122.aaa.10(3): 186 × 118 mm, trimmed; in volume of ten early eighteenth-century works; rebound 1932; *ECCO* copy
*BL, T.1107(23): 197 × 116 mm, trimmed; in volume of thirteen early eighteenth-century works; re-bound 1978
*§Bodl, G. Pamph. 825 (2): 177 × 114 mm, trimmed, with occasional loss of running titles; in volume of ten early eighteenth-century pamphlets, including first edition of *Conduct of the Allies* (optically collated with BL, 8122.aaa.10(3))

*Bodl, Pamph. 302 (8): 195 × 119 mm, trimmed; in volume of thirty-one c.1712 pamphlets, including sixth edition of *Conduct of the Allies*
*TCC, RW.62.63: 210 × 134 mm, untrimmed; stitched; no longer unopened as indicated in Rothschild Library, no. 2036
*§CUL, Williams 358: 189 × 119 mm, trimmed; re-bound (optically collated with BL, 8122.aaa.10(3))

Re-issue of London edition, 1712b

Title: [within double rules, 167 × 87 mm] SOME | REMARKS | ON THE | 𝕭𝖆𝖗𝖗𝖎𝖊𝖗 𝕿𝖗𝖊𝖆𝖙𝖞, | BETWEEN | HER MAJESTY | AND THE | States-General. | [rule] | By the AUTHOR of | *The Conduct of the ALLIES.* | [rule] | To which are added, | The said BARRIER-TREATY, | with the Two *Separate Articles*; Part of | the *Counter-Project*; The *Sentiments* of | Prince *Eugene* and Count *Sinzendorf*, | upon the said *Treaty*, And a *Represen-* | *tation* of | the *English* Merchants at *Bruges*. | [rule] | 𝕿𝖍𝖊 𝕾𝖊𝖈𝖔𝖓𝖉 𝕰𝖉𝖎𝖙𝖎𝖔𝖓. | [rule] | *LONDON,* | Printed for *John Morphew*, near *Stationers-* | *Hall*, 1712. Price 6 *d.*

Collation: 8°: A–F⁴

Pagination: *1–4*, 5–48

Contents: A1ʳ title page; A1ᵛ blank; A2ʳ⁻ᵛ preface; A3ʳ–C3ʳ text; C3ᵛ–E1ʳ Treaty; E1ᵛ–E2ᵛ Separate article; E2ᵛ–E3ʳ Second separate article; E3ᵛ–F1ʳ Articles of the Counter-Project; F1ᵛ–F3ᵛ Sentiments of Prince Eugene and Count Sinzendorf; F3ᵛ–F4ᵛ Representation of English Merchants

Typography: thirty-three lines per page (C2ʳ), type-page 155 (165) × 86 mm, twenty lines of roman type 93.5 mm; preface, twenty lines of italic type 93 mm; Counter-Project, twenty lines of roman type 81.5 mm

Failures of catchwords to catch:
A2ᵛ SOME] *Some*
B3ʳ rably,] ~;
C3ʳ *The*] The
D4ʳ [*om.*]] XIX. There

Copies examined:
*§Bodl, 8° K 102(6) Linc: 189 × 122 mm, trimmed; in volume of seven 1711–12 items on the war, including *Conduct of the Allies* (first edition); poorly folded, leading to poorly aligned pages; missing catchword 'ways' on E4^v (optically collated with BL, 8122.aaa.10(3)); one of registration copies deposited at Stationers' Hall (Chalmers, p. 424)
*§Bodl, Radcl. e. 133(7): 190 × 102 mm, trimmed; in volume of thirteen early eighteenth-century printed items (optically collated with BL, 8122.aaa.10(3))
*CUL, 7540.d.45 (4):186 × 112 mm, trimmed, with partial loss of first characters in lower half of C3^v; in volume of twenty-three early eighteenth-century printed tracts, including second edition of *New Way of Selling Places*
§CUL, Rel.f.1b.10: copy not physically examined; reproduction used (optically collated with BL, 8122.aaa.10(3))
§Senate House Library, University of London, [G. L.] 1712: copy not physically examined; reproduction used; ECCO copy (optically collated with BL, 8122.aaa.10(3))

Edinburgh edition, 1712c

Title: SOME | REMARKS | ON THE | 𝔅arrier 𝔗reaty, | BETWEEN | HER MAJESTY | AND THE | States-General. | [rule] | By the AUTHOR of | *The Conduct of the ALLIES*. | [rule] | To which are added, | The said BARRIER-TREATY, | with the two Separate Articles; Part of the | Counter-Project; The Sentiments of Prince | *Eugene* and Count *Sinzendorf*, upon the said | Treaty; And a Representation of the *En-* | *glish* Merchants at *Bruges*. | [rule] | *EDINBVRGH*: | Re-printed by Mr. *ROBERT FREEBAIRN*, | and sold at his Shop in the *Parliament-Closs*, 1712.

Collation: 8°: *A*⁴, B–D⁴

Pagination: *1–3*, 4–32

Contents: *A*1^r title page; *A*1^v blank; *A*2^r preface; *A*2^v–B3^v Remarks; B4^r–C4^r Barrier treaty; C4^v–D1^r separate article; D1$^{r–v}$ second separate article; D1^v–D3^r counter-project; D3^r–D4^r Sentiments; D4$^{r–v}$ Representation

Typography: A2^v–C3^r forty lines per page (B2^r; some pages thirty-nine lines), type-page 164 (171 or more) × 100 mm, twenty lines of roman type 82 mm; C3^v–D4^v forty-three lines per page (D3^v), type-page 158 or more (165 or more) × 100 mm, twenty lines of roman type 74 mm; preface, twenty lines of italic type 74 mm

Failures of catchwords to catch:
C1^r V.] And
C4^v and] for
D2^v [*om.*]] lan,
D3^v Ar] As

Copies examined:
*BL, 1572/722: 186 × 117 mm, trimmed; unbound
*CUL, Williams 409/29: 183 × 131 mm, most pages trimmed; disbound
[Bodl, Vet A4 e.2251: copy missing May 2005; not listed in *ESTC*]
†Houghton Library, Harvard, *EC7.Sw551.712s3f: copy not physically examined; reproduction used; *ECCO* copy

Dublin edition (Hyde), 1712d

Title: [within double rules, 161 × 85 mm] SOME | REMARKS | ON THE | Barrier Treaty | BETWEEN | HER MAJESTY | AND THE | States-General. | [rule] | By the AUTHOR of | *The Conduct of the ALLIES.* | [rule] | To which are added, | The said BARRIER-TREATY, | with the Two Separate Articles; | Part of the Counter-Project; The | Sentiments of Prince *Eugene* and | Count *Sinzendorf,* upon the said | Treaty; And a Representation of | the *English* Merchants at *Bruges.* | [rule] | *DVBLIN,* | Re-Printed for *John Hyde* Bookseller in | *Dames-street.* 1712.

Collation: 8°: A–D^4, E^2

Pagination: *1–2*, 3–36

Contents: A1^r title page; A1^v preface; A2^r–B4^r text; B4^v–C4^v Treaty; D1^{r-v} Separate article; D1^v–D2^r Second separate article; D2^v–D4^r Articles of the Counter-Project; D4^r–E1^v Sentiments of Prince Eugene and Count Sinzendorf; E2^{r-v} Representation of English Merchants

Typography: thirty-eight lines per page (A3^r), type-page 154 (164) × 86 mm, twenty lines of roman type 81 mm; preface, twenty lines of italic type 81 mm; Representation, twenty lines of roman type 67 mm

Failures of catchwords to catch:
A1^v SOME] *Some*
B4^r *The*] The
D4^r *First*] ∼,

Copies examined:
*Bodl, Vet.A4.e.1058: 175 × 106 mm, trimmed
*†NLI, LO Swift 114: 170 × *c*.100 mm, trimmed; re-bound (tightly) in twentieth century
*RIA, Haliday Pamph. 20, no. 6: 175 × 102 mm, trimmed; bound in volume of twelve 1712 political pamphlets (including Irish editions of *Some Reasons to Prove* and *Some Remarks on the Barrier Treaty*); part of Charles Haliday's library
Houghton Library, Harvard University, 310062: copy not physically examined; reproduction used; *ECCO* copy

Dublin edition (Waters), 1712e

Title: [within double rules, 145.5 × *c*.79 mm] SOME | REMARKS | ON THE | 𝕭arrier=𝕿reatp | BETWEEN | HER MAJESTY | AND THE | States-General | [rule] | By the AUTHOR of | *The Conduct of the ALLIES.* | [rule] | To which are added, | The said BARRIER-TREATY, with | the Two separate Articles; Part of the Coun- | ter-Project; The Sentiments of Prince Eu- | gene and Count Sinzendorf, upon the said | Treaty; And a Represen- tation of the English | Merchants at Bruges. | [rule] | Dublin: Re-printed by *E. Waters* at the New- | Post Office Printing House in *Essex-street*, at | the Corner of *Sycamore-Alley.*

Collation: 8°: *A*–D^4 (-B)

Pagination: *1–4*, 5–8, 17–32 (9–16 missing)

Contents: A1^r title page; A1^v blank; A2^{r-v} preface; A3^r–A4^v Remarks; C1^r–C4^r Barrier Treaty; C4^{r-v} Separate Article; C4^v–D1^r Second Separate Article (black-letter); D1^r–D2^v Counter-Project; D2^v–D4^r Sentiments of

Prince Eugene and Count Sinzendorf; D4^{r-v} Representation of English Merchants

Typography: A3^v–D4^v forty-one lines per page (A3^v; some pages are forty or forty-two lines), type-page 136 (145 or more) × 80.5 mm, twenty lines of roman type 67 mm; preface, twenty (leaded) lines of italic type c. 80 mm; C4^v, 20 lines of black-letter type, 65 mm

Failures of catchwords to catch:
A4^v [*none; B1^r missing*]
C2^r [*removed by trimming*]

Copy examined:
*†NLI, LO Swift 115: 155 × 95 mm, mostly trimmed with occasional loss of text; gift of E. R. McClintock Dix; re-bound (tightly) in modern binding

Dublin edition (Morphew & Waters), 1712f

Title: [within double rules, 148 × 86 mm] SOME | REMARKS | ON THE | 𝔅𝔞𝔯𝔯𝔦𝔢𝔯 𝔗𝔯𝔢𝔞𝔱𝔶, | BETWEEN | HER MAJESTY | AND THE | States-General. | [rule] | By the AUTHOR of | *The Conduct of the ALLIES.* | [rule] | To which are added, | The said BARRIER-TREATY, | with the Two Separate Articles; Part | of the Counter-Project; The Senti- | ments of Prince *Eugene* and Count *Sin-* | *zendorf*, upon the said Treaty; And | a Representation of the *English* Mer- | chants at *Bruges.* | [rule] | *London*, Printed for *J. Morphew*; And | Re-printed and Sold by *E. Waters* in | *Essex street*, at the *Corner* of *Sycamore-* | *Alley, Dublin*, 1712.

Collation: 8°: A–D^4 (A2 missigned 'A1')

Pagination: *1–4*, 5–32

Contents: A1^r title page; A1^v blank; A2^{r-v} preface; A3^r–B4^r Remarks; B4^v–C4^r Barrier Treaty; C4^{r-v} Separate Article; C4^v–D1^r Second Separate Article (black-letter); D1^r–D2^v Counter-Project; D2^v–D4^r Sentiments of Prince Eugene and Count Sinzendorf; D4^{r-v} Representation of English Merchants

Typography: A3ᵛ–D4ᵛ forty-one lines per page (A3ᵛ; some pages are forty or forty-two lines), type-page 136 (145) × 81 mm, twenty lines of roman type 67 mm; preface, twenty (leaded) lines of italic type c.80 mm; B2ʳ(from line 22)–B4ʳ, D1ʳ (from line 19)–D4ᵛ, twenty lines of roman type 68 mm; C4ᵛ, twenty lines of black-letter type 65 mm

Failures of catchwords to catch:
D1ʳ Towns] ~, [*there is blot after 's' on D1ʳ which may be a comma*]

Copies examined:
*†TCD, OLS B-9–951, no. 4 (formerly 192.S.1 no. 4): 160 × 103 mm, probably trimmed but outer and lower edges damaged; disbound; B1ʳ is mispaginated as '11' rather than '9'
*TCD, Gall.C.11.33 no. 2: 169 × 105 mm, untrimmed lower and outer edges; (tightly) bound in volume of twelve eighteenth-century pamphlets in English and French; some marginal marks and underlinings
*Royal Irish Academy, Haliday Pamph. 20, no. 7: 156 × 97 mm, some lower and outer edges trimmed; bound in volume of twelve 1712 political pamphlets (including Irish editions of *Some Reasons to Prove* and *Some Remarks on the Barrier Treaty*); part of Charles Haliday library

Emendations

131.11 unreasonable Obligation] 1712c; unreasonableObligation
133.5 he] 1712c; he he
136.26 *om.*] 1738; Davis; *to*
   Davis's suggestion that 'to' is unnecessary and hence an error of transcription is persuasive.
139.12 likewise] 1712c; likrwise
141.17 *States*] 1712c; *Scates*

Historical collation

123.12 *by*] *om.* 1712e
124.7 their] his 1738
124.22 together?] ~. 1712d, 1712e
124.24 to] with 1738

125.10 of] *om.* 1712d

125.13 tho'] although 1738

125.18 till] until 1738

125.26 the] *om.* 1712c

126.15 Chatellanies] Challanies 1712e

126.25 Duke] *om.* 1712e

127.2 above] *om.* 1712e

127.31 Gand] Grand 1738

127.32 *Masters*] *Master* 1712c

128.5 *of*] *om.* 1712e

128.10 Nations. This] Nations. [*new paragraph*] This 1712f; 1738

128.16 Qu——] Qu---- 1712c; QUEEN 1738

129.3 same] some 1712f

129.5 Qu——] Qu---- 1712c; QUEEN 1738

129.9 *What's*] *What* 1738

129.18 made] and made 1712c

129.22 *beneficial Bargains*] beneficial Bargains 1738

129.28 *own*] *om.* 1738

130.1 L——d Ch——f J——ce] L--- d Ch--- f J---- ce 1712c

130.10 though] although 1738

130.13 *Revolution-Principles*] Revolution-Principles 1738a–b; Revolution Principles 1738c

130.19 Q—— and M——ry] Q---- and M----ry 1712c; QUEEN and Ministry 1738

130.26 *common Honesty*, and *common Sense*] [common Honesty, and common Sense] 1738

131.11 Qu—] Qu--- 1712c; QUEEN 1738

131.11 unreasonable Obligation] unreasonableObligation 1712a–b

131.18 *except in a General Treaty*] except in a General Treaty 1738

131.20 though] although 1738

131.21 *Popish Princes*] Popish Princes 1738

131.22 *Protestant Succession*:] Protestant Succession. 1712c; Protestant Succession: 1738

131.24 Q——] Q---- 1712c; QUEEN 1738

131.29 'till] until 1738

132.2 giving] givien 1712f

132.3 *Why, Sirrah, are not we come here to protect you?*] Why, Sirrah, are we not come here to protect you? 1738

132.11 *Omission*] Omission 1738

132.13 *wilful Omission*] wilful Omission 1738

132.17 *some certain Persons*] some certain Persons 1738

132.18 *Omission*] Omission 1738

132.22 has] hath 1738

133.3 slowly] slow 1738c

133.3 after,] ~; 1738

133.10 that] *om.* 1712c

133.12 plain] very plain 1712c

133.13 thinks] think 1738a–b
> Presumably not a missetting: in 1738a, 'think' is the first word of 2B3^r; the catchword of the previous page also reads 'think'.

133.17 though] although 1738

133.23 *most Successful and Glorious War*] most Successful and Glorious War 1738

133.24 *Able, Diligent, Loyal Ministry; a most Faithful, Just, and Generous Commander*] able, diligent, and loyal Ministry; a most faithful, just, and generous Commander 1738

133.28 ——] ------- 1712c; *.* 1738

133.3 he] he he 1712a–b

134.13 *Answer-jobbers*] Answer-Jobbers 1738

134.15 *most Petty Princes*] most petty princes 1738

134.16 *Crowned Heads*] crowned Heads 1738

134.16 *the Soldiers of those Petty Princes are ready to rob or starve at Home*] the soldiers of those Petty Princes are ready to rob or starve at Home 1738

134.17 *Kings* and *Crowned Heads, Robbers* and *Highwaymen*] Kings and crowned heads, Robbers and Highwaymen 1738 [*1738b omits comma*]

134.20 *That the Business of* Thoulon *was discovered by the Clerk of a certain Great man, who was then Secretary of State*] That the Business of *Thoulon* was discovered by the Clerk of a certain Great man, who was then Secretary of State 1738

134.23 *that Secretary*, or of *that Clerk*] that Secretary, or of that Clerk 1738

135.3 the G——l] theG--l 1712c the General 1738

135.3 G——l:] ~. 1738

135.10 called] call 1712c

136.6 *said*] saids 1712c; *om.* 1738

136.13 *tho'*] *although* 1738

136.17 *Confederacy,*] ~; 1712c; 1738

136.19 *Wars*] *War* 1738

136.21 *has*] *hath* 1738

136.24 *of*] *to* 1738

136.26 *om.*] *to* 1712a–f

137.1 *Pensionary*] *Pentionary* 1712f

137.3 Spanbroek] Spanbrock 1738

137.5 Utrecht;] *Utrecht,* 1712c

137.6 Hessel] Hassel 1738

137.10 *part*] *one Part* 1738

137.12 Power] *Powers* 1712c

137.25 *greater Security of Her Majesty's Person and Government, and the Successionto the Crown of* Great Britain, &*c. in the Line of the most Serene House of* Hanover, *and in the Person of the Princess* Sophia, *and of Her Heirs, Successors and Descendants, Male and Female, already Born or to be Born*] greater Security of Her Majesty's Person and Government, and the Succession to the Crown of *Great Britain*, &c. in the Line of the most Serene House of *Hanover*, and in the Person of the Princess *Sophia*, and of Her Heirs, Successors and Decendants, Male and Female, already Born or to be Born 1738

137.28 though] although 1738

137.29 has] hath 1738

137.30 *Britain,*] ~; 1738

137.1 has] hath 1738

139.12 likewise] likrwise 1712a–b

139.24 exclusively] exclusive 1738

140.6 Livres] Livers 1712d

140.32 'till] until 1738

140.33 King *Charles*] K. Charles 1712e–f

141.16 *Swyn*] swan 1712e-f; *Swan* 1738

141.17 *States*] *Scates* 1712a–b

141.32 the] *om.* 1738

142.3 all] *om.* 1738

142.5 as favourably as the People the most favoured] as the People most favoured 1738

Eye-skip by compositor?

142.9 Kingdoms] Kingdom 1712c

142.10 settled] ~: 1712c (Houghton Library, Harvard, *EC7.Sw551. 712s3f); ~[reversed space] 1712c (CUL, Williams 409/29)

142.14 this] the 1738

143.8 Memory:] Memory, 1712c

143.10 likewise,] likewise; 1712c

143.17 nor] or 1738

143.31 [*signatories in different order*] 1738

144.4 [*separate article in italic*] 1738

144.13 'till] *until* 1738

144.30 Sovereignty,] ~; 1738

145.3 Herself] *her self* 1738a

145.5 has] *hath* 1738

145.5 Herself] *her self* 1738a

145.12 [*signatories in different order*] 1738

145.18 [*second separate article in italic*] 1738

145.22 it self] *itself* 1738

145.24 has] *hath* 1738

145.27 *Spain.*] ~: 1738

146.1 so] *om.* 1738

146.1 agreed,] ~. 1738

146.17 [*individual remarks not in italics*] 1738

146.22 *Perle,*] ~ˆ 1738a, 1738c

146.26 *to the*] *in the* 1712d

146.30 *of*] of of 1712e–f

147.5 Tack] Attack 1738

Davis follows 1738 here but 'tack' is noted (citing examples from 1720 and 1731) in OED (s.v. 'tack', v4) as an aphetic variant of 'attack'.

147.9 [*Article IX not in italics*] 1738

147.11 *Towns;*] ~, 1738

147.16 King of] K. of 1712e–f

147.17 *especially*] especially in 1738a, 1738c; especially, in 1738b

148.11 King of] K of 1712e–f
148.14 in] and 1738a, 1738c
148.27 Port;] ~, 1712c
148.13 *of*] *om.* 1738
150.15 *such Things, as the said Garrisons and Fortifications shall have need of*] such Things, as the said Garrisons and Fortifications shall have need of 1738
150.25 Consent,] ~; 1738
151.35 Interests:] ~. 1738
152.5 *represent,*] ~. 1738a-b; ~: 1738c
152.6 *Douay*] *Doway* 1712d
152.32 *Scotch*] *Scots* 1712c
152.33 *&c.* It is] &c. [*new paragraph*] It is 1712e–f

Word division (compounds only)

Copy text
123.20 like-wise
126.16 like-wise
130.6 when-ever
134.1 me-thinks
139.22 what-soever
140.30 fore-going
143.10 like-wise
144.23 above-mentioned
144.26 above-mentioned
145.7 under-written

Edited text
none

THE NEW WAY OF SELLING
PLACES AT COURT:
TEXTUAL ACCOUNT

Barber entered this work in the SR on 13 May 1712 and Morphew (who signed the entry on Barber's behalf) published an edition (hereafter 1712a) the same day (Woolley, 'Canon', endpaper table). (Confusingly, Woolley describes the work elsewhere in the same article as 'unregistered' (104).) Another issue (hereafter 1712b), with some minor variants, appeared as a 'second edition' in the same year. A Dublin edition also bearing 1712 in its imprint (hereafter 1712c) was (poorly) printed by the Tory printer and bookseller Cornelius Carter. Carter's usual standard of printing was 'deplorable' (Pollard, p. 92–3), but Carter at least followed 1712a very closely, varying substantively on only three occasions, and following spelling, punctuation and capitalization in all but thirteen cases.

The London edition, then, had evident links with Barber and Morphew; the latter advertised it with other Swift works at the end of *The Third Volume of the Examiners* in 1714 where it is mistitled as *New Method of Selling Places at Court* and priced at 2d (Woolley, 'Canon', 99 n.17, 104–5, and illustration 3a). Moreover, Swift referred to the events that formed the subject-matter of the work six weeks prior to that work's publication (Williams, *JSt*, p. 522). However, the work was not listed in Charles Ford's 1733 list of Swift's political writings (Woolley, *Corr.*, vol. III, p. 699). It was included by John Nichols – who based his attribution primarily on Morphew's advertisement – in *A Supplement to Dr. Swift's Works* (1776) as part of Hawkesworth's large octavo edition (TS, no. 88), reprinted in the 1779 first *Supplement* volumes of Hawkesworth's quarto and small octavo editions (TS, nos. 87 and 90), and retained in both Nichols's 1801 and 1808 *Works* (TS, nos. 129, 131). In each case, the work was prefaced by the relevant extract from *JSt*. Subsequent editors were more sceptical. Walter Scott included it in his 1814 and 1824 collected works but remarked that it had 'perhaps no very good title to be retained in Swift's works' (Scott

(1814), vol. VI, p. 175), and Temple Scott did not include it in his 1901 edition of Swift's *Prose Works*. Williams linked the work to Swift's account in *JSt* in a footnote but did not seek to attribute the work to Swift. Davis does not even mention the work in the relevant volume. Woolley, however, marshals a lengthy and persuasive case for attributing it to Swift, drawing on both the external evidence already noted and its stylistic characteristics ('Canon', 104–5, 111–17).

Textually 1712a and 1712b are printed using the same setting of type but issued with separate title pages. However, *pace* Woolley, there are at least three variants between the two issues. (These variants may, of course, be copy-specific as I have been able to examine only one copy of 1712b.) A variant on A4^r (1712a: 'Trouble'; 1712b: 'Touble') would seem to suggest that 1712b used uncorrected sheets: in other words, that 1712b (apart, obviously, from A1^r) represented an *earlier* state of the printing than 1712a. However, the appearance in 1712b of a comma immediately before 'at Mr. Vice-Chamberlain's Request' on A7^r, making the punctuation of that sentence more consistent than in 1712a, would perhaps seem to suggest otherwise. The remaining variant is more complex. Woolley, in his case for Swift's authorship, makes a particular point of the work's use of 'imposture'. Noting how the *Irish Spelling-Book* of 1740 suggested that 'imposture' was to be pronounced 'impostor', Woolley remarks: 'Swift had a weakness for phonetic spellings, and in this instance he is known [in a 1733 letter to Pope] to have *spelled* the word as in fact he pronounced it, "impostor", meaning not the deceiver but the deceit itself. On both occasions of its use in *The New Way*, "impostor" has been reproduced when "imposture" was intended' ('Canon', 116–17). Hence, according to Woolley, on the two occasions when 'impostor' is used in this work, the context dictates that the word should be 'imposture': the mistake is evidence that the printer was setting from Swift's holograph. Interestingly, while on A5^v 1712b agrees with 1712a's reading of 'Impostors' on A5^v), on A6^v 1712a's 'Impostor' becomes 'Imposture' in 1712b. In light of Woolley's comments, therefore, in this variant, 1712b is presenting a corrected state.

Taken together, these variant readings in 1712b would seem contradictory in consisting of what appear to be two readings subsequent to 1712a and one reading prior to 1712a. However, the paradox can be (at least partly) resolved when the spread of variants is considered in terms of the formes. *New Way* was printed on a single octavo sheet, using an outer (printing pages 1, 4, 5, 8, 9, 12, 13, 16) and inner (printing pages 2, 3, 6, 7, 10, 11, 14, 15) forme. The uncorrected reading appears on A4^r (p. 7) of the inner forme; the corrected readings on A6^v (p. 12) and A7^r (p. 13) of the outer forme. From this, it is possible to suggest the following hypothesis. The inner forme (bearing the uncorrected 'Touble') was printed first; during printing, the error was spotted and corrected on the press, and printing continued. Normally, once printing of the first side of the sheet was completed, the paper was turned over and the second side was printed (the 'perfecting' of the sheet); this would place the uncorrected sheets at the top of the pile. For some reason, however, the sheets were perfected either in an arbitrary manner or in reverse order and, as the outer forme was being printed, two further corrections (the change of 'Impostor' into 'Imposture' and the addition of the comma) were made (not necessarily at the same point in time). With printing over, the sheets were left to dry before being folded and stitched for sale; during this process, the pile of printed sheets was turned over so that the first sold copies were those that include the corrected 'Trouble' but the uncorrected 'Impostor' and omitted comma – in other words, 1712a. Not all the copies were sold so at some point the remaining sheets were re-issued with a new title page as a 'second edition', including those bearing the uncorrected 'Touble' and the corrected 'Imposture' and added comma – in other words 1712b.

It is, of course, possible that the outer forme was printed first but this is unlikely given English printers' 'strong tendency to print the inner forme first' (Gaskell, p. 127), which allowed the printer to leave until last not only the setting of the title page but also, in this particular case, the advertisements for books that appeared on A8^v. Moreover, while 'Impostor'/ 'Imposture' exists in both states in the outer forme, 'Impostors' was not corrected in the inner forme (at least in the copies examined), suggesting that the inner forme had already been printed by the time that the 'Impostor' error was noted.

The editorial consequences of this mean that 1712b cannot be considered as a separate edition but rather as a re-issue of the 1712a, exhibiting different states of both formes. Accordingly, it is difficult to identify readily which issue has the most authority; however, given that 1712b includes two corrected readings, including an 'accidental' variant (the comma), as opposed to 1712a's one corrected reading, I have chosen 1712b as copy text. The obvious error in 1712b's inner forme has been emended; moreover, in light of the correction made to 'Impostor', I have emended the other use of the word. The text has been collated against: copies of 1712a and Woolley's transcription (hereafter W) of 1712a (specifically Bodl, Vet. A4 c.107 (1)), in which he offers some possible emendations; the Dublin reprint (1712c) which offers no substantive variants; and the 1776 and 1779 reprints (both quarto (1779a) and octavo (1779b)). The 1776 and 1779 reprints expand the few elided nouns, change capitalization and punctuation and offer a number of substantive variant readings (including the corrected form of 'Imposture'). However, as most of these substantive changes in the 1776 and 1779b editions seem to have been made to 'improve' the prose, including the substitution of the slang term 'cully' with the somewhat more dignified 'dupe', I consider them to have insufficient authority to lead to any emendations of the copy text. (The 1779a edition, in contrast, retains many of the readings from the 1712 editions.) I have also checked the 1712a/b variant readings against BL's three copies of 1712a (C.108.bbb.37(10), T.1990 (16) and E.1984 (13)), all of which agree with the readings present in those copies of 1712a for which I have performed a full collation.

Copy text: CUL, 7540.d.45 (8)

References: Not in TS. Not in Davis. Woolley, 'Canon', no. 15 and Appendix A. Rothschild Library, nos. 2204–5. *ESTC* T43045 (first edition, listing twenty-five copies); T173476 ('second edition', listing two copies, the other at the Huntington Library); N10691 (Dublin edition, listing three copies, the third at University of Texas, Austin; the copy at TCC is listed erroneously as the copy in question is the London edition)

London edition, 1712a

Title: [Within double rules, 159 × 88 mm] THE | NEW WAY | OF | 𝔖elling 𝔓laces | AT | COURT. | IN A | LETTER from a SMALL | COURTIER to a GREAT | STOCK-JOBBER. | [rule] | ——*Omnia Romæ* | *Cum pretio*—— | [rule] | *LONDON*, | Printed for *John Morphew*, near *Stationer's-*[*sic*] | *Hall*, 1712. [flush right] Price 2 *d*.

Collation: 8°: A⁸

Pagination: *1–2*, 3–15, *16*

Contents: A1ʳ title page; A1ᵛ blank; A2ʳ–A8ʳ text; A8ᵛ advertisement (includes seventh edition of *Conduct of the Allies* and second edition of *Some Remarks on the Barrier Treaty*, both at 6d)

Typography: thirty lines per page (A3ʳ), type-page 141 (152) × 80 mm, twenty lines of roman type 94 mm

Failures of catchwords to catch:
none

Copies examined:
*BL, C.108.bbb.37(10): 188 × 120 mm, untrimmed; 'stitched as issued'
*†Bodl, Pamph. 304(3): 172 × 107 mm, trimmed; in volume of forty-five miscellaneous 1712 pamphlets (including *Some Reasons to prove*)
*†CUL, Ddd.23.5(3): 184 × 112 mm, lower edge untrimmed; folded incorrectly: A1, A2, A4, A3, A6, A5, A7, A8 (i.e., pp. *1–2*, 3–4, 7–8, 5–6, 11–12, 9–10, 13–15, *16*); in volume of fifteen 1712–13 printed items; bookplate: 'Academiæ Cantabrigiensis Liber'
*TCC, RW.24.12: 182 × 118.5 mm, some of lower edge untrimmed; disbound
*†NLS, 2.272 (9): 174 × 120 mm, trimmed; in volume of twelve miscellaneous items 1710–13; on fly-leaf, 'Ex Libris Bibliotheca Facultatis Juridica Edinburgi 1716'

Re-issue of London edition, 1712b

Title: [Within double rules, 159 × 87 mm] THE | NEW WAY | OF | 𝕾elling 𝕻laces | AT | COURT. | IN A | LETTER from a Sᴍᴀʟʟ | Cᴏᴜʀᴛɪᴇʀ to a Gʀᴇᴀᴛ | Sᴛᴏᴄᴋ-Jᴏʙʙᴇʀ. | [rule] | ——*Omnia Romæ* | *Cum pretio* —— | [rule] | 𝕿he 𝕾econ 𝕰ditiond. [*sic*] | [rule] | *LONDON*, | Printed for *John Morphew*, near *Stationer's-*[*sic*] | *Hall*, 1712. [flush right] Price 2 *d*.

Collation: 8°: A⁸

Pagination: *1–2*, 3–15, *16*

Contents: A1ʳ title page; A1ᵛ blank; A2ʳ–A8ʳ text; A8ᵛ advertisement (includes seventh edition of *Conduct of the Allies* and second edition of *Some Remarks on the Barrier Treaty*, both at 6d)

Typography: thirty lines per page (A3ʳ), type-page 141.5 (152) × 79 mm, twenty lines of roman type 94 mm

Failures of catchwords to catch:
none

Copy examined:
*†CUL, 7540.d.45 (8): 185 × 112 mm, outer edge (except A2, A3) trimmed; small tear in A7 and A8, with some loss of letters *c.* twelve lines down; in volume of twenty-three early eighteenth-century printed tracts, including second edition of *Some Remarks on the Barrier Treaty*; ex-libris C. Lacy Hulbert-Powell.

Dublin edition, 1712c

Title: THE | NEW WAY | OF | 𝔖𝔢𝔩𝔩𝔦𝔫𝔤 𝔓𝔩𝔞𝔠𝔢𝔰 | AT | COURT. | IN A | LETTER from a SMALL | COURTIER to a GREAT | STOCK-JOBBER. | [rule] | ——*Omnia Romæ* | *Cum pretio*—— | [rule] | *LONDON*: | Printed for *John Morphew* near *Stationer's*[*sic*] | *Hall*, | And Re-Printed in *Dublin*, by | *C. Carter*, in *Fishamble-street*, 1712.

Collation: 8°: *A* ⁸ (presumed)

Pagination: *1–2*, 3–15, *16*

Contents: *A*1ʳ: title; *A*1ᵛ blank; *A*2ʳ–*A*8ʳ text; *A*8ᵛ blank (not seen)

Typography: two sizes of roman type:
*A*2ʳ, *A*5ʳ–*A*7ʳ: larger (twenty-five lines per page)
*A*2ᵛ–*A*4ᵛ, *A*7ʳ(last seven lines)–*A*8ʳ: smaller (twenty-nine lines per page)

Failures of catchwords to catch:
none

Copies examined:
†Baker Library, Harvard University Graduate School of Business, Kress Room: copy not physically examined; reproduction used; *ECCO* copy (very poor reproduction)
†University of Illinois Library, Urbana, ×942.O69.N421 1712a: c.155 × c.98 mm, trimmed; copy not physically examined; reproduction used; measurement of title leaf deduced from ruler in image

Emendations

158.13 *Whitehall*] 1712c; *Whilehall*
159.19 Trouble] 1712a; Touble
160.18 Impostures] 1776; Impostors

Historical collation

157.2 A LETTER FROM A Sᴍᴀʟʟ Cᴏᴜʀᴛɪᴇʀ TO A Great Stock-Jobber] A LETTER TO A GREAT STOCK-JOBBER 1776+
158.5 Palace, can go] Palace, [and] can go W
Although the succession of clauses in this sentence seems to demand a conjunction, Woolley's 'and' changes the tenor of this sentence significantly by implying that the individual who lives in the palace can indeed walk unimpeded throughout the building and talk 'familiarly' with whom he meets.
158.9 Business.] business! 1776+
158.11 *Harry Killigrew, Fleet. Shepherd*] *Killigrew, Fleetwood Sheppard* 1776; *Killigrew, Fleetwood Shephard* 1779b
158.13 *Whitehall*] *Whilehall* 1712a–b; *White-Hall* W
Woolley silently corrects and adds an unnecessary hyphen.
158.26 'Tis true] It is true 1776+
159.5 own, said] own, and said 1776; 1779b
159.10 honest] *honest* 1776+
159.19 Trouble] Touble 1712b
160.8 given.] [*new paragraph after 'given'*] 1712c
The introduction of a new paragraph may have been an attempt to break up what was the longest paragraph in the work (stretching over three and a third pages in 1712a); alternatively, as it was made on a page which moved to

the larger type size, there may have been space reasons. Either way, the break seems to have been chosen with some attention to the text itself.

160.16 Cullies] dupes 1776; 1779b

160.18 Impostors] impostures 1776+

160.19 could be] were 1712c

This is the only substantive variant in the Dublin edition of any real significance; given that this edition was clearly set directly from a copy of 1712a, it is difficult to account for this different reading.

160.26 Hand] Hands 1712c

160.31 in very great haste] in a very great haste W

An uncharacteristic slip by Woolley.

161.8 it was wholly] it being wholly 1776; 1779b

161.19 Thousand Pound] thousand pounds 1776+

161.28 Imposture] Impostor 1712a; 1712c; W

161.29 lead] led 1776+

161.30 Cully-Sollicitor] solicitor 1776; 1779b

162.2 *t'other Thousand Pound*] the other thousand pounds 1776; 1779b

162.4 this] his 1712c

Given that this line includes two errors — 'Buisness' and 'immagine' — it is probable that this variant is also an error rather than a deliberately revised reading.

162.21 'Tis true] It is true 1776+

Word division (compounds only)

Copy text

162.22 where-ever

Edited text

SOME REASONS TO PROVE…IN A LETTER TO A WHIG-LORD: TEXTUAL ACCOUNT

Advertised in 29 May 1712 issue of *The Examiner* as due to be published 'On Saturday next', i.e. 31 May 1712 (Davis, vol. VI, p. xvi); Swift wrote on 31 May that he was 'printing a threepenny Pamphlet' (Williams, *JSt*, p. 536). Probably printed by Barber (Rivington, p. 248) and published by Morphew, it was not entered in the SR. Unusually for the works included in this present edition, the 1712 edition (hereafter 1712a) included an errata notice although I have only found two copies – both at CUL (Acton.d.25.1033/4 and Ddd.25.158/6) – in which readers actually amended the text. Swift urged Stella to '[r]ead the Lett[e]r to a Whig Lord' on 17 June (Williams, *JSt*, p. 542).

The Tory printer and bookseller Cornelius Carter printed a Dublin edition in the same year (hereafter 1712b). As with his reprint of *New Way of Selling Places*, this copy lives up to his usual 'deplorable' standard (Pollard, 92–3): misaligned lines and extremely poor inking in places, often rendering punctuation marks and letters wholly indiscernible. Carter, who followed 1712a closely but missed the errata note, evidently misjudged the length of the pamphlet: not only does sheet B have a larger number of lines per page than sheet A but from the bottom of B2^r Carter moved from using small pica to long primer, although this was insufficient to prevent him from having to use the whole of the direction line on the final page to set the last line of text.

The work was attributed to Swift by Charles Ford in his 1733 catalogue of Swift's political pamphlets (Woolley, *Corr.*, vol. III, p. 699). It was first collected and published in the 1752 *Supplement to the Works of Dr Swift* (TS, no. 83; hereafter 1752). It was reprinted in 1776 in Nichols's *Supplement to Dr Swift's Works* as part of Hawkesworth's large octavo edition (TS, no. 88; hereafter 1776) and in the 1779 *Supplement* volumes of Hawkesworth's quarto and small octavo (first volume) editions (TS, nos. 87 and 90); in each case, it was juxtaposed with the *Letter from the Pretender*. Both 1752 and 1776 fail to incorporate the errata changes. Temple Scott collated 1712a against the 1779 quarto edition; Davis, who applied his usual policy of expanding elided words, collated 1712a against 1752, incorporating one substantive variant. This edition collates 1712a against 1712b and 1752 (whose punctuation, spelling and capitalization differ considerably) for substantive variants; variants have also been cross-checked with 1776 (which followed 1752's readings in a number of places while expanding elisions and removing the capitalization of common nouns). (1712b follows the pattern of elisions in 1712a almost identically, although it occasionally uses hyphens where 1712a uses em-dashes and vice versa. In the collation, I have considered such variation – except where it uses a different pattern of letters and blanks – to be accidental and hence have not recorded it below.)

Copy text: CUL, Williams 357

References: TS, nos. 578 (London), 579 (Dublin). Davis, vol. VI, pp. 119–36, with facsimile of presumably Yale copy's title page on p. 123. Woolley, 'Canon', no. 17. *ESTC* T49355 (1712a, listing thirty-one copies); T155575 (1712b, listing seven copies). Rothschild Library, no. 2039

London edition, 1712a

Title: [within double rules, 161 × 87 mm] SOME | REASONS | *TO PROVE*, | That no Person is obliged by | his Principles, as a *Whig*, | To Oppose | *HER MAJESTY* | OR HER | Present Ministry. | [double rule] | 𝔍𝔫 𝔞 𝔏𝔢𝔱𝔱𝔢𝔯 𝔱𝔬 𝔞 𝔚𝔥𝔦𝔤=𝔏𝔬𝔯𝔡. | [double rule] | *LONDON*, | Printed for *John Morphew*, near *Stationers-* | *Hall*, 1712. Price 3*d*.

Collation: 8°: A–C⁴

Pagination: *1–2*, 3–24

Contents: A1ʳ title page; A1ᵛ blank; A2ʳ–C4ᵛ text; C4ᵛ 'ERRATA. Page 4. line 5. for *but* read *not*. Pag. 8. l. 23. read *Court*.'; C4ᵛ List of '*BOOKS Sold by* John Morphew, *near* Stationers-Hall'.

Typography: thirty-three lines per page (B1ʳ), type-page 155 (166) × 85.5 mm, twenty lines of roman type 94 mm

Failures of catchwords to catch:
A2^r: For,] ~^

Copies examined:
*†BL, T.1599 (8): 181 × 113 mm, some leaves trimmed; in volume of fifteen eighteenth-century pamphlets; re-bound 1978
*†Bodl, Pamph. 304 (37): 180 × 113 mm, tightly trimmed; in a volume of forty-five miscellaneous 1712 pamphlets
*†Bodl, G. Pamph. 1891 (16): 184 × 112 mm, outer edge trimmed on most leaves; in volume of twenty-nine 1712–13 pamphlets
*†CUL, Williams 357: 176.5 × 103 mm, trimmed; re-bound; no hand-written corrections
*TCC, Cambridge, RW.62.64: 187 × 116 mm, lower edge untrimmed; unbound; stitched

Dublin edition, 1712b

Title: [within single rules, 139 × 84 mm] SOME | REASONS | TO | PROVE, | That no Person is obliged by his Principles, | as a *Whig*, to Oppose | HER MAJESTY | OR HER | Present Ministry. | [rule] | *In a Letter to a Whig-Lord.* | [rule] | [inverted pyramid of ten printer's flowers, 18 × 31 mm] | [rule] | London. Printed; And Re-Printed in Dublin by *C.* | *Carter* in *Fish-shamble street*, 1712.

Collation: 8°: *A*^{4}, B^4

Pagination: *1–2*, 3–16

Contents: A1^r title page; A1^v blank; A2^r–B4^v text

Typography: A2^v–A4^v thirty-five lines per page (A4^v; except A3^v which has thirty-six lines), type-page 129.5 (137 or more) × 84 mm, twenty lines of roman type 74 mm; B1^r–B2^r thirty-six lines per page (B1^r; except B2^v which has thirty-seven lines), 133 (141) × 84 mm, twenty lines of roman type 74 mm; B2^r(bottom 4 lines)–B4^v forty-one lines per page (B3^r; except B4^v which has forty-two lines), 137 (144 or more) × 84 mm, twenty lines of roman type 67 mm.

Failures of catchwords to catch:
none

Copies examined:
*Codrington Library, All Souls College, Oxford, y.9.4(4): 152 × 95 mm, trimmed; in volume of sixteen 1711–15 political tracts
*†NLI, LO Swift 122: 154 × 94 mm, trimmed with loss of first letter in each line on A3ᵛ; re-bound (tightly) in 1912; gift of Duke of Leinster
*RIA, Haliday Pamph. 20, no.3: 156 × 94 mm, trimmed, lower edge damaged; bound in volume of twelve 1712 political pamphlets (including Irish editions of *Some Reasons to Prove* and *Some Remarks on the Barrier Treaty*); from library of Charles Haliday

Emendations

165.10 thoroughly] 1712b; thorougly
165.11 to be the only] 1752; to be only
165.13 not] 1712a *errata*; but
    This emendation follows the errata notice included in 1712a.
167.6 no Objection] 1712b; noObjection
168.15 Court] 1712a *errata*; Courts
    This emendation follows the errata notice included in 1712a.
168.14 from] 1712b; frem
178.18 Party] 1752; ~,
178.28 Realm] 1712b; Relam

Historical collation

165.11 to be the only] to be only 1712a–b
167.24 above] about 1752–76
168.12 M——ry] M----y 1712b; Ministry 1776+
168.15 Court] Courts 1712–52; courts 1776
168.17 than] that 1752
168.20 than] then 1752
170.23 into] in 1752–76
171.3 your own Thoughts] your Thoughts 1712b
171.7 M——y] M---y 1752; Majesty 1776+
171.13 Explanations] Explanation 1752–76
174.3 is cancelled] cancelled 1752–76

174.11 where] were 1752
   Clearly a typographic error in 1752 edition.
176.20 from] frem 1712a
178.28 Realm] Relam 1712a

Word division (compounds only)

Copy text
166.19 Lord-ship
168.24 Lord-ships
174.9 some-thing

Edited text
none

IT'S OUT AT LAST: OR,
FRENCH CORRESPONDENCE
CLEAR AS THE SUN:
TEXTUAL ACCOUNT

This, published by Morphew on or before 10 July 1712 and advertised in the 10, 17, 24, and 31 July issues of *The Examiner* (Woolley, 'Canon', 100 n. 19 and endpaper table), was not entered in the SR.

It does not seem to have been attributed to Swift until John Nichols included it in his list of items 'which have eluded his most diligent researches' (p. x in the 1776 *Supplement to Dr Swift's Works* (part of Hawkesworth's large octavo edition; TS, no. 88)). However, it was not until 1902 that a copy was first identified (although no location was given) and reprinted (without italicization or any small capitals) by Hamilton Lavers-Smith ('Swift's Political Tracts', *The Athenæum* 3915 (8 November 1902), 619–20). Lavers-Smith believed it to be one of Swift's famous '7 penny Papers' of July 1712 (Williams, *JSt*, p. 553):

> The suspiciously apposite quotation from the 'Swedish poet', the grave enumeration of the reasons for the surrender of Dunkirk, and the overwhelming evidence of the turpitude of the ministry which the author pretends to find in their readiness, nay, eagerness, to accept not only Dunkirk, but Toulon and St. Malo to boot – are not these all significant touches of the Dean's ironical pen?   ('Swift's Political Tracts', 620)

Williams, however, was sceptical – 'the style and choice of words do not suggest Swift' – and suggested that 'no ordinary reader of the day could take it for anything but an attack on the Ministry' (*JSt*, p. 554 n. 10). Davis was more equivocal, including it as an appendix (vol. VI, pp. 189–91). Woolley ('Canon', 106–9 and illustration 4) supports Lavers-Smith's attribution on the basis of Morphew's carefully laid-out advertisements and gives short shrift to Williams's reservations: 'every smallest thrust of political innuendo (with which [*It's out at last*] vibrates) will have been meaningful to the London coffee-houses *that week*, Tories "in the know", and Whigs smarting under the jeer' ('*Dialogue*', p. 216 n.1).

Copy text: Bodl, G.Pamph. 1680 (28)

References: Not in TS. Davis, vol VI, pp. 189–91 (Appendix B). Woolley, 'Canon', no. 19 and Appendix B(1). *ESTC* N17200, listing copies at Bodl (G. Pamph. 1680(28) only); TCC; Clark Library; and McGill University Library, Montreal

London edition, 1712

Title: It's Out at Last: | *OR*, | French Correspondence | Clear as the SUN.

Imprint: [rule] | LONDON: Printed in the Year M DCC XII.

Collation: half-sheet

Pagination: none

Contents: recto: text; verso: blank

Typography: printed in two columns of fifty-three lines lines each (the Latin quotation in the first column is leaded); column one 216.5 × 82.5 mm; column two 215.5 × 84 mm; twenty lines of roman type 80 mm.

Copies examined:
*†Bodl, Vet. A4 c.107 (1) (formerly Pamphlets 305 (50); re-catalogued July 1950): 319 × 190.5 mm, outer edge excessively trimmed with partial loss of some letters
*†Bodl, G. Pamph. 1680 (28): 338 × c.195 mm, outer edge trimmed; in volume of miscellaneous tracts 1700–14
*†TCC, RW. 70. 10 (Rothschild, 2041): 334 × 211 mm, untrimmed; unbound; reproduced in reduced facsimile in Woolley, 'Canon'.
†Clark Library, University of California University, Los Angeles, fPR3724.I891* (*not* *fPR3724.I891 as listed in *ESTC*): copy not physically examined; reproduction used; *ECCO* copy

Emendation

183.4 that the] *this edition*; thatthe

Historical collation

Word division (compounds only)

Copy text
none

Edited text
none

A DIALOGUE UPON DUNKIRK: BETWEEN A WHIG AND A TORY: TEXTUAL ACCOUNT

Woolley suggests this work was composed on 6–7 July 1712 and that Barber received it for the press on 8 July (*'Dialogue'*, 219–20 and n.3). It was published by Morphew on or before 10 July 1712 and advertised in the 10, 17, 24, and 31 July issues of *The Examiner* (Woolley, 'Canon', 100 n. 19 and endpaper table); it was not entered in the SR. In the 1776 *Supplement to Dr. Swift's Works* (part of Hawkesworth's large octavo edition; TS, no. 88), it was listed in John Nichols's catalogue of Swift items 'which have eluded his most diligent researches' (p. x). A copy was first identified at Chicago in 1974 by Frank H. Ellis, who considered it to have 'none of the marks of Swift' (*TLS* 3766 (10 May 1974), 506); Ellis suggested *A Description of Dunkirk* as an alternative candidate for the seventh of Swift's famous '7 penny Papers' of July 1712 (Williams, *JSt*, p. 553), a claim rebutted by Woolley in the following week's issue. Woolley later presented a more detailed case for the identification of *Dialogue* as one of Swift's seven on the basis of the following: the careful layout of Morphew's advertisements; the presence of internal historical and literary evidence; and the care taken over the printing ('Canon', 106–9 and illustration 4; *'Dialogue'*, 217–22). Woolley elsewhere noted the verbal parallels between it and a contemporaneous pamphlet, *Bouchain: In a Dialogue between the Late Medley and Examiner* (David Woolley, ' "The Author of The *Examiner*" and the Whiggish Answer-Jobbers of 1711–1712', *SStud* 5 (19901990), 109–11).

Copy text: Magdalen College, Oxford, Tb.4.8 (41).

References: Not in TS. Not in Davis. Woolley, 'Canon', no. 19 and Appendix B(2). *ESTC* N49709 (listing the copies above and one at McGill University Library, Montreal)

London edition, 1712

Title: A Dialogue upon Dunkirk, | between a *Whig* and a *Tory*, on *Sunday* Morn- | ing the 6th Instant.

Imprint: LONDON: Printed in the Year M DCC XII.

Collation: half-sheet

Pagination: none

Contents: recto: text; verso: blank

Typography: two columns of fifty-nine lines each; type-page (column 1) 240 × 83.5 mm, (column 2): 240 × 82 mm, twenty lines of roman type 82 mm

Copies examined:
*†Magdalen College, Oxford, Tb.4.8 (41): 305 × c.190, trimmed; in volume of miscellaneous works, 1677–1712; not listed by Woolley, 'Canon'.
†Regenstein Library, University of Chicago, f DA503 1712 .D5: copy not physically examined; reproduction used; facsimile reproduced in Woolley, 'Canon' (reduced) and '*Dialogue*' (slightly reduced and better quality)

Emendations

Historical collation

Word division (compounds only)

Copy text
189.4 out-witted

Edited text
none

A HUE AND CRY AFTER
DISMAL:
TEXTUAL ACCOUNT

One of Swift's '7 penny Papers' of late June and July 1712 (Williams, *JSt*, 553), this was published by Morphew on or before 17 July 1712; it was advertised in the 17, 24, and 31 July issues of *The Examiner* and mentioned to Stella as 'a Hue & Cry after Dismal' on 17 July (Woolley, 'Canon', 100 n.19 and endpaper table; Williams, *JSt*, 548). Rivington suggests Barber as the probable printer; it was not entered in the SR. Another edition, *Dunkirk to be Let*, was also printed in this year, presenting a slightly longer text (which involved two different sizes of type) and a large number of substantive and accidental variants. Neither edition was reprinted during the eighteenth or nineteenth centuries (Nichols, for one, was unable to locate a copy of *Hue and Cry* despite 'his most diligent researches'; see *A Supplement to Dr Swift's Works* (1776), p. x) and the existence of surviving copies was only confirmed in the early twentieth century (see Harold Williams, 'A Hue and Cry after Dismal', *RES* 6 (1930), 195–6). Williams, TS and Davis all considered *Dunkirk to be Let* to be a later edition, a view with which I agree. TS argued that the revised title and added verse indicated that this edition was a counter-response to some kind of printed reply to the original *A Hue and Cry*. Williams was tempted into suggesting the possibility that 'Swift re-touched his paper for a second edition'. He described *Dunkirk to be Let* as showing 'more typographical care' than *Hue and Cry*, presumably on the basis of the correction of one clear error, although Williams's judgement must be set against its lack of black-letter (evidence of a smaller printing house?), its misjudgement over type size and its introduction of a new error ('then' for 'than'). Williams claimed that *Dunkirk to be Let*'s verse 'may well be' by Swift and went so far as to include the lines in his edition of Swift's poems, albeit collected under 'Poems attributed to Swift': 'Are the added lines of verse by Swift? From their character they may be' (Williams, *Poems*, p. 1097). Although I recognize that *Dunkirk to be Let* does include a significant number of textual changes that indicate a reasonably careful revision of the text as printed in *Hue and Cry*, I feel that the evidence in favour of its authority is lacking. With the exception of *A Letter from the Pretender*, Morphew (and by extension Barber) can be associated with all of Swift's political publications in this period; it would seem unlikely that Swift would have collaborated with a different printer or publisher for a second edition. Morphew, as Woolley and others have pointed out, advertised a number of Swift's 'penny papers' in *The Examiner*, including *A Hue and Cry*. (Morphew didn't advertise *A Letter from the Pretender*, which may well indicate that he was not involved in what was a very poorly printed work.) At no point do these advertisements refer to *Dunkirk to be Let*; indeed, when Morphew re-advertised many of Swift's works at the end of *The Third Volume of the Examiners* in spring 1714, the work is still referred to as *Hue and Cry after Dismal* (Woolley, 'Canon', p. 99 n. 17 and illustration 3b). Swift does not mention a revised edition or title for this work in *JSt*, while Charles Ford's 1733 list of Swift's political writings from this period refers to the work as 'Hugh and Cry after Dismal' (Woolley, *Corr.*, vol. III, p. 699). Even the typography of *Dunkirk to be Let* – despite Williams's claim for its superiority – is suspicious: it does not make use of black-letter in the text in the meaningful way that *Hue and Cry* does. (Ross and Woolley, *Works*, while preferring *Dunkirk to be Let* as copy text, silently imported the use of black-letter from *Hue and Cry*.) While it is not impossible that Swift was responsible for the text that appeared in *Dunkirk to be let*, the weight of evidence at present resists such a view, suggesting instead that it was in fact an unauthorized embellishment of *Hue and Cry*. Accordingly, I have followed Davis in taking *Hue and Cry* as the copy text. *Hue and Cry* (1712a) and *Dunkirk to be Let* (1712b) have been collated with one another, and with Davis (which, as usual, silently expands all the elided names).

Copy text: CUL, Williams 389

References: TS, nos. 582–83. Davis, vol. VI, pp. 137–41. Woolley, 'Canon', no. 19. Rothschild Library, no. 2044. *ESTC* N16900 (*Hue & Cry*, listing three copies); no *ESTC* record for *Dunkirk to be Let*

London edition, 1712a

Title: 𝔄 𝕳𝖚𝖊 𝖆𝖓𝖉 𝖈𝖗𝖞 𝖆𝖋𝖙𝖊𝖗 𝕯𝖎𝖘𝖒𝖆𝖑; | *Being a full and true Account, how a* Whig *L–d* | *was taken at* Dunkirk, *in the Habit of a Chimney-* | *sweeper, and carried before General* Hill.

Imprint: London, Printed in the Year, 1712.

Collation: half-sheet

Pagination: none

Contents: recto: text; verso: blank

Typography: fifty-six lines (excluding title, subtitle and imprint), type-page 228 (276) × 139 mm, twenty lines of roman type 81 mm

Copies examined:
*†Bodl, MS Rawl D383 (135): 309.5 × 184.5 mm, untrimmed; in volume of early eighteenth-century manuscript and printed items; reproduced in reduced facsimile *Tracts 1*, frontispiece; copy not listed in *ESTC*
*†CUL, Williams 389: 309 × 192 mm, untrimmed; unbound; copy not listed in *ESTC*; copy purchased from Sotheby's by Bernard Quaritch Ltd in 1927, sold on to Jerome Kern, returned to Quaritch's possession by and of which Quaritch published a facsimile in *c.*1938 (Harold Williams, 'A Hue and Cry after Dismal', *RES* 6 (1930), 195; Woolley, '*Dialogue*', 216; Rothschild Library, no. 2044); copy not listed in *ESTC*
*†TCC, RW.70.12: 304 × 192 mm, possibly trimmed outer edge; unbound

?London edition, 1712b

Title: Dunkirk *to be Let,* Or, *A Town Ready Furnish'd.* | WITH | 𝕬 𝕳𝖚𝖊=𝖆𝖓𝖉=𝕮𝖗𝖞 after 𝕯𝖎𝖘𝖒𝖆𝖑: | *Being a full and true Account, how a* Whig *L–d was taken at* Dunkirk, | *in the Habit of a Chimney-Sweeper, and carried before General* Hill. | *To which is added the Copy of a* PAPER *that was found in his Pocket.*

Imprint: [in] the YEAR. M. DCXII [*loss through trimming*].

Collation: half-sheet

Contents: recto: text; verso: blank

Typography: sixty lines (incl. two blank lines), type-page 263 (325) × 161 mm; twenty lines of roman type (lines 1–42) 94 mm, (lines 43–60) 84 mm

Copy examined:
*†Bodl, Vet. A4 c.107 (2) (formerly Pamphlets 305 (53)): 336 × 191 mm, trimmed with partial loss of imprint

Emendation

197.13 plainly] 1712b; planly

Historical collation

195.1 *small*] *a small* 1712b
195.7 Bunch] a Bunch 1712b
196.8 That] This 1712b
196.15 Stobb] Hobb Davis
 Davis, who could 'make no sense of "each Stobb"', suggested a compositorial misreading of Swift's capital H 'which is not unlike St' *(vol. VI, p. 211), producing the plausible 'Hobb'. However,* OED *offers some support for the printed reading: a 'stob' was a stake or a post (s.v. 'stob', sb. 3).*
196.16 heap] deal 1712b
196.19 *om.*] [*After* 'about him.'] It is said, that he had the following Verses found in his Pocket, which he scatter'd up and down the Town. *Old* Lewis *thus the Terms of Peace to Burnish, | Has lately let out* Dunkirk *Ready Furnish'd; | But whether 'tis by* Lease, *or* Coppy-hold, | *Or* Tenure in Capite, *we've not been told. | But this we hope, if yet he pulls his Horns in, | He'll be oblig'd to give his Tenants Warning.* 1712b
197.1 no nor] nor no 1712b
197.3 than] then 1712b
197.6 (though that was too good a Trade for him)] *om.* 1712b
197.10 Pail full] Pail-full 1712b
197.10 Then they] They then 1712b
197.12 whispered] whispering 1712b
197.13 plainly] planly 1712a; plainly 1712b
197.19 L—d *Dismal*] L—d *Dismal* 1712b
197.20 The Governor then] Then the Governour 1712b
197.20 sorry] *very sorry* 1712b
197.27 hath] and hath 1712b

Word division (compounds only)

Copy text
195.1 Chimney-sweeper

Edited text
none

A LETTER FROM THE PRETENDER, TO A WHIG-LORD: TEXTUAL ACCOUNT

This was probably composed between 17 and 19 July 1712 (Woolley, 'Dialogue', 216; see also Woolley, 'Canon', 108 n. 67) and was published on 19 July 1712: 'To day there will be anothr Grub; a Letter from the Pretendr to a Whig Ld.' (Williams, *JSt*, pp. 550–1). Rivington suggests Barber as possible printer (p. 248); however, it is very poorly printed, with misaligned type, a mixed fount, and word repetitions and omissions, suggesting – from a charitable perspective – extreme haste. Unlike others of Swift's '7 penny Papers' of late June and July 1712 (Williams, *JSt*, p. 553), this work was not advertised by Morphew. It was not entered in the SR. Its authenticity is confirmed by its inclusion as 'Pretender's Letter to a Whig Lord' in Charles Ford's catalogue of Swift's political pamphlets which he sent to Swift in 1733; however, in an unexpected memory lapse, Swift confessed that he had no recollection of writing this and four other items listed by Ford (Woolley, *Corr.*, vol. III, pp. 699, 701–2). The work was collected by John Nichols, who first reprinted it in *A Supplement to Dr Swift's Works* (1776) as part of Hawkesworth's large octavo edition (TS, no. 88) rather than, as Davis claims (Davis, vol. VI, p. 211), in the first 1779 *Supplement* volume of Hawkesworth's quarto edition (TS, no. 87), although the latter edition does present a slightly more accurate text. (The work was also reprinted in the first 1779 *Supplement* volume of Hawkesworth's small octavo edition (TS, no. 90), varying only very slightly from the quarto edition.) Both 1779 editions identify a copy at Lambeth Palace Library; this copy, which was listed in *TS* and provided the copy text for Davis, was in a volume that has since been stolen from the library. The 1712 text has been collated for substantive variants against the 1776 and 1779 reprints and Davis; despite the poor setting I have resisted the temptation to emend anything other than obvious errors, meaning that possible mistakes of spelling and punctuation (such as 'Corresponddence' and 'oposeth') have been left untouched.

Copy text: NLS, Crawford MB 1064. (Text reproduced with permission of the Crawford (Bibliotheca Lindesiana) Collections in the National Library of Scotland.)

References: TS, no. 585. Davis, vol. VI, pp. 145–6. Woolley, 'Canon', no. 19. *Bibliotheca Lindesiana: Catalogue of English broadsides 1505–1897* (Aberdeen: Aberdeen University Press, 1898), no. 1064. *ESTC* T228339 (listing only NLS copy)

1712

Title: A *LETTER* from the | PRETENDER, | *To a Whig-Lord.*

Collation: half-sheet

Pagination: none

Contents: recto: text; verso: blank (presumed)

Typography: thirty-seven lines (including salutation but excluding signature), type-page 217.5 (276) × 139 mm, twenty lines of roman type 118 mm; signature (if extrapolated into twenty lines of roman type) 300 mm.

Copy examined:
*†NLS, Crawford MB 1064: 282 × 155, trimmed; mounted.

Emendations

201.1 ------] this edition; ----[ ]-
201.3 assured] 1776; assu[]ed
201.7 observe] 1776; obse[]ve
201.8 one Letter] 1776; *L*etter
201.11 Perhaps] 1776; Prehaps
201.14 a Year for Life, and a Dukedom.] Davis; a Year for a Year for Life, and and a Dukedom.
201.15 Secretary] 1776; S[]cretary
201.17 will] 1776; well
201.17 Exceptions] 1776; Exception[]
201.17 you, and] Davis; your add
   The compositor evidently intended to set eight not seven pieces of type here and given the proximities of the comma and 'r', and of 'n' and 'd' in the

standard English type-case lay (see Gaskell, 37), a garbled reading such as this is plausible.

202.2 other] 1776; o[]her

202.2 the] 1776; the the

202.6 tell me is what will] 1776; tell is what will

202.6 He] 1776; *H*e

202.6 first] 1776; fi[]st

Historical collation

201.1 *LETTER*]   SUPPOSED   LETTER   1776;   [SUPPOSED] LETTER 1779

201.15 a Year for Life, and a Dukedom.] a Year for a Year for Life, and and a Dukedom. 1712; six thousand pounds a year for life, and a dukedom. 1776–9

201.16 will] well 1712

201.18 Lord] 1712; a Lord 1776+

I am not convinced that an indefinite article is needed here.

201.18 you, and] your add 1712; you and 1776

See the relevant emendation for an explanation of this variant.

202.1 that] the 1776

202.2 tell me is what will] tell is what will 1712; tell me is what would 1776+

202.3 shall] should 1776

202.14 James R.] *om.* 1776

Word division (compounds only)

Copy text
none

Edited text
none

A DEFENCE OF ERASMUS LEWIS
OR THE EXAMINER
(2 FEBRUARY 1713):
TEXTUAL ACCOUNT

This issue of *The Examiner* was printed by Barber and published by Morphew on 2 February 1713. Swift had ceased as editor of *The Examiner* in June 1711 but apparently contributed at least two further occasional numbers: vol. 2, no. 34 (17–24 July 1712), known as 'Remarks on Fleetwood's Preface' and to be included in a later volume, and this issue. (One other issue, vol. 3, no. 16 (12–16 January 1713), the so-called 'Appendix' to *Conduct of the Allies* and *Some Remarks on the Barrier Treaty*, has been attributed to Swift in the past but will not be included in this edition: see the Textual Introduction, pp. 335–6.) Swift first mentioned the rumour of Erasmus Lewis's association with the Pretender's court on 26 January, declaring his intention to make Abel Roper's *Post Boy* 'give a Relation of it' (Williams, *JSt*, p. 609). A short paragraph duly appeared in *The Post Boy* for 27–29 January; a version of this account also appeared in the 29 January issue of *The Evening Post* and the 31 January issue of *The London Gazette* (Davis, vol. VI, p. xxvii). On 31 January Swift visited Barber 'in the City . . . to alter an Examiner about my Friend Lewis's story, which will be told with Remarks', and the following day, Barber returned the visit: 'I dictated to him what was fitt to be sd, and then Mr Lewis came and correctd as he would have it' (Williams, *JSt*, p. 612). Nichols included the issue (presumably in light of the entries in *JSt*) in *A Supplement to Dr Swift's Works* (1776) as part of Hawkesworth's large octavo edition (TS, no. 88) and reprinted it in the 1779 *Supplement* volumes of Hawkesworth's quarto and small octavo editions (TS, nos. 87 and 90; 1779a and 1779b respectively). Nichols entitled the work, *A Compleat Refutation of the Falsehoods alledged against Erasmus Lewis, Esq*, a title which, in modified forms, was used by editors up to the twentieth century, including Davis. (The running titles in the 1776 and 1779 editions read: 'VINDICATION OF

ERASMUS LEWIS, ESQ.'.) We have, however, adopted a more concise title, 'A Defence of Erasmus Lewis'. The work has been collated against *The Third Volume of the Examiners* (1714), where the issue is numbered as 10, the 1776 and 1779 editions (which, while following the 1714 edition for substantive readings, altered spelling, punctuation and capitalization throughout) and Davis.

Copy text: BL, Burney collection

References: TS, no. 525. Davis, vol. VI, pp. 171–8. Woolley, 'Canon', no. 24. *ESTC*, P1438 (see also P1437)

London edition, 1714

Title: Vol. III. [flush right:] Numb. 21. | The EXAMINER. | [rule] | From 𝕱𝖗𝖎𝖉𝖆𝖞 *January* 30, to 𝕸𝖔𝖓𝖉𝖆𝖞 *February* 2, 1712. | [rule]

Imprint: *LONDON*: Printed for JOHN MORPHEW, near *Stationers-Hall*, 1712.

Collation: half-sheet

Pagination: none

Contents: recto: headline; recto–verso: text; verso: '*ADVERTISEMENTS.*'; imprint

Typography:
recto: two columns, fifty-nine lines each, type-page 212 (290 or more) × 79 mm (col. 1), 78 mm (col. 2), twenty lines of roman type 72 mm
verso: two columns, seventy-seven lines each, type-page 276 (285 or more) × 78 mm, twenty lines of roman type 72 mm (except advertisements)

Failures of catchwords to catch:
none

Copies examined:
†BL, Burney collection: copy not physically examined; reproduction used from *Early English Newspapers* microfilm, reel 1062
*†Bodl, Hope. fol.17: 326 × c.198 mm, trimmed

Emendations

Historical collation

205.6 *Parva motu primo*] *Parva metu primo* Davis

Davis silently corrects the Latin tag taken from Virgil's description of rumours about Dido and Aeneas in Book IV of The Aeneid. *Interestingly, despite the fact that it was clearly an error (see for example, the relevant lines from 1701 Tonson edition of Virgil's works), this misquotation was not corrected in any of the subsequent eighteenth-century editions. Indeed,* ECCO *records only one other usage of this misquotation: on the title page of Carl Gyllenborg's* The Northern Crisis *(1716), which also bore Morphew's imprint.*

205.7 Service] good 1714; 1776; 1779b

208.16 *your self*] yourself 1776–9; Davis

208.32 Humane-kind] human-kind 1776–9

209.20 it self] itself 1776–9

209.25 whither] whether 1714; 1776–9

210.6 Third] third person 1714; 1776; 1779b

Word division (compounds only)

Copy text
none

Edited text
none

THE VOTE OF THANKS BY THE HOUSE OF LORDS (9 APRIL 1713) AND THE HUMBLE ADDRESS OF . . . THE LORDS (11 APRIL 1713): TEXTUAL ACCOUNT

These two works differ markedly from the other political works included in this volume, most notably in terms of their intended purpose. The 'Vote of Thanks' was the form of words agreed by the House of Lords following the Queen's Speech at the opening of Parliament. The 'Vote' prompted – and set the scope for – the slightly longer 'Address' from the Lords to the Queen in which the Lords formally and publicly thanked the Queen for her speech. The text of the 'Vote' was recorded only in the Lords' Journal and never printed; however, it was necessarily closely linked with the 'Address' as, understandably, there has to be a strong textual consistency between the two.

The brevity of the two works – the 'Vote' and the 'Address' – belies the complexity of their textual histories. In early Spring 1713, Robert Harley was making preparations for the opening of Parliament that would follow the anticipated conclusion of the negotiations over the Treaty of Utrecht. At dinner with Harley on 8 March 1713, Swift was shown a draft of the proposed Queen's Speech ('wch I corrected in sevrall Places'); he also noted that '[I] penned the vote of Address of thanks for the Speech' (Williams, *JSt*, p. 635). On 15 March, he 'had ready what [Harley] wanted, but he would not see it, but put me off till to morrow'; two days later, the prorogation of Parliament meant that Swift had to 'keep what I have till next week, for I believe he will not see it till just the Evening before the Session' (pp. 639–40). On 7 April, despite the imminent opening of Parliament, 'the Business' that Swift had with Harley was again 'put . . . off till to morrow' by the latter; consequently, it was only on 8 April that Swift was able to complete 'the

Business I had for him to his Satisfaction' (p. 656). The Queen delivered her speech to the newly convened Parliament on 9 April, after which the Lords agreed to prepare an address of thanks, appointing a committee for the purpose; the text of the address was approved by the House the following day, which was formally presented to Anne on 11 April (*LJ*, vol. XIX, pp. 511–16). On the same day (11 April), the Lords ordered that – as was usual with such addresses – the text, along with Anne's answer, be 'forthwith Printed and Published' by the Queen's Printing House.

The texts

Manuscript drafts of the 'Vote' and the 'Address', in Swift's hand with annotations by Harley, survive in Harley's papers at the BL (hereafter BL 'Vote' and BL 'Address' respectively). They survive on separate pieces of paper one after the other (although they have been re-ordered so that the 'Address' precedes the 'Vote'). The approved wording for the 'Vote' and the 'Address' was recorded in the manuscript journals of the House of Lords, session 1713 (hereafter *LJ* 'Vote' and *LJ* 'Address' respectively); these journals were later printed but I have consulted copies of the original manuscripts. The 'Address' as printed by the Queen's Printing House in 1713 survives as a printed bifoliam (hereafter 1713 'Address'), containing the Lords' license (dated 11 April), the text of the address (dated 10 April), and the Queen's response. (The 'Vote', as indicated above, was *not* printed.) Copies of the 1713 'Address' survive in at least two largely identical editions (one with a cancel title page); moreover, copies of the edition with the original title page bear different pressmarks, indicating that at least two separate pressmen or presses were involved in its production. However, the much larger size of the Queen's Printing House, the frequency and presumed speed with which such parliamentary addresses were produced, and the formulaic layout and design of these printed addresses suggests that such bibliographical variation reflects printing house practice rather than anything peculiar to this text. A version of the 'Address' was printed by Deane Swift in 1765 (hereafter 1765 'Address'): in volume VIII, part 1 (1765) of Hawkesworth's quarto edition of Swift's *Works* (TS, no. 87; hereafter 1765a 'Address'); in volume XV of Hawkesworth's large octavo (TS, no. 88; hereafter 1765b 'Address'), small octavo (TS, no. 90; hereafter 1765c 'Address'), and 18° editions (TS, no. 92; hereafter 1765d 'Address'); and in volume XII of Faulkner's octavo edition (TS, no. 47; hereafter 1765e 'Address'). It was also reproduced in the same year in volume XII of Faulkner's duodecimo and 18° editions (TS, nos. 52, 53, hereafter 1765f and 1765g); I am grateful to Daniel Traister of Van Pelt Library, University of Pennsylvania, for providing me with copies from these editions. Apart from a single substantive variant (recorded below, and clearly an error) and the occasional difference in punctuation, the 1765 editions follow each other closely, except that 1765d varies considerably in terms of punctuation and capitalization.

Differences

There are several substantive variations between the BL 'Vote' and 'Address' and the *LJ* 'Vote' and 'Address', the significance of which will be discussed below. Not surprisingly, the 1713 'Address' follows the *LJ* 'Address' closely; aside from minor differences in punctuation, capitalization and spelling, there is only one substantive but minor variant. In contrast, the 1765 'Address' differs from *both* the BL 'Address' and *LJ* 'Address'/1713 'Address', indicating the existence of a separate manuscript draft, since lost (see below).

The 'Vote'

Swift's specific claim of March 8 is that he wrote the 'Vote' (Ehrenpreis, for one, confused the 'Vote' with the 'Address' (Vol. II, p. 592)): in other words, the text of the vote taken in the Lords on 9 April and subject to an unsuccessful motion to strike out the reference to the Peace of Utrecht and the Protestant Succession. That Swift wrote the 'Vote' is supported by the BL 'Vote', written in Swift's hand with Harley's alterations although, interestingly, Harley's interlineation of a reference to the 'Harmony between her [Anne] & the House of Hannover' did not make it into the text recorded in the *LJ* (although a similar sentiment did appear in the text of the 'Address' as approved by the Lords). Despite Swift's unequivocal claim of authorship for the 'Vote' and its survival as a manuscript in Swift's hand, Davis did not print the 'Vote' (although he reproduced a photograph of the manuscript, facing p. 183), as he took the 1713 'Address' (i.e. the version printed by the Queen's Printing House) as his copy text, which does not include the text of the 'Vote'. Given this volume's editorial policy to prefer texts that had the most immediate public relevance and the lack of a contemporary printed edition of the 'Vote', I have taken the text of *LJ* 'Vote' as copy text, which has been collated with the BL 'Vote'. For readers interested in Swift's draft, a transcript of the BL 'Vote' has been included as an appendix.

The 'Address'

The case for Swift's authorship of the address is strong but not necessarily overwhelming. His references to his involvement with its composition are vague and inconclusive. As indicated above, a draft of the 'Address' itself in Swift's hand with Harley's corrections survives in Harley's papers (BL 'Address'). Harley underlined two passages, the first of which was omitted from the *LJ* 'Address'/1713 'Address' and the second substantially amended. Swift's additional claim that he corrected Harley's draft for the Queen's speech is substantiated by surviving manuscripts in Harley's papers, as J. A. Downie and David Woolley have demonstrated ('Swift, Oxford and the Composition of Queen's Speeches, 1710–1714', *BLJ* 8 (1982), 121–46, especially 125–9) and it is possible that his 'Business' with Harley in March and April included both the Queen's speech and the 'Address'. Swift was also involved with Harley during these months in the drawing-up of lists of the Lords assessing, it seems, their political loyalties (Clyve Jones, 'Swift, the Earl of Oxford, and the Management of the House of Lords in 1713: Two New Lists', *BLJ* 16 (1990), 117–30). Downie and Woolley are sceptical about Swift's actual authorship of the 'Address': 'it would seem that, with regard to *The Humble Address* . . . he acted as the Lord Treasurer's amanuensis' ('Swift, Oxford and the Composition', 123–4), although this did not prevent Woolley from later categorically including the 'Address' in his 'Canon' of Swift's pamphleteering between 1711 and 1714: '[Swift's] *authorship* of the Address, as well as the Vote, is confirmed by study of its textual history' ('Canon', 110, emphasis in original). Here Woolley draws his evidence from the version printed in the Hawkesworth edition (1765 'Address') which, he claims, was based on an 'earlier version' of the text drafted by Swift prior to the draft surviving in Harley's papers.

At first glance, Woolley's proposed straightforward textual progression from Swift's draft (lost but printed as 1765 'Address'), to second Harley-altered draft (BL 'Address'), to the text approved by the Lords (*LJ* 'Address') and subsequently printed by the Queen's Printing House (1713 'Address') is not supported by the surviving historical collations. There is clearly a close affinity between the BL 'Address' and the 1765 'Address', with both sharing a number of readings not present in the *LJ* 'Address' (and by extension the 1713 'Address'). But which came first? One way of answering this would be to consider the relationship between the BL 'Address' and the *LJ* 'Address'.

External evidence (Swift's account to Stella; Harley's annotations) coupled with their textual similarities indicates that a direct line of descent from the BL 'Address' to the *LJ* 'Address' can be identified. However, the differences between the two indicate that there must have been at least one interim draft. The passages in the BL 'Address' underlined by Harley correspond to those most significantly altered in the *LJ* 'Address'; similarly, Harley's change of 'Harmony' to 'friendshipp' is retained in the *LJ* 'Address'. The interim draft(s), then, would have included revised versions of the passages underlined in BL 'Address' and the word 'Friendship' along with a number of further changes that were not signalled by Harley in BL 'Address'. This would seem to rule out the text of the 1765 'Address' as a possible interim version: not only does this include 'Harmony' but it also does not contain certain readings shared by the BL 'Address' and the *LJ* 'Address'. The issue of priority is, however, muddied as there are two instances where the 1765 'Address' presents a reading that appears in the *LJ* 'Address' but which is at variance with BL 'Address'. The first of these (1765 'Address': 'humble'; BL 'Address': 'humblest') could perhaps be coincidence; the second (the phrase 'the success of your endeavours for a general peace' does not appear in the BL 'Address') would seem to imply a relationship between the 1765 'Address' and the *LJ* 'Address' that was *subsequent* to the BL 'Address'. However, the apparent anomaly is solved quite simply: the BL 'Vote' (the manuscript in Swift's hand in Harley's papers) includes those readings that appear in both the 1765 'Address' and *LJ* 'Address' and, in seeking to make the texts of the 'Vote' and 'Address' consistent with one another, someone – perhaps Harley, perhaps Swift – imported these phrases from the BL 'Vote' into the *LJ* 'Address'.

There are two further complicating factors: authorship and provenance. First of all, it would seem very difficult to claim Swift as the sole author of a work that was 'ghosted' upon the Lords' behalf and that was hence subject to the alterations of Harley and presumably the relevant members charged by the Lords 'to draw' up the 'Address' itself. (A similar point could be made about the 'Vote' although it is clear that the text of the 'Vote' had been prepared in advance of the debate.) Second, BL 'Address' survives in Harley's papers, while the 1765 'Address' must have been based on a manuscript that remained in Swift's possession and was subsequently passed down to Deane Swift, his cousin's son-in-law. While it is of course possible that this does not accurately reflect the exchange of drafts between Harley and Swift up to 9 April, it would seem that the 1765 'Address' was not a manuscript submitted to Harley (although it could have been a draft of one) and that, although the changes made by Harley to the BL 'Address' may have been made in Swift's presence or communicated to Swift afterwards, Harley did not return this manuscript to Swift.

I therefore propose the following hypothesis. Swift drafted at least two versions of the 'Address': the 1765 'Address' (which may or may not have been shown to Harley) and then, subsequent to that, the BL 'Address'. This version, along with BL 'Vote', was annotated by Harley and re-drafted, possibly by Swift, but, if so, Swift was not able to take away either BL 'Address' or BL 'Vote' to work from as they remained in Harley's possession. The revised 'Vote' and 'Address' may have been subject to further alterations but it was these (now lost) versions that were physically submitted to the Lords and Lords' committee respectively (on the grounds that no copy of the revised 'Address' or 'Vote' survives in Harley's papers), who in turn may or may not have made further changes. The approved versions were then entered in the journals of the House of Lords and a manuscript copy of the 'Address' (possibly the same one used to make the entry in the Lords' journals) was then passed to the Queen's Printing House.

The question for the textual editor of Swift's political works, however, is to which version of the 'Address' should primacy be given. (See the previous section for an account of the textual authority of the 'Vote'.) Davis, who did not consider the textual history of the 'Address' in any great detail (and completely omitted the 'Vote'), presented the 1713 'Address' as copy text. While it is possible that all or most of the substantive differences between the 1713 'Address' and the BL 'Address' were a consequence of Swift's own revision, the extent of Swift's hand in these differences is impossible to gauge; moreover, it would seem unlikely that Swift was able to retain any authority over the text once he had left it with Harley, let alone when it reached the Lords or the Queen's Printing House. However, in light of this volume's editorial decision to use, for works whose importance was directly linked to their immediate currency, the version that was publicly available (and hence able to have a direct bearing upon public debate), I have decided to follow Davis and take the 1713 edition as copy text. (I have chosen the CUL copy on the grounds that the one place where it varies from the other edition – a comma after 'Bound' in the final paragraph – seems slightly more grammatical; however, in contrast with the *LJ* version, all the 1713 copies are heavily punctuated.) It has been collated for substantive variants against the BL 'Address', the *LJ* 'Address', the 1765 'Address' (1765a–g) (although readers should bear in mind my belief that the 1765 'Address' represents an earlier manuscript draft) and Davis. The BL 'Address' has been supplied as an appendix.

Copy text:
- 'Vote': Parliamentary Archives, HL/PO/JO/1/84, p. 6
- 'Address': CUL, Broadsides B.71.42

References: Not in TS. SwJ, nos. 386–7. Both manuscripts transcribed (with very minor errors) in Williams, *JSt*, pp. 684–5. Davis vol. VI, p. 183; facsimile of manuscripts facing pp. xxviii, 183. Woolley, 'Canon', no. 25. *ESTC* N7192 (listing ten copies)

Manuscript (BL 'Vote' and BL 'Address')

Location: BL, Add. MS 70030, fos. 200–1 ('Address'); fo. 202^r ('Vote of Thanks')

Description:
- 'Address': holograph in Swift's hand with underlining and corrections by Robert Harley; in Harley Papers, vol. 30, October 1712–June 1713; no visible foliation (foliation taken from SwJ); bifoliam with page size: 196 × 155 mm; horizontal chainlines (i.e. a folio cut vertically in half); large 'Pro Patria' watermark in fold (see Heawood, nos. 3696–718).
- 'Vote of Thanks': Swift holograph with interlineation in another hand; in Harley Papers, vol. 30, October 1712–June 1713; no visible foliation (foliation taken from SwJ); single leaf, 158 × 196 mm; vertical chainlines; no watermark

Contents:
- 'Address': fo. 200^r (top) '[1713, April 9]' in pencil; fos. 200^{r-v} text written on right-hand half; fo. 201^r blank; fo. 201^v endorsed 'Address. &c'

- 'Vote of Thanks': fo. 202^r (top) '[1713, April 9]' in pencil; fo. 202^r text written on top half; fo. 202^v endorsed along right hand edge: 'Vote. &c'

Lords' Journal (LJ 'Vote' and LJ 'Address')

Location: Parliamentary Archives, HL/PO/JO/1/84, pp. 5–6 ('Vote'), 12 ('Address')

Description:
- 'Vote of Thanks': transcript of text as debated and approved by the House of Lords, 9 April 1713, and recorded in the Manuscript Journal of the House of Lords, Session 1713; copy supplied by the House of Lords Record Office
- 'Address': transcript of text to be presented to Queen by the House of Lords, 10 April 1713, and recorded in the Manuscript Journal of the House of Lords, Session 1713; copy supplied by the House of Lords Record Office

Contents:
- 'Vote of Thanks': p. 5 text as debated; p. 6 text as approved
- 'Address': p. 12 text as presented to Queen

London edition, 1713a ('Address')

Title: [within double rules, 246 × 144.5 mm] The Humble | ADDRESS | Of the Right Honourable the | Lords Spiritual and Temporal | In Parliament Assembled, | PRESENTED TO | HER MAJESTY | On *Saturday* the Eleventh Day of *April*, 1713.| [rule] | WITH | Her Majesties | MOST GRACIOUS | ANSWER. | [rule] | *LONDON*, | Printed by *John Baskett*, Printer to the Queens most Ex- | [indented] cellent Majesty, And by the Assigns of *Thomas New-* | [indented] *comb*, and *Henry Hills*, deceas'd. 1713. | [below double rules frame, flush right] (Price One Peny.)

Collation: 2°: A^2

Pagination: 1–2, 3–4

Contents: A1ʳ title page; A1ᵛ license; A2ʳ⁻ᵛ text; A2ᵛ Queen's answer.

Typography: type-page 261 × 141.5 mm, twenty lines of roman type 144 mm (no full page of text, measurements taken from running title to direction line)

Copies examined:
*†Bod, O.Pv.Eng (previously 22772 d.5): 301 × 177 mm, trimmed; in large volume of parliamentary votes and addresses, 1707–14 (arranged chronologically); copy not listed in *ESTC*
*†Bod, Pamph. 311 (44): 306 × 194 mm, trimmed; A1 and A2 detached from one another and separately tipped in; in volume of miscellaneous printed items from 1712–14; reduced facsimile of title page reproduced in Davis, vol. VI, p. 181
†Houghton Library, Harvard University, *fEC7.G798P.713h: copy not physically examined; reproduction used; presumed *ECCO* copy; price omitted possibly due to trimming or variant title page

London edition, 1713b ('Address')

Title: [within double rules, 253 × 146 mm] The Humble | ADDRESS | Of the Right Honourable the | Lords Spiritual and Temporal | In Parliament Assembled, | PRESENTED TO | HER MAJESTY | On *Saturday* the Eleventh Day of *April*, 1713.| [rule] | WITH | Her Majesties | MOST GRACIOUS | ANSWER. | [rule] | *LONDON*, | Printed by *John Baskett*, Printer to the Queens most Ex- | cellent Majesty, And by the Assigns of *Thomas Newcomb*, | and *Henry Hills*, deceas'd. 1713.

Collation: 2°: A²

Pagination: 1–2, 3–4

Contents: A1ʳ title page; A1ᵛ license; A2ʳ⁻ᵛ text; A2ᵛ Queen's answer

Typography: type-page 267 × 141.5 mm, twenty lines of roman type 144 mm (no full page of text, measurements taken from running title to direction line)

Copy examined:
*†CUL, Broadsides B.71.42: 281 × 171 mm, trimmed; unbound bifoliam; cancel title page; copy not listed in *ESTC*

Emendations

213.4 Communicating] *this edition*; Comunicating [*second 'm' interpolated from contraction mark over first 'm'*]

Historical collation

Vote of thanks
213.2 presented] made BL
213.2 Thanks] Most humble thanks BL
213.3 House] House to Her Majesty BL
213.4 Concluded] agreed on BL
213.8 Affection] Duty and Affection BL
213.9 due] that are due BL
213.9 an] the most BL

Humble Address
215.2 The Humble ADDRESS Of the Right Honourable the Lords Spiritual and Temporal in PARLIAMENT Assembled. *Die Veneris* 10 *Aprilis*, 1713. *Most Gracious Sovereign*] *om*. BL; Most Gracious Sovereign *LJ*; THE ADDRESS OF THE HOUSE of LORDS to the QUEEN. [Drawn up by Dr SWIFT, at the Command of the LORD TREASURER, and delivered by the DUKE of GRAFTON.] 1765
215.5 humble] humblest BL
215.6 Your Parliament] this House BL; 1765
215.7 a Peace] peace 1765
215.7 Concluded] concluded, so honorable to Your Majesty and safe and advantageous to Your Kingdoms BL; agreed on, so honourable to your Majesty, and safe and advantageous to your kingdoms 1765
   The BL variant reading is underlined, presumably by Harley and presumably to indicate a need for revision.
215.8 few Years] a few Years BL; 1765

215.9 And also do Congratulate Your Majesty upon the Success of Your Endeavours for a General Peace.] We likewise beg leave to congratulate with Your Majesty upon the generall Peace you have procured for all Your Allyes, wherein the true Interests and just Pretensions of each are so fully provided for that the Tranquillity and Welfare of Europe will be owing (next to the Divine Providence) to Your Majesty's Wisdom and Goodness. BL; We likewise beg leave to congratulate with your Majesty upon the success of your endeavours for a general peace; whereby the tranquillity and welfare of Europe will be owing (next to the Divine Providence) to your Majesty's wisdom and goodness. 1765

The BL variant reading is underlined, presumably by Harley and presumably to indicate a need for revision. 1765a ends 'to your your Majesty's wisdom and goodness'.

215.11 least] last BL

215.11 great Support and Ornament] greatest Ornament and Protector BL; 1765

215.12 Continue to take, as You have always done, the Wisest Measures] continue to take the wisest Measures BL; do every thing 1765

215.15 Friendship] Harmony BL; 1765

The BL variant reading is underlined and Harley has written 'friendshipp' in the margin.

215.16 we do humbly] we humbly *LJ*

215.16 Express] are pleased to express BL; 1765

215.18 strictest] greatest 1765

215.19 the Dutiful Returns] Returns BL; 1765

215.19 paid, by] due from BL; 1765

Word division (compounds only)

Copy text
none

Edited text
none

THE IMPORTANCE OF THE
GUARDIAN CONSIDERED:
TEXTUAL ACCOUNT

Entered by Barber in the SR on 2 November 1713 (although he did not sign the entry as was normal practice), this was printed by Barber and published by Morphew on the same day (Woolley 'Canon', endpaper table; Rivington, p. 252). Advertisements for it appeared in the 30 October and 2 November issues of *The Examiner* (Davis, vol. VIII, p. xiii), and it was also included among known Swift works in the first paragraph of Morphew's advertisements at the end of the 1714 *Third Volume of the Examiners* (Woolley, 'Canon', illustration 3a). Swift made no mention of the work in *JSt* but Charles Ford listed it in his 1733 catalogue of Swift's political pamphlets (Woolley, *Corr.*, vol. III, p. 699). Like *Letter from the Pretender* and *The New Way of Selling Places*, *The Importance of the Guardian Considered* was collected by John Nichols, who reprinted it first in *A Supplement to Dr Swift's Works* (1776), with copious footnotes, as part of Hawkesworth's large octavo edition (TS, no. 88; hereafter 1776) and again in the second 1779 *Supplement* volume of Hawkesworth's small octavo edition (TS, no. 90; hereafter 1779), this time with more modest footnotes. (Davis was apparently unaware of the 1776 reprint.) 1776 was prefaced by a footnote: 'This Tract is not inserted in its proper order; the Editor (who had in vain advertised for it in the public papers for some months) having been accidentally favoured with a copy of it whilst the preceding Letters were at the press' (p. 445). (Rather than being included in the opening section of collected prose, the work appeared about two-thirds through the volume between Swift's correspondence and poetry.) In the 1779 reprint, where the work sits at the beginning of volume two, Nichols expanded this footnote to explain the evidence for his attribution: he was unaware of Ford's catalogue but instead based his case upon Morphew's 1714 advertisement. Nichols – as Davis would do in the twentieth century – spelled out in full all the 'emvowelled' words even though the *Importance* includes a passage explicitly explaining this practice. Nichols did at least retain most of the marginal references to specific pages in Richard Steele's *Importance of Dunkirk Consider'd*, integrating them within the text; Davis excised these completely. Davis also, uncharacteristically, modernized the spelling on at least two occasions: 'hindred' became 'hindered', 'publick' became 'public'. Otherwise, apart from occasional mistranscriptions of punctuation and capitalization, he follows 1713. 1776 and 1779 regularized spellings, punctuation, capitalization and italicization (most notably romanizing the 1713's italic dedication and 'correspondence'). The 1713 edition has been collated against 1776 and Davis; the variants have been cross-checked with 1779.

Copy text: CUL, Williams 312

References: TS, no. 591. Davis, vol. VIII, pp. 1–25. Woolley, 'Canon', no. 26. Rothschild Library, no. 2048. *ESTC* T11780 (listing thirty-four copies)

London edition, 1713

Title: [within double rules, 156 × 87 mm] THE | IMPORTANCE | OF THE | GUARDIAN | Considered, in a Second | LETTER | TO THE | Bailiff of *Stockbridge*. | [rule] | By a Friend of Mr. *St---le*. | [double rule] | *LONDON*: | Printed for *John Morphew*, near *Stationers* | *Hall*. 1713. Price 6 *d*.

Collation: 8°: A–F⁴ (D2 missigned 'D3')

Pagination: 1 4, 5–46, *47 8*

Contents: A1ʳ title page; A1ᵛ blank; A2ʳ⁻ᵛ preface; A3ʳ–F3ᵛ text; F4ʳ⁻ᵛ blank

Typography: thirty lines per page (C4ʳ), type-page 141 (152) × 76 mm, twenty lines of roman type 94 mm; dedication and 'correspondence' on D4ʳ–E1ᵛ, twenty lines of italic type 118 mm; indented marginal notes (extrapolated measurements), twenty lines of roman type 70–80 mm

Failures of catchwords to catch:
none

Copies examined:
*†§Bodl, 8° M. 21 Linc.(3): 186 × 119 mm, trimmed, outer edge slightly damaged; in volume of five miscellaneous printed items from 1691 to 1717;

reduced facsimile of title page in Davis, vol. VIII, p. 3; one of registration copies deposited at Stationers' Hall (Chalmers, p. 422)

*§Bodl, Hope adds. 67(1): 177 × 118 mm, trimmed; in volume of nine Steele-related printed items 1713–14

*†Bodl, Pamph. 310(14): 179 × 115 mm, trimmed; A1 detached, A2, A3 very loose, F4 missing; in volume of twenty-eight miscellaneous printed items from 1713

*†CUL, Williams 312: 172 × 106 mm, trimmed; re-bound

*TCC, RW.62.68: 183 × 118 mm, untrimmed and all gatherings except D uncut; stitched

Emendations

227.20 to] 1776; too
237.21 P. 61] 1776; P, 61
239.1 Every] 1776; *Every*

Historical collation

219.1 THE PREFACE] THE AUTHOR'S PREFACE 1776–9
222.2 Pound] pounds 1776–9
222.3 Pound] pounds 1776–9
222.29 On the -------] In the beginning 1776–9
226.6 writ] wrote 1776–9
227.5 Dunkirk] *Dankirk* 1776
227.7 *Tugghe's*] *Tugghe* 1776–9
227.20 to] too 1713
229.24 *St—le*] *Steele* Davis

> *This edition has not made a point of noting the expansion of elisions in posthumous editions. However, at this point during Swift's discussion of the practice of eliding names, both the 1776 and 1779 use the elided form of Steele's name, along with a footnote: 'Thus, in the first Edition, the name was constantly contracted'. A similar footnote appears in Davis: 'The name in the original edition was regularly spelled with a dash, St—'. (Ross and Woolley,* Works *follows the same practice although no explanatory footnote is given.)*

However, such consistency of elision was not quite as constant or as regular as is evidenced in the text given in this volume.

236.3 forgot] forgotten 1776–9

239.26 *Latin*] the *Latin* 1776–9

239.34 a Jest] jest 1776–9

240.23 as long] so long 1776–9

Word division (compounds only)

Copy text

223.29 Corn-cutter

223.32 above-mentioned

230.26 when-ever

233.13 Stock-bridge

233.14 *Under-standing*

233.20 *with-out*

236.23 where-with

Edited text

THE PUBLICK SPIRIT OF
THE WHIGS:
TEXTUAL ACCOUNT

When Swift's *Publick Spirit of the Whigs* was reprinted in volume VI of his collected works, printed by Faulkner in 1738, it was prefaced by a short 'Advertisement':

> UPON the first Publication of this Pamphlet, all the *Scotch* Lords, then in *London*, went in a Body, and complained to Queen *ANNE* of the Affront put on them and their Nation, by the Author of this Treatise. Whereupon a Proclamation was published by her Majesty, offering a Reward of Three hundred Pounds to discover him. The Reason for offering so small a Sum was, that the Queen and Ministry had no Desire to have our supposed Author taken into Custody.   (p. 2)

This short account belies the real complexity of the publication history of the *Publick Spirit*, from its first publication in February 1714 to the attempts by the Lords to identify its author and to prosecute its printer, and the consequent reissuing of the work in a modified form. Quinlan's 1967 essay on the *Publick Spirit* was the first full description of the events surrounding its publication; his account was revised by Rivington and, more substantially, by Fischer ('Legal Response'), both writing in 1989. What is presented here draws heavily on those three accounts, especially Fischer.

Publication date
On 30 January 1714, advertisements for *The Publick Spirit of the Whigs* appeared in *The Post Boy* and *The Mercator*, followed by a 'substantively identical' advertisement in *The Examiner* two days later (Fischer, 'Legal Response', p. 22). The advertisement claimed the work would be published '[i]n a few Days', priced at sixpence 'but to the Subscribers Half a Crown'; its quarto format would make it 'fit to be bound up with the Crisis', a reference to Steele's *The Crisis* which had been published in mid-January. (Fischer believes that the absurd price for subscribers was a deliberate mockery of Steele's use of subscription in publishing *The Crisis*). By 4 February, the proposed price had been raised to a shilling, an indication, according

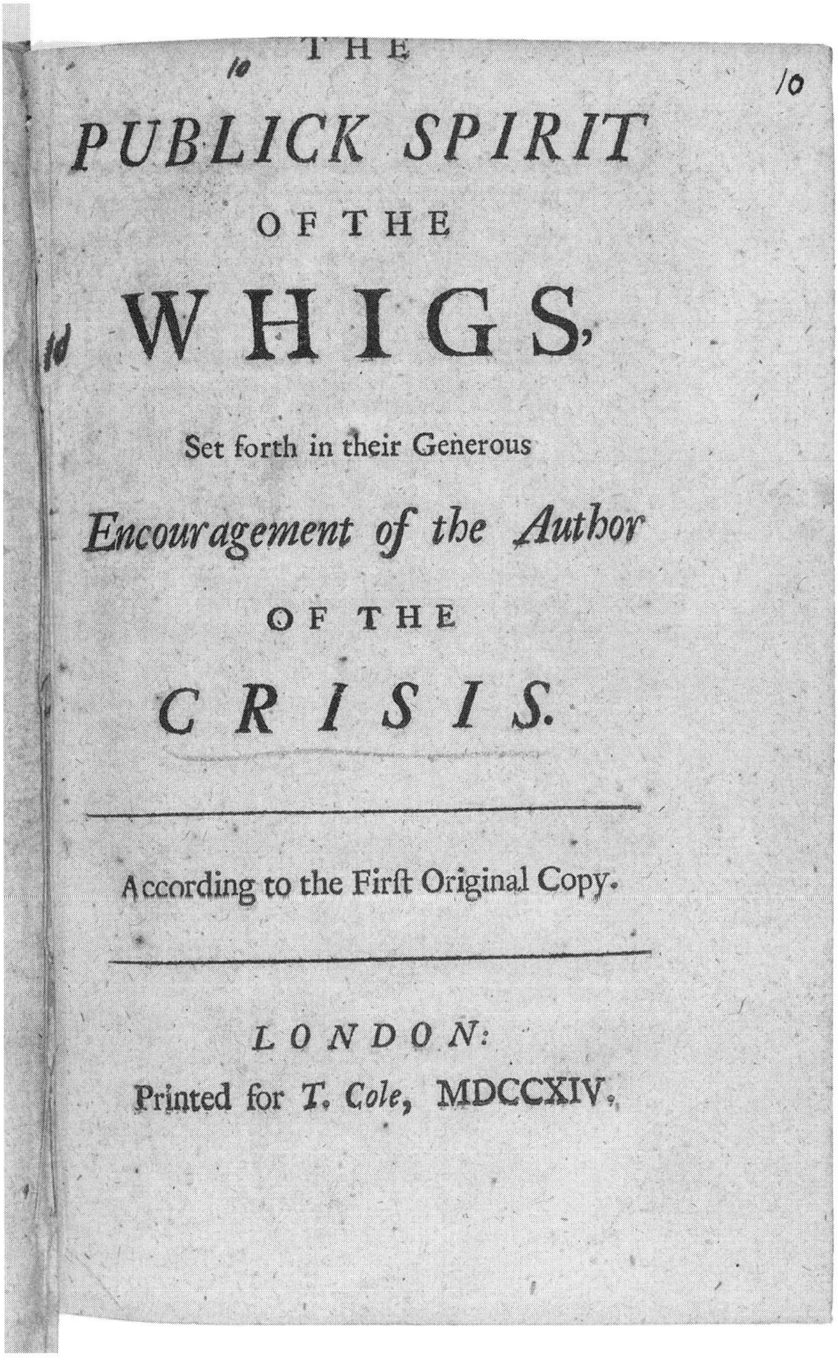

THE

PUBLICK SPIRIT

OF THE

WHIGS,

Set forth in their Generous

Encouragement of the Author

OF THE

CRISIS.

According to the First Original Copy.

LONDON:

Printed for *T. Cole,* MDCCXIV.

Figure 11. Title page of London edition bearing the false imprint 'T. Cole':
CUL, Ddd.25.144 (10).

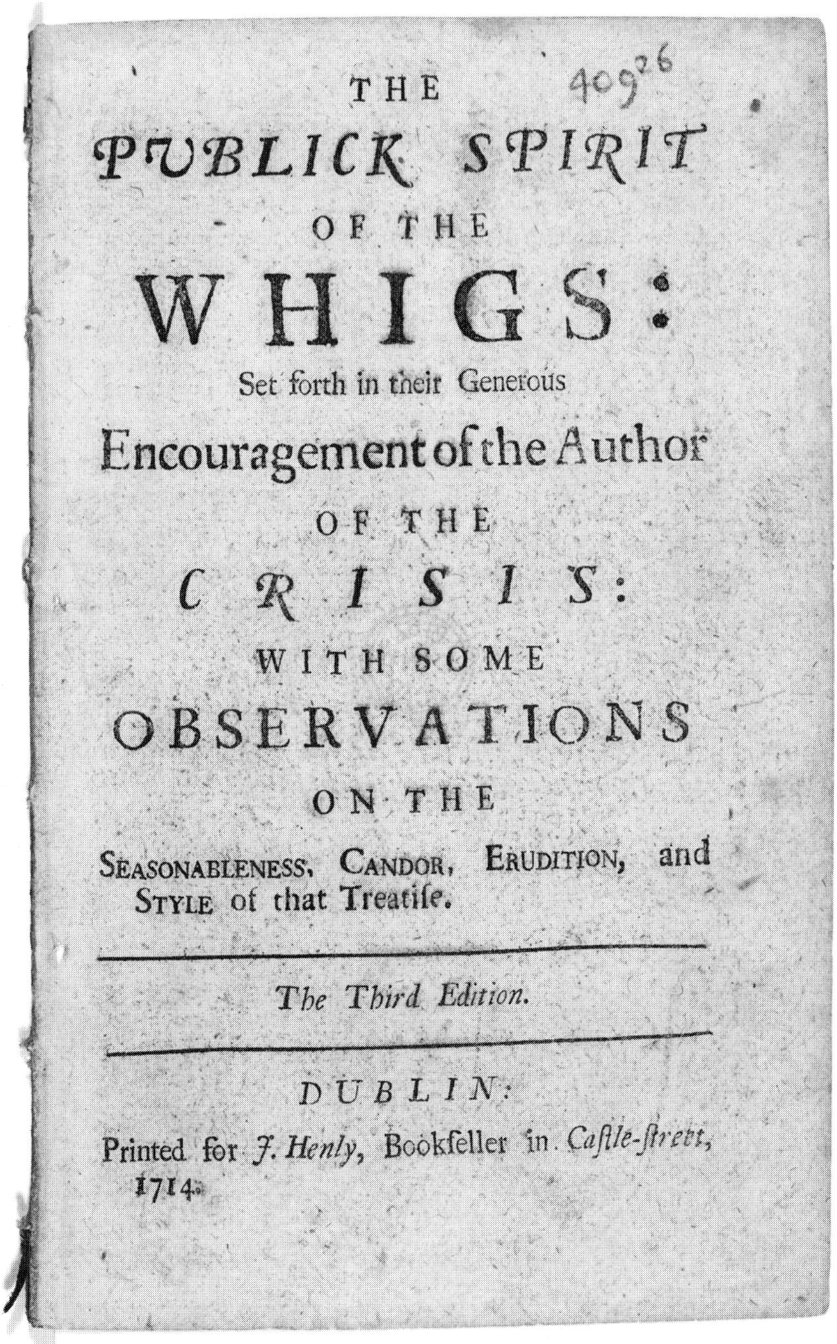

THE   409²⁶

PUBLICK SPIRIT

OF THE

WHIGS:

Set forth in their Generous

Encouragement of the Author

OF THE

CRISIS:

WITH SOME

OBSERVATIONS

ON THE

SEASONABLENESS, CANDOR, ERUDITION, and
STYLE of that Treatise.

The Third Edition.

DUBLIN:

Printed for *J. Henly*, Bookseller in *Castle-street*,
1714.

Figure 12. Title page of the John Henly Dublin edition: CUL, Williams
409 (26).

to Fischer, that Swift had initially misjudged the length of his response. Further advertisements appeared in all three newspapers although there was a hiatus of eleven and nineteen days in the advertisements carried by *The Examiner* and *The Post Boy* respectively – a sign that, Fischer suggests, Swift delayed publication in order to coincide with the probable date that the Queen would be sufficiently recovered from illness to deliver her speech at Parliament's new session. In apparent anticipation, advertisements re-appeared in *The Examiner* (19 and 22 February) and *The Post Boy* (23 February) and it is these that indicate a publication date of 23 February. (Ironically, Anne was still not able to attend Parliament on this date; the session was again adjourned, and Anne did not deliver her speech until 2 March.) The work was printed by Barber and published under Morphew's imprint; Morphew registered the copy, on Barber's behalf, in the SR on 27 February.

However, as Fischer argues, there is conflicting evidence about the advertised publication date of 23 February. Support for that date comes from the addition of three paragraphs at the end of *Publick Spirit* that explicitly engaged with Steele's *The Englishman*, which had been published on Monday 15 February. Swift claims in his closing paragraphs to have been brought Steele's pamphlet by his printer 'last *Wednesday*'; as Fischer notes, for this deixis to make sense, Swift had to believe that his work would have to be published before the following Wednesday (24 February). Yet, as Fischer indicates (and as will be detailed in the following section), there is apparently contradictory evidence, from the legal action that followed publication, that a version of the pamphlet, lacking these final three paragraphs, may have been already in some kind of printed form by 10 February. While textually this is plausible – without these three paragraphs, the text would have concluded 'And to Sum up all, an unlimited Freedom of reviling Her Majesty, and those She Employs' – no such version of the work survives.

Prosecution

On 27 February, John Barber was arrested on the orders of John Erskine, the Earl of Mar and Secretary of State for Scotland. Mar wrote to the Attorney-General and Solicitor-General on 1 March, enclosing a copy of the *Publick Spirit* 'which is found to contain several passages, highly reflecting on her Ma.[ties] Administration, and tending to creat[*sic*] uneasinesses in the minds of her Maties Subjects in both parts of the Kingdom, particularly in the 22.^d 23.^d and 24.th pages' (Fischer, 'Legal Response', p. 27). Mar had discovered 'upon Examination' that Barber had printed and published the work and consequently had been, 'by Her Maties express command', bound over to appear before the Queen's Bench at the start of the next legal term. Mar also declared his intention to prosecute and to seek out the author of the work. The following day, 2 March, Mar asked none other than Swift's friend Erasmus Lewis, secretary to William Bromley, Secretary of State in the Northern Department, to take recognizances to guarantee Barber's bail and sureties.

Although Mar had already moved against *Publick Spirit*, that same day (2 March) the pamphlet was also subject to complaint in the House of Lords. Lord Wharton's motion to condemn the work was carried and the Lords resolved that it was 'a false, malicious, and factious Libel, highly dishonourable and scandalous to the *Scotch* Nation, tending to the Destruction of the Constitution, and most injurious to Her Majesty'; the Gentleman Usher of the Black Rod was ordered to bring Morphew 'for whom the said Pamphlet is mentioned to be printed' before the House (*LJ*, vol. XIX, p. 628; Bond, p. 226; Ebenezer Timberland, *The History and Proceedings of the House of Lords* (1742), p. 404). Evidently, however, Barber had already managed to take evasive action: as Peter Wentworth wrote in a letter to his brother, the Earl of Strafford on 5 March, when Wharton attempted to read out the offending passage in the Lords, he discovered 'he had bought a second edition, w[h]ere those pages were left out, so he was forc't to call to some lords that had the first edition in their pockets' (*Wentworth Papers*, p. 359). Morphew was taken on 3 March and the Lords ordered that Barber too was to be attached; as the Lords were as yet still unaware of Mar's prosecution and, given what Morphew admitted in his examination three days later, it is probable that he revealed Barber as the printer (Bond, p. 226; *LJ*, vol. XIX, p. 630). (Timberland, *The History and Proceedings*, p. 406) reports that Morphew declared that 'an unknown Porter had brought to his House the Copies of the Pamphlet in question, from the House of *John Barber*'.) On the same day that the Lords ordered that Barber be attached (3 March), Harley wrote to Swift in a disguised hand, noting that 'some honest men who are very innocent are under troble[*sic*] touching a Printed pamphlet' and enclosing a bill for £100 to cover 'such exigencys as their case may immediatly require' (Woolley, *Corr.*, vol. I,

p. 589; the endorsed date of receipt of 14 March is probably erroneous). On 5 March, Mar reported to the House that he had already questioned Morphew and Barber; nonetheless, the Lords called both men before the House for examination. Morphew identified himself as the book's publisher (in the eighteenth-century sense) and said that the books had been brought by an unknown porter from Barber's (repeating his declaration of two days earlier); he claimed that he did not know the identity of the author or that he had not read the work before selling the copies on. Barber was briefly examined; his revelation that he was already 'under bail to answer at Queen's Bench' led to a debate among the Lords about how best to proceed (Bond, p. 227; Rivington, pp. 44–6, transcribes much of the original minutes that Bond calendars). It was during this debate, according to Oldmixon's 1735 account, that Wharton suggested that they should concentrate their efforts on identifying the author (Rivington, p. 47). Morphew was called in again and interrogated over an advertisement – presumably for the *Publick Spirit* – in *The Examiner*; particular reference was made to the authorship of a 'postscript', presumably that which appeared in the 1 March issue where Swift made some public corrections to the text of *Publick Spirit*. Morphew identified Barber as the printer of *The Examiner*, an allegation that Barber denied. The Lords then sent for two servants employed by Morphew and five journeymen and two apprentices of Barber's; in the meantime, both Barber and Morphew were held in custody 'to be kept asunder' and their servants were forbidden to visit them (*LJ*, vol. XIX, p. 631).

The servants, apprentices and journeymen were examined by the Lords the following day, 6 March; particular attention was paid to Barber's apprentices and journeymen, who were asked repeatedly about whether they had seen or been involved in the printing of *Publick Spirit*. Most revealed that they knew of the work but only the compositor Freeman Collins admitted having any hand ('very little part') in its production (Bond, p. 228; Rivington, p. 45). Interestingly, Collins and another of Barber's compositors, John Wright, both deflected attention away from the printing house by linking the work with Robert Lambourne (the manuscript minutes of the examination also name him erroneously as Lambert), a 'smouter' or freelance compositor who had been working for Barber for five weeks. With Barber and Morphew still in custody, Lambourne was called before the House on 9 March although, as Rivington acknowledges, he 'did not prove a very satisfactory witness from anyone's point of view'

(p. 46). His confused and contradictory answers ('I never saw such a thing' 'I composed something like this') proved inconclusive: 'I cannot tell anything' (Bond, p. 228). Thwarted, the Lords agreed to petition Anne to issue a proclamation seeking out the author of the work; Barber and Morphew were released (*LJ*, vol. XIX, pp. 633–4).

The wording of the Lords' address was agreed on 11 March and Anne issued a proclamation on 15 March, offering a reward of £300 'to any Person who shall Discover, and make due Proof against the Author or Authors' of the work (*LJ*, vol XIX, p. 635; Quinlan, p. 176). Swift, in the 1738 advertisement quoted above, felt the sum's size was evidence that the ministry had 'no Desire to have our supposed Author taken into Custody', a claim given some credence by Bolingbroke's letter of 13 March enclosing the draft of the proclamation to the Attorney-General which suggests that the reward may have been perceived as lenient: 'You will be pleased also to inform your self what Rewards have been usually offer'd on the like occasions, and acquaint the Lords therewith' (Fischer, 'Legal Response', p. 29). It seems that the reward tempted at least one informer, whose letter, dated 18 March, to Harley was apparently forwarded to Swift, although Swift was not named in it (Ball, *Correspondence*, vol. II, pp. 415–16). However, despite his authorship being presumed by many (such as Peter Wentworth, who had also heard 'if the worst comes to the worst . . . they have found out a man that will own, wch will save the Doctor's Bacon' (*Wentworth Papers*, p. 359)), Swift was never formally identified.

Mar continued to build a case against Barber. On 29 March he wrote to the Attorney-General, evidently believing that the testimonies of Lambourne, Collins and others would be sufficient to convict; however, in his reply, the Attorney-General argued that 'to convict Barber . . . the very Book to be produced in Evidence against him must be proved to have been printed by him, and his confession that he printed a book with that Title will not be sufficient'. Mar's copy of *The Publick Spirit* was 'not markt'; he had failed to follow the correct legal procedure of inscribing the relevant copy immediately on purchase and so as evidence it was non-admissible. Nonetheless, Mar persevered, examining twelve witnesses, mostly Barber's employees; Erasmus Lewis again was called upon to arrange the depositions. According to Mar, the witnesses 'seem all to agree, that a Book with this title was printed at Barber's printing house, and from a manuscript Copy'. On 14 April, the first day of Easter term, charges were brought against Barber and a trial date of 28 May was set; however, it appears that the Crown dropped the case (Fischer, 'Legal Response', 29–32). Curiously, though, Swift seemed to be unaware of Barber's pending legal case. In his letter to the Earl of Peterborough on 18 May, he alludes to the *Publick Spirit* furore but implies that the affair has now blown over: 'Barber the printer was, some time ago, in great distress, upon printing a pamphlet, of which evil tongues would needs call me the author: He was brought before your House, which addressed the Queen in a body, who kindly published a proclamation with 300*l.* to discover . . . So well protected are those who scribble for the Government' (Woolley, *Corr.*, vol. I, p. 602).

    This final observation by Swift suggests that we could read the actions of Mar, himself a member of the government on whose behalf Swift was writing, as protective – by thwarting the House of Lords' investigation – rather than aggressive. Fischer is dismissive of such a suggestion but the apparently careless oversight of having not marked the purchased copy is striking and may well have been deliberate: as Defoe wrote some years earlier, 'we have had some of the most considerable Trials in Matter of Misdemeanour, &c miscarried by the Mistakes of the Lawyers . . . Mistakes happening, as Mistakes will happen' (*Review* (7 December 1708), 435; I owe this reference and its interpretation to Alex Barber). The coincidence of Lewis's involvement is also intriguing, as is the fact that the information submitted to Queen's Bench on 14 April dated publication as 10 February, that is thirteen days before the usually accepted publication date. Fischer argues that this dating in the legal record is unlikely to have been an error (although, again, it is possible to interpret it as a deliberate mistake) and marshals supporting circumstantial evidence: Lambourne's commencement of employment at Barber's; the speed of Mar's initial examination of Barber; Swift's seeking renewal of his Letter of Absence from Dublin 'not [to] be limited in point of Place'; and a note by Harley on 20 February that the Scottish peers 'do all they can by their distrust to authenticate all the Scandals that their enemys cast on them'. Yet, as Fischer acknowledges, a publication date of 10 February runs counter both to the advertisements and to the textual evidence itself: no copy lacking Swift's response to Steele's *The Englishman* (published 15 February) is known to survive while first and second 'editions' of *Publick Spirit* published after 15 February retained the offending passage about the Scottish peers and the Union of the two kingdoms. Fischer is unwilling to speculate on how this evidence could be reconciled beyond suggesting that the work was 'produced and circulated in ways too complicated to reconstruct from the remaining evidence and too mercurial to fix within a single publication date' (pp. 33–4). While it is possible that Mar was acting upon good faith, I find the likelihood that a version of *Publick Spirit* was circulating publicly before 24 February far from convincing.

Boyer provided the first account of the parliamentary prosecution (although he was unaware of Mar's activities before and after Mar reported to the Lords, which he erroneously dated as 6 March) in 1719; he included the omitted passage (which follows the first edition's wording verbatim, with occasional variations in spelling, punctuation, capitalization, italicization and paragraphing) and also identified Swift 'the most *scandalous* and most *flagitious* of all *Libellers*' as the author (Boyer, *State*, vol. VII, pp. 230–6).

Printing history

Lord Wharton, in the House of Lords on 2 March, was the first of many to have been perplexed by the textual variations between the different editions of *The Publick Spirit of the Whigs*. At some point during the investigation into the pamphlet's publication, parts of the work were re-set. Up until 1978, scholars had assumed that Barber had simply cut the offending passage and re-set two sheets in such a way that the omission was not immediately apparent. However, with the discovery by John Harris of a variant copy at Lampeter, it became clear that, initially, Barber made only minor alterations, removing two sentences and amending a number of others. (It is perhaps to this version of the text that the account given in *An Impartial History of . . . John Barber*, published by Curll in 1741, is referring when it claimed that Barber retrieved the unsold copies of the original version from 'the *Publisher*'s' and, 'in an exceeding short space of Time', replaced the relevant passage with 'another Paragraph' composed by Bolingbroke, and delivered the altered copies back to the publisher (Rivington, p. 43; *Impartial History*, p. 6); however, the rest of the account given by the *Impartial History* is at odds with the surviving evidence.) As Harris noted, the bibliographical complexity of the various issues and states of the work belie the seemingly straightforward claims of the title pages ('Swift's *The Publick Spirit of the Whigs*: a Partly Censored State of the Scottish Paragraphs', *PBSA* 72 (1978), 92).

The quarto editions issued with Morphew's imprint (1714a–g) should be considered as a distinctive group. 1714a and 1714b (the latter described on the title page as the 'Second Edition') carry the unexpurgated text and are bibliographically identical (collation: A^1 B–F^4 G^3; A1 and G1 are conjugate, as G4 has been folded back to make A1). Either type was left standing or, more likely, existing sheets were simply re-issued under a new title page.

I have identified one copy of 1714a (BL, E.2004(10)) and one copy of 1714b (CUL, Williams 341(1)) that contain identical minor variants on E2^v: a full stop instead of a colon and 'accept' instead of 'receive'. (A terminal parenthesis on page 11 (C2^r) is also missing from the CUL copy.) Given the readings present in 1714c–g, it would seem that these variants represent an earlier state of this particular sheet.

1714c, the copy at Lampeter, bears a 'second edition' title page; D3,4 has been cancelled and replaced with a single folded half-sheet (collation: A^1 B–C^4 D^4 (–D3,4 +D3.4) E–F^4 G^3) but otherwise 1714c is identical to 1714a–b. The cancel incorporates a number of changes to the text; as there are some excisions, the type has been re-set to a narrower measure in order to maintain the book's pagination. The substantive changes are listed in the historical collations; there are also a handful of minor differences in spelling, capitalization and punctuation which have not been listed. (It has not been possible to optically collate 1714c against a copy of 1714a but careful comparison indicates that, in the case of the other sheets, either these were existing sheets or, less likely, printed from standing type.)

1714d–g represent the expurgated version in which the offending passage has been fully removed but bear a variety of title pages. 1714d carries a first edition title page, while 1714e–g claim to be second, third and fourth editions respectively. In each case, the passage 'After Two and twenty Pages . . . an Idea of', running to almost three pages in 1714a–b, has been excised. Rather than re-set the whole work, D3,4 and E1,2 have been cancelled and replaced with a three-quarter sheet; on this re-set sheet, the measure has been significantly narrowed, the page numbers altered (page numbers 22 and 25 are omitted), and new paragraph breaks inserted. Harris proposed A^1 B–C^4 D^4 (–D3,4) ^{x}E^4 (-^{x}E4) E^4 (–E1,2) F^4 G^3 for all the expurgated editions, a collation which is confirmed by examination of the untrimmed and unbound copy of 1714e in the Rothschild collection at

Trinity College, Cambridge. The signings and pagination, however, are intended to deliberately mislead the casual observer:

Actual Page	Pagination	Signed	Line Measure
D2^v	20	*unsigned*	110 mm
^{x}E1^r	21	*unsigned*	102 mm
^{x}E1^v	23	*unsigned*	102 mm
^{x}E2^r	24	E	97 mm
^{x}E2^v	26	*unsigned*	98 mm
^{x}E3^r	27	E2	97 mm
^{x}E3^v	28	*unsigned*	98 mm
E3^r	29	*unsigned*	110 mm
E3^v	30	*unsigned*	110 mm
E4^r	31	*unsigned*	110 mm
E4^v	32	*unsigned*	110 mm

Aside from the variant title pages, 1714d–f are identical to one another and, aside from the cancels, they are identical to 1714a–b; however, a few accidental variants and occasional different lineation indicate that the inner forme of ^{x}E (^{x}E1^v, ^{x}E2^r, and ^{x}E3^v) of two copies of 1714f (NLS, 1.178 (5), Bodl, F2.1(10) Linc.) have been re-set. 1714g is a new edition, following 1714e–f's lineation, spelling and capitalization for the most part and introducing only one substantive variant. However, optical collating reveals that the outer forme of ^{x}E and the inner forme of F in 1714g are identical to 1714d–f (although 'E2' on ^{x}E3^r has been moved); moreover, it seems that, but for some minor stop-press corrections, the inner forme of ^{x}E matches that of the NLS and Bodleian copies of 1714f (the corrections indicate that the inner forme of ^{x}E in 1714g is a later state). The outer forme of F of the NLS and Bodleian copies of 1714f, however, seems to be identical to the other copies of 1714f examined. This suggests that while the sheets that would be used in 1714d–f were being printed, the inner forme of ^{x}E was re-set; not all of the partially re-set ^{x}E sheets were used and so they were incorporated into the otherwise wholly re-set 1714g.

The 1 March issue of *The Examiner* carried a postscript claiming to have received a letter from the author of *Publick Spirit* in which the author 'owns himself in a Mistake in the 22d *Page*, where he says, *He doth not remember that an Union was ever thought on by any, except King* James I. *and the late King* William; for he hath been since told, That some Overtures were made to that End, in the Reigns of other Princes'. Aside from Swift's willingness to acknowledge publicly an error in his account, what is interesting about this admission is its date. The version of the *Publick Spirit* that Lord Wharton took from his pocket on 2 March did not include page 22 or the passage to which Swift alluded. Consequently, the changes must have been made very close to the date of 1 March: too late to amend *The Examiner* copy but early enough to be able to issue sufficient numbers of expurgated copies to have reached Lord Wharton's pocket. (Swift's postscript might have been a deliberate ploy to draw attention to the censored version but this would seem counter-intuitive given the lengths that Barber had gone to in order to hide his changes.) Swift's admission of error was not incorporated into editions of *Publick Spirit* until Faulkner's 1738, which carried a footnote: 'The Author's Memory failed him a little in this Assertion as one of his Answerers observed'.

The Examiner postscript concluded that the author 'complains likewise of some literal Mistakes of the Printer, particularly *P*.15. *L*.2. where, instead of *First Day in Lent*, it is printed, *First Sunday in Lent*: But these and the like Errors, a judicious Reader will easily correct.' This edition is the first to incorporate Swift's corrected reading in this instance. This postscript also explains – or at least acknowledges – the relatively numerous typographical errors (in comparison with the other texts Barber printed of Swift's work): not only obvious misspellings but also several apparently omitted definite articles which this volume has emended.

Two other London editions survive, one bearing Morphew's imprint and the other that of 'T. Cole'; the latter appears to be a false imprint as no T. Cole is known as an active member of the book trade in this period or indeed a member of the Stationers' Company. Both editions are octavos, both claim to have been printed during 1714 and both present the fully unexpurgated text of Swift's work. Morphew's edition (1714h) describes itself as the fourth edition (although no unexpurgated quarto fourth edition survives) while the other declares itself as 'According to the First Original Copy'. Given the fact that the prosecution of Barber was active until at least May, it is probable that these two editions appeared much later than the Morphew quarto editions, possibly even after the death of Anne in the summer. The Morphew octavo edition is also the only surviving edition whose imprint expressly echoed the facetious offer in the original advertisements in January and February: 'Price 1. s. But to Subscribers Half a Crown'. This edition follows the 1714a–b very closely (moving the marginal notes to the foot of the page) although it carries noticeably more misspellings and missettings. It is not clear whether Barber printed this edition; the quality of the paper is good and the setting is not cramped but its evident lack of sufficient 'sh' ligatures implies a limited fount. It includes only one significant variant, a rewriting of the conclusion of a paragraph on the Scottish peers (1714a–b, D4^v); this passage interestingly corresponds to the same lines that were removed in 1714c, suggesting that this edition had access to a version of the text that predated the changes made in 1714c. The 'T. Cole' edition (1714i) also follows 1714a–b closely, albeit with greater variation in capitalization, italicization, spelling and punctuation. In collating 1714h and 1714i for substantive variants, I have ignored obvious spelling errors and also the substitution of hyphens for em-dashes in elided names.

Two Dublin editions also survive with 1714 imprints; both carry the unexpurgated text. One (1714j), whose title page deliberately mimicked the title pages of the Morphew quarto editions and described itself as the 'third edition', was printed for John Henly, a bookseller in Castle Street; as Henly died in early June 1714 (Pollard, p. 283), it would seem that, in Dublin at least, it was still possible to read Swift's unexpurgated text prior to the Queen's own death on 1 August. This edition, for the most part, is well printed and follows 1714a–b's text closely (including its unusual spelling of 'indempnity'), although there are variations in capitalization, spelling, punctuation and (in one case) italicization. Another Dublin edition (1714k), describing itself as a 'fourth edition', was published anonymously in the same year; it follows the text of 1714a–b for the most part closely, including italicization, capitalization and spelling, although the printing quality is more variable than 1714j (reversed spaces, for example, on A2^r, A4^v and B1^r as well as a good number of composition errors). Interestingly, its text seems to have a direct relationship with 1714j as it shares substantive variant readings. However, 1714k also includes a number of variants ('perusing' for 'pursuing', 'tampering' for 'tempering', 'imperial' for 'impartial') that, while probable errors, suggest that it may have been set from a manuscript copy rather than another printed edition, in which case rather than 1714k directly descending from 1714j, both editions may have shared a common textual source. In both cases, I have collated for substantive variants but have excluded, where I believe it absolutely clear, errors of setting, regardless of whether they render the word nonsensical (e.g. 'infiitly' for 'infinintely') or manage to create a different word entirely (e.g. 'form' for 'from').

The full unexpurgated text of *Publick Spirit* was reprinted in 1738 by Faulkner in volume VI of his octavo (hereafter 1738a) and duodecimo (hereafter 1738b) editions of Swift's *Works* (TS, nos. 42, 50); both editions preface the work with a title page that claims, curiously, that the work was 'Written in the Year 1712'. As usual with Faulkner's reprints, Swift's style has been 'improved' ('hath' for 'has', 'although' for 'though', 'it is' for ''tis'), all elisions have been expanded and a few explicatory footnotes have been added. Punctuation, spelling and capitalization also differ and none of the original's marginal notes have been included. The text also includes a number of substantive variants which may have been authorial; however, given the Cambridge edition's editorial policy, these variants have not been incorporated as emendations. A near line-by-line reprint of Faulkner's octavo edition appeared in the second volume of Charles Davis's London edition of Swift's *Political Tracts* of the same year (TS, no. 25(7); hereafter 1738c). 1738a has been fully collated for substantive variants against 1714a, with all the variants cross-checked with 1738b–c. The text also appeared in volume VI of Faulkner's octavo edition of 1741 (TS, no. 44; hereafter 1741); this edition follows 1738a closely (to the point of reproducing one of 1738a's misreadings of 1714a) with a few minor differences in punctuation, but it also introduces a handful of substantive – but insignificant – variants.

Herbert Davis took 1738a as his copy text, although he retained 1714 readings in a number of cases; he also introduced one 1741 reading as an emendation ('the Mercy' for 'Mercy' on F4^v) which this edition rejects on the grounds that, while it does improve the syntax, no previous edition had considered the passage sufficiently problematic to need intervention. This edition takes 1714a as its copy text; this has been collated against 1714b–k, 1738a, 1741 and Davis.

Copy text: CUL, Syn. 5.71.21 (11)

References: TS, nos. 596 (1714a, 1714b, 1714d, 1714e, 1714f, 1714g (misidentifying a copy at TCD)), 597 (1714h), 598 (1714i), 599 (1714j), 600 (1714k); Davis, vol. VIII, pp. 27–68, 209–10 (notes). Woolley, 'Canon', no. 29. *ESTC* T46111 (1714a, listing over fifty copies); T223783 (1714d, listing four copies, of which TCC copy is misidentified); T26832 (1714e, listing twenty-nine copies, of which CUL copy is misidentified); T46112 (1714f, listing twenty copies); N39690 (1714g, listing five copies); T102767 (1714i, listing fourteen copies); T1863 (1714j, listing fifteen copies); T206601 (1714k, listing two copies); *ESTC* does not include entries for 1714b, 1714c or 1714h

London edition, first issue, 1714a

Title: THE | *PUBLICK SPIRIT* | OF THE | WHIGS: | Set forth in their Generous | Encouragement of the Author | OF THE | *CRISIS*: | WITH SOME | OBSERVATIONS | ON THE | Seasonableness, Candor, Erudition, |and Style of that Treatise. | [double rule] | *LONDON*: | Printed for *John Morphew*, near *Stationers-Hall*. | MDCCXIV. | [flush right] Price One Shilling.

Collation: 4°: A^1 B–F^4 G^3

Pagination: *i–ii*, 1–45, *46*

Contents: A1^r title page; A1^v blank; B2^r–G3^r text; G3^r Advertisement; G3^v blank

Typography: thirty-six lines per page (B1^v), although a number of pages are thirty-five lines, type-page 169.5 (181) × 110 mm, twenty lines of roman type 94 mm

Failures of catchwords to catch:
G1^v Well,] ~;

Copies examined:
*BL, E.2004(10): 202 × 142 mm, trimmed; laminated and remounted in 'new' gatherings on guards; bound with miscellaneous tracts 1714–15

*Bodl, G. Pamph. 1792 (8): 212 × 159 mm, trimmed; bound with miscellaneous political tracts 1713–58
*§CUL, Syn. 5. 71. 21 (11): 208 × 157 mm, trimmed
*§CUL, Williams 341: 233 × c.174 mm, trimmed outer edge, some trimming of lower edge; a second duplicate gathering of F has been erroneously bound inside F (collation: A^1 B–E^4 F^4 (F2+$^2F^4$) G^3); a small hole burned in ^{1}F2 and a burn mark (but no hole) in similar location on ^{2}F2 suggests that some damage happened to the sheets before folding
*TCC, RW.62.44: 236 × 182 mm, untrimmed; disbound; Rothschild Library, no. 2054; erroneously catalogued on *ESTC* as censored first edition (1714d)
*TCC, RW.62.45: 216 × 167 mm, trimmed; re-bound; Rothschild Library, no. 2055

London edition, first issue, cancelled title page, 1714b

Title: THE | *PUBLICK SPIRIT* | OF THE | WHIGS: | Set forth in their Generous | Encouragement of the Author | OF THE | *CRISIS*: | WITH SOME | OBSERVATIONS | ON THE | Seasonableness, Candor, Erudition, |and Style of that Treatise. | [rule] | 𝕿𝖍𝖊 𝕾𝖊𝖈𝖔𝖓𝖉 𝕰𝖉𝖎𝖙𝖎𝖔𝖓. | [rule] | *LONDON*: | Printed for *John Morphew*, near *Stationers-Hall*. | MDCCXIV. | [flush right] Price One Shilling.

Collation: 4°: A^1 B–F^4 G^3

Pagination: *i–ii*, 1–45, *46*

Contents: A1^r title page; A1^v blank; B2^r–G3^r text; G3^r Advertisement; G3^v blank

Typography: thirty-six lines per page (B1^v), although a number of pages are thirty-five lines, type-page 168.5 (181) × 110 mm, twenty lines of roman type 93.5 mm

Failures of catchwords to catch:
G1^v Well,] ∼;

Copies examined:
*Bodl, Pamph. 322(8): 207 × 161 mm, trimmed; title page damaged outer edge and price lost due to trimming; G3 leaf missing (not 'fo. 1' as given

on *ESTC* entry); erroneously classified by *ESTC* as 1714e; in volume of thirty-one miscellaneous items from 1714

*§CUL, Williams 342 (1): 218 × 161 mm, trimmed; bound with third edition (1714f); erroneously catalogued by *ESTC* as 1714e

*CUL, Syn.5.66.7 (25): 204 × c.152 mm, trimmed; in volume of twenty-eight printed pamphlets, 1663–1715; formerly U.24.8.25 (as listed in TS, no. 596)

London edition, second issue, 1714c

Title: THE | *PUBLICK SPIRIT* | OF THE | WHIGS: | Set forth in their Generous | Encouragement of the Author | OF THE | *CRISIS*: | WITH SOME | OBSERVATIONS | ON THE | Season-ableness, Candor, Erudition, |and Style of that Treatise. | [rule] | 𝕿𝖍𝖊 𝕾𝖊𝖈𝖔𝖓𝖉 𝕰𝖉𝖎𝖙𝖎𝖔𝖓. | [rule] | *LONDON*: | Printed for *John Mor-phew*, near *Stationers-Hall*. | MDCCXIV. | [flush right] Price One Shilling.

Collation: 4°: A^1 B–C^4, D^4 (–D3,4 +D3.4) E–F^4 G^3

Pagination: *i–ii*, 1–45, *46*

Contents: A1^r title page; A1^v blank; B2^r–G3^r text; G3^r Advertisement; G3^v blank

Typography: thirty-six lines per page (B1^v), although a number of pages are thirty-five lines

Failures of catchwords to catch:
G1^v Well,] ∼;

Copy examined:
†Lampeter, T.267, no. 59: copy not physically examined; reproduction used; see *A Catalogue of the Tract Collection of Saint David's University College, Lampeter* (London: Mansell, 1975), no. 5903 and John Harris, 'Swift's *The Publick Spirit of the Whigs*: a Partly Censored State of the Scottish Paragraphs', *PBSA* 72 (1978), 92–4. (I am grateful to Caroline Dery and Caroline Pilcher of the Founders' Library, Lampeter University, for their help in identifying and copying this item.)

London edition, third issue, 1714d

Title: [THE] *PUBLICK SPIRI[T]* | OF THE | WHIGS: | Set forth in their Generous | Encouragement of the Author | OF THE | *CRISIS*: | WITH SOME | OBSERVATIONS | ON THE | Seasonableness, Candor, Erudition, |and Style of that Treatise. | [double rule] | *LONDON*: | Printed for *John Morphew*, near *Stationers-Hall*. | MDCCXIV. | [flush right] Price One Shilling. [*First line of title lost due to trimming*]

Collation: 4°: A^1 B–C^4 D^4 (–D3,4) $^xE^4$ (–$^xE4$) E^4 (–E1,2) F^4 G^3

Pagination: *i–ii*, 1–21, 23–4, 26–45, *46*

Contents: A1^r title page; A1^v blank; B2^r–G3^r text; G3^r Advertisement; G3^v blank

Typography: thirty-six lines per page (B1^v), although a number of pages are thirty-five lines, type-page 168.5 (180) × 110 mm, twenty lines of roman type 94 mm; re-set sheets retain same number of lines (apart from D4^r, which has thirty-four lines) but line widths change (D4^{r-v} 102 mm; E1^r 97 mm; E1^v 98 mm; E2^r 97 mm; E2^v 98 mm)

Failures of catchwords to catch:
G1^v Well,] ~;

Copy examined:
*†NLI, LO Swift 128: 197 × 144 mm, trimmed all edges, tightly trimmed outer and top edges with occasional loss of page numbers; modern re-binding, with A and G remounted

London edition, 3rd issue, cancelled title page, 1714e

Title: THE | *PUBLICK SPIRIT* | OF THE | WHIGS: | Set forth in their Generous | Encouragement of the Author | OF THE | *CRISIS*: | WITH SOME | OBSERVATIONS | ON THE | Seasonableness, Candor, Erudition, |and Style of that Treatise. | [rule] | 𝕿𝖍𝖊 𝕾𝖊𝖈𝖔𝖓𝖉 𝕰𝖉𝖎𝖙𝖎𝖔𝖓 | [rule] | *LONDON*: | Printed for *John Morphew*, near *Stationers-Hall*. | MDCCXIV. | [flush right] Price One Shilling.

Collation: 4°: A^1 B–C^4 D^4 (–D3,4) $^xE^4$ (–$^xE4$) E^4 (–E1,2) F^4 G^3

Pagination: *i–ii*, 1–21, 23–4, 26–45, *46*

Contents: A1^r title page; A1^v blank; B2^r–G3^r text; G3^r Advertisement; G3^v blank

Typography: thirty-six lines per page (B1^v), although a number of pages are thirty-five lines, type-page 169 (180) × 110 mm (width: ^{x}E1^{r-v} 102 mm; ^{x}E2^r 97 mm; ^{x}E2^v 98 mm; ^{x}E3^r 97 mm; ^{x}E3^v 98 mm), twenty lines of roman type 93 mm

Failures of catchwords to catch:
G1^v Well,] ∼;

Copies examined:
*TCC, RW.62.46: c.233 × c.182 mm, untrimmed; unbound; stitched; Rothschild Library, no. 2056
†Spencer Research Library, University of Kansas, Prose 1769: *ECCO* copy examined:

London edition, third issue, cancelled title page, 1712f

Title: THE | *PUBLICK SPIRIT* | OF THE | WHIGS: | Set forth in their Generous | Encouragement of the Author | OF THE | *CRISIS*: | WITH SOME | OBSERVATIONS | ON THE | Seasonableness, Candor, Erudition, |and Style of that Treatise. | [rule] | 𝕿𝖍𝖊 𝕿𝖍𝖎𝖗𝖉 𝕰𝖉𝖎𝖙𝖎𝖔𝖓 | [rule] | *LONDON*: | Printed for *John Morphew*, near *Stationers-Hall*. | MDCCXIV. | [flush right] Price One Shilling.

Collation: 4°: A^1 B–C^4 D^4 (–D3,4) ^{x}E^4 (–^{x}E4) E^4 (–E1,2) F^4 G^3

Pagination: *i–ii*, 1–21, 23–4, 26–45, *46*

Contents: A1^r title page; A1^v blank; B2^r–G3^r text; G3^r Advertisement; G3^v blank

Typography: thirty-six lines per page (B1^v), although a number of pages are thirty-five lines, type-page 169 (180) × 110 mm (width: ^{x}E1^{r-v} 102 mm; ^{x}E2^r 97 mm; ^{x}E2^v 98 mm; ^{x}E3^r 97 mm; ^{x}E3^v 98 mm), twenty lines of roman type 93 mm

Failures of catchwords to catch:
G1^v Well,] ∼;

Copies examined:
BL, E.2004(10): 203 × 143 mm, trimmed; laminated and remounted in 'new' gatherings on guards (G1 reversed); bound with miscellaneous tracts 1714–15
*Bodl, F.2.1(10) Linc.: 222 × 163 mm, trimmed; in volume of nineteen miscellaneous late seventeenth- and early eighteenth-century items (TS erroneously gives shelfmark as Fr. 1. Linc. 10); one of registration copies deposited at Stationers' Hall (Chalmers, p. 424)
*§CUL, Williams 342 (2): 195 × 150 mm, tightly trimmed, with loss of direction line on F1^v
*TCC, RW.62.54: 196 × 150 mm, tightly trimmed with loss of upper and outer edge of title page; disbound; stitched; Rothschild Library, no. 2057
*TCD, OLS 192.n.62, no. 6: 231 × 187 mm, untrimmed; unbound; stitched; pencilled note on G3^v: 'Sotheby Hollick sale 19 May 1980 Lot 281 £25'
*NLS, 1.178 (5): 204 × 154 mm, trimmed; in volume of eleven early eighteenth-century works (^{x}E collated)

London edition, second edition, 1714g

Title: THE | *PUBLICK SPIRIT* | OF THE | WHIGS: | Set forth in their Generous | Encouragement of the Author | OF THE | *CRISIS*: | WITH SOME | OBSERVATIONS | ON THE | Seasonableness, Candor, Erudition, |and Style of that Treatise. | [rule] | The Fourth Edition. | [rule] | *LONDON*: | Printed for *John Morphew*, near *Stationers-Hall*. | MDCCXIV. | [flush right] Price One Shilling.

Collation: 4°: *A*^{1} B–C^4 D^4 (–D3,4) ^{x}E^4 (–^{x}E4) E^4 (–E1,2) F^4 G^3

Pagination: *i–ii*, 1–21, 23–4, 26–45, *46*

Contents: A1^r title page; A1^v blank; B2^r–G3^r text; G3^r Advertisement; G3^v blank

Typography: thirty-six lines per page (B1^v), although a number of pages are thirty-five lines, type-page 169 (180) × 110 mm (width: ^{x}E1$^{r–v}$ 102 mm; ^{x}E2^r 97 mm; ^{x}E2^v 98 mm; ^{x}E3^r 97 mm; ^{x}E3^v 98 mm), twenty lines of roman type 93 mm

Failures of catchwords to catch:
G1^v Well,] ∼;

Copy examined:
*§CUL, Williams 343: 227 × 169 mm, trimmed

London, octavo edition, 1714h

Title: THE | PUBLICK SPIRIT | OF THE | *WHIGS,* | Set forth in their generous encouragement, of | the Author of the CRISIS. | With some Observations on the seasonableness, | Candor, Erudition & Style of that Treatise. | [rule] | *The Fourth Edition.* | Price 1. s. But to Subscribers Half a Crown. | [rule] | [eight ornaments, arranged in two horizontal lines of four, 12 × 22.5 mm] | [rule] | *LONDON,* | Printed for JOHN MORPHEW,near| Stationers-Hall. 1714.

Collation: 8°: π^1 A–K^4

Pagination: *i–ii*, 1–80

Contents: π1^r title page; π1^v blank; A1^r–K4^v text

Typography: twenty-seven lines per page (B2^r), some pages have fewer, type-page 125 (135) × 83 mm, twenty lines of roman type 93 mm

Failures of catchwords to catch:
A3^r very] ∼,
C1^r them] ∼,
E1^r ge-] re
E3^v work] Work
F3^v vided] ded
K2^r liament] ∼,
K4^r in] a

Copy examined:
*†TCD, Fag.H.11.55(7): 173x 102, mostly untrimmed; tightly bound in volume of fifteen early eighteenth-century pamphlets

London edition (Cole), 1714i

Title: THE | *PUBLICK SPIRIT*| OF THE | WHIGS, | Set forth in their Generous | *Encouragement of the Author* | OF THE | *CRISIS.* | [rule] |

According to the First Original Copy. | [rule] | *LONDON*: | Printed for *T. Cole*, MDCCXIV.

Collation: 8°: A–E⁴

Pagination: *1–2*, 3–39, *40*

Contents: A1ʳ title page; A1ᵛ blank; A2ʳ–E4ʳ text; E4ᵛ blank

Typography: forty-two lines per page (A2ᵛ), type-page 138 (146.5) × 78.5 mm, twenty lines of roman type 65.5 mm

Failures of catchwords to catch:
none

Copies examined:
BL, 104.b.34: copy not physically examined; reproduction used; *ECCO* copy
†*CUL, Ddd.25.144 (10): 175.5 × 109 mm, trimmed (with occasional loss of running titles); in twelve printed items, 1702–27

Dublin edition, 1714j

Title: THE | *PVBLICK SPIRIT* | OF THE | WHIGS: | Set forth in their Generous | Encouragement of the Author | OF THE | *CRISIS*: | WITH SOME | OBSERVATIONS | ON THE | Sᴇᴀsᴏɴᴀʙʟᴇɴᴇss, Cᴀɴᴅᴏʀ, Eʀᴜᴅɪᴛɪᴏɴ,and| Sᴛʏʟᴇof that Treatise. | [rule] | *The Third Edition.* | [rule] | *DUBLIN*: | Printed for *J. Henly*, Bookseller in *Castle-street*, | 1714.

Collation: 8°: A–E⁴

Pagination: *1–2*, 3–38, *39–40*

Contents: A1ʳ title page; A1ᵛ blank; A2ʳ–E3ᵛ text; E4ʳ⁻ᵛ blank

Typography: forty-one lines per page (C4ʳ), type-page 139.5 (147) × 81 mm, twenty lines of roman type 67.5 mm

Failures of catchwords to catch:
A2ᵛ Project] ∼,
D4ʳ thank] the

Copies examined :

†*CUL, Williams 409 (26): 170 × 108 mm, trimmed; disbound
*TCC, RW.62.47: 159 × 95 mm, trimmed (with loss of running title on
D1ᵛ); rebound; Rothschild Library, no. 2058

Dublin edition, 1714k

Title: [within double rules 150 × 92 mm] THE | Publick Spirit | OF
THE | VVHIGS: | Set forth in their Generous | Encouragement of the
Author | OF THE | CRISIS: | WITH SOME | OBSERVATIONS |
ON THE | Seasonableness, Candor, Erudition, and Style | of that Trea-
tise. | [rule] | *The Fourth Edition.* | [rule] | *DVBLIN*: Printed in the
Year 1714.

Collation: 8°: A^4 B–E^4

Pagination: *1–2, 3–40*

Contents: A1ʳ title page; A1ᵛ blank; A2ʳ–E4ᵛ text

Typography: forty lines per page (B2ʳ), type-page 146.5 (154) × 85.5 mm,
twenty lines of roman type 73 mm; D4ᵛ–E2ᵛ(to line 24), E3ʳ(from line
20)–E4ʳ(to line 8), set in smaller roman type: forty-four lines per page
(E1ʳ), type-page 145.5 (153) × 86 mm, twenty lines of roman type 66 mm

Failures of catchwords to catch:
C1ᵛ *estimable*] *stimable*
C4ʳ *ment*] ~,
D1ʳ *ted*] ~;
E1ʳ Majestys] Majesty's
E4ʳ Throne] ~;

Copies examined:
*†NLI, LO Swift 129: 169 × 109 mm, mostly trimmed; re-bound; sheets
re-stitched into binding
*TCD, 91.q.57, no. 4: 159 × 98 mm, trimmed, with some loss of text
at lower outer edges; in volume of nine 1714 tracts; not listed in TCD's
annotated copy of TS

Emendations

244.3 the most] 1738; most
255.34 day] *this edition*; Sunday
  Swift's postscript in the 1 March issue of The Examiner *corrects this.*
266.18 Inconsistencies] 1738; Inconsistences
267.32 *Hand*] 1738; *Head*
  This obvious error – as Swift re-quotes the phrase correctly two lines later –
  was not corrected until 1738.
269.34 ever] 1714i; every
273.12 the same] 1714h; same
277.6 *the Encouragement*] 1738; *Encouragement*
278.2 Allegiance] 1714g; Allegiance
278.26 *Europe*] 1714h; *Eutope*
278.33 for] 1714g; fot

Historical collation

243.4 these] those 1741
243.21 *of*] *in* 1738, 1741
243.21 more conversant in Books than any of the Three, as well as] *om.*
  1714h
244.1 Politicks.] ~ˆ 1714k
  Presumably poor inking or a misprinting.
244.3 the most] most 1714
244.7 supposed] suppose 1738, 1741
244.8 E. of *N--t-ng---m*] Earl of *Nottingham* 1738, 1741
244.9 L--dsh-p's] Lordship's 1738, 1741
245.1 For] because 1738, 1741
245.4 Extract] Abstract 1714g
245.6 Authors] Author's 1714g; 1738, 1741
245.26 a Pamphlet, and a Pamphlet] a Pamphlet 1714h
245.29 inflame] enflame 1714g
245.29 Clamorous] Clamours 1714k
245.29 though] although 1738, 1741
246.13 E—— of *N--t--ng---m*] Earl of *Nottingham* 1738, 1741

247.7 hath been] had been 1714h

248.10 Tenths] tenth 1741

248.12 take it] take it in 1738, 1741

248.16 lost half] lost 1714h

248.17 but] except 1738, 1741

248.21 understands] understand 1738, 1741

249.2 B——p of S--r--m] Bishop of *Sarum* 1738, 1741

249.5 *enflaming*] *inflaming* 1738, 1741

249.19 this] his 1738, 1741

249.23 *Ireland?*] ~. 1741

250.3 Physicians:] ^. 1714h

250.8 *Ideas*] *Idea's* 1714g

250.13 for] against 1738, 1741

250.23 perusing] pursuing 1714k

250.25 present] *present* 1714i

251.20 ingenious] ingenuous 1741

251.23 B——p of S--r--m] Bishop of *Sarum* 1738, 1741

252.1 *L——d*] *Lord* 1714i; 1738, 1741

252.1 *Gentleman*] *Gentlemen* 1741

252.9 K.] King 1714i; 1738, 1741

252.9 received] receive 1714j

252.10 tampering] tempering 1714j; 1714k

252.14 Qu——] Q*ueen* 1738, 1741

252.28 Churches] Church's 1714i; 1738, 1741

253.2 *Powers*] *Power* 1738, 1741

253.10 them.] ~^ 1714j

253.13 in the] of the 1738, 1741

253.17 *enflame*] *inflame* 1738, 1741

253.25 to the Clergy from the *Whigs*] from to the *Whigs* the Clergy 1714h
   Garbled reading.

253.26 though] although 1738, 1741

253.27 S——le] *Steele* 1738, 1741

253.28 *Lechmere*] *Letchmere* 1714j

253.31 S——le] *Steele* 1738, 1741

254.6 St——le] *Steele* 1738, 1741

255.23 St——le] *Steele* 1738, 1741

255.25 *it's*] *its* 1714g; 1714i; 1738, 1741

255.25 *it's*] *its* 1738, 1741

255.27 *England;*] ˆ. 1714h

255.28 it's] its 1714i, 1738, 1741

256.6 *St——le*] *Steele* 1738, 1741

256.26 was never] never was 1738, 1741

256.30 *St--le's*] *Steele's* 1738, 1741

257.1 *St——le*] *Steele* 1738, 1741

257.6 *St——le*] *Steele* 1738, 1741

257.16 keeps] keep 1714j

258.3 though] although 1738, 1741

258.4 Humane] Human 1714i; human 1738, 1741

258.12 *NECESSITY*] *Necessity* 1738, 1741

258.20 *though*] *although* 1738, 1741

258.21 *St——le*] *Steele* 1738, 1741

258.31 good:] ˆ. 1714h

259.1 *St——le*] *Steele* 1738, 1741

259.4 come now] now come 1738, 1741

259.7 Blessing;] ˆ. 1714h

259.18 *St——le*] *Steele* 1738, 1741

259.28 [*marginal page reference*]] [*space made but text omitted*] 1714h

259.29 our] *or* 1738a–b

260.5 *Men's*] *Mens* 1714i

260.23 though] although 1738, 1741

260.25 St——le] Steele 1738, 1741

260.31 thus expound] expound 1714k

261.11 E. of *G-d--ph-n*] Earl of *Godolphin* 1738, 1741

261.13 *St——le*] *Steele* 1738, 1741

261.25 against] amongst 1714k

261.30 Printing] Printing of 1714c

262.1 After Two . . . Idea of.] *om.* 1714d–g

262.1 Parliament] Parliaments 1714k

262.5 though] although 1738, 1741

262.5 I] I [footnote: '*The Author's memory failed him a little in this Assertion, as one of his Answerers observed*'] 1738, 1741

262.21 poor, fierce] brave 1714c

262.23 till] until 1738, 1741

263.9 Person] Person [footnote: '*Lord* SOMERS'] 1738, 1741

263.11 E—— of G———] Earl of *Godolphin* 1738, 1741

263.15 the Island] this Island 1738, 1741

263.17 of a Year or two] dangerous to our own Liberties 1714c

264.2 *Union,*] ~. 1738a–b

264.8 till] until 1738, 1741

264.9 the greatest Part] many 1714c

264.10 I imagine . . . in his House] *om.* 1714c

264.20 the whole Body] many 1714c

264.22 I could point. . . .an Idea of.] *om.* 1714c

264.24 though their whole Revenues before that Period would have ill maintained a *Welch* Justice of the Peace; and have since gathered more Money than ever any *Scotchmen*, who had not travell'd could form an Idea of.] though they are known to have been great gainers by it; & their Revenues before that period were very inconsiderable, in regard to what they have been since. 1714h

264.24 though] although 1738, 1741

264.26 *Scotchmen*] *Scotchman* 1738, 1741

265.1 only one Thing more] one Thing 1714d–g

265.7 Publication:] ^. 1714k

265.8 *R——d St——le*] *Richard Steele* 1738, 1741

265.18 *Subject's*] *Subjects* 1714k

265.29 *Pretender:*] ^. 1714h

266.5 where] somewhere 1714h

266.7 Mind; tells us,] Mind. 1714h

266.7 tells us] tell us 1714f [BL, E.2004 (10*)], 1714g; He tells us 1738

266.8 Briton] Britain 1714i

266.11 *it's*] *its* 1714i; 1714j

266.16 *it's*] *its* 1714i

266.18 Inconsistencies] Inconsistences 1714

266.20 *Conduct of the Allies*] *Conduct to the Allies* 1714j; 1714k

266.28 *St——le*] *Steele* 1738, 1741

267.1 *St——le*] *Steele* 1738, 1741

267.10 Signs] Sign 1738, 1741

267.10 Kingdom or State] Kingdom of State 1714k

267.14 damnably] damnable 1714k

267.20 D—— of M———] Duke of *Marlborough* 1738, 1741

267.27 much;] ~ˆ 1714j

267.32 *Hand*] *Head* 1714

267.35 Intelligence?] ~: 1738, 1741

268.1 Advisers] Adviser 1738, 1741

268.4 receive] accept 1714a [BL, E.2004 (10)]; 1714b [CUL, Williams 342 (1)]

    Davis (vol. VIII, p. 203) identifies this BL copy, which has not been collated but all the variants have been checked.

268.5 *St——le's*] *Steele's* 1738, 1741

268.7 Dozen:] Dozen? 1714i

268.9 an Hundred] a Hundred 1714k, 1738, 1741

268.12 this] the 1738, 1741

268.16 *St——le*] *Steele* 1738, 1741

268.19 happens] happen 1738, 1741

269.5 I answer;] ˆ? 1714k

269.6 *France?*] *Fr.* 1714k

269.9 Humane] Human 1714i; 1738, 1741

269.12 though] although 1738, 1741

269.16 it led] he led 1714k

269.27 *impartial*] *imperial* 1714k

269.30 *St--le*] *Steele* 1738, 1741

269.34 ever] every 1714a–h

270.8 (of which . . . Instances.)] of which . . . Instances. 1714h

270.9 from our] from our own 1714k

270.17 *M——h's*] *Marlborough's* 1738, 1741

270.19 D——] Duke 1738, 1741

271.3 till] until 1738, 1741

271.10 tho'] although 1738, 1741

    Davis (vol. VIII, p. 203) claims a reading of 'though' in 1714b but does not specify the copy or copies consulted; I have not seen any copy of 1714 bearing this reading.

272.9 his Sovereign] this Sovereign 1714k

272.10 *St——le*] *Steele* 1738, 1741

272.11 *War!*] *War?* 1714j, 1714k

272.21 know that] know how 1738, 1741

273.3 *St——le*] *Steele* 1738, 1741

273.3 *a Truth*] *Truth* 1738, 1741

273.7 *a Truth*] *Truth* 1738, 1741

273.12 the same] same 1714a–g, 1714i–k

274.3 *St——le*] *Steele* 1738, 1741

274.12 till] until 1738, 1741

274.13 till] until 1738, 1741

274.15 till t'other] until the other 1738, 1741

274.25 *St——le*] *Steele* 1738, 1741

274.28 *St——le*] *Steele* 1738, 1741

274.29 it done] done it 1741

275.2 *St——le*] *Steele* 1738, 1741

275.5 GENTLEMEN BORN] GENTLEMEN BORN [footnote: '*Mr.*
   Steele *often stiles himself so*'] 1738, 1741

275.7 *St——le*] *Steele* 1738, 1741

275.13 though] although 1738, 1741

275.19 *St——le*] *Steele* 1738, 1741

275.20 *Hand*] *Hands* 1738, 1741

276.4 *St——le*] *Steele* 1738, 1741

276.8 t'other] the other 1738, 1741

276.11 *St——le*] *Steele* 1738, 1741

276.16 *it's*] *its* 1714i, 1714j, 1738, 1741; its 1714k

276.17 *till*] *until* 1738, 1741

276.25 till] until 1738, 1741

277.8 of the *Dutch*] to the *Dutch* 1714k

277.11 *Interest*] *the Interest* 1741

277.19 *the Encouragement*] *Encouragement* 1714

277.20 till] until 1738, 1741

278.9 tho'] although 1738, 1741

278.21 *the Doom be*] *be the Doom* 1741

278.23 are] be 1738, 1741

278.26 *St——le's*] *Steele's* 1738, 1741

278.26 *Europe*] *Eutope* 1714a–g

278.29 Pag. 32.] Pag. 22. 1714j, 1714k

279.12 for being *too far off*, and the *Chevalier de St. George*] om. 1738, 1741
   Presumed compositorial eye-skip, which 1741 preserves.

279.12 for] fot 1714a–f

279.13 *conquers*] *conquer* 1738, 1741

279.15 *Mercy*] *the Mercy* 1741

279.15 who] which 1738, 1741

279.15 his Back] its back 1738, 1741

279.20 dies] die 1738, 1741

279.20 for his] that his 1738, 1741

279.21 to torment] torment 1738, 1741

279.22 *St——le*] *Steele* 1738, 1741

279.25 *People*; because it seems a certain Sign that *the Generality of the People* are] *People* are 1714k
Eye-skip.

279.27 great] greater 1714k

280.2 *St——le*] *Steele* 1738, 1741

280.7 Jail] Jail [footnote: 'Upon his Conviction he was committed to the *Marshalsea*, and at his Sentence to the *Queen's Bench* for three Years'] 1738c

280.9 *Person*] *Person* [footnote: 'PARKER, *afterwards Lord Chancellor*'] 1738a–b, 1741

280.10 Knees] ~? 1714i, 1738, 1741

281.1 *St——le*] *Steele* 1738, 1741

281.8 *St——le*] *Steele* 1738, 1741

281.10 *S——m*] *Sarum* 1738, 1741

281.15 *Sunshiny*] *Sunshine* 1738, 1741

281.17 believes] believe 1738, 1741

281.18 *are*] *stand* 1738, 1741

281.25 are] be 1738, 1741

281.26 though] although 1738, 1741

281.26 asserts] assert 1738, 1741

282.4 feasible] feasibly 1741

282.13 *St——le*] *Steele* 1738, 1741

282.18 *St——le*] *Steele* 1738, 1741

282.20 *Crisis*;] ^? 1714k

283.2 Qu—n] QUEEN 1738, 1741

283.9 Dunkirk.] ^, 1714k

284.6 *St—le*] *Steele* 1738, 1741

284.15 till] until 1738, 1741

Word division (compounds only)

Copy text
245.31 Book-seller
249.20 *English-man*
254.21 *Self-denying*
257.16 *Brent-ford*
259.24 *under-stood*
266.25 *what-ever*

Edited text
none

A DISCOURSE CONCERNING THE FEARS FROM THE PRETENDER: TEXTUAL ACCOUNT

Only the two opening paragraphs of this work, which Swift began after finishing *The Publick Spirit of the Whigs* but prior to that work's publication, survive. Swift wrote to Charles Ford from Letcombe on 12 June 1714 that he was 'going on with the Discourse of which you saw the Beginning' (Woolley, *Corr.*, vol. I, p. 613), indicating that Ford had seen the draft at some point before Swift left London on 31 May. It seems that Swift abandoned the title and these paragraphs but not the topic, producing a manuscript of *Some Free Thoughts upon the Present State of Affairs* by 1 July (Davis, vol VIII, pp. xxii–xxiii). Both Ehrenpreis's account of *Some Free Thoughts* (vol. II, pp. 737–42) and Woolley's note to the Ford letter (*Corr.*, vol. I, p. 614, n. 2), conflate the compositions of the *Discourse* and *Some Free Thoughts* rather than considering them as separate entities. The text of *Discourse* (hereafter SwJ 403) was first printed in 1935 (*Ford*, pp. 216–17). Davis re-transcribed the manuscript for his edition, correcting Nichol Smith's transcript in two minor cases and as usual silently expanding elisions, but mysteriously inserted an unwarranted double-em dash in the second paragraph. Davis included the final cancelled sentence in his transcript; only in the textual notes (vol. VIII, pp. 204–5) did he indicate that this line had been cancelled in the manuscript. This cancelled sentence includes two largely illegible words for which Davis suggested '?both ?I . . . rs'. From a close examination of the manuscript, 'both' is possible although, compared with similar letter formations in the text, the initial letter may be an 'h'; moreover, the word looks very different to the 'both' in the first paragraph. The initial 'I' for the second word is fairly certain; the second letter is possibly a 'd' (albeit with a restrained looping ascender in comparison with others in the text); 'ers' looks a plausible reading for the remaining letters. For this edition, the manuscript has been re-transcribed and collated for both accidental and substantive variants against *Ford* and Davis.

Copy text: TCC, A.5.8

References: Rothschild Library, no. 2261. SwJ, 403. Davis, vol. VIII, pp. 69–72

Manuscript: SwJ 403

Location: TCC, A.5.8

Description: holograph of Swift, with minor revisions in same hand; bifoliam, of page size 304 × 189 mm; unpaginated; minor repairs to fold; vertical chainlines; watermark (fo. 2): royal coat of arms within circular motto, crowned (i.e. very similar to paper used for *Free Thoughts* but lacking monogram), 82 × 61 mm (compare Heawood, nos. 441, 445, 448); countermark (fo. 1): crowned 'AR', 28 × 25 mm.

Contents: fo. 1ʳ text, right-hand half only '(Feb. 20) [flush right] | A | Discourse concerning the Fears from | the Pretender'; fos. 1ᵛ–2ᵛ blank

Emendations

Historical collation

287.1 Feb.] Febr. *Ford*
287.1 Partyes.] ∼ — Davis
287.15 Qu—'s] Queen's Davis
288.3 Sincerity] ∼, *Ford*

Alterations to the manuscript

287.2 which in reason ought] *manuscript originally read 'which ought in reason'; the first 'ought' was cancelled and a second 'ought' interlined two words later*

287.4 were] *'were' interlined above a cancelled 'was'*

288.4 would] *'will' cancelled, 'would' written immediately afterwards*

288.6 Administration.] *the manuscript continues: 'I have therefore thought it may [two illegible words] be worth [of cancelled] some serious though[no terminal t] to examine.' This sentence was then cancelled*

Word division (compounds only)

Copy text
none

Edited text
none

SOME FREE THOUGHTS UPON THE PRESENT STATE OF AFFAIRS: TEXTUAL ACCOUNT

The attempt to publish in 1714

The textual origin of this work has been conflated with that of Swift's *Discourse concerning the fears from the Pretender* (see Ehrenpreis, vol. II, pp. 737–42 and Woolley, *Corr.*, vol. I, p. 614, n. 2) but this edition – following Davis – considers the two works to be distinct entities (one of which was not completed). On 12 June 1714, Swift wrote to Charles Ford from Letcombe that he was 'going on with the Discourse of which you saw the Beginning' (*Ford*, vol. I, p. 613). However, over the next fortnight he abandoned the title and the two paragraphs already drafted but not the topic. By Thursday 1 July 1714, this new work, *Some Free Thoughts*, was sufficiently complete for Swift to send it – a fair copy not in Swift's hand – to Ford along with detailed instructions:

> Here it is, read it, and send it to B— by an unknown hand, have nothing to do with it, thô there be no Danger. Contrive he may not shew it M^r L— yet how can You do that? for I would not have him know that you or I had any concern in it. Do not send it by the Penny post, nor your Man, but by a Porter when you are not at Your Lodgings. get some Friend to copy out the little Paper, and send it inclosed with the rest, & let the same Hand direct it, and seal it with an unknown Seal. If it be not soon printed, send it to Dunstons [coffee house] in the name desired. —Spend an hour in reading it, & if the same word be too soon repeated, vary it as You please, but alter Y^r Hand. adieu. Jul. 1. 1714. I would fain have it sent on Saterday night, or Sunday because of the date, that it might not be suspected to come from here. If You think any thing in the little Letter suspicious, alter it as you please.   (p. 627)

Swift's elaborate subterfuge – understandable given the problems over *Publick Spirit* – frustrated the publication process. (The most detailed accounts are given by Davis (vol. VIII, pp. xxiii–xxviii) and Rivington (pp. 62–8) although the interested reader can also trace developments through the relevant letters in Woolley, *Corr.*) Ford duly sent Barber (the 'B—' in Swift's letter) the copy on Sunday 4 July, writing to Swift on Tuesday that he hoped to 'soon send you a letter in print' (Woolley, *Corr.*, vol. I, p. 634). The 'little Paper' Swift mentions was evidently a brief covering note for Barber; it supplied a pseudonym ('Samuel Bridges'), using St Dunstan's Coffee House as a contact address. Barber's reply to 'Bridges' on 6 July, however, complicated the situation unexpectedly as he reported that he had 'shewn it only to one Person, who is charm'd with it, and will make some small Alterations and Additions to it, with your leave: You will the easier give leave, when I tell you, that it is one of the best Pens in England' (p. 645). At this stage, neither Ford nor Swift knew the identity of this 'one Person'; Ford sent Barber's note to Swift on Saturday 10 July (he only picked up the letter from the coffee house on the Friday), asking: 'What answer shall I send? I am against any alteration, but additions I think ought by no means to be allow'd . . . B. was a Blockhead to shew it at all, but who can help that? Write an answer either for yourself or me, but I beg of you to make no condescentions' (p. 643). The situation became more confused when, in a subsequent exchange of letters between Barber and 'Bridges', Ford discovered that Bolingbroke was the 'Person' advising Barber on the text ('how comicall a Thing', Swift wryly observed in a letter to Ford on 18 July, '[j]ust as if *the Public Spirit* had been sent to Argyle for his Approbation' (*Ford*, vol. II, p. 14)). As Ford reported to Swift on Thursday 15 July, he had stalled Barber by asking 'to see the alterations . . . If the alterations are material, shall I send it to some other printer as it was first written?' (p. 5). By Saturday, however, there had been no further word from Barber and Ford worried that the printer might not even return the original manuscript (p. 7). Swift's response on Sunday (presumably to Ford's 15 July letter) was simple: 'if you dislike the Alterations, take back the Thing, and either burn it or send it to some other Printer as you think best' (p. 14). However, Barber failed to return the manuscript. An increasingly agitated Ford urged Swift in three successive letters over the following week to send on his own personal copy of the text (pp. 15–16, 20–2). Swift did on Sunday 25 July – 'do with it as you please. It will now do nothing to the Cause' – but betrayed sufficient interest in its fate to draft a preface explaining the circumstances of publication: 'a very cautious Printer . . . The Person he showed them [the manuscript] to has kept them ever since . . . the time is almost lapsed wherein they might have done any

Service' (pp. 27–8). Ford probably transcribed a copy (at Swift's request) but Swift's hopes of publication were overtaken by events: Oxford was dismissed on Tuesday and by the following Sunday the Queen was dead.

The Rothschild manuscript

The subsequent history of the three copies is significant. Although Swift had first considered allowing Ford to burn the manuscript following the Queen's death, Ford returned Swift's own holograph copy during the second week of August as Swift felt 'I may have use for some Passages in it' (*Ford*, vol. II, pp. 45, 61, 66). Seven years later, in a letter to Ford in June 1721, Swift moots the possibility of publishing *Some Free Thoughts* along with *An Enquiry into the Behaviour of the Queen's Last Ministry* 'in a Volume by some Whig Booksell[er]' but nothing appears to have come of this (p. 384). Ford (as Woolley (*Corr.*, vol. II, p. 62 n. 8) suggests) appears to have retained his copy as he included 'Some Free Thoughts on the present State of Affairs, never printed' in his 1733 'Catalogue of Pamphlets and Papers, which I have bound' (vol. III, p. 699); its subsequent fate is unknown. In June 1737, Swift made fair copies of both the *Enquiry* and *Some Free Thoughts* for his cousin Martha Whiteway, evidently with a view to publication (Davis, vol. VIII, p. xxxvii); Swift wrote on the cover leaf of the latter: 'This is the Original Manuscript left in Possession of Mrs Martha Whiteway Corrected by me Jonath: Swift. Jun. 15th. 1737 – seven. I send a Fair Copy of this, to be printed in England. Jonath: Swift'. No copy, it seems, was printed from this manuscript (hereafter SwJ 474) in Swift's lifetime; the dashing of Swift's hopes of publication once again is presumably linked with the thwarting of the publication of Swift's *Four Last Years* (with which the *Enquiry* was closely associated) in 1736–8 (see Ehrenpreis, vol. III, pp. 804, 862–4; Davis, vol. VII, pp. xiii–xvi). In 1855, the Whiteway copy was sold, along with other Swift manuscripts, by Edmund Lenthal Swifte, Whiteway's great-grandson, to John Forster, who had been recently commissioned to write a biography of Swift by the publisher John Murray; Murray provided the cheque for £35. (Interestingly, although the manuscript would presumably have passed through the hands of Deane Swift, Edmund Lethal Swifte's grandfather, there is no evidence that Deane Swift, who was involved with the Hawkesworth and Nichols editions of Swift's works and correspondence, ever made his copy available to the publishers.) Of the manuscripts purchased, Murray evidently retained three, including *Some*

Free Thoughts; these were sold on in 1935 and are now in the Rothschild Collection in TCC (Woolley, 'Forster's *Swift*', 194–95, 201 n. 23). The manuscript of *Some Free Thoughts* was first printed by Davis, who incorporated Swift's revisions to the manuscript and made a number of silent minor changes (e.g. correcting 'Man' to 'Men').

Faulkner's 1741 edition
The other copy – the one sent by Ford to Barber – was evidently never returned either to Ford or Swift. On 22 July 1714, Ford reported that, according to Barber, the manuscript was still with Bolingbroke; Barber promised to return it as soon as it was 'restor'd to him' (Woolley, *Corr.*, vol. II, p. 20). Ford fretted to Swift in August about whether he should ask Barber for its return but it seems that he never did (Woolley, *Corr.*, vol. II, pp. 66–7). Woolley interprets the continued absence of the manuscript as a sign that it was still with Bolingbroke as late as 12 August (*Corr.*, vol. II, p. 62 n. 8) but as he points out elsewhere (vol. I, p. 610 n. 1), a note in volume XI of George Faulkner's 18mo *Works* (1762) demonstrates that Barber must have had the manuscript in his possession by the end of July: '[it] was ready for the Press when the Queen dyed: But, upon Messengers being sent to search [Barber's] Printing-Office, he and his Journeymen broke the Form[e]s to Pieces before the State Messengers got Admittance' (p. 220 n.). In the summer of 1741, Faulkner issued *Letters to and from Dr. J. Swift* in both octavo (20 June) and duodecimo (after 20 June) formats (TS, nos. 44 and 51), which included, at the end of each volume, a version of *Some Free Thoughts*; in both cases, a full divisional title and separate pagination allowed the work to be also issued separately. (As TS notes (p. 144), the collation of the octavo edition indicates that it was printed first.) The octavo edition (hereafter 1741a) differs slightly from the duodecimo edition (hereafter 1741b), mostly in matters of punctuation but there are two substantive variants. The two volumes prefaced the work with an identical 'Advertisement *to the* Reader', dated May 1741, which briefly outlined the circumstances of its composition and non-publication (making no mention of Bolingbroke) before explaining its appearance in this volume:

> in all Probability [it] would have been lost for ever, had not the Printer
> hereof been in *London* some Time ago, and got the original Manuscript
> from Alderman *John Barber*, formerly City-Printer, who had most carefully

preserved it, in Order to oblige the Publick some Time or other; which we here do in the most correct Manner, not doubting but it will be agreeable to all our Readers.   (1741a, sig. U2^r)

Exactly how or when Faulkner 'got' the manuscript is unclear, although the 1762 footnote quoted above claims that Faulkner 'had a Letter from the Author to the Alderman [i.e. Barber], to give him what Manuscripts he had of his, amongst which was [*Some*] *Free Thoughts*'; nonetheless, it seems striking that Barber died just over five months before *Letters* was published, suggesting that the manuscript may have only been retrieved immediately before or after his death. Nonetheless, I think it can be safely assumed that this was set from the copy – or a witness to the copy – that Ford originally sent to Barber and to which both Ford and Bolingbroke had apparently made alterations. (Ford, in his letter acknowledging receipt of the copy from Swift, had noted that he had made some minor changes of spelling and tense (Woolley, *Corr.*, vol. I, p. 634).)

Did Swift consent to – indeed did he even know of – Faulkner's publication of *Some Free Thoughts*? And, if so, did he make any changes to the text before it was published? The work's inclusion in Faulkner's edition of Swift's correspondence is significant. The complicated process by which Swift's correspondence was published during 1740–1 – which with its subterfuge, anonymous letters and hesitant printers is curiously reminiscent of the fate of *Some Free Thoughts* in July 1714 – has been summarised by Ehrenpreis (vol. III, pp. 883–98; see also TS, pp. 139–45) but the late addition of *Some Free Thoughts* (described 'as an afterthought' in TS, p. 144) indicates that it was not included in the correspondence as originally approved by Swift. Yet, Swift, despite his advancing years, was 'still competent enough' in the summer of 1741 (Ehrenpreis, vol. III, p. 908); moreover he commissioned Faulkner later that year to retrieve the manuscript of *Four Last Years* from Dr William King in England, to whom Swift had sent it in 1737 (Davis, vol. VII, p. xvi). How likely is it, therefore, that Faulkner would have put into press without Swift's consent a work with which the author had, twenty-seven years earlier and in admittedly a very different political climate, been scared of being associated? That the publishing of *Four Last Years* had been blocked due to political sensitivities in 1736–8 would presumably have added to the wariness of the author and his friends, if not the printer. Consent, however, does not necessarily mean that Swift read over, let alone revised the text; Faulkner's 'Advertisement', if anything, implies that the original manuscript has not been in any way retouched by the author.

Some Free Thoughts was reprinted separately in London bearing the imprints of Thomas Cooper (hereafter 1741c), which followed 1741b, and James Brindley and Thomas Cooper (hereafter 1741d), which was a near identical line-by-line resetting of 1741a. It also appeared in volume IX of the duodecimo *Miscellanies in Prose* (TS, no. 31(3)), published by Cooper in 1742. As TS notes (p. 23), the 1741 octavo *Letters* was volume VII of Faulkner's octavo *Works* in all but name; in 1746, it was reissued with a new title page bearing the correct volume number. (The same happened to the duodecimo edition in 1748.) *Some Free Thoughts* was included in all the major editions of Swift's works from the 1750s onwards. The large octavo Hawkesworth edition of 1754–5 (TS, no. 88) included the work in its third volume (1754) and expanded Faulkner's prefatory note, drawing virtually verbatim from Swift's account in a letter to Alexander Pope on 10 January 1721 (Woolley, *Corr.*, vol. II, 354–62); the delay in publication in July 1714 was blamed 'upon some difference in opinion between the author and the late Lord *Bolingbroke*' (*Works* (1754), p. 350). The volume also added a handful of explanatory footnotes. Hawkesworth's preface and footnotes were included in subsequent eighteenth-century editions; Nichols and Scott both included the preface in their early nineteenth-century editions. Temple Scott, in his 1901 edition, declared that he had been unable to locate a copy of the Faulkner 1741 edition (1741a–b) and so his text was based on Scott's 1824 edition, incorporating changes from the Cooper (1741c) edition 'which most nearly corresponds with that printed by Faulkner in 1746, in vol. vii. of his edition of Swift's works' (vol. V, p. 394); ironically, as TS (p. 33) notes, the 1746 edition was the 'same printing' as the 1741 edition with re-set preliminaries. Temple Scott seemed unaware of a manuscript copy.

Copy text

The identification of the appropriate copy text for this work, then, is the most ticklish of this volume. As noted elsewhere, for occasional (including polemical) works, this edition's editorial policy prefers the version of the work closest to the immediate circumstances of its original composition. The topicality of *Some Free Thoughts*, as Swift himself recognized, was

486 ENGLISH POLITICAL WRITINGS 1711–1714

strictly limited: barely three weeks after first dispatching a copy to London, he urged in his note to the would-be printer that 'the time is almost lapsed wherein [the work] might have done any Service' (Woolley, *Corr.*, vol. II, p. 28). Accordingly, a case could be made for 1741a–b as a witness of the fair copy of Swift's manuscript as sent to Ford on 1 July 1714, albeit one that by 1741 presumably bore the minor changes of Ford, the significant 'Alterations' of Bolingbroke, the possible further amendments of Barber and, of course, the editorial hand of Faulkner. Set against this, however, is SwJ 474, a manuscript bearing Swift's explicit authority, copied on his instructions – presumably from his own 1714 holograph or a corrected version of that – and corrected by him. The corrections could be considered, for the most part, to be stylistic although Swift did cancel a few phrases and lines. SwJ 474 does contain several passages not included in 1741a–b which, because of their content, seem to have been excised by Bolingbroke in 1714 – these include references to 'the uncertain timorous Nature of the Queen', 'some who have since affected great Fears of the Pretender, and quarrelled very much with the Treatise of Peace & Commerce with France', the belief 'that the Nation would humbly submit to their Sovereign's Pleasure, if Her Majesty conceived it proper upon certain Conditions to invite over the eldest Grandson of the present Elector, have a Maintenance allotted him by Parliament, and give him a Title' and a lengthy passage about the failings of unnamed political figures, including an allusion to those who 'deserted their Friends and Principles upon the Prospect of those Dangers which their own Instability or Ambition created'. Consequently, because of these omissions and the intervention by Bolingbroke, it is my belief that SwJ 474 represents a better copy text than 1741a–b. (Woolley agrees, describing the manuscript returned by Ford to Swift in August 1714 as 'the archetype' of 1737, 'representing the earlier and unrevised state'; 1741 is based on 'the later, revised state of the text' (*Corr.*, vol. II, p. 62 n. 8).) As this volume is more interested in Swift's intentions for this text in 1714 rather than any revisions he made in 1737, this edition takes as its copy text SwJ 474 *without* Swift's revisions (hereafter SwJ 474a); emendations based on the revised version (hereafter SwJ 474b) have been made only where there are good grounds to believe Swift was restoring an original reading or correcting a mistranscription. Consequently, 1741 has been used, where appropriate, as a form of 'verification' for Swift's 1714 intentions. The same principle, where possible, has been applied to punctuation, notwithstanding the obvious difficulties of identifying whether punctuation has been revised by Swift or not and of being unable to assume that 1741 accurately reflects the punctuation of the manuscript from which it was set. SwJ 474 has been collated with 1741a–d and Davis (I have included Davis's variant readings in the collations); italicization of words in 1741a–d has only been noted where it seems to be significant.

Copy text: TCC, A.5.10 (SwJ 474a)

References: SwJ, 474. Rothschild Library, no. 2263. TS, nos. 44, 62B, 778 (Faulkner octavo); 51, 64, 779 (Faulkner duodecimo); 780 (Cooper); 781 (Brindley & Cooper). Davis, vol. VIII, pp. 73–98; facsimiles of fo. 1^r and fo. 2^r facing vol VIII, pp. xxiv–xxv. *ESTC*, T219084 (section from Faulkner octavo edition as separate issue, listing copies at Auckland Public Library, New Zealand, and Bancroft Library, University of California, Berkeley); (section from Faulkner duodecimo edition as separate issue not listed in *ESTC*); T1078 (Cooper, listing sixteen copies); T98782 (Brindley and Cooper, listing twenty-two copies)

Manuscript: SwJ 474

Location: TCC, A.5.10

Description: Transcript in unidentified hand, with autograph revisions by Swift and some annotations in pencil; twenty-one leaves, 306 × c.183 mm; fos. 2^r–20^v paginated 1–38; foliation added later in pencil, lower left corner of recto; vertical chainlines; watermark visible on fos. 13–21: royal coat of arms within circular motto, crowned, with 'AR' monogram below, 99 × 67 mm (very similar to the watermark in *Discourse Concerning the Fears from the Pretender*; compare Heawood, nos. 441, 445, 448); countermark visible on fos. 1–12: crowned 'AR', 28 × 25 mm; bound in red morocco; front board: 'SOME FREE THOUGHTS | UPON THE | PRESENT STATE OF AFFAIRS | J. SWIFT | MS. WITH CORRECTIONS | IN THE AUTHOR'S HAND 1714'.

Contents: fo. 1^r 'Some Free Thoughts &c | May. 1714 | [*rest of page in different ink*] This is the Original Manuscript | left in Possession of Mrs Martha Whiteway | Corrected by me Jonath: Swift. | Jun. 15th. 1737 – seven. [*sic*] | I send a Fair Copy of this, to be | printed in England. Jonath:

Swift.'; fo. 1^v blank; fo. 2^r (left-hand column, in Swift's hand) 'Mem^{dm} | This discourse was written at | Upper Letcomb in Berkshire, about | two months before the Queens | Death, during my Retirement | upon finding it impossible ~ | after above two years endeavor | to [*letter cancelled*] reconcile My Lord ~ | Treasurer, and [*letter cancelled*] my Lord | Bolingbroke: from the quarrel | between which two great men | all our misfortunes proceeded. | The Papers were sent in an | unknown hand to Mr Barber ~ | the printer in London, who gave | them to My Ld Bolingbroke to | peruse, knowing nothing of the | Author, but by conjecture. [*full-stop could be semi-colon*] His | Lordship would have altered ~ | some passages; and during the | Delay and doubts he made, the | Queen dyed.'; fos. 2^r–20^v text on right-hand half of each page, in amanuensis's hand, with corrections by Swift mostly in left-hand column (ink darkens noticeably from fo. 7^v onwards, resulting in considerable bleed-through); fo. 21^r blank; fo. 21^v endorsed, top, right hand: (headed 'Some free thoughts upon the | Present State of Affairs | May —— 1714').

Faulkner octavo edition, 1741a

Issued separately and as part of Letters to and from Dr J. Swift *(Dublin, 1741) [TS, nos. 44, 62B]*

Divisional title: SOME | Free THOUGHTS | UPON THE | Present STATE | OF | AFFAIRS. | [rule] | Written in the YEAR 1714. | [rule] | [ornament, 22 × 33 mm] | [double rule] | *DUBLIN*: | Printed by and for GEORGE FAULKNER. | M,DCC,XLI. | U

Collation: 8°: U–X^8, C^2

Pagination: i–iv, 1–32

Contents: U1^r title page; U1^v blank; U2^r Advertisment to the reader; U2^v blank; U3^r–C2^v text; C2^v ornament 31 × 46 mm

Typography: thirty-two lines per page (U4^r), type-page 149 (160) × 83 mm, twenty lines of roman type 93.5 mm; advertisement, twenty lines of italic type 115.5 mm

Failures of catchwords to catch:
X8^r: not] ~,

Copies examined:
*†§BL, 12274.i.5: 196 × 125 mm, trimmed; *ECCO* copy
*†Bodl, Vet. A4 e.1280: 195 × 118 mm, trimmed
*†§CUL, Williams 218: 216 × 135 mm, trimmed; large paper copy; 'Doctor Swift's gift to Doc.ʳ Wilson'; bookplates of: Harold Williams, William Owen Mitchell, James Wilson, David Wilson
*CUL, Hib.7.741.22: 195 × 123 mm, trimmed

Faulkner duodecimo edition, 1741b

Issued separately and as part of Letters to and from Dr J. Swift *(Dublin, 1741) [TS, nos. 51, 64]*

Divisional title: SOME | Free THOUGHTS | UPON THE | Present STATE | OF | AFFAIRS. | [rule] | Written in the YEAR 1714. | [rule] | [ornament, 30 × 45] | [double rule] | *DUBLIN*: | Printed by and for GEORGE FAULKNER. | M,DCC,XLI. | N3

Collation: 12°: N3–N6, O⁶, P³

Pagination: i–iv, 1–22

Contents: N3ʳ title page; N3ᵛ blank; N4ʳ Advertisement to the reader; N4ᵛ blank; N5ʳ–P3ᵛ text

Typography: forty lines per page (O1ᵛ), type page 133 (141) × 70 mm, twenty lines of roman type 66.5 mm; advertisement, twenty lines of italic type 82 mm

Failures of catchwords to catch:
none

Copy examined:
*†BL, 1607/4628: 165 × c.92 mm, trimmed; *ECCO* copy

Cooper edition, 1741c

Title: SOME | FREE THOUGHTS | UPON THE | PRESENT STATE | OF | AFFAIRS. | [rule] | *By the Author of* GULLIVER'S TRAVELS. | [rule] | [ornament, 17 × 30 mm] | [double rule] | *DUBLIN* Printed: | LONDON,

Re-printed for T. Cooper, at the | *Globe* in *Pater-Noster-Row*. 1741. | [Price Six-Pence.] [square brackets in original]

Collation: 8°: A^2, B–D^4, E^2

Pagination: i–iv, 1–27, *28*

Contents: $A1^r$ title page; $A1^v$ blank; $A2^r$ Advertisement to the reader; $A2^v$ blank; $B1^r$–$E2^r$ text; $E2^v$ advertisement for Clarendon's *History of the Rebellion*

Typography: thirty-seven lines of type ($C3^r$), type-page 156 (167) × 80 mm, twenty lines of roman type 85 mm; advertisement to reader, twenty lines of italic type 93 mm

Failures of catchwords to catch:
none

Copies examined:
*†BL, 1093.d.77: 200 × 124 mm, trimmed; re-bound in 1947; *ECCO* copy
*BL, 08139.ccc.33(4): 199 × 123 mm, trimmed; contains numerous vertical pencil lines in the outer margins; in volume of seven tracts (1727–57); re-bound 1954

Brindley and Cooper edition, 1741d

Title: SOME | Free THOUGHTS | UPON THE | Present STATE | OF | AFFAIRS. | [rule] | Written in the Year 1714. | [rule] | [ornament: 29 × 46 mm] | [double rule] | *DUBLIN*, Printed: | *LONDON*, Reprinted for J. Brindley in | *New-Bond-Street*; and ſold by T. Cooper at the | *Globe* in *Pater-Noster-Row*. M,DCC,XLI.| [rule] | [Price Sixpence,] [square brackets in original]

Collation: 8°: A^2, B–E^4

Pagination: i–iv, 1–32

Contents: $A1^r$ title page; $A1^v$ blank; $A2^r$ Advertisement; $B1^r$–$E4^v$: text; $E4^v$: ornament, 26 × 49 mm

Typography: thirty-two lines per page ($B2^r$), type-page 149 (161) × 83 mm, twenty lines of roman type 93 mm; preface, twenty lines of italic type 118 mm

Failures of catchwords to catch:
E2^r: no[t]] not,

Copy examined:
*†BL, 101.g.38: 202 × 124 mm, trimmed; re-bound 1932; copy available on *ECCO*

Emendations

291.4 Qualities.] 1741 ~,
Although SwJ 474 clearly gives a comma, the sense demands a full stop.
291.15 Borgia] 1741; Bargis
This is how the word appears in the manuscript
291.18 have] SwJ 474b; then
Revised reading (made by amanuensis) is same as 1741 and as such can be seen to restore Swift's original intention.
291.23 Interests] 1741; Interest
There appears to be no terminal 's' in the manuscript; however, 1741's reading and the grammar of the sentence suggest a plural reading is correct
292.23 accounted] SwJ 474b; accouted
293.35 searching] SwJ 474b; seaching
294.2 which] SwJ 474b; & which
Revised reading is same as 1741 and as such can be seen to restore Swift's original intention.
294.10 the better, nor any Vice by which the Publick may not be] SwJ 474b; *om.*
The similarity of these words to 1741's reading suggests that Swift was restoring words that had been accidentally omitted by the amanuensis due to eye-skip over the repeated 'Publick may not be'.
294.14 intrepid] 1741; intreped
295.18 Majority] SwJ 474b; Maj[*unclear two or three letters*]ty
295.33 Foot] SwJ 474b; ?Sort
Revised reading is same as 1741 and as such can be seen to restore Swift's original intention.
296.1 Failures] SwJ 474b; certain Failures
Revised reading is same as 1741 and as such can be seen to restore Swift's original intention.

296.22 since affected great Fears of the Pretender, and] SwJ 474b; *om.*

These words have been interlined by the amanuensis and hence were pre-sumably present in manuscript from which SwJ 474 was copied; they are not present in 1741.

297.16 Changes] SwJ 474b; Changing

The change, as Davis suggests, may have been made by Swift; however, it is clearly a correction to an error of transcription rather than a revision.

298.31 their] SwJ 474b; the

Swift was evidently restoring an original reading as the 1741 reading con-firms.

299.10 unnecessarily] SwJ 474b; necessarily

Swift's interlineation corrects the amanuensis's error as the 1741 reading confirms.

300.10 impracticable:] SwJ 474b; ~,

Someone, perhaps Swift, added the colon later (without cancelling the comma); the sense here demands punctuation stronger than a comma.

301.4 preferred] SwJ 474b; prefered

301.19 Understanding to a Degree that in any other] SwJ 474b; *om.*

Swift's insertion is, as its appearance in 1741 indicates, a correction of the transcript not a revision.

301.26 entire] SwJ 474b; higher

As 'entire' is written immediately after the cancelled 'higher' by the amanuensis, this is evidently a transcription error; the 1741 reading confirms this.

302.27 or] SwJ 474b; nor

1741 reading indicates that 'or' was the probable original reading.

302.29 shall] SwJ 474b; *om.*

1741 reading indicates this was a transcription error.

303.9 to] SwJ 474b; that to

'that' is clearly ungrammatical.

306.1 they] SwJ 474b; the

Clearly a transcription error.

307.14 however,] 1741; ~.

A period here is clearly ungrammatical.

307.15 Choice:] SwJ 474b; ~,

The colon – more suitable for the grammar here – was added without cancelling the comma.

307.21 unnecessary] SwJ 474b; *om.*

Swift corrected the amanuensis's oversight.

308.12 Kingdom:] *manuscript reads 'Kingdom..'*

It is difficult to tell which mark here is the later but 1741 gives a colon.

309.12 the Threats] *not emended*

As my co-editor has pointed out, the sense of this passage seems to demand a negative phrase (e.g. 'not' or 'rather than') to be inserted before 'the Threats'. However, there is no evidence in the manuscript or in the 1741 edition to suggest that this reading was considered problematic and so we have not emended here.

309.25 Anti-Chambers] SwJ 474b; Ante-Chambers

1741 reads 'Anti', suggesting that Swift's correction to SwJ 474 was a restoration of the original reading.

Rejected revised readings in the manuscript

Except where noted, I have used 1741 readings to distinguish later Swift revisions of the original 1714 manuscript.

292.19 is] are

The revised reading here may well have been by Swift and as such, the balance of probability suggests it is a revision of the original manuscript (and hence post-1714 intention) rather than a correction of a transcription error. 1741 here differs from both readings.

292.20 so] so few

292.28 are] *cancelled*

293.18 any Man] most Man

294.1 &] and

Swift used ampersands elsewhere in SwJ 474; I have retained this one on the grounds that it reflects the original manuscript reading.

294.8 as] more

294.14 intrepid] disintrepid

295.15 will] must

295.35 as] or

Part of a phrase omitted from 1741; Swift's intervention would seem to suggest a later revision, which is why I have rejected the revised reading.

296.3 has] ?hath

*While there does seem to have been an attempt to overwrite the terminal 's',
I am not convinced by this reading. 1741 gives 'hath' but Faulkner often
changed 'has' to 'hath' in Swift's texts; SwJ 474's use of 'has' and 'hath' (it uses
both) is not sufficiently consistent to emend with confidence here.*

296.13 has] ?hath

see previous entry

296.15 in] in

296.23 Treatise] Treaty's

*It is tempting to ignore both the original and revised readings and emend
'Treaties' as in 1741; however, as the original reading is more likely to represent
Swift's original 1714 spelling, I have retained it here.*

296.28 that] this

*As 1741 indicates, a later revision by Swift. Davis links the change to the 'that'
later in the sentence, whose underlining suggests that Swift was conscious of
a repetition here.*

297.1 the] ?that

297.8 other] adverse

297.16 Office] Offices

298.17 tho'] although

*The printed editions of his other 1711–14 political writings suggest that Swift
appears to have preferred 'tho' to either 'though' or 'although'; that 1741 reads
'altho' here is I think a consequence of Faulkner's common practice of changing
Swift's 'tho'/'though' to 'although'.*

299.14 Though] Although

See previous entry.

299.16 usefull] true

302.18 though] although

I follow the uncorrected reading for reasons explained previously.

302.18 appears] appear

302.22 with] by

302.29 shall] may

303.1 though] although

I follow the uncorrected reading for reasons explained previously.

303.19 and with great Connivance leave it so long unsheathed till they
were got rid of their most formidable Adversaries] *cancelled*

304.16 pretended] would be thought
*Although 1741 does not match either reading, I have rejected Swift's interlin-
eation as a later revision (as this was presumably not an amanuensis error).*
306.10 passive Obedience, Non-Resistance and] *cancelled*
306.12 and must in their own Opinion renounce all those Doctrines by
setting up any other Title to the Crown] *cancelled*
307.7 Consequence] Moment
308.6 Treatise] Treatyes
See my previous comments about retaining 'Treatise' as a reading.
308.12 Kingdom:] Kingdom.:
309.3 Parties;] Parties;;
309.7 has] ?hath
For reasons given above I am reluctant to allow the revised reading here.
310.17 probably] *cancelled*
310.23 probably] *cancelled*
310.27 will probably] will[*sic*] may in all likelyhood
310.28 depress the Prerogative enough] enough depress the Prerogative
310.34 will not] may not perhaps
310.35 Party.] Party;.[*sic*]

Historical collation

291.2 never] hardly 1741
291.4 Qualities.] ~, SwJ 474
291.7 has] hath 1741
291.13 neither] nor 1741
291.14 Lewis the eleventh of France] *om.* 1741
291.15 Borgia] Bargis SwJ 474
291.16 Examples are not] Nor are Examples 1741
291.18 have] then SwJ 474a
291.23 Interests] Interest SwJ 474
291.26 Yet] *om.* 1741
292.8 practicing] employing 1741
292.9 those in Power] Ministry 1741
292.19 is generally supposed] are generally supposed SwJ 474b; we generally suppose 1741
292.20 so] so few SwJ 474b

292.22 point of Credit and Reputation] Decency 1741

292.28 Tis] It is 1741

292.28 are] *om.* SwJ 474b

292.30 deduce] deduct 1741a–c; Davis

Davis claims that the manuscript reads 'deduct' here but the final letter is, I believe, clearly an 'e'; of course, it is possible that the original 1714 reading was 'deduct' but that this was misread by the amanuensis of SwJ 474.

292.34 despises] despiseth 1741

293.11 Sessions] Session 1741

293.12 has] hath 1741

293.16 Dispositions] Disposition 1741

293.18 any Man] most Man SwJ 474b; most Men Davis

Davis follows SwJ 474b but corrects in order to preserve grammar.

293.22 Effects] Part 1741

293.35 deep. [*new paragraph*] And] deep. [*no new paragraph*] And 1741

294.1 &] and SwJ 474b+

294.2 which] & which SwJ 474a

294.6 Management] Administration 1741

294.7 virtues] great Abilities and Virtues 1741

294.8 as] more SwJ 474b; so 1741

294.9 has] hath 1741

294.10 the better, nor any Vice by which the Publick may not be] *om.* SwJ 474a; the better, nor any Defect by which the Publick is not certainly 1741

294.11 a very small Omission in Appearance] an Omission, in Appearance very small 1741

This stylistic change perhaps indicates that Swift may have edited his own 1714 manuscript before it was copied by the amanuensis.

294.14 intrepid] disintrepid SwJ 474b

294.15 that] and that 1741

294.15 that he loves his Prince and Country, and the Constitution in Church and State. I have seen all these Accomplishments unable to bear up their owner by the mixture of a few trifling Defects too inconsiderable to mention, and almost as easy to be remedied as related] *om.* 1741

294.23 And likewise because] Because likewise 1741

294.33 Concert] Love 1741

295.1 have] *have* 1741

295.1 Consequences] Consequence 1741

295.10 great a Number] many 1741

Davis interpreted the pencilled dashes beneath the two uses of 'great' in this sentence as a sign that Swift wanted to avoid repetition, prompting to inter-polate 1741's 'many' as a result. While it seems likely that Swift was noting repetitions, he did not seek to provide an alternative here; moreover, it may well be that the 'many' in 1741 was a stylistic correction by another hand – Swift himself advised Ford on receipt of his first copy of the manuscript to amend should 'the same word be too soon repeated'.

295.15 will] must SwJ 474b

295.15 Others] those who can better determine 1741

295.17 her Self] herself 1741

295.25 the chief Managers] those who were to have the chief Part in Affairs 1741

295.26 Friendship.] ∼, 1741a, d; ∼: 1741b–c

295.33 Foot] ?Sort SwJ 474a

295.33 The Cause of all] *om.* 1741

295.34 the uncertain timorous Nature of the Queen, as Obstructions from any private Remora about the Court] the uncertain timorous Nature of the Queen, or Obstructions from any private Remora about the Court SwJ 474b; *om.* 1741

296.1 Failures] certain Failures SwJ 474a; Failures among themselves 1741

296.2 Effects] their Effects 1741

296.3 has] ?hath SwJ 474b; hath 1741

296.4 which] who 1741

296.4 in] *om.* 1741b–c

296.4 forced ever since to act] acting ever since 1741

296.6 Sides] Side 1741

296.10 alone are] (or, if that was the Case) the *Minister* alone is 1741

296.13 has] ?hath SwJ 474b; hath 1741

296.15 upon which] whereon 1741

296.18 All which indeed arose from a very unjust, and perhaps an affected Diffidence towards those at the Helm.] *om.* 1741

296.21 no little] little 1741a, d; a little 1741b–c

296.22 (particularly some who have since affected great Fears of the Pretender, and quarrelled very much with the Treatise of Peace & Commerce
with France)] (particularly some who have since affected great Fears of
the Pretender, and quarrelled very much with the Treaty's of Peace &
Commerce with France) SwJ 474b *om.* 1741

296.24 a] *om.* 1741

296.28 Queen] – 1741

296.28 that] this SwJ 474b

297.1 the] that SwJ 474b

297.8 other] adverse SwJ 474b

297.16 Office] Offices SwJ 474b

297.16 Changes] Changing SwJ 474a

297.17 And that to] To 1741

297.20 dangerous] terrible 1741

297.26 in] *in* 1741

297.26 out] *out* 1741

297.27 Power] Assistance 1741

297.27 It was] And it is 1741

297.27 universall] general 1741

297.30 erecting] creating 1741

*It is possible, given the similarity of the letter formations, that the 1741 reading
is a misreading of a handwritten 'erecting'.*

298.1 is] was 1741

*Swift had urged Ford to make some stylistic changes to the manuscript he sent
in July 1714; on 6 July, Ford reported that 'in one Paragraph . . . I chang'd
the present to the past tence four times' (Woolley,* Corr., *vol. I, p. 634). This
is clearly one of those changes.*

298.1 may] might 1741

Presumably another change by Ford.

298.2 House] H. 1741a–b

298.2 Court and Country Party] *Court* and *Country* Parties 1741

298.3 can be never] could never be 1741

Presumably a Ford emendation.

298.4 have] had 1741

Presumably a Ford emendation.

298.6 proved] appeared to be 1741

298.17 tho'] although SwJ 474b; altho' 1741

298.31 their] the SwJ 474a

298.34 my self] myself 1741c

299.10 unnecessarily] necessarily SwJ 474a

299.10 Communication and Concert] *Communication* and *Concert* 1741

299.14 Though] Although SwJ 474b+

299.16 usefull] true SwJ 474b; useful 1741

299.18 who] who, at least 1741

299.20 Evil] Thing 1741

299.22 Comprehension] *Comprehension* 1741

299.22 moderate] *moderate* 1741

299.23 further] farther 1741

> *Presumably a Faulknerian stylistic improvement.*

299.30 Queen] – 1741a–c; ----- 1741d

299.31 (and I have good reason to be confident that not one of them was so)] *om.* 1741

300.7 too great a] very great 1741

300.8 too great a] very great 1741

300.8 (if we may believe generall Report, for I pretend to know no further)] if we may believe general Report (for I pretend to know no farther) 1741

300.10 impracticable:] impracticable:, SwJ 474b

300.17 faint] feint 1741

300.24 Operations:] ~. 1741

300.24 However . . . low] *om.* 1741

> *This passage includes a version of the line that Swift suggested to Ford on 18 July 1714 as being 'one of L^d B[olingbroke]'s alterations'; Swift quoted the line as 'Whether others have not contended for a greater Part in the Direction of Affairs, &c., than either Friendship, Gratitude or &c.' and suggested to Ford that 'Gratitude' could be dropped as it 'seems hard there' (Woolley, Corr., vol. II, p. 14). 'Gratitude' does not appear in SwJ 474; nor does the wording of the final part of Swift's quotation quite match SwJ 474. As Swift still had his own holograph copy at the time he wrote to Ford (the copy from which SwJ 474 derives), it is possible that he took the opportunity to amend this passage. Swift's suspicion that Bolingbroke might not like the reference may, if anything, have been an underestimation as it was presumably Bolingbroke who struck the entire passage from the copy from which 1741 derives.*

301.19 Understanding to a Degree that in any other] *om.* SwJ 474a

301.26 entire] higher SwJ 474a

302.11 that] *om.* 1741b–c

302.16 play with a Serpent] *play* with a *Serpent* 1741

302.18 though] although SwJ 474b; 1741

302.18 appears] appear Davis

302.21 formerly ruinous, and since very often dangerous] already very dangerous 1741

302.22 with] by SwJ 474b

302.27 or] nor SwJ 474a

302.28 till] until 1741

Presumably a Faulknerian 'improvement'.

302.29 shall] may SwJ 474b

303.1 though] although SwJ 474b; 1741

303.2 a] the 1741

303.3 necessary] very necessary 1741

303.4 the Officers of] *om.* 1741

303.5 many] most 1741

303.6 his] the 1741

303.9 to] that to SwJ 474a

303.19 and with great Connivance leave it so long unsheathed till they were got rid of their most formidable Adversaries] *om.* SwJ 474b; and with great Connivance leave it so long unsheathed, until they were got rid of their most formidable Adversaries 1741

303.23 Junta] *Junto* 1741d

304.16 pretended] would be thought SwJ 474b; seemed 1741

304.22 of] to 1741

305.6 changes] changeth 1741

305.22 now] now most 1741

306.1 Time] Times Davis

Davis misread the manuscript here.

306.1 they] the SwJ 474a

306.10 passive Obedience, Non-Resistance and] *om.* SwJ 474b; Passive-Obedience, Non-Resistance and 1741

306.12 and must in their own Opinion renounce all those Doctrines by setting up any other Title to the Crown] *om.* SwJ 474b

306.16 I am far from justifying] I do not pretend to justify 1741

306.19 Revolution-Principles.   Neither]   *Revolution-Principles.*   [*new paragraph*] Neither 1741

306.23 might have been laid hold on by] was offered to 1741

306.24 from] by 1741

306.28 all] all those 1741c

307.4 further] farther 1741

307.7 Consequence] Moment SwJ 474b

307.14 however,] ~. SwJ 474

307.15 Choice:] ~, SwJ 474a

The colon – more suitable for the grammar here – was added without cancelling the comma.

307.15 wherefore since the old Electrice is lately dead, I am apt to think, that the Nation would humbly submit to their Sovereign's Pleasure, if Her Majesty conceived it proper upon certain Conditions to invite over the eldest Grandson of the present Elector, have a Maintenance allotted him by Parliament, and give him a Title] *om.* 1741

307.21 unnecessary] *om.* SwJ 474a

307.24 be] to be 1741

308.1 Visits or Demands of Writs] *Visits* or *Demands of Writs* 1741

308.5 declare] *declare* 1741

308.6 Treatise] Treatyes SwJ 474b; Treaties 1741

308.8 Requests] Request 1741

308.9 all] *om.* 1741

308.12 Kingdom:] Kingdom.: SwJ 474

308.24 Parliament,] ~. 1741

308.24 her self] herself 1741d

308.26 in the same Interest] of the Number 1741

308.27 obstruct] *obstruct* 1741

308.27 bestow] *bestow* 1741

308.30 Thoughts] while 1741

308.33 Engagement] Engagements 1741

309.6 these] *These* 1741

309.7 others] *Others* 1741

309.7 true] *true* 1741

309.7 has] ?hath SwJ 474b; hath; 1741

309.10 Opinion] Esteem 1741

309.23 Refinements] *Refinements* 1741

309.24 any] an 1741

309.25 Anti-Chambers] Ante-Chambers SwJ 474a; Davis

309.25 at] of 1741

309.32 then] *om.* 1741

309.35 another] an other 1741a–c; another 1741d

310.5 may have] hath 1741

310.12 in the Wrong] *in the Wrong* 1741

310.17 probably] *om.* SwJ 474b

310.22 inconsiderable] small 1741

310.23 probably] *om.* SwJ 474b

310.27 will probably] may in all likelyhood SwJ 474b

310.28 depress the Prerogative enough] enough depress the Prerogative SwJ 474b

310.34 will not] may not perhaps SwJ 474b

310.34 consistent with her Safety and Honour] *consistent with her Safety and Honour* 1741

310.35 Hope] Hopes 1741

310.35 In such an improbable case] *om.* 1741

310.37 Alterations] Alteration Davis

Davis misread the manuscript at this point.

311.1 himself] *himself* 1741

311.2 latent unlimited] *latent, unlimited* 1741

311.4 such a] the 1741

311.4 not be of Persons] be of such 1741

311.5 might dispose] disposed 1741

311.5 confound] *confound* 1741

311.5 The late] *om.* 1741

311.10 we] one 1741

311.12 few] *few* 1741

311.12 Colleagues] *Colleagues* 1741

311.14 Dormant] *dormant* 1741

311.14 Pretences] Pretence 1741

311.15 any] *any* 1741

311.17 both] *both* 1741

311.19 it self] itself 1741d

311.23 very well] well 1741c

311.25 last] late 1741

Alterations to manuscript

291.18 have] *'have' interlined by amanuensis above cancelled 'then' (Davis read 'than')*

292.2 I remember a] *a cross is interlined above 'a', keyed to 'Monsiur Torcy' in Swift's hand in the left-hand column*

292.3 the Spirit of Negotiating] *'the Spirit of Negotiating' underlined; Davis believed the underlining to have been Swift's*

292.19 is] *'are' interlined, possibly by Swift, above cancelled 'is'*

292.20 so] *'few' interlined after 'so' in Swift's hand*

292.23 accounted] *'n' interlined by amanuensis*

292.30 are] *cancelled*

293.18 any Man] *Swift cancelled of 'any' and interlined 'most'; he did not correct 'Man'*

293.35 searching] *'r' interlined*

294.1 &] *Swift interlined 'and' over a cancelled ampersand*

294.2 which] *Swift cancelled an ampersand before 'which' and then interlined 'and' only to cancel it*

294.8 as] *Swift cancelled 'as' and added 'more'*

294.10 the better, nor any Vice by which the Publick may not be] *interlined by Swift in the margin of the manuscript*

294.14 intrepid] *Swift corrected the spelling and interlined 'dis' at the start of the word*

295.15 will] *Swift cancelled 'will' and interlined 'must'*

295.18 Majority] *two or three letters after 'Maj' cancelled; 'ori' interlined in different ink*

295.33 Foot] *Swift cancelled ?'Sort' in order to interlineate 'Foot'; Davis suggests ?'seat' as uncorrected reading*

295.35 as] *suggested reading of unclear original word; Swift cancelled this and interlined 'or'*

296.1 Failures] *'certain' (before 'Failure') cancelled; Davis suggests Swift's hand*

296.3 has] *Davis reads 'hath' as a revised reading and there does seem to have been an attempt to overwrite the terminal 's'*

296.7 losing] *a second 'o' has been interlined after the first 'o'*

296.13 has] *Davis reads 'hath' as a revised reading and there does seem to have been an attempt to overwrite the terminal 's'*

296.15 in] *'in' underlined; Davis believes the underlining to be Swift's*

296.22 since affected great Fears of the Pretender, and] *interlined by the amanuensis*

296.23 Treatise] *the final three letters are a suggested reading; these letters were overwritten by 'y's'*

296.28 that] *Swift cancelled 'that' and interlined 'this'*

297.1 the] *'the' is a suggested reading; Davis reads 'that' as an uncorrected reading but the formation of the 'at' and spacing between it and the following word suggests 'at' has overwritten a terminal 'e' in a different, presumably Swift's, hand*

297.8 other] *Swift cancelled 'other' and wrote 'adverse' in the left-hand margin*

297.16 Office] *A terminal 's' seems to have been added afterwards*

297.16 Changes] *'es' overwrites 'ing'*

298.17 tho'] *'al' interlined at start; both original word and interlineation cancelled; caret with 'although' written in left-hand margin*

298.31 their] *Swift cancelled 'the' and interlined 'their'*

299.10 unnecessarily] *Swift interlined 'un'*

299.14 Though] *'Al' written by Swift immediately before 'Though'*

299.16 usefull] *Swift interlined 'true' above a cancelled 'usefull'*

300.10 impracticable:] *original reading 'impracticable,'; someone, perhaps Swift, added colon immediately before comma without cancelling the latter*

301.4 preferred] *the third 'r' interlined, probably by the amanuensis*

301.19 Understanding to a Degree that in any other] *Swift inserted these words in the left-hand margin with a caret between 'mens' and 'Science'*

301.26 entire] *the amanuensis cancelled 'higher' and wrote 'entire' immediately afterwards*

302.18 though] *'al' written immediately before 'though'*

302.18 appears] *terminal 's' cancelled*

302.22 with] *Swift cancelled 'with' and interlined 'by'*

302.27 or] *An initial 'n' cancelled in pencil*

302.29 shall] *interlineation of 'shall' by amanuensis*

302.29 shall] *'shall' cancelled and 'may' interlined*

303.1 though] *'al' written immediately before 'though'*

303.9 to] *'that', immediately before 'to', cancelled*

303.19 and with great Connivance leave it so long unsheathed till they were got rid of their most formidable Adversaries] *cancelled, presumably by Swift*

304.16 pretended] *Swift cancelled 'pretended' and interlined 'would be thought'*

304.17 by a] *a cross interlined immediately above 'a', keyed to 'The Author means himself' in Swift's hand in the left-hand column*

306.1 they] *The 'y' added later*

306.10 passive Obedience, Non-Resistance and] *cancelled, presumably by Swift*

306.12 and must in their own Opinion renounce all those Doctrines by setting up any other Title to the Crown] *cancelled, presumably by Swift*

307.7 Consequence] *cancelled by Swift and 'Moment' interlined*

307.15 Choice:] *original reading 'Choice,'; someone, perhaps Swift, has added colon immediately after the comma without cancelling the latter*

307.21 unnecessary] *interlined by Swift*

307.23 *Expect*] *written in heavier ink, separated letters and underlined*

308.3 *expect*] *underlined*

308.6 Treatise] *'yes' overwrites last three letters, presumably by Swift*

308.12 Kingdom:] *manuscript reads 'Kingdom.:'*

309.3 Parties;] *manuscript reads 'Parties;;'; one of the semi-colons is in a lighter ink than the other but the duplication here is baffling*

309.7 has] *final letter appears to have been overwritten with 'th'*

309.25 Anti-Chambers] *'i' overwrites an 'e'*

310.17 probably] *cancelled, probably by Swift*

310.23 probably] *cancelled, probably by Swift*

310.27 German] *'?Tho ?the Author' written (by Swift?) and cancelled in left-hand column*

310.27 will probably] *Swift cancelled 'probably' and interlined 'may in all likelyhood' but failed to cancel the remaining 'will'*

310.28 depress the Prerogative enough] *Swift cancelled the 'enough' at the end of the sentence and interlined it three words earlier*

310.34 will not] *'may' interlined by Swift above a cancelled 'will' and 'perhaps' interlined after 'not'*

310.35 Party.] *Swift inserted a semi-colon after the period but did not cancel the latter*

311.2 empowering] *'i' overwrites the initial 'e'*

311.4 *Secret Committee*] *underlined; Davis presumes that the underlining was done by Swift rather than the amanuensis (although it appears in italic in 1741)*

Word division (compounds only)

Copy text
none

Edited text
299.3 Coffee-house

Note on transcript

The amanuensis did not always sufficiently distinguish between upper- and lower-case 'S' or 'M'; consequently, I have only capitalized *nouns* starting with these initial letters. The writer also did not always provide a cross-bar for 't', leading to clearly nonsensical readings such as 'sling' instead of 'sting'; I have here 'corrected' the manuscript's reading.

SOME CONSIDERATIONS UPON THE CONSEQUENCES: TEXTUAL ACCOUNT

On 7 August 1714, six days after Queen Anne had died, Swift wrote from Letcombe to Charles Ford in London that he was 'breeding anoth^r Pamphlet, but have not writt a Word of it. The Title will be something like this—Some Considerations upon th[e] Consequences apprehended by th[e] Qu—s Death. If I have hum[o]r, I will write it here & upon th[e] Road, & send it You from Ire^{ld}' (Woolley, *Corr.*, vol. II, pp. 60–1). The manuscript (hereafter SwJ 473) subsequently came into the possession of Mrs Martha Whiteway (Swift's cousin who nursed him during his final years), who bequeathed it to her son-in-law, Deane Swift, who in turn printed it in 1765: it appeared in volume VIII, part 1 (1765) of Hawkesworth's quarto edition of Swift's *Works* (TS, no. 87; hereafter 1765a); large octavo (TS, no. 88; hereafter 1765b), small octavo (TS, no. 90; hereafter 1765c), and 18° editions (TS, no. 92; hereafter 1765d); and in volume XII of Faulkner's octavo edition (TS, no. 47; hereafter 1765e). It was also reproduced in the same year in volume XII of Faulkner's duodecimo and 18° editions (TS, nos. 52, 53, hereafter 1765f and 1765g; I am grateful to Daniel Traister of Van Pelt Library, University of Pennsylvania, for providing me with copies from these editions). Apart from a very few substantive variants (recorded below and all of which are clearly errors on the part of the compositor) and the very occasional difference in punctuation, the 1765 editions follow each other closely, except that 1765d varies considerably in terms of punctuation and capitalization. The 1765 version followed the manuscript closely, with only one or two significant misreadings, but it did alter spellings, punctuation and capitalization; it also silently expanded all the elided names. In 1855, the manuscript was sold, along with twenty-five other Swift manuscripts, by Deane Swift's grandson, Edmund Lenthal Swifte, to John Forster, whom the publisher John Murray had recently commissioned to write a biography of Swift (Woolley, 'Forster's *Swift*', 194–5, 201 n. 24). Davis transcribed the manuscript with greater accuracy, allowing for his usual habit of silently expanding elided names. The manuscript has been re-transcribed for this edition and collated against all the 1765 editions (1765a–g) and Davis.

Copy text: National Art Library, Victoria & Albert Museum, Forster MS 515

References: SwJ, no. 473. Davis, vol. VIII, pp. 99–104; reduced facsimile of first leaf of manuscript, facing p. 101

Manuscript: SwJ 473

Location: National Art Library, Victoria & Albert Museum, Forster MS 515 (Pressmark F.48.G.6/2, item 3)

Description: holograph of Swift, with revisions in same hand; two separate leaves, mounted; fo. 1: c.310 × c.190 mm; fo. 2: c.307 × c.194 mm; vertical chainlines; large circular indistinct watermark in centre of fo. 1; indistinct counter-mark in centre of fo. 2; text only in right-hand half, left-hand half left blank; *pace* Davis (Davis, vol. VIII, p. 210), only fo. 2^r is paginated ('3'); endorsement in left-hand upper quarter of fo. 2^v; at one stage folded into sixteenths.

Contents: fos. 1^r–2^v text, headed 'Aug. 9. 1714 [flush right] | Some Considerations upon the Consequences | hoped and feared from the Death of the Queen.'; fo. 2^v endorsement, left-hand upper quarter reads 'Memoirs.', followed by (upside down) 'On the hopes & fears [*following word interlined*] by [of *cancelled*] the Queen's Death', and (in a different hand) two monograms(?) and '32' within an '>' symbol

Emendations

315.4 Reign.] 1765; ∼ˆ
316.18 contrary.] 1765; ∼ˆ
317.21 dispositions] 1765 [. . .] positions
    First three letters lost due to paper damage.

Historical collation

315.9 till] until 1765
315.13 larger] large 1765

315.17 utmost] the utmost 1765
315.21 though] although 1765
316.10 Dʳ] *om.* 1765d
316.21 that] the 1765f
316.28 D. of Marl—] *om.* 1765d
316.28 who intended it for the] *om.* 1765d
   Presumably an eye-skip on the part of the compositor.
317.9 to] of 1765f

Alterations to the manuscript

316.14 appeared] *following words 'to me in' cancelled*
316.15 E. of] *interlined*
316.23 united] *interlined*
316.25 her] *following word 'Hands' cancelled*
316.30 disposed of] *interlined above cancelled 'given'*
317.5 few] *interlined*
317.10 Dangers] *originally read '?Dangerous'; final letters cancelled; Davis suggests 'Dangerous'*
317.18 an] *following words 'Argument as an Incitement' cancelled*
318.1 running] *following word 'against' cancelled*
318.11 to] *interlined*
318.23 the] *interlined*

Word division (compounds only)

Copy text
none

Edited text
none

CONTRIBUTIONS TO THE POST BOY AND THE EVENING POST: TEXTUAL ACCOUNT

Introduction

Uncollected by Swift editors prior to Davis, these items from *The Post Boy* and *The Evening Post* were included in an appendix by Davis on the grounds that '[t]here can be no question about the[se] items . . . for Swift acknowledges that he was responsible for them' (vol. VI, p. xxiii). The thrice-weekly *Post Boy*, the leading Tory newspaper of the period, was edited by the bookseller and writer Abel Roper. It was printed by the little-known L. Beardwell, who was according to the imprint located 'next [to] the *Red-Cross-Tavern*, in *Black-friars*'. No 'L. Beardwell' appears to have been bound or freed by a member of London's Stationers' Company; however, he or she was probably related to Benjamin Beardwell, printer, who printed *The Post Boy* from 1697 and who freed one of Roper's apprentices in 1705, and to Edward Beardwell, who was bound to Roper in 1707 (H. Plomer and others, *A Dictionary of the Printers and Booksellers who were at Work in England, Scotland and Ireland from 1668 to 1725* (Oxford: Bibliographical Society, 1922), p. 27; McKenzie, *1701–1800*, p. 299). Swift had a low opinion of Roper's activities; he told Stella that his account of the Hamilton–Mohun duel was 'as malicious as possible, and very proper for Abel Roper t[h]e Printer of it' (Williams, *JSt*, p. 574). The less well-known tri-weekly *Evening Post* was printed by E. Berington, a printer active between 1711 and 1724 who apparently had Roman Catholic links; this was probably the Edward Berrington who was bound to Joseph Bennett in 1688 but never freed (Plomer, *Dictionary*, p. 32; McKenzie, *1641–1700*, p. 12). The periodical's imprint declared that it, like *The Examiner*, was published by Morphew.

1. Post Boy, 25–7 December 1711

Swift records Anne Long's death on 25 December: 'I have ordered a paragraph to be put in the *Post-boy*, giving an account of her death, and making
honourable mention of her' (Williams, *JSt*, p. 446).

2. Evening Post, 11–13 November 1712

On the morning of 4 November 1712, Robert Harley (in the presence of
Swift) received a booby-trapped box which, thanks in part to Swift's quick-
thinking, caused no injury to either man (Ehrenpreis, vol. II, p. 583). The
story of the so-called 'Bandbox plot' circulated swiftly: 'the Prints have told
a thousand Lyes of it', Swift wrote to Stella on 15 November, 'but at last
we gave . . . a true account of it at length, printed in the Evening: onely I
would not suffer them to name me, having been so often named before, &
teased to death with Questions' (Williams, *JSt*, p. 572). Swift's use of 'the
Evening' should be understood as referring to the newspaper rather than
the time of day. The account was also printed in the contemporaneous issue
of *The Post Boy*, with the near identical wording (but for the preamble),
punctuation and spelling, and it is possible that Swift himself may have
provided a copy to Roper as well; Swift noted about a month later that
'there is a particular Account of [the Bandbox episode] in the Post Boy, &
evening Post of that day' (Williams, *JSt*, p. 579). Woolley gives the date of
the event as 'variously 3/4 November' (*Corr.*, vol. I, p. 450 n. 2); however,
this would seem to be based on a misreading of the *Evening Post* account
which, although beginning, 'On the Third Instant', describes the delivery
of the box to Harley as taking place the 'next Morning'. Moreover, Swift
noted in January 1713 (Williams, *JSt*, p. 609) that, significantly, the box
had been received on King William's birthday, i.e. 4 November: William
was born on 14 November 1650 (new style). (William Wogan's dating of
the event as 'On Friday last', i.e. 7 November, in his letter to Sir John
Percival (Ehrenpreis, vol. II, p. 772) can be safely discounted.) *The Post
Boy* account of the episode was reprinted by Nichols in his quarto 1779
Supplement (TS, no. 87; pp. 24–5n.)

3. Post Boy, 15–18 November 1712

The duel between Hamilton and Mohun took place at 7 a.m. on
15 November; Swift provides a detailed account of the 'most terrible Accident that hath almost ever happened' and its immediate aftermath later

that same day (Williams, *JSt*, pp. 570–3). Two days later, Swift wrote that 'I have been drawing up a Paragraph for the Post boy, to be out to morrow, and as malicious as possible, and very proper for Abel Roper t[h]e Printer of it' (p. 574).

4. Post Boy, 18–20 November 1712

This account represents the 'further Particulars' promised in the previous issue. Davis described this report as 'even more malicious and not less likely to have come from Swift' (Davis, vol. VI, p. xxv).

5. Post Boy, 27–29 January 1713

A much abbreviated version of the account given by Swift in *The Examiner* on 2 February. On 26 January, Swift indicated his intention to 'make Abel Roper give a Relation' of this episode (Williams, *JSt*, p. 609). *The Evening Post* of 29 January carried the same account 'with minor changes', as did The *London Gazette* on 31 January (Davis, vol. VI, p. xxvii).

Copy texts and collations

The texts presented here are all taken from copies of the issues concerned. They have been collated against Davis; unusually for this edition, Davis's variants are included in the collations as he made a number of uncharacteristic transcription errors. The account of the band-box episode has also been collated against the account in *The Post Boy*.

1. The Post Boy, no. 2594 (25–7 December 1711)

Swift's contribution: verso, first column, paragraph beginning '*London*, Dec. 27.'

Copy examined: Bodl, Nichols collection: copy not physically examined; reproduction used from *Early English Newspapers* microfilm, reel 1197

References: TS, no. 556A. Davis, vol. VI, p. 196

Emendations

Historical collation

Word division (compounds only)

Copy text
none

Edited text
none

2. The Evening Post, no. 509 (11–13 November 1712)

Swift's contribution: recto, paragraph headed '*London, Nov. 13.*' (to verso)

Copy examined: BL, Burney collection: copy not physically examined; reproduction used from *Early English Newspapers* microfilm, reel 120

References: Not in TS. Davis, vol. VI, pp. 196–7

Emendations

322.2 from] Davis; form
322.5 fasten'd at] *Post Boy*; fasten at
    The tense of the sentence demands a 'ed' suffix and all the other past participles in this passage use an elided form.
322.6 two large] *Post Boy*; two-large
    The hyphen comes at the end of the line; it is clearly an error.

Historical collation

321.8 *London, Nov. 13*] *London*, Nov. 12 Davis
    Presumably a slip by Davis.
321.8 *London* . . . another Band-box] London, *Nov.* 13. *The Truth of the Fact concerning the Band-Box sent to the* Lord-Treasurer, *we are inform'd, is as followeth*: On Tuesday Morning, the 4th Instant, the Penny-Post-Man deliver'd a small Parcel at the Lord-Treasurer's House, directed

to his Lordship's Porter, in which, upon opening, was found enclos'd a Band-Box *Post Boy*

321.15 Causon] Carson Davis

Davis emends here without explanation. 'Carson' may have been a more common name but the text clearly reads 'Causon'. Moreover, there were at least a handful of Causon families in and around early eighteenth century London: for example, the International Genealogical Index *lists the christening of Sarah, daughter of John and Mary Causon of St Dunstan's parish, Stepney, in September 1714.*

321.18 lifting] stretching *Post Boy*

322.5 fasten'd at] *Post Boy*; fasten at *Evening Post*

Word division (compounds only)

Copy text
321.15 Post-man

Edited text
none

3. The Post Boy, no. 2734 (15–18 November 1712)

Swift's contribution: verso, second column, paragraph beginning: 'On Saturday Morning last'

Copy examined: BL, Burney collection: copy not physically examined; reproduction used from *Early English Newspapers* microfilm, reel 1197

Notes: Not in TS. Davis, vol. VI, pp. 197–8

Emendations

Historical collation

322.25 On Saturday Morning last] *London*, Nov 18. On Saturday Morning last Davis

Davies incorporates the location and date from the account immediately previous to this.

Word division (compounds only)

Copy text
322.31 down-wards

Edited text
none

4. The Post Boy, no. 2735 (18–20 November 1712)

Swift's contribution: recto, second column, paragraph beginning, '*London*, Nov. 20.' (to first column on verso)

Copy examined: BL, Burney collection: copy not physically examined; reproduction used from *Early English Newspapers* microfilm, reel 1197

References: Not in TS. Davis, vol. VI, pp. 198–9

Emendations

323.32 be came] *this edition*; became

Historical collation

323.32 became] *this edition*; be came
  Davis presumably overlooked the 'be', which had become detached from 'came' in the copy text.
324.3 B—llies.] B(u)llies. Davis
  A rare example of Davis visibly indicating his expansion of an elision.

Word division (compounds only)

Copy text
324.1 Lord-ship

Edited text
none

5. The Post Boy, no. 2765 (27–9 January 1713)

Swift's contribution: verso, second column, paragraph headed '*London*, Jan. 29'.

Copy examined: BL, Burney collection: copy not physically examined; reproduction used from *Early English Newspapers* microfilm, reel 1198

Reference: Not in TS. Davis, vol. VI, p. 200

Emendations

Historical collation

Word division (compounds only)

Copy text
none

Edited text
none

APPENDIX

These are inclusive-text transcripts, from BL, Add. MS 70030, of the 'Vote of Thanks' and 'Humble Address of the . . . Lords to the Queen' as drafted by Swift, with annotations by Robert Harley.

(Vote of Thanks; *BL, Add. MS 70030, fo. 202^r*)

Ordered that an humble Address be made to Her Majesty to return the Most humble thanks of this House to Her Majesty, for Her most gracious Speech from the Throne, and for Her Majesty's communicating to this House that a Peace is agreed on, and to congratulate Her Majesty upon the Success of her Endeavors for a generall Peace, and for what [*letters cancelled*] Her Majesty has done to secure the Protestant Succession; [& the Harmony between her & the House of Hannover *is interlined in a different hand after the semi-colon*] and to [*letters cancelled*] assure Her Majesty, that as She is pleased to express her Dependence next under God upon [*letters cancelled*] the Duty and Affection of her People, this House will make all Returns [*letters cancelled*] that are due from obedient Subjects to the most indulgent Soverain.

(Humble Address of the House of Lords to the Queen; *BL, Add. MS 70030, fos. 200^{r-v}*)

We Your Majesty's most dutifull and loyall Subjects the Lords Spirituall and Temporall in Parlm^t assembled, do with the greatest Joy and Satisfaction return our humblest Thanks to Your Majesty for Your most gracious Speech from the Throne, and for communicating to this House, that a Peace is concluded, so honorable to Your Majesty and safe and advantageous to Your Kingdoms; [*passage from* so honorable *to* Kingdoms; *underlined, presumably by Harley*] by which we hope with the Blessing of God, that your People will in a few Years recover themselves after so long and expensive a War, [*possibly a full-stop rather than a comma*] We likewise beg leave to congratulate with Your Majesty upon the generall Peace you have procured for all Your Allyes, wherein the true Interests and just Pretensions of each are so fully provided for that the Tranquillity and Welfare of Europe will be owing (next to the Divine Providence) to Your Majesty's Wisdom and Goodness. [*passage from* We likewise *to* and Goodness. *underlined, presumably by Harley*] We never had the least doubt, but that Your Majesty who is the greatest Ornament and Protector of the Protestant Religion, would continue to take the wisest Measures for securing the Protestant succession ['ion' *is blotted*]: towards which [*fo. 200ᵛ begins*] nothing can be more necessary than the perfect Harmony [Harmony *underlined, presumably by Harley, who wrote* friendshipp *on the left-hand side of the page*] there is between Your Majesty and the House of Hannover. And we do humbly assure Your Majesty, that as you are pleased to express Your Dependance (next under God) upon the Duty and Affection of Your People; we think our selves bound by the Strictest Tyes of Religion, Loyalty, and Gratitude, to make all Returns that can be due from the most obedient Subjects to the most indulgent Soverain.

BIBLIOGRAPHY

This bibliography excludes single-work editions of works included in this volume (except the Wheeler edition of The Conduct of the Allies) *but does include items listed in the abbreviations and the relevant Swift collected works (whose details have been taken from TS). Publishers' details have been omitted for all pre-1900 works.*

1. Primary Works

Addison, Joseph, *Letters of Joseph Addison*, ed. Walter Graham, Oxford: Oxford University Press, 1941

An Answer to the Examiner's Cavils Against the Barrier Treaty, London, 1713

Arbuthnot, John, *Law is a Bottomless Pit, Exemplify'd in the case of the Lord Strutt, John Bull, Nicholas Frog, and Lewis Baboon. Who spent all they had in a law-suit*, London, 1712

The History of John Bull, ed. Alan W. Bower and Robert A. Erickson, Oxford: Clarendon Press, 1976

Bancks, John, *The History of Francis-Eugene Prince of Savoy . . . by an English Officer*, 2nd edn, London, 1742

Beaumont, John, *Dutch Alliances: or, a Plain Proof of their Observance of Treaties*, London, 1712

Bolingbroke, Henry St John, Viscount, *Letters and Correspondence of Henry St John, Lord Viscount Bolingbroke*, ed. Gilbert Parke, 4 vols., London, 1798

Boyer, Abel (attrib.), *An Account of the State and Progress of the Present Negotiation of Peace*, London, 1711

Reflections upon the Examiner's Scandalous Peace, London, 1711

The Political State of Great Britain, 38 vols., London, 1711–29

A True and Impartial Account of the Duel . . . And, some Previous Reflections on Sham-plots, London, 1712

Boyle, John, Lord Orrery, *Remarks on the Life and Writings* of *Dr Jonathan Swift*, London, 1752, ed. João Fróes, Newark: University of Delaware Press, 2000

Burnet, Gilbert, *History of His Own Time*, 6 vols., London, 1724–34

Burnet, Thomas (attrib.), *The Thoughts of a Tory Author, Concerning the Press*, London, 1712

The Character and Declaration of the October Club, London, 1711

A Complete History of England, 3 vols., London, 1706

Considerations upon the Secret History of the White Staff, London, 1714

Curll, Edmund, *An Impartial History of . . . John Barber*, London, 1741

A Defence of the Allies and the Late Ministry: or, Remarks on the Tories New Idol, London, 1711

Defoe, Daniel, *Reasons why this Nation Ought to Put a Speedy End to this Expensive War*, London, 1711

    An Essay at A Plain Exposition Of That Difficult Phrase A Good Peace, London, 1711

    A Further Search Into the Conduct of the Allies, London, 1712

    (attrib.), *The Honour and Prerogative of the Queen's Majesty Vindicated and Defended Against the Unexampled Insolence of the author of the Guardian*, London, 1713

    (attrib.), *A Letter from a Member of the House of Commons to his Friend in the Country, Relating to the Bill of Commerce*, London, 1713

    Memoirs of Count Tariff, London, 1713

    (attrib.), *Reasons concerning the Immediate Demolishing of Dunkirk*, London, 1713

    (attrib.) *A Detection of the Sophistry and Falsities of . . . the Secret History of the White Staff*, Part II, London, 1714

    (attrib.), *The Scots Nation and Union Vindicated from the Reflections cast on them in an Infamous Libel*, London, 1714

    Letters of Daniel Defoe, ed. G. H. Healey, Oxford: Clarendon Press, 1955

    Defoe's Review, ed. Arthur W. Secord, 22 vols., New York: Columbia University Press for The Facsimile Society, 1937, 1965

The Description of Dunkirk with Squash's and Dismal's Opinion how easily Prince Eugene may Retake it, and many Other Matters of the Last Importance, London, 1712

Dryden, John, *The Satires of Decimus Junius Juvenalis*, 2nd edn, London, 1697

    The Works of Virgil containing his Pastorals, Georgics, and Æneis, London, 1697

Dunton, John, *Neck or Nothing: in a letter to the Right Honourable the Lord – – being [sic] a supplement to the Short history of the Parliament*, London, 1713

The Dutch Won't Let us Have Dunkirk, ?London, 1712

Encyclopédie de Diderot et d'Alembert, Paris, 1751

Ferguson, Robert, *An Account of the Obligations the States of Holland have to Great-Britain*, London, 1711

Foxe, John, *The Seconde Volume of the Ecclesiasticall Historie Conteyning the Acts and Monuments of Martyrs*, London, 1597

Fuller, William, *A Brief Discovery of the True Mother of the Pretended Prince of Wales known by the name of Mary Grey*, Edinburgh, 1696

A General Collection of Treatys, Declarations of War, Manifestos, and other Publick Papers, London, 1710

Grotius, Hugo, *De jure belli ac pacis*, Paris, 1625

Harbin, George, *The Hereditary Right of the Crown of England Asserted; the History of the Succession since the Conquest Clear'd; and the True English Constitution Vindicated from the Misrepresentations of Dr Higden's View and Defence*, London, 1713

Hare, Francis, *A Letter to a Member of the October-Club, Shewing, That to Yield Spain to the Duke of Anjou by a Peace, would be the Ruin of Great Britain*, London, 1711

   The Management of the War, London, 1711

   The Allies and the late Ministry Defended against France and the Present Friends of France, London 1711–12

   A Full Answer to the Conduct of the Allies, London, 1712

Hickes, George, *Some Queries Proposed to Civil, Canon, and Common Lawyers in London, July 1712. In order to prove the legitimacy of the Pretender*, London, 1712

Higgons, Bevil, *A Poem on the Peace*, London, 1713

The History of the Dutch Usurpations, London, 1712

Hobbes, Thomas, *Leviathan*, London, 1651

Jonson, Ben, *The Oxford Authors: Ben Jonson*, ed. Ian Donaldson, Oxford: Oxford University Press, 1985

Mabbot, Gilbert, *A Perfect Narrative of the Whole Proceedings of the High Court of Justice, In the Tryal of the King*, London, 1649

Macpherson, James, *Original Papers; Containing the Secret History of Great Britain, from the Restoration, to the Accession of the House of Hanover*, 2nd edn, 2 vols., London, 1776

Manley, Delarivier, *A Modest Enquiry into the Reasons of the Joy Expressed by a Certain Sett of People*, London, 1714

Marlborough, John Churchill, first Duke of, and Sidney, first Earl of Godolphin, *The Marlborough–Godolphin Correspondence*, ed. Henry L. Snyder, 3 vols., Oxford: Clarendon Press, 1975

Marlborough, Sarah Churchill, first Duchess of, *Private Correspondence of Sarah, Duchess of Marlborough*, London: Henry Colbourn, 1838

Maxwell, Henry, *Anguis in Herba; Or, The Fatal Consequences of a Treaty with France*, London, 1711

Maynwaring, Arthur, *Vindication of the Present M— —y, from The Clamours rais'd against them*, London, 1711

   The Life and Posthumous Works of Arthur Maynwaring, Esq; Containing Several Original Pieces and Translations in Prose and Verse, London, 1715

Milton, John, *The Poems of John Milton*, ed. John Carey and Alastair Fowler, Harlow: Longman, 1968

Oldmixon, John (attrib.), *Remarks upon Remarks*, London, 1711

   (attrib.), *The Dutch Barrier Our's*, London, 1712

Political Merriment: or, Truths told to Some Tune, London, 1714–15

Poyntz, Stephen, *The Barrier Treaty Vindicated*, London, 1712

Pufendorf, Samuel von, *De officio hominis ex civis juxta legem naturalem*, Cambridge, 1682

Rabelais, François, *The first book of the works of Mr Francis Rabelais*, tr. Thomas Urquhart, London, 1653

Remarks on a False, Scandalous, and Seditious Libel, Intituled, The Conduct of the Allies, and of the Late Ministry, London, 1711

Remarks on Mr. Steele's Crisis, &c.: By One of the Clergy In a Letter to the Author, London, 1714

Rogers, Woodes, *A Cruising Voyage Round the World; first to the South Seas; thence to the East-Indies, and homeward by the Cape of Good Hope; begun in 1708, and finished in 1711*, London, 1712; repr. Amsterdam: Da Capo Press, 1969

Some Remarks on the Letters Between the L–d T—nd, and Mr Se–tary B—le, London, 1712

The Spectator, ed. Donald F. Bond, 5 vols., Oxford: Clarendon Press, 1965

Steele, Richard, *The Importance of Dunkirk Consider'd: In Defence of the Guardian of August the 7th*, London, 1713

> *Correspondence of Richard Steele*, ed. Rae Blanchard, Oxford: Oxford University Press, 1941

> *The Tracts and Pamphlets of Richard Steele*, ed. Rae Blanchard, Baltimore: Johns Hopkins University Press, 1944

> *The Englishman: A Political Journal*, ed. Rae Blanchard, Oxford: Clarendon Press, 1955

> *The Guardian*, ed. John Calhoun Stephens, Lexington: University Press of Kentucky, 1982

Suidas, *Lexicon*, ed. Aemilius Portus, 2 vols., Geneva, 1619

Swift, Jonathan, *The Works of J.S, D.D, D.S.P.D.*, 4 vols., Dublin, 1737–8 (TS 50)

> *Political Tracts*, 2 vols., London, 1738 (TS 25 (6–7))

> *The Works of J.S, D.D, D.S.P.D.*, 6 vols., Dublin, 1738 (TS 42)

> *Letters to and from Dr J. Swift, D.S.P.D.*, Dublin, 1741 (TS 62B)

> *The Works of Jonathan Swift, D.D, D.S.P.D.*, 8 vols., Dublin, 1741–6 (TS 44)

> *The Works of Jonathan Swift, D.D, D.S.P.D . . . The Sixth Edition*, 8 vols., Dublin, 1741–8 (TS 51)

> *Miscellanies in Prose*, vol. 9, London, 1742 (TS 31(3))

> *A Supplement to the Works of Dr Swift*, London, 1752 (TS 83)

> *The Works of Jonathan Swift, D. D.*, 25 vols., London, 1754–79 (TS 88)

> *The Works of Jonathan Swift, D.D.*, 14 vols., London, 1755–79 (TS 87)

> *The Works of the Reverend Dr Jonathan Swift, Dean of St Patrick's, Dublin*, 19 vols., Dublin, 1756–68 (TS 53)

> *The Works of Dr Jonathan Swift, Dean of St Patrick's, Dublin*, 26 vols., London, 1760–79 (TS 90)

The Works of the Reverend Dr J. Swift, D.S.P.D., 20 vols., Dublin, 1763–71 (TS 52)

The Works of the Reverend Dr Jonathan Swift, Dean of St Patrick's, Dublin, 20 vols., Dublin, 1765–71 (TS 47)

The Works of Dr Jonathan Swift, Dean of St Patrick's, Dublin, 27 vols., London, 1765–79 (TS 92)

The Works of the Rev. Jonathan Swift, D.D., ed. John Nichols, 19 vols., London, 1801 (TS 129)

The Works of the Rev. Jonathan Swift, D.D., ed. John Nichols, 19 vols., London, 1808 (TS 131)

The Works of Jonathan Swift, ed. Walter Scott, 19 vols., Edinburgh, 1814 (TS 138)

The Works of Jonathan Swift, ed. Walter Scott, 2nd edn, 19 vols., Edinburgh, 1824

The Prose Works of Jonathan Swift, ed. Temple Scott, 12 vols., London, 1897–1908

The Correspondence of Jonathan Swift, D.D., ed. F. Elrington Ball, 6 vols., London: G. Bell & Sons, 1910–14

The Conduct of the Allies, ed. C. B. Wheeler, Oxford: Clarendon Press, 1916

Gulliver's Travels and Selected Writings, ed. John Hayward, London: Nonesuch Press, 1934

The Letters of Jonathan Swift to Charles Ford, ed. David Nichol Smith, Oxford: Clarendon Press, 1935

The Prose Writings of Jonathan Swift, ed. Herbert Davis *et al.*, 16 vols., Oxford: Basil Blackwell, 1939–74

Journal to Stella, ed. Harold Williams, 2 vols., Oxford: Clarendon Press, 1948

The Poems of Jonathan Swift, ed. Harold Williams, 2nd edn, 3 vols., Oxford: Clarendon Press, 1958

The Correspondence of Jonathan Swift, ed. Harold Williams, 5 vols., Oxford: Clarendon Press, 1963–5

A Discourse of the Contests and Dissentions between the Nobles and the Commons in Athens and Rome, ed. Frank H. Ellis, Oxford: Clarendon Press, 1967

Major Works, ed. Angus Ross and David Woolley, Oxford: Oxford University Press, 1984

Swift vs. Mainwaring: 'The Examiner' and 'The Medley', ed. Frank H. Ellis: Oxford, Clarendon Press, 1985

The Correspondence of Jonathan Swift, D.D., ed. David Woolley, 4 vols., Frankfurt am Main: Peter Lang, 1999–

Swift, Jonathan and Thomas Sheridan, *The Intelligencer*, ed. James Woolley, Oxford: Clarendon Press, 1992

The Taxes not Grievous, and therefore not a Reason for an Unsafe Peace, London, 1711

Timberland, Ebenezor (ed.), *The History and Proceedings of the House of Lords, from the Restoration in 1660, to the Present Time*, 8 vols., London, 1742

A True and Impartial Account of the Animosity, Quarrel and Duel . . . And, some Previous Reflections on Sham-plots, London, 1712

Two Letters concerning the Author of the Examiner, London, 1713

Wagstaffe, William, *The Character of Richard Steele, Esq; with some remarks. By Toby, Abel's kinsman*, London, 1713

Walpole, Robert, *A Short History of the Parliament*, London, 1713

2. Secondary works

Bailey, Nathan, *Divers Proverbs with their Explication and Illustration*, New Haven: Yale University Press, 1917

Ball, F. Elrington, 'Swift and Prince Butler,' *N&Q* 136 (1920), 404–5

The Bible: Authorized King James Version, ed. Robert Carroll and Stephen Prickett, Oxford: Oxford University Press, 1997

Bibliotheca Lindesiana: Catalogue of English Broadsides 1505–1897, Aberdeen: Aberdeen University Press, 1898

Bond, Maurice F. (ed.), *The Manuscripts of the House of Lords, Volume X: 1712–1714*, London: HMSO, 1953

Browning, Andrew (ed.), *English Historical Documents, 1660–1714*, London: Eyre & Spottiswoode, 1953

Cartwright, James J. (ed.), *The Wentworth Papers 1705–1739*, London: Wyman and Sons, 1882

A Catalogue of the Tract Collection of Saint David's University College, Lampeter, London: Mansell, 1975

Chalmers, John P., 'Bodleian Copyright Deposit Survivors of the First Sixteen Years of the Copyright Act of Queen Anne 10 April 1710 to 25 March 1726', unpublished M.Litt. thesis, University of Oxford (1974)

Cobbett, William, and John Wright, *Cobbett's Parliamentary History of England from the Norman Conquest in 1066 to the Year 1803*, 36 vols., London, 1806–20

Coombs, Douglas, *The Conduct of the Dutch*, The Hague: Nijhoff, 1958

Cotgrave, Randle, *A Dictionarie of the French and English Tongues*, London, 1611; facs. repr. Columbia: University of South Carolina Press, 1950

Coxe, William, *Memoirs of John, Duke of Marlborough, with his Original Correspondence*, London: Bohn, 1848
History of the House of Austria, 3rd edn, 3 vols., London: Bell and Daldy, 1868

Cruickshanks, Eveline, Stuart Handley and D. W. Hayton (eds.), *The History of Parliament. The House of Commons 1690–1715*, 5 vols., Cambridge: Cambridge University Press, 2002

Cullingford, Benita, *British Chimney Sweeps*, Lewes: Book Guild, 2000

Dane, Joseph A., *The Myth of Print Culture: Essays on Evidence, Textuality and Bibliographical Method*, Toronto: University of Toronto Press, 2003

Davies, G., 'The Seamy Side of Marlborough's War,' *HLQ* 15 (1951), 21–44

Dickinson, H. T., 'The October Club', *HLQ* 33 (1970), 155–73
  Bolingbroke, London, Constable, 1970

Downie, J. A., 'The Conduct of the Allies: The Question of Influence', in Clive T. Probyn (ed.), *The Art of Jonathan Swift*, London: Vision, 1978, pp. 108–28
  'Swift and the Oxford Ministry: New Evidence', *SStud* 1 (1986), 2–8
  'Swift and Jacobitism', *ELH* 64 (1997), 887–901
  Downie, J. A. and Woolley, David, 'Swift, Oxford and the Composition of Queen's Speeches, 1710–1714', *BLJ* 8 (1982), 121–46

Ehrenpreis, Irvin, *Swift: The Man, His Works, and the Age*, 3 vols., London: Methuen, 1962–83

Eighteenth Century Collections Online (Thomson Gale), online subscription database

Eilon, Daniel, 'Did Swift Write *A Discourse on Hereditary Right*?', *Modern Philology* 82 (1985), 374–92
  Factions' Fictions: Ideological Closure in Swift's Satire, Newark: University of Delaware Press, 1991

Ellis, Frank H., 'Swift's Seventh Penny Paper', *TLS* 3766 (10 May 1974), 506

Feiling, Keith, *A History of the Tory Party, 1640–1714*, Oxford: Clarendon Press, 1924

Ferguson, William, *Scotland's Relations with England: a Survey to 1707*, Edinburgh: Donald, 1977

Fischer, John Irwin, 'The Legal Response to Swift's *The Public Spirit of the Whigs*', in John Irwin Fischer, Hermann J. Real and James Woolley (eds.), *Swift and his Contexts*, New York: AMS Press, 1989, pp. 21–38

Furbank, P. N. and W. R. Owens, *Defoe De-Attributions*, London: Hambledon, 1994
  A Critical Bibliography of Daniel Defoe, London: Pickering and Chatto, 1998

Gaskell, Philip, *A New Introduction to Bibliography*, Oxford: Clarendon Press, 1972
  From Writer to Reader: Studies in Editorial Method, Winchester: St Paul's Bibliographies, 1978

Geyl, Pieter, *The Netherlands in the Seventeenth Century: Part Two*, London: Ernest Benn, 1964

Goldgar, B., *The Curse of Party*, Lincoln: University of Nebraska Press, 1961

Goslinga, Sicco van, *Mémoires*, ed. U. A. Evertsz and G. H. M. Delprat, Leefuwarden: Worcum, 1857

Gregg, Edward, *Queen Anne*, London: Routledge & Kegan Paul, 1980

Harris, John, 'Swift's *The Publick Spirit of the Whigs*: a Partly Censored State of the Scottish Paragraphs', *PBSA* 72 (1978), 92–4

Harris, Tim, *Politics under the Later Stuarts*, London: Longman, 1993

Hatton, R. M. *Charles XII of Sweden*, New York: Weybright and Talley, 1968

Hazen, Allen T. 'Eighteenth-century Quartos with Vertical Chain-lines', *The Library* 4th ser., 16 (1935), 337–42

Heawood, Edward, *Watermarks: Mainly of the 17th and 18th Centuries*, Hilversum: Paper Publications Society, 1950

Higgins, Ian, *Swift's Politics: A Study in Disaffection*, Cambridge: Cambridge University Press, 1994

Holmes, Geoffrey, *British Politics in the Age of Anne*, London: Macmillan, 1967
    The Trial of Doctor Sacheverell, London: Eyre Metheun, 1973

Hyland, P. 'A Breach of the Peace: the Controversy over the Ninth Article of the Treaty of Utrecht', *BJECS* 22 (1999), 51–66

Johnson, Samuel, *The Lives of the Poets*, ed. Roger Lonsdale, 4 vols., Oxford: Clarendon Press, 2006

Jones, Clyve, 'Swift, the Earl of Oxford, and the Management of the House of Lords in 1713: Two New Lists', *BLJ* 16 (1990), 117–30
    ' "Party Rage and Faction" – the View from Fulham, Scotland Yard, and the Temple: Parliament in the Letters of Thomas Bateman and John and Ralph Bridges to Sir William Trumbull, 1710–14,' *BLJ* 19 (1993), 148–80

Journals of the House of Commons, from November the 8th 1547, 101 vols., 1803–52

Journals of the House of Lords, Beginning Anno Primo Henrici Octavi, 79 vols., 1771

Jowitt, E., *The Dictionary of English Law*, 2 vols., London: Sweet & Maxwell, 1959

Kennedy, Máire, 'Reading Print, 1700–1800', in Raymond Gillespie and Andrew Hadfield (eds.), *The Oxford History of the Irish Book: Volume III, The Irish Book in English 1550–1800*, Oxford: Oxford University Press, 2006, pp. 146–68

Lavers-Smith, Hamilton, 'Swift's Political Tracts', *The Athenæum* 3915 (8 November 1902), 619–20

Lindsay, Alexander, *Index of English Literary Manuscripts, Vol. III, Part 4*, London: Mansell, 1997

Littré, E. *Dictionnaire de la langue française*, Paris: Libraire Hachette, 1885

McKenzie, D. F. (ed.), *Stationers' Company Apprentices 1641–1700*, Oxford: Oxford Bibliographical Society, 1974
    Stationers' Company Apprentices 1701–1800, Oxford, Oxford Bibliographical Society, 1978

Maner, Martin W., 'An Eighteenth-Century Editor at Work: John Nichols and Jonathan Swift', *PBSA* 70 (1976), 481–99

Meulen, David L. Vander and G. Thomas Tanselle, 'A System of Manuscript Transcription', *SB* 52 (1999), 201–12

Moore, J. R., 'Defoe, Steele, and the Demolition of Dunkirk', *HLQ* 13 (1950), 279–302

Nieuw Nederlandsch Biografisch Woordenboek VIII, Leiden: K. H. Kossmann, 1930

Plomer, H. R. *et al.*, *A Dictionary of the Printers and Booksellers Who Were at Work in England, Scotland and Ireland from 1668 to 1725*, Oxford: Bibliographical Society, 1922

Plomer, H. R., G. H Bushnell and E. R. McC. Dix, *A Dictionary of the Printers and Booksellers Who Were at Work in England, Scotland and Ireland from 1725 to 1775*, Oxford: Bibliographical Society, 1932

Pollard, M., *Dublin's Trade in Books, 1550–1800*, Oxford: Clarendon Press, 1989

   'George Faulkner', *SStud* 7 (1992), 79–96.

   A Dictionary of the Dublin Book Trade 1550–1800 Based on the Records of the Guild of St Luke the Evangelist, Dublin, London: Bibliographical Society, 2000

Pugh, Simon, 'A Variant Second Edition of Jonathan Swift's *The Conduct of the Allies*', *N&Q* 229 (1984), 388–9

Quinlan, Maurice J., 'The Prosecution of Swift's *Public Spirit of the Whigs*', *TSLL* 9 (1967), 167–84

Rivington, Charles A., *'Tyrant': the Story of John Barber*, York: William Sessions Limited, 1989

The Rothschild Library: A Catalogue of the Collection of Eighteenth-century Printed Books and Manuscripts Formed by Lord Rothschild, privately printed at Cambridge University Press, 1954

Smout, T. C., 'The Road to Union,' in Geoffrey Holmes (ed.), *Britain After the Glorious Revolution 1689–1714*, London: Macmillan, 1969, pp. 176–96

Szechi, D., *Jacobitism and Tory Politics 1710–14*, Edinburgh: John Donald, 1984

Tanselle, G. Thomas, 'The Concept of Format', *SB* 53 (2000), 67–116

Teerink, H., *A Bibliography of the Writings of Jonathan Swift*, 2nd edn, ed. Arthur H. Scouten, Philadelphia: University of Pennsylvania Press, 1963

Thompson, Paul V., and Dorothy J. Thompson (eds.), *The Account Books of Jonathan Swift*, Newark: University of Delaware Press, 1984

Tilley, Morris P., *A Dictionary of the Proverbs in England in the Sixteenth and Seventeenth Centuries*, Ann Arbor: University of Michigan, 1950

Treadwell, Michael, 'London Printers and Printing Houses in 1705', *Publishing History*, 7 (1980), 5–44

   'London Trade Publishers 1675–1750', *The Library* 6th ser., 4 (1982), 99–134

'Swift's Relations with the London Book Trade to 1714', in Robin Myers and Michael Harris (eds.), *Author/Publisher Relations during the Eighteenth and Nineteenth Century*, Oxford: Oxford Polytechnic Press, 1983, pp. 1–36

'Lists of Master Printers: The Size of the London Printing Trade, 1637-1723', in Robin Myers and Michael Harris (eds.), *Aspects of Printing from 1600*, Oxford: Oxford Polytechnic Press, 1987, pp. 141–70

'On False and Misleading Imprints in the London Book Trade, 1660- 1750', in Robin Myers and Michael Harris (eds.), *Fakes and Frauds: Varieties of Deception in Print and Manuscript*, Winchester: St Paul's Bibliographies, 1989, pp. 29–46

Trevelyan, George M., *England under Queen Anne*, 3 vols., London: Longman, 1930–4

Williams, Harold, 'A Hue and Cry after Dismal', *RES* 6 (1930), 195–6

Wolf, Henry W., 'The Pretender at Bar-le-Duc', *Blackwoods Edinburgh Magazine* 156 (1894), 220–46

Woolley, David, 'Forster's *Swift*', *The Dickensian* 70 (1974), 191–204

'Swift's Copy of *Gulliver's Travels*: The Armagh *Gulliver*, Hyde's Edition, and Swift's Earliest Corrections', in Clive T. Probyn (ed.), *The Art of Jonathan Swift*, London: Vision, 1978, pp. 131–78

'The Canon of Swift's Prose Pamphleteering, 1710–1714, and *The New Way of Selling Places at Court*', *SStud* 3 (1988), 96–123 (and foldout endpaper)

'"The Author of the *Examiner*" and the Whiggish Answer-Jobbers of 1711–1712', *SStud* 5 (1990), 109–11

'*A Dialogue upon Dunkirk* (1712) and Swift's "7 penny Papers"', in Hermann J. Real and Richard H. Rodino (eds.), *Reading Swift: Papers from the Second Münster Symposium on Jonathan Swift*, Munich: W. Fink, 1993, pp. 215–23

INDEX